30/5

A TRUE EUROPEAN

Judge David Edward has enjoyed a glittering career. After a substantial, successful period in Scotland, both as a practising advocate and professor of EC law, he was appointed to the Court of First Instance upon its creation in 1989. He was subsequently appointed to the Court of Justice where he has served for many years. This book has been prepared in honour of his retirement from that position in December 2003. The contributions reflect all aspects of Judge Edward's career as a lawyer, both in Scotland and in Luxembourg. In keeping with the respect with which he is held, contributions have been received from eminent members of the Scottish and Luxembourg judiciary, academics and practitioners. Not surprisingly, the main focus is on Community law, with important contributions on competition, institutional, substantive and remedial issues. This book will be an essential addition to the library of anyone with a genuine interest in Community law.

A True European
Essays for Judge David Edward

Edited by
MARK HOSKINS
&
WILLIAM ROBINSON

OXFORD AND PORTLAND, OREGON
2003

Published in North America (US and Canada) by
Hart Publishing c/o
International Specialized Book Services
5804 NE Hassalo Street
Portland, Oregon
97213-3644
USA

© The editor and contributors severally 2004

The editors and contributors have asserted their right under the Copyright,
Designs and Patents Act 1988, to be identified as the authors of this work

Hart Publishing is a specialist legal publisher based in Oxford, England.
To order further copies of this book or to request a list of other
publications please write to:

Hart Publishing, Salter's Boatyard, Folly Bridge,
Abingdon Road, Oxford OX1 4LB
Telephone: +44 (0)1865 245533 or Fax: +44 (0)1865 794882
e-mail: mail@hartpub.co.uk
WEBSITE: http//www.hartpub.co.uk

British Library Cataloguing in Publication Data
Data Available
ISBN 1–84113–447–3 (hardback)

Typeset by Hope Services (Abingdon) Ltd.
Printed and bound in Great Britain on acid-free paper by
Biddles Ltd, www.biddles.co.uk

Contents

Foreword	xi
Preface	xv
List of Contributors	xvii
Table of Cases	xix

Introduction

1 Tales from the Tartan Chambers 1
   Diane Hansen-Ingram

II The Scottish Perspective

2 What Waldemar Saw—A Young German's View of the
   Scottish Legal System 11
   Lord Rodger of Earlsferry

3 Justice Seen to be Done 21
   Lord Clyde

4 Unfinished Business 31
   Lord Clarke

5 Devolution and Community Law 47
   Christine Boch

III EU Institutional Issues

6 The Convention and the Court 69
   *President of the Court, Judge Rodríguez Iglesias and
   Julio Baquero Cruz*

7 The Judicial Architecture of the European Union—the Challenges
   of Change 81
   Judge Nicholas Forwood

8 Judge Edward Acting as Advocate General 91
   Professor Rosa Greaves

9 Enlargement of the European Union—the Council Process 99
   Elizabeth Willocks

IV EU Competition Issues

10 Certain Reflections on Recent Judgments Reviewing Commission Merger Control Decisions 117
    President of the Court of First Instance, Judge Vesterdorf

11 The National Courts and the Uniform Application of EC Competition Rules. Preliminary Observations on Council Regulation 1/2003 145
    Judge Sevón

12 The A M & S Judgment 153
    John Temple Lang

13 Collective Dominance—The Contribution of the Community Courts 161
    Mark Clough

14 Some Reflections on Procedure in Competition Cases 187
    Sir Christopher Bellamy QC

V EU Substantive Issues

15 Free Movement and the Environment: Seeing the Wood for the Trees 193
    Imelda Higgins and Marie Demetriou

16 The Dangers of too Much Precaution 203
    Ian Forrester QC

17 Different but (Almost) Equal—The Development of Free Movement Rights Under EU Association, Co-Operation and Accession Agreements 233
    Eleanor Sharpston QC

18 Diplomas and the Recognition of Professional Qualifications in the Case Law of the European Court of Justice 247
    Dr Dieter Kraus

19 The Transformation of the Rome Convention 257
    Richard Plender QC

20 Standard of Review in WTO Law 267
    Professor Claus Dieter Ehlermann and Nicolas Lockhart

VI EU Remedies Issues

21 Approaches to Interpretation in a Plurilingual System 297
    Advocate-General Francis G Jacobs

22 Private Enforcement—A Complete System of Remedies 307
    Anneli Howard and Deok Joo Rhee

Contents ix

23 Article 234: A Few Rough Edges Still 327
   Dr Robert Lane

24 Discretionary References: To Refer or not to Refer? 345
   Mark Hoskins

25 Direct Applicability or Effect 353
   Dr Joxerramon Bengoetxea

26 Du concept de l'effet direct à celui de l'invocabilité au regard de la jurisprudence récente de la Cour de justice 367
   Judge Melchior Wathelet

Index 391

Foreword

I must start this Preface with a confession and get it off my chest. I gave William Robinson a commitment, in deepest secrecy of course, to write a proper contribution to this book in honour of Judge David Edward. The topic that I chose was the existence of 'mandatory requirements' that stand to Article 81 (3), and, I think, also to Article 87 (3), of the European Community Treaty as 'mandatory requirements' stand to Article 30 (in view of Peter Oliver's view about the latter, I deliberately leave the nature of the relationship vague). Some of the established and potential mandatory requirements that apply in relation to the Treaty provisions on competition have their roots in other Articles of the Treaty (e.g. collective labour agreements; protection of human health and the environment); others (e.g. protection of the effective administration of justice) are rooted in 'the law' with which, over and beyond the Treaties, the Community was endowed, thanks to what is now Article 220 of the Treaty. And since the establishment of the Community, 'the law' has just been waiting to be uncovered through the exercise of their imagination by pleaders and through the percipient sagacity of the Community's Judges and Advocates General.

I even started to write my contribution, with assistance from Anneli Howard, another of David Edward's former Legal Secretaries and a walking encyclopaedia of Community law. But then, notwithstanding the polite reminders from William Robinson, the prior claims of the Clerks' Room (prior because the Clerks were closer than William and much less forbearing) resulted in my missing every deadline. Hence my present rôle as the man who comes on to the stage to utter the prologue before the play proper begins.

It is almost exactly fifty years since David Edward and I first met, as freshmen at University College, Oxford. People generally say to me, somewhat ungraciously I feel, 'Oh, but you must be much older than David.' I am older but by only two years and the reason why we went to Oxford at the same time was that he had not yet done his two years of National Service whereas I had. But even then he looked much, much younger than me, so I am reconciled to the unfavourable comparison.

Although David was reading Honour Mods (effectively Classical Literature) and I was reading for PPE Prelims (largely Logic and basic economic theory), we dined together most nights in Hall on the scholars' table, taking turns with the other scholars and exhibitioners to recite antiphonally with the Master, Arthur Goodhart, or Senior Fellow, what must be one of the longest Latin Graces in the world.

When, after seven Terms, David had completed Honour Mods, he wisely went off to do his National Service—in the Royal Navy: although one's

National Service could be a stimulating experience, it was best done before one completed one's University degree. When David returned to Oxford to do that, I was still about the place and it was probably then that our friendship was finally cemented.

With Greats behind him, David returned to Scotland and in due course was called to the Scottish Bar. Quite soon, as a busy Junior, he became Clerk of Faculty of Advocates. He took Silk in 1974, one year after the accession of the United Kingdom to the European Communities.

Until then, the opportunities for English and Scottish legal practitioners to work together had been limited. But with accession to the Communities, that changed and on two occasions I had the pleasure of working professionally with David. The first was the *AM&S* case,[1] about which Dr John Temple Lang has written in a paper published in this book.

In that case, I had the privilege of acting as Leading Counsel for AM&S with Christopher Bellamy (now Sir Christopher Bellamy QC) as my Junior and his fellow author, Graham Child, as my Instructing Solicitor.

The EC Commission was investigating certain believed arrangements relating to the marketing of zinc. On a visit to the company, Commission officials, armed with a Community warrant, had sought to inspect certain company files, the contents of which included legal advice. In fact, there was only one document that we really preferred not to produce—on account of its possibly prejudicial, rather than any evidentiary, value. But we could scarcely let the Commission officials inspect all the other legal advice, wholly irrelevant to the Commission's investigations and entirely innocuous, and withhold just that one document. So we claimed what a British lawyer would call 'legal professional privilege' for the legal advice documents as a whole. There being no Community law precedent to support our claim, the Commission understandably did not accept it. So our claim had to be tested in the European Court of Justice (this being in the days before there was a Court of First Instance). In the ECJ the Commission was represented by John Temple Lang, so we could be assured of a vigorous debate.

Now, the reason for this apparent digression is that the principal source of relevant legal material was a book written by David Edward and published in 1976; and by a stroke of good fortune—for AM&S—David was President of the EC Consultative Committee of Bars and Law Societies when we launched our application in the ECJ. David rightly perceived that the outcome of our application would have implications going far beyond the administration of competition law within the common market and, in particular, that unless something in the nature of legal professional privilege was recognised in the Community, West European lawyers would be ill-placed to support their colleagues in East Europe, behind what was then the Iron Curtain, if the police in those non-

---

[1] Case 155/79 *AM&S* v *Commission* [1982] ECR 1575.

democratic States, were free without restriction to raid law offices to collect material for use against the lawyers' clients.

At David's instance, therefore, the CCBE decided to apply to intervene in the *AM&S* case in favour of AM&S. The ECJ recognised that the CCBE had a sufficient interest in the subject matter of the case and granted the CCBE's application to intervene.

The CCBE's support was probably vital. Judge Bosco's initial reaction to AM&S's application was evidently that it was an Anglo-Saxon try-on (remember that the United Kingdom and Ireland had acceded to the Community only some six years before AM&S's application). But with the support of the CCBE and recognition by that great Advocate General, J-P Warner, that the claim raised issues of substantial constitutional importance, a full *plenum* of eleven Judges was assembled to hear the case. I believe that it was David's authoritative submissions that were probably decisive. Although AM&S was required to disclose the documents in issue to the Advocate General, Sir Gordon Slynn (as he then was) who had succeeded J-P Warner, to enable him to verify their contents, the principle of protection of legitimate legal confidence was established and AM&S was not required to disclose any of the documents to the Commission (and this, paradoxically, despite the fact that, although the ECJ did not recognise a privilege as attaching to the advice of in-house lawyers, the one potentially embarrassing document had emanated from an in-house lawyer).

David's valuable work as President of the CCBE was recognised in London by his appointment as a Companion of the Order of St. Michael and St. George and very gratifyingly also in Madrid, at a time when Spain was coming back into democratic Europe, with the Distinguished Cross, First Class, Order of St. Raymond of Penafort.

The other Community law case on which David and I worked together was the *IBM* case, of which only the tip of the iceberg found its way into the case law.[2] In that case David's knowledge of public international law as well as of Community law was of great value to other members of the legal team (one might almost say army of lawyers) working on the case.

In 1985, the year after I returned to England after seven years practice in Brussels, David took a step which is, I believe, regrettably rare in the United Kingdom: he gave up practice at the Bar to become Salvesen Professor of European Institutions in Edinburgh; a valuable by-product of that period has been his ability to recruit several of his Legal Secretaries in Luxembourg from amongst his former Edinburgh students.

In 1989, however, David was lured away from Edinburgh to become a Judge of the Court of First Instance of the European Communities on the formation of that Court; and in 1992, when most unusually the CFI appointed one of their number to act as Advocate General, he delivered a masterly Opinion.[3] Later in

---

[2] Joined Cases 60/81R & 190/81R *IBM v Commission* [1981] ECR 1857 and 2639.
[3] See Case T-24/90 *Automec srl v Commission* [1992] ECR II – 2283. See the contribution in this volume by Professor Rosa Greaves on this topic.

that year, when Sir Gordon Slynn, shortly to become Lord Slynn of Hadley, returned to London from the ECJ, there was speculation about who would succeed him. Perhaps mindful of the reproaches ('Another Scotch job') levelled by *The Times* at an earlier Scottish Lord Chancellor when he elevated, to the English High Court Bench, a fellow Scot (a great lawyer who in due course was to become a Lord of Appeal in Ordinary), the Lord Chancellor, Lord Mackay of Clashfern may have had a concern that the appointment to the ECJ of another Scot, so soon after Lord Mackenzie Stuart, could be resented by the English legal establishment. If so, inquiries would have swiftly and correctly dissipated any such concern. The esteem in which David is held by English Judges and practitioners is evidence by his election, which followed hard on the heels of his appointment to the ECJ, as an Honorary Bencher of Gray's Inn.

I believe that David's career is marked not just by its distinction but because of the great affection, as well as respect, that he has inspired from his professional colleagues and Judges of the Court of Session when he practised in Edinburgh as an advocate, from his academic colleagues and students when he occupied the Salvesen Chair and from his judicial colleagues, his Legal Secretaries and those who have appeared before him as a Judge of the Courts of the European Communities. I have no doubt that his knowledge, experience and judgment will continue to be in demand.

Sir Jeremy Lever
London
September 2003

Preface

Being part of the Edward Cabinet in Luxembourg was a great privilege…and also great fun. As anyone who has appeared in front of David Edward will know, he has exacting standards as a judge. Woe betide any lawyer who appeared in front of him without being fully prepared. However, his stern manner on the bench was quickly left behind when he returned to the Cabinet. It may sound clichéd, but the Edward Cabinet really was one, big happy family. The outward manifestation of that was clear to anyone who happened to lunch in the Court's canteen. The Edward clan was invariably there *en masse*, and would often depart on a quick walk round the Court buildings after lunch for a bit of fresh air before getting back to work.

When we learned that David, invariably addressed by all in the Cabinet as 'the Professor', was retiring from his position in Luxembourg, we knew we had to organise a book in his honour. Our task was made easier by the eagerness of the contributors to be involved in the project and to contribute essays, in English or French, on a wide variety of topics with which David has been closely associated. We are indebted to them all for their participation. We also wish to thank Freshfields Bruckhaus Deringer, and notably Rob Wills, Nicholas Gibson, David Ashton and Mark Boyle, without whose assistance we would not have been able to produce this book.

The first piece is by Diane Hansen-Ingram, who was the Professor's 'right-hand woman' for many years. Along with Liz Willocks, she formed part of the original Edward Cabinet when the Professor became the first British judge at the Court of First Instance in 1989. Both Liz and Diane were responsible for setting the high standards of friendliness and efficiency that have epitomised the Edward Cabinet throughout David's time in Luxembourg. It seemed only fitting that Diane should be asked to contribute the introductory piece to this book.

Of course, when one talks about the Edward Cabinet, it is impossible to omit mention of Mrs Edward, known to all, including the Professor, as 'the Boss'. Elizabeth was very much a member of the Cabinet. Great fun, great company and a tireless worker in entertaining visiting groups of judges, academics and students.

We would like to finish by indicating our own personal gratitude to the Professor. We have both benefited enormously from his learning, but most of all from his friendship. We are sure we speak for everyone in wishing both David, and Elizabeth, a long and happy retirement.

Mark Hoskins and William Robinson
London
August 2003

List of Contributors

Sir Christopher Bellamy QC, President of the Competition Appeal Tribunal, London, former Judge at the Court of First Instance of the European Communities

Joxerramon Bengoetxea, Ph.D. (Edinburgh), Professor Titular of Jurisprudence, University of the Basque Country in San Sebastian, référendaire to Judge Edward (1993–1998 and 2001–2004)

Christine Boch, Directorate of Legal Services, Scottish Parliament, formerly lecturer in the Europa Institute (University of Edinburgh)

The Honourable Lord Clarke, Judge of the Court of Session

Mark Clough QC, Partner, Solicitor Advocate, Ashurst Morris Crisp

The Right Honourable Lord Clyde, former Lord of Appeal in Ordinary

Julio Baquero Cruz, LL.M. (College of Europe, Bruges), Ph.D. (EUI, Florence), référendaire to President Rodríguez Iglesias, Court of Justice of the European Communities (2000–2003)

Marie Demetriou, Barrister, Brick Court Chambers, London, former référendaire to Judge Edward (1999–2001)

Claus-Dieter Ehlermann, Senior Counsel, Wilmer, Cutler & Pickering, Brussels, former Member and Chairman of the Appellate Body of the WTO, and Director-General of Competition and of the Legal Service, European Commission

Ian Forrester QC, White & Case LLP, Brussels, and Visiting Professor, University of Glasgow

Nicholas Forwood QC, Judge at the Court of First Instance of the European Communities

Professor Rosa Greaves, Allen & Overy Professor of European Law, Director of the Durham European Law Institute, University of Durham

Diane Hansen-Ingram, Secretary to Judge Edward (1989–1998)

Imelda Higgins, Barrister, Dublin, former référendaire to Judge Edward (1999–2000)

Mark Hoskins, Barrister, Brick Court Chambers, London, former référendaire to Judge Edward (1994–1995)

Anneli Howard, Barrister, Monckton Chambers, London, former référendaire to Judge Edward (2000–2003)

xviii *List of Contributors*

Gil Carlos Rodríguez Iglesias, President (1994–2003) and Judge (1986–2003) of the Court of Justice of the European Communities

Francis G Jacobs QC, Advocate General, Court of Justice of the European Communities

Dr Dieter Kraus, référendaire to Judge Edward (1998–2004)

Dr Robert Lane, School of Law (Europa Institute), University of Edinburgh

John Temple Lang, Cleary, Gottlieb, Steen and Hamilton, Brussels, Professor, Trinity College, Dublin and Senior Visiting Research Fellow, Oxford

Sir Jeremy Lever KCMG, QC, Monckton Chambers, London, and Fellow and Senior Dean of All Souls College, Oxford

Nicolas Lockhart, counsellor with the Appellate Body Secretariat of the WTO (currently on leave of absence) and former référendaire to Judge Edward (1995–1998)

Richard Plender QC, LLD (Cantab), Judge of the Employment Appeal Tribunal, Recorder, Senior Member Robinson College Cambridge, Visiting Professor, City University London, former référendaire, Court of Justice of the European Communities, Director of the Centre of European Law at King's College London and professeur associé, Université de Paris II

Deok Joo Rhee, Barrister, 11 King's Bench Walk Chambers, référendaire to Judge Edward (2003–2004)

William Robinson, Partner, Freshfields Bruckhaus Deringer, former référendaire to Judge Edward (1995–1999)

The Rt Hon Lord Rodger of Earlsferry, Lord of Appeal in Ordinary

Leif Sevón, President of the Supreme Court of Finland, and former Judge at the Court of Justice of the European Communities

Eleanor Sharpston QC, Hailsham Chambers, London, Fellow in Law, King's College Cambridge, and Senior Research Fellow, Centre for European Legal Studies, Cambridge

Judge Bo Vesterdorf, President of the Court of First Instance of the European Communities

Judge Melchior Wathelet, Professor of European Law at the Catholic University of Louvain (Belgium) and Judge at the Court of Justice of the European Communities

Elizabeth Willocks, Administrator, DG E I Enlargement, General Secretariat of the Council of the European Union, former référendaire to Judge Edward (1989–1992 (CFI) and 1992–1994 (ECJ)) and to President Gil Carlos Rodríguez Iglesias (1995- 2000)

Table of Cases

EUROPEAN COURT OF JUSTICE

Cases listed in numerical order

Case 13/61 *De Gens* v. *Bosch* [1962] ECR 45... 304
Case 25/62 *Plaumann* v. *Commission* [1963] ECR 95 312
Case 26/62 *van Gend en Loos* v. *Nederlandse Administratie der*
  Belastingen [1963] ECR 1 .... 54, 83, 235, 307, 311, 314, 327, 330, 365, 385
Joined Cases 28-30/62 *da Costa en Schaake NV and ors* v. *Nederlandse*
  Belastingsadministratie [1963] ECR 31.. 330
Case 6/64 *Costa* v. *ENEL* [1964] ECR 585..54, 327, 330–1, 333
Case 61/65 *Vaassen-Göbbels* v. *Management of the Beambtenfonds voor hat*
  Mijnbedrif [1966] ECR 261.. 262
Case 19/67 *Sociale Verzekeringsbank* v. *Van der Vecht* [1967] ECR 345 304
Case 34/67 *Firma Gebrüden Lück* v. *Hauptzollamt Köln-Rheinau*
  [1968] ECR 359, 372
Case 27/69 *Caisse de maladie des CFL "Enrt'aide medicale" and Société nationale des*
  chemins de fer luxembourgeois v. *Compagnie belge d'assurances générales*
  sur la vie et contre les accidents [1969] ECR 405 262
Case 77/69 *Commission* v. *Belgium* [1970] ECR 237 54
Case 78/70 *Deutsche Grammophon Gesellschaft mbH* v. *Metro-SB-*
  Großmärkte GmbH & Co KG [1971] ECR 487.. 342
Case 22/71 *Béguelin Import* v. *G.L. Import Export* [1971] ECR 949 166
Case 84/71 *Spot Marmet* v. *Ministero delle Finaze* [1972] ECR 89............................. 372
Case 93/71 *Orsohl Lenesio* v. *Ministero dell'agricoltura e foreste* [1972] ECR....287, 372
Case 5/72 *Fratelli Grassi* [1972] ECR 443... 348
Joined Cases 21-24/72 *International Fruit Company NV et al* v. *Produktschap voor*
  Groenten en Fruit [1972] ECR 1219 234
Case 81/72 *Commission* v *Council* [1973] ECR 575 45
Case 40/73 *Suiker Unie* v. *Commission* [1975] ECR 1663... 163
Case 127/73 *BRT* v. *SABAM* [1974] ECR 51.. 94
Case 166/73 *Rheinmülen* [1974] ECR 33 .... 346–7, 351
Case 167/73 *Commission* v. *France* [1974] ECR 359.. 372
Case 181/73 *Haegeman* v. *Belgium* [1974] ECR 449 235
Case 32/74 *Freidrich Haagen GmbH* [1974] ECR 1201 370
Case 41/74 *Van Duyn* v. *Home Office* [1974] ECR 1337... 359
Case 11/75 *Impresa Costruzioni comm Quirino Mazzalai* v. *Ferroria del*
  Penon [1976] ECR 657... 370
Case 43/75 *Defrenne* v. *SABENA* [1976] ECR 455.. 311
Case 11/76 *Netherlands* v. *Commission* [1979] ECR 245... 178
Case 26/76 *Metro* v. *Commission* [1977] 1875 94
Case 33/76 *Rewe-Zentralfinanz* [1976] ECR 1989 317

xx Table of Cases

Case 45/76 *Comet* [1976] ECR 2043 317
Case 51/76 *Verbond van Nederlandse Ondernemingen* v. *Inspecteur der
   Invoerrechten en Accijnzen* [1977] ECR 113 .... 309, 378
Case 52/76 *Benedetti* v. *Munari* [1977] ECR 163 341
Case 85/76 *Hoffman-La Roche* v. *Commission* [1979] ECR 461 .... 163, 175
Case 30/77 *Bouchereau* [1977] ECR 1999 .... 241, 305
Case 106/77 *Amministrazione delle Finanze dello Stato* v. *Simmenthal SpA*
   [1978] ECR 629 .... 327, 372
Case 83/78 *Redmond* [1978] ECR 2347 57
Case 92/78 *Simmenthal* v. *Commission* [1979] ECR 777 45
Case 93/78 *Mattheus* v. *Doego Fruchtimport und Tiefkülkost eG* [1978]
   ECR 2203 333
Case 120/78 *Rewe-Zentral* v. *Bundesmonopolverwaltung fur Branntwein*
   [1979] ECR 649 195
Case 125/78 *GEMA* v. *Commission* [1979] ECR 3173 94
Case 104/79 *Foglia* v. *Novello* (No 1) [1980] ECR 745 334–5
Case 105/79 *Preliminary Ruling by the Acting Judge at the Tribunal d'Instance,
   Hayange* (No. 1) [1979] ECR 2257 333
Case 109/79 *Maïseries de Beauce* v. *Office National Interprofessionnel des Céréals*
   [1980] ECR 2883 341
Case 149/79 *Commission* v. *Belgium* [1982] ECR 1845 54
Case 155/79 *AM & S Europe Ltd* v. *Commission* [1982] ECR 1575 .... x, xi, 153–60
Case 157/79 *Pieck* [1980] ECR 2171 239
Case 53/80 *Officier van Justitie* v. *Koninklijke Kaasfabriek Eyssen* [1981] ECR 409 ... 216
Case 66/80 *International Chemical Corporation (ICI)* v. *Amministrazione
   delle Finanze dello Stato* [1981] ECR 329
Case 68/80 *Preliminary Ruling by the Acting Judge at the Tribunal d'Instance,
   Hayange* (No. 2) [1980] ECR 771 333
Case 113/80 *Commission* v. *Ireland* [1981] ECR 1625 198
Case 126/80 *Salonia* v. *Poidomani and anor* [1981] ECR 1563 335
Case 158/80 *Rewe-Handelsgesellschaft* [1981] ECR 1805 318
Case 172/80 *Zuchner* v. *Bayerische Vereinsbank AG* [1981] ECR 2021 163
Case 244/80 *Foglia* v. *Novello* (No 2) [1981] ECR 3045 334
Case 270/80 *Polydor Limited and RSO Records Inc.* v. *Harlequin Records Shops
   Limited and Simons Records Limited* [1982] ECR 329 .... 236, 385
Case 59/81 *Commission* v *Council* [1982] ECR 3329 45
Joined Cases 60/81R to 190/81R *IBM* v. *Commission* [1981] ECR 1857 and 2639 xi
Case 65/81 *Reina & Reina* v. *Landeskreditbank Baden-Württemberg*
   [1982] ECR 33 332
Case 104/81 *Hauptzollamt Mainz* v. *Kupferberg & Cie KgaA*
   [1982] ECR 3641 .... 236, 385
Joined Cases 141/81 to 143/81 *Holdijk* [1982] ECR 1299 57
Case 210/81 *Demo-Studio Schmidt* [1983] ECR 3045 94
Case 266/81 *Società Italiana per l'Oleodotto Transalpino (SIOT)* v. *Ministero delle
   Finanze, Ministero della Marina mercantile, Circoscrizione doganale di Trieste
   and Ente Autonomo del Porto di Trieste* [1983] ECR 731 234
Case 283/81 *CILFIT* v. *Ministry of Health* [1982]
   ECR 3415 .... 301, 303, 329, 330, 346, 348–9

Table of Cases   xxi

Case 322/81 *Michelin* v. *Commission* [1983] ECR 3461 166
Case 169/82 *Commission* v. *Italy* [1984] ECR 1603 54
Case 327/82 *EKRO* v. *Produktschap voor Vee en Vlees* [1984] ECR 107 302
Case 14/83 *Von Colson and Kamann* v. *Land Nordrhein-Westfalen*
 [1984] ECR 1891..317–8, 370
Case 24/83 *Gewiese & Mehlich* v. *MacKenzie (PF Stornoway)* [1984] ECR 817 328
Case 97/83 *Criminal proceedings against CMC Melkunie BV* [1984] ECR 2367 216
Case 294/83 *Les Verts* v. *European Parliament* [1986] ECR 1339............................... 71
Case 298/83 *CICCE* v. *Commission* [1985] ECR 1105.. 94
Case 17/84 *Commission* v *Germany (beer)* [1987] ECR 1227 216
Case 152/84 *Marshall* v. *Southampton and South-West Hampshire Area Health
 Authority (Teaching)* [1986] ECR 723 .... 310, 376
Case 35/85 *Procureur de la République* v. *Tissier* [1986] ECR 1207 342
Case 54/85 *Ministère public* v. *Xavier Mirepoix* [1986] ECR 1067 216
Case 69/85 *Wünsche Handelsgesellschaft GmbH & Co* v. *Germany*
 [1986] ECR 947 341
Joined Cases 98, 162 & 258/85 *Bertini and ors* v. *Regione Lazio and anor*
 [1986] ECR 1885 331
Case 199/85 *Commission* v. *Italy* [1987] ECR 1039.. 54
Case 314/85 *Foto-Frost* v. *Hauptzollamt Lübeck-Ost*
 [1987] ECR 4199...83, 312, 319, 329–30, 346, 356
Joined Cases 372-374/85 *Ministére public* v. *Oscar Traen
 et autres* [1987] ECR 2141 376
Case 12/86 *Demirel* v. *Stadt Swäbisch Gmünd* [1987]
 ECR 3719 .... 235, 238, 385
Case 14/86 *Pretore di Salò* v. *Persons Unknown* [1987] ECR 2545 333
Case 66/86 *Ahmed Saeed Flugreisen and others* v. *Zentrale zur Bekämpfung
 unlauteren Wettbewerbs e.V.* [1989] ECR 803 171
Case 68/86 *United Kingdom* v. *Council* [1988] ECR 855 218
Case 79/86 *Hamilton (PF Dunfermline)* v. *Whitelock* [1987] ECR 2363 328
Case 80/86 *Kolpinghuis Nijmegen* [1987] ECR 3969 .... 314, 376
Case 118/86 *Nertsvoederfabriek Nederland* [1987] ECR 3883...................................... 57
Case 197/86 *Brown* v. *Secretary of State for Scotland* [1988] ECR 3205 328
Case 247/86 *Alcatel* v. *Novasam* [1988] ECR 5987 163
Case 30/87 *Bodson* v. *SA Pompes funèbres des regions libérées* [1988] ECR 2479.......167
Case 45/87 *Commission* v. *Ireland* [1998] ECR 4929... 54
Case 70/87 *Fediol* v. *Commission* [1989] ECR 1781 387
Case 380/87 *Enichen Base* v. *Comme di Cinisello Balsamo* [1989] ECR 2491 375
Case 103/88 *Fratelli Costanzo SpA* v. *Comune di Milano*
 [1989] ECR 1839..55, 363, 376
Joined Cases C-143/88 and C-92/89 *Zuckerfabrik Süderdithmarschen
 and Zuckerfabrik Soest* [1991] ECR I-415 319–20
Case 145/88 *Torfaen Borough Council* v. *B & Q plc* [1989] ECR 3851 340
Case C-221/88 *CECA* v. *Fillite Acciaierie e Ferriere Busseni SpA* [1990] ECR I-495...376
Case C-262/88 *Barber* v. *Guardian Royal Exchange Assurance Group*
 [1990] ECR I-1889 376
Case C-286/88 *Falciola Angelo SpA* v. *Comune di Pavia* [1990] ECR I-191 335
Joined Cases C-297/88 and C-197/89 *Dzodzi* v. *Belgium* [1990] ECR I-3763 333

Case C-326/88 *Hansen* [1990] ECR I-2911 312
Case 370/88 *Walkingshaw (PF Stranraer)* v. *Marshall* [1990] ECR I-4071 .... 328, 339
Case C-49/89 *Corsica Ferries France* v. *Direction générale des douanes Françaises*
   [1989] ECR I- 4441 195
Case C-69/89 *Nakajima All precision Co Ltd* v. *Council* [1991] ECR I-2069 387
Joined Cases C-100-101/89 *Kaefer & Procacci* v. *French State* [1990] ECR I-4647 332
Case C-106/89 *Marleasing* [1990] ECR I-4135 .... 300, 314, 364, 371
Case C-188/89 *Foster* v. *British Gas* [1990] ECR I-3313 309
Case C-192/89 *SZ Sevince* v. *Staatssecretaris van Justitie*
   [1990] ECR I-3461 .... 236, 238, 239
Case C-205/89 *Commission* v. *Hellenic Republic* [1991] ECR I-1361 195
Case C-213/89 *R* v. *Secretary of State for Transport*, ex parte *Factortame Ltd*
   [1990] ECR I-2433 .... 315, 317, 318, 319, 327
Case C-298/89 *Government of Gibraltar* v. *Council* [1993] ECR I-3605 63
Case C-340/89 *Vlassopoulou* v. *Ministerium für Justiz, Bundes- und
   Europaangelegenheiten Baden-Württemberg* [1991] ECR I-2357 .... 249-52, 254, 256
Case C-355/89 *Department of Health and Social Security* v. *Barr &
   Montrose Holdings Ltd* [1991] ECR I-3479 332
Case C-1/90 *Aragonesa de Publicidad Exterior SA and Publivia SAE* v. *Departmento
   de Sandidad y Seguridad Social de la Generalitat de Cataluña* [1991] ECR I-4151 ...55
Case C-2/90 *Commission* v. *Belgium* [1992] ECR I-4431 198
Joined Cases C-6/90 and C-9/90 *Francovich and Bonifaci* v. *Italy*
   [1991] ECR I-5357 .... 309, 314, 318, 327, 380, 381
Case C-18/90 *Office national de l'emploi* v. *Kziber* [1991] ECR I-199 386
Joined Cases C-87/90, C-88/90 and C-89/90 *Verholen* [1991]
   ECR I-3757 315
Case C-208/90 *Emmott* v. *Minister for Social Welfare* [1991]
   ECR I-4269 323
Joined Cases C-251 & 252/90 *Wither (PF Elgin)* v. *Cowie & Wood*
   [1992] ECR I-2873 328
Case C-260/90 *Leplat* v. *Territory of French Polynesia* [1992] ECR I-643 332
Case C-320/90 *Telemarsicabruzzo SpA and ors* v. *Circostel and ors*
   [1993] ECR I-393 336
Case C-343/90 *Lourenço Dias* v. *Director da Alfândega do Porto*
   [1992] ECR I-4673 335
Case C-69/91 *Decoster* [1993] ECR I-5335 373
Case C-83/91 *Meilicke* v. *ADV/ORGA AG* [1992] ECR I-4871 335
Case C-104/91 *Colegio Nacional de Agentes de la Propiedad Inmobiliaria* v. *Aguirre
   Borrell and Others* [1992] ECR I-3003 251
Case C-169/91 *Council of the City of Stoke-on-Trent* v. *B & Q plc*
   [1992] ECR I-6635 340
Case C-206/91 *Ettien Koua Poirrez* v. *Caisse d'allocations familiales de la region
   parisienne* [1992] ECR I-6685 262
Case C-212/91 *Angelopharm GmbH* v. *Freie und Hansestadt Hamburg*
   [1994] ECR I-171 .... 224, 225
Case C-237/91 *Kus* v. *Landeshauptstadt Wiesbaden* [1992] ECR I-6781 .... 238, 239
Joined Cases C-267/91 and 268/91 *Keck and Mithouard* [1993] ECR I-6097 ...... 194, 340
Case C-338/91 *Steenhorst-Neerings* [1993] ECR I-5475 323

Case C-11/92 *Secretary of State for Health, ex parte Gallaher Limited, Imperial Tobacco Limited and Rothmans International Tobacco (UK) Limited* [1993] ECR I-3545 65
Case C-91/92 *Faccini Dori* v. *Recreb Srl* [1994] ECR I-3325 .... 310, 314, 353, 371, 376
Case C-157/92 *Pretore di Genova* v. *Banchero ('Banchero I')*
[1993] ECR I-1085 .... 334, 336
Case C-188/92 *TWD Textilwerke Deggendorf GmbH* v. *Germany*
[1994] ECR I-833 335
Case C-262/92 *Sürül* v. *Bunlevanstalt für Arbeit* [1999] ECR I-2685 .... 244, 386
Case C-319/92 *Haim* v. *Kassenzahnärztliche Vereinigung Nordrhein*
[1994] ECR I-425 .... 250–1, 253
Case C-334/92 *Wagner Miret* v. *Fondo de garantia Salarial* [1993] ECR I-6911 371
Case C-386/92 *Monin Automobiles - Maison du Deux-Roues (No 1)*
[1993] ECR I-2049 336
Case C-393/92 *Almelo and others* v. *NV Energiebedrijf Ijsselmij* [1994]
ECR I-1477... 164, 167, 168, 171, 173
Case C-410/92 *Johnson* v. *Chief Adjudication Officer* [1994] ECR I-5483................. 323
Case C-431/92 *Commission* v. *Germany* [1995] ECR I-2189..................................... 354
Joined Cases C-46/93 and C-48/93 *Brasserie du Pêcheur and
Factortame* [1996] ECR I-1029 .... 309, 314, 318, 319, 321, 327, 381–4
Case C-52/93 *Commission* v. *Netherlands* [1994] ECR I-3591 373
Case C-154/93 *Tawil-Albertini* v. *Ministre des Affaires Sociales* [1994] ECR I-451 ... 251
Case C-297/93 *Grau-Hupka* v. *Stadtgemeinde Bremen* [1994] ECR I-5535................ 335
Case C-306/93 *SMW Winzersekt GmbH* v. *Land Rheinland-Pfalz*
[1994] ECR I-5555 334
Case C-312/93 *Peterbroeck* v. *Belgium* [1995] ECR I-4599.. 346
Case C-316/93 *Vaneetveld* v. *Le Foyer SA* [1994] ECR I-763 .... 336, 376
Case C-323/93 *Société Civile Agricole du Centre d'Insémination de la Crespelle* v.
*Coopérative d'Elevage et d'Insémination Artificielle du Département de la
Mayenne* [1994] ECR I-5077 167
Case C-355/93 *Eroglu* v. *Land Baden-Württemberg* [1994] ECR I-5131............. 240, 242
Case C-378/93 *La Pyramide SARL* [1994] ECR I-3999 336
Case C-387/93 *Criminal proceedings against Giorgio Domingo Banchero*
('Banchero II') [1995] ECR I-4663 334
Case C-392/93 *The Queen* v. *HM Treasury, ex parte British Telecommunications
plc* [1996] ECR I-1631 383–4
Case C-415/93 *Bosman* [1995] ECR I-4921 .... 168, 310, 335
Joined Cases C-418 etc/93 *Semeraro Casa Uno Srl and ors* v. *Comune di
Erbusco and ors* [1996] ECR I-2975... 340
Joined Cases C-430/93 and C-431/93 *van Schijndel* v. *SPF* [1995] ECR I-4705........... 346
Case C-434/93 *Bozkurt* v. *Staatssecretaris van Justitie* [1995] ECR I-1475 .... 237, 271
Case C-5/94 *The Queen* v. *Ministry of Agriculture, Fisheries and Food,
ex parte Hedley Lomas (Ireland) Ltd* [1996] ECR I-2553....................................... 384
Joined Cases C-68/94 and C-30/95 *France and Others* v *Commission*
[1998] ECR I–1375 .... 119, 121, 140, 143, 161–2, 173–9, 181–3
Case C-84/94 *United Kingdom* v. *Council* [1996] ECR I-5755 59
Case C-96/94 *Centro Servizi Spediporto Srl* v. *Spedizioni Marittima del
Golfo Srl* [1995] ECR I-2883 164

Case C-111/94 *Job Centre Coop. Sarl* [1995] ECR I-3361 335
Case C-129/94 *Ruiz Bernàldez* [1996] ECR I-8129 380
Joined Cases C-140/94, C-141/94 and C-142/94 *DIP SpA* v. *Comune di Bassano del Grappa and Comune di Chioggia* [1995] ECR I-3257 .... 164, 168
Case C-167/94 *Grau Gomis and ors* [1995] ECR I-1023 333
Joined Cases C-178/94, C-179/94, C-188/94, C-189/94 et C-190/94 *Dillenkofer and Others* v. *Germany* [1996] ECR I-4845 384
Case C-194/94 *CIA Security International SA* v. *Signalson SA & Securitel SPRL* [1996] ECR I-2201 .... 195, 309, 310, 354, 365, 373, 377, 379–80
Case C-253/94P *Roujansky* v. *Council* [1995] ECR I-7 333
Case C-277/94 *Taflan Met, Altun-Basar and Andal-Bugdayaci* v. *Bestuur van de Sociale Verzckeringsbank* [1996] ECR I-4085 243–4
Joined Cases C-283/94, C-291/94 and C-292/94 *Denkavit* v. *Bundesamt für Finazen* [1996] ECR I-5063 383
Case C-346/94 *City of Glasgow District Council* v. *Kleinwort Benson* [1995] ECR I-615 333
Case C-28/95 *Leur-Bloem* v. *Inspecteur der Belastingdienst/Ondernemingen Amsterdam* [1997] ECR I-4161 333
Case C-30/95 *Max Mara Fashion Group Srl* v. *Ufficio del Registro di Reggio Emilia* [1995] ECR I-5083 333
Case C-66/95 *R* v. *Secretary of State for Social Security, ex parte Sutton* [1997] ECR I-2163 323
Case C-72/95 *Kraaijeveld and Others* v. *Gedeputeerde Staten van Zuid-Holland* [1996] ECR I-5403 .... 309, 354, 365, 367
Case C-87/95P *CNPAAP* v. *Council* [1996] ECR I-2003 312
Joined Cases C-94/95 and C-95/95 *Bonifaci and Others* [1997] ECR I-4006 384
Case C-130/95 *Giloy* v. *Hauptzollamt Frankfurt am Main-Ost* [1997] ECR I-4291 ... 333
Case C-168/95 *Arcaro* [1996] ECR I-4705 .... 314, 376
Case C-171/95 *Recip Tetik* v. *Land Berlin* [1997] ECR I-329 240
Case C-178/95 *Wiljo NV* v. *Belgium* [1997] ECR I-585 335
Case C-261/95 *Palmisani* v. *INPS* [1997] ECR I-4025 .... 320, 384
Joined Cases C-267/95 and C-268/95 *Merck & Co. Inc. and Others* v. *Primecrown and others* [1996] ECR I-6285 178
Case C-285/95 *Kol* v. *Land Berlin* [1997] ECR I-3069 242
Case C-296/95 *R* v. *Commissioners of Customs and Excise, ex parte EMU Tabac and Others* [1998] ECR I-1605 304
Case C-299/95 *Kremzow* v. *Austria* [1997] ECR I-2629 333
Case C-337/95 *Parfums Christian Dior SA and anor* v. *Evora BV* [1997] ECR I-6013 332
Case C-338/95 *Wiener SI GmbH* v. *Hauptzollamt Emmerich* [1997] ECR I-6495 .... 330, 342, 349–51
Case C-351/95 *Kadiman* v. *Fieistaat Bayern* [1997] ECR I-2133 243
Case C-367/95P *Commission* v. *Sytraval et Brink's France SARL* [1998] ECR I-1719 ... 389
Case C-373/95 *Federica Maso and Others* [1997] ECR I-4051 384
Case C-386/95 *Eker* v. *Land Baden-Württemberg* [1997] ECR I-2697 240
Case C-388/95 *Belgium* v. *Spain* [2000] ECR I-3123 363
Case C-1/96 *Compassion In World Farming* [1998] ECR I-1251 57
Case C-36/96 *Günaydin* [1997] ECR I-5143 .... 241, 242

Case C-67/96 *Albany* [1999] ECR I-5751 201
Case C-85/96 *Maritínez Sala* v. *Freistaat Bayern* [1998] ECR I-2691 244
Joined Cases C-95 and C-96/96 *URSSAF des Bouches-du-Rhône* v.
    Clinique Florens SA, Order of 12 June 1996, unreported 333
Case C-98/96 *Ertanir* v. *Land Hessen* [1997] ECR I-5179 241
Case C-126/96 *Marie Brizard & Roger International SA* v. *Wm Grant and Sons
    (International) and anor* removed from the Register by Order of
    25 February 1997 328
Case C-129/96 *Inter-Environnement Wallonie ASBL* v. *Région Wallone*
    [1997] ECR I-7411 .... 362, 364, 365
Case C-149/96 *Portugal* v. *Council* [1999] ECR I-8395 .... 385, 387
Case C-157/96 *National Farmers' Union and Others* [1998] ECR I-2211 216
Case C-170/96 *Commission* v. *Council* [1998] ECR I-2763 235
Case C-171/96 *Pereira Roque* v. *HE The Lieutenant Governor of Jersey*
    [1998] ECR I-4607 332
Case C-176/96 *Lehtonen & Castors Canada Dry Namur-Braine ASBL* v. *Fédération
    Royale Belge des Sociétés de Basket-ball ASBL* [2000] ECR I-2681 336
Case C-203/96 *Chemische Afvalstoffen Dusseldorp* [1998] ECR I-4075 201
Case C-246/96 *Magorrian* v. *Eastern Health and Social Services Board*
    [1997] ECR I-7153 319
Case C-262/96 *Sürül* v. *Bundesanstalt für Arbeit* [1999] ECR I-2685 243
Case C-274/96 *Bickel and Franz* [1998] ECR I-7637 244
Case C-309/96 *Annibaldi* [1997] ECR I-7493 57
Case C-323/96 *Commission* v. *Belgium* [1998] ECR I-5063 54
Case C-326/96 *Levez* v. *TH Jennings (Harlow Pools) Ltd*. [1998] ECR I-7835 321–2
Case C-355/96 *Silhouette International Selmied GmbH & Co KG* v.
    Hartlauer Handelsgesellschaft GmbH [1998] ECR I-4799 376
Case C-389/96 *Aher-Waggon* [1998] ECR I-4473 199
Case C-394/96 *Brown* v. *Rentokil Ltd* [1998] ECR I-4185 328
Joined Cases C-395/96P and C-396/96P *Compagnie Maritime Belge SA and Dafra
    –Lines A/S* v. *Commission* [2000] ECR I-1365 ... 119, 161–2, 165, 169, 170–4, 177, 186
Case C–1/97 *Mehmet Birden* v. *Stadtgemeinde Bremen* [1998] ECR I-7747 241
Case C-95/97 *Région Wallonne* v. *Commission* [1997] ECR I-1787 62
Case C-104/97P *Atlanta* v. *Commission* [1999] ECR I-6983 383
Case C-126/97 *Eco Swiss China Time Ltd* v. *Benetton International
    NV* [1999] ECR I-3055 .... 145, 323
Case C-140/97 *Rechberger and Others* v. *Austria* [1999] ECR I-3499 383
Case C-180/97 *Regione Toscana* v. *Commission* [1997] ECR I-5245 62
Case C-185/97 *Cooke* [1998] ECR I-5199 .... 311, 371
Case C-210/97 *Akman* [1998] ECR I-7519 243
Case C-215/97 *Bellone* v. *Yokohama SpA* [1998] ECR I-2191 371
Case C-234/97 *Fernández de Bobadilla* v. *Museo Nacional del Prado*
    [1999] ECR I-4773 250
Case C-321/97 *Andersson & Wåkerås-Andersson* v. *Sweden* [1999] ECR I-3551 333
Case C-329/97 *Ergat* v. *Stadt Ulm* [2000] ECR I-1487 243
Case C-340/97 *Nazli* v. *Stadt Nürnberg* [2000] ECR I-957 241
Case C-355/97 *Landesgrundverkehrsreferent der Tiroler Landesregierung* v. *Beck
    Liegenschaftsverwaltungsgesellschaft mbH and anor* [1999] ECR I-4977 ...... 333, 336

Case C-394/97 *Heinonen* [1999] ECR I-3599 195
Case C-424/97 *Haim v. Kassenzahnärztliche Vereinigung Nordrhein*
  [2000] ECR I-5123 253
Case C-435/97 *World Wildlife Fund* [1999] ECR I-5613 378
C-440/97 *GIE Groupe Concorde and Others v. Master of the vessel "Suhadiwarno
  Panjan"* [1999] ECR I-6307 257
Case C-37/98 *R v. Secretary of State for the Home Department*, ex parte *Savas*
  [2000] ECR I-2927 242
Case C-65/98 *Eyüp v. Landesgeschäftsstelle des Arbeitmarktservice Vorarlberg*
  [2000] ECR 4747 243
Case C-78/98 *Preston and Fletcher* [2000] ECR I-3201, [2001]
  2 WLR 408 (HL) 318, 323, 325
Cases C-102/98 *Kocak v. Landesversicherungsanstalt Oberfranken und
  Mittelfranken* [2000] ECR I-1287 244
Case C-108/98 *RI.SAN. Srl v. Comune di Ischia, Italia Lavro SpA and
  Ischia Ambiente SpA* [1999] ECR I-5219 262
Case C-165/98 *Mazzoleni & Inter Surveillance Assistance* [2001] ECR I-7823 334
Joined cases C-174/98P and C-189/98P *Kingdom of the Netherlands and gerhard van
  der Wal v Commission* [2000] ECR I-1 148
Case C-195/98 *Österreichischer Gewerkschaftsbund, Gewerkschaft öffentlicher
  Dienst v. Austria* [2000] ECR I-1497 311
Case C-211/98 *Ramazan v. Bundesknappschaft* (C-211/98) [2000] ECR I-1297 244
Case C-224/98 *D'Hoop v. Office national de l'emploi* [2002] ECR I-6191 244
Case C-228/98 *Dounias v. Minister for Economic Affairs* [2000] ECR I-577 195
Case C-238/98 *Hocsman v. Ministre de l'Emploi et de la Solidarité*
  [2000] ECR I-6623 .... 250–2, 255–6
Joined Cases C-240/98 to C-244/98 *Océano Grupo Editorial SA v. Roció Murciano
  Quintero* [2000] ECR I-4941 .... 323, 371, 379–80
Case C-281/98 *Angonese v. Cassa di Risparmio di Bolzano SpA*
  [2000] ECR I-4139 336–8
Case C-287/98 *Grand Duchy of Luxemburg v. Linster and others*
  [2000] ECR I-6917 .... 309, 365, 378, 380
Joined Cases C-300/98 and C-392/98 *Parfums Christian Dior SA v. TUK
  Consultancy BV et Assco Gerüste GmbH* [2000] ECR I-11307 387
Case C-322/98 *Grimaldi v. Fonds des maladies professionnelles* [1989] ECR 4407 371
Case C-344/98 *Masterfoods Ltd v. HB Ice Cream Ltd* [2000] ECR I-11369 151
Case C-352/98 *Laboratoires pharmaceutiques Bergaderm SA and
  Jean-Jacques Goupil v. Commission* [2000] ECR I-5291 383
Case C-365/98 *Brinhmann Tabafabriken GmbH v. Hauptzollamt
  Bielefield* [2000] ECR I-4619 .... 371, 379
Case C-377/98 *Netherlands v. Parliament and Council* [2001] I-7079 .... 73, 387
Case C-379/98 *PreussenElektra* [2001] ECR I-2099 .... 199, 200, 201
Case C-381/98 *Ingmar GB Ltd v. Eaton Leonard Technologies Inc*
  [2000] ECR I-9305 265
Case C-387/98 *Coreck Maritime GmbH v. Handelsveem BV and others*
  [2000] ECR I-9337 257
Case C-410/98 *Metallgesellschaft & Hoechst v. Inland Revenue* [2001]
  ECR I-1727 321

Case C-443/98 *Unilever Italia Spa* v. *Central Food SpA* [2000]
ECR I-7535 .... 309, 310, 365, 376, 380
Case C-448/98 *Guimont* [2000] ECR I-10663 337
Case C-16/99 *Ministre de la Santé* v. *Erpelding* [2000] ECR I-6821 254
Case C-63/99 *R* v. *Secretary of State for the Home Department,*
ex parte *Gloszczuk* [2001] ECR I-6369 .... 237, 240–2, 386
Case C-74/99 *R* v. *Secretary of State for Health and ors,* ex parte
Imperial Tobacco and ors [2000] ECR I-8599 334
Joined Cases C-95/99 to C-98/99 and C-180/99 *Khali and others* v. *Bundesanstalt für
Arbeit* [2001] ECR 7413 262
Case C-184/99 *Grzelczyk* v. *Centre public d'aide social d'Ottignies-
Louvaine-la-Neuve* [2002] ECR I-6193 244
Case C-232/99 *Commission* v. *Spain* [2002] ECR I-4235 250
Case C-235/99 *R* v. *Secretary of State for the Home Department,* ex parte
Kondova [2001] ECR I-6427) 237, 240, 242, 386
Case C-257/99 *R* v. *Secretary of State for the Home Department,* ex parte *Barkoci
and Malik* [2001] ECR I-6557 .... 237, 240, 386
Case C-268/99 *Aldona Malgorzata Jany et al* v. *Staatssecretaris van
Justitie* [2001] ECR I-8615 241
Case C-306/99 *Banque Internationale pour l'Afrique Occidentale SA* v. *Finanzamt
für Großunternehmen in Hamburg* [2003] ECR I-1 333
Case C-307/99 *OGT Fruchthandelsgesellschanft mbH* v. *Hauptzollamt Hamburg-
St Annen* [2001] ECR I-3159 387
Case C-309/99 *Wouters* v. *Nederlandse Orde van Advocaten* [2002]
ECR I-1577 157
Case C-329/99 P(R) *Pfizer Animal Health SA and Others* v. *Commission*
[1999] ECR I-8343 204
Joined Cases C-414/99 to C-416/99 *Zino Davidoff SA* v *A&G Imports Ltd* and *Levi
Strauss & Co et al* v. *Tesco Stores Ltd et al* [2001] ECR I-8691 265
Joined Cases C-430 and 431/99 *Sea-Land Service Inc & Nedlloyd Lijnen
BV* [2002] ECR I-5235 335
Case C-453/99 *Courage* v. *Crehan* [2001] ECR I-6297 .... 308, 311, 318, 321, 342
Case C-459/99 *MRAX* v. *Belgian State* [2002] ECR I-6591 262
Case C-462/99 *Connect Austria Gesellschaft für Telekommunikation GmbH* v.
Telekom-Control-Kommission, judgment of 22 May 2003, not yet reported 327
Joined Cases C-515 etc/99 *Reisch and ors* v. *Bürgermeister der Landeshauptstadt
Salzburg and ors* [2002] ECR I-2157 337
Case C-1/00 *Commission* v. *France* [2001] ECR I- 9989 .... 61, 216
Case 3/00 *Denmark* v. *Commission,* judgment of 20 May 2003, not yet reported 216
Case C-17/00 *de Coster* v. *Collège des Bourgmestres et Echevins de Watermael-
Boitsfort* [2001] ECR I-9445 331
Joined Cases C-20/00 and C-64/00 *Booker Aquaculture Ltd* v. *The Secretary of State
for Scotland,* judgment of 10 July 2003, not yet reported 61, 328, 339
Joined Cases C-27/00 and C-122/00 *R* v. *Secretary of State for the
Environment, Transport and the Regions,* ex parte *Omega Air Ltd
and ors* [2002] ECR I-2569 334
Case C-31/00 *Conseil national de l'ordre des architectes* v. *Dreessen*
[2002] ECR I-663 .... 251–2, 254

Case 50/00P *Unión de Pequeños Agricultores* ('UPA') v. *Council*
[2002] ECR I-6677 .... 64, 76, 159, 308, 319, 339
Case C-60/00 *Carpenter* v. *Secretary of State for the Home Department* [2002]
ECR I-6279 262
Case C-62/00 *Marks & Spencer* [2002] ECR I-6325 314
Case C-64/00 *Hydro Seafoods GSP Ltd* v. *The Scottish Ministers*,
judgment of 10 July 2003, not yet reported 328, 339
Case C-86/00 *HSB-Wohnbau GmbH* [2001] ECR I-5353 335
Case C-94/00 *Roquette Frères SA* v. *Commission* [2002] ECR I-9011 74
Case C-99/00 *Lyckeskog* [2002] ECR I-4839 330
Case C-116/00 *Laguillaumie* [2000] ECR I-4979 .... 332, 334
Case C-153/00 *der Weduwe* [2002] ECR I-11319 335
Case C-162/00 *Land Nordrhein-Westfalen* v. *Beata Pokrzeptowicz-Meyer*
[2002] ECR I-1049 245
Case C-188/00 *Kurz, né Yüce* v. *Land Baden-Württemberg* [2002] ECR I-10691 241
Case C-253/00 *Muñoz* [2002] ECR I-7289 .... 308, 310, 313, 354
C-292/00 *Davidoff* v. *Gofkid* [2003] ECR I-389 298
Case C-300/00 P(R) *Federación de Cofradías de Pescadores de Guipúzcoa*
and others [2000] ECR I-8797 312
Case C-318/00 *Bacardi-Martini SAS and anor* v. *Newcastle United*
Football Company Ltd [2003] ECR I-905 .... 335, 338
Case C-326/00 *Idryma Koinonikon Asfaliseon* v. *Ioannidis*, judgment
of 25 February 2003, not yet reported 331
Case C-466/00 *Kaba* v. *Secretary of State for the Home Department*,
judgment of 6 March 2003, not yet reported 341
Case C-469/00 *Ravil SARL* v. *Bellon import SARL and Biraghi SpA*,
judgment of 20 May 2003, not yet reported 310, 311, 362
Case C-42/01 *Portugal* v. *Commission*, pending 119
Case C-108/01 *Consorzio del Prosciutto di Parma* v *Asda Stores Ltd and Hygrade*
Foods Ltd, judgment of 20 May 2003, not yet reported 310, 311, 362
Case C-110/01 *Tennah-Durez* v. *Conseil national de l'ordre des médecins*,
judgment of 19 June 2003, not yet reported 248, 254–5
Case C-189/01 *Jippes* v. *Minister van Landbouw, Natuurbeheer en Visserij*
[2001] ECR I-5689 329
Case C-206/01 *Arsenal Football Club plc* v. *Reed* [2002] ECR I-10273 341
Case C-224/01 *Köbler* v. *Austria*, pending 314–6, 318, 329
Case C-241/01 *National Farmers' Union* v. *Secrétariat Général du*
Gouvernement [2002] ECR I-9079 335
Joined Cases C-264/01, C-306/01, C-354/01 and C-355/01 *AOK Bundesverband*,
pending 311
Case C-265/01 *Pansard and ors* [2003] ECR I-683 342
Case C-300/01 *Doris Salzmann*, judgment of 15 May 2003, not yet reported 337
Case C-388/01 *Commission* v. *Italian Republic* [2003] ECR I-721 55
Case C-419/01 *Commission* v. *Spain*, judgment of 15 May 2003,
not yet reported 55, 252–3
Case C-462/01 *Ulf Hammarsten* [2003] ECR I-781 57
Case C-491/01 *R.* v. *Secretary of State for Health*, ex parte *British American*
Tobacco (Investments) Ltd and anor [2002] ECR I-11453 .... 73, 313, 334

Case C-24/02 *Marseille Fret SA* v. *Seatrano Shipping Co Ltd* [2002] ECR I-3383 332
Case C-93/02P *Biret International*, pending 386
Case C-94/02P *Etablissements Biret et Cie*, pending 386
Case C-122/02 *Commission* v. *Belgium* [2003] ECR I-833 55
Case C-138/02 *Brian Francis Collins* v. *Minister of State for Works and Pensions*,
  pending 244
Case C-190/02 *Viacom Outdoor Srl* v. *Giotto Immobilier SARL*
  [2002] ECR I-8289 336
Case C-263/02P *Commission* v. *Jégo-Quéré et Cie SA*, pending 339
Case C-281/02 *Jackson and Others* v. *Owusu*, pending 261
Case C-293/02 *Jersey Produce Marketing Organisation* v. *The States of Jersey*,
  pending 332
Case C-13/03P *Commission* v. *Tetra Laval*, pending 137
Case C-39/03P *Commission* v. *Artegodan GmbH et al*, judgment of 24 July 2003,
  not yet reported 142

EUROPEAN COURT OF JUSTICE

Cases listed in alphabetical order

Aher-Waggon Case C-389/96 [1998] ECR I-4473 199
Ahmed Saeed Flugreisen and others v. *Zentrale zur Bekämpfung
  unlauteren Wettbewerbs e.V.* Case 66/86 [1989] ECR 803 171
Akman Case C-210/97 [1998] ECR I-7519 243
Albany Case C-67/96 [1999] ECR I-5751 201
Alcatel v. *Novasam* Case 247/86 [1988] ECR 5987 163
Aldona Malgorzata Jany et al v. *Staatssecretaris van Justitie* Case
  C-268/99 [2001] ECR I-8615 241
Almelo and others v. *NV Energiebedrijf Ijsselmij* Case C-393/92
  [1994] ECR I-1477 .... 164, 167, 168, 171, 173
AM & S Europe Ltd v. *Commission* Case 155/79 [1982] ECR 1575 .... x, xi, 153–60
Amministrazione delle Finanze dello Stato v. *Simmenthal SpA* Case 106/77
  [1978] ECR 629 .... 327, 372
Andersson & Wåkerås-Andersson v. *Sweden* Case C-321/97 [1999] ECR I-3551 333
Angelopharm GmbH v. *Freie und Hansestadt Hamburg* Case C-212/91
  [1994] ECR I-171 224–5
Angonese v. *Cassa di Risparmio di Bolzano SpA* Case C-281/98 [2000]
  ECR I-4139 336–8
Annibaldi Case C-309/96 [1997] ECR I-7493 57
AOK Bundesverband, Joined Cases C-264/01, C-306/01, C-354/01 and C-355/01
  pending 311
Aragonesa de Publicidad Exterior SA and Publivia SAE v. *Departmento de Sanidad y
  Seguridad Social de la Generalitat de Cataluña* Case C-1/90 [1991] ECR I- 4151 55
Arcaro Case C-168/95 [1996] ECR I-4705 .... 314, 376
Arsenal Football Club plc v. *Reed* Case C-206/01 [2002] ECR I-10273 341
Atlanta v. *Commission* Case C-104/97P [1999] ECR I-6983 383

xxx *Table of Cases*

Bacardi-Martini SAS and anor v. *Newcastle United Football Company Ltd* Case C-318/00 [2003] ECR I-905 .... 335, 338
Banque Internationale pour l'Afrique Occidentale SA v. *Finanzamt für Großunternehmen in Hamburg* Case C-306/99 [2003] ECR I-1 333
Barber v. *Guardian Royal Exchange Assurance Group* Case C-262/88 [1990] ECR I-1889 376
Béguelin Import v. *G.L. Import Export* Case 22/71 [1971] ECR 949 166
Belgium v. *Spain* Case C-388/95 [2000] ECR I-3123 363
Bellone v. *Yokohama SpA* Case C-215/97 [1998] ECR I-2191 371
Benedetti v. *Munari* Case 52/76 [1977] ECR 163 341
Bertini and ors v. *Regione Lazio and anor* Joined Cases 98, 162 & 258/85 [1986] ECR 1885 331
Bickel and Franz Case C-274/96 [1998] ECR I-7637 244
Biret International, Case C-93/02P pending 386
Bodson v. *SA Pompes funèbres des regions libérées* Case 30/87 [1988] ECR 2479 167
Bonifaci and Others Joined Cases C-94/95 and C-95/95 [1997] ECR I-4006 384
Booker Aquaculture Ltd v. *The Secretary of State for Scotland*, Joined Cases C-20/00 and C-64/00 judgment of 10 July 2003, not yet reported 61, 328, 339
Bosman Case C-415/93 [1995] ECR I-4921 .... 168, 310, 335
Bouchereau Case 30/77 [1977] ECR 1999 .... 241, 305
Bozkurt v. *Staatssecretaris van Justitie* Case C-434/93 [1995] ECR I-1475 .... 237, 271
Brasserie du Pêcheur and Factortame Joined Cases C-46/93 and C-48/93 [1996] ECR I-1029 .... 309, 314, 318–9, 321, 327, 381–4
Brian Francis Collins v. *Minister of State for Works and Pensions*, Case C-138/02 pending 244
Brinhmann Tabafabriken GmbH v. *Hauptzollamt Bielefield* Case C-365/98 [2000] ECR I-4619 .... 371, 379
Brown v. *Rentokil Ltd* Case C-394/96 [1998] ECR I-4185 328
Brown v. *Secretary of State for Scotland* Case 197/86 [1988] ECR 3205 328
BRT v. *SABAM* Case 127/73 [1974] ECR 51 94
Caisse de maladie des CFL "Enrt'aide medicale" and Société nationale des chemins de fer luxembourgeois v. *Compagnie belge d'assurances générales sur la vie et contre les accidents* Case 27/69 [1969] ECR 405 262
Carpenter v. *Secretary of State for the Home Department* Case C-60/00 [2002] ECR 1-6279 262
CECA v. *Fillite Acciaierie e Ferriere Busseni SpA* Case C-221/88 [1990] ECR I-495 376
Centro Servizi Spediporto Srl v. *Spedizioni Marittima del Golfo Srl* Case C-96/94 [1995] ECR I-2883 164
Chemische Afvalstoffen Dusseldorp Case C-203/96 [1998] ECR I-4075 201
CICCE v. *Commission* Case 298/83 [1985] ECR 1105 94
CILFIT v. *Ministry of Health* Case 283/81 [1982] ECR 3415 .... 301, 303, 329, 330, 346, 348–9
City of Glasgow District Council v. *Kleinwort Benson* Case C-346/94 [1995] ECR I-615 333
CNPAAP v. *Council* Case C-87/95P [1996] ECR I-2003 312
Colegio Nacional de Agentes de la Propiedad Inmobiliaria v. *Aguirre Borrell and Others* Case C-104/91 [1992] ECR I-3003 251

Comet Case 45/76 [1976] ECR 2043 317
Commission v. Council Case 59/81 [1982] ECR 3329... 45
Commission v. Council Case 81/72 [1973] ECR 575 45
Commission v. Germany (beer) Case 17/84 [1987] ECR 1227................................... 216
Commission v. Artegodan GmbH et al, Case C-39/03P judgment of
  24 July 2003, not yet reported 142
Commission v. Belgium Case 149/79 [1982] ECR 1845 54
Commission v. Belgium Case 77/69 [1970] ECR 237 54
Commission v. Belgium Case C-122/02 [2003] ECR I-833... 5
Commission v. Belgium Case C-2/90 [1992] ECR I-4431 198
Commission v. Belgium Case C-323/96 [1998] ECR I-5063 54
Commission v. Council Case C-170/96 [1998] ECR I-2763 235
Commission v. France Case 167/73 [1974] ECR 359... 372
Commission v. France Case C-1/00 [2001] ECR I- 9989 .... 61, 216
Commission v. Germany Case C-431/92 [1995] ECR I-2189................................... 354
Commission v. Hellenic Republic Case C-205/89 [1991] ECR I-1361....................... 195
Commission v. Ireland Case 113/80 [1981] ECR 1625 198
Commission v. Ireland Case 45/87 [1998] ECR 4929.. 54
Commission v. Italian Republic Case C-388/01 [2003] ECR I-721 55
Commission v. Italy Case 169/82 [1984] ECR 1603 54
Commission v. Italy Case 199/85 [1987] ECR 1039 54
Commission v. Jégo-Quéré et Cie SA, Case C-263/02P pending 339
Commission v. Netherlands Case C-52/93 [1994] ECR I-3591 373
Commission v. Spain Case C-232/99 [2002] ECR I-4235 250
Commission v. Spain, Case C-419/01 judgment of 15 May 2003,
  not yet reported..55, 252–3
Commission v. Sytraval et Brink's France SARL Case C-367/95P [1998] ECR I-1719
Commission v. Tetra Laval, Case C-13/03P pending... 137
Compagnie Maritime Belge SA and Dafra –Lines A/S v. Commission
  Joined Cases C-395/96P and C-396/96P [2000]
  ECR I-1365...119, 161, 162, 165, 169, 170–7, 186
Compassion In World Farming Case C-1/96 [1998] ECR I-1251................................ 57
*Connect Austria Gesellschaft für Telekommunikation GmbH v. Telekom-Control-
  Kommission*, Case C-462/99 judgment of 22 May 2003,
  not yet reported... 327
Conseil national de l'ordre des architectes v. Dreessen Case C-31/00
  [2002] ECR I-663 .... 251–2, 254
Consorzio del Prosciutto di Parma v. Asda Stores Ltd and Hygrade Foods Ltd,
  Case C-108/01 judgment of 20 May 2003, not yet reported 310, 311, 362
Cooke Case C-185/97 [1998] ECR I-5199 .... 311, 371
Coreck Maritime GmbH v. Handelsveem BV and others Case C-387/98
  [2000] ECR I-9337 257
Corsica Ferries France v. Direction générale des douanes Françaises Case
  C-49/89 [1989] ECR I- 4441 195
Costa v. ENEL Case 6/64 [1964] ECR 585 ....54, 327, 330–1, 333
Council of the City of Stoke-on-Trent v. B & Q plc Case C-169/91
  [1992] ECR I-6635 340
Courage v. Crehan Case C-453/99 [2001] ECR I-6297 .... 308, 311, 318, 321, 342

xxxii Table of Cases

Criminal proceedings against CMC Melkunie BV Case 97/83
  [1984] ECR 2367 216
Criminal proceedings against Giorgio Domingo Banchero ('Banchero II')
  Case C-387/93 [1995] ECR I-4663 334
D'Hoop v. Office national de l'emploi Case C-224/98 [2002] ECR I-6191 244
Davidoff v. Gofkid C-292/00 [2003] ECR I-389 298
de Coster v. Collège des Bourgmestres et Echevins de Watermael-Boitsfort Case
  C-17/00 [2001] ECR I-9445 331
De Gens v. Bosch Case 13/61 [1962] ECR 45 304
Decoster Case C-69/91 [1993] ECR I-5335 373
Defrenne v. SABENA Case 43/75 [1976] ECR 455 311
Demirel v. Stadt Swäbisch Gmünd Case 12/86 [1987] ECR 3719 .... 235, 238, 385
Demo-Studio Schmidt Case 210/81 [1983] ECR 3045 94
Denkavit v. Bundesamt für Finazen Joined Cases C-283/94, C-291/94 and C-292/94
  [1996] ECR I-5063 383
Denmark v. Commission, Case 3/00 judgment of 20 May 2003, not yet reported 216
Department of Health and Social Security v. Barr & Montrose Holdings Ltd Case
  C-355/89 [1991] ECR I-3479 332
der Weduwe Case C-153/00 [2002] ECR I-11319 335
Deutsche Grammophon Gesellschaft mbH v. Metro-SB-Großmärkte
  GmbH & Co KG Case 78/70 [1971] ECR 487 342
Dillenkofer and Others v. Germany Joined Cases C-178/94, C-179/94,
  C-188/94, C-189/94 et C-190/94 [1996] ECR I-4845 384
DIP SpA v. Comune di Bassano del Grappa and Comune di Chioggia Joined
  Cases C-140/94, C-141/94 and C-142/94 [1995] ECR I-3257 .... 164, 168
Doris Salzmann, Case C-300/01 judgment of 15 May 2003, not yet reported 337
Dounias v. Minister for Economic Affairs Case C-228/98 [2000] ECR I-577 195
Dzodzi v. Belgium Joined Cases C-297/88 and C-197/89 [1990] ECR I-3763 333
Eco Swiss China Time Ltd v. Benetton International NV Case
  C-126/97 [1999] ECR I-3055 .... 145, 323
Eker v. Land Baden-Württemberg Case C-386/95 [1997] ECR I-2697 240
EKRO v. Produktschap voor Vee en Vlees Case 327/82 [1984] ECR 107 302
Emmott v. Minister for Social Welfare Case C-208/90 [1991] ECR I-4269 323
Enichen Base v. Comme di Cinisello Balsamo Case 380/87 [1989] ECR 2491 375
Ergat v. Stadt Ulm Case C-321/97 [2000] ECR I-1487 243
Eroglu v. Land Baden-Württemberg Case C-355/93 [1994] ECR I-5131 .... 240, 242
Ertanir v. Land Hessen Case C-98/96 [1997] ECR I-5179 241
Etablissements Biret et Cie, Case C-94/02P pending 386
Ettien Koua Poirrez v. Caisse d'allocations familiales de la region
  parisienne Case C-206/91 [1992] ECR I-6685 262
Eyüp v. Landesgeschäftsstelle des Arbeitmarktservice Vorarlberg
  Case C-65/98 [2000] ECR 4747 243
Faccini Dori v. Recreb Srl Case C-91/92 [1994] ECR I-3325 .... 310, 314, 353, 371, 376
Falciola Angelo SpA v. Comune di Pavia Case C-286/88 [1990] ECR I-191 335
Federación de Cofradías de Pescadores de Guipúzcoa and others
  Case C-300/00 P(R) [2000] ECR I-8797 312
Federica Maso and Others Case C-373/95 [1997] ECR I-4051 384
Fediol v. Commission Case 70/87 [1989] ECR 1781 387

Fernández de Bobadilla v. *Museo Nacional del Prado* Case
C-234/97 [1999] ECR I-4773... 250
Firma Gebrüden Lück v. *Hauptzollamt Köln-Rheinau* Case 34/67 [1968]
ECR 359.. 372
Foglia v. *Novello* (No 1) Case 104/79 [1980] ECR 745.......................... 334–5
Foglia v. *Novello* (No 2) Case 244/80 [1981] ECR 3045........................... 334
Foster v. *British Gas* Case C-188/89 [1990] ECR I-3313.......................... 309
Foto-Frost v. *Hauptzollamt Lübeck-Ost* Case 314/85 [1987]
ECR 4199 .... 83, 312, 319, 329, 330, 346, 356
France and Others v. *Commission* Joined Cases C-68/94 and C-30/95 [1998]
ECR I–1375... 119, 121, 140, 143, 161–2, 173–9, 181–3
Francovich and Bonifaci v. *Italy* Joined Cases C-6/90 and C-9/90
[1991] ECR I-5357 .... 309, 314, 318, 327, 380, 381
Fratelli Costanzo SpA v. *Comune di Milano* Case 103/88
[1989] ECR 1839 .... 55, 363, 376
Fratelli Grassi Case 5/72 [1972] ECR 443.. 348
Freidrich Haagen GmbH Case 32/74 [1974] ECR 1201 370
GEMA v. *Commission* Case 125/78 [1979] ECR 3173............................ 94
Gewiese & Mehlich v. *MacKenzie (PF Stornoway)* Case 24/83
[1984] ECR 817 328
GIE Groupe Concorde and Others v. *Master of the vessel "Suhadiwarno Panjan"*
C-440/97 [1999] ECR I-6307... 257
Giloy v. *Hauptzollamt Frankfurt am Main-Ost* Case C-130/95 [1997] ECR I-4291 333
Government of Gibraltar v. *Council* Case C- 298/89 [1993] ECR I-3705.................... 63
Grand Duchy of Luxemburg v. *Linster and others* Case C-287/98
[2000] ECR I-6917 .... 309, 365, 378, 380
Grau Gomis and ors Case C-167/94 [1995] ECR I-1023............................. 333
Grau-Hupka v. *Stadtgemeinde Bremen* Case C-297/93 [1994] ECR I-5535.............. 335
Grimaldi v. *Fonds des maladies professionnelles* Case C-322/98 [1989] ECR 4407 371
Grzelczyk v. *Centre public d'aide social d'Ottignies-Louvaine-la-Neuve*
Case C-184/99 [2002] ECR I-6193 244
Guimont Case C-448/98 [2000] ECR I-10663 337
Günaydin Case C-36/96 [1997] ECR I-5143 .... 241, 242
Haegeman v. *Belgium* Case 181/73 [1974] ECR 449 235
Haim v. *Kassenzahnärztliche Vereinigung Nordrhein* Case C-319/92
[1994] ECR I-425 .... 250–1, 253
Haim v. *Kassenzahnärztliche Vereinigung Nordrhein* Case C-424/97
[2000] ECR I-5123 253
Hamilton (PF Dunfermline) v. *Whitelock* Case 79/86 [1987] ECR 2363 328
Hansen Case C-326/88 [1990] ECR I-2911 312
Hauptzollamt Mainz v. *Kupferberg & Cie KgaA* Case 104/81 [1982]
ECR 3641... 236, 385
Heinonen Case C-394/97 [1999] ECR I-3599.. 195
Hocsman v. *Ministre de l'Emploi et de la Solidarité* Case C-238/98
[2000] ECR I-6623 .... 250–2, 255–6
Hoffman-La Roche v. *Commission* Case 85/76 [1979] ECR 461...................... 163, 175
Holdijk Joined Cases 141/81 to 143/81 [1982] ECR 1299............................ 57
HSB-Wohnbau GmbH Case C-86/00 [2001] ECR I-5353............................... 335

xxxiv Table of Cases

Hydro Seafoods GSP Ltd v. *The Scottish Ministers,* Case C-64/00
  judgment of 10 July 2003, not yet reported.. 328, 339
IBM v. *Commission* Joined Cases 60/81R to 190/81R [1981] ECR 1857 and 2639........ xi
Idryma Koinonikon Asfaliseon v. *Ioannidis,* Case C-326/00 judgment of
  25 February 2003, not yet reported... 331
Impresa Costruzioni comm Quirino Mazzalai v. *Ferroria del Penon*
  Case 11/75 [1976] ECR 657 370
Ingmar GB Ltd v. *Eaton Leonard Technologies Inc* Case C-381/98
  [2000] ECR I-9305 265
Inter-Environnement Wallonie ASBL v. *Région Wallone* Case C-129/96
  [1997] ECR I-7411.. 362, 364, 365
International Chemical Corporation (ICI) v. *Amministrazione delle*
  Finanze dello Stato Case 66/80 [1981] ECR 329
International Fruit Company NV et al v. *Produktschap voor Groenten*
  en Fruit Joined Cases 21-24/72 [1972] ECR 1219 234
Jackson and Others v. *Owusu,* Case C-281/02 pending....................................... 261
Jersey Produce Marketing Organisation v. *The States of Jersey,*
  Case C-293/02 pending 332
Jippes v. *Minister van Landbouw, Natuurbeheer en Visserij* Case C-189/01
  [2001] ECR I-5689 329
Job Centre Coop. Sarl Case C-111/94 [1995] ECR I-3361.................................... 335
Johnson v. *Chief Adjudication Officer* Case C-410/92 [1994] ECR I-5483............. 323
Joined Cases 28-30/62 *da Costa en Schaake NV and ors* v. *Nederlandse*
  Belastingsadministratie [1963] ECR 31.. 330
Kaba v. *Secretary of State for the Home Department,* Case C-466/00
  judgment of 6 March 2003, not yet reported... 341
Kadiman v. *Fieistaat Bayern* Case C-351/95 [1997] ECR I-2133........................... 243
Kaefer & Procacci v. *French State* Joined Cases C-100-101/89 [1990]
  ECR I-4647 332
Keck and Mithouard Joined Cases C-267/91 and 268/91 [1993] ECR I-6097...... 194, 340
Khali and others v. *Bundesanstalt für Arbeit* Joined Cases C-95/99 to
  C-98/99 and C-180/99 [2001] ECR 7413.. 262
Kingdom of the Netherlands and gerhard van der Wal v. *Commission*
  Joined cases C-174/98P and C-189/98P [2000] ECR I-1 148
Köbler v. *Austria,* Case C-224/01 pending... 314–6, 318, 329
Kocak v. *Landesversicherungsanstalt Oberfranken und Mittelfranken*
  Cases C-102/98 [2000] ECR I-1287 244
Kol v. *Land Berlin* Case C-285/95 [1997] ECR I-3069.. 242
Kolpinghuis Nijmegen Case 80/86 [1987] ECR 3969 .... 314, 376
Kraaijeveld and Others v. *Gedeputeerde Staten van Zuid-Holland* Case
  C-72/95 [1996] ECR I-5403... 309, 354, 365, 367
Kremzow v. *Austria* Case C-299/95 [1997] ECR I-2629....................................... 333
Kurz, né Yüce v. *Land Baden-Württemberg* Case C-188/00 [2002] ECR I-10691....... 241
Kus v. *Landeshauptstadt Wiesbaden* Case C-237/91 [1992] ECR I-6781 .... 238, 239
La Pyramide SARL Case C-378/93 [1994] ECR I-3999 336
Laboratoires pharmaceutiques Bergaderm SA and Jean-Jacques Goupil v.
  Commission Case C-352/98 [2000] ECR I-5291 383
Laguillaumie Case C-116/00 [2000] ECR I-4979 .... 332, 334

Land Nordrhein-Westfalen v. *Beata Pokrzeptowicz-Meyer* Case C-162/00
[2002] ECR I-1049 245
Landesgrundverkehrsreferent der Tiroler Landesregierung v. *Beck
Liegenschaftsverwaltungsgesellschaft mbH and anor* Case C-355/97
[1999] ECR I-4977 .... 333, 336
Lehtonen & Castors Canada Dry Namur-Braine ASBL v. *Fédération Royale Belge
des Sociétés de Basket-ball ASBL* Case C-176/96 [2000] ECR I-2681 336
Leplat v. *Territory of French Polynesia* Case C-260/90 [1992] ECR I-643 332
Les Verts v. *European Parliament* Case 294/83 [1986] ECR 1339 71
Leur-Bloem v. *Inspecteur der Belastingdienst/Ondernemingen Amsterdam*
Case C-28/95 [1997] ECR I-4161 333
Levez v. *TH Jennings (Harlow Pools) Ltd.* Case C-326/96 [1998] ECR I-7835 321–2
Lourenço Dias v. *Director da Alfândega do Porto* Case C-343/90
[1992] ECR I-4673 335
Lyckeskog Case C-99/00 [2002] ECR I-4839 330
Magorrian v. *Eastern Health and Social Services Board* Case C-246/96
[1997] ECR I-7153 319
Maïseries de Beauce v. *Office National Interprofessionnel des Céréals* Case
109/79 [1980] ECR 2883 341
Marie Brizard & Roger International SA v. *Wm Grant and Sons (International) and
anor* Case C-126/96 removed from the Register by Order of 25 February 1997 328
Maritínez Sala v. *Freistaat Bayern* Case C-85/96 [1998] ECR I-2691 244
Marks & Spencer Case C-62/00 [2002] ECR I-6325 314
Marleasing Case C-106/89 [1990] ECR I-4135 .... 300, 314, 364, 371
Marseille Fret SA v. *Seatrano Shipping Co Ltd* Case C-24/02 [2002] ECR I-3383 332
Marshall v. *Southampton and South-West Hampshire Area Health
Authority (Teaching)* Case 152/84 [1986] ECR 723 .... 310, 376
Masterfoods Ltd v. *HB Ice Cream Ltd* Case C-344/98 [2000] ECR I-11369 151
Mattheus v. *Doego Fruchtimport und Tiefkülkost eG* Case 93/78 [1978]
ECR 2203 333
Max Mara Fashion Group Srl v. *Ufficio del Registro di Reggio Emilia*
Case C-30/95 [1995] ECR I-5083 333
Mazzoleni & Inter Surveillance Assistance Case C-165/98 [2001] ECR I-7803 334
Mehmet Birden v. *Stadtgemeinde Bremen* Case C–1/97 [1998] ECR I-7747 241
Meilicke v. *ADV/ORGA AG* Case C-83/91 [1992] ECR I-4871 335
Merck & Co. Inc. and Others v. *Primecrown and others* Joined Cases
C-267/95 and C-268/95 [1996] ECR I-6285 178
Metallgesellschaft & Hoechst v. *Inland Revenue* Case C-410/98 [2001]
ECR I-1727 321
Metro v. *Commission* Case 26/76 [1977] 1875 94
Michelin v. *Commission* Case 322/81 [1983] ECR 3461 166
Ministére public v. *Oscar Traen et autres* Joined Cases 372-374/85
[1987] ECR 2141 376
Ministère public v. *Xavier Mirepoix* Case 54/85 [1986] ECR 1067 216
Ministre de la Santé v. *Erpelding* Case C-16/99 [2000] ECR I-6821 254
Monin Automobiles - Maison du Deux-Roues (No 1) Case C-386/92
[1993] ECR I-2049 336
MRAX v. *Belgian State* Case C-459/99 [2002] ECR I-6591 262

xxxvi Table of Cases

Muñoz Case C-253/00 [2002] ECR I-7289 .... 308, 310, 313, 354
Nakajima All precision Co Ltd v. Council Case C-69/89 [1991] ECR I-2069 387
National Farmers' Union and Others Case C-157/96 [1998] ECR I-2211 216
National Farmers' Union v. Secrétariat Général du Gouvernment
   Case C-241/01 [2002] ECR I-9079 335
Nazli v. Stadt Nürnberg Case C-340/97 [2000] ECR I-957 241
Nertsvoederfabriek Nederland Case 118/86 [1987] ECR 3883 57
Netherlands v. Commission Case 11/76 [1979] ECR 245 178
Netherlands v. Parliament and Council Case C-377/98 [2001] I-7079 .... 73, 387
Océano Grupo Editorial SA v. Roció Murciano Quintero Joined
   Cases C-240/98 to C-244/98 [2000] ECR I-4941 .... 323, 371, 379–80
Office national de l'emploi v. Kziber Case C-18/90 [1991] ECR I-199 386
Officier van Justitie v. Koninklijke Kaasfabriek Eyssen Case 53/80 [1981] ECR 409...216
OGT Fruchthandelsgeselhschanft mbH v. Hauptzollamt Hamburg-
   St Annen Case C-307/99 [2001] ECR I-3159 387
Orsohl Lenesio v. Ministero dell'agricoltura e foreste Case 93/71 [1972] ECR 287 372
Österreichischer Gewerkschaftsbund, Gewerkschaft öffentlicher Dienst v.
   Austria Case C-195/98 [2000] ECR I-1497 311
Palmisani v. INPS Case C-261/95 [1997] ECR I-4025 .... 320, 384
Pansard and ors Case C-265/01 [2003] ECR I-683 342
Parfums Christian Dior SA and anor v. Evora BV Case C-337/95
   [1997] ECR I-6013 332
Parfums Christian Dior SA v. TUK Consultancy BV et Assco Gerüste
   GmbH Joined Cases C-300/98 and C-392/98 [2000] ECR I-11307 387
Pereira Roque v. HE The Lieutenant Governor of Jersey Case C-171/96
   [1998] ECR I-4607 332
Peterbroeck v. Belgium Case C-312/93 [1995] ECR I-4599 346
Pfizer Animal Health SA and Others v. Commission Case C-329/99 P(R)
   [1999] ECR I-8343 204
Pieck Case 157/79 [1980] ECR 2171 239
Plaumann v. Commission Case 25/62 [1963] ECR 95 312
Polydor Limited and RSO Records Inc. v. Harlequin Records Shops Limited and
   Simons Records Limited Case 270/80 [1982] ECR 329 .... 236, 385
Portugal v. Commission, Case C-42/01 pending 119
Portugal v. Council Case C-149/96 [1999] ECR I-8395 .... 385, 387
Preliminary Ruling by the Acting Judge at the Tribunal d'Instance,
   Hayange (No. 1) Case 105/79 [1979] ECR 2257 333
Preliminary Ruling by the Acting Judge at the Tribunal d'Instance,
   Hayange (No. 2) Case 68/80 [1980] ECR 771 333
Preston and Fletcher Case C-78/98 [2000] ECR I-3201, [2001]
   2 WLR 408 (HL) 318, 323, 325
Pretore di Genova v. Banchero ('Banchero I') Case C-157/92 [1993]
   ECR I-1085 ....334, 336
Pretore di Salò v. Persons Unknown Case 14/86 [1987] ECR 2545 333
PreussenElektra Case C-379/98 [2001] ECR I-2099 .... 199, 200, 201
Procureur de la République v. Tissier Case 35/85 [1986] ECR 1207 342
R v. Commissioners of Customs and Excise, ex parte EMU Tabac
   and Others Case C-296/95 [1998] ECR I-1605 304

Table of Cases xxxvii

R v. *Secretary of State for Health and ors*, ex parte *Imperial Tobacco and ors* Case C-74/99 [2000] ECR I-8599 334
R v. *Secretary of State for Social Security*, ex parte *Sutton* Case C-66/95 [1997] ECR I-2163 323
R v. *Secretary of State for the Environment, Transport and the Regions*, ex parte *Omega Air Ltd and ors* Joined Cases C-27/00 and C-122/00 [2002] ECR I-2569 334
R v. *Secretary of State for the Home Department*, ex parte *Barkoci and Malik* Case C-257/99 [2001] ECR I-6557 .... 237, 240, 386
R v. *Secretary of State for the Home Department*, ex parte *Gloszczuk* Case C-63/99 [2001] ECR I-6369 .... 237, 240, 241, 242, 386
R v. *Secretary of State for the Home Department*, ex parte *Kondova* Case C-235/99 [2001] ECR I-6427) 237, 240, 242, 386
R v. *Secretary of State for the Home Department*, ex parte *Savas* Case C-37/98 [2000] ECR I-2927 242
R v. *Secretary of State for Transport*, ex parte *Factortame Ltd* Case C-213/89 [1990] ECR I-2433 .... 315, 317, 318, 319, 327
R. v. *Secretary of State for Health*, ex parte *British American Tobacco (Investments) Ltd and anor* Case C-491/01 [2002] ECR I-11453 .... 73, 313, 334
Ramazan v. *Bundesknappschaft* (C-211/98) Case C-211/98 [2000] ECR I-1297 244
Ravil SARL v. *Bellon import SARL and Biraghi SpA*, Case C-469/00 judgment of 20 May 2003, not yet reported 310, 311, 362
Rechberger and Others v. *Austria* Case C-140/97 [1999] ECR I-3499 383
Recip Tetik v. *Land Berlin* Case C-171/95 [1997] ECR I-329 240
Redmond Case 83/78 [1978] ECR 2347 57
Région Wallonne v. *Commission* Case C-95/97 [1997] ECR I-1787 62
Regione Toscana v. *Commission* Case C-180/97 [1997] ECR I-5245 62
Reina & Reina v. *Landeskreditbank Baden-Württemberg* Case 65/81 [1982] ECR 33 332
Reisch and ors v. *Bürgermeister der Landeshauptstadt Salzburg and ors* Joined Cases C-515 etc/99 [2002] ECR I-2157 337
Rewe-Handelsgesellschaft Case 158/80 [1981] ECR 1805 318
Rewe-Zentral v. *Bundesmonopolverwaltung fur Branntwein* Case 120/78 [1979] ECR 649 195
Rewe-Zentralfinanz Case 33/76 [1976] ECR 1989 317
Rheinmülen Case 166/73 [1974] ECR 33 .... 346–7, 351
RI.SAN. Srl v. *Comune di Ischia, Italia Lavro SpA and Ischia Ambiente SpA* Case C-108/98 [1999] ECR I-5219 262
Roquette Frères SA v. *Commission* Case C-94/00 [2002] ECR I-9011 74
Roujansky v. *Council* Case C-253/94P [1995] ECR I-7 333
Ruiz Bernàldez Case C-129/94 [1996] ECR I-8129 380
Salonia v. *Poidomani and anor* Case 126/80 [1981] ECR 1563 335
Sea-Land Service Inc & Nedlloyd Lijnen BV Joined Cases C-430 and 431/99 [2002] ECR I-5235 335
Secretary of State for Health, ex parte *Gallaher Limited, Imperial Tobacco Limited and Rothmans International Tobacco (UK) Limited* Case C-11/92 [1993] ECR I-3545 65

Security International SA v. *Signalson SA & Securitel SPRL* Case C-194/94
CIA [1996] ECR I-2201 .... 195, 309, 310, 354, 365, 373, 377, 379–80
Semeraro Casa Uno Srl and ors v. *Comune di Erbusco and ors* Joined
Cases C-418 etc/93 [1996] ECR I-2975 340
Silhouette International Selmied GmbH & Co KG v. *Hartlauer Handelsgesellschaft
GmbH* Case C-355/96 [1998] ECR I-4799 376
Simmenthal v. *Commission* Case 92/78 [1979] ECR 777 45
SMW Winzersekt GmbH v. *Land Rheinland-Pfalz* Case C-306/93 [1994]
ECR I-5555 334
Sociale Verzekeringsbank v. *Van der Vecht* Case 19/67 [1967] ECR 345 304
Società Italiana per l'Oleodotto Transalpino (SIOT) v. *Ministero delle Finanze,
Ministero della Marina mercantile, Circoscrizione doganale di Trieste and Ente
Autonomo del Porto di Trieste* Case 266/81 [1983] ECR 731 234
Société Civile Agricole du Centre d'Insémination de la Crespelle v. *Coopérative
d'Elevage et d'Insémination Artificielle du Département de la Mayenne*
Case C-323/93 [1994] ECR I-5077 167
Spot Marmet v. *Ministero delle Finaze* Case 84/71 [1972] ECR 89 372
Steenhorst-Neerings Case C-338/91 [1993] ECR I-5475 323
Suiker Unie v. *Commission* Case 40/73 [1975] ECR 1663 163
Sürül v. *Bundesanstalt für Arbeit* Case C-262/96 [1999] ECR I-2685 243
Sürül v. *Bunlevanstalt für Arbeit* Case C-262/92 [1999] ECR I-2685 .... 244, 386
SZ Sevince v. *Staatssecretaris van Justitie* Case C-192/89 [1990]
ECR I-3461 .... 236, 238, 239
Taflan Met, Altun-Basar and Andal-Bugdayaci v. *Bestuur van de Sociale
Verzckeringsbank* Case C-277/94 [1996] ECR I-4085 243–4
Tawil-Albertini v. *Ministre des Affaires Sociales* Case C-154/93 [1994] ECR I-451 251
Telemarsicabruzzo SpA and ors v. *Circostel and ors* Case C-320/90 [1993]
ECR I-393 336
Tennah-Durez v. *Conseil national de l'ordre des médecins*, Case C-110/01
judgment of 19 June 2003, not yet reported 248, 254–5
The Queen v. *HM Treasury, ex parte British Telecommunications plc* Case
C-392/93 [1996] ECR I-1631 383–4
The Queen v. *Ministry of Agriculture, Fisheries and Food, ex parte Hedley
Lomas (Ireland) Ltd* Case C-5/94 [1996] ECR I-2553 384
Torfaen Borough Council v. *B & Q plc* Case 145/88 [1989] ECR 3851 340
TWD Textilwerke Deggendorf GmbH v. *Germany* Case C-188/92 [1994]
ECR I-833 335
Ulf Hammarsten Case C-462/01 [2003] ECR I-781 57
Unilever Italia Spa v. *Central Food SpA* Case C-443/98 [2000]
ECR I-7535 .... 309, 310, 365, 376, 380
Unión de Pequeños Agricultores ('UPA') v. *Council* Case 50/00P [2002]
ECR I-6677 .... 64, 76, 159, 308, 319, 339
United Kingdom v. *Council* Case 68/86 [1988] ECR 855 218
United Kingdom v. *Council* Case C-84/94 [1996] ECR I-5755 59
URSSAF des Bouches-du-Rhöne v. *Clinique Florens SA*, Joined Cases
C-95 and C-96/96 Order of 12 June 1996, unreported 333
Vaassen-Göbbels v. *Management of the Beambtenfonds voor hat Mijnbedrif*
Case 61/65 [1966] ECR 261 262

Van Duyn v. *Home Office* Case 41/74 [1974] ECR 1337.. 359
van Gend en Loos v. *Nederlandse Administratie der Belastingen*
    Case 26/62 [1963] ECR 1 .... 54, 83, 235, 307, 311, 314, 327, 330, 365, 385
van Schijndel v. *SPF* Joined Cases C-430/93 and C-431/93 [1995] ECR I-4705........... 346
Vaneetveld v. *Le Foyer SA* Case C-316/93 [1994] ECR I-763 .... 336, 376
Verbond van Nederlandse Ondernemingen v. *Inspecteur der Invoerrechten en
    Accijnzen* Case 51/76 [1977] ECR 113 .... 309, 378
Verholen Joined Cases C-87/90, C-88/90 and C-89/90 [1991] ECR I-3757 315
Viacom Outdoor Srl v. *Giotto Immobilier SARL* Case C-190/02 [2002]
    ECR I-8189 336
Vlassopoulou v. *Ministerium für Justiz, Bundes- und Europaangelegenheiten
    Baden-Württemberg* Case C-340/89 [1991] ECR I-2357 .... 249-52, 254, 256
Von Colson and Kamann v. *Land Nordrhein-Westfalen* Case 14/83 [1984]
    ECR 1891 .... 317, 318, 370
Wagner Miret v. *Fondo de garantia Salarial* Case C-334/92 [1993] ECR I-6911 371
Walkingshaw (PF Stranraer) v. *Marshall* Case 370/88 [1990] ECR I-4071.......... 328, 339
Wiener SI GmbH v. *Hauptzollamt Emmerich* Case C-338/95 [1997]
    ECR I-6495..330, 342, 349–51
Wiljo NV v. *Belgium* Case C-178/95 [1997] ECR I-585 335
Wither (PF Elgin) v. *Cowie & Wood* Joined Cases C-251 & 252/90 [1992]
    ECR I-2873 328
World Wildlife Fund Case C-435/97 [1999] ECR I-5613... 378
Wouters v. *Nederlandse Orde van Advocaten* Case C-309/99 [2002] ECR I-1577 157
Wünsche Handelsgesellschaft GmbH & Co v. *Germany* Case 69/85
    [1986] ECR 947 341
Zino Davidoff SA v *A&G Imports Ltd* and *Levi Strauss & Co et al* v. *Tesco Stores
    Ltd et al* Joined Cases C-414/99 to C-416/99 [2001] ECR I-8691 265
Zuchner v. *Bayerische Vereinsbank AG* Case 172/80 [1981] ECR 2021..................... 163
Zuckerfabrik Süderdithmarschen and Zuckerfabrik Soest Joined Cases C-143/88
    and C-92/89 [1991] ECR I-415 319–20

COURT OF FIRST INSTANCE OF THE EUROPEAN COMMUNITIES

Cases listed in numerical order

Case T-64/89 *Automec I* [1990] ECR II-367 95
Joined Cases T-68/89, T-77/89 and T-78/89 *Società Italiano Vetro SpA* v.
    Commission [1992] ECR II-1403 .... 119, 121, 161–5, 167–9, 171–3, 179, 186
Case T-24/90 *Automec II* [1992] ECR II-2223 .... 91–2, 98
Case T-24/90 *Automec srl* v. *Commission* [1992] ECR II-2283 xi
Case T-28/90 *Asia Motor France* v. *Commission* [1992] ECR II-2285 .... 91, 93, 98
Case T-2/93 *Air France* v. *Commission* [1994] ECR II-323 181
Case T-115/94 *Opel Austria GmbH* v. *Council* [1997] ECR II-39 237
Case T-214/95 *Flemish Region* v. *Commission* [1998] ECR II-717.............................. 62
Case T-102/96 *Gencor Ltd* v. *Commission* [1999]
    ECR II-753 .... 120–2, 143, 161, 162, 174, 176, 179, 180–3, 185

xl *Table of Cases*

Joined Cases T-132/96 and T-143/96 *Freistaat Sachsen, Volkswagen AG and Volkswagen Sachsen GmbH* v. *Commission* [1999] ECR II-3663 62
Case T-238/97 *Communidad Autónoma de Cantabria* v. *Council* [1998] ECR II-2271 63
Joined Cases T-32/98 and T-41/98 *Government of the Netherlands Antilles* v. *Commission* [2000] ECR II-201 63
Case T-13/99 *Pfizer Animal Health* v. *Commission* [2002] ECR II-3305 .... 204, 205
Case T-70/99 *Alpharma Inc.* v. *Council* [2002] ECR II-3495 .... 204, 205, 224, 225
Case T-326/99R *Nancy Olivieri* v. *Commission* [2000] ECR II-1985 209
Case T-342/99 *Airtours plc* v. *Commission* [2002]
    ECR II-2585 .... 118, 119, 121, 122, 136, 138, 139, 140–3, 162, 180–6
Case T-74/00 *Artegodan GmbH et al* v. *Commission* [2002] ECR II-4945 142
Case T-174/00 *Biret International SA* v. *Conseil* [2002] ECR II-17 388
Case T-210/00 *Etablissements Biret et Cie SA* v. *Conseil* [2002] ECR II-47 388
Joined Cases T-377/00 etc *Philip Morris International Inc and ors* v. *Commission*, judgment of 15 January 2003, not yet reported 332
Case T-342/00 *Petrolessence and SG2R* v. *Commission*, judgment of 3 April 2003, not yet reported 125, 134, 137, 139, 143
Case T-342/00R *Petrolessence and SG2R* v. *Commission* [2001] ECR II-67 134
Case T-251/00 *Lagardère SCA and Canal+ SA* v. *Commission*, judgment of 20 November 2002, not yet reported 133
Case T-177/01 *Jégo-Quéré & Cie SA* v. *Commission* [2002] ECR II-2365 .... 63, 312
Case T-310/01 *Schneider Electric SA* v. *Commission* [2002] ECR II-4071 .... 118, 124, 136, 138, 139
Case T-5/02 *Tetra Laval BV* v. *Commission* [2002] ECR II-4381 .... 118, 125, 126, 131, 136, 138, 140, 141, 142
Case T-77/02 *Schneider Electric SA* v. *Commission* [2002] ECR II-4201 .... 118, 137, 143
Case T-80/02 *Tetra Laval BV* v. *Commission* [2002] ECR II-4519 ...... 118, 137, 142, 143
Case T-114/02 *BaByliss SA* v. *Commission*, judgment of 3 April 2003, not yet reported 118, 125, 128–31, 137, 140, 143
Case T-119/02 *Royal Philips Electronics NV* v. *Commission*, judgment of 3 April 2003, not yet reported 118, 125, 128, 130–2, 137

COURT OF FIRST INSTANCE OF THE EUROPEAN COMMUNITIES

Cases listed in alphabetical order

Air France v. *Commission* Case T-2/93 [1994] ECR II-323 181
Airtours plc v. *Commission* Case T-342/99 [2002]
    ECR II-2585 .... 118, 119, 121, 122, 136, 138–9, 140–3, 162, 180–6
Alpharma Inc. v. *Council* Case T-70/99 [2002] ECR II-3495 .... 204–5, 224–5
Artegodan GmbH et al v. *Commission* Case T-74/00 [2002] ECR II-4945 142
Asia Motor France v. *Commission* Case T-28/90 [1992] ECR II-2285 .... 91, 93, 98
Automec I Case T-64/89 [1990] ECR II-367 95
Automec II Case T-24/90 [1992] ECR II-2223 .... 91–2, 98
Automec srl v. *Commission* Case T-24/90 [1992] ECR II-2283 xi

BaByliss SA v. *Commission*, Case T-114/02 judgment of 3 April 2003,
  not yet reported 118, 125, 128–31, 137, 140, 143
Biret International SA v. *Conseil* Case T-174/00 [2002] ECR II-17............................ 388
Communidad Autónoma de Cantabria v. *Council* Case T-238/97 [1998]
  ECR II-2271 63
Etablissements Biret et Cie SA v. *Conseil* Case T-210/00 [2002] ECR II-47 388
Flemish Region v. *Commission* Case T-214/95 [1998] ECR II-717.............................. 62
Freistaat Sachsen, Volkswagen AG and Volkswagen Sachsen GmbH v. *Commission*
  Joined Cases T-132/96 and T-143/96 [1999] ECR II-3663...................................... 62
Gencor Ltd v. *Commission* Case T-102/96 [1999]
  ECR II-753 .... 120–2, 143, 161, 162, 174, 176, 179, 180–3, 185
Government of the Netherlands Antilles v. *Commission* Joined Cases T-32/98 and
  T-41/98 [2000] ECR II-201... 63
Jégo-Quéré & Cie SA v. *Commission* Case T-177/01 [2002] ECR II-2365 .... 63, 312
Lagardère SCA and Canal+ SA v. *Commission*, Case T-251/00 judgment of
  20 November 2002, not yet reported 133
Nancy Olivieri v. *Commission* Case T-326/99R [2000] ECR II-1985........................ 209
Opel Austria GmbH v. *Council* ase T-115/94 [1997] ECR II-39................................ 237
Petrolessence and SG2R v. *Commission* Case T-342/00R [2001] ECR II-67 134
Petrolessence and SG2R v. *Commission*, Case T-342/00 judgment of 3 April 2003,
  not yet reported 125, 134, 137, 139, 143
Pfizer Animal Health v. *Commission* Case T-13/99 [2002] ECR II-3305 .... 204, 205
Philip Morris International Inc and ors v. *Commission*, Joined Cases T-377/00 etc
  judgment of 15 January 2003, not yet reported 332
Royal Philips Electronics NV v. *Commission*, Case T-119/02 judgment of
  3 April 2003, not yet reported 118, 125, 128, 130–2, 137
Schneider Electric SA v. *Commission* Case T-310/01 [2002]
  ECR II-4071 ....118, 124, 136, 138, 139
Schneider Electric SA v. *Commission* Case T-77/02 [2002]
  ECR II-4201 .... 118, 137, 143
Società Italiano Vetro SpA v. *Commission* Joined Cases T-68/89, T-77/89 and
  T-78/89 [1992] ECR II-1403 .... 119, 121, 161–5, 167–9, 171–3, 179, 186
Tetra Laval BV v. *Commission* Case T-5/02 [2002]
  ECR II-4381 .... 118, 125, 126, 136, 138, 140–2
Tetra Laval BV v. *Commission* Case T-80/02 [2002] ECR II-4519 .... 18, 137, 42, 143

UNITED KINGDOM CASES

Allan v. *Patterson* 1980 JC 57... 302
Allinson v. *General Council of Medical Education and Registration*
  [1891-4] All ER 768 22
American Cyanamid v. *Ethicon Ltd* [1975] AC396.. 320
American Motor Insurance Co v. *Cellstar Corporation and another* [2003]
  EWCA Civ 206... 262
An Bord Bainne v. *Milk Marketing Board* [1985] 1 CMLR 6 346
Arsenal Football Club plc v. *Reed* [2002] EWHC 2695 (Ch), [2003] 1 All ER 137,
  [2003] EWCA Civ 96 (CA), [2003] All ER (D) 289 .... 313, 341

Associated Provincial Picture Houses Limited v. *Wednesbury Corporation*
[1948] 1 KB 223 38
Barrs v. *British Wool Marketing Board* 1957 SC 72 22
Boddington v. *British Transport Police* [1999] 2 AC 143 .... 43, 45
Bradford v. *McLeod* 1986 SLT 244. 22
Branwhite v. *Worcester Works Finance Ltd* [1968] 3 All ER 104 263
Brown v. *Hamilton District Council* 1983 SC (HL) 1 .... 31, 34–42
Bulmer Ltd v. *Bollinger SA (No 2)* [1974] Ch 401 .... 346, 348–9
Caledonia Subsea Ltd v. *Micoperi Srl* [2001] SC 716 261
Calvin v. *Carr* [1980] AC 574 44
Centralan Property Ltd v. *Customs and Excise Commissioners* [2003]
EWHC 44 (Ch), [2003] All ER (D) 186 351
Connor v. *Strathclyde Regional Council* 1986 SLT 530 38
Courage v. *Crehan* [2003] EWHC 1510 (Ch) 342
Crédit Lyonnais v. *New Hampshire Insurance Company* [1997]
2 Lloyd's Rep 1 258
Customs and Excise Commissioners v. *BAA plc* [2002] EWCA Civ 1814,
[2003] STC 35 351
Customs and Excise Commissioners v. *Littlewoods Organisation plc* [2001]
EWCA Civ 1542, [2001] STC 1568 350
Dickson v. *Murray* (1886) 4 M 797 33
Flores v. *Workmen's Compensation Appeals Board* (1974) 11
Cal 3d 171 300
Forbes v. *Underwood* (1886) 13 R 465 .... 32, 33, 35, 38, 40, 41
Garden Cottage Foods v. *Milk Marketing Board* [1984] AC 130 321
Hazell v. *Hammersmith and Fulham LBC* [1992] 2 AC 1 263
Import Export Metro Ltd and another v. *Compañia Sud Americana de
Vapores SA* [2003] EWHC 11 (Comm) 262
Lesotho Highlands Development Authority v. *Impreglio SpA and others*
[2002] EWHC 2435 (Comm) 262
Litster v. *Forth Dry Dock Ltd* 1989 SC 96, [1990] 1 AC 546 (HL) 328
Marodi Service di D Mialich & Co sas v. *Mikkal Myklesbuthaug Rederi A/S*
[2002] GWD 13-398 261
Marubeni Hong Kong and South China Ltd v. *Mongolian Government*
[2002] 2 All ER (D) 09 (Aug) 262
Metropolitan Properties Co. (FGC) Ltd v. *Lannon* [1969] 1 QB 577 (CA),
[1968] 1 WLR 815 (QBD) 22
O'Reilly v. *Mackman* [1983] 2 AC 237 31
Pepper v. *Hart* [1993] AC 593 301
Percy v. *Hall* [1997] QB 924 44
Preston v. *Wolverhampton NHS Trust* [1998] 1 WLR 280 (HL) 318, 321
Professional Contractors' Group v. *Commissioners of Inland Revenue*
[2001] EWCA Civ 1945 .... 350, 352
R (on the application of the Professional Contractors' Group) v. *Commissioners of
Inland Revenue* [2002] EWCA. Civ. 1945, [2002] STC 165 352
R v. *Bow Street Metropolitan Stipendiary Magistrate and Others*, ex parte *Pinochet
Ugarte (No.2)* [2000] 1 AC 119 22
R v. *Gough* (1993) AC 646 .... 22, 23

R v. Her Majesty's Advocate and The Advocate General for Scotland
[2003] 2 WLR 317 .... 49, 51
R v. Murphy [1980] QB 434 302
R v. Papadopoulos (No.2) 1979 1 NZLR 629 23
R v. Pharmaceutical Society of Great Britain, ex parte *Association of*
Pharmaceutical Importers [1987] 3 CMLR 348
R v. Secretary of State, ex parte *Trade Union Congress* (2000) IRLR 565 (CA) 320
R v. Secretary of State for Transport, ex parte *Factortame (No.2)*, (1991)
1 AC 603 320

R v. Secretary of State for Transport, ex parte *Factortame* (No 5) [1999]
3 WLR 1062 321
R v. Secretary of State, ex parte *Imperial Tobacco & ors* [2001] 1 WLR 127 319–20
R v. Stock Exchange, ex parte *Else Ltd* [1993] QB 534 348–52
R v. Sussex Justices, ex parte *McCarthy* [1924] 1 KB 256 21
Re Castioni [1891] 1 QB 149 300
Re Harrods (Buenos Aires) Ltd [1992] Ch 72 261
Roe v. Russel [1928] 2 KB 117 301
Roylance v. GMC (No 2) [2000] 1 AC 311 22
Safeway Foodstores Limited v. Scottish Provident Institution 1989 SLT 131 38
Salvesen (or Van Lorang) v. Austrian Property Administrator [1927] AC 641 258
Starrs v. Ruxton 2000 JC 208 24
Stevenson v. Midlothian District Council 1983 (HL) 50 37
Taff Vale Railway Co v. Amalgamated Society of Railway Servants
[1901] AC 426 19
Trinity Mirror plc v. Commissions of Customs & Excise [2001] 2 CMLR 759;
[2001] EWCA 65 .... 350, 352
Tullis Russell & Co Ltd v. Eadie Industries Ltd [2001] GWD 28-1122 262
Van Nievelt, Goudrian and Co's Stromvaartmij v. NV Hollandische Assurantie
Societeit and Others (1967) 56 Rev. crit. Dr.int.priv. 522 263
Vaughan Engineering Limited v. Hinkins & Frewin Limited 2003 SLT 428 ...... 40, 42
Vtech Electronics (UK) plc v. Commissioners of Customs & Excise [2003]
EWHC 59 (Ch) 351–2
Wandsworth London Borough Council v. Winder [1985] AC 461 .... 42, 43
Webb v. The Queen (1994) 181 CLR 41 23
Welex AG v. Rosa Maritime Ltd [2002] EWHC 2033 (Comm) 262
West v. Secretary of State for Scotland 1992 SC 385 38

European Court of Human Rights

Findlay v. UK (1997) 24 EHRR 221 24
James and others v. UK (1986) 8 EHRR 123 299
Piersack v. Belgium (1982) 5 EHRR 169 23
Rekvényi v. Hungary [1999] EHRLR 114 311

United States

Brazos River Authority v. City of Graham 354 SW 2d 99 (Tex 1961) 300

xliv Table of Cases

Chevron USA., Inc v. Natural Resources Defense Council, In, 467 U.S. 837 (1984) ... 275
Daubert v. Merrell Dow Pharmaceuticals 509 US 579 (1993) 213
Industrial Union Department, AFL-CIO v. American Petroleum Institute et al.
　448 US 607 (1980) 213
Kumho Tire Co v. Carmichael 526 US 137 (1999) 213
Railroad Commission of Texas v. Miller 434 SW 2d 670 (Tex 1968) 300
State ex rel Vance v. Hatten 600 SW 2d 828 (Tex Cr App 1980) 300
Tennessee Valley Authority v. Hill 437 US 153 (1978) 214

Other

Société Nouvelle des Papéteries de l'Aa v BV Maschinenfabriek BOA Hoge Raad,
　NJ1992/750 258
Van Nievelt, Goudrain and Co's Stromvaartmij v NV Hollandische Assurantie
　Societeit and Others (1967) 56 Rev. crit. Dr.int.priv. 522 263

Introduction

1

Tales From The Tartan Chambers

DIANE HANSEN-INGRAM*

1. MONDAY

Drive over the red bridge, round the Court of First Instance (CFI) building and turn left, past a Henry Moore statue into the Court's underground car park. Try to get to the office as early as possible. Otherwise risk 20 pages of shorthand notes before I can get my coat off. Though it's a rare thing for the Professor[1] to arrive first these days—his daily bike ride around Flaxweiler[2] (before breakfast, in all weathers) has put an end to that. Take the lift up to the third floor, to office P/314.[3] We're well located—right next to the President's *cabinet*[4] and the toilets. Most important task first—put on the tea machine. Check telephone, fax and e-mail. Run through latest developments (and gossip) with Christèle and Gaby. Ready for (just about) anything.

Professor (dressed in brown corduroys, blue shirt, tartan tie, Harris Tweed[5] jacket and newly polished[6] Church's English shoes) arrives, slightly breathless after taking the stairs from the car park (four flights, including basement to ground floor, and they're double height), bursts into our office and sinks down into the chair opposite my desk. Begins handing over papers, some from his giant leather school satchel, some from the pockets of his jacket. Graham[7] arrives close behind, cooler than the proverbial cucumber, carrying a box filled with more papers, books and case files in various colours.[8] If the Professor has

---

* Secretary to Judge Edward from 1989 to 1998. Shared office (and spent far too much time chatting) with Dominique Verdon (1991–1994), Christèle Courtin (1992–1995), Gabriella Carta-Paganoni (1994–present) and Nathalie Grosjean (1996–present).

[1] Judge Edward is called 'Professor' by his staff and 'Judge' or 'Professor' by his children. Mrs Edward is called 'The Boss' by everyone.

[2] Small farming village (pop. 338), 14 kms northeast of Luxembourg city, where Judge and Mrs Edward live.

[3] From 1989 to 1992, office A/0024 in the CFI.

[4] Chambers.

[5] The world's only commercially produced handwoven tweed, Harris Tweed is a trademark. Judge Edward was a director of the Harris Tweed Association Ltd (1984–1989).

[6] One of the Judge's *bête noires* is unpolished shoes, no doubt dating back to his time in the navy (HMS Hornet, 1956–1957).

[7] Graham Paul, Judge Edward's driver (1992–present).

[8] Case files are colour-coded: red files are to be read first, then blue, then green. A tremendous amount of paper comes into chambers each week: judgments, pleadings, translations, reports and memos. The Judge loves good order and has devised numerous systems (and bought countless gadgets) to keep himself organised.

just returned from a trip, the box will also contain souvenirs for all of us.[9] Professor fishes out a few things and hands them over with detailed instructions. Then looks out his notepad[10] and does a final run through. Everything is beautifully written: nothing *ever* scribbled, though he has been known to doodle during the longueur of monotonous pleadings.

Supply the Professor with a cup of tea[11] and call everyone into his office for our Monday morning meeting: three secretaries, three *référendaires*[12] and any *stagiaires*[13] or visitors who happen to be with us. The Professor takes off his jacket and puts on a wool cardigan. When we are all seated (on the black leather sofa and armchairs,[14] or the umpteen standard issue swivel chairs), he begins. He runs through his diary for the week, so we all know where he is, what he is doing and when we can expect to have some time with him. Then he runs through the weekly list. This is a list of cases where he is Reporting Judge (around 40 cases), or sitting in plenum or chamber (another 80). The list gives a complete overview of work-in-hand and, perhaps more importantly, work overdue (the refs often refer to it as the 'List of Shame').

With the unpleasant part over, it's time for a general chinwag: from the latest sexy (i.e. interesting) cases we have been allocated, to the fantastic meal someone had at the *Auberge de la Klauss*,[15] or the *Maison des Baillis*.[16]

But the highlight of the meeting (indeed, of the week) is when the Professor tells one of his tales. It could be something which happened to him over the weekend, or an old favourite.[17] But whatever it is, he's in his element and we sit, enchanted. I've seen him work his magic on schoolchildren, academics and giants of industry. Whenever he speaks, everyone else stops and, for some reason, people expect him to have the answer to everything—not just the law, but history, geography, art and music. The annoying thing is, he normally does.

For the finale, there's invariably a recommendation: the Professor's latest gadget/most recent read/cheap-at-twice-the-price wine discovery. We all nod and dutifully note down the name of the shop/publication/vineyard, as everyone really should buy it/read it/drink it as soon as possible.

---

[9] Judge and Mrs Edward are generous to a fault. The Judge always brings back small gifts from his business trips and holidays, and is a prolific postcard writer. Staff birthdays are marked with a gift and a slap-up lunch at a restaurant of the birthday boy/girl's choosing. There are also countless *cabinet* lunches and dinners at Flaxweiler, to which both staff and their partners are invited.

[10] Always *Economist* notepads.

[11] Black, no sugar or milk, in a breakfast cup from Villeroy & Boch's *Vieux Luxembourg* series.

[12] Legal Secretaries or 'refs' for short.

[13] The Court offers a limited number of paid traineeships (*stages*) to young European lawyers. Occasionally, judges and advocates general take on unpaid trainees in their chambers.

[14] Designed by Børge Mogensen (1914–1972), Denmark.

[15] http://www.auberge-de-la-klauss.com.

[16] http://www.les-baillis.com.

[17] Like the time he stayed at a rather run-down gentlemen's club in New York. Tired and hungry after a long flight, he entered the dining room and, not sure if he should merely sit down or wait to be seated, asked the waiter, 'What's the form here?' To which the waiter replied, 'The form, Sir, is that you go back to your room and put on a tie!'

It's noon precisely[18] and the whole *cabinet* (Judge, refs and secretaries) is off to the *cantine*. We were the first *cabinet* to dine *en masse*, but the Sevóns and the Ragnemalms[19] followed suit. The *cantine* food is pretty good, though after dining there five days a week, most weeks of the year, you can pretty well be sure that if it's Monday, it must be *potage parmentier*.[20] After lunch, we have a brisk walk round the Kirchberg,[21] then it's down to business.

The main bulk of the afternoon is spent in the company of the refs. First of all, there is a brainstorming session with all three taking part. The Professor is giving two talks next week (a conference in Brussels and a lecture in Trier), one of which will require a written text for publication. And he has just agreed to provide an article for a *Festschrift*, so will need a few ideas for that, too. Two of the refs depart—the third stays to look at a draft judgment (deliberated by the plenum on Friday) which needs careful rewording in French.[22] Christèle and Gaby are drafted in to help, and arrive brandishing copies of *Le Petit Robert* and the *Dictionnaire Bordas des pièges et difficultés de la langue française*.

Finally it's my turn. We try to get through as many piles of paper as time allows (the Professor is hoping for a fairly early getaway tonight as his son, John,[23] is visiting) and are just tidying up when one of the other judges pops his head round the door, on the pretext that he wants to borrow a British law journal. I can sense that he actually wants a private word with the Professor, so make my excuses and leave them to it. Graham takes a box of files down to the car, and I phone Mrs Edward to tell her that the Professor will soon be on his way.

2. TUESDAY

Professor (in navy suit, pale blue shirt, blue tie and newly polished Church's English shoes) arrives after taking the stairs, whizzes past our office and into his own, calling for one, two, three refs and myself. Graham arrives carrying a box filled with papers and files. Professor calls out instructions and, before we have a chance to reply, he's off and running, down the stairs to the *grande salle d'audience*[24] for the first plenary hearing of the day. Desperate for answers, I chase him out into the corridor, notebook in hand.

---

[18] Generally speaking, staff from Northern Europe lunch between noon and 1 pm, and those from the South between 1 and 2 pm.
[19] The cabinets of Judge Leif Sevón (Finland) and Judge Hans Ragnemalm (Sweden). All grades lunching together seems to be a Northern thing.
[20] Potato soup. Antoine Parmentier (1737–1813) introduced the potato to France.
[21] A plateau where the European institutions are clustered.
[22] French is the official working language of the Court and the main language of communication between staff (from the courtroom to the *cantine*).
[23] Judge and Mrs Edward have four children: Giles, Anne, John and Katherine.
[24] Main courtroom.

The second plenary case didn't start until after lunch, so it's late afternoon before I have a chance to have a quick session with the Professor. I've got letters for signing, draft judgments from the English translation department which need approval, the seventh version of an article he is writing (I know he's a perfectionist, but if he makes any more changes, I'll scream) and over 10 telephone messages. He takes off his jacket, puts on his cardigan and we sit down at the desk (me on a swivel chair, he's perched on his Robert Thompson[25] stool).

His office is an Aladdin's cave, though the cleaning lady would probably describe it as a junkshop. There are papers, books and files everywhere. The Professor has had bookshelves built into every available space—a sea of blue and purple ECRs. Photos of friends and family stare back at you from the bookshelves and walls and desk. The biggest desk you have ever seen, with two writing surfaces, a computer section and a conference table. That is, if you could get a glimpse of the desk, which groans under the weight of articles and case files, rows of post-it pads (in several sizes), paperclip containers (in various shapes), pen and pencil pots, blotting paper (as much as he loves his computer, all personal correspondence is written in fountain pen), bottles of ink (all blue, all *Montblanc*), highlighter pens (in all the colours of the rainbow), computer disks and various gadgets for stamping, stapling, punching and labelling. Plus the computer, CD player, humidifier and purifier. Anything not in constant use is resigned to the drawers below: stamps (various denominations and from several countries), a set of scales, notebooks and jotters, envelopes (white, manila, padded), plastic files (in various colours), personal notepaper (Flaxweiler and Edinburgh), stacks of postcards (for writing personal messages to friends and family), photos, medicines (headache tablets and Olbas oil), wetwipes and stain-remover cloths (for those days when the *cantine* is serving *moules et frites*).

When we're through, the refs arrive to brief the Professor for tonight's *réunion générale*[26] at 6 pm. Given that he read the Reports (15 cases) over the weekend, it doesn't take them too long to get through the dossier. He puts on his jacket, combs his hair and, with a quick 'toodle-oo' to all of us, is off.

The Professor comes back to the office at the *pause technique*,[27] signs a few more documents and makes changes to a dozen more (drat). He tells Graham that the meeting should easily be over by 8 pm.

---

[25] A furniture maker from Kilburn, known as 'Mousey Thompson' and 'The Mouseman' (1876–1955). If you look closely you will find a small hand-carved mouse on all his work: chair legs, bed heads, etc. He chose this as his trademark because he was 'as poor as a church mouse' when he got his first commission. http://www.robertthompsons.co.uk.

[26] General Meeting of the Court (judges, advocates general and registrar). Preliminary Reports are presented, and the Court decides whether the case should be dealt with by the whole Court, a *petit plenum*, a chamber of five or a chamber of three.

[27] Court terminology for toilet break during the *Réunion générale*.

3. WEDNESDAY

The Professor is away at the *Comité administratif*[28] for most of the morning, so get on with the organisation of the visit by British judges to Luxembourg next week. Their two-day guided tour of the European Court of Justice (ECJ) includes hospitality[29] at the Edwards' home. Phone 'The Boss' and give her the final numbers for the sit-down dinner (28 this time). Then the dietary requirements: one gluten-free, one kosher, two vegetarian and one allergic to seafood. Mrs Edward doesn't flinch—she's being doing this so long, she could cater for a black-tie reception using a camping stove.

Professor comes back and I follow him into his office, bearing tea and biscuits (it's going to be a long session) and my shorthand notebook. We work through piles of paper, top to bottom, from left to right.[30]

After lunch (and another brisk walk), we manage to get through another two towering piles of paperwork, i.e. it's moved from his desk to mine, before the arrival of a language teacher.[31] These lessons always start with the Professor apologizing for not doing his homework, and the teacher telling him not to fret.

Just over an hour later the Professor is off and running again, this time to a meeting of the Court's computer committee, of which he is the chairman. He's not sure how long it will take, so we agree to meet downstairs at a drinks reception for Court staff in the *salle des pas perdus*.[32] It's an occasion to catch up with former colleagues from the CFI and to find out what's really going on in-house.[33] I love the *salle des pas perdus*. Where else can you place your drink on the plinth of a Miró[34] or touch a Rodin statue[35] (which I do, whenever I'm on my way to the library) without an alarm ringing somewhere?

4. THURSDAY

The Professor is in a bit of a rush this morning. He's giving a talk to students from a UK university before the First Chamber case starts in the *salle*

---

[28] Administrative Committee.
[29] The three British members of the ECJ and CFI split the cost of food and drink. Mrs Edward, with a little help from her trusty assistant, Graham, does all the baking (she makes the world's best bread), cooking, serving and washing up.
[30] If I've learnt one thing from the Judge, it's never to put off a task (however unpleasant) until later. The longer you leave it, the worse it gets.
[31] Margit Pfänder (German), Luisella Piccoli (Italian), plus Greek and Spanish teachers.
[32] Main hall in the Palais building.
[33] The drivers and internal mailmen are always first with the latest scandal.
[34] 'Bird nesting on flowering fingers' by Joan Miró (1969).
[35] 'Bronze Age' by August Rodin (1876).

Grieshaber[36] at 9.30 am, so doesn't come up to the office but sends Graham instead with a list of things that need doing.

The hearing is over fairly quickly (the parties kept to their 15 minute slots)[37] and the Professor looks in on us to find out if anything requires his urgent attention. He manages a quick meeting with the refs before he's required in one of the conference rooms downstairs. A Minister of Justice is visiting the Court today, and all the members of the ECJ are expected to attend a round table discussion followed by an official lunch.

We are all queueing up to see him when he returns, but will have to wait a little longer. The Professor closes the door to his office[38] and gets ready for his nap. He used to sleep on the floor of his office in the CFI, but his elevation to the ECJ in 1992 meant a larger office and more furniture, so he now uses the sofa.[39] I wake him up after 20 minutes (eight out of ten times he snores through the alarm) and tell him there's fresh tea. His hair is standing on end, so he wanders off in the direction of the toilets, combing his hair as he goes. Supply him with more tea and he's bright as a button. Liz[40] and I tried powernapping once and were exhausted for the rest of the day.

We're in and out of the Professor's office for the next hour and he's probably glad to leave at 3.30 pm for the relatively peaceful deliberations of the First Chamber (three straightforward cases today). He returns half an hour later to find that an old friend has popped in to say hello—an English barrister who is in Luxembourg pleading a case over in the the CFI.[41]

The next couple of hours should be fairly quiet. So he dons his favourite cardigan, puts on some music and comfies himself in an armchair. Cup of tea on the table beside him and a pile of Reports for the Hearing, draft judgments and the minutes of various Court committees on his lap.

Phone Graham just before 7 pm to say that the Professor is ready to go home. Before leaving, try to make my desk look a little less like a mini version of the Professor's.

5. FRIDAY

Deliberations of the full Court start at 10 am and there are 9 cases up for discussion today. The Professor arrives at 8.45 am to find four new notes for

---

[36] In my opinion, the most exciting courtroom (metal walls, peacock blue chairs and wooden boxes hanging from the ceiling), now sadly closed. The Palais building was evacuated in July 1999, due to the discovery of asbestos, and is currently under reconstruction.

[37] Generally 30 minutes each, but 15 minutes in hearings before the small chambers of three judges and for interveners in direct actions.

[38] Judge Edward works with an open door. It is only closed for two reasons: his after-lunch nap and serious gossip.

[39] Look underneath the cushions and you'll find a newspaper for putting his feet on.

[40] Elizabeth Willocks, the Judge's first Legal Secretary (1989–1994).

[41] It is customary for counsel not to approach members of the Court when pleading before them that day.

deliberation on his desk and three restless *référendaires* ready for action. They spend the next quarter of an hour with their heads bent over the desk, skimming through ECRs, checking references, consulting CELEX and bouncing ideas off each other. Meanwhile, there is a great noise coming from the corridors where a flock of refs from other *cabinets* are trying to lobby their own judge's idea.

The Professor sits down at the screen and starts drafting a reply. The refs huddle round and every word is carefully weighed. Christèle and Gaby proofread the note, print it, then all three of us are out of the door at full speed. Gaby and I take the *cabinets* on the third floor, Christèle those on the second. We weave in and out of offices, hoping to deliver the note before the judges make their way to the deliberation room. On our way, we meet secretaries from the other *cabinets* on the same mission.

10.05 am and it's all quiet in the corridors. The judges are behind closed doors in the *salle des délibérés* and an air of quiet respectability has once again descended over the court. We're not quite sure how heated the discussions are inside the deliberation room, but at least the language used will be polite.[42]

Two hours pass and we're beginning to wonder if the Professor is going to get away in time. He's booked on Luxair flight LG403 to London at 12.50 pm (he's giving a speech there tonight, then going on to Edinburgh tomorrow for two trustee meetings).

At 12.15 pm he bursts into our office, grabs his ticket, passport and some last paperwork from the waiting refs, and runs off down the stairs, not to the car park but the main Palais entrance. Graham is waiting for him on the concourse, with the engine running and the Professor's satchel on the back seat. The Professor jumps into the front passenger seat and they're off.

The secretaries breathe a sigh of relief and the refs collapse into chairs. We're damn glad to get him out of our hair. But—to tell you the truth—we're actually looking forward to his return on Monday morning, when he bursts through the door, breathless, but raring to go. As Robert Burns[43] might have said, 'Here's tae him, Wha's like him, Damn few, And they're a' deid! (Mair's the pity)'.

---

[42] The members of the Court usually address each other by their first names, and use the first person singular (*tu*). However, in deliberations, the judges use surnames and the polite form (*vous*).

[43] Scotland's national poet (1759–1796).

II. The Scottish Perspective

2
What Waldemar Saw: A Young German's View of the Scottish Legal System

ALAN RODGER

ALTHOUGH THESE ESSAYS mark David Edward's retirement from his office as a judge of the Court of Justice, his Scottish friends still think of him, perhaps first and foremost, as a powerful figure on the Scottish legal scene. In the 1960s and 1970s, first as Clerk and then as Treasurer of the Faculty of Advocates—the Scottish Bar—he transformed its administration, reorganised its finances and set it on an entirely new path. In campaigning for these reforms, David forced members of Faculty, almost for the first time, to look critically at an institution that was both familiar and comfortable. Later, in the Council of the Bars and Law Societies of the European Union (the CCBE) and in the Court of Justice, he cast a critical eye over the legal and other institutions of the various member states. He may therefore find some interest in this account of what a young German thought of the legal institutions he found on a visit to Scotland in 1906.

In Germany the Bürgerliches Gesetzbuch (the BGB) had entered into force on 1 January 1900, bringing the same system of substantive law to the whole of Germany. Although this monumental reform carried with it the risk of legal isolationism, there were some at least in Germany who thought that lessons could still be learned from experience in other countries. In the field of public law Rudolf von Gneist's work comparing the 'English' and German systems of constitutional and administrative law[1] had long been influential, not least because it showed the working of another modern state with a monarchical constitution. As the twentieth century opened, there was a feeling that, while the new civil code had brought the system of German private law up to date, the law of procedure remained in need of revision to meet the challenges of the new century and of the new Empire. Could lessons be learned from Britain?

---

[1] R von Gneist, *Das englische Verwaltungsrecht der Gegenwart in Vergleichung mit den deutschen Verwaltungssystemen* (Berlin, Springer 3rd edn, 1883–84).

One man, at least, thought so. He was Franz Adickes,[2] the hyperactive Liberal Mayor of Frankfurt-am-Main. Now aged about 60, he had had a legal education and had at one time contemplated a life in academic law, but had instead forged an outstanding career in local government. During his twenty-one years as mayor, by improvements in education, housing and town planning, he did much to make Frankfurt a modern city. Just as the First World War broke out, he was to achieve perhaps his greatest triumph when the Johann Wolfang Goethe-Universität, the university for the city of Frankfurt, came into existence. In the midst of this welter of activities, on 30 March 1906, Adickes found the time to make a speech to the Upper House of the Prussian Parliament advocating far-reaching reforms to what he saw as wasteful aspects of the German justice system. In particular, he pointed out that, under the law of 1879 which governed court procedures, the only people who could pronounce orders having legal effect were the judges. In practice this meant that the judges spent much of their time doing work which could have been done by less highly qualified officials. If some of this work were to be offloaded onto other officials, the number of judges could be reduced. Similarly, there were too many layers of appeals, all of them requiring to be manned by judges. If the appeals were rationalised, again the number of judges might be reduced and a more efficient and economical system would result.

His speech attracted attention. Adickes followed it up immediately with a book, 'Basics of a Thorough Reform of the Justice System'[3] in which he identified the problems and suggested that lessons could be learned from the English and Scottish legal systems. Both the speech and the book were the result of his own reflexions on the British legal system, based partly on Gneist's famous book but more particularly on a study of the relevant official statistics and the discussions which he had had with judges, lawyers and lay people during a visit to England. While careful to avoid the pitfall of praising the British system extravagantly, Adickes noted that in the English courts Masters relieved the English judges of much of the routine procedural work, while the use of lay magistrates and juries allowed the legal system to operate with very many fewer judges than in Germany. His and similar criticisms bore fruit when in 1909 legislation was passed to relieve the judges of some routine work. After the War more radical measures were adopted in the interests of economy.

Before launching his campaign, Adickes had not been able to go to Britain for long. He certainly spent time in England, but it is not clear whether he visited Scotland. His book did, however, include a considerable amount of information about the Scottish legal system, derived apparently from official publications

---

[2] See article on Adickes, Franz in *Neue Deutsche Biographie* Vol 1 (Berlin, Duncker & Humblot, 1953).

[3] F Adickes, *Grundlinien durchgreifender Justizreform* (Berlin, Guttentag, 1906). The preface is dated Palm Sunday (8 April) 1906, just over a week after his speech to the Herrenhaus.

and two recent works on Scots law.⁴ Adickes suggested that others might carry on and, where necessary, correct his work.⁵ Quickly taking up the challenge, some time later in 1906 a young Prussian lawyer, Waldemar Peters, set off to Scotland to study the legal system there. The very next year, a book based on his experience appeared under the title 'The Scottish Legal System in the Past and the Present'.⁶

Not much is known about Peters. Like the young man in Zarah Leander's hit song of 1940, *er heisst Waldemar*, he was called Waldemar. He came from a protestant Prussian family, both his father, Wilibald, and his grandfather being judges.⁷ Since he had published his doctoral thesis in 1902,⁸ it seems likely that Waldemar was born about 1880 and so would have been roughly 26 or 27 at the time of his trip to Scotland. He was the eldest of the three children of Wilibald and Marie Vogelsang, the other two being girls. Hela, who was born in 1885 and lived on until 1973, was a portrait-painter and engraver.⁹ She enjoyed a certain celebrity during her lifetime, being the subject of an article in *The German Woman* in 1914. Waldemar's father had worked his way up through the Prussian court system and eventually, on 1 January 1900, the day when the BGB came into force throughout Germany, he became a member of the Imperial Supreme Court, the Reichsgericht. He served on the Third Senate, dealing chiefly with cases involving public officials.¹⁰ At the time of the publication of his Scottish book Waldemar was a Gerichtsassessor,¹¹ a trainee judge, but, not surprisingly, he seems to have spent time later working as a Regierungsrat, a civil servant roughly equivalent to an Assistant Principal in the British civil service. Unfortunately, and almost inevitably, he served as a regimental captain in the First World War and was killed in 1915.¹² His father outlived him, dying in 1926.

While Adickes had quite openly put forward the institutions of British law as models which might be copied, Waldemar Peters disavowed any such intention. His aim, he tells us, was to give a 'purely objective description' of the Scottish system, leaving it to others to decide whether the Scottish institutions contained

---

⁴ J W Brodie-Innes, *Comparative Principles of the Laws of England and Scotland. Courts and Procedure* (Edinburgh,, Greens, 1903); J Chisolm (ed), *Green's Encyclopaedia of the Law of Scotland* (Edinburgh, Greens, 1896–1904).
⁵ Above n3, at III.
⁶ W Peters, *Der schottische Rechtskörper in Vergangenheit und Gegenwart* (Berlin, Franz Vahlen, 1907).
⁷ See H A L Degener's article on Peters, Friedrich Albert Emil Wilibald, in *Wer ist's?* (Leipzig, H. A. Ludwig Degener, 1922).
⁸ W Peters, *Die Klagenkonkurrenz im römischen, gemeinen und neuen bürgerlichen Rechte* (Berlin, Häring, 1902).
⁹ See article on Ebbecke, Hela Peters in *Degeners Wer ist's?* (Berlin, Hermann Degener, 10th edn, 1935).
¹⁰ A Lobe, *Fünfzig Jahre Reichsgericht* (Berlin, W de Gruyter, 1929) 368, 390–92 and 24.
¹¹ Above n6, at title page.
¹² Above n7. Wilibald's last published work was on the defence of German borders against French Lorraine: W Peters, *Die Sicherung der deutschen Grenzen gegen Französisch-Lothringen im Licht der Geschichte* (Dresden and Leipzig, Bibliothek für Volks- und Weltwirtschaft Heft 56, 1918).

anything worth copying.[13] His professed attitude was timely since by 1906 Britain and Germany were eyeing one another warily. The Entente Cordiale had been concluded in 1904 and in February 1906 the first Dreadnought was launched. Not surprisingly perhaps, Adickes' promotion of Britain as the fount of wisdom on procedural matters was meeting with resistance.[14] Peters might therefore not have wished to be seen as openly advocating a British model. None the less it is noteworthy that his book is dedicated to his father, Wilibald, who was a prolific writer on legal topics, not least on aspects of procedure. In particular, he had written what sounds like a somewhat dry commentary on the regulations on the powers of clerks of court in the Prussian Amtsgericht (roughly equivalent to the County Court).[15] At this time he was actively interested in advocating reforms to cut delays in proceedings[16] and in considering whether lessons could be learned from the experience in England.[17] This suggests that Adickes' speech would have struck a particular chord within the Peters family and that Waldemar's trip to Scotland may have been prompted, or at the very least encouraged, by his father.

Waldemar's book runs to 135 pages. Consistently with its purpose, it deals only with the legal institutions—the courts, the judges, court officials, prosecutors and the legal profession—not at all with substantive Scots law. The year after his visit, the Sheriff Courts (Scotland) Act 1907 was to adjust the balance between the Court of Session and the Sheriff Court by removing the last vestiges of the Court of Session's monopoly of jurisdiction in cases relating to land, which had once been the very core of its work. So his book describes the system just before that important reform. A reader today is unlikely to be able to spot inaccuracies in the details of his account but the author of a contemporary notice in the *Law Magazine and Review* rightly remarked that 'there is many an advocate in Edinburgh who might learn a good deal from it.'[18] Not only was his book unique in its time, but no convenient systematic account of the legal institutions of Scotland was to appear in English until more than fifty years later.[19]

As its title makes clear, the book covers the Scottish legal system in the past as well as in the present, since Peters thought that the current institutions could not be understood without some knowledge of their history. Therefore the first 60 pages are historical, starting with the position up until the sixteenth century and then going on to cover developments after that. This later period of history

---

[13] Above n6, at Preface, VI.
[14] See, eg, K von Lewinski, *England als Erzieher?* (Berlin, Franz Vahlen, 1907).
[15] W Peters, *Die Geschäftsordnung für die Gerichtsschreibereien der preussischen Amtsgerichte* (Berlin, Siemenroth & Worms, 1894; 3rd edn, with W Boschan 1901).
[16] W Peters, *Prozessverschleppung, Prozessumbildung und die Lehren der Geschichte* (Berlin, Häring, 1904); *Die Beschleunigung und Vereinfachung des bürgerlichen Streitverfahrens und der Entwurf zur Justiznovelle* (Berlin, Franz Vahlen, 1908).
[17] W Peters, *Das englische bürgerliche Streitverfahren und die deutsche Zivilprozessreform* (Berlin, Franz Vahlen, 1908).
[18] (1907) 32 *Law Magazine and Review* 510.
[19] D M Walker, *The Scottish Legal System* (Edinburgh, Greens, 1959).

is broken down into sections on the lower courts (the Sheriff Courts etc.), the higher courts (the Court of Session, the High Court of Justiciary and the House of Lords), and finally a miscellaneous group such as the Court of Exchequer, the Bill Chamber and the Jury Court. Although the *Law Magazine* reviewer particularly commended this historical section, it is very obviously derivative and is less interesting for a reader today. The second part on the contemporary legal system starts by describing the professional bodies and then goes on to deal with the various lower courts, the supreme courts and the House of Lords, followed by a number of other legal institutions including the public prosecutors.

On the whole the author abides by his self-imposed rule of strict objectivity. The institutions are described very precisely. If his account was going to be useful for reformers in Germany, they had to be able to assess not only how the system operated but how much it cost. So he is careful to give details, in both Pounds Sterling and German Marks, of the salaries paid to even quite minor officials. The high status of the post of Lord Advocate, the principal Scottish law officer and head of the prosecuting system, can be seen from the fact that at that time he was paid the same as the head of the judiciary, the Lord President of the Court of Session. Today, by contrast, his successor gets little more than half the Lord President's salary. Peters lists all the relevant positions but, in conformity with his scientific purpose, never gives the names of any of those who held them at the time. As a result, the work has a certain timeless quality.

Only rarely does he let his own views show through. When he does so, however, they are especially interesting precisely because he must have felt strongly about the matter in order to break his self-imposed rule of strict objectivity. So, for instance, in the historical section he cannot resist saying that section 2 of the Court of Session Act 1839, which vested the right of appointing the Clerk of Justiciary in the Crown instead of the Lord Justice-Clerk, had to be passed after Lord Justice-Clerk Boyle had nominated his ten-year old son to the vacancy.[20]

Such abuses may more easily arise in a small system and Peters obviously felt that they had not been entirely eliminated in the system that he was studying in 1906. At that time the Faculty of Advocates, whose members enjoyed a monopoly of practice before the higher courts, was in many ways an exclusive club. An insuperable bar to entry for most people lay in the capital sum which new members had to pay to the Faculty before they could be admitted to practice. Peters was rightly amazed at the size of this entry money and had no doubt of its effect. He comments that:

> persons without means scarcely feature in the advocates' profession since the fees for admission to the Faculty are extraordinarily high. They amount to £339 10s. (= around 6800 Marks), of which £50 are Stamp Duty, £50 go to the Widows' Fund, while almost all the rest goes straight into the coffers of the Advocates Library![21]

---

[20] Above n6, at 130–31.
[21] *Ibid*, at 65.

This most restrained of authors actually permits himself an exclamation mark. Elsewhere Peters records that the salary of a judge of the Court of Session, the equivalent of an English High Court judge, was £3600 per annum.[22] So, in order to become an advocate, you had to pay a lump sum of just under 10% of a judge's salary: if it still existed, the equivalent entry fee today would be about £15,000. Although the sum did not increase greatly, the entry money remained a significant deterrent to entry until the 1960s when a reform promoted by David Edward as Clerk of Faculty allowed it to be paid in instalments. Inflation did the rest.

Not only the Faculty of Advocates had erected a financial barrier to entry. When Peters comes to the exclusive body of Edinburgh solicitors, the Writers to the Signet, he notes that the entry money is £486 2s. 9d. One must 'buy the glory' of becoming a Writer to the Signet by paying 'enormous fees that all go into the coffers of the Society and exceed even those of the advocates.'[23]

Another point on admission to the Faculty of Advocates struck Peters. He notes that all the Court of Session judges and all the Sheriffs, who deal with certain appeals from the Sheriff Court, are chosen from the Faculty. The Faculty in turn has a completely independent right to decide whom to admit to membership, with the result that members of Faculty 'have it in their power to keep the more important judicial positions free from such elements as do not meet with their approval.'[24] Peters then goes through the various regulations on admission, ending up with the ballot in which members of Faculty must vote to admit the new member. This ballot means, he says, that the Faculty can at will restrict the size and composition of the membership.[25] In this respect, at least, Peters probably misread the situation and exaggerated the importance of the ballot which was, by this date, little more than an amusing formality. There is little to suggest that it was actually used as a means of keeping people out. On the other hand, the hurdles to be crossed before admission—the university courses, the unpaid period of training and, above all, the entrance money—were so substantial that few 'undesirables' could ever have presented themselves for admission.

For present purposes, the interesting point is that Peters was clearly very surprised to find that the arrangements for admission to the Scottish professional bodies were so strongly biased in favour of the wealthy, and so clearly designed to keep power within the hands of a moneyed elite. This was not the reaction of a radical observer from republican France or from the democratic United States, but of a young man from Prussia, the most conservative part of the conservative German Empire where the institutions were deliberately designed to be anything but democratic. Basically, his perception of the Bar was surely correct, even though the published memoirs of Scottish judges such as Lord Shaw of

---

[22] Above n6, at 84.
[23] Ibid, at 67.
[24] Ibid, at 63.
[25] Ibid, at 65.

Dunfermline and Lord Alness often strive to present a rather different, more homely or couthy, picture of life at the Bar as being in tune with the social and religious life of the wider Scottish community. There were undoubtedly close ties with the Scottish churches since many advocates were sons of ministers of one denomination or another. But this fact does not point to humble origins. Rather it serves to highlight the wealthy background of many ministers of those days who could afford to support their sons in this way. The very real barriers to entry that Peters observed had a lasting influence. As judges, advocates admitted under the regulations of those days were to continue to dominate the Scottish legal system well into the second half of the twentieth century.

Another point which clearly intrigued Peters was the amount of time during which the Court of Session judges actually worked. This would plainly have been of interest to any of his readers who were considering ways to make the German judicial system more efficient. He goes into the matter in considerable detail, giving the statutory rules for the sessions and for the breaks at Christmas and in February.[26] His conclusion is that in any year the total working time of a Court of Session judge comes to less than seven months and the total vacation time to more than five months. Not content with this, he points out that the court does not usually sit on Mondays (when the judges may be required to do criminal work), nor on 15 May or 11 November, nor indeed on certain other days such as the King's Birthday. Somewhat remorselessly, he adds that, since there are 4 judges in each Division and only 3 usually sit, this allows the Inner House appeal judges to have every fourth day free, while the five first instance Lords Ordinary have a blank day every fifth day. He tells us that sittings usually begin at 10 and finish at 3.30, on Saturday by 1 p.m. It is difficult to conclude that Peters was striving to impress his readers with the arduous nature of the work of the Court of Session judges in those far-off days. With studied restraint, he does not spell out the lessons which his German readers might draw from these facts. Certainly, any overworked German judges might well have been attracted by the picture which he drew.

The absence of any system of administrative law in Britain was as familiar a theme to German lawyers as it was to Dicey.[27] Not surprisingly, therefore, Peters notes that there are no separate administrative courts in Scotland: the principle is that all, including officials, are equal before the law.[28] For the rest, he obviously found the somewhat haphazard structure of the Scottish court system strange. He himself came from a logical system with first instance courts over which there lay a pyramid of appeal courts. By contrast in Scotland he found a series of overlapping jurisdictions—with the Court of Session having exclusive first instance jurisdiction in certain matters, but sharing jurisdiction

---

[26] Ibid, at 95–96.
[27] See, for example, G Anschütz, 'Verwaltungsrecht' in R Stammler *et al*, *Systematische Rechtswissenschaft* (Berlin and Leipzig, B G Teubner, 1906) 377–81: the English and Contintental systems are said to be 'completely incommensurable'.
[28] Above n6, at 68–69.

with the sheriff courts in many others. Then there was the system of appeals to the Sheriffs from their substitutes or in certain situations to the Court of Session, but in the case of the Small Debt Courts appeals lay to the Justiciary Court—which otherwise dealt only with criminal cases. On the criminal side the same kind of confusion could be seen, for example, with the overlapping jurisdiction of the High Court and the Sheriff Court in jury trials. He notes that, if someone were convicted in the Justiciary Court, which dealt with the most serious charges, he could not appeal.[29] The difference in the approach to appeals between Britain and Germany had, of course, struck Adickes. In accordance with his strictly objective approach Peters makes no comment on the Scottish position. But in Britain the lack of any proper system of appeals in criminal cases, especially in cases of murder carrying the death penalty, was already being called into question. Indeed in England the Criminal Appeal Bill setting up a Criminal Appeal Court was going through Parliament as Peters was writing his book. The equivalent reform in Scotland had to wait until the scandal of the Oscar Slater case eventually forced a change in the Criminal Appeal (Scotland) Act 1926.

Peters seems to have been interested in the historical reasons for the existence of these various courts with their overlapping jurisdictions. In particular he investigates the steps by which the Sheriff Court in its present form came into existence and by which in 1868 the machinery of advocation was largely superseded by a system of appeals to the Court of Session. It is not difficult to find the source of all this material in the Historical Introduction to John Dove Wilson's work on Sheriff Court practice, where he lovingly examines all these issues.[30] Without having to abandon his stance of neutrality Peters is able to indicate a view about the Scottish structure by citing[31] the prediction—Peters calls it 'the wish'—of Dove Wilson that some day at last the Court of Session and sheriff courts

> will stand to each other as courts of higher and lower instance, with their relative powers and jurisdictions as sharply defined as if they were to be found in a code framed with the wonderful foresight of continental jurists.[32]

This is a classic piece of Dove Wilson. He had attended Berlin University in the 1850s and ever since had been a rather uncritical admirer of Continental codes and advocate of codification in Britain.[33] Not surprisingly Peters picks this up, but he would not so readily appreciate that, although Dove Wilson's book was highly regarded, his views on the virtues of logical codes were not widely shared and so, to this day, his prediction of an orderly system has not come to pass.

---

[29] Above n6, at 99.
[30] J Dove Wilson, *The Practice of the Sheriff Courts of Scotland in Civil Causes* (Edinburgh, Bell & Bradfute, 4th edn, 1891).
[31] Above n6, at 23–24.
[32] Above n30, at 27.
[33] A Rodger, 'Codification of Commercial Law in Victorian Britain' (1992) 108 *Law Quarterly Review* 570.

A Young German's of the Scottish Legal System 19

We may also notice that Peters takes particular interest in the law-making function of the courts—especially in the difference which he sees in the way the House of Lords makes law and the Court of Session and High Court of Justiciary make law.[34] Those brought up in the system take the rôle of case law for granted. Coming from outside, Peters adopts a more theoretical and analytical approach. So, for instance, he points out that, of the purely Scottish courts, only those with jurisdiction over the whole of Scotland can make law in this way since only their decisions apply throughout the country. The lower courts, with their limited territorial jurisdiction, cannot perform this function.[35] The Court of Session and High Court make law by laying down principles which, through repeated use, become part of the settled store of objective law which the lower courts must apply.[36] In the case of the Court of Session, however, this objective law can be set aside by a decision of the House of Lords, which Peters thinks may be influenced by the political outlook of members of the House.[37] It looks as if he found it hard to accept that the House of Lords in its judicial capacity would act in a judicial rather than in a political fashion. Moreover he was plainly puzzled by the fact that, in the end, one House of Parliament had the right to determine the correct interpretation of a statute which had required to be passed by both Houses.[38] This leads Peters to raise the spectre of the House of Lords in its judicial capacity taking the same approach as it had adopted in its legislative capacity, as opposed to the approach which the Commons had taken. Although all British lawyers know that the system does not in fact work in this way, it obviously appeared strange and fraught with potential dangers to someone looking at it from outside. These fears and dangers about the independence of the judicial decisions of the House of Lords may have seemed more substantial to a foreign observer in 1906. As he would read in the newspapers, after the General Election in January, the historic struggle between the two Houses of Parliament was building up, especially in relation to trade union reform to deal with the judgment of the House of Lords in *Taff Vale Railway Co v. Amalgamated Society of Railway Servants*.[39] Peters' theoretical concerns will only finally be laid to rest if the proposals to set up a Supreme Court take effect.

Last and not least interestingly, it should be noted that Peters sees Scots Law as very much a case law system as opposed to a system developing from antecedent principles. The purpose of statutes, he says, is usually to give a more coherent and comprehensive form to rules that have been worked out by the courts: 'more of an editorial than of a creative activity'.[40] The courts make the

[34] Above n6, at 110–19.
[35] *Ibid*, at 112.
[36] *Ibid*, at 112–13.
[37] *Ibid*, at 111.
[38] *Ibid*, at 111–12.
[39] [1901] AC 426.
[40] Above n6, at 113.

law on a very practical basis. Indeed the leading characteristic of the law made by the courts is its very practicality. The courts first decide the answer in the individual case and then ask what principle can be derived from it. In this way the courts avoid laying down principles as opposed to law. Peters observes that, because of the variety of circumstances in everyday life, general principles can constitute a great danger to the administration of justice. Under the Scottish system the public is in no danger of having the workability of legal theories tried out on its legal assets. There is no conflict between law and the practical requirements of everyday life, for the highest law is to be true to those requirements.[41]

While Peters' view of Scots Law as essentially a case law system with no great attachment to principle may be a little over-simplified, it probably reflected the view of practitioners of the time. It is also much nearer the truth than is admitted by those who like to portray Scots Law as somehow peculiarly based on a set of defined principles which the judges apply in preference to precedent.[42] While Peters obviously sees the advantages in the very practical approach of the Scottish courts, he is not blind to possible disadvantages. Their approach may lead to uncertainty, as a result of which members of the public may have difficulty in forming a clear view of the consequences of a decision. He also thinks that the Scottish approach frequently allows the judges to decide on the basis of general considerations and on the basis of discretion, instead of having to go back to the more difficult task of laying down a rule of positive law.[43] One suspects that he might assess the advantages and disadvantages in much the same way today.

It seems unlikely that Peters' book had any significant influence on the debate on procedural reforms in Germany. Nor would it be sensible to attach undue weight to the observations of a foreign observer who could not have immersed himself in the Scottish legal system. Nonetheless, with all its limitations, the book stands as a friendly, but candid, assessment of some aspects of the Scottish legal system in the opening decade of the twentieth century. In the opening decade of the twenty-first century, under the auspices of the British Council, many young European lawyers, known as 'Eurodevils', come to spend six months studying aspects of the Scottish legal system and working with practitioners and judges. David Edward has long been one of the greatest supporters of the programme. What these latter-day Waldemars learn and report about the Scottish system when they return home we can never be sure. But it cannot all be bad, since every year new faces appear to take the course—presumably to their benefit, but certainly to the benefit of the members of the Scottish legal profession and judiciary, *der schottische Rechtskörper* of today.

---

[41] Above n6, at 114.
[42] A Rodger, 'Thinking about Scots Law' (1996) 1 *Edinburgh Law Review* 1, 11.
[43] Above n6, at 114.

3

Justice Seen To Be Done

THE RT. HON. THE LORD CLYDE

JUSTICE IS NORMALLY nowadays represented as a female figure holding in one hand an upraised sword and in the other a pair of scales. The sword represents her power and the scales are said to signify her impartiality.[1] There is a blindfold wound around her eyes. But the addition of a blindfold is a relatively recent feature, dating back only to the sixteenth century. In antiquity Justice was distinguished by her clear-sightedness and in the older tradition[2] Justice would normally be represented in painting and in sculpture without a blindfold.[3]

In the generality blindfolding is a symbol of moral or spiritual blindness, of the darkness of sin and ignorance, or the arbitrary randomness of chance.[4] To those who do not understand the symbolism it might seem that without being able to see it would be impossible for Justice to discover whether her scales have reached an equilibrium or to know who it is that falls victim to her sword. Or one might be led to think that Justice is to be blind to the realities of life. The symbolic purpose of the blindfold is evidently to represent a judicial impartiality, but the scales alone should suffice to show that and a total deprivation of sight seems a somewhat extreme way of representing impartiality. But the difference in tradition may reflect a tension between the necessity for judges to be independent and impartial and the desirability for judges to have contact with the real world.

Justice should not only see what she is doing but should be seen to be doing it. The judicial process requires not only that justice should be done but that justice 'should manifestly and undoubtedly be seen to be done'.[5] With regard to the substance of the decision there may be occasions when a court's vision may be thought to have waivered. But appeal courts and if necessary legislation may avail to put that right. However, the requirement that justice must be seen to be done looks principally to the mechanisms and procedures of the whole process

---

[1] JA Hall, *Dictionary of Subjects and Symbols in Art* (Boulder, Co, Westview Press, 1986), 183.
[2] *Ibid* at 183.
[3] Examples can be found in Bernini's Tomb of Pope Urban VIII and Veronese's Homage to Venus.
[4] Hall, note 1, above, at 49. Nemesis and Fortuna are both represented with blindfolds at 221. So also are Ignorance and Avarice.
[5] R v. *Sussex Justices, ex parte McCarthy* [1924] 1 KB 256, Hewart CJ at 259.

of decision-making. The procedural right to a fair trial does not carry with it any protection against judicial error, but is concerned with the question whether the tribunal has dealt fairly and equally with the parties. In Scotland, where Judge Edward first qualified and practised, the test has been said to be not 'Has an unjust result been reached?', but 'Was there an opportunity afforded for injustice to be done?'.[6]

In exploring how much transparency is required for justice to be seen to be done one obvious starting point is the matter of impartiality and independence on the part of any person or body acting judicially.[7] Partiality may be actual or apparent. The principle underlying the rule about actual partiality is that no man may be judge in his own cause. This means that the judge is disqualified if he or she is a party to the dispute or stands personally to gain by the outcome of it. Disqualification has also now been recognised to apply where the judge is involved personally or as a director of a company in promoting the same cause in the same organisation as a party to the case.[8] But this cannot be developed too far. Where there is no involvement in positive promotion private beliefs should not readily be elevated into a partiality warranting disqualification. Judges are human beings with an education and experience of life which will inevitably have moulded their attitudes and beliefs. They will have their own views on society and their own values. Their personal beliefs may have to be made subservient to the law which it is their primary duty to administer. They may still be able to act impartially despite the potential influences caused by their individual experience of life or their own personal beliefs.

But for justice to be seen to be done the judge or tribunal must be seen to be impartial. This is not strictly an application of the principle that a man may not be judge in his own cause. It is more simply an ingredient of the over-ruling requirement for fairness. But a problem arises in this context in the precise definition of the measure by which the appearance is to be tested. Is it the court's view of the risk of bias, or is it the court's view of the public perception of the risk? In England it was earlier observed[9] that any person taking part in the administration of justice should not be in such a position that he might be suspected of being biased: but more recently the test has been formulated as one of a 'real danger of bias'.[10] The test adopted in Scotland has been of a suspicion of bias raised in the mind of a reasonable man.[11] The test in New Zealand for determining the impartiality of a juror has been formulated in these terms:

---

[6] *Barrs v. British Wool Marketing Board* 1957 SC 72, 82.

[7] The principle is set out in Article 6(1) of the European Convention on Human Rights and Fundamental Freedoms.

[8] *R v. Bow Street Metropolitan Stipendiary Magistrate and Others, ex parte Pinochet Ugarte (No.2)* (2000) 1 AC 119.

[9] Lord Esher MR in *Allinson v. General Council of Medical Education and Registration* [1891–4] All ER Rep 768 at 771.

[10] *R v. Gough* [1993] AC 646.

[11] *Bradford v. McLeod* 1986 SLT 244. See *Roylance v. GMC (No 2)* [2000] 1 AC 311.

Whether there is reasonable ground of suspecting that the verdict might have been influenced by bias.[12]

The jurisprudence of the European Court of Human Rights recognises that impartiality for the purposes of Article 6(1) must be resolved first by a subjective test, whether in fact the judge was personally impartial, and then also by an objective test, whether there is or is not a reasonable doubt about his or her impartiality. If there is such a reasonable doubt and the fear of impartiality can be objectively justified, then the judge must be disqualified, because the public must have confidence in the courts.[13]

At the heart of the matter is the necessity to preserve public confidence in the machinery of justice. In *Metropolitan Properties Co. (FGC) Ltd* v. *Lannon*[14] it was said:

> Justice must be rooted in confidence: and confidence is destroyed when right-minded people go away thinking 'the judge was biased'.

The possibility of bias is an issue which has to be decided by a court. But if the test is one which should satisfy public confidence, then it should be a test which looks not simply to what the court thinks of the risk of bias but to what the court thinks a member of the public might think of the risk of bias. In Canada, in *Webb* v. *The Queen*,[15] the formulation of the House of Lords in *Gough* was rejected and the wider test was preferred of a reasonable apprehension or suspicion on the part of a fair-minded and informed member of the public that the judge or juror would not discharge their task impartially. In the leading judgment given by Mason CJ and McHugh J it was said that the rejection by the House of Lords of the need to take account of the public perception of the possibility of bias rested on the assumption that public confidence would be maintained because the public would accept the conclusions of the judge. But they continued 'the premise on which decisions in the court are based is that public confidence in the administration of justice is more likely to be maintained if the court adopts a test that reflects the reaction of the ordinary reasonable member of the public to the irregularity in question.'[16]

An approach which looks to the viewpoint of the bystander has much to commend it. The court is well used to deciding what view a reasonable man would take of a given state of affairs. The ubiquitous reasonable man is a constant point of reference for judicial thinking. The suspicion which a reasonable man would or would not hold of the situation in question is something which a court can readily assess. This approach recognises the importance of the public perception of justice and the necessity of retaining public confidence.

---

[12] *R* v. *Papadopoulos (No.2)* 1979 1 NZLR 629, 634.
[13] *Piersack* v. *Belgium* Series A no 53 (1983) 5 EHRR 169.
[14] [1968] 3 All ER 304 at 310 Lord Denning MR.
[15] *Webb* v. *The Queen* (1994) 181 CLR 41.
[16] *Ibid* at 51.

The factors which go to make up independence and impartiality may overlap with each other. Structural independence can be identified as one element. The connection between the officer convening a disciplinary hearing and the prosecution may be too close to be acceptable.[17] The control of the tenure of temporary sheriffs in Scotland by the Lord Advocate who also promoted the criminal proceedings to be heard by them was a structural shortcoming which proved fatal to the continuance of the prosecution of the charge.[18] So regard has to be given to the method of appointment of judges in order to secure their independence.

It is easy to say that judges should be recruited from persons of intelligence and calibre and that there must be no discrimination on grounds of sex, race, religion or ideology. But it is far less easy to define the precise factors which go to compose the characteristics of judicial competence. It is easy to say that the test for appointment to the bench should be the test of merit. But that may re-state the problem rather than answer it. Moreover not only may opinions differ on the ingredients which constitute merit but particular characteristics may be of more particular importance in different levels of the judicial hierarchy. Merit here has to be assessed and understood in the context of the particular appointment. Article 223 of the Treaty of Rome states that the judges and Advocates General of the European Court of Justice,

> shall be chosen from persons whose independence is beyond doubt and who possess the qualifications required for appointment to the highest judicial offices in their respective countries or who are jurisconsults of recognised competence.

Undoubted independence is of course an essential and the professional qualification or the academic standing are particularly appropriate for a supreme court. Judge David Edward's own qualifications unquestionably made him a distinguished candidate for the European Court. But especially at lower levels other qualities may be of special value. For example in addition to the necessary intellectual qualities—and a degree of physical fitness and stamina—the ideal ingredients might well be thought to include elements of courtesy, patience, sensitivity and common sense. Moreover greater public confidence in the judiciary may be established when, so far as maybe practicable, all sectors of the community can be seen to be represented.

Apart from such characteristics the essence of a judicial ability is not easy to define. The duty of a judge, according to Cardozo,

> becomes itself a question of degree, and he is a useful judge or a poor one as he estimates the measure accurately or loosely. He must balance all his ingredients, his philosophy, his logic, his analogies, his history, his customs, his sense of right, and all the rest, and adding a little here and taking out a little there, must determine, as wisely as he can, which weight shall tip the scales.[19]

---

[17] *Findlay* v. *UK* (1996) 21 EHHR CD7.
[18] *Starrs* v. *Ruxton* 2000 JC 208.
[19] BN Cardozo, *The Nature of the Judicial Process* (8th edn, New Haven, Yale University Press, 1985), 162.

One has only to start such an analysis of the judicial function to see at once how hard it may be to identify the ability to make the accurate estimate of where the balance should lie.

The major problem is how to devise a system of appointment which secures that the 'right people' are chosen. It has been observed that 'the dislike of closed more or less hereditary judicial castes is widespread'.[20] But to exclude all candidates simply on the ground of relationship might be unfortunate. Something of a judicial ability may sometimes be carried down by a genetic inheritance. Quite apart from that consideration, if the selection is entrusted to senior officials whose enquiries are secret and whose processes are unknown, there may well be a suspicion that decisions are influenced by considerations which do not directly attach to the particular calibre and ability of the individual and a fear that there is a lack of objectivity in the choice. A process of making appointments behind closed doors may often be successful in identifying the right person to be appointed, but it does not nowadays carry with it the confidence which a more transparent process may achieve. On the other hand processes which are open to a degree of scrutiny in a public process carry their own problems.

The American system for the appointment of the judges of the Supreme Court of Justice consciously spreads the responsibility between the President and the Senate. The former nominates and the latter advises and consents.[21] But the Constitution is short in giving guidance as to how these respective functions are to be carried out. The system is thus open to the influence of political considerations. It is understandably tempting for a President to nominate candidates whose views and inclinations will help to advance the President's own policies. The Court will frequently have to resolve issues of constitutional importance and those issues may well be important for the development of the President's own aims for the future direction of the country.

The current view is that the appointment of judges should be more transparent than it has been in the past. The United Kingdom is moving towards a system of assessment and even interviews by a special committee, like the Judicial Appointments Commission which has already been set up in Scotland. Such a panel has even been suggested for the appointment of judges to the European Court of Justice.[22] The idea of public advertisement for applications and interviews before committees is a relatively recent development in the United Kingdom and is a major change from former practice. But it is not without its problems. The interviews will be conducted in private so that the process is not wholly open. The identities of the members of the committee should be matters open to public knowledge, but the question arises how far should it be proper to disclose the names of those who have applied or the names of those rejected

---

[20] RC Van Caenegem, 'Judges, legislators and professors: chapters in European legal history' *Goodhart Lectures 1984–1985* (Cambridge University Press, 1987).
[21] Article 11.2 of the Constitution.
[22] Arnull, 'Judicial Architecture or Judicial Folly?' in A Dashwood and A Johnston (eds), *The Future of the Judicial System of the European Union*, (Oxford, Hart Publishing, 2001) 48.

or at least not immediately chosen. These difficulties should not be too great where the system operates on the basis of a career judiciary, but is more significant where judges are selected from the practising legal profession. It may be thought that there is a particular sensitivity for a practitioner for it to be known that he has applied for a judicial appointment, or has applied and not been chosen. However, it may be that a revised attitude to the new practice will remove such sensitivity. In other contexts there is no disgrace in being an unsuccessful candidate in an open competition, such as an election to Parliament. It may be recalled that in former times a person nominated as an Ordinary Lord of the Court of Session in Scotland, the supreme court in that country, was required by statute to undergo an examination before the court before he was admitted.[23] This served as a protection against improper crown nominees but when that threat diminished the examination was recognised to be an empty formality[24] and was abolished.[25]

While there may be problems in deciding the degree of transparency which can be achieved in judicial appointments a corresponding difficulty may arise in the allocation of judges to particular cases. Where there is one local court and one local judge the problem will not arise, although there may be difficulties in finding a substitute if for any reason the single judge is disqualified or unable to sit. It is in the larger courts, and particularly supreme courts, that the problem becomes more acute.

There may be considerable advantage in a supreme court always sitting in plenary session. Such a course provides a sufficient answer to the complaint that a differently constituted tribunal might have returned a different result. It may be that if the appellate committee of the House of Lords was a to be transformed into a new supreme court, and perhaps merged with the judicial committee of the Privy Council, the practice should be for the new court to sit at least in the normal course *en banc*. But that course considerably restricts the amount of business which the judges can achieve. A much harsher selection of cases to be taken to such a court would have to be introduced. It is easy to see the course as a desirable one but it faces distinct practical problems. It is to be noticed that in relation to the European Court of Justice Article 221 of the Treaty of Rome as amended in Nice reversed the mandatory sitting in plenary session subject to an option to sit in chambers to a provision that the Court shall sit in chambers but may sit as a full court.

Where the volume of business makes it impractical for all the judges to sit in every case it probably has to be left to the court to decide the composition of the bench for particular cases. Individual expertise in a particular field may be one factor which assists such a choice. But the choice will not be a very public affair. It may be that informally the parties may perfectly properly advise the court

---

[23] Court of Session Act 1723, c 19, 81.
[24] Report of the Royal Commission on the Court of Session, 1927, 795.
[25] Administration of Justice (Scotland) Act 1933, c 41, sl.

administration of a particular expertise which their case demands which may guide the administration in the selection of the most appropriate judge or judges to hear the case. But wherever there is room for a choice to be made regarding the particular individuals who are to compose the panel to hear a particular case the anxiety may remain on the part of the litigant that a differently composed tribunal might have produced a different result. The known expertise in a particular field on the part of one member of the judicial body might be thought to have swayed the decision if only he had been sitting. Again, it would not be impossible for those who formed a minority in one case to find themselves with different colleagues in a later case and be unanimously of the view that the earlier decision was wrong. These kinds of difficulties provide some ground for uncertainty or even lack of confidence in the decision. But so long as practical considerations necessitate the selection of particular judges to hear particular cases such uncertainty and lack of confidence are likely to remain.

The choice of judge may be a matter which is substantially beyond the control of the litigant and not be open to much in the way of transparency. But the proceedings which take place before him or them, and in particular the hearing of the case, will be open to public scrutiny. While the preliminary stages of a litigation, such as the lodging of documentation and the communications with the officials of the court, may be private, the hearing of the parties by a judge is something which fairness requires must be seen. It is a public hearing to which everyone with a civil dispute or a criminal charge to be determined is entitled. The right to a public hearing embodied in Article 6(1) of the European Convention for the Protection of Human Rights and Fundamental Freedoms requires that the judgment shall be pronounced publicly but makes express exceptions for the exclusion of the press and the public in relation to the trial. Subject to such exceptional cases the courtroom must be open to the public so that they may enter and hear and see what is going on, and it must be open to the press so that they can report to a wider public on the course of the hearing. In some jurisdictions and subject to certain safeguards television cameras may even be permitted to film and record the proceedings or parts of them. The appeal in the Lockerbie trial provides one example.

But unrestricted coverage of trials may still carry with it risks that the consciousness of the presence of cameras may affect the behaviour of the lawyers, the witnesses and the jury. There are limits which may have to be imposed in the interests of the judicial process on the extent to which the publicity of the hearing may be allowed to go. Even the filming of an appellate process is open to hazard. Parts of the argument taken out of context and parts of the questions or observations made by individual judges during the argument may easily be misunderstood or given an exaggerated importance which they do not deserve. Nor will many visitors attend the whole course of the hearing. They will come for a part of the time and only hear part of the proceedings. Indeed since in many cases members of the public will be sitting behind the counsel who are speaking it may be difficult for them to hear all that is said. The judges may speak in their direction but since they are addressing the counsel their voices may not be so pitched as to carry to the members of the public sitting a the back of the courtroom. But even with these limitations there is a sufficient transparency in the process. It is not that justice, like a child in the Victorian era, should be seen and not heard. What matters in the public hearing is that people are at least permitted to see and hear what goes on. The important thing is that the proceedings are conducted openly. There should then be no opportunity for injustice to be done.

The judgment in the case must be pronounced publicly. But all that has passed between the conclusion of the public hearing and the public pronouncement of the judgment is not open to view. The process of judicial thought which culminates in the published determination cannot always be thoroughly transparent. What passes through the judicial mind cannot be totally open to scrutiny. Indeed both before and after the public hearing there may be processes which affect the final determination which are not open to the public view. In systems where there is a *juge d'instruction* the steps he or she may take in preparation for the trial may not be evident. How far any judge may have investigated the case prior to any public hearing may not always be disclosed. So also the process of reaching a determination after the hearing may be secret. The eventual course of reasoning will be disclosed in the terms of the judgment. But preliminary views which may have been favoured during the course of the hearing, may have become past history by the time the final decision is reached and ideas earlier discarded may revive.

Practice may vary from country to country on the style in which a judgment may be prepared and pronounced. Some countries require their supreme courts to issue a single judgment with no disclosure of even a strongly held dissenting view. In others the expression of a variety of views whether agreeing with or dissenting from the view held by the majority is allowed. In the latter case the public can understand more fully the detail of the process of reasoning which has been accepted by individual judges. Where each judge involved in the decision gives his or her own opinion in a separate judgment there is room for individuality of style and presentation. Sometimes the style may be so characteristic as at once to disclose the identity of its author.[26] Some may have a literary elegance. Some may be illuminated by poetic quotations or references culled from sources far outside the field of law. The personality of the judge which may peep through such work may give a more human face to the decision which a rigid standardised format for the giving of a decision may lack.

Where several judges are sitting and all are able to give individual judgments it is sometimes practice for some simply to concur with the reasoned judgment prepared by one of their number. This may not represent historically all that has happened. It may be that the one judge has circulated his or her opinion before the others and the others are so satisfied with the expression and the reasoning

---

[26] The judgments of Lord Denning are an obvious example.

of the decision that they may feel it unnecessary to add further words of their own. Or there may have been a discussion about the case among the judges before anything has been written, the result and the grounds of the decision have been from the start unanimous, and it has been agreed from the start that one of their number will write the judgment with which they all agree. Sometimes this can be presented as the decision of the whole court. Alternatively it may appear as a single judgment by one of them with separate consents from all the others. The substance of the position is the same in each case. But to the reader it may seem different. In the latter kind of case the judge who produces the judgment may be thought to have some individual responsibility for the whole decision, while the truth is that all the members of the court who took part and agreed with the particular text are equally responsible and all may have in fact contributed some of their own thinking to it.

In collegiate decisions the thoughts and discussions which take place after the public hearing may be of enormous significance in both the form and the substance of the final decision. Opinions voiced initially may change. A minority view may eventually be adopted by a majority. Where only a single judgment is to be issued the process of working out the form of a collegiate judgment may be influenced even by the views of those who would if they could dissent from it. As Judge Edward has himself observed:

> Even more than in those national systems where it is indigenous, the process of judicial debate behind closed doors is one of the most important ways in which Community judges adapt their own habit of mind to a developing legal system in which the doctrinal position is seldom clear and even more rarely settled.[27]

A truly transparent system should perhaps allow all the course of thinking to be disclosed. Such a course was introduced into early procedure for a period in Scotland by the Court of Session Act 1693.[28] That Act required that all reports, debates, proofs and suchlike should be considered, reasoned and determined with open doors so that the parties and their advocates and all others that please might be present when the judges were arguing and voting. The innovation caused Viscount Stair some concern.[29] He believed that the parties would have the greater irritation towards the judges when they heard the judges reason and vote against their interest, 'but there will be much less reasoning amongst the Lords than behoved to be formerly; and their prudence and generosity will oblige them to forbear all heats in reasoning'. In a later age debate between the judges, even coolly conducted, came to be managed in private.

The fact is that even if the judge's mind is disposed towards a particular conclusion at the close of the hearing, he may at that stage be unsure how best to express his thinking or to present his reasoning. There is a question how far

---

[27] In the epilogue to BS Markesinis, *The Gradual Convergence: Foreign Ideas, Foreign Influences, and English Law on the Eve of the 21st Century* (Oxford, Oxford University Press, 1994), 267.
[28] 1693 C26, APS ix, 305, c42.
[29] Stair, *Institutes*, Appendix, VII.

there is any merit in a disclosure of the details of the actual decision-making process. Judges may prepare draft opinions which they later partly or entirely reject. They may change their minds the more they think about the case. They may have assistants or clerks to help in research and talk about the case with them. In America the law-clerks in the Supreme Court may have a substantial contribution to make to the eventual judgment and there has been a remarkable degree of disclosure recently on the methods and practices of the American Supreme Court.[30] Law-clerks have in recent years been introduced to assist the work of the Law Lords in the House of Lords, but are engaged strictly on research and take no part in the preparation of judgments. But the contribution resulting from their research may remain an element in the thinking expressed in the eventual judgment. Correspondingly the legal assistants in courts outside the United Kingdom may play a significant part in the judge's work. But so long as the decision is the decision of the judge appointed to make it there should be no need for disclosure of the details of the process by which he came to the particular decision. It is matter for scholastic research to explore how great works of art, music or literature were crafted. The notebooks of Beethoven or the manuscripts of Scott may disclose details important for scholars of how great musical themes were created or how the style of the Waverley novels was perfected. But the public are not immediately interested in how many draft judgments were prepared and what convolutions of thought were experienced before a decision was reached. That may be material for academic study if they ever become available, but in the absence of any grounds for suspecting that the judge is not acting fairly it is not necessary for that part of the judicial process to be seen.

The need for transparency in the judicial process is to secure public confidence in the process of decision-making. One critical reason for giving reasons is to secure the confidence of the public in the judicial system. Where there is a greater public confidence in the system the necessity for transparency will be the less acute. Members of the public attend trials and hearings more through an interest or a curiosity to see what is going on, perhaps because of an interest in the facts, or conceivably the law, and in some cases because of what is regarded as the sensational nature of the litigation. They do not usually attend because they are anxious about the conduct of the system of justice. The mere fact that the proceedings are open to the public should serve as a sufficient safeguard against oppression or injustice. It is only where there is a lack of public confidence that blindfolds should be removed and the process be thrown open to greater public scrutiny.

---

[30] For example in B Schwartz, *Decision: How the Supreme Court Decides Cases* (Oxford, Oxford University Press, 1996).

4

Unfinished Business

THE RT. HON. THE LORD CLARKE

ON 4 OCTOBER 1982, at about 11 am, David Edward QC rose to address the House of Lords for the first time, I believe, in his career as an advocate. The case in question was *Brown* v. *Hamilton District Council*.[1] David was assisted by two junior counsel, the writer of this piece and Mr SA Bennett, Advocate. The decision of the House of Lords in the case resulted in the birth of the modern law in relation to judicial review in Scotland.[2] This was the first occasion on which I had been instructed to appear in the House of Lords. It was a revelatory experience, not least because of David's performance. I do not think that the word 'performance', in this context, is inappropriate. An advocate on top form before the House of Lords can, in my view, be said to be involved in giving a performance which is the product, like that of any great actor or musician, of intense preparation, careful thought and judging his audience perfectly.

In the weeks leading up to the hearing in *Brown,* David had researched, along with junior counsel, the law relating to the case and the issues that arose therefrom and engaged his juniors in deep discussion about these issues. It is impossible for me to describe adequately what I learned from him during that time. One thing I will mention is that David has, as all really great jurists, in my experience, have, an acute sense of history and its importance. Such jurists bring illumination to present day problems in the law by understanding intensely the historical process in which they are set. They also have a respect for and understanding of historical development which means that they avoid the too ready, superficial and slick solution to a particular new problem. The case of *Brown* gave David full reign to exploit his formidable talents in these respects.

The issue in *Brown* was this. The Scottish legal system had for centuries recognised that the Supreme Court in that jurisdiction had a special jurisdiction, exclusive to it, to review the legality of the acts and decisions of persons and bodies who themselves were charged with administering the law and exercising powers conferred on them for the public good, and in the interests of others. The classic description of the nature and scope of this jurisdiction was to be

---

[1] 1983 SC (HL) 1.
[2] The case was heard at about the same time as the English case of *O'Reilly* v. *Mackman* [1983] 2 AC 237 which itself had a significant impact on the development of procedural law in England in relation to judicial review.

found in the opinion of Lord President Inglis in the case of *Forbes* v. *Underwood*.[3] That case involved an attack on a decision of an arbiter. Lord President Inglis in the following passage provided a comprehensive definition of the extent of this jurisdiction. At page 467 he said this:

> The position of an arbiter is very much like that of a Judge in many respects, and there is no doubt whatever that whenever an inferior Judge, no matter of what kind, fails to perform his duty, or transgresses his duty, either by going beyond his jurisdiction, or by failing to exercise his jurisdiction when called upon to do so by a party entitled to come before him, there is a remedy in this court, and the inferior Judge, if it turns out that he is wrong, may be ordered by this Court to go on and perform his duty, and if he fails to do so he will be liable to imprisonment as upon a decree *ad factum praestandum*. The same rule applies to a variety of other public officers, such as statutory trustees and commissioners, who are under an obligation to exercise their functions for the benefit of the parties for whose benefit these functions are entrusted to them, and if they capriciously and without just cause refuse to perform their duty they will be ordained to do so by decree of this Court, and failing their performance will, in like manner, be committed to prison. Now, all this belongs to the Court of Session as the Supreme Civil Court of this country in the exercise of what is called, very properly, its super-eminent jurisdiction.

The willingness of courts, in the United Kingdom, to review the acts and decisions of government bodies, whether central or local, and to review decisions and actings of other bodies and persons who perform administrative functions began to grow significantly in the 1960s as a counterpart to the considerable growth in government itself and administrative agencies. A body of administrative law began to be developed for the modern age by judges such as Lord Reid and Lord Wilberforce in the House of Lords and Lord Denning. The principles of that law were being developed, but the procedures suitable for their application in modern conditions were not, at least in Scotland, being equally developed. Essentially a person who sought to challenge a decision or act of a public authority, or the like, had to use the ordinary procedures of ordinary civil litigation to have the act or decision declared null and void by the court together with any consequential remedy he might seek. This usually involved a time consuming and expensive procedure, ill-suited to obtaining any quick redress, where *ultra vires* acts had been carried out, and equally producing considerable uncertainty and delay in government and administration while the issue in question was being litigated. Mr Brown, in bringing his action against Hamilton District Council, sought to establish that it ought not, at least, to be necessary to have such issues raised in the Supreme Court. They should be capable of being dealt with in the local court, that is the Sheriff Court.

The context in which this issue was raised was a piece of social welfare legislation which had as its objective the creation of certain rights, in certain conditions.

---

[3] (1886) 13 R 465.

The operation of the legislation was bestowed upon local government bodies. The measure was the Housing Homeless Persons Act 1977. The legislation, in broad terms, provides for homeless persons who have not become intentionally homeless, to be provided with accommodation. The arbiter as to whether any such person has become homeless intentionally, or not, is, in terms of the legislation, the relevant local authority. There is no right of appeal from any decision in that respect. Mr Brown brought an action in his local Sheriff Court in which he complained that he was a homeless person who should have been provided with accommodation in terms of his rights under the legislation, by the local authority, but that they had held him to be intentionally homeless when they ought not to have done so. The local authority, in defending the action brought against them, argued that the Sheriff had no jurisdiction to entertain the complaint. Mr Brown, they contended, was seeking to invoke the jurisdiction of review, which was described by Lord President Inglis in *Forbes* v. *Underwood* and which, as his Lordship had pointed out, was exclusive to the Supreme Court in Scotland, the Court of Session. The case raised a further question of procedure and practice. What Mr Brown sought was a declarator by the Sheriff that the decision of the local authority was unlawful, an order against the authority to perform its statutory duty and damages for loss and suffering he claimed they had caused him. While declaratory remedies were available in the Sheriff Court, it was settled that in Scots Law the remedy of reduction was not. That remedy could only be obtained in the Court of Session—*Dickson* v. *Murray*.[4] The remedy of reduction is the remedy which is appropriately sought when it is necessary to have a decision or written document, *ex facie* valid and otherwise having legal effect, set aside or quashed. The local authority attacked the competency of Mr Brown's Sheriff Court action on the further ground that, however it had been framed, it was, in effect, an action to have the decision of the local authority reduced and such an action was competent only in the Court of Session.

The arguments of the local authority based on competency did not succeed before the Sheriff who held that Mr Brown's action was perfectly competent. The local authority appealed to the Inner House of the Court of Session. The majority of their Lordships in the Second Division of that court, reached the conclusion that the decision of the local authority complained of was purely administrative in character. It was not a judicial or quasi-judicial decision. The previous authorities, the majority held, including the judgment of Lord President Inglis in *Forbes* v. *Underwood*, as to the exclusive supervisory jurisdiction of the Court of Session, was confined, when properly understood, to the review of decisions of persons or bodies who were acting in a judicial or quasi-judicial capacity. There was nothing, therefore, to prevent decisions of persons and bodies, which decisions could be properly categorised as only administrative in character, being reviewed by the local courts. As to the second point taken in relation to the competency of the proceedings, the majority of the court

[4] (1866) 4 M 797.

took the view that the question at issue could be determined by the pronouncement of a suitable declarator in the Sheriff Court. It was to be assumed that the local authority, faced with such a declarator, would return to the question which they had decided and would reconsider their decision. The judge in the minority, Lord Dunpark, put his position on the jurisdiction question in the following terms:

> Every wrong must have a remedy. Where an applicant for housing accommodation is deprived of his rights under this Act by a decision of a housing authority which is fundamentally null, or so obviously wrong that no reasonable housing authority could have reached it on the facts before it, he is entitled to apply to the courts for enforcement of his rights. As the Act has failed to provide a remedy for him, his only recourse is to the equitable jurisdiction of the courts. For the reason which I have given, I find that the Sheriff has no jurisdiction to review and quash decisions of housing authorities, purporting to act in pursuance of this Act, on the ground of fundamental nullity. That is the sole prerogative of the Court of Session in the exercise of its super-eminent jurisdiction by providing a remedy where no other exists.[5]

His Lordship was not impressed by the submission that convenience, expediency and economy were factors which might suggest that it would be desirable for Sheriffs to have jurisdiction to review such decisions, particularly as there was no guarantee that a sheriff's decision would be accepted as final and, if it was not, review of his decision would require to be sought in the Court of Session. His Lordship, on the other hand, reached the view that, had he considered that the Sheriff Court had jurisdiction to review such decisions, the absence of the remedy of reduction in that court would not have meant the action was incompetent.[6] Nevertheless, Lord Dunpark remarked that the absence of the remedy of reduction in the Sheriff Court was supportive of his view that that court had no power of review of such decisions.[7]

The majority decision of the Inner House in the case of *Brown*, had it stood, would, in the writer's view, have resulted in a serious wrong turning for administrative law in Scotland, particularly with regard to the distinction upon which it was based between decisions and acts which could be categorised as judicial or quasi-judicial, on the one hand, and those which could be categorised as administrative on the other. It was for David Edward to persuade the House of Lords of this and that he did with style and aplomb. He was, I have to say, and I am sure he would admit, a little fortunate, in one way, as one of the five law Lords hearing the case was Lord Fraser of Tullybelton, a known expert in the field of Scots constitutional and administrative law. The thorough and perceptive review of the history of the supervisory jurisdiction of the Court of Session which David presented to their Lordships was familiar to Lord Fraser as was apparent in his speech, with which the other four law Lords agreed. Lord Fraser,

---

[5] 1983 SC (HL) 1 at 30–31.
[6] *Ibid* at 31.
[7] *Ibid* at 29.

having referred to the passage cited above from the judgment of Lord President Inglis in *Forbes* v. *Underwood*, swiftly exposed, and then put to death, the error in the reasoning of the majority of their Lordships in the Inner House. He did so in the following words:

> I accordingly regard the passage that I have quoted as authority for two propositions relevant to this appeal; first, the Court of Session has a supervisory jurisdiction over decisions of administrative bodies such as local authorities, whether the decisions are administrative, judicial or quasi-judicial; and secondly, the supervisory jurisdiction is privative to the Court of Session and is not shared by the Sheriff Court.[8]

His Lordship went on to emphasise that he did not consider that, in this context, the distinction between administrative and judicial decisions was helpful. Lord Fraser, in taking up David Edward's submissions in this respect, pointedly remarked that the local authorities could clearly be seen as the historical successors, in many respects, to the commissioners to whom reference was made by Lord President Inglis in the passage from *Forbes* v. *Underwood*.

David Edward, in presenting the appeal, was keen to stress the second and, perhaps, subordinate part of the appellant's case as to competency, namely that what was required in such a case was for the act or decision which was complained of, and which was found to be invalid or illegal to be quashed, set aside, or in Scottish remedial language, reduced. A mere bare declarator by a lower court that an act or decision was illegal, or otherwise null and void, did not have the required legal effect. That argument also found favour in the House of Lords in the speech of Lord Fraser. His analysis of the position was as follows:

> There is also a separate, and narrower, reason why the appellants are in my opinion entitled to succeed on the issue of competency and jurisdiction. It is this. The Sheriff Court has no jurisdiction to grant decree of reduction of the appellant's decision. It has a limited jurisdiction to reduce deeds or decisions *ope exceptionis* under Rule 5 of Sched. 1 to the 1907 Act but it has no general power to grant decrees of reduction. The Second Division recognised that, and no argument to the contrary has been submitted to the House. Yet the majority of the Second Division held that decree of declarator that the decision of the housing authority was one they were not entitled to reach was enough to dispose of the principal issue in the case, and that it was unnecessary for the decision to be reduced or set aside. I am unable to agree with that view. The decision on whether the respondent was a homeless person and if so whether he had become homeless intentionally is one which in terms of the Act of 1977 is entrusted to the housing authority and to them alone. Their decision effectively determines whether the authority has the duty of making accommodation available for the respondent. If the authority is 'satisfied' that he became homeless intentionally that is conclusive— s.4(3). So long as their decision stands, the necessary consequence is that the appellant's duty is only to furnish him with 'appropriate assistance' in accordance with subs.(3) of s.4. They have no duty to secure that accommodation becomes available for him, as they would have under subs. (5) of s.4 if they had not been so satisfied. A

---

[8] *Ibid* at 44.

mere declarator that the decision was one which they were not entitled to reach does not get rid of the decision, nor can it open the way for the housing authority to reach a different decision if, on further consideration of the matter in light of the court's direction on matters of law, it thinks fit to do so. In a case such as this, where the housing authority is both the decision-making authority, and the decision-implementing authority, the proper procedure is for the decision to be reduced so that a different decision, creating different legal rights for the private party in the position of the respondent, can be made. The view which was taken by the majority of the Second Division involves a decree of declarator by the Sheriff either as being in substance a decree of reduction, in which case it will be granted without jurisdiction, or as a mere *brutum fulmen*, having no compulsive force, in which case it would be futile and ought not to be pronounced. I am of the opinion on this ground also that this action is not competent in the Sheriff Court.[9]

It will have been noticed that, in the course of that passage, Lord Fraser refers to the limited jurisdiction in the Sheriff Court to reduce deeds or decisions in *'ope exceptionis'*. Essentially that jurisdiction allows persons who find themselves being sued in the Sheriff Court, on the basis of a deed or decision, which they claim to be illegal or invalid in some way, to plead the illegality or invalidity as a defence, without the need of going to another court ie the Court of Session to have the deed or decision reduced. The significance of that power in the context of the modern law of judicial review will require to be considered later, as will be seen.

It is not an overstatement to say that David Edward and the House of Lords, in particular Lord Fraser, in *Brown,* ensured that the modern law of judicial review was set on the appropriate jurisdictional direction and drawn back from the wrong turning to which their Lordships in the Inner House had led it. Having regard particularly to the expansion, in the last few decades, of the challenges to acts and decisions of central government, local government and other administrative bodies it would have been surely constitutionally inappropriate for these challenges to be available, as a matter of course, in all the local courts. As the authors of the leading textbook in Scotland on Judicial Review, Clyde and Edwards point out in the opening passage of their work:

> This book is concerned with the power of a Supreme Court to ensure that all those vested with a legal authority exercise that authority lawfully and properly. Historically, the supervisory jurisdiction of the Court of Session has been the means by which the Supreme Court in Scotland has achieved this objective. As elsewhere, the term 'judicial review' is now used to refer to this jurisdiction, the essential purpose of which is to ensure that the law is observed. The existence of a supervisory jurisdiction is a fundamental element of a constitution which is based on respect for the rule of law. It is an inherent jurisdiction of a Supreme Court and cannot be taken away consistently with respect for the rule of law.

---

[9] 1983 SC (HL) 1 at 45–46.

As the writers in their work go on to demonstrate, the exclusivity of the Supreme Court's jurisdiction in this respect had been recognised from earliest times and was reaffirmed loudly in *Brown*.[10]

There remained, after *Brown,* however, unfinished business. *Brown* settled the jurisdictional question, but the procedural difficulties which had driven Mr Brown to attempt to seek his remedy in his local court were recognised. They were acknowledged by Lord Fraser himself, in *Brown,* towards the end of his speech, where he recognised the need to make available remedies in this branch of the law which were 'speedy and cheap and which protected public authorities from unreasonable actions'.[11] His Lordship repeated the need in Scotland for an expeditious procedure in a subsequent Scottish case before the House of Lords, namely *Stevenson* v. *Midlothian District Council*.[12] His Lordship's words did not fall on deaf ears. A committee was established under the chairmanship of Lord Dunpark, (suitably enough having regard to the part he played in the case of *Brown*) to study the question. Equally suitably, a member of that committee was David Edward QC. The committee came forward with a recommendation which included a proposed new procedure embodied in draft Rules of Court. The committee's proposals were adopted virtually without change. The procedure which the committee in substance recommended has proved to be, on the whole, highly successful, having, in-built, the requirements of speed, relative simplicity and flexibility and also a certain protection against wholly unreasonable actions getting very far. For Scotland they also introduced, pretty well for the first time, a move away, to some extent, from the traditional common law adversarial system of litigation to a procedure where the judge has overall control of the procedure. The beneficial effects of such procedures have been seen to be such that they have been taken up and adapted in other forms of procedure in Scotland eg commercial action procedure. The combination of the decision in *Brown,* and the new Rules of Court, provided well for the growth of administrative law cases that were being brought in Scotland and could, indeed, be said to have contributed themselves to that growth. But still there was unfinished business.

While the jurisdictional question itself had been settled and the procedural means for invoking that jurisdiction had been dealt with satisfactorily, the scope of that jurisdiction, in modern times, was a question waiting to be decided. To a large extent, the context in which that question arose, in Scotland, was due to the fact that it was recognised, not least in *Brown,* that the substantive law, as opposed to jurisdictional and remedial law, to be applied in judicial review was

---

[10] I should commend to the reader David Edward's own description of how the case of *Brown* came to be argued and decided in his essay 'Administrative Law in Scotland; the Public Law/Private Law Distinction Revisited' which is included in D Curtin and D O'Keeffe (eds), *Constitutional Adjudication in European Community and National Law: Essays for the Hon. Mr Justice T.F. O'Higgins* (Dublin, Butterworths, 1992).
[11] Above n 9, at 49.
[12] 1983 SC (HL) 50 at 59.

the same whether one was litigating in Scotland or in England. So the decision, for example in *Associated Provincial Picture Houses Limited* v. *Wednesbury Corporation*[13] was regarded as good law for Scotland. In English administrative law, however, there was a distinction drawn between public and private law acts and decisions. The former were amenable to judicial review, the latter were not. For a time in Scotland, after *Brown*, the Court of Session was seduced by that distinction in a number of cases. (See for example *Connor* v. *Strathclyde Regional Council*[14] and *Safeway Foodstores Limited* v. *Scottish Provident Institution*.[15]) In being so seduced, the judges deciding those cases conveniently overlooked the fact that in the classic formulation of the jurisdiction given by Lord President Inglis in *Forbes* v. *Underwood* no such distinction was drawn and, indeed, the case of *Forbes* itself was concerned with the review of an arbiter in a private arbitration.

Another wrong turning in the administrative law in Scotland was, however, corrected by the decision in the case of *West* v. *Secretary of State for Scotland*.[16] The case involved a dispute between a prison officer and his employer, the Secretary of State, as to the prison officer's terms and conditions of employment. The prison officer sought to have a decision of the employer regarding the operation of his terms and conditions of employment made the subject of judicial review proceedings. At first instance, the court dismissed the application as being incompetent, as being a matter of private contract between the parties. That decision was upheld, on appeal, by the First Division of the Court of Session. In so doing Lord President Hope sought to set out and define, authoritatively, the scope of the supervisory jurisdiction of the Court of Session in judicial review. He did so in a number of propositions, which have proved, after subsequent scrutiny and application in other cases, a wholly satisfactory basis for describing and marking the limits and extent of the supervisory jurisdiction. The propositions in question were put in the following words by Lord President Hope:

(1) The Court of Session has power, in the exercise of its supervisory jurisdiction, to regulate the process by which decisions are taken by any person or body to whom a jurisdiction, power or authority has been delegated or entrusted by statute, agreement or any other instrument.

(2) The sole purpose for which the supervisory jurisdiction may be exercised is to ensure that the person or body does not exceed or abuse that jurisdiction, power or authority or fail to do what the jurisdiction, power or authority requires.

(3) The competency of the application does not depend upon any distinction between public law and private law, nor is it confined to those cases which English law has

---

[13] [1948] 1 KB 223.
[14] 1986 SLT 530.
[15] 1989 SLT 131.
[16] 1992 SC 385.

accepted as amenable to judicial review, nor is it correct in regard to issues about competency to describe judicial review under Rule of Court 260B as a public law remedy.[17]

What has led to some subsequent criticism, or controversy, was one of a number of remarks Lord President Hope made by way of explanation of the reasoning lying behind those propositions. The observation in question was as follows:

> Contractual rights and obligations, such as those between employer and employee, are not as such amenable to judicial review. The cases in which the exercise of the supervisory jurisdiction is appropriate involve a tripartite relationship, between the person or body to whom the jurisdiction, power or authority has been delegated or entrusted, the person or body by whom it has been delegated or entrusted and the person or persons in respect of or for whose benefit that jurisdiction, power or authority is to be exercised.[18]

The need for the identification of the existence of a tripartite relationship, which Lord President Hope appeared to require in that *dictum*, before judicial review was available, has been the subject of considerable academic discussion, and it has been questioned in some subsequent cases as to whether or not it is a feature which <u>must</u> be present in all cases. As the writer has suggested elsewhere, the difficulty would not have arisen had Lord President Hope simply inserted the words 'will normally' before the word 'involve' in the passage in question. The insertion of those words would have done, otherwise, no material damage to the overall scheme of his judgment. The approach taken in that judgment in respect of the inappropriateness of the public law/private law distinction as the test for judicial review has been approved of by writers of the highest reputation in English law.[19]

The relevant Rule of Court in Scotland governing applications for judicial review, in its present form, states as follows: 'An application to the supervisory jurisdiction of the court . . . shall be made by petition for judicial review'.[20] It will be recalled that the effect of the decision in *Brown* was to confirm that such an application could not be made to the Sheriff Court. It will also be recalled, however, that Lord Fraser, in his speech, made reference to the Sheriff Court having a statutory jurisdiction to 'reduce' deeds and decisions, *ope exceptionis*. The Rules of the Court of Session also provide that:

> Where, in an action, a deed or other writing is founded on by a party any objection to it may be stated by way of exception, unless the Court considers that the objection would be more conveniently disposed of in a separate action of reduction.[21]

---

[17] *Ibid* at 412–13.
[18] *Ibid* at 413.
[19] See Wade and Forsyth, *Administrative Law* (8th edn Oxford, Oxford University Press, 2000) at 634–35 and 650–51.
[20] RC 58.3(1).
[21] RC 53.8.

Another piece of unfinished business, a question remaining to be asked and answered after *Brown* and the promulgation of the Rules of Court in relation to the supervisory jurisdiction, which followed thereon, was whether the combined effect of the decision in *Brown,* and the provisions of the new Rules, was that what is sometimes described as a 'collateral attack' on the validity of an act or decision may be taken by a defender in an action, either in the Sheriff Court, or in the Court of Session, without the need of seeking to have the decision or act declared invalid and reduced (quashed) by invoking the supervisory jurisdiction, which the Rules of Court say can only be done by way of an application brought under that rule. Similar questions had been, as shall be seen, troubling English law for some time. The writer found himself recently, in his judicial capacity, having the question, as it arises in Scotland, raised before him and was required to provide an answer to it.

In the case of *Vaughan Engineering Limited* v. *Hinkins & Frewin Limited*[22] the question arose in this way. By legislation of 1996 a scheme was introduced, for building and civil engineering contracts, whereby disputes which arose during the currency of such contracts might be resolved, on an interim basis, by reference to an 'adjudicator' in a process that was designed to be speedy. The policy of the legislation was to improve the cash flow problems of contractors who might be held out of substantial sums of money, due to be paid under their contract during the currency of the contract, pending the resolution of a dispute between themselves and the employers which may not take place until the completion of lengthy and complicated litigation or arbitration. The legislation, the Housing Grants, Construction and Regeneration Act 1996, and the scheme made thereunder, provide that the adjudicators' decisions are to be regarded as binding and any award of money made as a result requires to be paid forthwith. The matters adjudicated on, however, by the adjudicator may be reopened later and determined in litigation or arbitration. The legislation provides for no right of appeal against, or review of, the adjudicators' decisions.

In a series of decisions, courts in Scotland held that the decisions of those adjudicators could not be distinguished, in principle, from decisions of arbiters. As has been seen in the case of *Forbes* v. *Underwood*, which itself was a case involving the decision of an arbiter, the supervisory jurisdiction of the Court of Session has been held to be competently invoked to review the decisions of such persons. The courts in Scotland, in the cases just referred to, accordingly, accepted that the decisions of adjudicators were amenable to attack by way of judicial review in the Court of Session. In the case of *Vaughan Engineering,* contractors who had obtained a decision in their favour from an adjudicator for payment of certain sums sought enforcement of payment of those sums by raising an action for payment of those sums in the Court of Session. The employer defended the action on the basis that the adjudicator in question had failed to exhaust his jurisdiction by failing to take into account the employers'

[22] 2003 SLT 428.

counterclaim, a well established basis for seeking to have an arbiter's award reviewed. The employer, in effect, claimed that the decision of the adjudicator was *ultra vires*. They sought to have the action against them sisted (stayed) to enable themselves to bring a petition for judicial review to have the decision of the adjudicator reduced. The pursuers in the action, the contractors, opposed this application on the basis that the defenders did not require to raise separate proceedings to protect themselves. They could as well in their defences to the action plead the alleged invalidity of the adjudicator's decision by way of exception, *ope exceptionis*, under Rule of Court 53.8. A review of the authorities, prior to the promulgation of the modern Rules of Court regarding judicial review, amply demonstrated that, side by side with the supervisory jurisdiction of the Court of Session, it had been held competent, for over 100 years at least, for a defender to an action for enforcement of an arbiter's award against him to plead, by way of defence, that the decision was *ultra vires* or otherwise was fundamentally invalid, without the need of raising an action of reduction of the decision in the Court of Session. All the modern textbook writers, since the promulgation of the Rules of Court, who had looked at the question, had appeared to consider that that remained the position after the decision in *Brown* and the promulgation of the new Rules of Court. The writer was, therefore, not persuaded that, as a matter of competency, it was necessary for the defenders to make an application to the supervisory jurisdiction of the court in terms of Rule of Court 58.3 in order to defend themselves from the enforcement of the adjudicator's decision. I observed, however, that as the previous authorities had held, there may be situations where it would be preferable that such a course be followed and the court might have a discretion to decide that this should be done in the circumstances of a particular case. The two key issues, however, that the case raised, in my judgement, were expressed in the following terms:[23]

> Counsel for the pursuers was well founded in submitting that in seeking to defend an action by challenging the validity of an act or decision upon which it is based, a party, like the defenders is not making an application to the supervisory jurisdiction of the Court of Session. It is important, in this respect, to keep in mind what is embraced in and what is meant by the expression 'supervisory jurisdiction'. As is clear from the judgment of Lord President Inglis in *Forbes* v. *Underwood* it is the jurisdiction which embraces the power of one court, and one court alone, to direct decision makers and decision takers and certain other bodies to carry out their duty and to carry them out according to their power. Only the Court of Session has that power. As it is put in Clyde & Edwards at para. 8.15, page 329: 'Undoubtedly it is competent for a Sheriff to rule on the *ultra vires* acts of a public authority in order to dispose of the action before the Sheriff Court. But in doing so, the Sheriff is not exercising a power of review. The Sheriff cannot instruct the decision maker on what the law requires, quash decisions which it has made, or stop it from taking steps beyond its powers. These remedial actions are exclusively for the Court of Session in the exercise of its supervisory jurisdiction in judicial review.'

[23] *Ibid* at 441.

The writer then went on to set out the second point which the case raised and did so in the following terms:

> The second reason for holding that the defenders' position is misconceived is this. It focused on the need for reduction, or as counsel for the defenders put it, 'proper' reduction, but such a focus can distract from what is the real question, viz. whether the defender **needs** to invoke the supervisory jurisdiction of the Court of Session to defend himself in the present action. Once again the writers of Clyde & Edwards illuminate our path and they do so at para. 8.14 at page 328. There they opine that there is nothing to prevent a person from raising an action for damages for loss, injury or damage arising out of alleged unlawful decisions or acts by a body which is subject to the supervisory jurisdiction of the Court of Session, even though Rule 58.4 provides that the remedy of damages is available in judicial review proceedings. The writers then state: 'The problem of the remedy of damages exemplifies that the nature of the remedy is an unsure guide to the scope of judicial review.' In a case like the present the defenders, in my judgement, do not **need** the decision to be quashed by way of its reduction. They simply need to have available to them the shield that has been available in the courts in Scotland for at least well over 100 years (and in the Court of Session for over 150 years) by pleading, in defence, its invalidity.

If, however, the decision or act is not reduced as a result of an application to the supervisory jurisdiction of the Court of Session, the decision itself, technically speaking, is not deprived of all legal validity. The position remains as Lord Fraser put it in *Brown*:

> The proper procedure is for the decision to be reduced so that a different decision, creating different legal rights for the private person in the position of the respondent, can be made.

In the course of the review of the Scottish position in relation to such matters which took place in the case of *Vaughan Engineering*, the position in England was noted. In the case of *Wandsworth London Borough Council* v. *Winder*[24] a defendant had been sued for arrears of rent in respect of a flat let to him by a local authority. The local authority also sought repossession of the premises. The defendant sought to defend the proceedings on the basis that the resolutions which the authority had passed in relation to the current rent, which they sought to recover, were invalid and void. The Council sought to have this defence struck out as involving an abuse of process since the challenge to the conduct of a public authority could only be made by an application for judicial review under the relevant rules of the Supreme Court.[25] The House of Lords held that there was no merit in the Council's application to have the defence struck out. They held that there was nothing in the provisions regulating applications for judicial review in England and Wales, which prevented a defender contesting the validity of the resolutions without making an application for judicial review.

---

[24] [1985] AC 461.
[25] (RSC Ord 35).

(It is of passing interest at least to note that the main speech in that case was given by Lord Fraser.)

Subsequent to the decision in *Winder* the English court had indulged in an exercise whereby a distinction was drawn between acts and decisions which might be described as 'substantively invalid' on the one hand, and 'procedurally invalid' on the other. The consequence of that distinction was that in a case of 'procedural invalidity' where what was being attacked was, for example, a bye-law or other piece of subordinate legislation, the legislation remained valid until set aside in judicial review, whereas if the invalidity was identified as being of a substantive character, the invalidity might be pointed to by way of defence to an action based on the measure in question. In the case of *Boddington* v. *British Transport Police*[26] the House of Lords held that a defendant was not precluded from raising, in a criminal prosecution, a defence that a bye-law or an administrative act carried out under it was *ultra vires* and unlawful and in that regard there was no distinction to be drawn between substantive and procedural invalidity. What should not be lost sight of, at least in the law of Scotland, is that while the defender is entitled to protect himself from the effects of the decision or act by establishing its invalidity by way of defence, the act or decision is not thereby quashed and may continue to have legal force and effect where it is addressed not just to the defender but to other persons. It is for the decision-maker or law maker then to revisit the matter and to issue a new decision or law. As David Edward pointed out in his essay referred to above[27] this is an approach well understood by Community lawyers and underlies Articles 33 and 34 of the ECSC Treaty.

The case of *Boddington*, furthermore, leaves open the related question as to what effect the court's upholding of a defence to a criminal charge that the measure upon which it is founded is invalid, has in relation to things done and persons affected by it in the past. Lord Browne-Wilkinson in *Boddington*,[28] having indicated that he agreed with the leading speech given in the case by the Lord Chancellor, save for one point, said this:

> The Lord Chancellor attaches importance to the consideration that an invalid bye-law is and always has been a nullity. The bye-law will necessarily have been found to be *ultra vires*; therefore it is said it is a nullity having no legal effect. I adhere to my view that the juristic basis of judicial review is the doctrine of *ultra vires*. But I am far from satisfied that an *ultra vires* act is incapable of having any legal consequence during the period between the doing of that act and the recognition of its invalidity by the court. During that period people will have regulated their lives on the basis that the act is valid. The subsequent recognition of its invalidity cannot re-write history as to all the other matters done in the meantime in reliance on its validity. The status of an unlawful act during the period before it is quashed is a matter of great contention and of

[26] [1999] 2 AC 143.
[27] Above n 10, D Edward, 'Administrative Law in Scotland; the Public Law/Private Law Distinction Revisited' at 294.
[28] See n at 164.

great difficulty: see *Percy* v. *Hall* [1997] QB 924, 950–952, *per* Schiemann L.J. and the authorities there referred to; de Smith, Woolf & Jowell, Judicial Review of Administrative Action, 5th Ed. (1995), paras. 5.04–5.048 and *Calvin* v. *Carr* [1980] AC 574, 589–590.

I prefer to express no view at this stage on these difficult points. It is sufficient for the decision of the present case to agree with both my Lords in holding that a man commits no crime if he infringes an invalid bye-law and has the right to challenge the validity of the bye-law before any court in which he is being tried.

Lord Slynn of Hadley dipped his toe, somewhat gently, into this intellectual whirlpool. At page 165 his Lordship said:

> I consider that the result of allowing a collateral challenge in proceedings before courts of criminal jurisdiction can be reached without it being necessary in this case to say that if an act or bye-law is invalid it must be held to have been invalid from the outset for all purposes and that no lawful consequences can flow from it. This may be the logical result and will no doubt sometimes be the position but courts have had to grapple with the problem of reconciling the logical result with the reality that much may have been done on the basis that an administrative act or a bye-law was valid. The unscrambling may produce more serious difficulties than the invalidity. The European Court of Justice has dealt with the problem by ruling that its declaration of invalidity should only operate for the benefit of the parties to the actual case or of those who had begun proceedings for a declaration of invalidity before the court's judgment. In our jurisdiction the effect of invalidity may not be relied on if limitation periods have expired or if the court in its discretion refuses relief, albeit considering that the act is invalid. These situations are of course different from those where a court has pronounced subordinate legislation or an administrative act to be unlawful or where the presumption in favour of the legality has been overruled by a court of competent jurisdiction. But even in these cases I consider that the question whether the acts or bye-laws are to be treated as having at no time had any effect in law is not one which has been fully explored and is not one in which it is necessary to rule in this appeal and I prefer to express no view upon it. The cases referred to in Wade & Forsyth, Administrative Law 7th Ed. (1997), pages 323–324, 342–344 lead the authors to the view that nullity is relative rather than an absolute concept (page 343) and that 'void' is meaningless in any absolute sense. Its meaning is relative. This may all be rather imprecise but the law in this area has developed in a pragmatic way on a case by case basis. The result, however, in the present case is clear that the validity of the administrative act may be challenged by way of defence.

The problem discussed by Lord Browne-Wilkinson and Lord Slynn in the passages just cited, does not seem to have ever been the subject of judicial discussion far less judicial decision in Scotland. The question is formulated by Clyde and Edwards in the following way:

> If a decision or deed is reduced, the effect is retrospective in that it falls to be treated as null from the start. It follows that reduction of the deed or decision will nullify anything which has followed on it. But this logical approach gives rise to considerable problems. Many things may have been done in reliance upon the validity of the decision and it seems unattractive to ignore the reality of history. But the question then

sharply arises whether the court can consistently with the view that a decision is invalid nevertheless preserve it as a valid basis of rights in respect of some past period.[29]

After having referred to the case of *Boddington* and to other English authorities the writers continue:

> The precise analysis of the status of an act or decision which is later found to be a nullity remains uncertain. It will be necessary before too long either to reconsider the retrospectivity of judicial decisions or to devise some satisfactory analysis of the extent to which the validity for some purposes of past actings may still be recognised where they have proceeded on what turns out to be a nullity.

Yet more unfinished business, therefore, remains in this area of the law. In the meantime Clyde and Edwards assert that: 'A decision or a deed which could be open to reduction will require to be regarded as valid if no reduction is sought or if the attempt to reduce it fails.'

There would seem, possibly, to be some attraction, following the approach suggested by Lord Slynn in *Boddington* that principle should sometimes give way, to some extent at least, to pragmatism in this field. As Clyde and Edwards note: 'By virtue of section 102 of The Scotland Act 1998 where a court or tribunal decides that an Act of the Scottish Parliament or any subordinate legislation made by the Scottish Executive is *ultra vires* the court or tribunal may remove or limit any retrospective effect of the decision or suspend its effect in order to allow the defect to be corrected.' Such an approach would be quite familiar to judges of, and practitioners before, the European Court of Justice, as the passage from Lord Slynn's speech in *Boddington* confirms.[30] In cases such as those noted below and in *Simmenthal* v. *Commission*[31] the principle of legal certainty has been upheld, rather than observance of the strict theoretical consequences of the court having exercised its Article 230 function in declaring a measure to be void. When the question does come up for determination in Scotland one might anticipate a solution will require to be found having regard to European and other experience.

I conclude on a personal note. It is very difficult to contemplate David Edward in retirement. I am pretty sure that by him, work and life will continue to be regarded, like the title of this contribution in his honour, as very much 'unfinished business.'

---

[29] At para. 14.16.
[30] *Cf.* Case 81/72 *Commission* v. *Council* [1973] ECR 575, and Case 59/81 *Commission* v. *Council* [1982] ECR 3329.
[31] Case 92/78 [1979] ECR 777.

5
Devolution and Community Law

CHRISTINE BOCH

'La particularité des problèmes que pose la combinaison des droits nationaux et du droit communautaire vient de ce qu'il s'agit, non seulement d'ordres juridiques distincts avec des fondements différents, mais, en outre, de droits nationaux différents qui tous doivent être, en même temps, combiné de façon suffisamment différenciée pour respecter les sphères d'autonomie des Etats membres, mais de façon suffisamment coordonnée voire uniformisée pour assurer le degré d'application uniforme nécessaire à la réalisation des objectifs de l'intégration communautaire'[1]

These remarks from a former President of the Court, highlight the problems of articulation between Community law and the legal systems of the Member States and capture neatly one of the challenges of integration.[2] Apart from enhancing its effectiveness, legitimacy and transparency, the Union must also ensure that it respects the autonomy and diversity of its constituent parts. In this stage of its development, the conundrum for the Union is how to accommodate diversity, inter alia through allowing exemptions and derogations, while at the same time ensuring that the Union's capacity to act as a single entity is strengthened in order to enable it to be equipped to meet the rigours of global competition. This is no easy task, particularly if one also considers the internal structures of Member States. In Member States where powers are devolved and territories are given a degree of autonomy, those territories may press a legitimate case that the Union ought to recognise and respect their spheres of devolved competence. This raises the question as to the extent to which the Union should develop direct relations with autonomous territories rather than an indirect relationship through the Member States.

This contribution will look at the place and role of Community law in the UK devolution settlement. It will also discuss the place of devolved institutions in Community law. As a preliminary point, it should be explained why throughout the paper the term Community law will be used. The Scotland Act 1998 (hereafter the '1998 Act') does not make any reference to EU law, but only to

---

[1] J Mertens de Wilmar, 'Réflexions sur le système d'articulation du droit communautaire et du droit des Etats membres' in *L'Europe et le droit. Mélanges en hommage à Jean Boulouis* (Dalloz, Paris, 1991).
[2] And one which enlargement shakes to the core. It hardly seems possible to maintain the paradigm of the uniform application of Community law in a Union of 25.

Community law. Section 126(9) of the 1998 Act defines Community law by reference to the Community Treaties.[3]

1. COMMUNITY LAW IN THE DEVOLUTION SETTLEMENT

A restraint on the devolved powers.

The Scottish Parliament (hereafter 'SP') has no power to legislate in a way which is incompatible with Community law; and similarly the Scottish Executive has no power to make subordinate legislation or to take executive action which is incompatible with Community law. It is possible to challenge such legislation and actions in the Scottish courts on the ground that the SP or Executive has exercised its powers incompatibly. If the challenge is successful then the legislation or action would be held to be unlawful.

Limitation on legislative competence

The 1998 Act limits the legislative competence of the SP. Some of these limitations can be regarded as having an EC dimension. First, the SP cannot legislate on reserved matters.[4] A number of the reserved matters relate to Community law.[5] They are defined by a specific[6] or general reference to Community law[7] or by specific reference to the subject matter of UK legislation which has a principal purpose of implementing Community obligations[8] or by a descriptive reference to an area of law with a significant Community law content.[9] Secondly, in respect of devolved matters, the SP cannot enact legislation which is incompatible with Community law.[10] Finally, the legislative capacity of the UK Parliament to make law for Scotland be it in relation to reserved or devolved

---

[3] The European Communities Act 1972 (as amended) (the 'ECA') continues, post Nice, to draw a distinction between EC and EU law. Section 1(2) only gives effect to the law contained and arising under the 'Community Treaties', and therefore continues to exclude Title V and Title VI of the Treaty on European Union (the 'TEU'), or as they are commonly known the second and third pillars. Accordingly the domestic effect of Title V TEU and anything done under it does not flow from the European Communities Act, but is dependent on further specific enactment—but Article 61 EC *communautarises* most measures which would be taken under Title VI TEU.

[4] Section 29(2) (b) of the 1998 Act provides that a provision is outside legislative competence in so far as it 'relates to reserved matters'.

[5] T StJ N Bates, 'Domestic Implementation of European Law in the context of Devolution' in J Usher (ed), *The State of the EU* (London, Longman, 2000).

[6] Schedule 5, Part II, section B2(b) of the 1998 Act, for example, reserves the subject matter of Council Directive 95/46/EC on the protection of individuals with regard to the processing of personal data and on the free movement of such data.

[7] Schedule 5, Part II, section C(8) of the 1998 Act.

[8] Schedule 5, Part II, section L2 of the 1998 Act.

[9] Schedule 5, Part II, section C1 of the 1998 Act.

[10] Section 29(2)(d) of the 1998 Act.

matters[11] is preserved by virtue of section 28(7) of the 1998 Act, and a decision by the UK Parliament to exercise such a power may be motivated by the necessity to ensure that Community obligations are adhered to.

Limitation on the Scottish Ministers

The competence of Scottish Ministers to make subordinate legislation, including subordinate legislation relating to Community obligations, is similarly subject to limitations and control. A Scottish Minister can competently make subordinate legislation only where it is within the legislative competence of the SP;[12] there is no competence to make subordinate legislation which is incompatible with Community law.[13] Section 57(1) of the 1998 Act[14] in effect preserves the competence of UK Ministers to make subordinate legislation implementing Community obligations under the European Communities Act 1972 on a UK wide basis.[15] Finally, it is not just the capacity to make subordinate legislation that is limited by Community law. The Scottish Executive exercises a wide variety of administrative functions relating to Community obligations. These need to be exercised in conformity with Community law as section 57(2) of the 1998 Act provides a general rule which applies to the exercise of all functions by Scottish Ministers, no matter how they are acquired. It is ultra vires for Scottish Ministers to 'do any act' which is incompatible with Community law.[16] The 1998 Act similarly prohibits the SP legislating in a manner incompatible with Convention Rights and prevents the Executive from taking executive action or making subordinate legislation incompatible with Convention Rights. However, notwithstanding that both Community law and Convention Rights are used as limitations on legislative competence, there is no

---

[11] There is however an 'understanding' whereby the Westminster Parliament will not normally seek to legislate on devolved matters without first obtaining the consent of the SP.
[12] Section 54 of the 1998 Act
[13] Section 57(2) of the 1998 Act provides that 'A member of the Scottish Executive has no power to make any subordinate legislation, or to do any other act, so far as the legislation or act is incompatible with any of the Convention rights or with Community law'.
[14] It provides that 'despite the transfer to the Scottish Ministers by virtue of section 53 of functions in relation to observing and implementing obligations under Community law, any function of a Minister of the Crown in relation to any matter shall continue to be exercisable by him as regards Scotland for the purposes specified in section 2(2) of the European Communities Act 1972.'
[15] In this sense it has been said that the observance and implementation of Community obligations in Scotland can be regarded as shared competence: J Convery, *The Governance of Scotland, A Saltire Guide* (Edinburgh, the Stationery Office, 2000), at 312; Clyde and Edwards, *Judicial Review* (Edinburgh, Green, 2000), at 298.
[16] Guidance as to what constitutes and does not constitute an 'act' within the meaning of section 57(2) of the 1998 Act was provided in the case *of R v. Her Majesty's Advocate and The Advocate General for Scotland* [2003] 2 WLR 317. It is now clear that the term 'act' in section 57(2) does not include a failure to act. Failure by a member of the Scottish Executive to carry out one of his functions, however, carries legal consequences under the 1998 Act. So failure to implement a Community obligation would be a devolution issue under paragraph 1(e) of Schedule 6.

scope for developing an isolated UK based jurisprudence[17] on Community law,[18] whereas there is such scope in relation to Convention Rights,[19] and to this extent there is a fundamental difference between the status of Community law and Convention Rights in the devolution settlement.

Community law as a Driving force

On the other hand Community law does not act as a limitation, but can also be seen as a driving force. In other words, the acquired capacity to legislate or act is not simply limited by Community law. Part of the devolved institutions' legislative programme and general activity can be seen as mobilised and driven by Community law. In many areas, primary or secondary legislation has to be made for the sole purpose of giving effect to, applying or implementing Community obligations.[20] In this respect too, Community law has a fundamentally different significance in the devolution settlement from Convention Rights.

Observing and implementing obligations under Community law is not reserved, and the Scottish Ministers have been given powers to implement Community obligations in devolved matters.[21] They may decide to implement such obligations by making secondary legislation or by introducing primary legislation in the SP. For example, the purpose of Part I of the Water Environment and Water Services (Scotland) Act 2003, which makes provision for protection of the water environment ,is to implement the Water Framework Directive.[22]

---

[17] Section 3(1) of the ECA goes well beyond any of the duties created for the courts under the Human Rights Act 1998 (the 'HRA'). While section 2(1) of the HRA provides that the European Court of Human Rights' case law must be 'taken into account', section 3(1) of the ECA states that 'for the purposes of all legal proceedings any question as to the meaning or effect of any of the Treaties, or as to the validity, meaning or effect of any community instrument, shall be treated as a question of law (and if not referred to the European Court), *be for determination as such in accordance with the principles laid down by and any relevant decision of the European Court or any court attached thereto.*'

[18] This is a requirement of primacy. See C Boch, *EC Law in the UK* (Harlow, Longman, 2000) at 20–36.

[19] And on one view, even a Scottish based one, see Clyde and Edwards, above n15, at 302, who argue that: 'within the UK, the distinct identity of the component parts has not only long been recognised, but is now being fortified by devolution. In particular, the existence of the Scottish Parliament has its origins, perceived or real, between Scotland and other parts of the UK. Accordingly it may well be that the distinct powers of the courts over Scottish legislation justify granting a margin of appreciation to the SP'.

[20] So for example in the first session of the SP 148 SSI were made for the purpose of implementing Community obligations using the powers conferred by section 2(2) of the ECA. This figure does not give a comprehensive picture, as a number of Community obligations are given effect through the use of domestic powers.

[21] Schedule 5 of the 1998 Act reserves international relations, which includes relations with the European Communities and their institutions, but excepts from the reservation 'observing and implementing obligations under Community law'. However it does not give responsibility directly to the Executive for this function. This is done by virtue of the transfer of functions in section 53 of the 1998 Act.

[22] Directive 2000/60/EC of the European Parliament and of the Council of 23 October 2000 establishing a framework for Community action in the field of water policy.

Community law may have a significant impact on most devolved matters. The devolved areas with the greatest European dimension are agriculture and fisheries policy, rural development, environmental policy, transport policy, land use,[23] competition and industrial policy, and Justice and Home Affairs. Community law also has an impact on matters which, although reserved, have a particular Scottish dimension. These include developing the potential of financial services, exploiting Scotland's stake in electronics and commitment to e-commerce, the whisky industry's interest in the elimination of tax barriers and the mutual recognition of qualifications. It can be seen from the foregoing that the distinction between devolved/reserved matters is not ideally suited to Community obligations. Community legislation ignores that dichotomy, and, to the extent that some Community obligations may straddle the divide, the limits on the capacity to implement separately are just ill-suited to the task at hand.

EC Policy and Legislation imposed on the new institutions?

As far as the EU is concerned, it is only the UK which is a Member State, and it is only the UK Government or a representative authorised to commit the UK Government that can represent the UK in its dealings with the Community institutions.[24] Under the 1998 Act, relations with the European Communities and the institutions are expressly reserved although reference is made to the capacity of the Scottish Ministers to be involved.[25] As a result, the devolved institutions are in the position of being bound by, and having to give effect to, Community obligations, that they had little or no opportunity to influence.

So, while it has been said that 'the 1998 Act is a major constitutional measure which altered the government of the United Kingdom',[26] it should be borne in mind that the new UK constitutional structure cannot be fully understood unless account is taken of the EU and how this both circumscribes and mobilises[27] the devolved institutions.

The extent to which the devolved institutions can influence the content of Community obligations which will bind them and/or to which they will have to give effect is examined next.

---

[23] Land use may be influenced by Community law in a variety of ways, including the effects of the Directives on environmental impact assessment (Directive 2001/42/EC and Directive 85/337/EEC) or the incidental influence of EC water legislation, the Birds Directive, and the Habitats Directive. The CAP is a major driver of rural land use in Scotland etc . . . .

[24] Article 203 EC Treaty

[25] Above n21.

[26] Lord Rodger of Earlsferry in *R v. Her Majesty's Advocate and the Advocate General for Scotland*, above n16, at para 121.

[27] This in many ways is an understatement given the Union legislative capacity, and the vast number of Community instruments adopted every year.

Guarantees for involvement with EU affairs.

The 1998 Act provides that Members of the Scottish Executive may assist UK Government Ministers in the negotiation of Community obligations.[28]

In addition, the Memorandum of Understanding and supplementary agreements between the United Kingdom Government and the Scottish Ministers, collectively known as 'the concordats',[29] also address the Scottish Ministers' involvement in European matters.[30] They provide that, although relations with the EU remain the responsibility of the UK Government and the UK Parliament, the Government recognises the particular interest of the devolved administration in many aspects of EU business which affect devolved areas. They further provide that, while the determination of the policy to be pursued at such negotiation would be for the UK Government and any rôle which the Scottish Executive would play would have to be within policy so determined, the UK Government will involve the devolved administration as fully as possible in discussions about the formulation of the UK policy position on all EU issues which touch on devolved matters. Lastly, they provide that the devolved administrations are responsible for implementing EU obligations which concern devolved matters. In this respect, the concordats assert that, together with the responsibility for implementing Community obligation comes the corresponding accountability for shortcomings in the implementation or application of Community obligations, and that:

> to the extent that financial penalties are imposed on the UK as a result of any failure of implementation or enforcement, responsibility for meeting them will be borne by the administration responsible for the failure.[31]

Section 57(1) of the 1998 Act gives the UK Government the capacity to intervene at any point to implement Community obligations. Given that this is so, it has been suggested that the extent to which the Scottish Ministers could be held liable for breaches of Community law is questionable, and that it is possible to

---

[28] Schedule 5 of the 1998 Act.

[29] The 1997 White Paper *Scotland's Parliament* provided that Departments in both the UK and Scottish Administration should develop mutual understandings for matters including exchange of information and joint workings. These negotiations bore fruit and led to the publication of the 'concordats' in October 1999. http://www.scotland.gov.uk/library2/memorandum/#B1.

[30] The Memorandum of Understanding and other agreements are just that: an *understanding* between the UK Government and the devolved administrations of the principles that will underlie relations between them. They are statements of political intent and should not be interpreted as a binding agreement or as a document which creates legal obligations between the parties. However, it has been suggested that, if the concordats are not legally contractual in character, they may in effect be enforceable in an application for review of an act or decision which has failed to comply with them. For example, a concordat may create a legitimate expectation of consultation and so in effect be enforced by a third party who was relying on its provisions being observed. Clyde and Edwards, above n15, at 308.

[31] The Memorandum of Understanding and supplementary agreements between the United Kingdom Government, Scottish Ministers and the Cabinet of the National Assembly for Wales SE/99/36, at para 20.

consider that the UK Government has in fact a residual liability based on its failure to make use of its powers under section 57(1) of the 1998 Act to remedy breaches of Community law occasioned by the Scottish Ministers.[32] The concordats also take stock of the fact that Community law is principally enforced through domestic courts, and remind the devolved administrations that:

> they are directly accountable through the domestic courts, in the same way as the UK Government is, for shortcomings in their implementation or application of EC law.[33]

Debates and inquiries

The 1998 Act does not seek to limit the capacity of the SP to hold inquiries or debate.[34] Thus, the SP can use debates to focus attention on the ways in which particular Community policies or obligations may adversely affect Scottish interests. In this way, influence may be brought to bear on the UK Government in its negotiations on EU policy and legislation as they affect Scotland, whether the effect of these obligations relates to devolved matters or not.

In contrast to the debating function, the 1998 Act appears to restrict the power of the SP to inquire into issues in respect of reserved matters. The SP may only require the attendance of persons and the production of documents relating to devolved matters concerning Scotland and matters where statutory functions are exercisable by Scottish Ministers.[35] Nonetheless, EU Commissioners (and members of their staff), and MEPs (including those from other Member States), have often given evidence to UK Parliamentary Committees even though Westminster has no power to compel them to do so. Indeed, such voluntary appearances have also taken place before the SP.

In summary, from the perspective of the devolved institutions, Community law plays a dual rôle. It acts as a limit on the legislative capacity of the devolved institutions, but it also mobilises and drives much of their activities. Under the devolution settlement there is scope for the devolved institutions to influence the making of Community law, both at the direct level, involving inter-governmental relationships, and at the indirect level, by Parliamentary debate.

2. THE PLACE OF DEVOLVED INSTITUTIONS IN COMMUNITY LAW.

The Union is currently undertaking a large scale process of institutional reform, yet finalisation of this process is still some way off.[36] This part of the contribution

---

[32] J Convery, above n15, at 312.
[33] Above n31.
[34] Provided the methods of discussion do not offend the Standing Orders. See section 22 of the 1998 Act.
[35] Section 23 of the 1998 Act.
[36] The Intergovernmental Conference to discuss the proposals for reform has yet to be convened, and any new Treaty or Constitution which might be agreed then will have to be ratified in each

examines the way devolved institutions fit into the current Treaty structure. It is useful in this context to consider Scotland as an autonomous region.

The Member States as main protagonists

The debate on the European Constitution, the fact that the EC Treaty affects individuals directly,[37] that it has been considered to be more than an agreement creating mutual obligations between the contracting States, and that the Court characterised the Community legal order as a new legal order of international law[38] makes it difficult to treat the Treaties as ordinary international treaties. Yet, at a formal level, the Treaties are simply international agreements signed by the Member States and binding on the Member States. As a result, European policy has been treated in the Member States as foreign policy, traditionally the prerogative of the central State. The fact that the Member States are the contracting parties means that, from a Union perspective, national constitutional arrangements are irrelevant. Internal matters are of no concern to the Union, which remains in the main blind towards the internal distribution of powers within the Member States. Consequently, Member States are not allowed to justify non-compliance with their Community obligations by reference to difficulties arising from national constitutional arrangements. The ECJ has consistently held that while each Member State was free to allocate areas of internal legal competence as it sees fit, the fact still remains that it alone is responsible towards the Community under Article 226 EC for compliance with its obligations. A Member State cannot plead conditions existing within its own legal system as a justification for its failure to comply with obligations arising under Community law.[39]

Member State in accordance with their respective constitutional requirements (Article 52 TEU) before it can enter into force. On average the process of ratification has taken 20 months.

[37] Case 26/62 *van Gend en Loos* v. *Nederlandse Administratie der Belastingen* [1963] ECR 95; Case 6/64 *Costa* v. *ENEL* [1964] ECR 585, at 593.

[38] *Ibid.*

[39] The principle was set out in Case 77/69 *Commission* v. *Belgium* [1970] ECR 237: 'the liability of a Member State arises whatever the agency of the State whose action or inaction is the cause of the failure to fulfil its obligations'. A Member State can be answerable, in proceedings for failure to fulfil obligations under Article 28 EC, for measures implemented by one of its local authorities (Case 45/87 *Commission* v. *Ireland* [1998] ECR 4929). Other illustrations of circumstances where Member States have been held to have failed to fulfil their obligations on account of acts or omissions attributable to decentralised institutions include Case 169/82 *Commission* v. *Italy* [1984] ECR 1603, where the region of Sicily adopted legislation incompatible with a Community regulation; and also where the municipality of Milan failed to publish a contract notice in the OJEC, contrary to Directive 71/305/EEC (Case 199/85 *Commission* v. *Italy* [1987] ECR 1039). Likewise, Belgium was held to have failed to fulfil its obligations because the municipalities of Brussels and Auderghem made Belgian nationality a condition of entry for certain municipal posts contrary to Article 39 EC (Case 149/79 *Commission* v. *Belgium* [1982] ECR 1845) and because the Flemish Parliament breached the procurement rules when building its own premises in Brussels (Case C-323/96 *Commission* v. *Belgium* [1998] ECR I-5063); and also because some of the Belgian regions had just sent preliminary draft legislation for the purpose of implementing Directive 98/83/EC

In the same way that Member States cannot rely on local government reorganisation, or constitutional reform, as a way to avoid their Community obligations, decentralised authorities, as emanations of the State, have been compelled by individuals to deliver the obligations contained in Directives even where the responsibility for implementation was with the central Government:

> all organs of the administration, including *decentralised authorities* regional or local such as municipalities, are obliged to apply those provisions.[40]

In *Aragonesa de Publicidad* v. *Departamento de Sanidad*,[41] the Court held that Article 28 EC may apply to measures adopted by all authorities of the Member states, be they central authorities, the authorities of a federal State, or other territorial authorities.

Given the strict approach of the ECJ to Member State liability for belated, or incorrect implementation of Community obligations, there is every reason for Member States with developed institutions to put in place adequate mechanisms to ensure that devolved competences are exercised in accordance with Community obligations.[42]

The impact of integration on the internal structure of the Member States

Whenever Member States transfer powers to the Community, this has an impact on domestic constitutional arrangements. Whenever the Community acquires competences in areas such as economic development, town and country

(Case C–122/02 *Commission* v. *Belgium* [2003] ECR 0). In Case C–419/01 *Commission* v. *Spain* [2003] ECR 0, Spain was found to be in breach of its obligations under Directive 91/271/EEC, because some of the Autonomous Communities had failed to designate sensitive zones. In Case C-388/01, *Commission* v. *Italian Republic* [2003] ECR 0, the ECJ, on being invited to consider the legality of preferential rates granted by local or decentralised State authorities for admission to museums, monuments, galleries, archaeological digs, parks and gardens classified as public monuments, rejected a defence based on the autonomy of such authority and found Italy in breach of its obligations.

[40] Case 103/88 *Fratelli Costanzo SpA* v. *Commune di Milano* [1989] ECR 1839, at para 31.
[41] Case C–1/90 *Aragonesa de Publicidad Exterior SA and Publivia SAE* v. *Departmento de Sandidad y Seguridad Social de la Generalitat de Cataluña* [1991] ECR I–4151, at para 45. The legislation at issue in the domestic proceedings had been enacted by the Autonomous Community of Catalonia.
[42] In the 1998 Act, various mechanisms are in place are available to ensure implementation and compliance with Community obligations. These include the power to legislate on behalf of or instead of the devolved institutions in devolved matters (section 28(7) and section 57(1); the power of the Secretary of State for Scotland—a UK Minister—to make an Order prohibiting a bill from being sent for Royal Assent (section 35), or an Order revoking secondary legislation (section 58(4)) or preventing or directing certain action to be taken (section 58(1)) or not to be taken by the Scottish Ministers (section 58(2)); the UK Ministers' powers to make subordinate legislation to amend an Act which is beyond the legislative competence of the SP or correct any action taken by a Member of the Scottish Executive in the exercise of its functions (section 107). Finally there are all the informal mechanisms established under the Concordats. For the most these envisage negotiations, co-operation and exchange of information, but also refer to financial penalties where the devolved institutions fail to discharge their responsibilities.

planning, land use, transport infrastructure, environment, consumer protection, management of water resources, industrial restructuring, employment policy—areas which in many Member States are decentralised—this has an impact for these decentralised authorities. They will need to comply with the Community obligations resulting from intervention by the Community institutions. As Community law has evolved beyond laying down rules for the establishment of the common market and more areas of social regulation became subject to Community influence, decentralised authorities have been forced to pursue policies in these areas in accordance with or with due regard for priorities set elsewhere, depending on the nature of Community competence.[43] This is true even in situations where Community instruments leave Member States some discretion as to means to achieve a particular objective. Indeed, while such discretion can be used to accommodate regional or local differences, the implementing measures must be in conformity with the Community objective.

Still, there is a discernible pattern, whereby more flexibility is fed into Community decision making in the form of derogations,[44] exemptions and options.[45] This in turn means that there are different ways in which Community obligations can leave a margin of discretion. These include the capacity to maintain or introduce national legislation in areas where the Community has legislated,[46] to set higher standards than those laid down in a Community measure,[47] the possibility of delaying the entry into force of the Community measure,[48] or the use of options and exemptions.[49]

---

[43] The nature and intensity of Community interventions vary. At times, it takes the form of very detailed, binding legislation; on other occasions it takes the form of financial assistance; in others still the Community might simply be encouraging the adoption of best practices.

[44] For example, by resort to Article 15 EC.

[45] M Dougan, 'Minimum Harmonisation and the Internal Market' (2000) 32 *CMLRev* 853; PJ Slot, 'Harmonisation' (1996) 21 ELRev 378; S Weatherill, 'Beyond preemption? Shared competence and constitutional change in the European Community' in O'Keeffe and Twomey (eds), *Legal Issues of the Maastricht Treaty* (Wiley, 1994).

[46] Provided for in Article 95(4) EC.

[47] Article 8 of the Directive on Unfair Terms in Consumer Contracts provides that 'Member States may adopt or retain the most stringent provisions compatible with the Treaty in the area provided by this directive, to ensure a maximum degree of protection for the consumer'.

[48] The Protection of Young People at Work Directive provided that Member States should adopt the measures necessary to prohibit work by children. Yet, Article 4(2) permitted this prohibition to be set aside in certain circumstances, eg for light work, and left considerable scope for differing national legislation. In addition, delayed implementation was possible for some Member States. Thus, the United Kingdom was permitted a further four years. Similar provisions were included in the Directive providing for a general right of information and consultation of workers.

[49] The Product Liability Directive includes a provision which states that 'the producer shall be liable for damage caused by a defect in his product'. The Directive also provides that Member States can decide whether or not a defence should be available. Accordingly Member States were free to decide whether or not to adopt a system of strict liability for producers. Article 7 of Directive 90/220/EEC (now repealed by Directive 2001/18/EC) on the deliberate release into the environment of genetically modified organisms ('GMO') provided that 'where a Member State considers it appropriate, it may provide that groups of the public shall be consulted on any aspect of the proposed deliberate release'. Thus Member States could, subject to respect for the other conditions laid down in the Directive, authorise a release of GMO without holding a consultation process.

Where Community intervention led to the adoption of harmonisation measures, the extent to which 'differential implementation' of Community obligations is permitted depends primarily on the legal basis of the harmonisation measure.

Even in areas where Community intervention appears exhaustive, there may be residual competence. So for example.

> Where there is a regulation on the common organisation of the market in a given sector the Member States are under an obligation to refrain from taking any measures which might undermine or create exceptions to it.[50]

However:

> the establishment of a common organisation of the agricultural markets does not prevent the Member States from applying national rules intended to attain an objective relating to the general interest other than those covered by the common organisation even if those rules are likely to have an effect on the functioning of the common market in the sector concerned.[51]

On occasion, establishing that the general interest pursued by the implementing measure is not one of the objectives already covered by the Community measure can be a difficult task.[52] In matters such as social protection—health and safety, working conditions, information and consultation of workers, integration of people excluded from the labour market—consumer protection and environmental protection, the Treaty[53] now expressly leaves Member States the freedom to maintain or introduce more stringent measures than those laid down in the Community harmonisation measures. So it is no longer necessary in these fields to have minimum harmonisation clauses included in specific Community instruments.

Where the Community legislature leaves some discretion to a Member State, and where the constitutional arrangements of that Member State provide for implementation of Community obligations by devolved institutions, there does not appear to be any reason why each of the devolved institutions should not be entitled to exercise this discretion separately. Therefore, Scotland could implement Community obligations in devolved areas differently from the rest of the UK. In fact, differential implementation has already taken place.[54] Thus, some of the support schemes under the common agricultural policy (the 'CAP'), and in particular those related to the application of the Rural Development Regulation[55] have been implemented separately in the different parts of the UK.

---

[50] Case 83/78 *Redmond* [1978] ECR 2347, at para 56; Case C-1/96 *Compassion In World Farming* [1998] ECR I–1251, at para 41.
[51] Joined Cases 141/81 to 143/81 *Holdijk* [1982] ECR 1299, at para 12; Case 118/86 *Nertsvoederfabriek Nederland* [1987] ECR 3883, at para 12; and Case C–309/96 *Annibaldi* [1997] ECR I–7493, at para 20.
[52] Case C–462/01 *Ulf Hammarsten* [2003] ECR 0.
[53] Respectively, Articles 137(5), 153(5) and 176 EC.
[54] Even before devolution.
[55] Regulation 1259/99 EC.

Some questions as yet remain to be addressed in Community law. Let us consider the following scenario: in a Member State, devolved institutions make use of their power to implement the same Community obligations separately. If this power to implement the same Community instrument resulted in differential implementation and was challenged, as breaching inter alia the EC general principle of equal treatment, would devolution itself be seen as constituting an objective justification? Would the fact that different parts of the UK have devolved decision making powers in areas occupied by Community law provide a justification for the difference in treatment resulting from the exercise by these different parts of their power to implement differently the same Community instrument? Would the ECJ consider that, in the matter of legislation, the decisions of one legislative body cannot be a comparator with another legislative body? Would it say that the principle of equal treatment is not breached because conditions in each jurisdiction differ and the legislative response will reflect those differences?

The devolved institutions strategy to (re)gain power[56]

In Member States with a 'federalised' structure—Germany and Belgium—transfers of powers to the EU and the consequential impact on domestic constitutional arrangements lead to changes in constitutional arrangements.[57] In addition, steps to try and protect devolved competences directly at Community level were taken.

This is one of the reasons why the principle of subsidiarity found its way into the Treaty. Certainly the principle is a mechanism to control the expansion of Community activity, designed to identify the appropriate level at which action should be taken, but it was developed to entrench national constitutional arrangements.

Subsidiarity

Subsidiarity is now a value of the Union and a general principle of Community law. The TEU makes reference to decisions being taken 'as openly and as closely as possible to the citizens',[58] and the TEC provides that:

> In areas which do not fall within its exclusive competence, the Community shall take action in accordance with the principle of subsidiarity only if and in so far as the objectives of the proposed action cannot be sufficiently achieved by the Member States and

---

[56] The various initiatives taken to strengthen sub-national representation at Community level are detailed in J Kottman, 'Europe and the Regions' (2001) 26 *ELRev* 160.

[57] An illustration is provided by Article 23 of the German Basic Law, which limits the types of powers that can be transferred, guarantees that transfer of sovereign powers must be authorised by the Bundesrat, and guarantees for involvement in European affairs.

[58] Article 1 TEU.

can therefore by reasons of the scale and effects of the proposed action be better achieved by the Community.[59]

The Treaty of Amsterdam also appended a protocol on the application of the principle of subsidiarity and proportionality to the EC Treaty. The protocol provides that national constitutional arrangements need to be considered in the application of the principle of subsidiarity—a formulation which is noteworthy, since this is the first reference to the need to consider national constitutional arrangements. The ECJ, however, has never been called upon to consider the implications of this particular aspect of the protocol. Nor is it known how the Court will treat arguments to the effect that the requirements of the protocol have not been respected by the Community institutions. Similarly, the degree of control that the Court will be prepared to exercise over the statement of reasons to be supplied by the Commission is necessarily a matter of speculation at this stage.

On the other hand, there is some guidance available. First, while the protocol provided that 'compliance with the principle of subsidiarity shall be reviewed in accordance with the rules laid down in the Treaty', this point had already been established by the Court.[60] Moreover, even before subsidiarity was introduced in the Treaty, Community legislation has been challenged for lack or competence and/or violation of the principle of proportionality. In other words, Community law has for some time recognised that Member States and other actors could challenge the competency and/or intensity of Community intervention. In this respect, the *Tobacco Advertising* case is of particular interest, for the Court signalled a rather significant departure from its traditional approach to scrutiny of the exercise of Community competences:[61]

> the measures referred to in Article 95 of the Treaty are intended to improve the conditions for the establishment and functioning of the internal market. To construe that article as meaning that it vests in the Community legislature a general power to regulate the internal market would not only be contrary to the express wording of the provisions cited above but would also be incompatible with the principle embodied in Article 5 EC that the powers of the Community are limited to those specifically conferred on it.

Furthermore that 'a mere finding of disparities between national rules and of the abstract risk of obstacles to the exercise of fundamental freedoms or of distortions of competition liable to result therefrom were sufficient to justify the choice of Article 95 as a legal basis, judicial review of compliance with the proper legal basis might be rendered nugatory.'

---

[59] Article 5 EC.
[60] Eg in Case C-84/94 *UK v Council* [1996] ECR I–5755.
[61] For a different view, see P Oliver and M Jarvis (eds), *Free movement of goods in the European Communities* (London, Sweet and Maxwell, 2003), at 444, who consider that the Court has not to date treated the principle of subsidiarity as a significant fetter on the discretion of the Community institutions.

Access to the Council of Ministers

Another change to the Treaty was the insertion of Article 203(1) EC, which provides that the Council shall consist of a representative of each Member State at ministerial level authorised to commit the Government of that Member State. This provision enables Member States to delegate their vote in the Council to a ministerial representative of the devolved tier of government. Accordingly, there can only be one view coming from any given Member State. So, while a Scottish Minister can sit in the Council for the UK, there still has to be just one UK position on any given proposal.

Consultation

A Committee of the Regions ('COR') was established, consisting of representatives of regional and local bodies appointed for four years by the Council acting unanimously on proposals from the respective Member States. At Nice it was decided that it should be composed of representatives who either hold a regional or local authority electoral mandate or are politically accountable to an elected assembly. The link with sub-national tiers of government was further reinforced by the fact that the membership of COR is now explicitly dependent on that electoral mandate. At the same time, and rather paradoxically, the Treaty provides that Members of COR cannot be bound by mandatory instructions, and that they must be completely independent in the performance of their duties, in the general interest of the Community. Therefore, COR Members have an obligation to perform their duties not in the interests of the specific level of government which elected them, but in the general interest of the Community. COR is consulted by the Council or the Commission where the Treaty specifically provides for such consultation. It is also consulted 'in all other cases, in particular those which concern cross-border co-operation, in which one of these two institutions considers it appropriate'. Finally, it may be consulted by the European Parliament and may issue an opinion on its own initiative.[62] So in practice, while COR's rôle remains advisory, it has the capacity to deliver an opinion in relation to draft legislation whenever local or regional interests are affected. At the same time, the role of COR has not developed as anticipated, as it still does not have the status of an institution. Perhaps this can be explained by the fact that COR makes no allowances for the fact that the constitutional position of sub-national levels of government and institutional structures differ radically from one Member State to another.[63] COR also attempted to be recognised as a privileged applicant for the purpose of challenging the legality of Community legislation, where the principle of subsidiarity had been breached.

---

[62] Article 265 EC.
[63] COR is composed of elected representatives from regions with and without legislative powers, and of elected representatives from local authorities. As a result, the mayor of a small French *commune* sits with the Ministerpräsident of a German *land*.

No such amendments were made to the Treaty at Amsterdam, and the issue was not dealt with at Nice.

Challenging Community legislation.

Devolved institutions are affected by decisions taken and legislation made by the Community institutions, and the extent to which they have the capacity to challenge the legality of Community measures is of some importance. The Belgian delegation, in the framework of the last Inter-Governmental Conference ('IGC') argued that direct access to the ECJ should be given to entities which have their own law making powers conferred on them under national constitutional law. The rationale for this proposal was that it would be the counterpart to the legal obligations put on the constitutional entities to transpose Community law.[64]

The next section examines the extent to which challenges to Community legislation can be brought by devolved institutions[65] in their capacity as such.[66]

Only Member States are privileged applicants

At present, only the Member States have the right to challenge the legality of any binding act of a Community institution, including measures of general application, without proving that they have an interest in bringing proceedings and regardless of the position they took when the measure being challenged was adopted.[67] By contrast, devolved institutions have no direct right of access to the Court to challenge Community legislation. The only route open to them is that open to natural or legal persons.[68] Their attempts to be treated as Member States for the purpose of challenging Community measures were unsuccessful. The Court held:

> it is apparent from the general scheme of the Treaties that the term Member State . . . refers only to Government authorities of the Member States of the European

---

[64] The proposed amendment to Article 230 EC did not gather sufficient support at Nice.

[65] Provided of course that they have legal personality under national law. Both the Scottish Ministers and the SP have legal personality. In the case of the SP, section 40 of the 1998 Act provides that proceedings shall be instituted by or against the Scottish Parliamentary Corporate Body on behalf of the Parliament.

[66] Devolved institutions can obviously already find themselves before the ECJ as a result of being involved in an indirect challenge to the validity of Community legislation in the domestic courts. However, in these circumstances they appear in their capacity as a party to the proceedings in the domestic courts. As such, the devolved institutions have the opportunity to present their own observations independently from those of the central Government which may present its own observations like other Member States and the Community institutions. For an illustration in the Scottish context see Joined Cases C–20/00 and C–64/00 *Booker Aquaculture Ltd* v. *The Secretary of State for Scotland* [2003] ECR 0.

[67] With this privilege comes a corresponding responsibility. If they do not challenge a Community measure under Article 230, Member States are barred from raising its invalidity in a defence to infringement proceedings or later in preliminary rulings, see Case C–1/00 *Commission* v. *France* [2001] ECR I–9989 and Case C–241/01 *NFU* v. *France* [2002] ECR.

[68] Under the very strict conditions laid down in Article 230(4) EC.

Communities and cannot include the Governments of regions or autonomous communities irrespective of the powers they may have.[69]

There is a contradiction in the case law. On the one hand, the Court is prepared to consider that regions constitute the State for the purpose of forcing compliance with Community law. On the other hand, it refuses to consider they are the State for the purpose of challenging Community legislation. The objective justification for this difference of approach is not clear. It may be a matter of legal policy, although the Court has not expressly approached it in this way.

In spite of their limited rights of access, a number of actions have been brought by regional authorities. Most actions held admissible challenged Commission decisions that refused or restricted State aids granted by the authority in question, or that denied or reduced Community contributions through structural funds.

Individual decisions

A region can challenge a decision addressed to it or a decision which, although addressed to another person, is of 'direct and individual concern' to it.

As the authority submitting a programme, a devolved institution can challenge the Commission decision approving, rejecting or amending the programme. So the Scottish Ministers could challenge a Commission decision approving, rejecting or amending the Structural Funds Programme, or the Commission's decision approving or rejecting the Rural Development Programme. Commission decisions in State aid matters which alter or refuse a State aid granted by a region are not addressed to the regions.[70] Still, the CFI found it to be of direct and individual concern to the region granting the aid.[71] It held that although the Commission decision is addressed to the central Government of that Member State, it is communicated in that form to the region that granted the aid, and is therefore truly addressed to that region. Moreover, the aid is granted by the region from its own resources and it is the region which will have to initiate the procedure for recovery of the aid, and the Commission's decision is as an interference with that region's capacity to exercise its autonomous powers.

---

[69] The ECJ and CFI have on a number of occasions made it clear that self-governing communities and autonomous regions cannot be equated to a Member State for the purpose of challenging the legality of Community measures. See Case C–95/97 *Région Wallonne* v. *Commission* [1997] ECR I–1787, at para 6; Case C–180/97 *Regione Toscana* v. *Commission* [1997] ECR I–5245, at para 6; and Case T–214/95 *Flemish Region* v. *Commission* [1998] ECR II–717, at para 28.

[70] The procedure established in the Treaty regarding the application of the State aid rules only envisages a relationship between the Member States and the Commission.

[71] Joined Cases T–132/96 and T–143/96 *Freistaat Sachsen, Volkswagen AG and Volkswagen Sachsen GmbH* v. *Commission* [1999] ECR II–3663.

Measures of general application

Measures of general application can also be challenged, but regions have great difficulty in doing so, for they have to establish that the measures are of direct and individual concern to them. The requirement of 'individual concern' is only considered to be met where a Community measure affects the position of a region by reason of certain attributes peculiar to it or by reason of factual circumstances which differentiate it from all other regions. However it does not appear that the existence of different geographical and/or climatic conditions would be sufficient to meet this requirement. The fact that a Community measure has certain adverse socio-economic effects in the territory of a particular region will not be sufficient to give a region title and interest to challenge a Community Regulation laying out the conditions under which aid could be granted to certain shipyards under restructuring.[72] Nor is it possible for a region to challenge the provisions of a directive which regulates scheduled interregional air services and modifies the system of authorisation of such services, even though the airport of the relevant region is excluded from the scope of the directive, if other regional airports have also been excluded.[73]

By contrast, the involvement of a region in the procedure leading up to the adoption of a Community measure has been treated as differentiating that region from all other regions. So where the Commission is, by virtue of specific provisions, under a duty to take account of the consequences of a measure which it envisages adopting for the situation of certain territories,[74] these territories are then treated as being individually concerned by this measure.[75]

Current developments in the case law

Because 'direct' and 'individual concern' are traditionally construed restrictively, any change of interpretation is of interest. In *Jégo Quéré*,[76] the CFI decided that the existing test of individual concern should be reconsidered, and that a natural or legal person should be regarded as individually concerned by a measure of general application 'if that measure affected its legal position, in a manner that is both definitive and immediate, by restricting his rights or imposing obligations upon him'. This decision could have been significant for the regions to the extent that they have responsibility for implementation of Community legislation.

---

[72] Case T–238/97 *Communidad Autónoma de Cantabria* v. *Council* [1998] ECR II–2271, at para 50.
[73] Case C– 298/89 *Government of Gibraltar* v. *Council* [1993] ECR I–3605.
[74] Joined Cases T–32/98 and T–41/98 *Government of the Netherlands Antilles* v. *Commission* [2000] ECR II–201.
[75] Perhaps a way forward for devolved institutions is to ensure that, whenever a Community instrument is being drafted, an explicit reference is made to a duty on the Commission specifically to take account of their particular situation.
[76] Case T–177/01 *Jégo-Quéré & Cie SA* v. *Commission* [2002] ECR II–2365.

However, in *UPA*,⁷⁷ the Court refused to depart from its traditional interpretation of the concept of individual concern. The ECJ held that while individual concern had to be interpreted in the light of the principle of effective judicial protection, for example by taking into account the various circumstances that may distinguish an applicant individually, such interpretation could not have the effect of rewriting the text of the Treaty. The Treaty required that a measure of general application could only be challenged where it was of individual concern to the applicant. The Court could not ignore an explicit Treaty requirement without going beyond its jurisdiction as established under the Treaty. The ECJ then added that, while the system of judicial review of the legality of Community measures of general application might very well be in need of reform to accommodate the various developments which had taken place since it was established, such a reform had to be undertaken by the Member States, following the procedure for Treaty amendments.

In sum, while there are a number of situations where it is open to the regions to challenge the legality of Community measures, some real obstacles remain, as it now seems clear that the ECJ will not extend the existing opportunities to challenge measures of general application.

What then might be the way forward? Devolved institutions could try to broaden the range of circumstances where they could challenge the legality of Community measures through suggesting appropriately scoped amendments to the Treaty, and in the UK context a change in the concordats.

Modifications of the concordats

Consideration could be given to a modification of the concordats. They at present are silent on the issue of challenge to the legality of Community legislation.⁷⁸ The concordats, if modified, could provide that, in well-defined circumstances, the devolved administration would have the capacity to act as an agent for the UK for the purpose of challenging the legality of Community legislation.

The advantage of such an arrangement would be that, in such circumstances, the devolved administration would be acting *qua* Member State. Whenever a national mechanism entitles decentralised authorities to bring an action on behalf of the Member States, then the ECJ would have to declare that action admissible.⁷⁹ The concordats, if modified, could also provide the devolved administrations with the opportunity, in well-defined circumstances, to request the UK to bring an action for annulment before the ECJ on their behalf.⁸⁰

---

⁷⁷ Case C–50/00 P *Unión de Pequeños Agricultores* v. *Council* [2002] ECR I–6677.

⁷⁸ They only set out mechanisms for the handling of infringement proceedings and requests for preliminary rulings.

⁷⁹ P van Nuffel, 'What's in a Member State? Central and decentralised authorities before the Community courts' (2001) 38 *CMLRev* 871.

⁸⁰ The UK Government obligation to defend the devolved institutions interests would be the counterpart of the UK Government internally holding the devolved institutions responsible for any infringement, above n31. P van Nuffel, *ibid*, at 881, describes how in Germany the Federal Government can be obliged by the Bundesrat to bring an action before the ECJ, while in Austria and Belgium a single region can compel the Federal Government to bring such a suit.

Co-operation with other devolved institutions

Another possible area of activity is continuing to build links[81] with other devolved institutions in order to convince Member States to amend the Treaty. However, it is not only the principle of amendment, but the detail of any such amendments which needs to be considered. What devolved institutions need to ensure is that they are in a position to challenge the validity of any Community legislation, the subject matter of which falls within the devolved legislative competence.

In response to the impact of integration on their areas of competence, devolved institutions have at a domestic level tried to ensure that national constitutional arrangements are put in place to guarantee their involvement in European affairs. They have also tried to increase their participation in European affairs at EU level. There have been changes to the original Treaty framework. These include the capacity of sub-national ministers to represent Member States in Council, the establishment of an advisory COR, and the inclusion of the principle of subsidiarity in the Treaty. There is also widespread recognition in political declarations that regions with legislative powers are playing an increasing rôle in the implementation of Union policies. However, the EU remains, in the main, wedded to a conception of the Member States as unitary States. This explains why, given that institutional reform is again on the agenda, devolved institutions are actively trying to increase the limited rôle presently given to them under the current Treaties.

The fact that the TEU provides little opportunity for involvement of devolved institutions, and that Member States remain the main protagonists, points to the need for further development of national constitutional guarantees for involvement in European affairs.

At a broader level, one must bear in mind that accommodating a multitude of interests has costs. Thus, the discretion left by Community instruments and their consequences has on occasion been challenged on the basis that it leads to discrimination, creates distortions of competition, and jeopardises the free movement of products which the Community measure is designed to facilitate.[82] On this occasion, the ECJ had the opportunity to highlight that the less favourable treatment for national products in comparison with imported products and the inequalities in conditions of competition are consequences attributable to the degree of harmonisation sought by the provisions in question, which lay down minimum requirements.

An important dimension to devolved governance is the 'rights' dimension. Community law does not just impose new obligations, it also creates new rights. What perhaps is missing in the debate today about the way in which the various

---

[81] See the Flanders and Florence declarations.
[82] Case C–11/92 *Secretary of State for Health, ex parte Gallaher Limited, Imperial Tobacco Limited and Rothmans International Tobacco (UK) Limited* [1993] ECR I–3545, at para 22.

tiers of government interlock is this 'rights' dimension. The transfer of competences to the EU level brings benefits to citizens.[83] To the extent that the devolved institutions have a duty to comply with Community law, the devolution settlement can be regarded as ensuring that rights that stem from the EU will be guaranteed. The devolution settlement assures the people of Scotland that neither the UK nor the Scottish institutions can deny them their rights as EU citizens.

In some Member States, devolved institutions have buttressed their own national constitutional arrangements by ensuring that they have a degree of control over the ratification process after any Treaty is agreed. This has been treated as important given that, at present, any Treaty change has to be ratified by all the Member States in accordance with their own constitutional requirements. In fact, the ratification process is the only time the Treaty recognises that national constitutional requirements can effectively control the process of integration.[84] A way forward for devolved institutions might be to ensure involvement in the process of ratification of the Treaty. There is no barrier in the TEU to the development at national level of constitutional arrangements for increased scrutiny over the way EU business is handled, including the ways in which governments conduct IGC negotiations. Internal arrangements in individual Member States may even be seen as a system of checks and balances.

Devolved institutions have tried to gain explicit recognition in the new Constitutional Treaty. This has been resisted by those who consider that the internal organisation of the Member States should not be a matter for the Union. Their position can be summarised as follows—it is one thing to recognise that the Union may impact on the division of powers as enshrined in national constitutions, it is quite another to entrust the EU with the task of interfering with national constitutional arrangements. Time will tell.

---

[83] C Boch, 'The Iroquois at the Kirchberg' in J Usher (ed), *The State of the EU* (Longman, 2000).
[84] Article 313 EC, and Article 48 TEU.

III. EU Institutional Issues

6

The Convention and the Court

GIL CARLOS RODRÍGUEZ IGLESIAS
JULIO BAQUERO CRUZ

1. INTRODUCTION

THE CONVENTION ON the future of the European Union, which at the time of writing has just completed its work,[1] has made an important proposal to provide the Union with a more stable and perfect constitutional framework. This highly complex and difficult exercise involved the codification and development of existing constitutional principles and rules, the introduction of new principles and their inclusion in a comprehensive constitutional document.

In principle, the Court of Justice seems to be less affected by the Convention's proposals than other institutions of the European Union. This is due to three main reasons. First, institutional issues such as the future role, size and appointment procedure of the Commission and its President, the possibility of creating a Foreign Minister of the Union or the proposal for a more permanent President of the European Council, could significantly alter the current institutional balance and thus have a political momentum that leaves judicial issues on a secondary plane.[2] Second, since the inception of the Communities, the Court has had a distinct and clearly defined role in the institutional framework: that of ensuring, in accordance with Article 220 EC, that the law is observed in the interpretation and application of the Treaty. Unlike other institutions, the Court has never sought to change its institutional position, but rather to adapt itself to evolving circumstances in order to continue to fulfil the same role. Third, the Treaty of Nice has already introduced several adaptations to allow the Court to face the challenge of enlargement. In particular, the Treaty of Nice has made the judicial system of the Community more flexible, allowing the

---

[1] This article was completed on 25 June 2003.
[2] See, for example, Arts I–21 (The European Council Chair) and I–27 (The Union Minister of Foreign Affairs) of the draft Treaty establishing a Constitution for Europe, submitted by the Chairman of the Convention to the European Council meeting in Thessaloniki on 20 June 2003 (CONV 820/03, of 20 June 2003). According to a report of the Select Committee on the European Union of the House of Lords, 'it is clear that the balance of power in the European Union is going to shift from the Commission in favour of the Member States if the proposals [. . .] are adopted'; '[t]he proposal for a President of the European Council is clearly intended to alter the institutional balance in the European Union' (Session 2002–03, 21st Report, *The Future of Europe: Constitutional Treaty—Draft Articles on the Institutions*).

Council to modify by unanimity various aspects for which a Treaty revision used to be required.[3] Besides, the division of jurisdiction between the Court of Justice and the Court of First Instance as amended in Nice tends to reinforce the supreme and constitutional character of the Court of Justice, while the Court of First Instance appears as the general administrative jurisdiction of the Community, in charge of the review of the legality of Community measures.[4] Moreover, almost any competence, including the competence to give preliminary rulings in specific areas, may now be transferred to the Court of First Instance. Another important element of flexibility introduced by the Treaty of Nice is the possibility of creating judicial panels that can be attached to the Court of First Instance to judge the legality of measures taken in specific areas.

The Court is not explicitly mentioned in Declaration No 23 on the future of Europe, annexed to the Final Act of the Treaty of Nice, nor in the Laeken declaration of 15 December 2001,[5] the political moments that paved the way for, and established, the Convention. Nevertheless, it is clear that several issues at the heart of the Convention's discussions will undoubtedly have an influence on the judicial system of the European Union. Particularly, the issues related to the monitoring of the application of the subsidiarity principle and to fundamental rights protection clearly have a judicial dimension. In addition, a discussion circle specifically focused on the Court of Justice was established within the Convention in February 2003. After discussing several issues, the circle gave its final report on 25 March 2003.[6]

The creation of this discussion circle on the Court and the reference to the Court in various debates of the Convention bears witness to the centrality of the judiciary in the current and future constitutional system of the European Union. A strong and independent judiciary is a key factor in the health and life of any constitutional system. Thus, in spite of the changes due to the Treaty of Nice, it is important that the constitutional Convention has given due consideration to the Community judiciary as such and as a dimension of other constitutional issues. The rule of law is an essential part of any constitutional system and it is the Court's responsibility to ensure that it is observed. Indeed, it is the Court's case law that first began to confer a constitutional character on the Community legal order and that referred to the Treaty as the constitutional charter of a

---

[3] Following the line of flexibility of the Treaty of Nice, the discussion circle of the Convention on the Court of Justice has proposed to provide that the Parliament and the Council may take by qualified majority and through the legislative procedure the decisions foreseen in Arts 225a (creation of judicial panels), 229a (conferral of jurisdiction on the Court with regard to disputes relating to Community industrial property rights) and 245 (amendment of the Statute of the Court, with the exception of Title I) of the Treaty (CONV 636/03, of 25 March 2003). This proposal has been included in the Convention draft Constitution (CONV 802/03, of 12 June 2003, 147, 149 and 153).

[4] See, in this regard, the draft Council resolution amending Arts 51 and 54 of the Protocol on the Statute of the Court of Justice (available at www.curia.eu.int/en/instit/txtdocfr/index.htm).

[5] In the Laeken declaration there is a reference to the *acquis jurisprudentiel* relating to Arts 95 and 308 EC. It also foresaw that the Praesidium of the Convention could invite the President of the Court to address the Convention.

[6] CONV 636/03, of 25 March 2003.

Community based on the rule of law.⁷ So it seems natural for the European Convention, whose task was to draw up a constitutional framework for the Union, to have taken an interest in the Court.

This article does not mean to provide for an exhaustive treatment of the issues discussed at the Convention that may have a bearing on the Court. Among these, we shall concentrate on two of them which appear to be quite significant: the mechanisms to ensure respect for the principle of subsidiarity and the protection of fundamental rights—including a reference to the issue of access of individuals to the Community courts. The conclusion will briefly reflect upon the future of the Court and that of the *acquis jurisprudentiel*.

2. THE PRINCIPLE OF SUBSIDIARITY

Declaration No 23 annexed to the Final Act of the Treaty of Nice made clear that one of the questions to be addressed in the 'deeper and wider debate about the future of the European Union' would be 'how to establish and monitor a more precise delimitation of powers between the European Union and the Member States, reflecting the principle of subsidiarity'.⁸ The Laeken declaration of 15 December 2001 emphasised that 'the important thing is to clarify, simplify and adjust the division of competence between the Union and the Member States in the light of the new challenges facing the Union.' The aim of the Convention would be to make the division of competence 'more transparent' and to ensure both 'that a redefined division of competence does not lead to a creeping expansion of the competence of the Union or to encroachment upon the exclusive areas of competence of the Member States' and that 'the European dynamic does not come to a halt'.

These political statements reflect a degree of dissatisfaction about the current situation regarding the division of powers between the Union and its Member States. Issues of division of powers in divided-power or federal systems are often difficult, sometimes even intractable. It is indeed quite complex to devise the legal principles and institutional mechanisms that ensure what is sought by the Laeken declaration: 'the search for unity, combined with genuine respect for the autonomy and the legitimate interests of the participant entities.'⁹ The constitutional orders of divided-power systems normally try to preserve this balance through a mixture of political and legal mechanisms, but ultimately everything will depend on the actual operation of those mechanisms.

No wonder, then, that this has been one of the major issues of the Convention, which has precisely focused on the political and judicial mechanisms to ensure

---

⁷ Case 294/83 *Les Verts* [1986] ECR 1339, para 23; Opinion 1/91 (European Economic Area) [1991] ECR I–6079, para 21.

⁸ Paras 3 and 5 of Declaration No 23.

⁹ P Pescatore, Foreword to T Sandalow and E Stein (eds), *Courts and Free Markets: Perspectives from the United States and Europe* (Vol I, Oxford, Clarendon Press, 1982), x.

respect for the principle of subsidiarity. The final report of the Working Group on subsidiarity states that since the principle of subsidiarity is,

> a principle of an essentially political nature, implementation of which involve[s] a considerable margin of discretion for the institutions (considering whether shared objectives could 'better' be achieved at European level or at another level), monitoring of compliance with that principle should be of an essentially political nature and take place before the entry into force of the act in question.[10]

In accordance with these premises, the Working Group proposes to establish a political 'early warning mechanism', intended to reinforce the monitoring of compliance with the principle of subsidiarity by national parliaments, who could make the Commission reconsider its legislative proposals in the light of this principle.

The Protocol on the application of the principles of subsidiarity and proportionality, which is annexed to the draft Treaty establishing a Constitution for Europe submitted by the Chairman of the Convention to the European Council meeting in Thessaloniki on 20 June 2003, develops and articulates the political and *ex ante* 'early warning mechanism' proposed by the Working Group.[11] According to the draft protocol, the Commission shall consult widely before proposing legislative acts, except in cases of exceptional urgency, and it shall send all its legislative proposals and its amended proposals to the national Parliaments at the same time as to the Union legislator. The Parliament and the Council shall also send their legislative resolutions and common positions to the national Parliaments. Legislative proposals of the Commission must contain a detailed statement making it possible to appraise compliance with the principles of subsidiarity and proportionality. Within six weeks from the transmission of a legislative proposal, any national Parliament or any chamber of a national Parliament may send to the Presidents of the Parliament, the Council and the Commission 'a reasoned opinion stating why it considers that the proposal in question does not comply with the principle of subsidiarity'. The Union institutions shall take account of the reasoned opinions issued by the national Parliaments. When these opinions represent at least one third[12] of the votes allocated to the national Parliaments (unicameral Parliaments have two votes while in bicameral systems each chamber has one vote), 'the Commission shall review its proposal.' 'After such review the Commission may decide to maintain, amend or withdraw its proposal', giving reasons for its decision.

As regards the judicial dimension of the control for respect of the principle of subsidiarity, the final report of the Working Group proposed that the principle of subsidiarity should remain subject to *ex post* judicial review by the Court of Justice, rather than to the *ex ante* review by the Court itself or by a separate constitutional or 'subsidiarity' court that would hear and determine cases concern-

---

[10] CONV 286/02, of 23 September 2002, 2.
[11] CONV 820/03, of 20 June 2003, 65 to 67.
[12] A quarter in the case of proposals concerning the area of freedom, security and justice.

ing the division of competences between the European Union and the Member States.¹³ This is in tune with a resolution of the European Parliament, based on the Lamassoure report, in which the Parliament considered 'that the Court of Justice is, in many respects, the Union's Constitutional Court.'¹⁴ In addition, the Working Group states quite clearly that the institutional and procedural improvements in respect for the principle of subsidiarity 'should not make decision-making within the institutions more cumbersome or lengthier, nor block it' and that 'the creation of an *ad hoc* body responsible for monitoring the application of the principle of subsidiarity should be ruled out.'¹⁵

This position seems to have met with the consensus in the Convention, and it tends to confirm the current constitutional role of the European Court of Justice as the final arbiter of the division of powers between the Community and the Member States. As is well known, the Court is already competent to examine compliance with the principle of subsidiarity in actions for annulment brought under Article 230 EC, and it has done so in certain cases.¹⁶ The extension of standing to bring a judicial action for breach of the principle of subsidiarity to bodies other than those mentioned in Article 230 EC has also been considered by the Working Group. In its final report, it proposed that a national parliament which has delivered a reasoned opinion under the early warning mechanism and the Committee of the Regions, if it has raised objections based on subsidiarity as regards a legislative proposal, should be allowed to bring the matter to the Court for violation of the principle of subsidiarity.

Following the final report of the Working Group, the Protocol on the application of the principles of subsidiarity and proportionality annexed to the draft Treaty establishing a Constitution for Europe proposed by the Convention enshrines an *ex post* review by the Court. Concerning procedural issues and the standing before the Court, it has chosen to give the Court jurisdiction to hear actions on grounds of infringement of the principle of subsidiarity by a legislative act, 'brought in accordance with the rules laid down in Article III–266 [currently Article 230 EC] by Member States, or notified by them in accordance with their legal order on behalf of their national Parliament or a chamber of it.' It has also kept the proposal to give standing to the Committee of the Regions.¹⁷

---

¹³ For proposals of this kind, see, for example, J H H Weiler, 'A Constitution for Europe? Some Hard Choices', *Journal of Common Market Studies* (2002) 555, 573–74; in the Convention, E Teufel, Member of the European Convention on behalf of the Bundesrat, WG I–WD 6, of 9 July 2002. See also U Goll and M Kenntner, 'Brauchen wir ein Europäisches Kompetenzgericht? Vorschläge zur Sicherung der mitgliedstaatlichen Zuständigkeiten', *Europäische Zeitschrift für Wirtschaftsrecht* (4/2002) 101; N Reich, 'Brauchen wir eine Diskussion um ein Europäisches Kompetenzgericht?', *Europäische Zeitschrift für Wirtschaftsrecht* (9/2002) 257.
¹⁴ See A5–0133/2002, of 24 April 2002, para 37. The report is somewhat different from the resolution on this point, as the former stated that 'the Union needs a real Constitutional Court' that 'could be based on the existing Court of Justice' (*ibid*, point 8).
¹⁵ CONV 286/02, of 23 September 2002, 2.
¹⁶ For example, in a judgment of 10 December 2002, Case C–491/01, *British American Tobacco*, not yet reported; or in Case C–377/98 *Netherlands v Parliament and Council* [2001] I–7079.
¹⁷ CONV 820/03, of 20 June 2003, 67, para 7.

According to the Praesidium, this proposal tries to find a balanced solution to the question of standing to bring issues of subsidiarity before the Court: while giving Member States' national Parliaments the right to bring [an] action before the Court of Justice on grounds of infringement of the principle of subsidiarity, [the proposal] leaves it to the legal orders of the Member States to determine the arrangements for exercising that right, including the question of granting it to each of the chambers of national Parliaments.[18]

It seems, therefore, that in the blueprint put forward by the Convention the Court will continue to fulfil the role it has fulfilled so far with regard to the principle of subsidiarity and, more generally, to the division of powers between the European Union and its Member States. In this field, the Court has always had to strike a balance between the protection of the legitimate prerogatives of the Member States and those of the Community, which represents the common interest of all of them. Indeed, the case law of the Court already bears witness to the consolidation of its role as guardian of the distribution of competences. The novelties introduced by the Convention in this regard would be mainly political and procedural, and they would not affect the position of the Court. Indeed, if seen in the context of the various proposals to create a distinct 'subsidiarity' or 'competence' court, the Convention's results reinforce the Court of Justice by confirming it as the judicial body that ensures compliance with the principle of subsidiarity. This can be seen as a constitutional acknowledgement of this important role of the Court.

3. FUNDAMENTAL RIGHTS

Another issue discussed at the Convention that may have an influence on the Court of Justice is the protection of fundamental rights. Declaration No 23 annexed to the Final Act of the Treaty of Nice raised the question of the legal status of the Charter of Fundamental Rights. The Laeken Declaration added a complementary issue: whether the European Union should accede to the European Convention on Human Rights.

As is well known, in the absence of a catalogue of fundamental rights, it was the Court of Justice which developed a comprehensive body of case law in this field. According to this settled jurisprudence,

> fundamental rights form an integral part of the general principles of law observance of which the Court ensures. For that purpose, the Court draws inspiration from the constitutional traditions common to the Member States and from the guidelines supplied by international treaties for the protection of human rights on which the Member States have collaborated or to which they are signatories. The [European Convention on Human Rights] has special significance in that respect.[19]

---

[18] CONV 724/1/03 REV 1, of 28 May 2003, 144.
[19] See, for example, Case C–94/00 *Roquette Frères* [2002] ECR I–9011, paras 23–24.

The basic principles established by that case law are now set out in Article 6(2) EU.

The adoption of the Charter of Fundamental Rights in Nice constituted a new element in this field. If the Charter is given binding force, as the Working Group of the Convention in charge of these issues has recommended,[20] its provisions will become the central point of reference for the protection of fundamental rights in the European Union. The draft Treaty establishing a Constitution for Europe proposed by the Convention follows this suggestion. The text of the Article I–7 is quite clear:

1. The Union shall recognise the rights, freedoms and principles set out in the Charter of Fundamental Rights which constitutes Part II of this Constitution.
2. The Union shall seek accession to the European Convention for the Protection of Human Rights and Fundamental Freedoms. Accession to that Convention shall not affect the Union's competences as defined in this Constitution.
3. Fundamental rights, as guaranteed by the European Convention for the Protection of Human Rights and Fundamental Freedoms, and as they result from the constitutional traditions common to the Member States, shall constitute general principles of the Union's law.[21]

Among the options that were open in order to incorporate the Charter into the Constitution, the Convention has opted for the incorporation into the text of the Constitution, instead of adding it as an annex. It is perhaps the clearest option, giving fundamental rights their deserved status and visibility.

With regard to fundamental rights, the question has also been raised as to whether a specific judicial procedure for the protection of fundamental rights should be established.

Such a procedure does not seem necessary in order to improve the protection of fundamental rights in the European Union, and the final report of the Working Group in charge of these issues has not recommended its introduction.[22] It would indeed be rather difficult to distinguish fundamental rights issues from other legal problems, because they normally come bundled together. Besides, it might be a better approach to ensure the legal protection of fundamental rights within the general framework of actions and procedures. If these procedures were considered to be insufficient, they could be improved as regards the protection of all subjective rights, not just for fundamental rights. This is indeed the route that the Convention has chosen. Instead of proposing a separate procedure for the protection of fundamental rights, it seems to favour a limited opening of direct access for individuals to the Court of Justice.

This topic has been examined in the discussion circle on the Court of Justice. As is well known, Community law is generally applied by national courts, and they can make a reference to the Court for a preliminary ruling on issues of Community law. Thus, the judicial protection of individuals is mainly ensured

---

[20] CONV 354/02, of 22 October 2002.
[21] CONV 820/03, of 20 June 2003, 9.
[22] CONV 354/02, of 22 October 2002, 15.

within the framework of national court systems, while individuals can only attack before the Community Courts decisions of the EU institutions which are addressed to them and general measures which are of 'direct and individual concern' to them (this is the condition currently imposed by the fourth paragraph of Article 230 EC).[23] The discussion circle has analysed whether this situation could be improved in the future Constitution.

According to the final report of the discussion circle, a majority of members of the group were in favour of amending the fourth paragraph of Article 230 EC to allow individuals to attack general measures which are of direct concern to them without entailing implementing measures. This development would clearly facilitate individual access to the Community courts. Whether this will apply to all general measures or only to regulatory measures was expressly left open by the discussion circle. The draft Articles on the Court of Justice proposed by the Convention make it clear however that the easier test (acts of direct concern to the individual without entailing implementing measures) is limited to regulatory acts, to the exclusion of legislative acts, with regard to which the traditional test will continue to apply (direct *and* individual concern).[24] The introduction of this truncated test for individual access to the Court of Justice would be made possible by the introduction of the distinction between legislative and non-legislative acts, an important innovation proposed by the Convention.[25] This approach aims to ensure that the extension of the right to institute proceedings would apply only to those cases in which the individual concerned would have to infringe the regulatory act in order to obtain access to justice. In our view, it seems appropriate to continue to take a restrictive approach to actions by individuals against legislative measures and to limit the more open approach to actions against regulatory measures. This could indeed be a way to facilitate the access of individuals to the Court in certain problematic cases without radically departing from the basic fundamental principle that their judicial protection should generally be ensured by national courts.

With regard to the issue of the accession of the Community to the European Convention on Human Rights, the Working Group in charge of this question has recommended 'that a legal basis should be inserted at an appropriate place in the Constitution which would authorise the Union to accede to the [European Convention on Human Rights].'[26]

---

[23] See Case C–50/00P *Unión de Pequeños Agricultores* [2002] ECR I–6677.

[24] CONV 802/03, of 12 June 2003, 149: 'Any natural or legal person may, under the same conditions, institute proceedings against an act addressed to that person or which is of direct and individual concern to him, and against a regulatory act which is of direct concern to him without entailing implementing measures' (Art III–266, para 4; ex-Art 230, para 4, EC).

[25] This distinction between legislation and non-legislative acts is contemplated in the Final Report of Working Group IX 'Simplification' (CONV 424/02 of 29 November 2002); it has been introduced by Art I–32 of the draft Treaty establishing a Constitution for Europe (see CONV 820/03, of 20 June 2003, 28).

[26] CONV 354/02, of 22 October 2002, 13.

This is an important political decision which is reserved by the Working Group to the plenary of the Convention. The Convention's draft Treaty establishing a Constitution for Europe, as we have seen, has proposed to introduce a provision to the effect that the European Union '*shall seek* accession to the European Convention for the Protection of Human Rights and Fundamental Freedoms' (emphasis added). This language is clearly stronger than simply foreseeing the possibility of accession. If such a provision were adopted, it would be clear that the Constitution mandates, and not merely allows for, accession to the European Convention on Human Rights.

Accession to the Convention system is clearly a good idea to ensure coherence to the European system for the protection of fundamental rights. It is the merit of the Laeken Declaration and of the Convention to have underlined the complementary, not alternative, character of the Charter and the accession to the European Convention on Human Rights. Both the Charter of Fundamental Rights and the European Human Rights Convention could complement each other and make a significant contribution towards strengthening the protection of fundamental rights in the European Union, and beyond. Thus, rather than competing with each other, the European Convention on Human Rights and the Charter should serve to enrich one another. In the same vein, the Court of Justice and the European Court of Human Rights will cooperate and complement each other in the protection of fundamental rights in Europe. It is clear, moreover, that the possibility of submitting judgments of the Court of Justice to the European Court of Human Rights for review on fundamental rights issues does not undermine the institutional position of the Court of Justice. Indeed, the Court of Justice would remain in a position equivalent to those of the constitutional and supreme courts of the High Contracting Parties of the European Human Rights Convention. In sum, the accession of the Union to the system of the Convention would provide for a formal normative link between the Union and the Convention and prevent potential divergences.

It is to be noted, finally, that the issue of the status of the Charter remains a politically sensitive issue. The fact that the Convention has incorporated it in the draft Treaty establishing a Constitution for Europe does not mean that this position is accepted by all the members of the Convention.[27] Even though the proposals of the Convention reflect a high degree of consensus among its members, certain objections may be raised in the intergovernmental conference to be convened in October 2003.

---

[27] See CONV 659/03, of 14 April 2003, a contribution of representatives of the UK, Denmark, Ireland, Latvia, the Netherlands and Sweden, making the consensus on the incorporation of the Charter subject to the completion of work on the horizontal clauses of the Charter. See also the letter of P. Hain to the Chairman of the Convention, repeating that those governments 'cannot agree a specific method of incorporation without seeing the whole technical package' (CONV 736/03, of 13 May 2003).

4. CONCLUDING REMARKS: THE FUTURE OF THE COURT AND THE FUTURE OF THE *ACQUIS JURISPRUDENTIEL*

In these and other areas, it seems that the Convention has fulfilled its role of proposing a more perfect and stable constitutional framework for the Union. It is to be noted, however, that according to the Laeken Declaration, '[t]ogether with the outcome of national debates on the future of the Union, the final document [presented by the Convention] will provide *a starting point* for discussions in the Intergovernmental Conference, which will take *the ultimate decisions*.'[28] In the same vein, the Presidency Conclusions of the European Council meeting at Thessaloniki (19 and 20 June 2003), highlight that 'the text of the Draft Constitutional Treaty is *a good basis for starting in the Intergovernmental Conference*',[29] language which does not exclude the possibility of changes to the blueprint proposed by the Convention. The weight of the proposals presented by the Convention, both as a whole and as regards each of its novelties, will ultimately depend on the degree of support it receives in the conference. The last stage of the Convention, in particular, became more and more 'intergovernmentalised', and the existence of an overlapping consensus with regard to some of the salient institutional issues referred to in the introduction is doubtful. Thus, the content of the draft Constitution should not be taken for granted, and several things may be changed during the intergovernmental conference.

In contrast, the role and position of the Court of Justice in the institutional system of the European Union seems to receive a broad consensus on the part of the Convention. The final report of the discussion circle of the Convention on the Court of Justice already highlighted that 'the Court of Justice would remain at the centre of the Union's judicial system.'[30] The draft Treaty establishing a Constitution for Europe presented by the Convention confirms the function that the Court has had since the inception of the Community: to ensure that the law is observed in the legal order of which it is the highest judicial authority. It would also consolidate the constitutional functions of the Court, which are an increasingly important part of its activities, in addition to those of a supreme jurisdiction.[31]

A word of caution must nonetheless be voiced with regard to the continuity of the Court's case law, which is one of its most important assets and explains in part the strength of its institutional position. According to the Schuman Declaration of 9 May 1950, the founding constitutional document of European

---

[28] Laeken Declaration of 15 December 2001, SN 273/01 (emphasis added).
[29] SN 200/03, para 5 (emphasis added).
[30] CONV 636/03, of 25 March 2003, 6.
[31] See CONV 820/03, of 20 June 2003 (draft Treaty establishing a Constitution for Europe, Art I–28, para 1): 'The Court of Justice [. . .] shall ensure respect for the law in the interpretation and application of the Constitution [. . .].'

integration, 'Europe will not be made all at once, or according to a single plan', but 'through concrete achievements which first create a de facto solidarity.' The same applies indeed to its law: the Community legal order was not built all at once, but through a slow and gradual process of Treaty amendments, legislative measures and jurisprudence. In this context, the Convention's task seemed to be closer to the exercise of bringing the legal order to completion rather than proposing a brand-new legal order. To this end, it may be convenient to avoid an outcome where the degree of legal certainty ensured through the jurisprudence built up over the last fifty years (the *acquis jurisprudentiel*) is put into a state of uncertainty or even jeopardy as a result of radical changes in the wording or the structure of the law. In this regard, Article IV–2, paragraph 1, of the Convention's proposal provides that '[t]he case-law of the Court of Justice of the European Communities shall be maintained as a source of interpretation of Union law.'[32] While the wording of this provision is not the happiest of wordings, it clearly reveals an intention to respect the *acquis jurisprudentiel*.

Finally, it is to be hoped that the central character of the basic economic provisions of the Treaty, the rules on free movement and competition, will be maintained in the future Constitution.[33] As David Edward has emphasised, these provisions constitute the 'kernel' of the Community legal order.[34] They have indeed a constitutional nature, and should not be seen as something of secondary importance.

---

[32] CONV 802/03, of 12 June 2003, 185.

[33] The draft Treaty establishing a Constitution for Europe (CONV 820/03, of 20 June 2003) provides, in Art I–4, para 1, that '[f]ree movement of persons, goods, services and capital, and freedom of establishment shall be guaranteed within and by the Union, in accordance with the provisions of this Constitution.' The establishment of the competition rules necessary for the functioning of the internal market is mentioned as an exclusive competence of the Union in Art I–12.

[34] DAO Edward, 'What Kind of Law Does Europe Need? The Role of Law, Lawyers and Judges in Contemporary European Integration', *Columbia Journal of European Law* (1998) 1, 8: 'we must first understand and value the law we already have. The kernel is the Internal Market [. . .]. Put shortly, the task of those who wrote the EEC Treaty was to create an enforceable Commerce Clause without the rest of the Constitution. [. . .] Thus, the Treaty has *some* of the characteristics of a federal constitution, in the sense that it establishes an autonomous institutional framework, and *some* of the characteristics of a bill of rights, in the sense that it guarantees individual economic rights: the right to trade, the right to work, the right to move and the right to invest. For the average citizen in a Western democracy, who is more likely to lose his job than his liberty, enforceable economic rights are every bit as important as the rights guaranteed by a conventional bill of rights.'

7

The Judicial Architecture Of The European Union— The Challenges Of Change

THE HON. JUDGE NICHOLAS FORWOOD QC

ON 9TH MAY 1950, Robert Schuman delivered the famous speech in which he set out his proposals for establishing a European Community founded on bringing the coal and steel industries of France and Germany under the supervision of a single supranational High Authority. The plan embodied Schuman's firm conviction that permanent peace in Europe could only be assured by establishing a close and enduring political and economic union between the states of Europe.

That idea was not a new one, however, as Schuman himself acknowledged two years earlier when he attended the opening of a museum in honour of the French poet and philosopher Victor Hugo, in the town of Vianden in the Grand Duchy of Luxembourg. The museum, in the house where Hugo had lived during part of his long exile from France between 1851 and 1870, commemorates Hugo not only as a man of letters but also as one of the first true Europeans.

Schuman and Hugo had much in common, even though Schuman was born in 1886, the year after Hugo's death. Hugo, son of the French general who had defended Thionville in 1814, saw five of his relations killed in the war of 1870. Schuman was born and brought up in Clausen, in Luxembourg, to where his Lorraine-born father had fled after that same Prussian invasion and occupation. Returning to Metz in 1912 to practice law, he entered politics after the First World War, serving as a deputy in the French National Assembly until 1940. Arrested and imprisoned by the Gestapo, he escaped in 1942 to join the resistance. Both men had thus experienced the futility of war, and both had found refuge in Luxembourg. But more importantly, as he acknowledged in his Vianden speech, Schuman's own inspiration for a united Europe drew largely on Hugo's own visions of a United States of Europe, formed a century earlier.

Victor Hugo was not just the greatest French poet of his age. After the tragic death of his daughter and son-in-law in a boating accident, he turned to politics, and by 1850 was a deputy in the Assemblée Nationale. In 1851, during a debate on a proposed revision of the constitution, Hugo referred to the revolution which, three years earlier, had resulted in the French 2nd Republic, and continued,

> The people of France have thereby fashioned from indestructible granite, and placed in the very middle of this old monarchist continent, the foundation stone of the immense building that is our future, and which one day will be called the United States of Europe.

According to contemporary records of the debates, this pronouncement was accompanied by murmurs of discontent from the right and cries of approval from the left—a pattern that could have been repeated, at least in the parliament of my own country, at almost any time over the last twenty-five years.

Hugo later noted: 'These words, the United States of Europe, had an astonishing effect. It was new; it was in this speech that they were pronounced for the first time', but in fact the words were not new, even for Hugo. At the 1849 peace congress in Paris, which he chaired with the renowned English economist and free trader Richard Cobden—an early recognition of the close link between free trade and political union—Hugo had predicted in his opening speech that:

> The day will come when bombs and bullets are replaced by votes and by the universal suffrage of peoples, and by the wise decision making of a sovereign senate, which will be to Europe what the Parliament is in England, the Diet in Germany and the Legislative Assembly in France. One day will come, when we see these two immense groups, the United States of America and the United States of Europe face to face extending their hands across the sea, exchanging their products, their trade, their industry and their geniuses, cultivating the globe, colonising deserts, improving creation under the eye of the Creator, and combining together those two unlimited forces, the brotherhood of man and the power of God.

Hugo's far-sightedness was, moreover, not limited to predicting the economic imperatives of a European Union. In 1876, the town of Balak in Serbia, in a chilling precursor of the events of recent years in the Balkans, sustained a massacre in which the population was reduced from 9 000 to just 1,300. Hugo remarked:

> What is happening in Serbia demonstrates above all the necessity for a United States of Europe. . . .

Even if, some hundred and twenty years later, it still took too long for the European Union to respond collectively and effectively to the situation in first Bosnia and then Serbia, we can but hope that the measures belatedly taken, and the prospects of future EU membership, will bring to this region a real chance of permanent stability, and even peace.

But while we may, therefore, safely assume that Hugo would have approved of the European Union's new competences in the field of Foreign and Security Policy, we cannot be so certain how he would have viewed its other characteristics.[1]

---

[1] In one important respect at least, the European Union is very different from that for which Hugo campaigned. Hugo envisaged a single government of Europe—based, perhaps unsurprisingly, in Paris—the existence of which would render national governments superfluous. A state in which, as

Certainly, few in Hugo's 19th century France could have envisaged the importance of Community law in the political and economic structure of today's united Europe, still less the significance of the role played by the Court of Justice, particularly in the formative years of the Communities, in ensuring that the political commitments undertaken by politicians were transformed into enforceable rights and obligations for the citizens of Europe. Schuman, by contrast, clearly saw the central place of Community law, and thus the role of the Community judges, in bringing about the social and economic integration that would be necessary if the political aims of the Treaties were to be achieved.

That role was embedded from the outset in the Treaty of Paris, and later reinforced in the Treaties of Rome. The 'new legal order of international law' created by these treaties[2] was vital in underpinning those political aims, by ensuring that the rights and obligations flowing from Community law could, when appropriate, be invoked by companies and individuals before their own national courts and tribunals, even against their own national governments and despite inconsistent provisions of national law.

In entrusting the task of giving effect to that new legal order jointly to the judges of the Member States and to the Community judges, the treaties created a distinctive judicial architecture. National courts were to be primarily responsible for giving effect to the rights and obligations created by Community law, both as between individuals, and as between individuals and Member States. Meanwhile, the first task of the Community judges, for which their jurisdiction is—and has to be—exclusive,[3] was to control the legality of the acts of the Community institutions. In its other main tasks, however, namely ensuring the correct and uniform application of Community law both by Member States (through infringement proceedings under Article 226 EC) and by national courts (through preliminary rulings under Article 234 EC on questions of interpretation of Community law), the task of the Community judges is shared with national judges.

So long as it was possible for a single Community court to carry out all these tasks, there was no need to prioritise them. Even though the progressive transfer of first instance jurisdiction in direct actions to the Court of First Instance (CFI), over the period 1989 to 1994, has involved a major handover of judicial function, particularly for cases requiring extensive fact-finding, the Court of Justice (ECJ), by virtue of the unrestricted right of appeal to it on points of law from all CFI decisions, and of its exclusive jurisdiction in preliminary ruling

he put it, 'there are no longer French or Belgians or British or Germans'. Instead, the basis of the three Communities and their progressive evolution to today's Union, and even tomorrow's Convention, has been firmly rooted resulted in a very different model, one of sovereign nations pooling sovereignty in certain areas in pursuit of their own interests and the common good (the order of priority being debatable), while nevertheless retaining their national identity.

[2] Case 26/62 *Van Gend en Loos* [1963] ECR 1.
[3] Such is the combined effect of Article 240 EC for direct actions and, in regard to validity issues arising in proceedings before national courts, the judgment in Case 314/85 *Foto-frost* v. *HZA Lübeck-Ost* [1987] ECR 4199.

cases, remains today the one, and only, court in the Community legal order that can be called on **in every case**, if the litigant is sufficiently determined, to give a definitive ruling on a question of Community law that, whatever its nature or importance in the broader scheme of things, happens to be decisive for all or part of the case in hand.

However, for several years before the run-up to the Nice Inter-Governmental Conference (IGC), it was clear from the ECJ's increasing backlog of work and the ever-rising time taken to deal with all parts of its caseload, but particularly with preliminary rulings, that this situation could no longer continue. The point had long since been reached when it was simply impossible for one single court to carry out all these tasks. The legal issues to be resolved in its traditional areas of jurisdiction were becoming technically more complex, and new areas of competence were being added continuously. The ECJ could not, at one and the same time, be expected to render judgments within the time frames reasonably expected by litigants and by national courts, whilst continuing to devote to each case, in a formation appropriate to a supreme court where uniformity and consistency are vital, the time for reflection and debate that the cases required.

By Articles 225 and 225a EC, as amended at Nice, the judicial architecture of the Community courts has now been modified in a way that will permit a more rational allocation of judicial resources, and allow the workload of the ECJ to be reduced to a level more appropriate to a supreme court. The structure involves two key elements. The first is the creation of a new third tier of Community specialised courts—somewhat unimaginatively called 'judicial panels' in the Nice Treaty, though this will not stop them being given the name of courts when they are created—to be 'attached' to the CFI, in the same way that in 1989 the CFI was attached to the ECJ. Each specialised court, once formed, will take over the CFI's current direct action jurisdiction in the specific area or areas defined in the Council decision creating it.

The second element is a major redefinition of the role of the CFI, both by enlarging its existing competences in the field of direct actions, and by conferring on it two new competences: first as an appellate court from decisions of the new specialised courts, and second as a court capable of dealing with preliminary rulings in certain, though yet to be defined, areas of Community law. Reflecting its new, broader role, the CFI is no longer formally 'attached' to the Court of Justice, though together with the ECJ it remains part of a single institution, also entitled the 'Court of Justice'.[4]

In deciding how best to implement this new structure, it is however vital to rethink, and if necessary to redefine, the role of the ECJ so as better to reflect its position in the judicial hierarchy, composition and methods of work, and then to reallocate competences as between the various courts in the light of that redefined role. In order to understand the choices that have to be made, it

---

[4] The draft Constitution prepared by the European Convention would remove the current ambiguity, by using the title 'Court of Justice' to refer exclusively to the Institution, and by renaming the ECJ, its highest court, the 'European Court of Justice'.

is necessary to look in more detail at the basic elements of the new structure in force since 1st February 2003.

Article 225 EC, first paragraph, as amended by Nice, now establishes a general presumption in favour of CFI competence in direct actions brought against any Community institution, irrespective of the category or status of the applicant. This general presumption applies to all actions for annulment, actions for failure to act and actions for damages, all staff cases (at least until a judicial panel is set up) and all actions brought under arbitration clauses in contracts with a Community institution. The presumption is, however, subject to specific and limited exceptions, to be defined by the Council, on the one hand for those cases to be reserved to the ECJ, and on the other hand for cases assigned to one of the new judicial panels.

The other significant changes to the CFI's judicial status are brought about by paragraphs 2 and 3 of Article 225 EC. First, under paragraph 2, the CFI will have sole competence to hear appeals from the judicial panels, with no further appeal to the ECJ as of right from the CFI's judgments, but only the possibility of an 'exceptional review'. The CFI will, notwithstanding its increasingly inappropriate name,[5] in fact be for such cases an appeal court of last resort.

Secondly, under Article 225 EC, paragraph 3, it will be possible for the first time for the CFI to be given jurisdiction in preliminary ruling cases in 'specific areas', to be laid down in the Statute of the Court. Revisions of the Statute to confer and extend jurisdiction in these yet to be defined 'specific areas' will require the unanimous decision of the Council, acting on a proposal of the Court or the Commission. Rulings by the CFI will not be subject to an appeal to the ECJ, but will, again, be subject to the possibility of an 'exceptional review'.

While some of the conditions for such a review are laid down by Article 225 EC and by Article 62 of the Statute, others have still to be determined. It is nevertheless clear that the possibility of a review will only arise 'where there is a serious risk of the unity or consistency of Community law being affected', and that the review will not be an appeal in any conventional sense, whether 'as of right' or 'by leave'. Under the new procedure, if the First Advocate General of the ECJ, within one month following the delivery of the CFI's decision, considers that such a 'serious risk' is present, he may (but need not) propose to the Court that it should review the judgment. If, but only if, such a proposal is made, the ECJ will then have one further month to decide whether or not it should accept the proposal, and undertake the review. While the precise role of the parties to the litigation in this review process has yet to be clarified, it is clear that their views, and even their participation in the review process, are in no way to be determinative. Thus a review will be possible even though none of the parties to the litigation in the lower court requests or supports it. Nor will the scope or outcome of the Court's review be limited, let alone defined, by the submissions of the parties.

---

[5] The Convention has proposed that the CFI should be renamed 'the High Court of the European Union'.

In deciding what changes to the Statute should be made to give effect to this new structure, the proposals from the Court, or Commission, and the decisions of the Council will to need to be guided by a number of factors.

1) A cardinal feature of this new structure is that, for the first time, it will be possible for certain points of Community law to be definitively resolved in a particular case without the 'quasi-automatic' possibility of allowing the dissatisfied party to bring the issue before the ECJ—whether by way of an appeal from the CFI, or, in the case of national proceedings, by way of an 'obligatory' reference under Article 234(3).
2) The situations in which this possibility will arise, namely under Article 225(3) (preliminary rulings) and under Articles 225(2) and 225a (appeals from decisions from judicial panels), will in each case be delimited by reference to one or more 'specific areas' of Community law.
3) In the specific areas of Community law for which such a transfer is made, it will be primarily for the CFI to exercise the general supervisory and coordinating function currently exercised by the ECJ, subject only to the 'exceptional' possibility of review by the latter in strictly limited circumstances.
4) In deciding whether a specific area is appropriate for such a transfer of responsibility from ECJ to CFI, a primary consideration should therefore be whether Community law in a particular area has become sufficiently 'mature' to be susceptible to such a transfer. Such maturity is the implicit corollary of the idea that recourse to the review procedure to ensure uniformity or consistency should truly be 'exceptional'. Among some of the suggestions as to suitable areas for transfer, being those where the basic principles of Community law are now well established and where request for preliminary rulings tend to raise questions of a purely technical nature, are company law, VAT and social security.
5) A further consideration in the choice of suitable specific areas may also be the relative importance of the area, or lack of it, within the overall framework of the Community legal order. However, the mere fact that an area of law is regarded as important, even central, in the Community legal order (for example, competition law, or free movement of goods) should not necessarily preclude a transfer.
6) By contrast, transfers of primary responsibility would normally be inappropriate in areas of Community, or Union, law that are still in an early stage of development (for example, immigration and asylum policy, concept and implications of Union citizenship).
7) It may be particularly desirable, in order to ensure the harmonious development and application of Community law, to coordinate transfers of responsibility under the two mechanisms. Thus, establishment of judicial panels for trade mark cases under Council Regulation No 40/94,[6] with the consequence

---

[6] Council Regulation (EC) No 40/94 of 20 December 1993 on the Community trade mark (OJ 1994, L 11/1).

of establishing the CFI as the usual final court of appeal, should ideally be accompanied by a transfer of competence in relation to preliminary rulings concerning the interpretation of First Council Directive 89/104/EEC.[7]
8) In view of the unrestricted right of appeal to the ECJ, the transfer of direct action competence to the CFI should in principle be as extensive as possible.
9) Consideration should also be given to extending CFI direct action jurisdiction to infringement proceeding under Article 226 EC. The risk of Member States abusing rights of appeal to the ECJ, merely in order to postpone a definitive judgment finding an infringement, can be prevented or minimized by appropriate procedural measures.

1. FOUR CANDIDATES FOR JUDICIAL PANELS

So far as the possible jurisdiction of the judicial panels is concerned, four immediate candidates have emerged:

Staff cases

The Final Act of the Nice IGC contains a declaration calling upon the ECJ and the Commission to submit, as swiftly as possible, a draft decision establishing a judicial panel competent to deliver judgments at first instance on disputes between the Community and its servants. Staff cases are by no means always trivial, and it is important that any judicial panel that is set up should have sufficient authority, and independence, to supervise the proper functioning of the Community's civil service. However, most staff cases are relatively straightforward and raise no point of principle. There is also a settled body of ECJ and CFI case law. It should therefore be possible for the new judicial panels to handle those disputes effectively within that existing legal framework, subject of course to an appropriate right of appeal to the CFI.

Trade mark cases

It has been suggested[8] that the Boards of Appeal which already exist at the Office for Harmonisation in the Internal Market (OHIM) in Alicante, Spain, could be also given the status of judicial panels within the meaning of Articles 220 and 225a EC.

---

[7] First Council Directive 89/104/EEC of 21 December 1988 to approximate the laws of the Member States relating to trade marks (OJ 1989, L 40/1).
[8] This possibility was also envisaged in the declaration of Luxembourg annexed to the Treaty of Nice.

An alternative, and preferable, approach is to leave the Boards of Appeal to continue to provide a valuable internal review procedure within the OHIM, and to transfer the CFI's present competence to a judicial panel.

Such a panel might also have jurisdiction in other related fields, such as design and plant protection rights, as well as patent cases under the new regime for Community patents, discussed below.

Patent cases

In March 2003, the industry Council decided, in principle, to adopt a Community patent regime, which would include the creation of new Community courts with Community-wide jurisdiction in cases of alleged infringement of a Community patent. Behind this proposal is the idea that remedies and procedures in the event of infringements of Community patents should not vary from state to state, and should cover the whole Community. A common court system should also ensure a more harmonised approach to validity issues, at least to the extent that these are raised in the context of infringement proceedings rather than at the stage of grant.[9] All this can be achieved by having Community courts decide such cases, though the judges in such courts would almost certainly be chosen from existing national patent judges.

The proposal will involve a major new development in the role of the Community courts. For the first time, Community judges will be directly resolving disputes between Community citizens, a task to date reserved exclusively to the national courts. For this purpose, Article 229a EC has been added to the EC treaty (though not the Euratom treaty) allowing the Council to confer jurisdiction on the Court of Justice 'in disputes relating to the application of acts adopted on the basis of this Treaty which create Community industrial property rights.' In principle, this provision could be used to create Community courts for resolving *inter partes* civil litigation disputes over trade marks and other Community IP rights, such as design rights and, perhaps in future, even copyright.

While these latter possibilities may be some way off, there seems to be substantial agreement that these specialised patent courts would take a position in the judicial architecture as judicial panels, with a single appeal from their decisions lying as of right to the Court of First Instance, where a specialised chamber will be created.

---

[9] Disputes in relation to grant would continue to be dealt with by national courts or, in the case of a European Patent, by the Boards of Appeal set up under the European Patent Convention.

Competition Cases

A late entrant into the judicial panel stakes is the suggestion that a specialised competition court should be established, with competence to deal with annulment actions against Commission decisions in merger cases and in proceedings finding unlawful agreements or abuses of a dominant position. The idea, which is still at a formative stage, has also formed part of Commissioner Monti's reflections on the future of Commission merger policy.

The suggestion is an interesting one, and not without its merits. Competition law, though economically important, is not at the centre of the constitutional debate. Any such proposal would undoubtedly have a major effect on the existing workload of the Court of First Instance, where cartels and concentrations form the single largest source of work for the CFI in terms of judicial demands, and even more in terms of pages of pleadings filed. Looking further ahead, however, if such a proposal were to be coupled with a transfer of jurisdiction to the CFI in preliminary rulings in competition cases, the result would be to create the CFI as the primary, and normally final, court to adjudicate on all competition law questions. This could be an important means of reducing the caseload of the ECJ once the new decentralised regime created by Council Regulation No 1/2003[10] comes into force from May 2004.

Finally, with regard to direct actions, the IGC invited the ECJ and the Commission to submit detailed proposals for the redistribution of direct action jurisdiction between the two courts as a priority. At the time of writing, a broad consensus appears to have been reached, to the effect that only those cases seen as having an essentially 'inter-institutional' character, and those involving challenges by Member States or Community institutions to Community acts of a truly legislative character, should be reserved to the ECJ. Infringement proceedings against Member States would, for the present at least, continue to be heard exclusively by the ECJ.

2. CONCLUSION

Whatever the criticisms that can be, and have been, made of the other provisions of the Nice Treaty, there can be no doubt that one of its main achievements is that it has made it possible to restructure the 'judicial architecture' of the European Community so as to enable the Community courts, or rather the courts of the Union, to carry out effectively the role that Schuman foresaw as essential to the success of the European adventure. While the Convention IGC

---

[10] Council Regulation (EC) No 1/2003 of 16 December 2002 on the implementation of the rules on competition laid down in Articles 81 and 82 of the Treaty (Text with EEA relevance) (OJ 2003, L 1/1).

next year may provide the opportunity for minor adjustments to some parts of the Nice package, and there are respects in which this is desirable, the general shape is unlikely to change. The overall package of proposals to implement these new provisions will set the framework for, and thus determine—for better or worse—the efficiency of, the Community's judicial system for the foreseeable future. It is to be hoped that those responsible for taking these decisions will be as bold and far-sighted as Schuman, and Hugo, were in their own times.

8

Judge Edward Acting As Advocate General

ROSA GREAVES

1. INTRODUCTION

ONE OF THE frustrations for a common law scholar when analyzing the case-law of the two European Courts (The Court of Justice of the European Communities (ECJ) and the Court of First Instance (CFI)) is the inability to identify the position taken on important issues of Community law by individual judges. It is perhaps easier to feel slightly more certain where a judge is the Reporting Judge in a given case but, even then, the nature of the collegiate decision-making involving the consensus approach undoubtedly undermines that confidence to a significant extent. UK and Irish lawyers have been trained to evaluate carefully the words used in legislative measures and in judgments of our national judges. Dissenting judgments are closely perused seeking persuasive reasoning which may be successfully pleaded in future litigation. This tool is denied to us in the Community legal system where not only a single judgment is delivered by the Court but, in the majority of cases, it is a translation of the judgment that is accessible to most readers. A third party, the translator, is a factor to be considered in the communication of the judgment to the reader. It is not surprising therefore that the Opinion of the Advocate General (AG), written by one individual in his/her mother tongue, is often seen as much more coherent, persuasive and logical exposition of reasoning than the judgment itself.

In a few rare cases, an opportunity arises to find out the views of an individual judge on some issues of Community Law and to consider the approach taken to the role of Advocate General. This occurs where the CFI appoints one of their brethren as 'acting' Advocate General in a specific case. This happens exceptionally, in cases where either due to the complexity of the facts, or to the nature of the Community Law issues which the CFI has to address, the Court decides it would be helpful to have an independent, logically argued Opinion delivered by a member of the Court. Such an opportunity arose in *Automec* v. *Commission* and *Asia Motor France and Others* v. *Commission*[1] where Judge

---

[1] Case T–24/90 (known as 'Automec II') [1992] ECR II–2223 and Case T–28/90 [1992] ECR II–2285.

David Edward, then a member of the CFI, acted as the Advocate General. Although the cases were not formally joined, AG Judge Edward delivered a single Opinion since he considered the cases raised a common issue of principle. The Opinion was delivered to a full CFI Court.

In this paper various aspects of AG Judge Edward's Opinion will be highlighted as a demonstration of how a particular judge approaches certain issues of Community law. Judge Edward's background both as a practitioner with considerable experience of the Commission's investigative practices in the competition field, and as an academic, adds another dimension to his Opinion. He is in a privileged position, as a former practitioner, of being familiar with the problems that complainants/applicants experience vis-à-vis Commission investigations and the difficulties they encounter in litigation before a Community court operating within an embryonic legal system. There are many uncertainties both as to the nature and scope of the relevant substantive and procedural rules, and there are insufficient procedural safeguards for litigants. To a great extent this is an exercise in speculation but, given that the opportunity to have a judge acting as Advocate General is so rare, I hope I may be forgiven for this indulgence.

As these issues were raised in the context of the two above-mentioned cases, the facts are briefly summarized below.

2. THE FACTS: *AUTOMEC II /ASIA MOTOR FRANCE*

In *Automec II* the applicant/complainant was an Italian car distributor whose non-exclusive concession to distribute BMW cars in the north of Italy was not renewed by the relevant Italian BMW subsidiary. The business relationship between the parties had lasted over 10 years and Automec had adapted its business practices so as to comply with the contractual requirements of BMW. The applicant/ complainant brought an action for damages against BMW before an Italian court alleging breach of Article 81(1) EC Treaty. Additionally, Automec lodged a complaint with the Commission under Article 3(2) of Regulation 17.[2] It requested the Commission to investigate the alleged infringement and asked the Commission to compel BMW to resume supplies of cars. The Commission rejected the complaint by letter indicating that it had no powers under Article 81(1) to force an undertaking to supply, unless that undertaking was in a dominant position within the meaning of Article 82 EC Treaty. No allegation of a breach of Article 82 had been made nor evidence provided. In addition, as Automec had already initiated national proceedings against BMW alleging an infringement of Article 81(1), the Commission concluded there was no sufficient

---

[2] [1959–62] OJ Spec. Ed. p87. Article 3(1) provides that the Commission 'may by decision require the undertakings. . . . to bring such infringements to an end.' Under the corresponding Regulation in the transport field, Articles 10 and 11 of Regulation 1017/68, OJ 1968 L175/1 imposes a duty on the Commission to act on a complaint but confers a discretion as to the taking of a decision.

Community interest to justify a deeper examination of the facts. Automec appealed to the CFI seeking annulment of the Decision.

In *Asia Motor France* the applicants/complainants were engaged in importing, marketing and distributing Japanese cars in France which had been imported from other Member States where they were in free circulation. The Commission received a complaint from *Asia Motor France* in respect of an agreement reached between the French Government and five Japanese car manufacturers. The agreement concerned an agreed quota of imported Japanese cars equal to 3% of national sales. The quota was to be shared by the five Japanese car manufacturers. The French Government agreed in return that no new Japanese car manufacturer would be accredited. In addition the French Government introduced a number of discriminatory measures to prevent parallel imports of Japanese cars. The Commission requested information from the major importers of Japanese cars and from the French Government but failed to take a decision or any other action. The Commission had been informed of national litigation where the national judges had stayed proceedings pending a decision by the Commission. Having failed to obtain a response, the applicant brought an Article 232 action ('failure to act') against the Commission.

3. THE ISSUE OF PRINCIPLE

The common issue of principle raised in both cases concerned the nature and extent of the Commission's duty to act on a complaint by a private party under Article 3 of Regulation 17. Regulation 17 sets out the means of enforcing EC Competition Rules (Articles 81 and 82 EC Treaty) at Community level.[3] The Commission is granted powers to initiate, investigate and terminate infringements of these Articles, and duties are imposed on the Commission when acting as a competition authority. Although the Commission has the power to initiate investigations, most cases are brought to their attention by complainants/applicants.

Having identified this issue of principle, AG Judge Edward proceeded by posing a series of questions and proposing reasoned appropriate answers to the Court:

> Must the Commission investigate? If so, in what depth? Does it have a discretion not to proceed on the ground that it is not opportune to do so? Must it take a decision which the complainer can challenge before the Court under Article 173 [now Article 230]? Can the complainer use Article 175 [now Article 232] to prod the Commission into action? Can the Commission justify inaction on the ground that relief is available in the national courts, that there is insufficient Community interest in pursuing the case, or that the Commission does not have the staff to deal with minor complaints?[4]

---

[3] Regulation 17 has now been replaced by Regulation 1/2003 OJ 2003 L1/1 which enters into effect on 1 May 2004.

[4] Above n1, at para 2, II–2226.

The questions identified by AG Judge Edward for consideration can be reformulated into two fundamental issues: first, whether and to what extent does the Commission have a duty to act under Article 3(1) of Regulation 17; secondly, under what circumstances may a complainant rely on Article 232 ('failure to act' action) to force the Commission to act?

The Commission's duty to investigate a complaint

This issue was dealt with in a very straightforward manner. Relying on Articles 211 and 85 EC Treaty,[5] AG Judge Edward concluded that 'the Commission has an active and positive duty of ensuring compliance with its [the Treaty] terms and, as one aspect of that general duty, the duty of ensuring that the competition rules are applied,'[6] which is shared with the national courts since Articles 81(1) and 82 are directly effective.[7] But is there a duty on the Commission to act on a complaint? Given that there was nothing in the EC Treaty to impose such a duty on the Commission, AG Judge Edward looked to secondary legislation and relevant case-law for guidance. He not only looked at Regulation 17 itself but also at the equivalent measure in the field of transport,[8] and at the anti-dumping regulation where a duty to act on complaints where they contain sufficient evidence is imposed on the Commission. Finally, relevant case-law[9] was analyzed and used in support of his view that the Commission does not have a duty to take a decision on the alleged infringement of the competition rules itself, but it must take complaints seriously and respond to the complainant/applicant by taking a reviewable decision if the latter insists. Furthermore, the exercise of its discretion as to what kind of action to take is not unfettered.

The methodology used to come to this conclusion is a common one: taking the treaty and secondary legislation first to establish the duty, and then the case-law, to define the extent of the duty.

---

[5] Article 211 imposes on the Commission the duty to ensure that the provisions of the EC Treaty are observed and Article 85(1) obliges the Commission to investigate cases of suspected infringements of the Competition Rules.

[6] Above n1, at para 7, II–2227.

[7] Case 127/73 *BRT v. SABAM* [1974] ECR 51.

[8] Regulation 1017/68, OJ 1968 L175/1.

[9] Case 125/78 *GEMA v. Commission* [1979] ECR 3173 (Commission has a discretion but no duty to issue a Decision); Case 26/76 *Metro v. Commission* [1977] 1875 (complainant's right to institute proceedings if their request is not complied with); Case 210/81 *Demo-Studio Schmidt* [1983] ECR 3045 (Commission's duty to examine the facts put forward by applicant in order to decide whether [the conduct complained of] was capable of distorting competition); and Case 298/83 *CICCE v. Commission* [1985] ECR 1105 (Commission's duty to examine facts brought to its attention).

Can the complainant/applicant use Article 232 to compel the Commission to act?

The ruling in *Automec I*[10] made it clear that the so-called 'Article 6 letter' of Regulation 99/03[11] is not a reviewable decision since it is deemed to be a preparatory administrative stage with no legal consequences. Such a letter is issued where the Commission considers that there are insufficient grounds for acceding to a complaint. The letter informs the complainant of the Commission's reasons and asks for written comments within a specified period. Although this type of letter cannot be reviewed by the Court it is not necessarily the end of the matter. AG Judge Edward had no hesitation in reaching the conclusion that if the Commission remained inactive the complainant/applicant would have recourse to a failure to act action under Article 232 EC Treaty. Although the Commission may not have a duty to adopt a decision after issuing an Article 6 letter, the Commission cannot remain inactive after receiving the complainant/applicant's observations in reply to that letter.

However, an Article 232 action can only arise once the procedural preconditions of paragraph 2 have been met. First, the relevant institution must have been called to act and secondly, the institution must have failed within two months to 'define its position'. AG Judge Edward considered different approaches to the meaning of these procedural requirements and concluded that the paragraph merely lays down a 'purely procedural precondition designed to avoid unnecessary action'.[12]

AG Judge Edward's choice of approach to the interpretation of the procedural requirements of paragraph 2 of Article 232 demonstrates his concern to allow 'both the Commission and the Court to deal with each case on its own terms without excessive formalism and without depriving the private party of the protection of judicial control'.[13] Thus, judicial means are provided to enable a complainant/applicant to ensure that the Commission does not simply ignore the complaint.

Substance of Automec II: can the Commission justify inaction on the ground that relief is available in the national courts, insufficient Community interest, or that the Commission does not have the staff to deal with minor complaints?

As far as the reasons given by the Commission for rejecting the complaint were concerned the AG rejected firmly any notion that the Commission had an

---

[10] Case T-64/89 [1990] ECR II-367.
[11] [1963] OJ Spec. Ed. 47.
[12] Above n1, at para 30, II-2231.
[13] Above n1, at para 34, II-2232.

unfettered discretion to deal with competition complaints. Similarly, excuses based on a shortage of staff were dismissed as not justifying a refusal to fulfil a legal obligation.

As to the Commission's argument that there was an absence of 'Community interest' in this case, the AG gave this issue greater attention. He rejected the idea of a vague concept defined by the Commission on a case by case basis and argued for transparency and objectivity in the criteria adopted for establishing the absence of Community interest. The absence of Community interest must be clearly evidenced if it is to have the effect of ousting a review of the decision by the Community Courts.

The substantive reason given by the Commission to reject the claim was the fact that the case was already before the Italian courts. Here the AG detailed the difficulties that complainants/applicants experience if they can only resort to national courts. The detailed manner in which the AG went into these practical difficulties which litigants encounter is a reminder that this AG is a former practitioner, who specialized in competition law and had often advised on these matters. AG Judge Edward's detailed analysis of procedural matters and the workings of national courts undoubtedly reflect his considerable experience as a practitioner and his sympathy for the litigant in these circumstances.

4. PROCEDURAL ISSUES

Can an action under Article 232 be converted into an action for annulment under Article 230 of an Article 6 letter?

Even though it was clear that the answer to the above question should be given in the negative since the established case-law clearly confirmed that an Article 6 letter is not a reviewable act as it lacks legal effect, AG Judge Edward also rejected this proposition on grounds of principle. He admitted that national procedural rules allow amendments to pleadings after the initiation of an action but he rejected this option for the Community legal system. The reasoning was as follows. First, the Treaties, the Statute of the Court and the Rules of Procedure lay down precise details of what is required in a writ initiating an action. These details of the action are published in the Official Journal. It is on the basis of this published information that Member States, institutions and interested parties decide whether to intervene. If changes of plea were unrestricted this would undermine the Community system and could even encourage interventions as an insurance policy. Here we see recognition that a less restrictive procedural rule, which may function well in a national legal order is deemed inappropriate for the Community legal order. There is an implied recognition that not all national procedural rules are appropriate for transplanting into the Community's legal system. The Community legal order is a supranational system which requires its own procedural rules.

Secondly, the relevant rules of the Court's Rules of Procedure could not be interpreted as permitting the introduction of new issues in the course of proceedings, except under extremely restrictive circumstances. Such a restrictive interpretation is necessary so that the other party to the proceedings is not taken by surprise. Procedural certainty is the most significant way of safeguarding the interests of all parties. Once again recognition that the Community's legal system is different from the national legal systems seems to underpin the reasoning.

Admissibility of Asia Motor France's Article 232 action

When dealing with this matter each of the Commission's three reasons in favour of inadmissibility were considered. The first two reasons were dismissed easily allowing for a more detailed consideration of the third one. In the Commission's view the purpose of the action had been exhausted as it had now defined its position. What are the consequences when an Article 232 action is admissible when initiated but the Commission subsequently defines its position? The AG took the view that since the purpose of an Article 232 action is to get the institution concerned to take some action, it would no longer serve any purpose to carry on the action once the Commission has indeed defined its position under Article 232(2). However, in his opinion this argument is not relevant to the question of admissibility since that issue must be determined at the moment the action is initiated. The question is not one of admissibility but whether the action has lost its purpose. In his opinion this was indeed so. But what is the court to do? Dismiss the action or suspend the action until the outcome of the Commission's investigation into the complaint is known? On this issue AG Judge Edward decided not to express his view as he considered it was not necessary to answer the question in order to deal with the costs of the action. The Commission's delay in taking action was enough to justify his recommendation that the Commission be ordered to pay the costs.

Here AG Judge Edward seems to be acting more like a judge than an Advocate General. He did not see the necessity of deciding the point in order to dispose of the issue of costs and so, he merely highlighted the problem and refrained from offering advice on the appropriate solution.

5. CONCLUDING OBSERVATIONS

The structure and style of the Opinion

A striking feature of the Opinion is its structure. It is so unlike a CFI judgment. The two cases were direct actions where the parties set out pleas and evidence in support of their case. The structure of a CFI judgment in a direct action is, normally, as follows: the facts are first set out and then the Court systematically considers each plea (summarizing the arguments of the parties and setting out the findings of the Court). The approach taken by AG Judge Edward is rather different. He takes the issue of principle first, then sets out the facts of each case, and only then proceeds to deal with specific issues such as admissibility and the substance of each case. The first part of the Opinion, therefore, deals with issues of principle in the abstract. The second part summarizes the facts of both cases and deals with the issues of admissibility and the possibility of converting an Article 232 action for failure to act into an Article 230 action for annulment. Finally, having concluded that the *Asia Motor France* Case is inadmissible he addressed the substance of *Automec II* Case.

Why this approach? Was it the advocate's training in drafting opinions for clients where precision, simplicity and identification of the key issues is paramount? Was it awareness that in the creation of a new legal order the principles of law must be firmly established before they can be applied to a given set of facts? Was it that Judge Edward primarily perceived the role of AG as defining the existence and scope of the issue of principle, rather than to arbitrate between the two contesting parties? It is interesting that, unlike the judgment in these cases, the Opinion relies much less on the facts and arguments of the parties. AG Judge Edward argued from basic general principles of law and relied mostly on primary sources. The CFI judgments closely follow the pleas of the applicant and do not go beyond what evidence and arguments are put forward by the parties. The Opinion, on the other hand, is an expression of AG Judge Edward's view on the issue of principle he identified as relevant to these cases. In the second part of the Opinion he considered and rejected most of the arguments raised by the Commission in their defence. One gets the impression that matters of procedure matter very much to this Judge. Perhaps one should not expect any less from a UK- trained advocate.

Given that the issues considered in this Opinion were of great importance in the development of a Community system granting substantive and procedural rights to complainants in the competition field, it is interesting that the Opinion is reasonably short. The practitioner in the Judge is reflected in the reasoning and in the succinct manner in which he deals with the issues. For example, by examining the principle first he was able to establish clearly the parameters which were later used to deal with the question of converting one type of action for another.

The result is an Opinion which is focused, carefully reasoned and aimed at assisting the court to reach a consensus judgment.

9

Enlargement of the European Union—the Council process

ELIZABETH WILLOCKS*

1. INTRODUCTION

ON 1 MAY 2004 ten new Member States join the European Union.[1] The process leading up to this ambitious enlargement was unprecedented and the purpose of this short paper is to shed some light on that process from a Council Secretariat point of view, on how the negotiations were organised and on how the Accession Treaty was drafted.

But before going into the detail, a little about why I chose this topic for David Edward.

As a student at the University of Edinburgh in the Honours EC Law classes and then as a trainee solicitor in an Edinburgh law firm, Professor Edward[2] took a great interest in me and in my hopes of a career in European law. In this respect he gave me two opportunities of a lifetime. Coincidentally both came about in 1989—the year of the fall of the Berlin Wall.

In the early part of that year on the Professor's recommendation I was awarded the 'Joseph Bech-Preis Reisestipendium' by the Stiftung FVS in Hamburg. This travel stipend was one of three awarded to young Europeans on the occasion of the award of the Joseph Bech Prize to Lord Mackenzie Stuart[3] for his contribution to European Unity. In deciding how to use the stipend the Professor suggested I complete my traineeship at the Bundeskartellamt (Federal Cartel Office) in West Berlin. This was a wonderful opportunity. As a 'Praktikantin' it gave me the opportunity to learn about German competition law. Moreover the experience of living and working in West Berlin during the last summer of the Wall was unforgettable.

---

* The views expressed in this paper are purely those of the writer and may not in any circumstances be regarded as stating an official position of the Council. The writer is very grateful for the help of David Johns, Christos Katharios and Heather Taylor who provided some sound advice and useful comments in the preparation of this paper. Any errors or omissions are, of course, the writer's own.

[1] The Czech Republic, Cyprus, Estonia, Hungary, Latvia, Lithuania, Malta, Poland, Slovenia and Slovakia.

[2] Salvesen Chair of European Institutions, Europa Institute, University of Edinburgh.

[3] President of the Court of Justice of the European Communities (1985-1988).

The Professor's keen interest in my training in competition law had another aspect which I was thrilled to realise when he appointed me as his Référendaire (legal assistant) upon taking up his post as Judge at the new EC Court of First Instance.

And so we started in Luxembourg in September 1989. It was an exciting and challenging experience, and in many ways an adventure. We worked very hard and over the years I was able to appreciate his many qualities as a lawyer, linguist, tutor and chief. Fired with his enthusiasm we used our spare time to the full, discovering the peculiarities and very particular identity of the country we had come to live in and of its neighbours; countries which were at the heart of the conflict 50 years earlier and at the centre of the Community set up to ensure that there would be no repeat.

In 1990, the Professor was invited to serve as member of the board to re-establish the European University of Viadrina (1506-1811) at Frankfurt (Oder), a town situated about 100 km east of Berlin on the Polish border. The objective was to set up a truly European University offering an interdisciplinary education to students of all nationalities in Law, Economics and Management, and Cultural Studies in at least two languages. We travelled to Frankfurt a number of times to attend the intensive weekend discussions. Work finished in 1991 and that autumn the University opened its doors to its first students, 40% of whom were non-Germans and many of whom came from neighbouring Poland. Today the University is home to 3000 students. For me this experience brought home the enormity of what reuniting Europe was all about, its importance and the fact that so much of it comes down to the vision, commitment and effort of the individuals involved. David Edward is one of those individuals.

2. THE ENLARGEMENT PROCESS

The fifth enlargement of the European Union involves thirteen candidate countries: the Czech Republic, Cyprus, Estonia, Hungary, Latvia, Lithuania, Malta, Poland, Slovenia, Slovakia, Bulgaria, Romania and Turkey. Should negotiations be concluded successfully with the remaining two negotiating candidates (Bulgaria and Romania), the European Union will increase from 15 to 27 Member States; its population will increase from 375 million to just under half a billion, and its land mass will increase by a third. Should negotiations be opened and closed successfully with Turkey, the Union's population will increase to 550 million inhabitants and its landmass will increase by half its present size. Given the state of economic, administrative and judicial development in most of the candidate countries, and the developed nature of the '*acquis communautaire*' (*acquis*) now comprising around 80,000 Official Journal type pages, this enlargement process was bound to be a challenge.

So how has the Union gone about organising this enlargement and ensuring its successful conclusion?

3. THE POLITICAL PROCESS

Following the applications for membership[4] and the Commission's opinions on these applications, successive decisions of the European Council between 1993 and 1999 set out the strategy and the means for preparation for accession.

The Copenhagen European Council of June 1993 set out the conditions on which applicants could become members. These are known as the 'Copenhagen criteria':

—the political criteria: stability of institutions guaranteeing democracy, the rule of law, human rights and respect for and protection of minorities. These are a pre-requisite for opening negotiations;
—the economic criteria: the existence of a functioning market economy as well as the capacity to cope with competitive pressure and market forces within the Union;
—the ability to take on the obligations of membership, including adherence to the aims of political, economic and monetary union and the administrative and judicial capacity to effectively apply and implement the acquis.

The Luxembourg European Council in December 1997 then took the concrete decisions on the process. This enlargement was to be comprehensive, inclusive and ongoing and would take place in stages; each of the candidates proceeding at its own rate, depending on its degree of preparedness.

There was to be an enhanced pre-accession strategy which was to comprise four aspects: the existing Europe/Association Agreements, Accession Partnerships,[5] increased Pre-accession financial assistance and Regular Reports.[6] Its objective was to target Community funds towards each candidate's specific needs with a view to developing its capacity to implement and enforce the acquis and to strengthen and reform its administrative and judicial structures.

Agreement at the Berlin European Council in March 1999 then provided the framework for financing enlargement and finally, in June 1999, the Cologne European Council convened the Intergovernmental Conference to ensure the efficient working of the institutions following enlargement.

---

[4] The Central and Eastern European countries lodged their applications between April 1994 and June 1996. Malta and Cyprus had already lodged their applications in July 1990. The Commission gave positive opinions on all of these applications. Turkey lodged its application in 1987 but has yet to fulfil all the Copenhagen political criteria. For this reason negotiations have not yet been opened.

[5] Accession Partnerships, which take the form of Council Decisions, set out the specific tasks to be tackled by the candidate in the short and medium term. These are updated on a regular basis. In response candidates draw up National Programmes for the Adoption of the Acquis.

[6] Regular Reports, prepared annually by the Commission, assess progress in meeting the Copenhagen criteria and the Accession Partnership targets.

4. THE OPENING OF NEGOTIATIONS

The Luxembourg European Council opened negotiations with six of the candidates: Cyprus, the Czech Republic, Estonia, Hungary, Poland and Slovenia (the *'Luxembourg six'*) in March 1998. The Helsinki European Council (December 1999) opened negotiations with Bulgaria, Latvia, Lithuania, Malta, Romania and Slovakia (the *'Helsinki six'*) in February 2000.

At the first meeting (Accession conference) held with each of the candidates, the Union outlined what accession meant and what were the Union's expectations. Membership would imply nothing less than full acceptance of the actual and potential rights and obligations attaching to the Union and its institutional framework, and effective implementation of the acquis. No opt in/opt out offers were on the table.

The negotiations were to be divided into discussions on 31 acquis chapters.[7] These were to take place in bilateral, intergovernmental Accession Conferences between the Union and each candidate. Their objective was to discuss whether an agreement could be reached on the Union's 'Common Position' drawn up in response to the candidate's negotiating position on a particular chapter. The outcome of the discussions was to be recorded in Summary Conclusions agreed upon between the two sides. Taken together, the agreed Common Positions and Summary Conclusions would then serve as the basis for drawing up the Accession Treaty.

As regards the internal procedure for the Union to reach its Common Position, the Member States conferred the power on the Council bodies (the Council Enlargement Working Group and Coreper[8]) to prepare the Union's position for presentation by the Presidency to the candidate. Negotiations on the Union's position were conducted in the Enlargement Group comprising senior diplomats from the 15 Member states and chaired by the Presidency. Strictly speaking, since the negotiations were intergovernmental, the Commission had no role to play. But in line with previous accessions, the Member States gave the Commission the right of initiative and requested it to assist and to prepare the draft Common Positions. At the outset this competence was limited to those chapters concerning the EC Treaty. However, as negotia-

---

[7] 1. Free movement of goods, 2. Freedom of movement for persons, 3. Freedom to provide services, 4. Free movement of capital, 5. Company law, 6. Competition policy, 7. Agriculture, 8. Fisheries, 9. Transport policy, 10. Taxation, 11. Economic and monetary union, 12. Statistics, 13. Social policy and employment, 14. Energy, 15. Industrial policy, 16. Small and medium-sized undertakings, 17. Science and research, 18. Education and training, 19. Telecommunications and information technologies, 20. Culture and audiovisual policy, 21. Regional policy and coordination of structural instruments, 22. Environment, 23. Consumers and health protection, 24. Cooperation in the fields of justice and home affairs, 25. Customs union, 26. External relations, 27. Common foreign and security policy, 28. Financial control, 29. Financial and budgetary provisions, 30. Institutions, 31. Other.

[8] Committee of Permanent Representatives (Ambassadors) of the EU Member States. Coreper sits in two parallel formations Coreper I and Coreper II.

tions progressed, the Commission was requested to prepare the positions on all matters including the Common Foreign and Security Policy (*CSFP*), External Relations as well as the Justice and Home Affairs chapters (*JHA*).

5. THE NEGOTIATIONS FOR THE FIRST TEN

Screening

Prior to drafting a Common Position in a particular chapter, the Commission first had to 'screen' the candidate. This involved explaining what the EU policy and legislation in that chapter was about and then making a thorough assessment of the candidate's ability to adopt and implement it; an important exercise since it was the only way to be sure that the candidate was fully aware of the acquis it was supposed to accept.

The draft Common Position

Once the Commission and the Presidency were satisfied that the candidate's negotiating position was robust enough to allow the Union to propose the opening of negotiations in that chapter, the Commission presented the Enlargement Group with a draft Common Position (*DCP*).

The Enlargement Group met two or three times a week (with increasing intensity as the negotiations progressed) to discuss the DCPs. Where amendments were agreed upon, the General Secretariat amended the text making sure that it found a formula of words agreeable to all delegations. The General Secretariat also ensured consistency with other Common Positions already established by the Union in that chapter for other candidates and with Positions taken on related chapters. Most importantly it involved ensuring that the Common Position was a complete self-standing document, which contained all the essential elements for the conclusion of the negotiations, the key passages of which were sufficiently clear to enable their transposition into the Accession Treaty.

In this way, over the course of the negotiations a model type Common Position emerged. In its structure it was usually between 5 and 15 pages long (acquis heavy chapters excepted). The main part comprised a record of the commitments made by the candidate to implement, apply and enforce the acquis according to the detailed timetables provided, and the Union's requests for any further information and for clarifications, as well as the Union's reasoned response on all outstanding requests for transitional measures. The Common Position concluded with the Union's assessment on whether negotiations should remain open on the chapter, or whether they could be provisionally closed.

On the more straightforward chapters the Enlargement Group would normally reach agreement on the DCP over a period of two to three weeks. Others, particularly those involving requests for transitional measures could take much longer.

Having reached agreement, the Enlargement Group presented the Common Position to Coreper II for approval. Invariably it was considered as an 'I' point, ie a point for approval not requiring further discussion. Once approved, the Common Position became the Union's position in the Accession Conference and was submitted to the candidate.

The Accession Conference

Accession Conferences were held shortly thereafter, usually at Deputy ie Ambassador level. Meetings of the Accession Conferences were presided over by the Presidency (the Permanent Representative) as the host delegation. Delegates from the 15 Member States were present as well as the Commission. The candidate delegation consisted of the Chief Negotiator, the Ambassador, and a team of about five to ten from the Mission in Brussels and from the Ministry of Foreign Affairs. The meetings generally lasted about 45 minutes. The Presidency, followed by the Director General of Enlargement at the Commission, would present the Common Positions to be agreed upon and the Presidency would then request the Chief Negotiator to accept the positions as they stood. Where agreement was reached, the Conference would conclude. Where agreement was not reached, the Conference would agree to discuss the Common Position again at a later stage. After the meeting, the Summary Conclusions recording the exact terms of the agreement (adding to or subtracting from the Common Position as necessary) were exchanged between the General Secretariat and the candidate delegation so that they could be agreed upon formally at the next Accession Conference.

Before the end of each Presidency, all of the Common Positions adopted by Coreper during that Presidency were presented to the General Affairs and External Relations Council for formal approval as 'A' points, ie a point for approval not requiring further discussion. Thereafter each Accession Conference also met at Ministerial level (Ministers of Foreign Affairs or their deputies) formally to approve the work done by the Deputies over the last six months. There were rarely any surprises at these meetings. Nonetheless they were important politically; a televised press conference followed each of them which contributed to raising public awareness of progress in the negotiations.

A total of 260 meetings of the Accession Conferences were held in the course of the negotiations with the ten. The period of time between the opening of negotiations on a chapter and its provisional closure was roughly a year, depending on the candidate's rate of progress. The acquis heavy chapters, such as Agriculture and Environment, required more time and up to eight or nine successive Common Positions was not uncommon. In total, 3,646 documents were considered by the ten Accession Conferences, 2,825 of which were negotiating positions submitted by the candidates and 821 of which were Common Positions submitted by the Union (averaging 82 Common Positions per candidate and 2/3 Common Positions per candidate per chapter).

Working methods and language

The Accession Negotiations were essentially conducted in one language. The candidates' negotiating positions, the Common Positions, and the Summary Conclusions were all drawn up and agreed upon in English. For the purposes of the Union, the Common Positions to be agreed upon by Coreper and the Summary Conclusions were translated into the ten other Community languages.

The Accession Conferences followed the linguistic practice of the Council. Thus, at Deputy level, as for Coreper, either party could speak in either English, French or German, and at Ministerial level any one of the eleven Community languages could be used.

Discussions in the Enlargement Group used the special interpretation Coreper regime of English, French and German. Moreover, each revised DCP constituted the outcome of proceedings in the Group, thus dispensing with the need to draw up minutes.

The principles governing the negotiations

Negotiations were conducted on the basis of commitments. Candidates were not expected to have done all that was required by the end of the negotiations. However, they had to provide the necessary commitment to do so. This led to the use of the concept of provisional closure. The Union was able to close negotiations with a candidate on a particular chapter on a provisional basis if it was satisfied that the candidate had:

—accepted all of the requirements laid down by the acquis;
—adopted all relevant legislation in the field, or provided a clear commitment and timetable to do so by the date of accession;
—demonstrated on the basis of clear and detailed timetables, accompanied by finance plans, that it would have the administrative capacity to implement the acquis effectively by the date of accession; and that
—it would have the judicial and regulatory capacity to enforce the acquis by the date of accession.

Failure to respect the commitments could lead to re-opening of negotiations on the chapter with all the political consequences that this would entail. Thus provisional closure allowed progress to be made on all fronts in the negotiations whilst sending a warning signal that this had to be reflected by progress on the ground.

The concept of provisional closure was also useful because of the close interdependency between different chapters as it allowed for sufficient flexibility up until the conclusion of the final deal. One of the basic negotiating principles agreed upon at the outset of the negotiations was that agreements, even partial, reached during the course of the negotiations on chapters to be examined successively could not be considered as final until an overall agreement had been established. Finally, it was useful for making progress on those chapters where the ultimate financial decisions could only be taken at the end of the negotiations. Thus common positions on Agriculture, Financial and Budgetary Provisions, Regional Policy and Co-ordination of Structural Instruments were agreed upon well ahead of the 2002 Copenhagen European Council.

There were occasions however, where despite all the commitments given the Union did not feel sufficiently confident to close the chapter provisionally preferring instead to keep the chapter open. This was particularly the case where it wanted to keep the pressure on the candidate until key measures had been adopted/implemented.

Re-opening of a chapter remained an exceptional measure. In practice, the threat of re-opening was sufficient for the candidate to take the necessary measures. There were also other options, such as raising the matter and passing a firm message in the Accession Conference, or calling upon the Commission to step up the monitoring exercise. Where new matters came to light, such as new acquis upon which the Conference had to decide on the candidate's position and which might have entailed re-opening, the preference was to deal with the matter separately, for example under chapter 31 'Other'.

Despite repeated messages by successive Presidencies and by the Commission that the number of chapters provisionally closed was not an indication of actual progress in the negotiations (some chapters being more complex than others) or on the ground (the negotiations being closed on the basis of commitments), the importance of provisional closure of a chapter stuck and it became common to compare candidates on the basis of the scoreboard of chapters opened and provisionally closed with each of them.

In finding solutions to the problems in the negotiations, the Union agreed on some basic parameters: the outcome of the negotiations always had to respect the acquis, respect the equality of the candidates and their equality with the Member States, be consistent, not prejudge the future development of the acquis and be applicable in practice.

In no circumstances could the outcome of the negotiations involve amendments to the rules or policies of the Union, disrupt its proper functioning or lead to significant distortions of competition. Transitional measures therefore had to be limited in time and in scope and be accompanied with a plan with clearly defined stages for the gradual implementation of the acquis. During the screening process the Commission worked hard to find alternative solutions to requests for transitional periods and to ensure that those transitional measures requests which remained complied with these criteria. In the end, transitional measures were negotiated on both sides. The Union obtained important concessions on the free movement of workers as well as on cabotage in the road transport market. The concessions granted to the candidates vary between them and across the chapters. Most concern environmental, agricultural and road transport legislation. Others include the ownership of land and secondary residences, pharmaceutical marketing authorisations, the provision of financial services, fish stocks, taxation on cigarettes and minimum levels of oil stocks.

In finding solutions to almost all problems, the Enlargement Group achieved remarkable results considering that almost all of the Common Positions were agreed upon at its level. In this respect it set the example for agreed and advocated best practice at the Council. There were very few occasions where the Group had to turn to Coreper II for political guidance. This was crucial for the momentum of the process.

Monitoring

A core element of the Common Positions, and a central factor for the success of the enlargement process, were the commitments made by the candidates to develop adequate administrative and judicial capacity to implement and enforce the acquis. Progress in the negotiations was not a theoretical exercise, it had to be matched by progress on the ground. For the purpose of the ongoing negotiations the Enlargement Group wanted to monitor progress made in meeting these and other commitments.[9] To this end, discussions on monitoring were included on the agenda. These concentrated on tables drawn up by the Commission on the basis of data already available as well as on the basis of specific peer review missions involving experts from the Member States. As the date of accession grew closer, the monitoring exercise extended beyond its original purpose as a negotiating tool towards ensuring, up until the date of accession, that the outcome of the negotiations was effective and that the new Member States would be integrated smoothly into the Union. Moreover, and increasingly importantly, it reassured public opinion in the current Member States that credible preparations were underway in the candidate countries. Further to the Brussels European Council (October 2002), the monitoring exercise was bolstered by the decision to include provisions in the Accession Treaty on safeguard measures, should monitoring reveal a breach in the commitments undertaken concerning the internal market and JHA acquis.

---

[9] This was a related but not identical exercise from monitoring of implementation of the pre-accession strategy on the EU side which is performed by two (since merged) Council Working Groups: the South East Europe Working Group (for Cyprus, Malta and Turkey) and the Central Europe Working Group (for the Central European candidates). The Union's position as prepared in these Working Groups is then discussed with the candidate in the relevant Association sub-Committees, Association Committee and Association Council.

How the negotiations were concluded

The negotiations for the ten spanned ten Presidencies and about as many European Council Summit meetings. In the same way as they were important in the run up to the opening of negotiations, the European Councils were instrumental in driving the process forward to its conclusion.

At the outset, the emphasis was very much on encouraging the candidates to make sufficient progress in order to allow for the opening of negotiations on all of the straightforward chapters. The Luxembourg six, having started negotiations in 1998, had a head start and by December 1999 had on average opened 23 chapters. However it was made clear once the Helsinki six started negotiating, that each candidate was to be judged on its own merits and the pace of and progress in negotiations was driven by each candidate's own achievements. This opened the possibility for the Helsinki candidates to 'catch up', or even overtake, the progress made by the Luxembourg candidates.

By December 2000, the more advanced Helsinki candidates had opened negotiations on 17 chapters. It was at this point that the European Council took up the Commission's 'roadmap' for the completion of negotiations with all twelve candidates. This roadmap was designed to ensure that the negotiations moved ahead according to a realistic timetable. The aim was to complete as much work as possible and to push ahead on provisional closure of identified chapters with each of the candidates in each of the next three Presidencies (Swedish, Belgian and Spanish until June 2002), so as to avoid leaving all of the difficult issues to the end. This provided a boost to the negotiations and sent a clear signal to the candidates of the Union's commitment to complete negotiations provided the candidates completed the necessary hard preparatory work. The Union had already seen a slowdown in 2000 as the going got tough in the national Parliaments on the more sensitive reform issues.

The Swedish Presidency got through the bulk of the work in early 2001 involving the Enlargement Group in marathon sessions. By the Gothenburg European Council in June the distinction between the Helsinki and Luxembourg candidates was no longer discernible. Lithuania and Latvia had caught up with Estonia and Slovakia had caught up with the Czech Republic on almost all issues. Thus the Gothenburg European Council was able to conclude that the road map had provided an ambitious and realistic framework for the negotiations and that this should make it possible to conclude negotiations by the end of 2002 for those candidates which were ready so that they could participate as members in the European Parliament elections as of 2004.

Six months later the European Council in Laeken examined progress and declared that negotiations could be concluded within the next year with the Czech Republic, Cyprus, Estonia, Hungary, Latvia, Lithuania, Malta, Poland, Slovenia and Slovakia, provided they were ready.

The Spanish Presidency then pulled off all possible remaining discussions with the candidates on the Agriculture, Regional Policy and Coordination of

Structural Instruments, Financial and Budgetary Provisions and Institutions. The most sensitive financial issues (CAP direct payments, structural funds appropriations and budgetary compensation) were decided by the union at the Brussels European Council under the Danish Presidency in October 2002. These were then submitted to the candidates in November. After intensive negotiations in the interim, negotiations concluded in Copenhagen on 13 December 2002. The ten candidates became 'acceding States'.

6. THE ACCESSION TREATY FOR THE FIRST TEN

The Laeken and Seville European Councils set the timetable for drafting the Accession Treaty. Work was to begin in the first half of 2002 and signature was set for 'spring 2003'. This meant that drafting work would need to be completed very soon after the conclusion of the negotiations—around January 2003.

A special drafting group was set up in parallel to the Enlargement Group and the Commission was charged with the preparation of draft texts. The Drafting Group worked in much the same way as the Enlargement Group, most importantly as 15. This was for two main reasons: first, the EU 15 had to reach an agreement on the draft texts before presenting them to the candidates; and second, because accession negotiations were ongoing it was not considered appropriate for draft Treaty texts for one candidate to be seen by the others. A multilateral drafting forum would therefore not only have been unmanageable but also politically impossible.

In line with previous accessions, one single Treaty document was drawn up for the ten. Separate treaties would have run the risk of the so-called 'à la carte' approach which would have hampered the ratification process. As a single document, the Treaty could only be approved or rejected in its entirety—consistent with the political will to have an inclusive accession process.

The structure of the Accession Treaty was worked out at an early stage so that as the individual texts were agreed upon they could be slotted in and gradually build up the final work in all 21 languages.[10] Whilst previous accession treaties provided a framework, more definition was necessary in order to ensure that the final work was consistent and clear. Thus the main body of the Treaty and the Act of Accession were kept as short as possible. All adaptations, transitional measures texts, and so on, were contained in structured Annexes. This resulted in a Treaty which consists of three Articles and an Act which consists of 62 Articles, 18 Annexes and 10 Protocols. 44 Declarations were included in the Final Act.[11]

---

[10] The 12 Community Treaty Languages including Gaelic and the nine acceding States languages.
[11] OJ L236 of 23.9.03 (Community Treaty Language versions). Other language versions in special Edition OJ of 23.9.03.

Work started in April 2002 on the texts adapting the acquis as a consequence of accession. Whilst on the whole an uncontroversial task, it was an unprecedented exercise given the volume of texts involved, the complexity of the acquis, the number of candidates, and the problems encountered not least because of the diversity of the new candidate languages and the constant evolution of the acquis. When examining the texts the Group bore two points in mind. First, the adaptations exercise only concerned those pieces of Community legislation which had to be adapted to take account of enlargement; the presumption being that all Community legislation automatically applied to new Member States. Second, the legislation had to be adapted as it stood. No improvements could be made to take account of developments since the legislation had been adopted. The texts resulting from the negotiations started to be fed into the drafting exercise towards the end of May 2002. These were drafted in the same style as for previous accession treaties and followed the wording of the Common Positions and Summary Conclusions agreed at the Accession Conferences very closely. By the end of July 2002 the Commission had presented the bulk of the draft Treaty text to the Group. This was with a view to meeting the Danish Presidency's aim of having an almost complete Treaty text by the Copenhagen Summit, thus leaving the remaining time in January 2003 to draft the items resulting from the final package.

The procedure for agreeing the texts was straightforward. As soon as the Group had agreed on the text, it was sent by email as an EU Agreed text to the candidates with a two-week silent deadline. Any comments received were considered in the Group. The text then shuttled between the Group and the candidate(s) until an agreement was reached. The text then became a Final text. On this basis, translations were finalised by the States of the language concerned, again with a two-week silent deadline. The complicating factor was that negotiations were still ongoing. Whilst texts adapting the acquis were sent to all candidates for their agreement (unless specifically negotiated in the individual Accession Conferences), texts drafted as a result of negotiations, typically on transitional measures, could only be sent to and agreed upon by the candidate concerned. This meant that the whole text, as well as its translation, was not available to the candidates until after the conclusion of the negotiations.

On 31 January 2003, the Group concluded its work on schedule. It had held a total of 67 meetings and at its peak had met three times a week, with some meetings involving no less than 80 documents, some of which were hundreds of pages long. In total 3,133 documents had been considered. In the fortnight that followed, Coreper II formally agreed upon the 250 agreed documents making up the Accession Treaty. The acceding States then gave their agreement and during a somewhat intensive period all final outstanding matters were resolved. Under Article 49 of the Treaty on European Union, the Commission gave its Opinion on the applications and conditions for membership on 21 February 2003. On 14 April 2003 the European Parliament gave its Assent. As for previous accessions this took the form of Legislative Resolutions—one for each acceding State. The

Council then adopted its decision admitting the applications for membership and the conditions for membership on 14 April 2003. The Accession Treaty was signed in Athens on 16 April 2003.

Drafting the Accession Treaty was the single biggest task ever undertaken by the General Secretariat and the enormity of the task required a number of changes to traditional working methods. The Drafting Group operated almost exclusively in one language. All drafting was done and agreed upon in the Group and with the candidates on the basis of the English text. In the meeting room there was no interpretation. Moreover communication was entirely electronic; no paper copies were delivered to delegations or to candidates.

Whilst translation of the Accession Treaty was not the concern of the Group, it also required exceptional measures. The newly developed TRADOS translation system at the Council Secretariat was put into full operation. Special programmes had to be drawn up to monitor the production of texts in the 20 translated versions, and new systems had to be developed to cope with the peculiarities of the candidate language alphabets. Jurist Linguists from each of the candidate countries had to be recruited. They were required to produce texts in their own language, which ultimately would be the focus of scrutiny during the ratification procedure—a challenge, not least because of problems of terminology since translation of EU secondary legislation was still ongoing.

The approval of the text also required novel procedures. Time was short and the text was long. The 250 constituent documents making up the 4,800 A4 pages approved by Coreper, were consolidated and put onto CD-ROM by the Council Secretariat Agreements Office. These CD-ROMs were distributed to the acceding States, to the Commission and to the European Parliament for their respective approval under Article 49 TEU. No paper copies of the Accession Treaty prior to signature were ever required.[12] The Jurist Linguist meetings to finalise the text were also quite exceptional—completing examination of the text in all 21 language versions in less than a week, and holding meetings with the 25 States around the table for the first time.

7. RATIFICATION OF THE ACCESSION TREATY

With the exception of Cyprus, where the Parliament ratified the Treaty unanimously, referenda prior to ratification were held in each of the acceding States between April and September 2003. In some instances a referendum was constitutionally required, and in others there was a political commitment to do so. No referenda were held in the Member States. The scheduling of the referenda was worked out to take account of elections being held in some of the acceding States in 2003, as well as to allow those countries with the most popular support to go

---

[12] In its 21 languages in the unpublished version, the Accession Treaty stands 11m55cm high, and if each page is placed end to end it measures almost 30 kilometres long.

to the polls first. At the time of writing, all of the referenda have been positive, the main concern having been to achieve the minimum voter turnout required. The ratification procedure is currently on track.

8. THE CYPRUS PROBLEM

Throughout the accession negotiations, parallel negotiations were conducted under the auspices of the United Nations to find a political solution to the Cyprus problem. The European Council consistently supported these negotiations, indicating its preference for the accession of a reunited island. Nonetheless, it was made clear that reunification was not a precondition to enlargement.

In anticipation of a settlement, the accession negotiations were conducted on the basis of the whole island joining the Union. On a practical level this was done on the basis of data available for the Republic of Cyprus on the assumption that upon a solution being found, the necessary decisions adjusting the figures would be taken. There was also an open invitation to representatives of the Turkish Cypriot community to take part in the negotiations as part of the Cypriot delegation, although this was never taken up.

At the date of signature there was still no settlement. A Protocol on Cyprus was therefore included in the Accession Treaty, providing for the suspension of application of the acquis in those areas of the Republic of Cyprus in which the Government of the Republic of Cyprus does not exercise effective control. It also conferred the power upon the Council to decide unanimously on the basis of a Commission proposal to withdraw the suspension and, in the event of a settlement, to decide on the necessary adaptations of the Accession Treaty with regard to the Turkish Cypriot Community.[13]

9. POST SIGNATURE, PRIOR TO ACCESSION—THE INTERIM PERIOD

Special measures were agreed concerning the period between conclusion of negotiations and accession.[14] This was a time when the acceding States had to complete the fulfilment of their commitments made during the negotiations. It was also the time for the Member States to get used to their future new partners, and for the acceding States to make the mental leap from behaving as candidates in negotiations to new Member States.

---

[13] At the time of writing no solution has yet been found. In line with the Copenhagen European Council's request, the Commission paper on ways of promoting economic development of the northern part of Cyprus and bringing it closer to the Union (COM(2003) 325 final) is now under consideration in the Council.

[14] See for example the Exchange of Letters attached to the Final Act to the Treaty of Accession as well as Arts 37–39, 55 and 57 of the Act of Accession.

Upon conclusion of negotiations, an information and consultation procedure was put into effect whereby the acceding States were informed of all measures (proposals, communications, recommendations, initiatives, etc.) which might lead to an EU decision, and were consulted on all draft measures about to be adopted. Where a draft measure was about to be adopted, it was classified as an 'orientation commune' and a deadline was set for the acceding State to submit any request for consultation. Typically such 'orientations communes' concerned draft Community legislation on which the Council or the Council and the Parliament had reached a position.[15] Consultations on these measures took place within seven days, in the 'Interim Committee' convened for this purpose. The Interim Committee consisted of the members of Coreper and representatives of the acceding States. Given that the legislation was to be adopted in any event, the purpose of the exercise was limited although it did have the benefit of allowing the acceding States to be heard around the one table. Where an acceding State had a concern requiring more than consultation, under Articles 55 and 57 of the Act of Accession it could request the Commission to make a proposal to the Council either for the adaptation of that legislation once adopted, or for a temporary derogation to be granted from its application.

Immediately after signature, the acceding States became active observers in the work of the Council at all levels. Thus, as of 17 April 2003, the Council working groups, the Antici and Mertens groups, Coreper and the Council all sat as 25. The acceding States had the right to speak on any point concerning the development of the acquis, as well as on all questions likely to have an impact after accession. Whilst the working languages remained at 11, the impact of enlargement was already a reality. Acceding State administrations had to learn to cope with the volume of legislative work and Council working group meetings, dramatically stepping up the number of personnel based in Brussels. Given the challenges of decision making among a group of 25, long advocated working methods gradually took hold. A Code of Conduct was adopted in order to improve the efficiency of the preparation and conduct of meetings of the Council and its preparatory bodies. New guidelines were also introduced on seating arrangements in the Council meeting rooms, which were being stretched to capacity.

There were only a few Groups where the acceding States did not participate as active observers. These included the Schengen Collective Evaluation Group, as well as the Working Groups dealing with relations with the candidate/acceding States under the Association and Europe Agreements, and the Enlargement Group still working on the ongoing monitoring process of the ten as well as on the accession negotiations with Bulgaria and Romania.

---

[15] They could also concern common strategies (Art. 13 TEU), joint actions (Art. 14 TEU) and draft Council common positions (Art. 15 TEU), as well as draft Council common positions, framework decisions and decisions (Article 34 TEU). The consultation procedure varied according to the legal basis of the act.

Another aspect of the interim period was the final assessment of the acceding States' respect of their commitments. As mentioned above, the Act of Accession (Articles 38–39) set out the provisions on safeguard measures which could be invoked against a new Member State. The 2002 Copenhagen European Council charged the Commission with preparing a Final Monitoring Report, scheduled for 5 November 2003, as a basis for any further Commission decision in this respect.

10. THE PROCESS CONTINUES

As indicated at the beginning of this paper, the fifth enlargement is an inclusive process which also involves Bulgaria, Romania and Turkey. Bulgaria and Romania are continuing negotiations on the same basis as before and the 2002 Copenhagen European Council underlined the importance of making sure that the pace of negotiations is maintained. To this end, the Commission prepared revised roadmaps,[16] funding was increased and the Accession Partnerships were updated. Provided Bulgaria and Romania are ready, the Thessaloniki European Council in June 2003 announced its intention to complete negotiations in 2004, with 2007 as the target date for accession.

Turkey remains a candidate with whom negotiations have yet to start. Despite pressure from other parts of the world, the Union has insisted that, as for the other candidates, there has to be prior fulfilment of the Copenhagen political criteria prior to opening negotiations. Since 1999, Turkey has been involved in its own pre-accession process which includes screening by the Commission, pre-accession financial assistance, an Accession Partnership and Commission Regular Reports. Progress, particularly since the new government under PM Erdogan (AKP) took office, has been made. In an effort to move things forward, the 2002 Copenhagen European Council requested the Commission to draw up a report for December 2004, together with a recommendation as to whether Turkey fulfils the political criteria. If the Commission's findings are positive, the Union will open negotiations without delay. Top of the Accession Partnership list of tasks is the issue of the Cyprus problem, and it seems that without a settlement it would be difficult to open negotiations.

The countries of the Western Balkans, namely Albania, Bosnia Herzegovina, Croatia, the Former Yugoslav Republic of Macedonia, Serbia and Montenegro are all earmarked as 'potential candidates for EU membership'. The Thessaloniki European Council in June 2003 decided to strengthen the Stabilisation and Association Process with these countries which will provide the framework for future accession. Croatia already lodged its application on 20 February 2003, and the procedure under Article 49 TEU was launched by the Council on 14 April 2003, with an Opinion from the Commission expected by early 2004.

---

[16] COM(2002) 624 final of 13 November 2002.

11. THE EU'S NEW NEIGHBOURS

And a final word about the countries bordering on the new enlarged Europe. At the European Conference held the day after the signature of the Accession Treaty in Athens, the forty members, comprising the EU Member States, the acceding States, the European Economic Area (*EEA*) Member States, Switzerland, the countries of the Western Balkans, Moldova, and Ukraine, as well as Russia, reaffirmed:

> their determination not to tolerate any new dividing lines, to agree to promote policies of political rapprochement and gradual integration in social and economic structures between the enlarged European Union and its neighbours and to accelerate the political, economic and cultural dynamism on the European continent and beyond.

The Commission's new neighbourhood initiative of 11 March 2003[17] was discussed, whereby an arrangement with Moldova, Ukraine and Russia, ultimately leading to an arrangement resembling the links between the Union and the countries of the EEA, is proposed. The Commission makes clear that the aim of the policy is to provide a framework for the development of a new relationship, which would not, in the medium term, include a perspective of membership or a role in the Union's institutions.

12. CONCLUSION

As anyone who knows the man would agree, the Professor is an enthusiast, has a tremendous sense of fun and possesses an insatiable curiosity for all things. He is also a very generous man. Few, if any, could surpass his kindness and his willingness to devote his time. He is finally, and perhaps less surprisingly for a Judge, a man of justice who firmly believes in the equality of man, and a man of clear logic, once described to me by Lord Rodger (another contributor to this book) as 'a lawyer's lawyer'. He has a gift for rendering the complicated simple and has taken great efforts to demystify the law and its procedure, often referring to the 'boiler room perspective'. This paper was inspired by his approach. It is a very modest tribute to a great man from whom I have learned a tremendous amount, who has my utmost respect and who I consider as a very good friend. I would like to thank him for all that he has given me.

---

[17] COM(2003) 104 final of 18 June 2003—'Wider Europe—Neighbourhood: A New Framework for Relations with our Eastern and Southern Neighbours'.

IV. EU Competition Issues

10

Certain Reflections on Recent Judgments Reviewing Commission Merger Control Decisions

JUDGE BO VESTERDORF*

1. INTRODUCTION

JUDGE DAVID EDWARDS'S interest in competition law extends back beyond our initial appointment on 25 September 1989 as two of the first twelve judges of the fledgling Court of First Instance ('CFI'), a court over which I now have the privilege of presiding. That it is an interest that survived his subsequent elevation to the Court of Justice on 10 March 1992 is amply demonstrated by a number of the other essays in this most deserving of collections. One of the important spheres of competition law that has attracted 'the Professor's' (the title by which, I believe, he is usually known within his chambers and amongst the Edward 'diaspora') attention over the years is that concerning the control of mergers. Being an area where the contribution of the Community judicature and particularly of the CFI has in recent years become noticeably more apparent, I am sanguine that a discussion of some salient features of that developing case-law will constitute a fitting tribute to the independence, competence and, above all, manifest enthusiasm for European law that has characterised David Edward's important contribution to the work of that judicature since 1989.

2. INTRODUCTION

The advent of the expedited (or fast-track as it is colloquially known) procedure before the CFI has radically changed the landscape of judicial review of Commission merger-control decisions.[1] In proposing the rule change that

---

* The opinions expressed throughout this contribution are entirely personal and in no way represent those of the Court of First Instance. I would like to thank Noel Travers, legal secretary in my chambers, for his assistance.
[1] See Article 76a of the Rules of Procedure of the Court of First Instance, which came into effect on 1 February 2001.

became that procedure, the CFI was conscious of the particular need for expedition in the treatment of challenges to Commission merger decisions. Few would contest that, in the area of merger control, expedition is of especial importance in ensuring the existence of a system of effective judicial review. The capacity of the CFI, in appropriate cases, to be able rapidly to adjudge challenges to such decisions is essential if one is to provide a convincing response to criticism of the Commission's current role of investigator, prosecutor and decision-maker in respect of concentrations having 'a Community dimension' and, thus, falling within its competence under Article 1 of the Merger Control Regulation ('MCR').[2] By the end of 2002, of the 14 cases where applications for an expedited procedure had been accepted, some 11 thereof concerned annulment actions in respect of Commission merger-control decisions. Indeed, this trend reflects the significant recent upturn in the willingness of undertakings affected by such decisions, whether positive or negative, to contest them. Of the 44 merger cases lodged with the Community judicature by 31 December 2002, some 23 thereof date from the period 2000 to 2002, with 13 cases lodged in 2002 alone.[3] I am particularly pleased to observe that of the six cases which have gone to judgment by the time of writing (June 2003) where the expedited procedure has been applied (ie in the *Schneider*[4] and *Tetra Laval* cases,[5] as well as the *BaByliss*[6] and *Philips*[7] cases), the procedure has enabled those cases to be adjudged within a commercially useful (if not necessarily ideal) period of time. Thus, the (four in total) *Schneider* and *Tetra Laval* cases were adjudged by the CFI within ten months of their introduction (in the *Schneider* cases, judgments were actually delivered a little over seven months after acceptance by the CFI of the applicability of the procedure), while the judgments in *BaByliss* and *Philips* were both given within a year of those cases being lodged (and only nine months after the granting of the expedited procedure).

In this article, conscious of the editors' expressed desire for shorter contributions, I will concentrate on examining some of the substantive-law points developed in those cases, with particular emphasis on the nature of the judicial control exercised by the CFI. In the context of a tribute to David Edward, it is fitting, I believe, to start with the notion of collective dominance, whose application to mergers has again been considered by the CFI in the *Airtours* case.[8]

---

[2] Council Regulation 4064/89/EEC of 21 December 1989 on the control of concentrations between undertakings (OJ 1989 L 395/1, corrected version in OJ 1990 L 257/13), as amended by Council Regulation 1310/97/EEC of 30 June 1997 (OJ 1997 L 180/1).

[3] So far, by 18 June 2003, five new cases concerning the MCR have been lodged in 2003. In one of these fresh cases an application for an expedited procedure has also been lodged.

[4] Case T–310/01 *Schneider Electric SA* v. *Commission* [2002] ECR II–4071 and Case T–77/02 *Schneider Electric SA* v. *Commission* [2002] ECR II–4201.

[5] Case T–5/02 *Tetra Laval BV* v. *Commission* [2002] ECR II–4381 and T–80/02 *Tetra Laval BV* v. *Commission* [2002] ECR II–4519.

[6] Case T–114/02 *BaByliss SA* v. *Commission* (judgment of 3 April 2003, not yet reported).

[7] Case T–119/02 *Royal Philips Electronics NV* v. *Commission* (judgment of 3 April 2003, not yet reported).

[8] Case T–342/99 *Airtours plc* v. *Commission* [2002] ECR II–2585.

This is because it is perhaps one of the most open secrets in the relatively short history of the CFI that 'the Professor' was the CFI's Judge Rapporteur in the celebrated *Flat Glass* case, where the Community judicature for the first time sought to grapple with the legal significance of the complex and somewhat esoteric economic notion of collective dominance.[9] He was also a member of the plenary formation of the Court of Justice which later (31 March 1998) adjudged the *Kali and Salz* case,[10] that Court's only judgment to date in respect of the MCR.[11] The notion of collective dominance is therefore one in respect of whose Community law definition David Edward has had a very direct input.[12] Without wishing to trespass too much upon what I understand will be the subject of Mark Clough's essay, I would like to begin by briefly commenting on collective dominance and *Airtours*, which, as the first judgment annulling a Commission MCR prohibition decision, is obviously worthy of comment in its own right.

3. COLLECTIVE DOMINANCE AND MERGER CONTROL

In *Kali and Salz*, the Court of Justice decided that concentrations that would lead to the creation or strengthening of a collective dominant position ('CDP') fell within the scope of the MCR.[13] If the result of such a creation or strengthening is that effective competition on a substantial part of the common market would be impeded, the concentration in question must be prohibited. In this respect the Court stated:

> In the case of an alleged collective dominant position, the Commission is therefore obliged to assess, using a prospective analysis of the reference market, whether the concentration which has been referred to it leads to a situation in which effective competition in the relevant market is significantly impeded by the undertakings involved in the concentration and one or more other undertakings which together, in particular because of factors giving rise to a connection between them, are able to adopt a common policy on the market and act to a considerable extent independently of their competitors, their customers, and also of consumers.[14]

Although hardly very specific from an economic perspective, the Court's formulation was careful not to limit the scope of the factors that could be taken

---

[9] Joined Cases T–68/89, T–77/89 and T–78/89 *Società Italiana Vetro SpA et al v. Commission* [1992] ECR II–1403.
[10] Joined Cases C–68/94 and C–30/95 *France et al v. Commission* [1998] ECR I–1375.
[11] The oral hearing in Case C–42/01 *Portugal v. Commission*, which is likely to result in the Court of Justice's second judicial pronouncement in this area, is scheduled to take place on 9 September 2003 before the Court's plenary formation.
[12] He was also, of course, the Judge Rapporteur in Joined Cases C–395/96 P and C–396/96 P *Compagnie maritime belge transports SA et al v. Commission* [2000] ECR I–1365, where the Court of Justice most recently considered the notion of collective dominance in the context of Article 82 EC.
[13] Above n10, especially paras 171, 172 and 178:
[14] *Ibid*, para 221.

into account by the Commission to concrete, structural links.[15] Instead, it held that the approach to be adopted by the Commission 'warrants close examination in particular of the circumstances which, in each individual case, are relevant for assessing the effects of the concentration on competition in the reference market.'[16]

Recognising that the MCR confers 'a certain discretion, especially with respect to assessments of an economic nature' on the Commission, such that 'review by the Community judicature of the exercise of that discretion, which is essential for defining the rules on concentrations, must take account of the discretionary margin implicit in the provisions of an economic nature which form part of the rules on concentrations,' the Court of Justice still signalled, in finding that the analysis effected in that case 'was flawed in certain respects which affect the economic assessment of the concentration,' the existence of clear limits to that discretion.[17] Thus, it concluded, among others, that the Commission had erred in finding that a market share of approximately 60% held by K+S (the merged entity) and SCPA (the third party with which, according to the Commission, it would hold a CDC) could not 'of itself point conclusively to the existence of a collective dominant position on the part of those undertakings'[18] and that 'the cluster of structural links between K+S and SCPA' which allegedly constituted the core of the contested decision, were not, in the end, 'as tight or as conclusive as the Commission sought to make out.'[19] Moreover, the Commission had underestimated the competitive pressure which the merged entity's competitors would still be able to exert.[20] These flaws in the Commission's positive, but conditional, competitive assessment of the concentration resulted in the complete annulment of the contested decision.

The judgment of the CFI the following year in *Gencor* is worthy of particular note.[21] In that case the CFI confirmed the Commission's far from uncontroversial thesis that a concentration between two parties active on an oligopolistic market could give rise to a CDP by creating a duopoly between them and a third player in the market (Amplats in that case). The CFI held that, although '[i]t is true that, in the context of an oligopoly, the fact that the parties to the oligopoly hold large market shares does not necessarily have the same significance, compared to the analysis of an individual dominant position, with regard to the opportunities for those parties, as a group, to act to a considerable extent independently of their competitors, their customers and, ultimately, of consumers,' it added that, in the

---

[15] This formulation in the English text, ie "because of factors giving rise to a connection between them," of the notion, expressed in French (the language of the case) as, "en raison des facteurs de corrélation existant entre elles" would seem to be intended to convey the generality of the type of potentially relevant factors at issue, which a more literal translation of the French text such as "because of correlative factors which exist between them" might not have conveyed.

[16] Ibid, para 222.
[17] Ibid, paras 223 to 225.
[18] Ibid, para 226.
[19] Ibid, para 232.
[20] Ibid, paras 242 to 248.
[21] Case T–102/96 *Gencor Ltd* v. *Commission* [1999] ECR II–753.

particular case of a duopoly, 'a large market share is, in the absence of evidence to the contrary, likewise a strong indication of the existence of a collective dominant position.'[22] In that case, the parties would, following the concentration, have had a market share of 'about 30% to 35%, that is to say [together with Amplats] a combined market share of approximately 60% to 70%, in the world PGM [platinum group metal] market and approximately 89% of the world PGM reserves,' while the next major player, Russia, was likely to dispose of its stocks within two years.[23] In these circumstances, the CFI was satisfied that, 'having regard to the allocation of market share between the parties to the concentration and to the gap in market share which would open up following that concentration between, on the one hand, the entity arising from the merger and Amplats and, on the other, the remaining platinum producers, the Commission was entitled to conclude that the proposed concentration was liable to result in the creation of a dominant position for the South African undertakings.'[24]

As regards the type of links required to establish collective dominance, the applicant, relying on the *Flat Glass* case, interpreted the CFI's reference in that case to economic links as requiring, in effect, the presence of at least some structural links between the supposedly collective dominant parties. This interpretation (of the much-discussed paragraph 358 of the *Flat Glass* judgment) was rejected as misplaced by the CFI in *Gencor*. It held instead, in two important paragraphs (276–277), that:

> [T]here is no reason whatsoever in legal or economic terms to exclude from the notion of economic links the relationship of interdependence existing between the parties to a tight oligopoly within which, in a market with the appropriate characteristics, in particular in terms of market concentration, transparency and product homogeneity, those parties are in a position to anticipate one another's behaviour and are therefore strongly encouraged to align their conduct in the market, in particular in such a way as to maximise their joint profits by restricting production with a view to increasing prices. In such a context, each trader is aware that highly competitive action on its part designed to increase its market share (for example a price cut) would provoke identical action by the others, so that it would derive no benefit from its initiative. All the traders would thus be affected by the reduction in price levels.
>
> That conclusion is all the more pertinent with regard to the control of concentrations, whose objective is to prevent anti-competitive market structures from arising or being strengthened. Those structures may result from the existence of economic links in the strict sense argued by the applicant or from market structures of an oligopolistic kind where each undertaking may become aware of common interests and, in particular, cause prices to increase without having to enter into an agreement or resort to a concerted practice.

These principles have been, it seems to me, confirmed by *Airtours*. The CFI, in that case, first sets out the general criterion established in *Kali and Salz*, namely

---

[22] *Ibid*, para 206.
[23] *Ibid*, para 207.
[24] *Ibid*, para 208.

that effective competition may be significantly impeded by the undertakings involved in a concentration and a (or several) third party undertaking(s) 'which together, in particular because of factors giving rise to a connection between them, are able to adopt a common policy on the market,'[25] before quoting in full from the above-quoted paragraph 276 of the *Gencor* judgment.[26] The CFI then fleshes out the explanation offered in *Gencor* (paragraph 277) as follows:[27]

> A collective dominant position significantly impeding effective competition in the common market or a substantial part of it may thus arise as the result of a concentration where, in view of the actual characteristics of the relevant market and of the alteration in its structure that the transaction would entail, the latter would make each member of the dominant oligopoly, as it becomes aware of common interests, consider it possible, economically rational, and hence preferable, to adopt on a lasting basis a common policy on the market with the aim of selling at above competitive prices, without having to enter into an agreement or resort to a concerted practice within the meaning of Article 81 EC . . . and without any actual or potential competitors, let alone customers or consumers, being able to react effectively.

This is followed by what is arguably the most significant passage of the *Airtours* judgment (paragraph 62) where the CFI enumerates the steps which the Commission must undertake in future decisions in order to establish that a collective dominant position with significant anti-competitive effects is likely to result from a concentration. It will, in essence, have to prove that three conditions are met: *first* that there is sufficient market transparency so that each member of the dominant oligopoly will be aware, sufficiently quickly and precisely, of the way in which the other members' market conduct evolves; *second* there must be a long-term incentive not to depart from the common policy (ie a real risk of retaliation); *third* that the foreseeable reaction of current and future competitors of the merged entity, as well as of consumers, will not jeopardise the results expected from the common policy.

As regards the burden of proof incumbent on the Commission when seeking to rely on an essentially prospective analysis of the likely effects of a particular merger, the CFI requires it to produce 'convincing evidence.'[28] In the context of the foreseen creation of a CDP, the 'evidence must concern, in particular, factors playing a significant role in the assessment of whether a situation of collective dominance exists, such as, for example, the lack of effective competition between the operators alleged to be members of the dominant oligopoly and the weakness of any competitive pressure that might be exerted by other operators.' Nevertheless, the CFI confirms that the Commission enjoys a 'certain discretion' in applying the economic rules which underlie the MCR, especially Article 2, such that the 'Community judicature must take account of the discretionary

---

[25] Above n8, para 59.
[26] *Ibid*, para 60.
[27] *Ibid*, para 61.
[28] *Ibid*, para 63.

margin implicit in the provisions of an economic nature which form part of the rules on concentrations.'[29] However, the detailed examination carried out in the remainder of the judgment of the evidence relied upon by the Commission (correctly or incorrectly), and of other relevant factors found by the CFI to have been overlooked, shows that the Commission's discretion, far from being unlimited, is subject to effective judicial control.

The CFI, in brief, held, first, that the Commission had wrongly assessed that the three major tour operators remaining after the merger would have an incentive to cease competing with one another, stressing that the Commission had not sufficiently proved a tendency in the industry towards collective dominance, had not properly taken into account the demand volatility in the market and had not demonstrated a sufficient degree of market transparency;[30] second, that the retaliatory measures which could be taken against a member of the oligopoly if it departed from the common policy were neither clearly identified nor established;[31] and, third, that the Commission had wrongly assessed the possible reaction of smaller tour operators, potential competitors and consumers as a countervailing force capable of counteracting the creation of a collective dominant position.[32] No appeal having been lodged by the Commission against this judgment, the judgment is now definitive.[33]

4. HORIZONTAL MERGERS: THE RELEVANCE OF TRANS-NATIONAL CONSIDERATIONS FOR NATIONAL SECTORAL MARKETS

In the main *Schneider* case there were essentially two aspects of particular interest to the decision of 10 October 2001[34] by which the Commission prohibited the merger between Schneider and Legrand, two very large, internationally active, French-based, manufacturers of low voltage electrical equipment. First, the Commission found that the concentration would create a dominant position on certain of the various sectoral markets at issue in Denmark, Spain, France, Greece, Italy, Portugal and the United Kingdom and, second, it would strengthen the pre-existing dominant position of the parties on no fewer than

---

[29] *Ibid*, para 64.

[30] *Ibid*, paras 79 to 182. The CFI referred notably to the fact that the main tour operators' market shares had been volatile in the past. Moreover, the fact that such volatility was linked to the circumstance that the large operators had made numerous acquisitions could, it held, be taken to be indicative of strong competition between the operators, such further acquisitions being made to avoid being outdistanced by their main competitors in key areas and to take full advantage of economies of scale (see paras 109 to 113).

[31] *Ibid*, paras 183 to 207.

[32] *Ibid*, paras 208 to 277.

[33] Indeed, in its XXXII Annual Report on Competition Policy for 2002, the Commission states (point 234) that, "[d]espite its negative finding, the judgment should be welcomed as a significant step forward in that it brings clarity as to what are the *necessary standards of proof* in cases of creation of collective dominance" (emphasis in original).

[34] Case COMP/M.2283 *Schneider Electric/Legrand*.

five sectoral markets in France, thereby significantly impeding competition on those relevant product markets. Schneider contested the decision.

The CFI found that, with the exception of the French markets, the Commission's economic analysis contained errors and omissions which led it to overestimate the economic power of the new entity and consequently to exaggerate the impact of the concentration on each of the affected national sectoral markets.

First, as regards the analysis of the geographic coverage of the merged entity (the applicant's third plea), the CFI found that, while the Commission had identified the national dimension of the various sectoral markets concerned, it had nevertheless relied upon trans-national or global factors in assessing the competitive impact of the merger and thus gleaned evidence of economic power from an overview of each of the various relevant national sectoral markets, but especially the French ones. Although confirming that it is open to the Commission to take account of trans-national effects which may increase the impact of a concentration on each of the national sectoral markets at issue, the CFI found that the existence of those effects had not been established to the requisite legal standard on the latter markets.[35] It was inconsistent to rely upon the overall position the merged entity would enjoy in the EEA when the Commission had, itself, accepted that the merger would only create specific competition problems on some product markets in France and in six other Member States.

Second, the CFI found, regarding the fourth plea, that, given certain errors in the analysis of the distribution structure, it had not been properly established that the new entity would be an unavoidable trading partner for wholesalers, or that the latter would be incapable of exercising any competitive restraints on it.[36] The CFI elaborated on this, in dealing with the fifth plea, holding that the analysis of the merged entity's economic power on the affected national sectoral markets was incorrect. It found, inter alia, that the Commission was not entitled, in this respect, to make an abstract appreciation of the notifying parties' product range and wide variety of brands in the EEA; since the merged entity did not necessarily supply the whole range of products on each of the various national sectoral markets concerned, it would not necessarily offer in those markets all the brands which it owned throughout the EEA.[37] In upholding the sixth plea, the CFI rejected as unconvincing the Commission's rejection of the significance of integrated sales made by the merged entity's main competitors, ie of sales made by them to electrical-installation companies within their own groups. By its seventh and eighth pleas, the applicant challenged certain specific errors and omissions in the Commission's approach to the Danish and Italian markets, which were largely upheld by the CFI.

---

[35] Case T–310/01 *Schneider Electric SA v. Commission* [2002] ECR II–4071 at paragraphs 170 to 192.
[36] *Ibid*, paras 198 to 230.
[37] *Ibid*, paras 257 to 258.

As regards the French market, the applicant did not, in its ninth plea, fundamentally dispute the negative analysis of the impact of the concentration. The decision was therefore not vitiated by any errors regarding the Commission's economic analysis in this respect. However, because the notifying undertakings' rights of the defence were infringed by a misleading ambiguity in the statement of objections issued by the Commission during 'Phase 2' of the procedure, the contested decision was annulled in its entirety. The judgment constitutes an important confirmation of the specific importance of the statement of objections for fair proceedings in Phase 2 of those merger cases which go to that stage, in particular because of its importance for the notifying parties in deciding which, if any, commitments (ie remedies) they should offer to present to the Commission so as to overcome the latter's objections to the proposed merger.

5. CONGLOMERATE AND PORTFOLIO EFFECTS

The issue of 'leveraging' in the context of merger control fell to be considered by the CFI for the first time in the main *Tetra Laval* case.[38] It concerned a concentration which was 'conglomerate' in type, ie a merger of undertakings which do not have a pre-existing competitive relationship, either as direct competitors or as suppliers and customers of each other. Conglomerate-type portfolio issues also arose in two of the three most recent CFI merger judgments, given on 3 April 2003, namely in the *BaBylis*[39] and *Philips*[40] cases. The third, *Petrolessence*, concerned the implementation of the conditions set by the Commission for approval of what was a classic horizontal merger.[41]

In its decision of 30 October 2001,[42] the Commission declared incompatible with the common market and the EEA the acquisition by Tetra Laval (a company belonging to a group whose name is well known to readers of the European Court Reports and which holds an uncontested dominant position on the markets for aseptic carton packaging machines and for the corresponding packaging material and related equipment as well as a strong position on the corresponding non-aseptic carton packaging markets) of Sidel, a French plastics company. Sidel holds a leading position on the market for stretch blow moulding ('SBM') machines used for manufacturing plastic bottles/containers made from a type of plastic known as polyethylene terephthalate ('PET'). The Commission took the view that, notwithstanding the commitments proposed by the notifying parties and the resulting lack of any substantive horizontal or vertical effects, the concentration would, due largely to the growing competitive

---

[38] Case T–5/02 *Tetra Laval* v. *Commission* [2002] ECR II–4381.
[39] Above n6.
[40] Above n7.
[41] Case T–342/00 *Petrolessence and SG2R* v. *Commission* (judgment of 3 April 2003, not yet reported).
[42] Case COMP/M.2416 *Tetra Laval/Sidel*.

relationship between carton and PET packaging, have harmful effects on competition on both the various PET packaging equipment markets and the aseptic carton packaging markets. This was because it would allegedly enable Tetra to leverage its market power on the latter to assist Sidel to acquire dominance on the former, while permitting Tetra concomitantly to reinforce its dominance on the latter.

By judgment of 25 October 2002, the CFI annulled that decision, holding that the Commission had erred in its assessment of the effects of the merger, as modified by the parties' commitments. In relation to the first substantive plea, the CFI rejected as unjustified the regard (whose precise nature and significance remained undefined in the contested decision) had by the Commission, notwithstanding the commitments offered, to the modified merger's supposed residual horizontal (on the markets for low-capacity SBM machines, aseptic PET filling machines and barrier technology) and vertical (the risk of creating a vertically integrated market structure in respect of PET bottle 'performs') effects.[43]

In relation to the second substantive plea, the CFI examined if the Commission was justified in prohibiting the merger by reference to certain feared, anticompetitive conglomerate effects. The judgment contains a series of observations of general interest in this respect since they essentially confirm the basis of the 'leveraging' thesis underlying the Commission's decision. *First*, it confirms that the Commission is fully entitled to consider potential conglomerate effects of a merger. Such effects may be structural, ie arising directly from the creation of an economic structure, or behavioural, ie occurring only if the entity resulting from the merger engages in certain commercial practices.[44] *Second*, even if the proposed merger does not result in the immediate creation of a dominant position in favour of the merged entity, the judgment confirms that it falls to be prohibited if the Commission establishes that a dominant position would, in all likelihood, be created or strengthened 'in the relatively near future'[45] and would, as a result, lead to effective competition on the market being significantly impeded.[46] By declining to define this crucial temporal concept, the CFI has left the Commission with a considerable margin of discretion. In the case at hand, the CFI was willing to accept the relatively long five-year timeframe which apparently, as explained particularly in the Commission's oral pleadings, underlay the analysis contained in the contested decision. *Third*, since the effects of a conglomerate-type merger are generally considered to be neutral, or even beneficial, for competition, a claim that such effects will, in fact, be sufficiently anti-competitive to justify prohibiting a merger calls for a precise examination by the Commission, supported by convincing evidence, of the circumstances which will, within the relatively near future, allegedly produce those effects.[47]

---

[43] Above n38, paras 119 to 141.
[44] *Ibid*, paras 146 to 147 and 155.
[45] *Ibid*, para 148.
[46] *Ibid*, paras 148 to 153.
[47] *Ibid*, para 155.

As regards the degree of evidence needed to establish the likely future conduct of the merged entity, the CFI held that the Commission must take into account the extent to which the economic incentives to engage in anti-competitive practices would be reduced, or even eliminated, by the illegality of the conduct in question, the likelihood of its detection, action taken against it by the competent authorities, both at Community and national level, and the financial penalties which could ensue from such action. Since the Commission did not carry out any such assessment in the contested decision, but merely referred to the economic incentives of the merged entity to engage in anticompetitive practices, the CFI rejected those parts of the Commission's conclusions which were predicated on, what would in all likelihood, constitute illegal conduct and especially conduct likely to violate Article 82 EC.[48] The CFI noted, inter alia, that Tetra Pak, following the Commission's earlier *Tetra Pak (II)* decision,[49] had expressly undertaken not to engage in the very type of anticompetitive behaviour apprehended by the Commission in the contested decision.[50]

The CFI next examined if the Commission had proved to the requisite legal standard that the merger would: (i) enable the merged entity to use its dominant position on the global carton packaging market as a 'lever' in order to achieve a dominant position, 'in the relatively near future,' on the PET packaging equipment markets to which the contested decision referred and, thereby, significantly to impede competition on those markets; (ii) reinforce the current dominant position of Tetra on the markets for aseptic carton packaging equipment and aseptic cartons by eliminating (or at least reducing significantly) the competitive constraint, largely in the form of Sidel, coming from the neighbouring PET packaging equipment markets and, thereby, significantly to impede competition on those markets; and (iii) generally strengthen the overall position of the merged entity on the markets for packaging of 'sensitive' products with similar perceived effects on competition.

The CFI found, having regard to the merger, as amended by the commitments and excluding post-merger conduct that would in all probability constitute an abuse by Tetra Laval of its pre-existing dominant position on the aseptic carton markets, that the Commission had made a number of errors of assessment in concluding that a dominant position would be created on the PET equipment markets, especially the SBM machine markets, at issue. In this respect, the CFI assumed that the commitments, and especially the commitment not to bundle sales of carton equipment with sales for SBM machines, dismissed effectively as being impossible to monitor by the Commission, would be respected.[51] The errors related, as regards the PET markets, inter alia, to: the assessment of the

---

[48] *Ibid*, paras 159 to 162.
[49] See Commission Decision 92/163/EEC of 24 July 1991 relating to a proceeding under Article [82 EC] (IV/31043 *Tetra Pak II*) (OJ 1992 L 72/1). It was uncontested before the CFI that Tetra Laval was bound by this decision.
[50] Above n38, paras 219 to 224.
[51] *Ibid*, paras 221 and 222.

level of likely growth in the use of PET for packaging particularly aseptic milk and juices;[52] the insistence that SBM machines could be defined by reference to their end-use notwithstanding the Commission's own recognition[53] that the 'majority' of such machines were 'generic';[54] the general overestimation of Tetra's alleged first-mover advantage vis-à-vis its existing carton customers[55] and underestimation of the competitive influence exerted on PET by other forms of plastic packaging, especially high density polyethylene (HDPE) on the vital (having regard to the quantities at stake) milk-packaging markets and by glass on the juices-packaging markets (particularly on very large German market) where, moreover, certain of Tetra's competitors, rather than Tetra, would have a first-mover advantage.[56] The CFI was also unconvinced by the decision's refusal to explain why the growth potential for use of PET in the beer market where Tetra had no presence and could not therefore engage in leveraging was not relevant to the possibility of the merged entity being able, within five years, to acquire through leveraging a dominant position on the SBM machine markets.[57] The Commission's analysis of the likely future acquisition of dominance also suffered from the absence of an 'adequate analysis of the competition which Sidel must face in the market for high-capacity [SBM] machines.'[58]

As the judgment and the related judgment concerning the divestiture decision have both been appealed, I do not feel it would appropriate to discuss in greater detail these or the other various errors or inadequacies found by the CFI in the contested decision. In essence, the CFI found that the sum of those errors amounted to a manifest error of assessment on the Commission's part as to the likely creation by 2005 of a dominant position for the merged entity on the PET packaging equipment markets, especially the low- and high-capacity SBM machines markets and as to the likely strengthening of Tetra Laval's position on the aseptic carton markets. Consequently, the Commission's semi-autonomous third-pillar conclusion that the overall position of the merged entity on the markets for packaging of 'sensitive' products would be enhanced fell to be rejected.[59] The CFI, like the Court of Justice in *Kali and Salz*, did not therefore have to reach the stage of formally considering the extent to which a significant impediment to competition could be caused by the merger as amended. It is submitted that it is at this latter level that the Commission should enjoy its widest margin of discretion.

I would also like to mention, in this context, the *BaByliss*[60] and *Philips*[61] cases. They concern a Commission decision of 8 January 2002 approving the

---

[52] Above n38, , paras 201 to 206.
[53] Above n42, recital 177.
[54] Above n38, paras 258 to 269.
[55] Ibid, paras 288 to 293.
[56] Ibid, para 290.
[57] Ibid, paras 278 and 303.
[58] Ibid, para 294.
[59] Ibid, paras 334 and 335.
[60] Above n6.
[61] Above n7.

merger between SEB (French producer manufacturing small, electrically-powered household equipment marketed under worldwide-known brands like Tefal and Rowenta) and its direct, but effectively insolvent, competitor Moulinex.[62] Although the sector of small household electric goods comprises thirteen discrete categories of products, the kitchenware range, with which the contested decision was concerned, accounts for 11 of these. The other two categories are irons and ironing stations and what are known as personal care appliances (ie health and beauty appliances). Furthermore, not even all of the kitchenware range of products was relevant in each of the geographic markets considered in the decision.

The acquisition by SEB of certain assets of Moulinex took place in the framework of a receivership procedure which had been opened against Moulinex in France. The Commission approved the concentration at the end of Phase I on the basis of Article 6(1)(b) of the MCR. This approbation decision was unconditional in relation to five EEA countries (United Kingdom, Italy, Spain, Finland and Ireland). As regards a further nine other EEA states (Germany, Austria, Denmark, the Netherlands, Belgium, Greece, Norway, Portugal and Sweden), the approval of the concentration was conditional on a number of commitments offered by SEB, including the granting of an exclusive license to a third party for the use of the Moulinex trade mark for a period of five years in order for the latter to use that brand together with its own brand (co-branding) so as (hopefully) to be able to become a real competitor for SEB on those markets. Moreover, SEB was required to refrain from using the brand for a further period of three years after the expiry of the licence. It is noteworthy that the final version of these undertakings had been proposed by SEB and Moulinex only after the expiry of the deadline imposed by the Merger Regulation.

Regarding France, upon receipt of a request from the French competition authorities, the Commission referred the notified concentration, as regards its effects on the relevant French markets, by a second decision ('the referral decision') to those authorities.[63] On 8 July 2002, the French authorities approved the merger for the various French markets without imposing any conditions on the basis of the so-called 'failing firm' defence. This was notwithstanding the considerable market power of the parties on many of the relevant French markets.

The Commission's positive decision regarding the five markets and the positive conditional decision regarding the nine others were challenged before the CFI by BaByliss, a French undertaking active on the markets for the health-and-beauty-appliances category of products and which had made an unsuccessful bid in the context of the receivership for a part of the activities of Moulinex. Although the Commission unsuccessfully challenged the admissibility of BaByliss' action,[64] it did not seriously dispute that it was at least a potential

---

[62] SG(2002)D/228078 in Case COMP/M.2621 *SEB/Moulinex*.
[63] Commission Decision C (2002) 38 of 8 January 2002.
[64] Above n6, paras 87 to 117.

competitor of SEB-Moulinex in respect of the kitchenware range of products. Indeed Babyliss' United States parent, Conair, was active in the latter range.[65] In its action, Philips, an existing direct competitor of SEB, in addition to challenging the substantive decision, also contested the validity of the referral decision.

As regards the nine geographical markets where commitments had been made, the CFI found that the commitments offered (which the Commission was entitled to accept notwithstanding the expiry of the delay for their submission since the latter only bound the parties but not the Commission[66]) sufficed to dissipate all serious doubts as to the compatibility of the concentration with the common market. It noted, in particular, that the eight-year duration of the commitments was sufficient to enable a third party to drive customers away from the Moulinex brand and towards its own brand, given in particular the fact that the life cycle of the products in question was only three years.

These judgments, although involving what was a horizontal merger as between the parties themselves, endorse the application of the MCR to mergers having potential conglomerate-type portfolio effects. The potential lever for the exercise of portfolio effects was, given the nature of the products at issue, the unique collection of trade marks that would be available to the merged entity.[67] Thus, in requiring SEB-Moulinex to agree that it could not compete on those markets using the Moulinex brand, even in respect of those products where, on a particular geographic market, no particular competitive concerns were raised by the merger, the Commission relied upon the need effectively to eschew the occurrence of what was described as 'portfolio effects' to the detriment of the licensees of the brand on those markets.[68]

However, as regards the five geographical markets not covered by the commitments, the CFI found that the Commission had not sufficiently demonstrated the absence of serious doubts as to the merger's unconditional compatibility with the common market. The CFI held, in particular, that the Commission had not sufficiently demonstrated that no additional restriction of competition arose from the 'portfolio effects' of the merger. Accordingly, although there were no significant overlaps in the product markets, the Commission should have taken into account the increased strength of the new entity in relation to its direct customers, the resellers of the goods, which normally buy the full range of products offered by this entity. According to the Commission, since SEB-Moulinex would not be dominant on the product markets where it generates the most significant part of its turnover, it would not be possible for it to abuse its position on the dominated markets (where it generated less than 10% of its overall turnover), without its being punished by the resellers shifting their purchases to products manufactured by other producers. The risk of such 'punishment' would, according to the Commission, deter SEB-Moulinex from committing an abuse

---

[65] Above n6, para 12.
[66] Ibid, paras 127 to 151.
[67] Above n62, recital 52, referred to in the BaByliss judgment (above n6, para 345).
[68] Above n7, paras 166 to 168.

on the dominated markets. The CFI found this assessment to be unconvincing; ie that the Commission had not established to a sufficient legal standard its conclusion as to the absence of serious doubts regarding the effects of the concentration in the countries not covered of the commitments.[69]

In this respect, the CFI noted that the argument advanced at the oral hearing by the intervener, De'Longhi, an Italian-based competitor of the parties, to the effect that the hypothesis envisaged by the Commission of a conflict between the merged entity and its resellers was no more plausible than that of collusion between them designed to maximise their respective interests.[70] It also criticised the fact that the Commission had only taken into account the possibility of SEB-Moulinex committing an abuse through implementing a price increase, without taking into account other forms of possible anti-competitive behaviour.[71] This point is not, it seems to me, meant to modify the (abovementioned) position adopted by the CFI in *Tetra Laval*, to the effect that the Commission had incorrectly failed to assess if the merged entity would be discouraged from engaging in anticompetitive practices as a consequence of the merger due, inter alia, to the risk of detection and the imposition of fines. At issue in *Tetra Laval* was the potential relevance of the strong countervailing economic incentive for Tetra Laval not to engage in abusive behaviour. This had been relied upon by it both before the Commission and the CFI and, although its potential relevance was effectively overlooked by the Commission in its decision, it was considered by the CFI in its judgment The reverse was the case in BaByliss; in effect, the Commission simply assumed in its decision in that case, equally incorrectly according to the CFI, that no anticompetitive conduct would occur on the markets for which no commitments were required.

6. WITHER THE ONE-STOP-SHOP

One of the Commission's core objectives in proposing the adoption of the MCR was to guarantee the application of a one-stop regulatory procedure to companies involved in mergers having a Community dimension. This is, of course, reflected in Recital 9 in the preamble to the MCR, pursuant to which the MCR ought to be the only legal instrument applicable to concentrations having a Community dimension. The inclusion of Article 9 in the text of the regulation as adopted ensures, however, that the MCR only partially respects the 'one-stop-shop' principle heralded by that recital. The *Philips* case serves graphically to emphasise the regulation's shortcomings in this respect. In its decision in *SEB/Moulinex*, the Commission examined the impact of the concentration on the various national markets other than France, the examination of which was,

---

[69] Above n6, general considerations at paras 353–365, followed by an examination country by country.
[70] *Ibid*, para 356.
[71] *Ibid*, para 360.

as noted above, referred back to the French authorities by virtue of a separate decision adopted, on the same day as the main decision, on the basis of Article 9(3) of the MCR. Philips challenged the legality of the latter 'referral' decision.[72]

Consequently, of particular note is the CFI's finding that the Commission's referral decision, which concerned the merger's effects on the French markets where SEB and Moulinex enjoyed, pre-merger, their strongest positions, was in conformity with Article 9 of the MCR. Philips alleged essentially that there was no evidence that the interests of France could only be adequately protected by a referral to the French authorities. The situation on the French market was not structurally different from that on the other relevant markets and there was no justification for fragmenting the assessment of the merger.

The CFI had little difficulty agreeing with the Commission that the threat to competition on the French market was particularly acute given the 60% market share that the merged entity would enjoy on some 11 of the relevant product markets. In applying the second condition, namely whether the French market presented the characteristics of a distinct market, the CFI held that the Commission must take account of the various criteria laid down in Article 9(7) of the MCR. In this respect, the CFI recognised the Commission's margin of discretion in this respect.[73] Having decided that the conditions for a transfer under Article 9(2)(a) MCR were satisfied, the CFI then examined whether, 'by actually referring the examination of the effects of the concentration on the relevant markets in France to the French competition authorities,'[74] the Commission had correctly applied Article 9(3) thereof. In this respect the CFI recalled that under that provision the Commission is not obliged to refer a case: on the contrary, the provision 'confers on the Commission broad discretion as to whether or not to refer a concentration, [but] it cannot decide to make such a referral if, when the Member State's request for a referral is examined, it is clear, on the basis of a body of precise and coherent evidence, that such a referral cannot safeguard or restore effective competition on the relevant markets.'[75] However, the CFI will only exercise a limited review of referral decisions and the legality of a decision must be assessed at the moment of its adoption.[76] In the present case, the CFI was satisfied that the Commission had had no reason to foresee, when adopting the contested referral decision, the result of the examination by the French competition authorities, whose subsequent (questionable) treatment of the case could not call into question, in effect retroactively, the legality of that decision. Although such referrals compromise the one-stop-shop principle underlying the objectives of the MCR, this problem is inherent in the referral procedure and should be resolved, the CFI found, by the legislature and not the community

---

[72] Above n7.
[73] *Ibid*, especially paras 335 to 337.
[74] *Ibid*, para 341.
[75] *Ibid*, para 343.
[76] *Ibid*, para 347.

judiciary.[77] The CFI was thus unwilling to adopt an especially narrow interpretation of the scope of Article 9. However, it signalled for the future, I believe quite correctly, to the Commission that apprehension as to the appropriateness of the criteria that national authorities propose to apply when assessing the merger might well justify the latter's refusing a referral request.

7. ANCILLARY RESTRAINTS

The Commission's merger control *annus horribilis* in 2002 culminated on 22 November 2002 with the judgment in *Lagardère and Canal+*, a case which concerned the creation of two joint ventures between Lagardère SCA and Canal+ SA in the area of special-interest channels and interactive television services.[78] The Commission had first adopted a decision authorising this concentration, wherein it held certain restrictions to be directly related and necessary to the implementation of the two concentrations at issue. 18 days later it withdrew that decision and notified to the parties a new decision, which, although still clearing the mergers, now considered none of the restrictions contained in the agreements to be ancillary thereto.

Under Article 6(1)(b) of the MCR, a 'Phase I' decision clearing a concentration that falls within the scope of the regulation 'shall also cover restrictions directly related and necessary to the implementation of the concentration,' ie the so-called 'ancillary restraints' that would otherwise fall to be considered under Article 81 EC. It therefore reflects the logic of the one-stop-shop principle, whereby all matters directly related to a concentration having a Community dimension are to be regulated by the Commission. However, before the CFI, the Commission argued that it had never been under a legal obligation to assess and formally address ancillary restraints in its MCR decisions. Any statements made in past decisions concerning such restraints were therefore of a purely declaratory nature, ie they had no legally binding effects on the parties or for national courts. It relied upon its new 'Notice on ancillary restraints' pursuant to which it had decided, in particular in view of the strict deadlines and the need to simplify procedures, no longer to appraise whether any restrictions in the context of a merger were ancillary.[79] According to the Notice (particularly point 3), disputes between the parties to a concentration as to whether restrictions are automatically covered by a positive decision fall under the jurisdiction of national courts.

This view was categorically rejected by the CFI. It observed that the exclusive competence conferred on the Commission in respect of the supervision of

---

[77] *Ibid*, para 356.
[78] Case T–251/00 *Lagardère SCA and Canal+ SA v. Commission* (judgment of 20 November 2002, not yet reported).
[79] See Commission Notice on restrictions directly related and necessary to concentrations (OJ 2001 C 188/5).

concentrations with a Community dimension fell to be interpreted as imposing an obligation to assess whether restrictions to a concentration are directly related and necessary to its implementation, thus escaping an appraisal under Article 81 EC, so as to ensure the efficiency of its control of concentrations and legal certainty for the undertakings subject to this control.[80] The strict deadlines imposed on the Commission did not excuse it from adopting a legally binding assessment of ancillary restrictions contained in a notified operation; only the Community legislature and not the Commission may change the scope of the MCR.[81] The CFI concluded that, where the Commission has, in a decision approving a concentration, classified the restrictions notified by the parties to that concentration as being ancillary, it has made a legal assessment which, pursuant to the said provision, determines the substance of the operative part of that decision.[82] As to the question, in the case at hand, whether the Commission was entitled to revoke the first decision and replace it by the second, the CFI formulated a cautious, but positive, response relying largely on the principle of the protection of legitimate expectations. It held that a Community institution may, in exceptional circumstances and within a reasonable time, withdraw an unlawful act. The Commission having neither proved that the revoked decision was unlawful, nor stated adequate reasons for its revocation in the second decision, the latter was annulled.

As notifying undertakings will often insist upon the direct necessity of various restraints in an effort to preclude future consideration thereof, particularly under Article 81 EC, the import of the judgment is that the Commission must examine them and take a decision in their respect unless it is satisfied, and provides reasons therefore, that they are not 'directly related and necessary for the implementation of the concentration.' In the context of 'Phase I' investigations, this may place a not inconsiderable burden on the Commission. It has, however, not appealed this judgment.

8. IMPLEMENTATION OF COMMITMENTS UNDERLYING CONDITIONAL POSITIVE DECISIONS

Penultimately, might I turn to the third of the recent decisions of 3 April 2003 which was given in the *Petrolessence* case.[83] At issue in *Petrolessence* was a Commission decision of 13 September 2000 refusing initially to approve a list of purchasers for 70 of its service stations proposed by TotalFina/Elf in implement-

---

[80] Above n78, paras 90 to 107.
[81] *Ibid,* para 108.
[82] *Ibid,* para 109.
[83] Above n41. In Case T–342/00 R *Petrolessence and SG2R v. Commission* [2001] ECR II–67, I had occasion, on 17 January 2001 sitting as the judge hearing interlocutory applications, to reject an application for suspension of the contested decision in that case, lodged with the main application on 13 November 2000, on the basis of the applicants' failure to satisfy the condition of urgency.

ation of the conditional positive decision adopted by the Commission in February 2000 in respect of the merger of Elf with TotalFina.[84] The sell-off was deemed necessary as the merger would create a dominant position and a resulting strong incentive for the merged entity to raise prices and reduce the quality of the services offered at its service-stations in respect of the supposed discrete market for the sale of petroleum fuels at motorway service-stations in France. An amended list, ie excluding the applicants, was approved on 20 October 2000 by the Commission. TotalFina and Elf had proposed to sell six stations to the applicants, who intended to adopt an attractive price policy to attract customers which they hoped to be able in the longer term to sustain, in part by business synergies expected between the sale of fuels and the provision of restaurant services, at the six stations. The Commission, in essence, regarded the 18 months it would take the applicants to develop restaurants on the sites in question as being too long and their capacity to negotiate good purchase prices with French oil refineries too uncertain. It concluded that the applicants would be unable to develop and provide effective competition for the merged entity on the relevant market. This approach was upheld in a judgment which cannot be said to perform an especially critical review of the Commission's analysis.

Thus, in response to the applicant's argument that they would be in a position at their stations to charge attractive retail prices, as there was no real price competition as regards the price at which service-stations purchases their fuel supplies and that the current difference in the retail prices practised by large and small operators was minimal,[85] the CFI declared that the importance of the latter difference, relied upon in the contested Commission decision, had to be accepted (even though it amounted to a difference of about two old French centimes, or about a third of a euro cent per litre, and then assuming the independent operator had only one service-station).[86] Pointing to the Commission's finding that price competition was the predominant form of competition, the CFI states that, 'contrary to what the applicants assert, it must be found that the Commission can validly use as a basis for the decision rejecting the applicants' candidacy the argument that the applicants would be incapable of resisting reprisals by French refiners if they, the applicants, were to follow an active pricing policy' and finds that '[a] prospective analysis by the Commission can be challenged as vitiated by a manifest error of assessment only on the basis of concrete evidence adduced by the applicants, which is lacking in this case.'[87] In this respect the CFI added that 'the applicants' argument that the banks consider the project to be profitable is not relevant in this case [and that] [t]he banks' approach concentrates on the applicants' solvency, whereas that of the

---

[84] Commission Decision 2001/402/EC of 9 February 2000 in Case COMP/M.1628 *TotalFinal/Elf* (OJ 2001 L143/1).
[85] Above n41, para 111.
[86] *Ibid*, para 74.
[87] *Ibid*, para 112.

Commission is based on the aim of maintaining effective competition on the market in question.'[88]

The production of some concrete evidence that the French refineries would seek to punish a small operator, such as the applicant, if it pursued an active pricing policy was seemingly not required of the Commission. That such conduct, were it to occur, could be incompatible with both national and Community competition law would seem not to have been considered by the Commission. In this respect, I note that, following an investigation of alleged price fixing on the motorway service-station market in France by the major players, including the largest TotalFina/Elf, the *Conseil de la concurrence* has recently imposed fines of some €27 million.[89]

One might also have thought that the solvency of a project, clearly a prerequisite for its subsequent competitiveness if implemented, would have been considered a factor that weighed, at least prima facie, in the applicant's favour when considering whether it might be able to provide effective competition, at least in the area where its six stations would be situated, to the merged entity. However, the fact that the CFI was unwilling seriously to question the basis of the Commission's analysis in this case, should, I believe, be considered in the light of the fact that at issue was the degree of competition which the applicant undertakings might be capable of exercising against the merged entity so as, along with others (including the owners of the other 64 stations to be divested by the merged entity), to render acceptable with the common market a concentration that would otherwise clearly have generated unacceptable adverse effects on competition. At this level of the analysis of a concentration, the Community judge will only rarely upset what is manifestly a highly economic assessment on the Commission's part.

9. BURDEN OF PROOF AND THE RECENT CASE-LAW

A lot of media and academic attention has already been devoted to discussing the allegedly scathing assessment by the CFI in *Airtours* of the Commission's economic analysis.[90] In the immediate aftermath of the judgment, a lot (undue it seems to me) media focus was placed on the CFI's conclusion regarding the 'undoubted gravity' of the 'errors, omissions and inconsistencies' which it had 'found in the Commission's analysis of the impact of the merger.'[91] The *Tetra*

---

[88] Above n41, para 114.

[89] See Press Release No 31/2003 of 1 April 2003 of the French *Conseil de la concurrence* (*'Distribution de carburants sur les autoroutes: le Conseil de la concurrance sanctionne les principaux groupes pétroliers'*). Of the total of the fines in question, TotalFina/Elf was fined some €12 million for its part in the concerted behaviour which centred on exchanging information regarding prices.

[91] Above n8, para 404. This paragraph seems to have been latched onto by certain sections of the media as a result of the court's own press release in relation to its *Schneider* judgment (above n32). (Press Release No 84/02 of 22 October 2002) which, alluding to that paragraph referred to 'several obvious errors, omissions and contradictions in the Commission's economic reasoning.'

Laval prohibition-decision judgment is, I understand, under appeal in large part because the appellant believes the CFI paid lip service only to the margin of appreciation usually accorded to the Commission. Contrariwise, the Commission is reported, I understand, to be content with the *BaByliss* and *Philips* judgments, even though its economic analysis was again, albeit only in part, rejected by the CFI. Finally, in *Petrolessence*, the CFI was clearly conscious of the Commission's margin of appreciation in respect of economic analyses, mentioning, as it did, the need to respect that margin of appreciation no fewer than seven times in the relevant part of its judgment.[92] At the time of writing, no appeals have been lodged in the latter three cases.

In the second *Schneider* and *Tetra Laval* cases concerning the legality of the divestiture decisions adopted by the Commission in those cases,[93] the issue of the scope of the margin of appreciation to be allowed to the Commission when the latter determines, for the purposes of Article 8(4) of the MCR, the extent to which the restoration of effective conditions of competition requires the complete separation of the undertaking involved in the relevant merger was central.[94] The CFI found that the annulment of the contested divestiture decisions resulted directly from the annulment in the main cases of the prohibition decisions. The CFI was more explicit in *Tetra Laval* than in *Schneider* stating in the former that 'the separation of the undertakings involved in a concentration is the logical consequence of the decision declaring the concentration incompatible with the common market.'[95] Given that separation will, in such circumstances, be the rule, it follows, in my view, that the Commission's margin of discretion in such cases will, by force of consequence, be wide. It could not really be otherwise if there exists no basis for calling into question the validity of the prohibition decision. The Community judicature should allow the Commission a wide, but clearly not unfettered, margin of appreciation in determining the scope and modalities of the divestiture and/or other appropriate action required to restore effective conditions of competition.

I would reject the charge that the CFI has adopted a new approach to reviewing substantive Commission MCR decisions. It has, rather, adjusted the normal approach to reviewing Commission competition decisions so as to take account of the peculiarities of merger cases. The latter, it must be recalled, focus on a prospective analysis of the relevant markets. Nevertheless, this prospective analysis cannot be carried out in a vacuum. It must therefore be based on present facts. Thus, in any merger case, the Commission, before it can take a decision either to approve a merger following its notification ('Phase I') or to

---

[92] Above n41, paras 100 to 123.
[93] Commission Decision of 30 January 2002 in Case COMP/M.2283 *Schneider/Legrand*, and Commission Decision of 30 January 2002 in case COMP/M.2416 *Tetra Laval/Sidel*.
[94] Cases T–77/02 *Schneider Electric SA* v. *Commission* [2002] ECR 11–4201 and Case T–80/02 *Tetra Laval BV* v. *Commission* [2002] ECR 11–4519.
[95] Case T–80/02 *Tetra Laval* v. *Commission* [2002] ECR II–4519 at paragraph 76. This judgment is under appeal in Case C–13/03 P *Commission* v. *Tetra Laval*, lodged on 14 January 2003.

move to a full Phase 2 examination and final decision in respect thereof, needs, first, to ascertain and base its assessment of that merger, and of its potential effects on competition, on already existing material facts. These include the present position and market shares of the undertakings in question on one or more precisely defined and analysed relevant product or service market, as well as the present position and market shares of competing undertakings and the likely capacity of the merged entity's actual or potential suppliers or customers to resist any future nefarious conduct on its part. The Commission must, second, having ascertained such primary facts, evaluate the likely effects of the merger on the competitive situation on the market(s) concerned. This is where the twofold prospective analysis is required: essentially, the Commission needs to ascertain, in application of the criteria set down in the merger regulation, *first*, whether the merger will create or reinforce a dominant position and, *second*, whether it will have significant negative effects on competition on the market(s) concerned, or, alternatively, whether it will not have such effects.

In this respect, I would, by way of parenthesis, observe that one of the significant aspects of the *Tetra Laval* case is, in my view, the emphasis it places on the cumulative nature of these two conditions. To prohibit a concentration under the MCR, unlike for example under the significant lessening of competition (SLC) test that now applies within the EU in a number of national competition laws, *both* conditions must formally be satisfied. On the basis of *Tetra Laval,* this must occur in conglomerate mergers within an acceptable timeframe. Although the same formally applies, given the parallel wording of Article 2(3) and (4) of the MCR, for a positive decision, ie both conditions must not be satisfied, it is clear that a merger that might, for example, have a significant adverse effect on competition but which was unlikely to lead to the creation or strengthening of a dominance position would ultimately have to be approved (perhaps after the Commission had extracted certain commitments from the undertakings involved), simply because the dual conditions for adopting a prohibition decision could not be satisfied. In many respects, it seems to me that the *Tetra Laval* conglomerate type of case is precisely where this situation may occur: the merging of parties on different but closely related markets such that, because especially of the overlap in the potential customer base, the possibility of future anticompetitive conduct cannot be excluded, even in the absence of the foreseeable creation or strengthening of a dominant position.

How then does the CFI proceed in respect of reviewing the abovementioned two different types of examination that must be effected by the Commission? As regards, first, the assessment of the present market situation, the CFI will, as it appears clearly from the case-law, for example, *Airtours* and *Schneider*, examine closely, and without restraint, whether the Commission has got the core, material facts right. Thus, for example, in *Schneider* the Commission relied, in its analysis of the structure of competition at wholesaler level, on their limited capacity to exert competitive pressure on manufacturers such as the merged entity. Referring to some of the markets, notably Spain and Portugal where a

Judgments Reviewing Commission Merger Control Decisions   139

large proportion of distribution was controlled by a limited number of wholesalers, the CFI found that the Commission had failed to establish that the strong level of competition existing between the large wholesalers active on those markets would not also affect manufacturers by pressurising them to lower their prices.[96] The Commission's conclusion that the merged entity would be the unavoidable supplier for most wholesalers was insufficiently established. Permit me to refer to one of the relevant figures. The mere fact that the merged entity would supply 30 to 40% of the sales of a particular major Italian wholesaler did not, the CFI found, suffice to establish what, if any, would be the real economic power which it would enjoy vis-à-vis distributors in that national market.[97] This was because, first, that wholesaler only supplied 4% of the panel-board components (one of the important types of product at issue) sold in Italy and, second, a consultant's report submitted by the applicant showed that over 800 wholesalers were active in the supply of electrical equipment downstream from final panel-boards, ie ultra-terminal equipment such as switches.[98] A second example may be drawn from *Airtours* where, although agreeing with the Commission that 'the stability of historic market shares [would be] a factor conducive to the development of tacit collusion,'[99] the CFI found, on examining the market share figures (relied upon in the notification and in the Article 230 EC application by Airtours) that the Commission had simply entirely excluded market shares acquired through acquisitions, ie external growth, on the spurious, at least as a general proposition, basis that a merger did not necessarily result in the merged entity enjoying the arithmetic combined market share of its component undertakings. In my view, these two examples (among the various others that could be drawn from those two cases alone) demonstrate that it is essential for the CFI carefully to review the facts presented as material by the Commission, as well as the direct factual inferences drawn therefrom, if effective judicial control of the latter's MCR decisions is to be a reality.

Regarding the second part of the assessment, namely the examination of what will be the likely effects of the merger on the competitive situation on the market, the CFI has stated that, as long as the facts regarding the existing situation have been proved satisfactorily, the Commission enjoys a certain margin of appreciation regarding its analysis of the immediate or future effects of the merger in question. This means in particular, as the CFI stated clearly in *Petrolessence*, that, when reviewing 'complex economic assessments made by the Commission in exercising the discretion conferred on it by Regulation No 4064/89,' the control exercised by the Community judicature 'must be limited to ensuring compliance with the rules of procedure and the statement of reasons, as well as the substantive accuracy of the facts, the absence of manifest

---

[96] Above n35, paras 203 to 216.
[97] *Ibid,* para 220.
[98] *Ibid,* paras 221 to 225.
[99] Above n8, para 117.

errors of assessment and of any misuse of power'; it must in particular not 'substitute its own economic assessment for that of the Commission.'[100] The margin of appreciation is, however, clearly a function of the degree of discretion involved. Thus, as regards the first stage of the prospective analysis, a certain margin of appreciation will, in accordance with *Kali and Salz* (paragraph 226), be attributed by the Community judicature to that part of the Commission's assessment of the likely creation or strengthening of a dominant position (or the absence thereof) that is based upon inferences drawn from primary facts, while a greater margin will be allowed to pure economic assessments. In so far as a case turns on the competitive impact of the merger (the creation or strengthening of a dominant position having been established) the margin of appreciation accorded is likely to be large as, by definition, the Community judicature will almost invariably be examining complex economic assessments made by the Commission. These principles have been unequivocally stated and, I suggest, correctly applied by the CFI in the recent cases, in only one of which (to date) have appeals been lodged. When the CFI refers, as it has done in particularly in the *Airtours*, *Tetra Laval* and *BaByliss* cases to the Commission's not having proved a claim to a sufficient legal standard or to the absence of 'convincing evidence,' it is quite clear that the CFI means that, having regard to primary facts and the direct inferences made therefrom, the particular prospective positive or negative analysis of the Commission decision at issue is so uncertain as to amount to, or form part of what amounts overall to, a manifest error of appreciation. I do not see any difference of substance between this approach and that of the Court of Justice, upon which it is based, in *Kali and Salz*.

This may be amply illustrated by two further examples from *Airtours*. The first concerns the CFI's rejection of the Commission's analysis of the significance of what it perceived would be the moderate growth of the relevant British shorthall, package-holidays market. Having requested production of the market 'study' to which the Commission referred in its decision in partial justification of this conclusion, the CFI found that it comprised a single page extract prepared at an unknown date.[101] On examination, the CFI observed that it was 'apparent from a cursory examination of that document that the Commission's reading of it was inaccurate,'[102] the author actually having emphasised the massive growth in the market in the previous 20 years! The Commission was, therefore, 'not entitled to conclude that market development was characterised by low growth, which was, in this instance, a factor conducive to the creation of a collective dominant position.'[103] Second, as regards demand volatility, the contested decision (paragraphs 92 and 93) found that, although a degree of such volatility existed, it did not preclude the creation of a collective dominant position but quite the reverse; ie in the circumstances of that case it would encour-

[100] Above n41, para 101.
[101] Above n8, para 129.
[102] *Ibid*, para 130.
[103] *Ibid*, para 133.

age a 'wait and see' conservative approach to capacity-planning decisions by the remaining post-merger major operators. The CFI found that the Commission's acknowledgement that a certain degree of demand volatility is characteristic of the relevant market was understated as 'several of the documents' on the case-file indicated 'that there is a considerable degree of volatility in the market.'[104] The Commission retorted that this was not relevant in the case at hand as 'operators tend to be cautious to protect themselves against any volatility.'[105] The manifest incorrectness of this assessment and thus the correctness of the CFI's rejection thereof emerge clearly, in my view, from paragraph 142 which I quote:

> However, the Commission is not entitled to rely on the fact that tour operators, to protect themselves against sudden downward volatility in demand, plan capacity cautiously, preferring to increase it later if demand proves to be particularly strong (Decision, paragraph 97), for the purpose of denying the relevance in this instance of a factor which is significant as evidence of oligopolistic dominance, such as the degree of market stability and predictability. Although it is certainly the case that the caution inherent in the way the market normally operates means that account must be taken of the need to make the best possible estimates of the way in which demand will develop, the planning process remains difficult, because each operator must anticipate (some 18 months in advance because of the market's distinctive features) how demand will evolve—demand being distinguished by its considerable volatility and thus entailing a degree of speculation. Furthermore, the Commission did not regard either the operators' caution or demand volatility to be restrictive of competition in the pre-merger market. Caution cannot therefore be interpreted, as such, as evidence of a collective dominant position rather than as a characteristic of a competitive market of the kind that existed at the time of the notification.

The *Airtours* and *Tetra Laval* cases also illustrate, I believe, that the scope of the margin of assessment allowed to the Commission should be a function of the novelty and/or controversial or contested nature of the economic theory(ies) upon which it bases its assessment. Thus, in *Airtours*, the CFI observes that the Commission recognises 'economic theory regards volatility of demand as something which renders the creation of a [CDP] more difficult' before it concludes, after a detailed analysis of the Commission's analysis, that the latter 'has failed to establish that economic theory is inapplicable in the present case' and, hence, 'was wrong in concluding that volatility of demand was conducive to the creation of a dominant oligopoly by the three remaining major tour operators.'[106] In *Tetra Laval*, the CFI held that

> [s]ince the effects of a conglomerate-type merger are generally considered to be neutral, or even beneficial, for competition on the markets concerned, as is recognised in the present case by the economic writings cited in the analyses annexed to the parties' written pleadings, the proof of anti-competitive conglomerate effects of such a merger

---

[104] *Ibid*, para 140.
[105] *Ibid*, para 141.
[106] *Ibid*, paras 139 and 147.

calls for a precise examination, supported by convincing evidence, of the circumstances which allegedly produce those effects.[107]

This approach is consistent with the history of the development of competition law and particularly Article 82 EC. Thus, the notion of dominance was initially based on crude market share assessments but has developed to encompass more complex economic notions such as real market power, barriers to entry and the effects/influence of intellectual property rights. When new theories advanced by the Commission in the context of the exercise of its merger control function are contested before the Community judicature, it is, in my view, the duty and responsibility of the CFI, so as to ensure effective judicial review, closely to scrutinise the convincing nature of the evidence relied upon in the contested decision in support of such theories.

It remains to be seen whether the Court of Justice confirms the *Tetra Laval* judgments which, like the *Airtours* judgment, found squarely in favour of an applicant whose notified concentration had been prohibited by the Commission. In its appeal against the main judgment, ie that dealing with the prohibition decision, the Commission claims, inter alia, that the CFI, although ostensibly accepting the principle of a certain margin of appreciation for the Commission as regards its economic assessments, has nevertheless in reality failed to respect that margin and, in so doing, allegedly raised the level of proof required. The Commission contends that the test effectively applied is no longer whether the applicant has established that the Commission has committed a manifest error of appreciation in the contested decision but whether it has cast sufficient doubts regarding the convincing nature of the Commission's case. In effect, the Commission would appear to be contending that the CFI has effectively substituted its own appreciation for that of the Commission regarding the likely effects of the merger on competition on the markets concerned.[108] Judgments in the *Tetra Laval* appeals will probably not be given until the later part of next year (2004) at the earliest, as the Commission has not requested the application by the Court of Justice of an expedited procedure under Article 62a of the Court's Rules of Procedure.[109] One might have expected such an application from the Commission given that the Commission stated, on adopting a

---

[107] Above n38, para 155.

[108] For a more detailed summary of the pleas in law advanced by the Commission in its appeals, see the notice regarding the appeals against the judgment in Cases T–5/02 and T–80/02 (above n5) published at OJ 2003 C70/3 and C70/5 respectively.

[109] The first such request in an appeal case was lodged recently by the Commission in the *Artegodan* case (see Case C–39/03 P *Commission* v. *Artegodan GmbH et al*, lodged on 3 February 2003, concerning an appeal against the judgment of 26 November 2002 in Case T–74/00 *Artegodan GmbH et al* v. *Commission* (not yet reported)). It was accepted by the President of the Court of Justice and an oral hearing has already taken place (on 10 June 2003) in the appeal, at the end of which AG Alber immediately delivered an oral Opinion (in favour of rejecting the appeal) and a judgment is, I understand, due to be delivered by end-July 2003. Consequently, it is clear that the Court of Justice is capable of dealing very expeditiously with appeals where required in exceptionally urgent cases.

conditional positive decision (to date unpublished on its website or in the Official Journal) the day after lodging its appeal in respect of the re-notification of the merger by the parties, that the new decision 'could be affected by the outcome of the Commission's appeal and an eventual re-examination of the Commission's earlier decision in the event that the matter would be referred back to it by the Court of Justice.'[110]

My impression, as one of the judges responsible for *Gencor* and the *Schneider* cases, as Judge Rapporteur (almost all third parties interested in the matter seem already to be aware of this formally undisclosed fact) in the *Tetra Laval* cases and as a very interested reader of the judgments in *Airtours*, *BaByliss/Philips* and *Petrolessence*, is that, with the possible exception of *Petrolessence*, the CFI has simply been more exacting latterly than it arguably was previously when applying the well-established principles to which I have referred. It has also, I believe rightly, required convincing proof for findings based on novel or contested economic theories. This follows, it must be recalled, considerable adverse academic analysis, as well as persistent criticism from practitioners representing parties involved in or interested by merger notifications, particularly in recent years, of the Commission's perceived unparalleled role as investigator, prosecutor and judge in such cases. This is particularly significant when one takes account of the fact that many mergers with a Community dimension are, of course, often of critical economic and social importance for the parties involved or affected thereby, including quite often Member States, as illustrated tellingly by France's multi-level intervention the *Schneider* case. In so doing, I think the CFI has correctly taken its lead from the approach adopted by the Court of Justice itself in *Kali and Salz*, where, having recalled the Commission's margin of assessment, the Court of Justice had little hesitation (see above) in annulling the Commission decision once it detected 'flaws' affecting the economic assessment carried out by the latter. Consequently, if the Commission presents a case for or against a merger (and/or commitments offered by the parties thereto) in a contested decision in which, for example, it has clearly overlooked, underestimated or exaggerated the relevant economic data, drawn unconvincing, in the sense of implausible, direct inferences from primary material facts or adopted an erroneous approach to assessing the material facts, such failings may, depending on their cumulative effect in the context of the circumstances of the case viewed as whole, suffice to constitute, for the purpose of the CFI's review of the relevant overall economic analysis, a manifest error of assessment. On the other hand, if no such (or very few or insignificant such) errors are found, then the CFI, even if it would not itself have subscribed to the Commission's economic assessment of the foreseeable effects of the merger and/or the adequacy of the commitments offered, should uphold the Commission's findings.

---

[110] See Commission press release IP/03/36 of 13 January 2003.

10. CONCLUDING REMARKS

This account of some of the more interesting features of the recent case-law should, I feel, provide an overall indication of the developing nature of the MCR litigation and the complexity of the issues now coming before the CFI. It is obvious as that litigation increases that the Court of Justice will increasingly be called upon to adjudicate as final arbiter of some of the important legal questions raised. David Edward's retirement will mean that he will no longer be a member of the Court that deals with these future cases. However, I have little doubt that he will, for some time to come, maintain a close eye over, and a keen academic interest in, the area. Let us hope that the judgments of those of us who remain for the time being, and who in future become, judges of the Community courts are sufficiently well reasoned to withstand possible future 'professorial' censure.

11
The National Courts and the Uniform Application of EC Competition Rules. Preliminary Observations on Council Regulation 1/2003

LEIF SEVÓN

WORKING WITH DAVID Edward has always been a pleasant and rewarding experience. David Edward can always identify the relevant problems of a case. He seeks solutions to those problems that are fair and just as well as workable in practice. It is regrettable that he leaves the Court of Justice at a time when the Court will be faced with several new challenges needing pragmatic solutions. May it suffice to mention the problems arising out of enlargement and those inherent in the extension of Community law into new fields of criminal law.

In this paper I shall deal with yet another challenge, namely that posed by Council Regulation 1/2003 on the implementation of the rules laid down in Articles 81 and 82 of the Treaty.[1] However, the Regulation may be a lesser problem for the Court of Justice than for the courts of the Member States. Nevertheless, the Regulation concerns a field of law crucial to the Community. In *Eco Swiss China Time*[2] the Court of Justice remarked that Article 85 (now Article 81) of the EC Treaty constitutes a fundamental provision which is fundamental for the accomplishment of the tasks entrusted to the Community and, in particular, for the functioning of the internal market.[3] It seems that this statement would also apply to provisions that are essential for the functioning of Articles 81 and 82 such as those on the implementation and operation of these Articles. Thus the present Regulation 17 and its successor Regulation 1/2003 would be equally fundamental. This idea is reflected in the first indent of the preamble of Regulation 1/2003 according to which competition rules must be effectively and uniformly applied in the Community even if the statement would probably apply to all instruments on Community law.

---

[1] Council Regulation (EC) No 1/2003 of 16 December 2002 (OJ 2003 L1/1).
[2] Case C–126/97 *Eco Swiss China Time Ltd* v. *Benetton International NV* [1999] ECR I–3055.
[3] *Ibid*, at para 36.

However, Regulation 1/2003 introduces a new system for the operation of those Articles. It does so by introducing a decentralised system instead of the previous centralised system. Hence, the Regulation poses challenges different in nature from those arising out of Regulation 17, in particular as regards the uniform application of Community competition rules. The measures taken in order to meet those challenges are essential for the functioning of the Regulation, the Community competition policy as a whole as well as for the internal market.

The Regulation has been criticised for being vague and leaving a number of questions unanswered. It has been asked whether the Regulation is sufficiently clear in order not to endanger legal certainty for enterprises. In that respect two points may be made.

Firstly, I have so far not come across any piece of legislation that would not be susceptible of raising questions of interpretation. Certainly Regulation 1/2003 has already posed and will pose problems of interpretation. Some of the questions that have been raised concerning the meaning of certain provisions of the Regulation are clearly relevant, others probably less so. Some of the questions posed may never require an answer. On the other hand, any legislation, Community legislation as well as national legislation, seems in due time to present problems that were not envisaged during the preparation of it.

Secondly, any piece of legislation attempting to answer all conceivable—and inconceivable—questions would be a disaster. What is important is that the Regulation settles a sufficient number of relevant questions and provides workable solutions to those questions. It seems that it does. In any case, the Regulation exists and will apply from 1 May 2004. At this stage it is less useful to discuss what should have been done but has not been done. What may be useful is to make a few observations on issues that may still be settled.

Still another remark is that no legal system is capable of ensuring perfect uniformity. There are several reasons for this. For instance, judgments are not always appealed against with the consequence that disparate rulings may be left in force. When cases are decided it is far from always possible to see all implications a judgment may have. Seeing the results of a ruling may convince the Judge of the necessity to seek a subtler solution to the problem or even to reverse the previous case law. Consequently, the new ruling would not be coherent with previous case law.

Perfect coherence is thus not obtainable, nor desirable. What may be achieved is a system that offers sufficient tools in order to have a reasonable degree of uniformity.

This brings me to the question whether Regulation 1/2003 meets such a more modest objective.

In the Regulation a number of measures have been adopted in order to enhance uniformity. Two mechanisms are fundamental in that respect.

Firstly, the Regulation provides in Article 3 that where the competition authorities of the Member States or the national courts of Member States apply national competition law to agreements and practices or abuses, which may affect trade between the Member States, they shall also apply Articles 81 and 82. The effect of the word 'also' is that the national courts shall apply these Articles instead of national provisions that would otherwise have been applicable. The reasons for the provision are stated in the 8th recital of the preamble: only thus can the objective of creating a level playing field for agreements, decisions by associations of undertakings and concerted practices within the internal market be achieved. Only thus can one ensure that the application of national competition laws will not lead to the prohibition of agreements, decisions and concerted practices that are not also prohibited under Community competition law.

Applying the same law thus promotes uniformity. Applying the same law in accordance with the case law of the Court of Justice promotes it further.

The second fundamental measure is the creation of a network consisting of the Commission and the competent authorities of the Member States. The purpose of the network is to ensure the effective enforcement of the Community competition rules and, consequently, to promote uniformity and efficiency. It aims to do so through division of work and avoidance of duplication of work. It is stated in the Commissions proposal,[4] *inter alia*, that effective case allocation makes it necessary that the members of the network should inform each other of all new cases and exchange relevant case-related information.

The success of Regulation 1/2003 will depend on the efficiency of this network. It is stated in the 15th recital of the preamble that the modalities of the networking are not set out in detail but will be laid down and revised by the Commission. It seems that an intense exchange of information is called for.

The Regulation also contains a number of provisions aimed at ensuring uniform application of the competition rules when applied by the national courts. Decentralisation implies an important role for the courts of the Member States. That is due, in particular, to the fact that national courts may also apply Article 81(3). The extended role clearly implies a risk for diverging case law in the Member States. The Regulation endeavours to diminish that risk by four methods.

The first method has already been mentioned. The national courts apply Articles 81 and 82, not provisions of national law. In addition, they apply them in accordance with the case law of the Court of Justice. The application of the same law will in itself promote consistency throughout the single market.

The second method is laid down in Article 15(1). Courts of the Member States may ask the Commission to transmit to them information in its possession or its opinion on questions concerning the application of the Community competition rules. During the preparation of the Regulation the question was raised whether the information provided by the Commission should be confidential or whether the public should have access to it. I believe that this query has been settled by a

---

[4] OJ 2000 C365 E/284.

ruling of the Court of Justice.[5] In that ruling it was held that a lawyer having a competition case is entitled to information on opinions of the Commission.

An opinion of the Commission on questions concerning the application of Community competition rules referred to in Article 15(1) is not an assessment of the specific case in question and thus not an opinion, much less a suggestion, on how the national court should decide the case. It is rather a statement on the actual state of Community law as the Commission sees it. As it reflects the Commission's view the opinion it is, of course, not binding on the national courts. That is not to say that the national Judge may not find the opinion persuasive.

Since the opinion reflects the views of the Commission on the state of Community law, there seem to be no valid reasons why an opinion should be confidential. Not being confidential may well have a purifying effect on the contents of the opinion. In addition, confidentiality would hardly be compatible with the European Convention on Human Rights and the EU Charter on Fundamental Rights if confidentiality would extend to the parties in the proceedings for which the opinion has been sought. A court cannot take into account an opinion that has not been communicated to the parties and on which the parties have not had an opportunity to express themselves.

The third method is to be found in Article 15(2) and (3). Under Article 15(2) Member States shall forward to the Commission a copy of any written judgment deciding on the application of Article 81 or 82. In Article 15(3) it is stated that where the coherent application of Article 81 or 82 so requires, the Commission, acting on its own initiative, may submit written observations to courts of the Member States. With the permission of the court in question, it may also make oral observations. For the purpose in the preparation of their observations only, the Commission may request the relevant court to transmit or ensure the transmission to it of any documents necessary for the assessment of the case.

This gives rise to a number of reflections. Firstly, the observations by the Commission envisaged in Article 15(3) are of a different nature to those envisaged in Article 15(1). What is now in issue is a statement intended to influence the outcome of a specific case. The views are those of an *amicus curiae*. Secondly, the provisions in question are cast in general terms. The right of the Commission to submit observations concerns, in principle, all courts and is not affected by the fact that the national competition authorities may submit their own observations on the case if that is envisaged under national law. Thirdly, no obligation is imposed on a court before which a case is brought to inform the Commission of the fact that a competition case has been brought before it, nor to inform the Commission directly about the outcome of the case. There is only an obligation to transmit, or ensure the transmission of, documents to the Commission upon request, as well as an obligation on the Member State con-

---

[5] Joined cases C–174/98P and C–189/98P *Kingdom of the Netherlands and Gerhard van der Wal v Commission* [2000] ECR I–1.

cerned to transmit a copy of its judgments. It is for the national law to provide the necessary tools for the Member State to obtain the information that it is obliged to transmit to the Commission. Fourthly, the modalities necessary in order to enable the Commission to act in accordance with Article 15(3) must be provided for in national law. That might well lead to different solutions in the Member States.

There is a further consequence of the system envisaged in Article 15(3). The provisions will obviously operate quite differently in different kinds of cases. If in a case before the national court a decision by the national competition authorities is challenged, the network may well provide the Commission with information of that case. The Commission may then be in a position to intervene immediately before the court first hearing the case. On the other hand, if the case is brought by one economic operator against another and concerns, for example, damages for breach of competition rules, it is less likely that the Commission will be informed of the fact that such a case is pending. At least in Finland the competition authorities are not automatically informed of such a case and are not involved in the case. In view of the presently limited number of cases of the latter category that difference may be unimportant.

Unless the network has provided the Commission with sufficient information on cases brought for the Commission to present its observations before the court initially hearing the case, the emphasis of the system in Article 15(3) seems to be on appeals. Observations by the Commission may be triggered by the communication of a judgment under Article 15(2). But then again, there is nothing in Regulation 1/2003 to suggest that the Commission itself is entitled to appeal against a decision by a court that has applied Articles 81 or 82. It would, indeed, be somewhat strange to attribute such a right to someone who has so far not been a party to the procedure. In addition, as drafted, Article 15(3) seems to presuppose that observations may be submitted in pending cases. If none of the parties appeal the case, there is nothing on which to submit observations.

Once again, the rules may function differently in cases where a decision of the national competition authorities has been challenged, and in those where the case has been brought by one private party against another. In the former case the Commission may be aware of the case thanks to the network and may persuade the competition authorities to appeal against the judgment. In the latter case that possibility would not exist.

Nor is there any provision indicating the time within which observations should be submitted by an *amicus curiae*. That is a question regulated by national law.

In any case, even where the Commission would be allowed to appeal against a judgment, its position may be difficult. It would be faced with the following scenario. The time allowed for appeals is normally relatively short. A part of it will be consumed before the Member State gets hold of the judgment and transmits it to the Commission. The Commission services will then have to assess whether the case is sufficiently important for it to submit observations. What has been transmitted to it would be a judgment in any of the future official languages of the Community. In cases of necessity the Commission would have to request the court concerned to transmit any document necessary for the assessment of the case. The observations of the Commission must then be formulated in the language used by the services and in many cases translated into the language of the case before the national court. There seems to be little time to be lost at any of these stages.

It is thus inherent in the system that national procedural provisions are applicable in cases envisaged by Article 15(3). The Regulation provides little guidance as to the requirements to be put on the national provisions. National provisions are thus likely to be highly divergent. This is likely to create a considerable pressure to provide further guidance to the national legislator. That again is likely to create pressure towards a further harmonisation of national procedural rules in competition cases. It might be preferable to proceed with caution in that minefield. Any harmonisation may easily upset procedural rules other than those harmonised.

It is difficult to assess the effects of Article 15 on a uniform application of competition rules. But one should not lose sight of the fact that presently the Commission is reluctant to embark on a considerable number of cases for the reason that the Community interest is not sufficiently important for it to act. The fact that cases may be brought before national courts may thus lead to an increase in the number of competition cases that are brought. If the Commission manages to intervene under the Regulation in cases that it has deemed not to be of such an importance for it to take over the case, where that is possible, but which are still interesting from the point of view of Community interest, this might well result in an improvement compared to the present state of affairs. The right of the Commission to submit observations might have a discouraging effect on any tendency of what is called the homeward trend in courts favouring national interests at the expense of the interests of competitors from the other Member States. Where decisions by national competition authorities are challenged, the Commission is likely to be in a better position to submit observations than in competition cases between private parties.

The fourth method is the existing one, according to which national courts may, and are in certain cases obliged to, make a reference for a preliminary ruling to the Court of Justice. In this respect one may ask whether the new competencies of national courts pose particular problems. They probably do. What I have in mind is the competence under Article 81(3) on exemptions. One may then ask if the preliminary ruling procedure is capable of providing sufficient guidance in that respect. I am not convinced that the situation in that respect is any worse than on many other points of Community law. One may further ask if these cases are more urgent than others. They probably are, but not likely to such an extent that they would systematically have to be treated under the accelerated procedure.

The Regulation also codifies a limitation on the discretion of the national court concerned. Article 16 provides that where national courts rule on agreements, decisions or practices which are already the subject of a Commission decision, they cannot take a decision running counter to the decision adopted by the Commission. They must also avoid giving decisions which would conflict with a decision contemplated by the Commission in proceedings it has initiated.

That Article broadly reflects the judgment of the Court of Justice in *Masterfoods*.[6] That judgment makes it clear that the rule also applies in cases where the Commission decision has been challenged before the Community courts in Luxemburg. Until definitively overruled, a decision by a Community institution is presumed to be legal. Thus the options of the national court in a case where the same issue as the one decided by the Commission has been brought before it, is either to suspend the case or to suspend and make a reference for a preliminary ruling. What it cannot do is to decide the case before it and take the risk that its judgment will be in conflict with the final outcome concerning the Commission decision.

A number of questions concerning Regulation 1/2003 have been raised in this paper. They are certainly not the only ones that one could pose. In spite of this there seems to be little room for doubt that the Regulation may function. It most likely will, and better than one may fear.

---

[6] Case C–344/98 *Masterfoods Ltd* v. *HB Ice Cream Ltd* [2000] ECR I–11369.

12

The A M & S Judgment

JOHN TEMPLE LANG

THERE CAN BE few lawyers who have contributed as much to a single judgment on which so many lawyers all over Europe rely every day as David Edward contributed to the *A M & S*[1] judgment.

1. THE *A M & S* JUDGMENT

The case began as a challenge by *A M & S* to a Commission competition decision requiring the company to disclose to Commission inspectors a number of documents requesting or providing legal advice. The case was argued by both parties on the assumption that the issue was procedural: how should it be decided whether documents of this kind were really what they were said to be? However, David Edward had written a book *The Professional Secret, Confidentiality and Legal Professional Privilege in the Nine Member States of the European Community* which the Consultative Commission of the European Bars and Law Societies (known as the CCBE on the basis of its title in French) had published in 1976. When I suggested that the CCBE should intervene, David Edward was the President of the CCBE, and he appeared for that organisation. The intervention convinced the Court of Justice that it was impossible to deal with the procedural question without first deciding whether Community law contained a substantive rule guaranteeing the confidentiality of communications between lawyers and clients requesting and giving legal advice. The Court re-opened the case after the conclusions of Advocate General Warner, there was a second oral argument and a second set of conclusions, this time from Advocate General Slynn, and the Court finally gave judgment.

As is well known, the Court said that written communications which relate to the subject-matter of a current or subsequent Commission procedure are confidential and need not be disclosed to the Commission. The Court however said that this applied only if the lawyer was an independent lawyer in private practice (and not an in-house lawyer employed by his client) and if he or she was entitled to practice in a Member State and to benefit from the Directive on the provision of legal services.

[1] Case 155/79 *AM & S Europe Ltd* v. *Commission* [1982] ECR 1575.

This limitation was stated on the initiative of the Court. The Commission had said that an in-house lawyer should be entitled to the confidentiality if he or she was effectively subject to a regime of legal ethics and discipline comparable to that of a lawyer in private practice. This view had already been expressed, on a personal basis, by the then Director General of the Legal Service of the Commission at the conference of FIDE, the *Fédération Internationale pour le Droit Européen*, at its conference in Copenhagen in 1978.

2. THE RATIONALE OF *A M & S*

The judgment said that communications concerning legal advice with lawyers in private practice in the then Member States, and no others, were entitled to confidentiality. The Court said that the counterpart of that confidentiality lies in the rules of professional ethics and discipline, but did not elaborate. It has always been assumed, but more as a matter of logic than because of anything said by the Court or even the Advocates General, that this was on the assumption that all lawyers in the Member States of the Community had a professional duty not to help their clients to do anything which the lawyer knew or believed to be unlawful, and had a duty not to mislead a national or Community court which also prohibited him from misleading a competition authority such as the Commission. It was also assumed, again implicitly, that the rules of ethics of all Bars and Law Societies would be effective, when necessary, in enforcing these rules. The FIDE report had suggested that confidentiality would not apply if the lawyer was assisting the client's illegal activities. The rationale for confidentiality, that law-abiding citizens must be free to obtain legal advice about what they may or may not legally do without creating evidence which might be used against themselves, would not apply if the lawyer was helping the client to break the law. The rights of the defence, of which the confidentiality forms part, are usually considered not to entitle the lawyer knowingly to mislead a court, or a public authority with more or less quasi-judicial functions.

Assuming that these are necessary conditions for confidentiality, several questions arise. Are they fulfilled by the rules of all the Bars? And if they are necessary conditions, are they sufficient conditions or, to be more precise, what additional conditions, if any, might employed lawyers or lawyers in private practice in a non-Member State be able to fulfil which would make the confidentiality rule applicable to their communications with their clients? The Court simply said that their communications were not entitled to confidentiality, but gave no clear reason.

Rather surprisingly, even the answer to the first question is not clear: not all Bars have explicit rules saying that it is unprofessional to help a client to do something known to be unlawful, or to mislead a competition authority such as the Commission. The CCBE, after David Edward ceased to be President, was asked to confirm that all its member organisations do in fact regard both these kinds of conduct as unprofessional, and has consistently failed to do so.

3. EMPLOYED LAWYERS

Looking first at the question of employed or in-house lawyers, several arguments have been suggested for the view that their communications should not be entitled to confidentiality. First, it is said in some Member States that an employed lawyer has not got the necessary characteristic of independence from the client which, it is said, is essential for a lawyer to fulfil his duties properly. Second, it is said (though without evidence) that an employed lawyer is likely to be so dependent on the client that he would not be able when necessary to advise that the client's proposed course of action was unlawful and should not be adopted. These are, essentially, a formal and a sociological argument for the same conclusion.

The formal argument is now substantially weaker than it was at the time of the *A M & S* judgment. Then only two Member States (Ireland and the United Kingdom) formally recognised employed lawyers as capable of being full members of their professions. Since then, several other Member States (Belgium, Denmark, Germany, the Netherlands) have enacted legislation which either brings about that result or gives employed lawyers, on certain conditions, a status essentially equivalent to that of independent lawyers in private practice.

What I have called the sociological argument is also weaker than it was in 1982. This is largely because there are now several national associations and one European association of employed lawyers, the *Association Européenne de Juristes d'Entreprises*, which have their own rules of ethics and discipline, which are intended to be as strict as those of the Bars in the Member States in question. Indeed, they are stricter, because they expressly state that there is a duty not to help the client to do something clearly unlawful, and not to mislead the Commission or any national competition authority. It is also weaker for several other reasons. The first of these is that there are now a great many more employed lawyers in the Member States of the European Union than there were in 1982. They are giving legal advice, although because of the *A M & S* judgment they are giving it in unsatisfactory conditions. Many, though of course not all, of these are fully qualified to practise as independent lawyers in at least one Member State in every respect except their employment.

The second reason why the sociological argument has recently become weaker concerns Regulation 1/2003, the Community Regulation by which the application of EU competition law is decentralised, with effect from May 2004. This Regulation has several consequences which are relevant to the question of employed lawyers. The first is that notifications to the Commission will no longer be made. So each company must decide, with whatever legal advice it prefers. Community competition law will rely entirely, in the first place, on voluntary compliance. This means that it should be Community policy to encourage companies to consult lawyers. If they have in-house lawyers, they are the lawyers most likely to be consulted, and the lawyers best acquainted with the company's affairs. Independent lawyers are much less likely to be routinely consulted. So a Community policy which discourages consultation of employed lawyers is self-defeating, because it makes satisfactory voluntary compliance less likely, more difficult and more expensive. Companies with in-house lawyers are in general the companies with most numerous and most complex legal problems, which wish to act within the law. It does not make sense to discourage such companies from getting legal advice in the way they find most efficient. Even if granting confidentiality were to allow a couple of in-house lawyers to act unprofessionally, the overall benefit of encouraging all in-house lawyers to write freely and firmly, knowing that they were not creating evidence which could be used against their companies, would far outweigh any harm which might occur. Antitrust advice often needs to be in writing, and it is bad policy to discourage in-house lawyers from putting their opinions in writing when they think that is necessary. Discouraging in-house lawyers from putting their advice in writing would also be inconsistent with the Commission's leniency policy, which is also intended to promote voluntary compliance.

The second consequence of Regulation 1/2003 is that national competition authorities will be obliged to apply Community competition law in all cases in which there is an effect on trade between Member States. Where there is no effect on that trade, and for some other purposes, they may also apply national competition law. Presumably, insofar as they are applying Community law, they will be obliged to recognise the confidentiality guaranteed by the *A M & S* judgment, even if it is not recognised by their national law. But when they apply their national laws, widely different results will occur: some national laws recognise confidentiality for communications with in-house lawyers, others apparently do not recognise confidentiality for legal advice, even from independent lawyers, except for advice given after proceedings have begun. So documents which would be treated as confidential by the U.K competition authorities would not be treated as confidential by the French authority. This will not only lead to inconsistencies and anomalies: it will mean that the rights of defendants and complainants depend on which authority deals with the case, and this will lead to decisions to transfer cases being open to challenge in national or Community courts. It will also lead to inextricable complications: what should be the status, before the UK competition authority, of a document written by a French in-house lawyer, when the UK authority is applying either Community law or UK law? The confidentiality of legal advice, and the usefulness of lawyers, should not depend on which jurisdiction a case falls into.

So far, the Commission has claimed that in-house lawyers are likely to help their employers to break the law, and so their advice should not be confidential. This is naïve, and it is static and unconstructive. It is naïve, because a client company can stop instructing an independent lawyer whose advice it dislikes at any time: employed lawyers cannot have their employment terminated without risking claims for wrongful dismissal, in which the reasons for the dismissal would be likely to emerge. A strategic policy would be for the Commission to devise or support rules which would ensure that in-house lawyers who did help their employers to break the law would be disciplined, so as to strengthen the position of in-house lawyers telling their employers that certain conduct would be illegal. The Commission's position is unconvincing because, as far as is known, the Commission has never complained to any Bar or lawyers' organisation about any lawyer, independent or employed, who was thought to have helped a client to break the law. The Commission's position is also weakened by the fact that it has not consistently put pressure on the CCBE to get its member organisations to confirm that their rules make it unethical knowingly to help a client to break the law, or to mislead the Commission or any national competition authority. With ten or more new Member States, with Bar rules which are no clearer than those of the other Member States, it is time for the Commission to adopt a clear and constructive policy on these issues.

4. NON-EUROPEAN UNION LAWYERS

Analogous but rather different considerations apply to non-EU lawyers (or, more accurately, to non-EEA lawyers: presumably the Community confidentiality rule applies to communications with lawyers qualified to practise in the EEA States). If, as is suggested here, it is a necessary condition for confidentiality to apply that the lawyer is bound by the two rules of professional ethics mentioned above, and is subject to effective professional discipline, then communications with a non-EU lawyer who was not so bound would not be confidential. But if a non-EU lawyer is bound by rules of ethics which are clearer in these respects than those of some of the Bars of EU Member States, and to at least as strict a professional discipline, it is not easy to see why the non-EU lawyer's communications should not be confidential also. There seem to be only two possible reasons. The first is that EU lawyers communications might not be treated as confidential in the non-EU country, so that reciprocity was not given. Since this does not seem to be true of the USA, the most important non-EU country in this context, that sounds like an excuse for inaction rather than the real reason. The second possible reason is that EU Member States, but not non-EU countries, have duties under EU law which apply even when they have in effect delegated to lawyers' professional organisations some of the responsibility for regulating the profession.[2] This also sounds like an excuse: the Commission has never called on any Member State to do anything to enforce principles of professional ethics in this context, in spite of the fact that the Commission claims to be aware of some cases of unprofessional conduct.

---

[2] See in this connection Case C–309/99 *Wouters v. Nederlandse Orde van Advocaten* [2002] ECR I–1577.

On this question also, the European institutions should consider what solution is best calculated in the long term to maximise voluntary compliance with EU competition law. Non-EU lawyers often have occasion to give advice on EU competition law, usually in the course of advising on their own national laws. They are less likely than EU lawyers to give advice when they are not well enough informed to do so. But US lawyers in particular are acutely conscious of the need to obey antitrust laws, since the penalties and costs of non-compliance (including triple damage actions) are more severe under US law than in Europe. They are therefore likely to be the allies of the Commission in informing companies of their duties under EU competition law. There is certainly no obvious competition policy reason why their advice should not be confidential.

5. ARE THERE UNADMITTED REASONS?

Apart from the Commission's prejudice against in house lawyers (which is almost certainly unjustified insofar as it applies to lawyers subject to rules of ethics and discipline at least as strict as those of some EU Bars) there may be several other reasons why the short-sighted policy of defending the illogical compromise set out in the *A M & S* judgment has lasted so long. One reason is, in short, protectionism: denying confidentiality to in-house lawyers and non-EU lawyers protects the interests of independent EU lawyers. This is certainly true, and this was one of the reasons why a tentative Commission proposal in the 1980s to extend confidentiality was unfavourably received. But that is not a valid competition policy reason to refuse confidentiality for these two classes of lawyers, provided that it is accompanied by suitable safeguards. Another reason is that it seems that some of the Bars of EU Member States do not, in fact, regard it as unprofessional to mislead a competition authority or knowingly to help a client to break the law, and the Bar or Bars in question are well aware that if this became clear, their lawyers' claim to confidentiality would be unjustified. This seems to be the only possible explanation for the CCBE's complete failure to respond to the Commission's long standing request for confirmation that all its member organisations regard these two kinds of conduct as unethical. It is certainly impossible to believe that none of the CCBE organisations knew whether they regard such conduct as unethical or not, and that none of them were able to make up their minds. The Commission may have been unwise in not asking the appropriate questions directly to the national Bars, which could hardly have failed to respond.

6. WHAT CAN BE DONE?

In the absence of any initiative from the Commission, and unless the issue is raised in the WTO as an obstacle to the provision of legal services in the EU by non-EU lawyers, there are several possible courses of action available to interested parties. The most obvious, of course, is for a company which has been required by the Commission to disclose communications with an in-house lawyer or a non-EU lawyer to challenge the Commission's decision under Article 230 EC Treaty, and argue in the Court of First Instance, and if necessary in the Court of Justice, that circumstances have now altered so much that confidentiality should now be regarded as applying to these kinds of lawyers. There are certainly lawyers who are ready and willing to act in proceedings of this kind, when a suitable case arises. If and when proceedings of this kind are brought, at least some lawyers' organisations may intervene in the case before the Court of First Instance, as they would be entitled to do. The fact that no such case has been brought so far may merely indicate that companies are reluctant to quarrel with the Commission over questions of principle when little is otherwise at stake. It may also mean that the Commission has exaggerated the problem, and that the Commission in practice rarely finds communications of kinds which it regards as non-confidential and which it wishes to use as evidence. Certainly, the Commission's suggestion that it would not use legal advice which it regards as non-confidential as a reason for increasing the amount of a fine is a wholly illogical compromise which cannot provide a long term solution.

It now appears that there is another procedure which might be used for this purpose, by an appropriate company. The Court of Justice has decided, in *Unión de Pequeños Agricultores*[3] that a private party which has no standing under Article 230 to challenge a Community Regulation may go before a national court, and that the national court must enable the private party to challenge any national decision based on the Community regulation in question. It therefore seems clear that if a national competition authority applying Community competition law decided to treat as non-confidential a communication with an in-house lawyer or with a non-EU lawyer, the national decision could be challenged in the national courts on the grounds that the national authority had acted incorrectly, and that Community law protects the confidentiality of these lawyers' communications after all. The national court would then refer to the Court of Justice under Article 234 the question whether the rule stated in the *A M & S* judgment should now be understood and applied differently. There are also strong arguments for saying that this kind of procedure should be available when there is no national decision to be challenged, but the private party is directly (though not 'individually') harmed by the Community measure. If these arguments are correct, it would seem to be open to a company with an in-house legal department in Europe concerned with, among other things, Community competition law to ask a national court for a declaration that communications with its in-house counsel were protected by confidentiality under Community law. The national court would then refer that question to the Court of Justice under Article 234.

---

[3] Case C–50/00 *Unión de Pequeños Agricultores* [2002] ECR I–6677.

7. NEW MEMBER STATES

Clarification of the rules of ethics and discipline needed to justify confidentiality for lawyer-client communications will be particularly necessary in those of the new Member States where the legal profession in its present form is comparatively recent, and where the relevant rules may not be as comprehensive as they are, or should be, in the present Member States. This is yet another reason why an initiative by someone, if the Commission declines to deal with any of these issues, is needed.

8. CONCLUSION

Nothing would be gained by bringing these issues before the Court again unless the Court altered its conclusions, as it might well do in the light of all the new considerations outlined here. No initiatives are to be expected from either the Commission or the CCBE. Members and former members of the Community Courts have informally and extra-judicially indicated that reconsideration was appropriate. It is surprising and unfortunate that the Commission's views have altered and become opposed to any extension of confidentiality, although the arguments for extending it have strengthened. Another lawyer with the stature and knowledge of David Edward is needed to convince the Courts that confidentiality should be extended, not merely to promote a more effective Community competition policy, but because, as David Edward argued twenty years ago, the freedom to consult the lawyer one chooses without creating admissible evidence is a fundamental human right in a society based on the rule of law.

13

Collective Dominance—The Contribution of The Community Courts

MARK CLOUGH QC

1. INTRODUCTION

THIS PAPER reviews the main case law of the European Court of Justice (*ECJ*) and Court of First Instance (*CFI*) on collective dominance. The topic has been selected in recognition of the major contribution to the decisions of both Courts by DAOE.[1] He launched the debate about the definition of the concept of collective dominance under Article 82 EC when the CFI confirmed the principle of collective dominance in its 1992 judgment in the *Flat Glass* case.[2] More recently, DAOE was the *Judge Rapporteur* in the leading judgment of the ECJ on collective dominance under Article 82 EC in the *Cewal* case.[3]

The concept of collective dominance under the EC Merger Regulation (*ECMR*) has been developed in parallel in the case law of the ECJ and CFI. In particular, the ECJ cited the *Kali & Salz* case[4] (where DAOE was a member of the Court) as a precedent in *Cewal*[5] and the CFI followed it in the *Gencor/Lonhro* case.[6] The CFI has now confirmed the economic tests required to be satisfied in order to establish collective dominance under the ECMR in the

---

[1] Judge David Edward QC CMG.
[2] Joined Cases T-68/89, T-77/89 and T-78/89 *Società Italiano Vetro SpA v. Commission* [1992] ECR II-1403, (hereafter, *Flat Glass*) para 358; DAOE was the President of the First Chamber and the *Judge Rapporteur*.
[3] Joined Cases C-395/96 P and C-396/96 P *Compagnie Maritime Belge SA, Compagnie Maritime Belge SA and Dafra –Lines A/S v. Commission* [2000] ECR I-1365, (hereafter *Cewal*) para 36, where the ECJ Fifth Chamber, of which DAOE was President, defined the concept of collective dominance under Art. 82 thus: 'a dominant position may be held by two or more economic entities legally independent of each other, provided that from an economic point of view they present themselves or act together on a particular market as a collective entity'.
[4] Joined Cases C-68/94 and C-30/95 *France and Others v Commission* [1998] ECR I–1375 (hereafter, *Kali & Salz*).
[5] *Cewal*, para 41.
[6] Case T-102/96 *Gencor Ltd v. Commission* [1999] ECR II–753 (hereafter, *Gencor*).

Airtours case[7] where the CFI has defined the concept of collective dominance under the ECMR in a way that is consistent with that of the ECJ in *Cewal*.[8]

The first part of this paper examines the development by the Community courts and the European Commission of the legal concept of collective dominance under Article 82 EC (Article 86 of the EC Treaty) from *Flat Glass*[9] to *Cewal*. The second part discusses the refinement of the approach to collective dominance by the Community courts and European Commission under Article 2 ECMR and the economic tests for establishing collective dominance in an oligopolist market from *Nestlé/Perrier*[10] to *Kali & Salz*, *Gencor* and *Airtours*.

There is much overlap in the case law under Article 82 EC and the ECMR suggesting that the principles applied in the most recent cases such as *Cewal*, *Gencor* and *Airtours*[11] will apply to the retrospective analysis under Article 82 as much as to the prospective assessment under the ECMR. However, while the prospective assessment inevitably requires more attention to the dynamic features of the market, the Court has applied a strict standard of forecasting under the ECMR which requires the prediction of uniform conduct or common policy to be 'sufficiently likely' on the basis of the structural features of the relevant market.[12]

2. COLLECTIVE DOMINANCE UNDER ARTICLE 82

This part analyses the judgments of the Community courts identifying the definition of collective dominance given in those decisions. By way of back-

---

[7] Case T-342/99 *Airtours plc* v. *Commission* [2002] ECR II–2585 (hereafter, *Airtours*).
[8] *Cewal*, at para 36.
[9] *First Glass*, at para 358.
[10] Case No.IV/M.190–*Nestlé/Perrier*, 22 July 1992 [1992] OJ L356/1.
[11] Above n7. See also: Case IV/M.1524–*Airtours/First Choice*, Commission Decision 2000/276/EC of 22 September 1999 [2000] OJ L93/1; P Chistensen and V Rabassa, 'The Airtours Decision: Is There a New Commission Approach to Collective Dominance?' 2001 ECLR 227; Briones and Padilla, 'The Complex Landscape of Oligopolies under EU Competition Policy—Is Collective Dominance Ripe for Guidelines?' [2001] 24 World Competition 307 at 308 *et seq.*; C Withers and M Jephcott, 'Where to now for E.C. oligopoly control?' 2001 ECLR 295 at 301 *et seq.*; M Motta, 'E.C. Merger Policy and the Airtours Case' 21 (2000) ECLR 199 at 204 *et seq.*; S Stroux, 'Is EC Oligopoly Control outgrowing Its Infancy?' World Competition 23 (2000) at 35 *et seq.*; B Etter, 'The Assessment of Mergers in the EC under the Concept of Collective Dominance: An Analysis of the Recent Decisions and Judgments—an Economic Approach' World Competition 23 (2000) 3, 103 at 133 *et seq.*; R Whish, *Competition Law* (Butterworths Tolley, 4th edn, 2001), at 490 *et seq.*
[12] *Kali & Salz*, at para 246. See, for discussion of the relevant economic principles: H Haupt 'Collective Dominance under Article 82 EC and EC Merger Control in the light of the Airtours Judgment' (2002) ECLR 434, at 435–36; and on the theory of oligopolistic interdependence, see Whish, above n17, at 460 *et seq*. In legal literature, the term 'tacit co-ordination' is used as a paraphrase for oligopolistic inerdependence in order to emphasise the distinction between non-collusive market interaction and 'explicit' collusion in the sense of Art. 81(1) E.C.: see Whish, above n17, at 459 and 462; see also Caffarra and Kühn, 'Joint Dominance: The CFI Judgment on Gencor/Lonrho' (1999) ECLR 355 at 356; P Christensen and V Rabassa, above n17, at 228.

ground, it starts with a short overview of the historical development of the concept in the Commission's practice, the wording of Article 82 EC, and the relationship between Articles 81 and 82.

Non-collusive parallel behaviour and the development of collective dominance

One of the reasons for the development of the concept of collective dominance was the limited scope for applying the concept of concerted practice under Article 81 EC (ex Article 85) to oligopolistic parallel behaviour. The Commission can generally only control such behaviour in situations where it can prove deliberate or express collusion. The well defined concept of concerted practice does not extend to non-collusive parallel behaviour in an oligopolistic market. The principle of collective dominance under Article 82 EC, therefore, where the conditions are satisfied, may fill the perceived gap in regulatory control.

In one early decision, *European Sugar Industry*, the Commission found that measures taken by three companies (Raffinerie Tirlemontoise, Suiker Unie and Centrale Suiker Maatsachappij) comprised infringements of Article 86 of the EC Treaty (now Article 82 EC). Certain behaviour, close co-operation in all activities together with a 85% market share of Suiker and Centrale, were found to constitute an abuse of a jointly held dominant position.[13] However, the development of the scope of the concept of collective dominance was blocked until the late 1980s due to the ECJ, which sought to maintain a distinction between the application of Articles 85 of the EC Treaty (now Article 81 EC) and 86 of the EC Treaty (now Article 82 EC) in, for instance, the *Zuchner* and *Hoffman-La Roche* cases.[14]

In the late 1980's, after a period of reticence with regard to the scope of collective dominance in the case law, the Commission raised the issue of collective dominance in its written observations in the *Alcatel* case.[15] The Commission submitted that where undertakings within the same group of undertakings adopt an agreement, decision or concerted practice amongst themselves, together they have the power to impede competition in a substantial part of the relevant market.[16] The Court did not reply, and it was not until the *Flat Glass case* that the concept of collective dominance was recognised by the Court.

---

[13] IV/26 918–*European Sugar Industry*, OJ 1973 L140/17.
[14] Case 172/80 *Zuchner* v. *Bayerische Vereinsbank AG* [1981] ECR 2021, para 10. The same approach can be found in Case 85/76 *Hoffman-La Roche* v. *Commission* [1979] ECR 461, para 39, where the Court held: 'a dominant position must also be distinguished from parallel courses of conduct which are peculiar to oligopolists in that in an oligopoly the courses of conduct interact, whilst in the case of an undertaking occupying a dominant position the conduct of the undertaking which derives profits from that position is to a great extent determined unilaterally' See also Case 40/73 *Suiker Unie* v. *Commission* [1975] ECR 1663.
[15] Case 247/86 *Alcatel* v. *Novasam* [1988] ECR 5987.
[16] Ibid, at 5993–5994.

Abuse by one or more undertakings

The *Flat Glass* case put to rest the linguistic disputes about the meaning of the provision in Article 82 that 'abuse by one or more undertakings' of a dominant position will be prohibited, confirming that it expressly provides for a situation where the dominant position is held by more than one undertaking.[17] The ECJ has also accepted the term collective dominance as the normal label for the concept.

Relationship between Articles 81 and 82: no recycling of Article 81 infringement

Articles 81 and 82 are entirely separate provisions. In order to find infringements of either prohibition it is necessary to assess the facts of any given situation by applying two different and distinct sets of rules. Neither the Treaty nor Community legislation preclude the application of both articles at the same time to the same facts.

In the *Almelo* case, the ECJ held that:

(a) Article 85 of the Treaty precludes the application, by a regional electricity distributor, of an exclusive purchasing clause contained in the general conditions of sale which prohibits a local distributor from importing electricity for public supply purposes and which, having regard to its economic and legal context, affects trade between Member States; and

(b) Article 86 of the Treaty precludes the application, by a regional electricity distributor where it belongs to a group of undertakings occupying a collective dominant position in a substantial part of the common market, of an exclusive purchasing clause contained in the general conditions of sale which prohibits a local distributor from importing electricity for public supply purposes and which, in view of its economic and legal context, affects trade between Member States.[18]

In *Flat Glass* the CFI, having found an infringement of Article 85 of the EC Treaty (now Article 81 EC), went on to say that '[t]here is nothing, in principle, to prevent two or more independent economic entities from being, on a specific market, united by such economic links that, by virtue of that fact, together they hold a dominant position vis-à-vis the other operators on the market.'[19] The CFI found support for this view in the wording of Article 8(2) of Council Regulation 4056/86 which provides that 'the conduct of a liner conference

---

[17] *Flat Glass* at para 358.
[18] Case C-393/92 *Almelo and others* v. *NV Energiebedrijf Ijsselmij* [1994] ECR I-1477, para 42; Case C-96/94 *Centro Servizi Spediporto Srl* v. *Spedizioni Marittima del Golfo Srl* [1995] ECR I-2883, para 33; and Joined Cases C-140/94, C-141/94 and C-142/94 *DIP SpA* v. *Comune di Bassano del Grappa and Comune di Chioggia* [1995] ECR I-3257, para 51.
[19] *Flat Glass*, at para 358.

benefiting from an exemption from a prohibition laid down by Article 85(1) EEC may have effects which are incompatible with Article 86 EEC.'[20]

These judgments clearly envisage the possibility of the abuse of a collective dominant position being established in parallel with an infringement of Article 81 on the basis of the same facts. Therefore, it is possible to establish an abuse of a collective dominant position on the basis of facts which also constitute an infringement of Article 81.

It is equally clear from the decisions in the CFI and ECJ in the *Flat Glass* and *Cewal* cases that the exception to finding infringements of both Articles 81 and 82 on the basis of the same facts is that of 'recycling' the Article 81 infringement.

The CFI in *Flat Glass* stated that 'for the purposes of establishing an infringement of Article 86 EEC, it is not sufficient . . . to **'recycle' the facts constituting an infringement of Article 85**, deducing from them the finding that the parties to an agreement or to an unlawful practice jointly hold a substantial share of the market, that **by virtue of that fact alone they hold a collective dominant position**, and that their unlawful behaviour constitutes an abuse of that collective dominant position' (emphasis added).[21] These words were repeated by the CFI in the *Cewal* case.[22] In other words, an infringement of Article 82 cannot be found solely on the basis of an infringement of Article 81 simply because the parties to the agreement have a high market share. That does not mean that such a situation excludes a finding of dominance or abuse. However, there has to be a further assessment of the specific market situation in order properly to establish the existence of a collective dominant position and, from there, an abuse of that collective dominant position.

In *Flat Glass* the CFI found that the Commission had not conducted a proper assessment of either the product or the geographical market in question[23] nor had the Commission substantiated the assertion that 'the undertakings present themselves on the market as a single entity and not as individuals'.[24] The CFI went on to say that 'even supposing the circumstances of the present case lend themselves to application of the concept of 'collective dominant position' (in the sense of a position of dominance held by a number of independent undertakings), the Commission has not adduced the necessary proof.'[25]

Therefore, in order to establish infringements of Article 82, on the basis of facts capable of constituting an infringement of Article 81, it is vital to show all of the individual elements required for establishing an infringement of Article 82 on its own, in addition to all of the elements of the infringement of Article 81. The ECJ has clarified the relationship between Articles 81 and 82 in the *Cewal* case, where it makes it clear that facts may be reused in establishing infringements

---

[20] Ibid, at para 359.
[21] Ibid, at para 360.
[22] *Cewal*, at para 67.
[23] *Flat Glass*, at paras 363–364.
[24] Ibid, at para 365.
[25] Ibid, at para 366.

of both prohibitions but (facts constituting) an infringement of Article 81 may not be reused to establish an infringement of Article 82, since the prohibitions, and the criteria for establishing an infringement of each, are entirely separate:

32. The second and third grounds of appeal, which should be examined together, relate essentially to the issue whether the Commission is entitled to base a finding that there is abuse of a dominant position solely on circumstances or facts which would constitute an agreement, decision or concerted practice under Article 85(1) of the Treaty, and therefore be automatically void unless exempted under Articles 85(3) of the Treaty.

33. It is clear from the very wording of Articles 85(1)(a), (b), (d) and (e) and 86(a) to (d) of the Treaty that the same practice may give rise to an infringement of both provisions. Simultaneous application of Articles 85 and 86 of the Treaty cannot therefore be ruled out a priori. However, the objectives pursued by each of those two provisions must be distinguished.

34. Article 85 of the Treaty applies to agreements, decisions and concerted practices which may appreciably affect trade between Member States, regardless of the position on the market of the undertakings concerned. Article 86 of the Treaty, on the other hand, deals with the conduct of one or more economic operators consisting in the abuse of a position of economic strength which enables the operator concerned to hinder the maintenance of effective competition on the relevant market by allowing it to behave to an appreciable extent independently of its competitors, its customers and, ultimately, consumers (see Case 322/81 *Michelin* v. *Commission* [1983] ECR 3461, paragraph 30).

35. In terms of Article 86 of the Treaty, a dominant position may be held by several 'undertakings'. The Court of Justice has held, on many occasions, that the concept of 'undertakings' in the chapter of the Treaty devoted to the rules on competition presupposes the economic independence of the entity concerned (see, in particular, Case 22/71 *Béguelin Import* v. *G.L. Import Export* [1971] ECR 949).

...

43. The mere fact that two or more undertakings are linked by an agreement, a decision of associations of undertakings or a concerted practice within the meaning of Article 85(1) of the Treaty does not, of itself, constitute a sufficient basis for such a finding.

44. On the other hand, an agreement, decision or concerted practice (whether or not covered by an exemption under Article 85(3) of the Treaty) may undoubtedly, where it is implemented, result in the undertakings concerned being so linked as to their conduct on a particular market that they present themselves on that market as a collective entity vis-à-vis their competitors, their trading partners and consumers.

45. The existence of a collective dominant position may therefore flow from the nature and terms of an agreement, from the way in which it is implemented and, consequently, from the links or factors which give rise to a connection between undertakings which result from it. Nevertheless, the existence of an agreement or of other links in law is not indispensable to a finding of a collective dominant position; such a finding may be based on other connecting factors and would depend on an economic assessment and, in particular, on an assessment of the structure of the market in question.

Article 82 collective dominance case law and the definition of 'economic links'

In 1988 the Commission adopted the Flat Glass decision, in which it considered that the producers had a collective dominant position by maintaining very close and structural links in respect of production through systematic exchange of products. In the *Flat Glass* judgment,[26] the CFI accepted for the first time the concept of 'collective dominance' under Article 86 of the EC Treaty (now Article 82 EC). The Commission Decision alleged that the three producers held a 'collective dominant position' whereby they enjoyed a degree of independence from competitive pressure that enabled them to impede the maintenance of effective competition, notably by not having to take account of the behaviour of the other market operators.[27] The CFI broke new ground in accepting the concept of collective dominance.

The Court held that two or more independent economic entities may be united by economic links and together hold a dominant position in relation to other participants on a specific market.[28] However, as the Commission did not adduce the necessary evidence, the CFI annulled the decision.[29]

The *Almelo* case[30] concerned the question of whether the regional electricity distributors in the Netherlands held a collective dominant position on the market for the public supply of electricity in the Netherlands to local distributors. The ECJ found that independent licensees could be considered as being collectively dominant. The ECJ's conclusion in *Almelo* was that in order for a collective dominant position to exist, the undertakings in the group have to be linked in such a way that they adopt the same conduct on the market. Apart from suggesting that these links should be 'sufficiently strong',[31] the ECJ did not discuss whether the links must be 'economic' links, as required by *Flat Glass*.

The same view is found in a later case, *La Crespelle*.[32] This case concerned the question whether French insemination centres acting in their own territories and exercising their exclusive rights to store semen and carry out insemination had abused their dominant position by charging additional costs to users who requested them to supply semen from insemination centres in other Member States.

---

[26] *Flat Glass*, at para 358. For comment on the *Flat Glass* judgment, see D Pope, 'Some reflexions on Italian Flat Glass' (1993) ECLR 172.

[27] Point 78 of the Decision.

[28] This situation is distinguished from Case 30/87 *Bodson* v. *SA Pompes funèbres des regions libérées* [1988] ECR 2479, in which the ECJ held that agreements between undertakings belonging to the same group do not fall within the scope of Article 85(1).

[29] The CFI overturned the Commission's decision on the ground that there were insufficiencies in the definition of the relevant market; *Flat Glass* at para 330.

[30] Above n18.

[31] Ibid, at para 43. For comment on the *Almelo* case, see L Hancher 'Case C-393/92' (1995) CMLR 32, at 305.

[32] Case C-323/93 *Société Civile Agricole du Centre d'Insémination de la Crespelle* v. *Coopérative d'Elevage et d'Insémination Artificielle du Département de la Mayenne* [1994] ECR I-5077. This case, like the *Almelo* case, also raised Article 90 issues.

In the joined cases *DIP* v. *Comune di Bassano del Grappa and others*,[33] the ECJ ruled that national Italian legislation requiring the licensing of retail outlets did not violate Articles 30, 85 and 86. (The Commission considered that the retailers, which held trading licences, did not limit competition between themselves, and since the application of the relevant Italian law was always at a local level there was no dominant position in a substantial part of the Common market). The ECJ referred to paragraph 42 in *Almelo*, stating that undertakings must be linked in such a way that they adopt the same conduct on the market without further developing the definition of links.[34]

The *Bosman*[35] case deals with issues concerning the application of Articles 48, 85 and 86 of the EC Treaty to the rules on foreign football players and the rules on transfers of football players to other Member States. In this case, Advocate General Lenz raised the concept of collective dominance when considering whether professional clubs in the Community together occupy a dominant position and whether this position could be assessed collectively. The Advocate General stated that it could very well be assumed that professional football league clubs are united by such economic links referred to in the *Flat Glass* case and that together they are to be regarded as having a dominant position.[36] As the ECJ found the relevant rules to be contrary to Article 48, it did not find it necessary to rule on the interpretation of Articles 85 and 86.[37]

The importance of the *Flat Glass* judgment for liner conferences and shipping is illustrated by the four Commission decisions relating to maritime transport, in which the concept of collective dominance is applied: *French-West African Shipowners' Committees*, *Cewal*, *Rødby* and the *TACA* decision.

French-West African Shipowners' Committees

In the *French-West African Shipowners' Committees* decision, the Commission considered that the dominant position held by the shipping companies that were members of the Committees had to be assessed collectively because of structural links between the companies and the methods of sharing business and control of cargo. These two elements had the effect of eliminating all effective competition within the Committees and the Commission concluded that the members were collectively dominant.[38]

---

[33] Above n18.
[34] Ibid, at para 26.
[35] Case C-415/93 *Union Royale belge des sociétés de football association, ASBL* v. *Jean-Marc Bosman* [1995] ECR I-4921.
[36] Ibid, Opinion of Advocate General Lenz, at paras 283–85.
[37] Ibid, Judgment, at para 138.
[38] IV/32.450—*French-West African shipowners' committees*, OJ 1992 L 134/1.

Rødby

The Rødby decision related to the application of Article 90(1) of the EC Treaty (now Article 86(1) EC) and a refusal to grant access to the port and the route of Rødby. The Commission held that the two ferry companies who operated services on the Rødby-Puttgarden route were jointly dominant where they co-ordinated their timetables, fixed common rates and undertook joint marketing for the service. According to the Commission, the joint operation of the Rødby-Puttgarden service was sufficient to constitute the requisite economic link for the purposes of a joint dominance assessment.[39]

TACA

In the TACA decision,[40] the Commission imposed fines (totalling ECU 273 million) on the parties to the Trans-Atlantic Conference Agreement (TACA). The parties to the TACA, who had a joint market share exceeding 60%,[41] applied in 1994 for an exemption under Article 85(3). The Commission decided that the TACA did not qualify for the liner conference block exemption under Regulation 4056/86, nor for the individual exemption sought.

It also held that the TACA parties had abused their joint dominant position in two ways. First, by restricting the availability of individual service contracts. Individual contracts were openly banned by the TACA parties in 1995 and even after 1995 all service contracts were only available under highly restrictive conditions. Second, by actively discouraging independent market entry by potential competitors and coercing them to join the TACA, they thereby altered the competitive structure of the market. This was achieved particularly through agreements with shipping lines which were not traditionally conference members which were allowed to charge a lower price in service contracts than the price charged by the traditional conference members. According to the Commission, the purpose and effect of the TACA's entering into dual rate service contracts was to limit competition from independent shipowners by bringing them inside the conference.[42]

In the TACA decision, the Commission analyses the concept of collective dominance and gives concrete examples of the economic links between the TACA parties. Referring to *Flat Glass* and the *Cewal* case, the Commission states that the CFI has:

---

[39] Commission Decision of 21 December 1993 concerning a refusal to grant access to the facilities of the port of Rødby (Denmark), OJ 1994 L 55/52.

[40] Commission Decision of 16 September 1998 relating to a proceeding pursuant to Articles 85 and 86 of the EC Treaty (Case No IV/35.134–Trans-Atlantic Conference Agreement 'TACA') (notified under document number C(1998)2617), OJ 1999 L 95/1.

[41] Ibid, at paras 85–88. Such a large market share gives rise to a strong presumption of a dominant position according to the Commission (ibid, at para 534).

[42] Commission press release, IP/98/811, 16 September 1998.

confirmed that liner shipping conferences are an example of agreements between economically independent entities which enable economic links to be formed that can give those entities jointly a dominant position in relation to other operators on the same market and found support for that conclusion in the wording of Article 8 of Regulation 4056/86.[43]

The considerable number of economic links that support the finding of a collective dominant position between the TACA parties are, according to the Commission, the following:

(i) a requirement to adhere to a tariff, the failure of which can result in civil liabilities;
(ii) extensive enforcement provisions, including the setting up of an enforcement authority which surveys the duties of the parties, which has total access to all documents and which is authorised to impose fines for any breach of the agreement. Also, policing in the form of the payment of substantial guarantees and fines for exceeding quotas;
(iii) adoption of measures which are intended to present the TACA parties as a single united body, for instance the important rôle of the TACA secretariat and the publication of annual business plans; and
(iv) reinforcement of the economic links between the TACA parties by the economic links between individual TACA parties resulting from their various consortia arrangements.[44]

Cewal

Following receipt of several complaints, the Commission opened an inquiry into the practices of the various liner conferences involved in trade between the Community and West African ports. In its decision, the Commission concluded that the Cewal liner conference and its individual members had abused their joint dominant position.[45]

The Commission considered that the members of the Cewal conference had abused their collective dominant position in the following three ways:

(i) by implementing a co-operation agreement with the Zairean shipping authority, Ogefrem, which required all goods shipped between Cewal ports to be carried by Cewal members;
(ii) by using 'fighting ships' to undermine the only independent competitor, which involved lowering the conference's freight rates in order to compete with those charged by the independent competitor for ships sailing on the same or similar dates; and
(iii) by using loyalty contracts, imposing certain contract terms and thus requiring customers to accept a loyalty obligation and establishing black lists of 'disloyal shippers'.[46]

[43] TACA decision, above n40, at para 521.
[44] Ibid, at paras 526–531.
[45] Decision 93/82/EEC, OJ 1993 L 34/20.
[46] See the Commission's own summary of the *Cewal* Decision, and paras 70–91 and 523–24 of the *TACA* Decision. For an analytical comment, see P Treacy and T Feaster, 'Compagnie Maritime Belge SA & Others v. Commission' [1997] ECLR 467.

An action for annulment of the Cewal decision was brought by *Compagnie Maritime Belge SA and others*[47] against the Commission. The CFI found that three liner shipping conferences, Cewal, Cowac and Ukwal, had infringed Article 85(1) and that the members of Cewal had abused their collectively held dominant position contrary to Article 86.[48]

Given the links between the shipping companies, the CFI agreed with the Commission that the parties' dominant position had to be assessed collectively and that the shipping companies presented themselves as a single entity on the relevant market adopting the same conduct and acting unilaterally in order to eliminate competition.[49]

In the light of the Decision as a whole the CFI stated that the Commission had 'sufficiently shown that it was necessary to assess the position of the Cewal members on the relevant market collectively'.[50] The CFI went on to repeat the prohibition against 'recycling' contained in *Flat Glass*, and said that 'quite apart from the arrangements concluded between the shipping companies creating the Cewal conference . . . there were links between the companies such that they **adopted uniform conduct on the market**' and 'The Commission was fully entitled to consider that Article 86 could apply, subject only to the other requirements laid down by that provision being met.'[51]

A further appeal to the ECJ concerning the CFI's judgment on the infringement of Article 86 was brought on behalf of Cewal etc, *Compagnie Maritime Belge NV and Dafra-Lines v. Commission*,[52] presenting the Court with its first opportunity to consider the application of the competition rules to conference shipping lines. In his opinion, Advocate General Fennelly rejected the parties' arguments on the substance but recommended that the fines should be lifted as a result of procedural irregularities.[53]

According to Advocate General Fennelly, the *Almelo* case contained the clearest statement to date on the concept of collective dominance (undertakings . . . must be linked in such a way that they adopt the same conduct on the market). Referring to *Ahmed Saeed*,[54] he concluded that such conduct may in principle infringe both Articles 85 of the EC Treaty (now Article 81 EC) and 86 of the EC Treaty (now Article 82 EC), although it is not sufficient to support a

---

[47] Joined Cases T-24/93, T-25/93, T-26/93 and T-28/93, [1996] ECR II-1201; on appeal to the ECJ, see Joined Cases C-395/96P and C-396/96P.

[48] Articles 85 and 86 apply to maritime transport by virtue of Council Regulation 4056/86 which lays down substantive and procedural rules for the application of Article 85 and 86 to maritime transport services. Article 8 of the Regulation provides that the abuse of a dominant position within the meaning of Article 86 shall be prohibited without any prior decision.

[49] Joined Cases T-24-26/93 and T-28/93, above n47, at para 67.

[50] Ibid, at para 66.

[51] Ibid, at para 67.

[52] *Cewal*, above n3. See also Opinion of Advocate General Fennelly delivered on 29 October 1998.

[53] Ibid, at para 197.

[54] Case 66/86 *Ahmed Saeed Flugreisen and others v. Zentrale zur Bekämpfung unlauteren Wettbewerbs e.V.* [1989] ECR 803, para 37; *Cewal* Opinion, at para 22.

finding of a collective dominant position with a finding of concerted behaviour. Where sufficient economic links are established, he said independent firms may be collectively dominant when acting on the market as a single entity.[55]

Advocate General Fennelly took the analysis of links further than the previous case law by giving the following examples of economic links which are to be defined by establishing a situation where a group of independent undertakings act as a single market entity:

- use of model conditions of supply drawn up by a common trade association;
- cross-share holdings, common directorships or even family links with economic consequences;
- pursuit of a common marketing strategy or sales policy;
- the links found by the CFI which each constitute an economic link *with the result that Cewal presented itself on the market as one single entity*: the committees of Cewal members, the common structure to define and apply uniform freight rates; and
- the absence of competition.[56]

Advocate General Fennelly supported dismissing the appeal against the findings of collective dominance, rejecting the claim that the reasoning of the Commission did not establish that the members of Cewal behaved as a single or common entity on the market concerned, even though it did not address more explicitly the issue of economic links.[57]

Links and other connecting factors

In *Flat Glass*[58] the CFI had confirmed for the first time that one or more legally independent economic undertakings could enjoy a position of dominance within the meaning of Article 82 EC collectively if they were 'united by such economic links'.[59] However, the CFI did not address the issue as to whether 'economic links' were limited to an agreement or other links in law, or could depend on an economic assessment of other connecting factors, including the structure of the market in question, which would allow the court to recognise the concept of 'oligopolistic inter-dependence'.

In the *Cewal* case, the ECJ defined the legal concept of collective dominance under Article 86 of the EC Treaty (now Article 82 EC) as 'a dominant position . . . held by two or more economic entities legally independent of each other, provided that from an economic point of view they present themselves or act together on a particular market as a collective entity. That is how the expression

---

[55] *Cewal* Opinion, at paras 23 and 28–29.
[56] Ibid, at paras 31–32 and 34.
[57] Ibid, at paras 41–42.
[58] *First Glass*, at para 358.
[59] Ibid, at para 358.

'collective dominant position' as used in the remainder of this judgment, should be understood.'[60]

The court continued by indicating that 'a finding that two or more undertakings hold a collective dominant position must, in principle, proceed upon an economic assessment of the position on the relevant market of the undertakings concerned, prior to any examination of the question whether those undertakings have abused their position on the market.'[61]

It is necessary, therefore, first 'to consider whether the undertakings concerned together constitute a collective entity vis-à-vis, their competitors, their trading partners and consumers on a particular market. It is only where that question is answered in the affirmative that it is appropriate to consider whether that collective entity actually holds a dominant position and whether its conduct constitutes abuse.'[62]

The ECJ then explains how to satisfy the test relating to a 'collective entity':

> In order to establish the existence of a collective entity as defined above, it is necessary to examine the economic links or factors which give rise to a connection between the undertakings concerned (see *inter alia*, Case C-393/92 *Almelo* [1994] ECR I–1477, paragraph 43, and Joined Cases C-68/94 and C-30/95 *France and Others* v. *Commission* [1998] ECR 1–1375, paragraph 221).[63]

On the one hand, the mere fact that two or more undertakings are linked by an agreement, a decision of associations of undertakings or a concerted practice within the meaning of Article 85 (1) of the EC Treaty (now Article 81(1) EC) does not, of itself, constitute a sufficient basis for such a finding. On the other hand, an agreement, decision or concerted practice (whether or not covered by an exemption under Article 85(3) of the Treaty (now Article 81(3) EC) may undoubtedly, where it is implemented, result in the undertakings concerned being so linked as to their conduct on a particular market that they present themselves on that market as a collective entity vis-à-vis their competitors, their trading partners and consumers.

The Court recognises the importance of the existence of an agreement or other links in law since it held that 'the existence of a collective dominant position may therefore flow from the nature and terms of an agreement, and the way it is implemented, consequently from the links or factors which give rise to a connection between undertakings which result from it.' However, the Court equally makes it clear that such links are 'not indispensable to a finding of a collective dominant position; such a finding may be based on other connecting factors and would depend on an economic assessment and, in particular, on an assessment of the structure of the market in question.'[64]

---

[60] *Cewal*, at para 36.
[61] Ibid, at para 38.
[62] Ibid, at para 39.
[63] Ibid, at para 41.
[64] Ibid, at para 45.

The reference to the *Kali & Salz* case endorses the importance of factors giving rise to a connection between the undertakings concerned which are able to adopt a 'common policy on the market' and adopts the test used by the ECJ in the context of the ECMR.

It follows that a collective dominant position may be established by a connecting factor which causes the undertakings either to present themselves on the market as a collective entity or to behave on the market as a collective entity. This approach, which is based on the economic links or factors having the result or effects of collective dominance, supports the extension of the concept of collective dominance to the members of a tight oligopoly, even if there are no contractual or structural links between them. Further, the ECJ's reference to the *Kali & Salz* judgment indicates that the Court considers the test under Article 82 EC to be the same as that under Article 2 ECMR, subject (presumably) to the difference between retrospective and prospective assessments. It is not surprising, therefore, that while there has been no case in the context of Article 82 in which the Community courts or European Commission have considered the connecting factor required for collective dominance as existing solely in oligopolistic market interaction, the CFI has extended the concept of collective dominance to a tight oligopoly under the ECMR.[65] In the *Gencor* case, the CFI justified the extension in the following way:

> There is no reason whatsoever in legal or economic terms to exclude from the notion of economic links the relationship of interdependence existing between the parties to a tight oligopoly within which, in a market with the appropriate characteristics, in particular in terms of market concentration, transparency and product homogeneity, those parties are in a position to anticipate one another's behaviour and are therefore strongly encouraged to align their conduct on the market, in particular in such a way as to maximise their joint profits by restricting production with a view to increasing prices. In such a context, each trader is aware that highly competitive action on its part designed to increase its market share (for example, a price cut) would provoke identical action by the others, so that it would derive no benefit from its initiative. All the traders would thus be affected by the reduction in price levels.[66]

Members of a tight oligopoly, therefore, may be linked by structural factors revealed by an assessment of the market structure and found to be collectively dominant because their reactions to the market structure are likely to make their impact on the market as a collective entity.[67] As the CFI recognised in the *Gencor* case, in an oligopoly 'each undertaking may become aware of common interests and, in particular, cause prices to increase without having to enter into an agreement or resort to a concerted practice.'[68]

The following can be said to be the three requirements for the abuse of a collective dominant position under Article 82 EC, in the light of the case law:

---

[65] *Gencor*.
[66] Ibid, at para 276.
[67] G Monti, 'The Scope of Collective Dominance under Article 82 EC' (2001) 38 CML Rev 131.
[68] *Gencor*, at para 276.

(i) it is necessary to consider whether the undertakings concerned together constitute a collective entity with regard to their competitors, their trading partners and consumers on a particular market. To establish the existence of a collective entity, it is necessary to examine the economic links or factors which give rise to a connection between the undertakings concerned. In particular, it should be possible to demonstrate the absence of effective internal competition between the legally independent economic entities, which will be the case if they act as a collective entity on the relevant market due to the economic links existing between them. The economic links or factors may flow from the nature and terms of an agreement, from the way in which it is implemented and from other links or factors which give rise to an internal connection between the undertakings which result from it, such as the inter-dependence in a tight oligopoly;[69]

(ii) the collective entity must be shown to enjoy a dominant position in accordance with the general criteria for establishing dominance, and in particular it must be shown that there is no external competition with their competitors, trading partners or consumers on a particular market. It is necessary, therefore, to assess whether the undertakings concerned have the power to behave to an appreciable extent independently of their competitors, their customers and, ultimately, their consumers;[70]

(iii) third, there must be convincing evidence of an abuse of the collective dominant position so established.[71]

1. COLLECTIVE DOMINANCE UNDER THE ECMR

The Commission has considered the existence of a collective dominant position in over 80 merger cases[72] starting with the decision in *Nestlé/Perrier*.[73] Other

---

[69] *Cewal*, at paras 36,39,41 and 45.
[70] *Flat Glass* at para 358 regarding the ECJ's general formula for market dominance in Case 85/76 *Hoffman La Roche v. Commission* [1979] ECR 461 at paras 38 and 48.
[71] H Haupt, above n12.
[72] For example, Case IV/M.619 *Gencor/Lonrho*, 24 April 1996, OJ (1997) L11/30, [1999] 4 CMLR 1076; Case IV/M.1524 *Airtours/First Choice*, 22 September 1999, OJ (2000) L93/1, [2000] 5 CMLR 494; Case COMP/M.1741 *MCI WorldCom/Sprint*, 28 June 2000, [2000] 5 CMLR 198; Case COMP/M.2097 *SCA/Metsä Tissue*, 31 January 2001, OJ (2002) L57/1.
[73] Case IV/M.190 *Nestlé/Perrier*, 22 July 1992, OJ L56/1, point 108 *et seq*. See also Case IV/M.308 *Kali & Salz/MdK/Trehand*, 14 December 1993, OJ (1994) L186/38; Case IV/M.358 *Pilkington-Techint/SIV*, 21 December 1993, OJ (1994) L158/24; Case IV/M.315 *Mannesmann/Vallourec/Ilva*, 31 January 1994, OJ L102/15; Case IV/M.484 *Krupp/Thyssen/Riva/Falck/Tadfin/AST*, 21 December 1994 OJ (1995) L251/18; Case IV/M.477 *Mercedes-Benz/Kässbohrer*, 14 February 1995, OJ L211/1; Case IV/M.580 *ABB/Daimler-Benz*, 18 October 1995, OJ (1997) L11/1; Case IV/M.603 *Crown Cork & Seal/CarnaudMetalbox*, 14 November 1995, OJ (1996) L75/38; Case IV/M.1016 *Price Waterhouse/Coopers & Lybrand*, 20 May 1998, OJ (1999) L509/27; Case IV/M.1225 *Enso/Stora*, 25 November 1998, OJ (1999) L254/9; Case IV/M/ 1313 *Danish Crown/Vesjyske Slagterier*, 9 March 1999, OJ (2000) L20/1; Case IV/M.1532 *BP Amoco/Arco*, 29 September 1999, OJ (2000) L18/1; Case IV/M.1383 *Exxon/Mobil*, 29 September 1999 (not yet published); Case COMP/M.1663 *Alcan/Alusuisse*, 14 March 2000, OJ (2002) L90/1; Case COMP/M. 1673 *VEBA/VIAG*, 13 June 2000, OJ (2001) L188/1; Case COMP/M.1882 *Mobil/JV Dissolution*, 2 February 2000, OJ C112/6; Case COMP/M.2201 *MAN/Auwärter*, 20 June 2001, OJ (2002) L116/35; Case COMP/M.2314 *BASF/Eurodiol/Pantochim*, 11 July 2001, OJ (2002) L132/45; Case COMP/M.2434 *Grupo Villar Mir/EnBW/Hidroeléctrica del Cantábrico*, 26 September 2001; Case COMP/M.2498

key decisions include *Price Waterhouse and Coopers & Lybrand*[74] and the second *Kali & Salz* decision in 1998 replacing its previous 1993 decision annulled by the ECJ in *France* v. *Commission*.[75] The Commission and the CFI have also dealt with this issue in *Gencor/Lonhro*.[76] The *Kali & Salz*[77] and *Gencor*[78] cases have made an important contribution to the debate about collective dominance under Article 2, ECMR, paving the way for the landmark CFI judgment in *Airtours*.

In these cases, the Commission has applied the concept of collective dominance to 'structural' situations of market dominance in merger cases. The *Nestlé/Perrier* decision concerned a merger in the market of bottled still and sparkling water. The Commission obliged Nestlé to sell brands amounting in total to 20% of the combined capacity of Nestlé before authorising the merger. The Commission stated that the 'ECMR' applies to oligopolistic as well as to single firm dominance in cases where effective competition on the market is significantly impeded.[79]

In the merger between Price Waterhouse and Coopers & Lybrand, the Commission assessed whether it resulted in collective as well as single dominance. With regard to collective dominance, the Commission found that the relevant market was characterised by elements which indicated collective dominance such as slow demand growth and relative insensitivity to price, the homogenous nature of the service, a transparent market characterised by a low rate of innovation, interlinking of suppliers via self-regulatory professional organisations, and the tendency to lock clients in to auditors for long periods

---

UPM-Kymmene/Haindl, 21 November 2001, OJ (2002) L233/38; COMP/MDEA2499 *Norske Skog/Parenco/Walsum,* 21 November 2001, OJ (2002) L233/38; Case COMP/M.2389 *Shell/DEA,* 20 December 2001, OJ (2003) L15/35; COMP/M.2533 *BP/E.ON* 20 December 2001, OJ (2002) L276/31.

[74] Commission press release, IP/98/454.

[75] *Kali and Salz/Mdk/Treuhand,* above n73. On 9 July 1998, the Commission decided to clear the concentration on the basis of a second examination of it after the earlier decision from 1993 was annulled by the ECJ in, Case C-68/94, of 31 March 1998.

[76] *Gencor,* above n6.

[77] Above n4. See also González-Díaz, 'Recent Developments in EC Merger Control Law—The Gencor Judgment'; Korah, 'Gencor v. Commission: Collective Dominance' [1999] ECLR 337; Caffarra and Kühn, above n12; Elliott, 'The Gencor judgment: collective dominance, remedies and extraterritoriality under the Merger Regulation' (1999) 24 ELRev. 638; Christensen and Owen, 'Comment on the Judgment of the CFI of 25 March 1999 in the merger case IV/Sache M.619–Gencor/Lonrho' (1999) Competition Policy Newsletter 19; Bavasso, 'Gencor: A Judicial Review of the Commission's Policy and Practice—Many Lights and Some Shadows' *World Competition* 22 (1999) 45; Stroux, above n11, 34 et seq.; Etter, above n11, at 131 *et seq.*; Briones and Padilla, above n11, at 316 *et seq.*; Whish, above n11, at 487 et seq.

[78] Above n6. See also Venit, 'Two steps forward and no steps back; Economic analysis and oligopolistic dominance after Kali & Salz' (1998) 35 CML Rev 110; García Pérez, 'Collective Dominance under the Merger Regulation' (1998) 23 EL Rev 475; Ysewyn and Caffarra, 'Two's Company, Three's a Crowd: The Future of Collective Dominance after the Kali & Salz Judgment' (1998) ECLR 468; Bishop, 'Power and Responsibility: The ECJ's Kali-Salz Judgment' [1999] ECLR 37; Stroux, 30 et seq.; Etter, above n11, at 127 et seq.; Briones and Padilla, above n11, at 315 *et seq.*; Whish, above n11, at 484 *et seq.*

[79] For a comment on the decision, see JF Briones Alonso 'Economic Assessment of Oligopolies under the Community Merger Control Regulation' (1993) ECLR 118.

because of significant switching costs. However, despite these market characteristics, the Commission held that there was no conclusive evidence that the merger strengthened a position of collective dominance and cleared the merger.[80]

In *Kali & Salz*, the ECJ considered whether a proposed concentration would result in a collective dominant position on the market for potash-salt-based products for agricultural use. The test applied by the ECJ was to assess whether the concentration would lead to a situation in which effective competition was significantly impeded because of factors giving rise to a connection between the undertakings concerned which were capable of adopting a common policy on the market and acting to a significant extent independently of their competitors. The Court found, when applying this test, that some of the applicants' criticisms of the supposed structural links relied upon by the Commission were well founded.[81]

In its judgment, the ECJ confirmed that the concept of collective dominance is applicable to analysis under the ECMR,[82] stating that it is necessary to assess whether effective competition is impeded because of 'correlative factors' which exist between the parties, which make them adopt a common policy and not act independently. The ECJ ruled that the Commission's evidence of structural links was not sufficient to establish to the 'necessary legal standard that the concentration would give rise to a collective dominant position liable to impede significantly effective competition in the relevant market.'[83] In particular, the following findings were not sufficiently well established:

(i) a causal link between K+S and SCPA's membership of the export cartel and their anticompetitive behaviour on the relevant market; and
(ii) the specific distribution link alleged between K+S and SCPA relating to supplies by K+S in France since it only concerned a product not forming part of the relevant product market and it is thus apparent that the parties did not have a privileged relationship for the distribution of potash-based products.[84]

In the light of the ECJ judgment, the fact that K+S was active as an independent competitor in the French market, and that the combined market share of K+S and SCPA had fallen to below 50%, the Commission cleared the concentration on 9 July 1998.[85]

Starting with the *Nestlé/Perrier* decision, the Commission has in a number of decisions considered that a concept of collective dominance was included in the ECMR in the absence of its explicit exclusion. This has now been confirmed by the CFI in *Gencor*.

[80] Commission press release, IP/98/454.
[81] *Kali & Salz*; above n4 and see Advocate General Fennelly's Opinion in *Cewal*, above n3, at para 26.
[82] *Kali & Salz*, at paras 220–21.
[83] Ibid, at paras 221 and 249.
[84] Ibid, at paras 227–231.
[85] Case No. IV/M.208–*Kali & Salz/MDK/Trenhand*, OJ 1998 C 275/3.

The Commission examined the possible creation or strengthening of collective dominance in its decision on *Gencor/Lonrho*, which concerned the platinum market.[86] The Commission rejected a merger between the two companies because it considered that such an operation would involve the creation of a duopoly dominating the world markets for platinum and rhodium, for the following reasons:

(i) the merger would have enabled Gencor and Lonrho to be equal in the platinum market (28%) with the other South African group, Amplats (Anglo American Platinum Corporation, 35%), with Russia being a major supplier (23%). Together, the South African groups control 90% of the world platinum market;
(ii) PGMs (platinum, palladium, rhodium, iridium, ruthenium and osmium) are not sufficiently interchangeable to be considered to form a single product market and therefore each PGM by itself constitutes a product market;
(iii) the world platinum and rhodium markets are characterised by product homogeneity, high market transparency, price-inelastic demand in the current price range, moderate growth in demand, mature production technology, high entry barriers, a high level of concentration of undertakings, financial links and contacts between suppliers on a number of markets, a lack of negotiating power for purchasers, and a low level of competition with only a few elements of competition in the past;
(iv) following the operation, Implats/LPD and Amplats would have similar cost structures;
(v) the concentration would definitively remove the competitive threat previously posed by LPD in the market;
(vi) following the concentration, Russia would be only a minor player in the market;
(vii) the sources of supply outside the oligopoly would not be able to thwart the economic power of the duopoly comprising Implats/LPD and Amplats; and
(viii) new entrants in the platinum and rhodium markets were unlikely.

The CFI upheld the Commission Decision in a leading judgment on the concept of collective dominance and mergers.

In particular, the CFI has assessed whether Article 2 ECMR is applicable to concentrations which create or strengthen a collective dominant position. According to the CFI, the question is whether the words 'dominant position' in Article 2(3) cover only an individual dominant position, or also refer to a collective dominant position. Referring to *Kali & Salz*, the CFI held that in view of the neutral nature of the wording in Article 2 and the general scheme of the ECMR, the scope of the Article covers both an individual and a collective dominant position.[87] Further, the Commission's competence to control the anticompetitive behaviour of members of an oligopoly under Article 86 of the EC

---

[86] Commission Decision *Gencor/Lonrho* of 24 April 1996, OJ 1996 L11/30.
[87] *Gencor*, paras 124–126 and 132. The CFI refers to Case 11/76 *Netherlands* v. *Commission* [1979] ECR 245, at para 6, Joined Cases C-267/95 and C-268/95 *Merck & Co. Inc. and Others* v. *Primecrown and others* [1996] ECR I-6285, at paras 19–25; and *Kali & Salz*, at para 168.

Treaty (now Article 82 EC), did not raise doubts about the applicability of the ECMR to cases of collective dominance resulting from a concentration.[88]

The CFI, referring to *Kali & Salz*, stated that in assessing whether collective dominance exists, the Commission must establish whether the concentration would lead to a situation in which effective competition is significantly impeded by the undertakings involved in the operation and one or more other undertakings, which together, in particular because of factors giving rise to a connection between them, are able to adopt a common policy on the market and act to a considerable extent independently of their competitors, their customers and, ultimately, of consumers. The CFI also noted that Article 2 ECMR confers on the Commission a certain discretion with respect to assessments of an economic nature.[89]

In its assessment of the alleged joint control of Gencor and Lonrho over LPD, used to justify a finding of collective dominance, the CFI analysed the evidence submitted to the Commission prior to the concentration, such as the structural links existing between Implats and LPD before the concentration, and the impact of the concentration on the structure of competition in the platinum market. From the Commission's analysis, it followed that Lonrho was able exclusively to control its marketing policy without the agreement of Gencor. Following the concentration, that aspect of LPD's commercial policy would be under the joint control of Lonrho and Gencor.[90] The CFI agreed with the Commission's analysis that the concentration was liable to alter significantly the degree of influence that the applicant (Gencor) could exercise over LPD, and thereby would alter the conditions and structure of competition in the platinum and rhodium markets.[91]

Referring to the *Flat Glass* case, the CFI stated that for findings of collective dominance, it is necessary for there to be structural links between the two undertakings, for instance through a technological lead by agreements or licences, which give them the power to behave independently of their competitors, of their customers and, ultimately, of consumers.[92] The question that arises, according to the CFI, is whether the Commission has succeeded in demonstrating the existence of structural links, or in proving that the merged entity and Amplats intended to behave as if they were a single dominant entity. The Commission referred to the following structural links between the merged entity and Amplats: (i) links in certain industries; and (ii) Anglo American Corporation's (*AAC*) recent purchase of 6% of Lonrho with a right of first refusal over a further 18%.[93] The CFI stated that it could not be deduced from

---

[88] *Gencor*, at paras 132–152.
[89] Ibid, at paras 163–164.
[90] Ibid, at paras 178–179.
[91] Ibid, at paras 170–194.
[92] Ibid, at para 264.
[93] Ibid, at para 265. On 23 April 1997, the Commission cleared AAC's purchase of Lonrho shares subject to the condition that it reduced its shareholding in Lonrho form 27.5% to 9.99%, Commission press release IP/97/338.

Flat Glass that it had not laid down the existence of economic links as a requirement, or restricted the notion of economic links to structural links, as argued by the applicant. Therefore, the Commission is entitled, according to the CFI, to interpret this notion as including the relationship of interdependence which exists between the members of a tight oligopoly. The members within such a relationship are in a position to anticipate each other's behaviour, and are therefore strongly encouraged to align their conduct in the market so as to maximise their profits by restricting production in order to increase prices.[94]

The CFI said that this conclusion is important in relation to the ECMR, whose objective is to prevent anti-competitive market structures from arising or being strengthened. Such structures result from the notion of economic links in the strict sense, or from market structures of an oligopolistic kind where each undertaking may become aware of common interests and, in particular, align pricing without having to enter into an agreement or resort to a concerted practice.[95] Clearly, this judgment has clarified a number of key issues which will encourage the Commission to use the concept of collective dominance in the context of oligopoly and duopoly.

Airtours

On 6 June 2002, the CFI overturned the Commission Decision of September 1999 blocking the acquisition of First Choice by Airtours. The Commission had prohibited the Airtours/First Choice merger on the ground that it would have created a collective dominant position between the three largest short-haul package holiday companies in the UK (previously the Commission's collective dominance cases had only involved two firms—this was the first time the Commission applied the collective dominance theory to three firms).

The CFI has shown that it is willing to apply the same rigorous review that it applies in ordinary EC competition cases to Commission Decisions under the ECMR, while recognising the margin of discretion that the Commission retains in reaching economic decisions whether or not to approve a merger. It is the first time that the CFI has scrutinised in such detail the factual as well as the legal assessment by the Commission of a merger decision, following a Phase II investigation under the ECMR. In particular, the Court identified from the documents and evidence before it which factors the Commission took into account, and then determined whether the Commission made a manifest error of assessment in the conclusions that it made on the basis of those factors.

Before outlining the way the CFI reviewed the Commission's decision in *Airtours*, it is necessary to set out the substantive legal approach applied by the

---

[94] *Gencor* at para 276.
[95] Ibid, at para 277.

Court which contains the tests against which the findings and reasoning of the Commission's decision were reviewed by the Court: [96]

> Where, for the purposes of applying Regulation No 4064/89, the Commission examines a possible collective dominant position, it must ascertain whether the concentration would have the direct and immediate effect of creating or strengthening a position of that kind, which is such as significantly and lastingly to impede competition in the relevant market (see, to that effect, *Gencor* v. *Commission*, paragraph 94). If there is no substantial alteration to competition as it stands, the merger must be approved (see, to that effect, Case T-2/93 *Air France* v. *Commission* [1994] ECR II-323, paragraphs 78 and 79, and *Gencor* v. *Commission*, paragraph 170, 180 and 193).
>
> It is apparent from the case law that 'in the case of an alleged collective dominant position, the Commission is . . . obliged to assess, using a prospective analysis of the reference market, whether the concentration which has been referred to it leads to a situation in which effective competition in the relevant market is significantly impeded by the undertakings involved in the concentration and one or more other undertakings which together, in particular because of factors giving rise to a connection between them, are able to adopt a common policy on the market and act to a considerable extent independently of their competitors, their customers, and also of consumers' (*Kali & Salz*, cited above, paragraph 221, and *Gencor* v. *Commission*, paragraph 163).
>
> The Court of First Instance has held that: 'There is no reason whatsoever in legal or economic terms to exclude from the notion of economic links the relationship of interdependence existing between the parties to a tight oligopoly within which, in a market with the appropriate characteristics, in particular in terms of market concentration, transparency and product homogeneity, those parties are in a position to anticipate one another's behaviour and are therefore strongly encouraged to align their conduct in the market, in particular in such a way as to maximise their joint profits by restricting production with a view to increasing prices. In such a context, each trader is aware that highly competitive action on its part designed to increase its market share (for example a price cut) would provoke identical action by the others, so that it would derive no benefit from its initiative. All the traders would thus be affected by the reduction in price levels.' (*Gencor* v. *Commission*, paragraph 276).
>
> A collective dominant position significantly impeding effective competition in the common market or a substantial part of it may thus arise as the result of a concentration where, in view of the actual characteristics of the relevant market and of the alteration in its structure that the transaction would entail, the latter would make each member of the dominant oligopoly, as it becomes aware of common interests, consider it possible, economically rational, and hence preferable, to adopt on a lasting basis a common policy on the market with the aim of selling at above competitive prices, without having to enter into an agreement or resort to a concerted practice within the meaning of Article 81 EC (see, to that effect, *Gencor* v. *Commission*, paragraph 277) and without any actual or potential competitors, let alone customers or consumers, being able to react effectively.
>
> As the applicant has argued and as the Commission has accepted in its pleadings, three conditions are necessary for a finding of collective dominance as defined:

---

[96] *Airtours*, paras 58–62.

—first, each member of the dominant oligopoly must have the ability to know how the other members are behaving in order to monitor whether or not they are adopting the common policy. As the Commission specifically acknowledges, it is not enough for each member of the dominant oligopoly to be aware that interdependent market conduct is profitable for all of them but each member must also have a means of knowing whether the other operators are adopting the same strategy and whether they are maintaining it. There must, therefore, be sufficient market transparency for all members of the dominant oligopoly to be aware, sufficiently precisely and quickly, of the way in which the other members' market conduct is evolving;

—second, the situation of tacit co-ordination must be sustainable over time, that is to say, there must be an incentive not to depart from the common policy on the market. As the Commission observes, it is only if all the members of the dominant oligopoly maintain the parallel conduct that all can benefit. The notion of retaliation in respect of conduct deviating from the common policy is thus inherent in this condition. In this instance, the parties concur that, for a situation of collective dominance to be viable, there must be adequate deterrents to ensure that there is a long-term incentive in not departing from the common policy, which means that each member of the dominant oligopoly must be aware that highly competitive action on its part designed to increase its market share would provoke identical action by the others, so that it would derive no benefit from its initiative (see, to that effect, *Gencor* v. *Commission*, paragraph 276);

—third, to prove the existence of a collective dominant position to the requisite legal standard, the Commission must also establish that the foreseeable reaction of current and future competitors, as well as of consumers, would not jeopardise the results expected from the common policy.

In addition to the substantive tests applied by the CFI, which provide a blue print for collective dominance in oligopolistic markets under the ECMR, it is also essential to set out the legal standard that the CFI expects the Commission to meet in terms of evidence and reasoning in its decisions where it seeks to prohibit a merger on the ground that it creates or strengthens a collective dominant position: [97]

> The prospective analysis which the Commission has to carry out in its review of concentrations involving collective dominance calls for close examination in particular of the circumstances which, in each individual case, are relevant for assessing the effects of the concentration on competition in the reference market (*Kali & Salz*, paragraph 222). As the Commission itself has emphasised, at paragraph 104 of its decision of 20 May 1998 *Price Waterhouse/Coopers & Lybrand* (Case IV/M.1016) (OJ 1999 L 50, p. 27), it is also apparent from the judgment in Kali and Salz that, where the Commission takes the view that a merger should be prohibited because it will create a situation of collective dominance, it is incumbent upon it to produce convincing evidence thereof. The evidence must concern, in particular, factors playing a significant role in the assessment of whether a situation of collective dominance exists, such as, for example, the lack of effective competition between the operators alleged to be members of the dominant oligopoly and the weakness of any competitive pressure that might be exerted by other operators.

[97] *Airtours*, paras 63–64.

Furthermore, the basic provisions of Regulation No 4064/89, in particular Article 2 thereof, confer on the Commission a certain discretion, especially with respect to assessments of an economic nature, and, consequently, when the exercise of that discretion, which is essential for defining the rules on concentrations, is under review, the Community judicature must take account of the discretionary margin implicit in the provisions of an economic nature which form part of the rules on concentrations (Kali & Salz, paragraphs 223 and 224, and Gencor v. Commission, paragraphs 164 and 165).

Therefore, it is in the light of the foregoing considerations that it is necessary to examine the merits of the grounds relied on by the applicant to show that the Commission made an error of assessment in finding that the conditions for, or characteristics of, collective dominance would exist were the transaction to be approved.

There are two main approaches pursued in its review on appeal under Article 230 EC. First, the CFI reviews the evidence to verify carefully if the factual findings are based on cogent evidence. Second, it checks whether the reasons for conclusions are consistent with those factual findings and, without substituting its own judgment for the assessment resulting from the Commission's exercise of its discretion, confirms whether it has made any manifest errors.

This approach can be illustrated by the following extracts from the Court's judgment:

> it follows from the foregoing that the Commission made errors of assessment in its analysis of competition obtaining in the relevant market prior to the notification. First, it did not provide adequate evidence in support of its finding that there was already a tendency in the industry to collective dominance and, hence, to restriction of competition, particularly as regards capacity selling (paragraph 120);
>
> the Court holds that the Commission's findings are based on an incomplete and incorrect assessment of the data submitted to it during the administrative procedure (paragraph 127);
>
> however, it is apparent from a cursory examination of that document that the Commission's reading of it. . . . It follows that the Commission construed that document without having regard to its actual wording and overall purpose, even though it decided to include it as a document crucial to its finding that the rate of market growth was moderate in the 1990s and would continue to be so (paragraph 130);
>
> As regards volatility linked to the business cycle, the Commission cannot just conclude as it does . . . that 'it is likely that all tour operators will have similar views as to the market development' without producing any evidence in support of that statement, given that capacity is set initially some 18 months before the start of the season (paragraph 144);
>
> it follows from all of the foregoing that the Commission wrongly formed a view that market transparency is high for the four major integrated operators during the planning period. Accordingly, it appears that it wrongly concluded that the degree of market transparency was a characteristic which made the market conducive to collective dominance . . . (paragraph 180); and
>
> . . . the Court finds that the Commission has failed to prove that the result of the transaction would be to alter the structure of the relevant market in such a way that the leading operators would no longer act as they have in the past and that a collective dominant position would be created (paragraph 293).

As a result of its searching analysis of the findings in the Commission's Decision, the evidence taken into account by the Commission, and the available evidence which it either did not take into account or had misunderstood, the Court concluded:

> that the Decision, far from basing its prospective analysis on **cogent evidence**, is vitiated by a series of **errors of assessment** as to factors fundamental to any assessment of whether a collective dominant position might be created. It follows that the Commission prohibited the transaction without having proved to **the requisite legal standard** that the concentration would give rise to a collective dominant position of the three major tour operators, of such a kind as to significantly impede effective competition in the relevant market (paragraph 294) (emphasis added).

The reason, therefore, that the Court overturned the Commission's Decision is not that it rejected the theory of collective dominance in the form of collusion on capacity through tacit collusion. In laying down three conditions to establish collective dominance or tacit collusion, the Court found the Commission wanting in its treatment of the facts rather than the theory. The three conditions identified by the Court were transparency, the possibility of retaliation, and the absence of actual and potential external constraints on competition. While these three conditions are a helpful guide to future collective dominance cases and go beyond the checklist approach followed by the Commission to date, the Court's judgment is taken up with testing the Commission's Decision in the context of each of the three conditions and concluding that the Commission's analysis was at fault on each. In particular, the Commission wrongly found that the package travel market characteristics were conducive to passive collusion since there was insufficient market transparency for all firms in the oligopoly to be aware, sufficiently precisely and quickly, of the way in which the other firms' market conduct would develop. Second, any tacit co-ordination would not be sustainable over time, since the retaliatory measures identified by the Commission are not capable of acting as adequate deterrents in that way. The Commission also underestimated the counter-balance of competitors as well as customers to destabilise any expected collusion.

The three Airtours conditions for collective dominance

On the basis of the *Airtours* decision, the conditions for collective dominance under Article 2 ECMR may be summarised by reference to the three conditions set out in paragraph 62 of the CFI's judgment. It was agreed by the applicant and the Commission that three conditions are necessary for a finding of collective dominance as defined:

> (i) each member of the dominant oligopoly must have the ability to know how the other members are behaving in order to monitor whether or not they are adopting the common policy. As the Commission specifically acknowledges, it is not enough

for each member of the dominant oligopoly to be aware that the interdependent market conduct is profitable for all of them but each member must also have a means to acknowledging whether the other operators are adopting the same strategy and whether they are maintaining it. **There must, therefore, be sufficient market transparency for all members of the dominant oligopoly to be aware, sufficiently precisely and quickly, of the way in which the other members' market conduct is evolving;**

(ii) the situation of tacit co-ordination must be sustainable over time, that is to say, there must be an incentive not to depart from the common policy on the market. The notion of retaliation in respect of conduct deviating from the common policy is thus inherent in this condition. **For a situation of collective dominance to be viable, there must be adequate deterrents to ensure that there is a long-term incentive in not departing from the common policy,** which means that each member of the dominant oligopoly must be aware that highly competitive action on its part designed to increase its market share would provoke identical action by the others, so that it would derive no benefit from its initiative (see, to that effect, *Gencor* v. *Commission*, paragraph 276);

(iii) to prove the existence of a collective dominant position to the requisite legal standard, the Commission **must also establish that the foreseeable reaction of current and future competitors, as well as of consumers, would not jeopardise the results expected from the common policy.**

European Commission Guidelines on Horizontal Mergers and Collective Dominance

As part of its review of the ECMR the Commission has published draft guidelines on horizontal mergers in which it deals with collective dominance post *Airtours*. The Commission clearly adopts the approach of the Court of First Instance in *Airtours* at paragraph 4 of the proposed guidelines. The Commission states that three conditions must be fulfilled in order to establish collective dominance as a result of the merger: 1) the co-ordinating firms must be able to monitor to a sufficient degree whether the terms of co-ordination are being adhered to; 2) there must be credible deterrent mechanisms; 3) the actions of outsiders, such as current and future competitors, as well as customers, should not be able to jeopardise the results expected from co-ordination.

Under point (1) (monitoring the terms of co-ordination), the first issue is whether the terms of co-ordination themselves may be established. The more complex the market, the more difficult it is to establish the terms of co-ordination. The Commission points to some elements that show a sufficient degree of stability in the market, namely:

- homogeneous v differentiated products;
- single v numerous products;
- stable v volatile demand;
- stable v volatile supply;

- characteristics of customers (geographic markets, firm/product loyalty); and
- symmetry v asymmetry of the firms.[98]

The Commission points out that even in volatile and unstable markets the oligopolists may find ways of agreeing and monitoring the terms of co-ordination. Such ways are:

- simple pricing rules;
- transparency of the cost structure;
- structural links such as cross-shareholdings or participation in joint ventures; and
- public exchange of strategic information through the press.

The need for an effective deterrent presupposes two conditions:

- effective monitoring; and
- deterrent mechanisms.

Finally, and consistently with the judgment of the Court of First Instance in *Airtours*, at paragraph 69 the Commission considers the reactions from outsiders, and in particular customers, by reference to buyer power. At paragraphs 75-77 of the proposed Guidelines, the Commission addresses the countervailing effect of buyer power in the post-merger scenario.

1. CONCLUSIONS

The review of the ECMR, and in particular the issues raised by the proposed new definition of the legal test for merger assessment in Article 2 ECMR, are outside the scope of this paper. However the *Airtours* judgment has played a major role in this context. It remains to be seen whether the Community Courts will recognise that there is a 'gap' not covered by Article 82 EC or Article 2 ECMR collective dominance. In particular, it remains to be seen what test the Member States will agree for the new ECMR text. What is clear is that the case law has developed enormously from *Flat Glass* through *Cewal* to *Airtours*.

---

[98] *Airtours*, para 62.

14

Some Reflections on Procedure in Competition Cases

SIR CHRISTOPHER BELLAMY QC

IT WAS A great honour to be present on 10 March 1992 when David Edward was sworn in as a judge of the Court of Justice of the European Communities. It is also a great honour to be asked to contribute to this *Liber Amicorum*. David's contribution to the development of Community law as practitioner, academic and judge—of both the CFI and the ECJ—has indeed been outstanding.

In paying tribute to his achievement, I have chosen to devote a few words to the largely neglected, and in my view, underrated, subject of procedure, with particular reference to competition law. As every student learns, but soon forgets, the development of substantive law is highly influenced by procedure.[1] An obvious example, in the field of competition law, is whether the role of the court in a particular case is to review the legality of the decision of the competition authority, or to conduct an appeal on the merits.[2] The result could be very different, depending on the procedural context in question.

Under the Competition Act 1998 the United Kingdom carried out its first reform of competition law for over 40 years, introducing a domestic system modelled on Articles 81 and 82. When I had the great privilege of being asked to set up and run the new Competition Appeal Tribunal (CAT)[3] created by that Act, several possible models presented themselves. Should the new system follow the traditional 'litigation' model of English and American courts, with the emphasis on adversarial proceedings, oral evidence, and extensive disclosure of

---

[1] The high point is Maine's striking phrase in *Early Law and Custom*, 389: 'So great is the ascendancy of the Law of Actions in the infancy of Courts of Justice, that substantive law has at first the look of being gradually secreted in the interstices of procedure'. Despite substantial procedural reform in England, in 1830 and 1875, which swept away the ancient 'forms of action' governing civil procedure, F W Maitland could still say, in his famous lectures published in 1909, 'the forms of action we have buried, but they still rule us from their graves'.

[2] Contrast Art. 234 of the EC Treaty with the UK Competition Act 1998, Sch. 8, para 3 ('appeal on the merits'), The Enterprise Act 2002, s.120 ('review' of decisions in merger cases) and s. 195(2) of the Communications Act 2003 ('appeal on the merits').

[3] Then known as the Competition Commission Appeal Tribunal, but renamed the Competition Appeal Tribunal under Part 2 of the Enterprise Act 2002.

documents? Or should the system be a written procedure, with more of an inquisitorial emphasis, with the Tribunal undertaking its own inquiries, rather than simply relying on the parties? Or should it be somewhere in between?

In making that choice, the eternal elements of time and cost inevitably loomed large. The traditional system of litigation *à l'anglaise* undoubtedly enables the court to get to the bottom of the facts, to root out dishonest conduct and to expose rival expert hypotheses to the rigours of cross examination. But it is expensive: some cases may last many days, with very heavy costs to the parties. On the other hand, a system that does not depend on the testing of evidence in court, or which does not do so in the same way, may also be unsatisfactory in certain respects, at least to English eyes. So a balance has to be struck, taking notably into account costs and time.

In addition, all legal systems need to focus on how to avoid delays. To some extent, a certain amount of delay is endemic in the legal process. However, if one moves from Bar to the bench, one of the first things that strikes one, at least in my case, is the sudden absence of imperative deadlines. In terms of creating the new CAT, this gave rise to two ideas. First, the CAT should work to an internally set timetable, as a proxy for the external deadlines found in normal legal life. Secondly, instead of adopting a certain procedure and then finding that it was very time consuming, one should look at the matter through 'the other end of the telescope'. In other words, one should *first* ask oneself how long in general the appeal process should aim to take, and *then* adapt the procedure accordingly, rather than the other way round. Of course, such an approach is much easier if one is starting with 'a clean sheet', as was the case with the new CAT.

In the event, it was decided that 'a straightforward' case in the CAT should take around six months, although the CAT was careful not to define what was meant by a 'straightforward' case. On that basis, it became possible to set a 'target' date for judgment right at the outset of the case. Once such an anticipated 'target' date for judgment is set, the CAT is then able to work back, as it were, in fixing hearing dates and case management conferences in a way that facilitates the meeting of the target.

One other consideration strongly influenced the way the CAT was eventually structured. In my own view, one of the deep truths of litigation, and the legal process generally, is that for many parties the ultimate outcome of the case is not necessarily the most important consideration. Leaving aside the litigants who, in one way or another abuse the legal system, and who deserve no judicial sympathy, there are nonetheless many litigants whose chief concern is to find someone who will listen to the arguments they are making in an open and impartial way. In other words, 'having one's day in court' is an essential aspect of the legal landscape, irrespective of the final outcome. A judicial tribunal which, however briefly, gives the impression of having listened courteously, and having grappled with the points made, before giving a reasoned decision, is a major foundation of a developed legal system. This aspect, in my view, is particularly important in competition law systems based on the European model. In such systems, the competition authority inevitably combines the roles of investigator, prosecutor and judge. However much the competition authority seeks to be fair, those on the receiving end sometimes seem to feel that the authority 'is just not listening'. To correct this impression, and to ensure public confidence in the fairness of the system as a whole, there is perhaps a particular premium on transparency and fairness when a competition case reaches whatever court is dealing with it.

Taking all these considerations in mind, an obvious model for the CAT presented itself: the Court of First Instance of the European Communities (*CFI*). The CFI is a court which specialises in competition cases. The procedure is written. It does, however, have case management powers (known as 'measures for the organisation of the procedure') which were highly innovative when they were introduced. It also has a lively oral stage of the procedure, in which the court is able to test the theses of the opposing parties. If not quite 'a hail of judicial grapeshot', as one hearing in the English Court of Appeal was recently described, the oral stage in the CFI does enable at least some Socratic dialogue to take place between the Court and the parties, despite the limitations of simultaneous translation. The judgments of the CFI are fully reasoned, notably so as to be able to withstand the scrutiny of the Court of Justice.

So it was that the CAT was, in the event, modelled on the CFI. The CAT's current rules of procedure[4] envisage that an appeal against a decision taken by the competition authority under the domestic equivalent of Articles 81 and 82 must be lodged, with full supporting arguments and documents, within 2 months of the relevant claim. There is then a defence, which is filed within 6 weeks, a procedure for intervention, and an oral hearing which is structured on similar lines to those of the CFI. In the majority of cases the oral hearing lasts a day, or at the most 2 days, although two cases so far have lasted for 4 days. But this may be seen against the background of the English system, where heavy cases may easily last for 4 to 6 weeks in court, perhaps longer.

It is true that the opportunity has been taken to modify the CFI procedures in some respects. One round of pleadings may if necessary 'reformulate' the decision, by itself making any decision which the competition authority could have made, or indeed making 'such directions' or taking 'such steps' as the competition authority could have taken. In these respects the power of the CAT is wider than that of the CFI. However, in merger cases the CAT is limited to a 'review' of the decision of the competition authority, where the CAT must 'apply the same principles as would be applied by a court on an application for judicial review'. In merger cases, therefore, the powers of the CAT are similar to those of the CFI under Article 234.

To give some flavour of the way the CAT Rules operate, the Tribunal's current *Guide to Appeals under the Competition Act 1998* sets out the principles as follows:

[4] The Competition Appeal Tribunal Rules 2003 SI 2003/1372.

'2.3. The five main principles of the Rules are as follows.

Early disclosure in writing

2.4. Each party's case must be fully set out in writing as early as possible, with supporting documents produced at the outset.

Active case management

5. The proceedings will be actively case managed by the appeal tribunal, the objective being to identify and concentrate on the main issues at as early a stage as possible, to avoid undue prolixity or delay, and to ensure that evidence is presented in an efficient manner.

Strict timetables

6. The tribunal will indicate, as early as possible, a target date by which the tribunal's decision on the appeal is to be given, together with the date for the main hearing. The main stages of the case, and the internal planning of the tribunal's work, will be geared to meeting this timetable. **In general the tribunal will aim to complete straightforward cases in less than six months.** This target will be reviewed in the light of experience.

Effective fact-finding procedures

7. The tribunal will pay close attention to the probative value of documentary evidence. Where there are essential evidential issues that cannot be satisfactory resolved without cross-examination, the tribunal may permit the oral examination of witnesses. As regards expert evidence, the tribunal will expect the parties to make every effort to narrow the points at issue, and to reach agreement where possible.

Short and structured oral hearings

8. The structure of the main oral hearings of the tribunals will be planned well in advance, in consultation with the parties, with a view to avoiding lengthy oral argument. Since the written arguments of the parties will have already been set out, and since the main issues will have been identified prior to the main oral hearing, this hearing will normally be conducted within short defined time limits, in accordance with established practice in the CFI.'

So far, the CAT has managed, more or less, to stick to its self imposed deadline. As at 5 August 2003, the CAT had given about 30 judgments on interlocutory and substantive matters. Details are on the website: www.catribunal.org.uk.

That brief description of the CAT leads me on to particular points, which I hope demonstrate why the CAT should figure at all in a *Liber Amicorum* in honour of David Edward.

The first point is that the CAT represents, in my view, an interesting and, so far, unique example of 'soft harmonisation' in the area of European procedural law. The model of the CFI, of which of course David was a judge from 1989 to 1992, has proved transposable to the soil of the United Kingdom, where it has taken root and, so far at least, flourished.

The second point is that both the traditional procedures of the common law, and what may be loosely described as 'Continental-style' procedures have strengths and weaknesses. It is, however, possible in my view to harmonise them, at least in the field of competition law, drawing on the best of both systems. The CAT is not a 'clone' of the CFI, nor has it entirely followed the model of the English High Court or the former Restrictive Practices Court, albeit that close attention has been paid to the systems of civil procedure which followed the Woolf Report. It is, I hope, the product of both systems.

That, of course, leads me to the third point, which is the most important point to be made in this brief homage to David Edward. David too is, if he will forgive me saying so, also the product of both systems. With his background in Scots law, itself subject to Continental influence, his knowledge of the common law, and his deep understanding of Continental legal systems, David also combines, in his own person, the collective strength which the different systems can together bring to bear, to the great benefit of Community law. But in the present context, the point is even more specific. David Edward has not only been a judge of the Court of Justice for 11 years; from 1989 to 1992 he was also a judge of the CFI. He played a vital role in shaping the procedures which that court adopted, particularly in the spheres of case management and the conduct of the oral hearing. It is, I think, a fitting tribute to the founding work of David and his original colleagues that the CFI has grown in stature and importance since 1989. It is also, I hope, at least in a small way, a tribute to his influence that, a decade after the establishment of the CFI, the CAT was conceived along similar lines. I hope, therefore, that I may be permitted to salute David Edward, not only as a distinguished judge of the CFI, and of the Court of Justice, but also as an 'honorary grandfather' of the CAT.

V. EU Substantive Issues

15

Free Movement and the Environment: Seeing the Wood for the Trees

MARIE DEMETRIOU AND IMELDA HIGGINS

1. INTRODUCTION

THE PROFESSOR NEVER misses the wood for the trees. There are numerous areas in which he has made a valuable contribution to Community law by stepping back from unnecessarily complicated legal argument and asking the question: 'What is the Treaty trying to achieve?' We have chosen to address one such example.

With increasing frequency, the European Court of Justice (ECJ) and national courts are asked to resolve problems arising out of conflicts between two or more Community objectives. Does an agreement which pursues social policy objectives but has an anti-competitive effect contravene Community law? Are national measures designed to protect the environment or consumer welfare, but which restrict imports, compatible with the Treaty? Judge Edward has long emphasized that such questions should be resolved by 'looking at the Treaty', an approach initially shared by the ECJ. Thus in resolving conflicts between objectives central to the achievement of the Common Market, such as the free movement of goods, and other objectives, such as environmental or consumer protection, the ECJ has given precedence to the needs of the Common Market. However, while this precedence was justified under the original Treaty of Rome, subsequent amendments to that Treaty have ostensibly changed the relationship between the fundamental policies and other policies. In particular, the Treaty of Maastricht appears to have abolished any precedence between the various Community policies. Thus the Treaty is no longer built around the four fundamental freedoms. Instead, the Treaty contains a number of non-hierarchical 'Community policies'.

In this article, we consider the implications of this approach for one of the original foundations of the Community, namely the free movement of goods, and environmental protection, one of the recently promoted policies. Judge Edward takes the view that proper account should be taken of the evolved structure of the Treaty when resolving conflicts between different Community policies. To date the ECJ has failed to follow this advice. We respectfully submit that by failing to take into account the equalising of the various Community policies, the ECJ is placing an unjustifiable emphasis on the free movement of goods at the cost of other policies. On the other hand, the ECJ's attempts to incorporate the rôle of the new policies into its traditional case-law on the free movement of goods are causing significant confusion.

We will first consider the treatment of the free movement of goods and environmental protection in the Treaty of Rome. We will then look at the changes that successive Treaty amendments have introduced in both of these areas and the difficulties that the ECJ's failure to take account of such amendments has caused. In conclusion we argue for a fundamentally new approach in the assessment of restrictions on trade resulting from environmental protection measures.

2. THE CHANGING STRUCTURE OF THE TREATY

Free movement of goods

As befitted the original aims of the Community which focused on the removal of barriers to trade, the provisions guaranteeing the free movement of goods occupied a very privileged position in the Treaty. The establishment of a 'common market' featured first in the list of tasks assigned to the Community by Article 2 of the Treaty. The provisions on the free movement of goods contained in Articles 30 to 36 of the EEC Treaty were central to the achievement of the common market.

Articles 30 and 34 EEC (now 28 and 29 EC) contained a broad prohibition on quantitative restrictions and measures of equivalent effect on imports and exports between the Member States. Article 36 EEC (now Article 30 EC) defined the limited grounds on which Member States could derogate from this prohibition. These grounds reflected the concerns of the Member State at the time the provision was drafted: public morality, public policy and public security; the protection of health and life of humans, animals or plants; the protection of national treasures possessing artistic, historic or archaeological value; and the protection of industrial and commercial property.

The fundamental position of the free movement of goods in the Treaty of Rome also owes much to the case-law of the ECJ. The ECJ has construed broadly the concept of 'measures having equivalent effect' to quantitative restrictions on imports and exports. In addition, it has applied Article 28 so as to prohibit not only discriminatory barriers to trade but also indistinctly applicable measures (other than selling arrangements)[1] which nevertheless present obstacles to the free movement of products between Member States. Consistently with its aim of giving the greatest possible effect to the free movement of goods provisions, the Court has construed narrowly the express derogations in Article 30.

[1] See Joined Cases C-267/91 and 268/91 *Keck and Mithouard* [1993] ECR I-6097.

However, the ECJ has also recognised that certain measures which restrict the free movement of goods may be justified if those measures are necessary in order to achieve objectively justifiable purposes. Thus, in a series of cases, starting with *Cassis de Dijon*,[2] the ECJ recognised a number of 'mandatory requirements'[3] in addition to the express grounds of justification set out in Article 30. However, reliance on such mandatory requirements is also tightly controlled.

In a number of cases, the ECJ has given express recognition to the privileged position that the free movement of goods enjoys in the scheme of the Treaty, referring to it variously as 'a fundamental freedom',[4] 'one of the fundamental principles of the common market',[5] a 'fundamental Community provision',[6] 'one of the foundations of the Community'[7] and a 'fundamental right'.[8]

Aside from being renumbered, Articles 28 and 30 have not themselves been amended since the adoption of the Treaty of Rome. However, pursuant to amendments introduced by the Maastricht Treaty, the old Part II of the Treaty of Rome which had been entitled 'Foundations of the Community' and covered the four freedoms together with agriculture and transport was merged with the old Part III into a new Part Three entitled 'Community Policies'. Ostensibly, the free movement of goods was thus placed on the same footing as other Community policies.

Protection of the environment

In contrast to the elevated position of the free movement of goods, the original Treaty had no express provisions relating to environmental protection, largely because, at that time, such issues were not of significant concern.[9] Nevertheless, until the adoption of the Single European Act (SEA), Articles 100 and 235 were used as a legislative basis for Community action in this field.[10] These two Articles provided the legal framework for an extensive body of substantive environmental rules covering, inter alia, air, water, noise quality, waste and hazardous substances.[11]

---

[2] Case 120/78 *Rewe-Zentral* v. *Bundesmonopolverwaltung fur Branntwein* [1979] ECR 649.
[3] Sometimes referred to by the Court as 'overriding requirements of general public importance.'
[4] Case C–394/97 *Heinonen* [1999] ECR I–3599, at para 38.
[5] Case C–205/89 *Commission* v. *Hellenic Republic* [1991] ECR I–1361, at para 9.
[6] Case C–49/89 *Corsica Ferries France* v. *Direction générale des douanes Françaises* [1989] ECR I- 4441, para 8.
[7] Case C–194/94 *CIA Security* v. *Signalson* [1996] ECR I–2201, at para 40.
[8] Case C–228/98 *Dounias* v. *Minister for Economic Affairs* [2000] ECR I–577, para 64.
[9] L Krämer, *EC Environmental Law*, (Sweet & Maxwell 4 edn, 2000); D Geradin, 'Trade and Environmental Protection: Community Harmonization and National Environmental Standards' (1993) *YELR* 151.
[10] Now Articles 94 and 308 EC.
[11] Geradin, above n9, at 162.

The SEA resulted in the inclusion of a new Title VII entitled 'Environment' in Part III of the EEC Treaty which dealt with the 'policies of the Community'.[12] Title VII consisted of Articles 130r to 130t (now Articles 174 to 176) which set out a number of provisions relating to environmental protection. Of particular relevance to the status of Community environmental policy was the requirement in Article 130(r)(2), that environmental protection become a component of the Community's other policies. Other significant changes from the perspective of the status of environmental protection included Article 100a(3), which required the Commission, in its proposals concerning inter alia, environmental protection, to take as a base a high level of protection. Moreover, under Article 100a(4), Member States were given the right to derogate from a Community measure adopted by qualified majority voting 'on grounds of major needs . . . related to the protection of the environment'.

The provisions relating to environmental protection introduced by the SEA were amended within the space of a few years, in 1993, by the Maastricht Treaty on Political Union.[13] The Maastricht Treaty strengthened and deepened the role of environmental policy at Community level, placing it at the heart of the Community's role and purpose.[14] In particular, this Treaty amended both Articles 2 and 3 of the EEC Treaty, neither of which had been amended by the SEA. Article 2 of the Treaty defined the tasks of the Community, and provides that:

> the Community shall have as its task . . . by establishing a common market and an economic and monetary union and by implementing the common policies and activities referred to in Article 3 and 3a, to promote throughout the Community a harmonious and balanced development of Economic activities, *sustainable* and non inflationary growth *respecting the environment*.

By altering the fundamental task of the Community and referring to 'sustainable growth . . . respecting the environment'[15] this amendment of Article 2 represented a greening of the Treaty.[16] In addition, as mentioned above, the Maastricht Treaty merged the old Parts II and III of the EC Treaty into a new

---

[12] D Vandermeersch, 'The Single European Act and the Environmental Policy of the European Economic Community' (1987) 12 *CML Rev* 407; L Krämer, 'The Single European Act and Environmental Protection: Reflections on Several New Provisions in Community Law' (1987) 24 *CML Rev* 659.

[13] M Hession and R Macrory, 'Maastricht and the Environmental Policy of the Community: Legal Issues of a New Environment Policy', in O'Keeffe and Twomey (eds) *Legal Issues of the Maastricht Treaty* (John Wiley, 1994).

[14] *Ibid*, at 167.

[15] According to Kramer, above n9, at 7, sustainable growth incorporates the idea of a 'development which meets the needs of the present without compromising the ability of future generations to meet their own needs'. Moreover, in Regulation 3062/95 on operations to promote tropical forests (OJ 1995 L327/9, Art 2(4)), the related concept of 'sustainable development' is defined as 'the improvement of the standard of living and welfare of the relevant populations within the limits of the capacity of the ecosystems by maintaining natural assets and their biological diversity for the benefit of present and future generations'.

[16] Hession and Macrory, above n13, at 153.

Part Three ('Community Policies'). Ostensibly, environmental protection was now placed on the same footing as free movement of goods and the other three original fundamental freedoms. The Maastricht Treaty also introduced other significant changes. Thus, the requirement in Article 130(r)(2) that environmental considerations be a component of other policies was strengthened into a requirement that it be integrated into the definition and implementation of other policies (Article 3c).

Subsequent Treaty amendments have consolidated the position of environmental protection within the Treaty by extending the environmental areas covered by majority voting.

It is clear from the above that, since the foundation of the European Economic Community, the role of the environment has undergone a substantial change. At best an after-thought in the earlier years of the Community, the environment now occupies a key place at its very heart.

As a result of these changes it is no longer legitimate to treat environmental objectives as 'second class'. It is clear that this objective should no longer be seen as an element outside the Common Market that may be taken into consideration only if it does not interfere with the achievement of economic objectives.[17] In particular the ascending status of environmental protection demands that:

> in any case where a conflict between the Community's economic and environmental objectives arises, the interests involved must be reconciled insofar as possible, in accordance with the principle that all Community purposes and interests set out in Article 2 are of equal value.[18]

3. FREE MOVEMENT OF GOODS VERSUS ENVIRONMENTAL PROTECTION

Having considered the changing position of environmental protection in the Treaty, the question arises as to how those changes have impacted on the ECJ's treatment of environmental protection measures which restrict the free movement of goods: to what extent does the ECJ look at these amendments when balancing these policy objectives?

As remarked above, the ECJ has played an active rôle in promoting Articles 28–30 as constituting a broad prohibition on quantitative restrictions and measures having an equivalent effect with a narrow range of permitted derogations. The ECJ was prepared to recognise that environmental protection measures could constitute a mandatory requirement and thus legitimately impact on inter-state trade. However, in keeping with the ECJ's case-law on mandatory requirements, such a derogation is subject to the usual restrictions. In particular, and in contrast, to the Article 30 derogations, the measure has to be indistinctly

---

[17] M Wasmeier, 'The Integration of Environmental Protection as a General Rule for Interpreting Community Law' (2001) 38(1) *CML Rev* 159.
[18] *Ibid*, at p 160.

applicable in the sense that it does not discriminate directly or indirectly against imported goods.[19] Moreover, like the Article 30 derogations, the national measure must be necessary in order to achieve the aim in question; must be proportionate to that aim; must not constitute arbitrary discrimination; and must not constitute a disguised restriction on trade between Member States. Despite the significant amendments to the Treaty of Rome, as outlined above, there has been no overt change to the ECJ's approach when balancing environmental objectives and the free movement of goods.

The Court's approach has given rise to difficulties. Measures of environmental protection are inherently likely to discriminate against goods or undertakings established in other Member States, as it is well-recognised that pollution is best tackled at source. But even though a measure of environmental protection may be necessary and proportionate, it will quite simply be prohibited if it is directly or indirectly discriminatory. This is hardly compatible with the position of environmental protection as an equal policy to that of the free movement of goods.

In order to close the gap, the ECJ, rather than revise its earlier case-law in the light of the Treaty amendments, has chosen to resort to creative interpretive techniques. In particular, confined by the strait jacket of its earlier case-law, the ECJ has classified blatantly discriminatory measures as 'indistinctly applicable' to enable them to benefit from derogations on the basis of one of the mandatory requirements. Perhaps the most striking example of this occurred in the *Walloon Waste* case.[20] That case concerned legislation which amounted to a ban on the importation of all waste products into Wallonia. The ECJ held that the legislation fell within Article 30 (now Article 28) of the Treaty and then went on to consider its potential conformity with the mandatory requirement of environmental protection. The ECJ found that the legislation was justified by that requirement. In response to the Commission's argument that mandatory requirements could not be relied upon, as the measure discriminated against waste originating in other Member States, the ECJ pointed out that:

> in assessing whether or not the barrier in question is discriminatory, account must be taken of the particular nature of waste. The principle that environmental damage should as a matter or priority be remedied at source, laid down by Article 130(r)(2) of the Treaty as a basis for action by the Community relating to the environment, entails that it is for each region, municipality or other local authority to take appropriate steps to ensure that its own waste is collected, treated and disposed of: it must accordingly be disposed of as close as possible to the place where it is produced, in order to limit as far as possible the transport of waste.

The Court thus found that the Wallonian measures were not discriminatory because waste produced in different places was different because of the connection it had with its source of production.

---

[19] See, for example, Case 113/80 *Commission* v. *Ireland* [1981] ECR 1625.

[20] Case C–2/90 *Commission* v. *Belgium* [1992] ECR I–4431. For a commentary see L Hancher and H Sevenster, 'Case Comment on Case C–2/90 *Commission* v. *Belgium*' (1993) 30 *CML Rev* 351.

This classification of the Wallonian measures as indistinctly applicable has been widely criticised on the basis that 'a measure which clearly favours waste produced in one region of a Member State is plainly not an indistinctly applicable measure'.[21]

Nevertheless, in subsequent cases, the ECJ has again applied the mandatory requirements case-law to measures which appear to be clearly discriminatory. Thus in *Aher-Waggon*[22] the ECJ once more upheld a discriminatory environmental protection measure. That case concerned German legislation restricting noise emissions from aircraft. Pursuant to the legislation, aircraft which had obtained German registration before the implementation of the German measure were exempted from the new standards while aircraft registered in other Member States before that date did not benefit from the exemption. The ECJ held that the German legislation could be justified by considerations of public health and environmental protection. This time, in its short judgment, the Court simply did not enter into any discussion of whether the measure was discriminatory; it avoided the issue by proceeding on the basis that the measure 'restricted' the free movement of goods.

Rather than resorting to some far-fetched—not to say exotic—devices so as to maintain the façade that the 'mandatory requirements' only apply to 'indistinctly applicable measures, various commentators have suggested a fundamental change of approach. In particular, Oliver has suggested that the mandatory requirements should be subsumed under Article 30 and be subject to the exact same test as these express derogations.[23] Similarly, Advocate General Jacobs, in *PreussenElektra*[24] called upon the ECJ to take a more flexible approach in respect of the mandatory requirement of environmental protection. At issue in that case was the compatibility with Article 28 EC of German legislation designed to increase the proportion of electricity produced from renewable energy sources. The legislation placed obligations upon electricity supply undertakings to purchase electricity produced from renewable sources *in their region* at fixed minimum prices. Given that suppliers were thereby required to buy a certain proportion of their electricity from *national* sources, they were limited in the quantity of electricity they were able to import. The legislation therefore restricted the free movement of goods in a discriminatory manner.

In his Opinion, Advocate General Jacobs took the view that the legislation should nonetheless be capable of justification on grounds of environmental protection.[25] He argued as follows:

---

[21] *Ibid*, at 361. See also P Oliver, *Free Movement of Goods in the European Community* 3rd edn (Sweet & Maxwell, 2003) at 219.
[22] Case C–389/96 *Aher-Waggon* [1998] ECR I–4473.
[23] Oliver, above n21, at 217.
[24] Case C–379/98 *PreussenElektra* [2001] ECR I–2099.
[25] *Ibid*, Opinion of Mr Advocate General Jacobs, at paras 225–33.

To hold that environmental measures can be justified only where they are applicable without distinction risks defeating the very purpose of the measures. National measures for the protection of the environment are inherently liable to differentiate on the basis of the nature and origin of the cause of harm, and are therefore liable to be found discriminatory, precisely because they are based on such accepted principles as that 'environmental damage should as a priority be rectified at source' (Article 130r(2) of the Treaty).

He added that:

In view of the fundamental importance for the analysis of Article 30 of the Treaty of the question whether directly discriminatory measures can be justified by imperative requirements, the Court should, in my view, clarify its position in order to provide the necessary legal certainty.[26]

However, the ECJ did not follow that suggestion. In its judgment, the ECJ held that the German legislation was not incompatible with Article 28 EC. However, its reasons are a little difficult to discern. The Court did refer to the greater prominence given by the Treaty to the goal of environmental protection.[27] However, the Court also noted that the German legislation was 'designed to protect the health and life of humans, animals and plants', thereby leaving open the possibility that its conclusion of compatibility was based on the express derogation contained in Article 30 EC. In any event, there is no indication in that case that the ECJ intended to abandon the distinction between express derogations and mandatory requirements.

4. EQUAL VALUES FOR EQUAL POLICIES?

The existence of a fundamental tension between the economic objective of the free movement of goods and the socio-political objective of environmental protection is inevitable. Environmental protection is inherently likely to necessitate trade barriers. As the ECJ itself recognised in *PreussenElektra*, environmental initiatives taken by the Member States may well be legitimate and desirable even though they impede the free movement of goods.

In resolving this conflict we take the view that the ECJ should follow Judge Edward's sound advice and look to the Treaty. The protection of the environment has evolved into a key Community objective. As outlined above, this has been reflected by a succession of amendments to the Treaty. Environmental protection has been elevated to one of the 'Community policies' contained in Part III of the EC Treaty. The Treaty contains no hierarchy of policies; on its face, it gives them equal priority.

This fundamental change ought to inform the way the Court seeks to reconcile the free movement provisions with the protection of the environment. The

[26] Case C–379/98 *PreussenElektra* [2001] ECR I–2099, at para 229.
[27] Above n24, at para 76.

Court's rather artificial efforts to shoehorn environmental initiatives taken by the Member States into its traditional analysis of permissible derogations from Article 28 miss the point. They start from a presumption that no longer holds good; namely, that the Treaty values the free movement provisions above all others. Nor do we think that the answer necessarily lies in the approach advocated by Oliver and by Advocate General Jacobs in *PreussenElektra*.[28] In our view, the lack of certainty arising from the ECJ's case-law is due not so much to the fact that it has not adapted its traditional case-law on the interpretation of Article 28, but rather to its failure properly to reflect the changing priorities of the EU as set out in the Treaty. We consider that the Court ought to start from a position of no hierarchical presumption. The question should not be whether a measure is discriminatory or non-discriminatory or whether it interferes to the least possible degree with imports, but whether it is proportionate in light of the equal but competing aims of environmental protection and free movement.

The Court has already adopted such an approach in another area. In *Albany*,[29] the Court had to consider the compatibility with the Treaty's competition provisions of a decision by the Dutch public authorities making it compulsory for all undertakings in a particular sector to join a single sectoral pension scheme. The Court held that the decision fell outside the scope of Article 81(1) of the Treaty. The Court's analysis did not follow its traditional case-law on Article 81 EC. Instead, the Court stepped back and considered the competing policy interests at stake. It referred to the fact that, under Article 3(1)(g) and (j) of the Treaty, the activities of the Community are to include not only a 'system ensuring that competition in the internal market is not distorted' but also a 'policy in the social sphere'. The Court went on to hold:

> It is beyond question that certain restrictions of competition are inherent in collective agreements between organisations representing employers and workers. However, the social policy objectives pursued by such agreements would be seriously undermined if management and labour were subject to Article 81(1) of the Treaty when seeking jointly to adopt measures to improve conditions of work and employment.
>
> It therefore follows from an interpretation of the provisions of the Treaty as a whole which is both effective and consistent, that agreements concluded in the context of collective negotiations between management and labour in pursuit of such objectives must, by virtue of their nature and purpose, be regarded as falling outside the scope of Article 81(1) of the Treaty.[30]

There is, in our view, every reason why the Court should adopt a similar analysis in relation to environmental policy and the free movement of goods.

---

[28] See also Case C–203/96 *Chemische Afvalstoffen Dusseldorp* [1998] ECR I–4075.
[29] Case C–67/96 *Albany* [1999] ECR I–5751.
[30] *Ibid*, at paras 59 and 60.

16

The Dangers of too Much Precaution

IAN S. FORRESTER QC

Hecate: 'For you all know, security
Is mortals' chiefest enemy'[1]

ONE OF THE pleasures of being a member of the Edward professional family is the hospitality. As an intermittently hungry devil,[2] I was treated to frequent, regular food in Heriot Row, a phenomenon whose human and material generosity seemed at the time merely delightful, but which now seems truly prodigious in light of my own experience of juggling the demands of parenthood, a busy practice and the other preoccupations of legal life. In honour of the many teas, lunches, dinners, whiskies and other organoleptic delights I have enjoyed over the years *chez* Edward, this article considers how lawyers, officials, government ministers and judges handle controversies about food safety. I wish to voice some doubts about the precautionary principle, and to submit that it is an imperfect basis for regulating controversies in a society dependent on technology and governed by law.

I enjoy cooking. If I could knowingly choose between cooking a piece of a chicken reared by a farmer who used no antibiotics in his feedstuffs, and a piece of chicken produced in a factory farm with no light, no freedom for the birds and no nourishment which I would naively regard as normal chickenfeed, I would choose the former. My choice would be guided by what I might call commonsense and instinct, not scientific knowledge. I would prefer 'natural' raw materials when cooking.

However, animals raised for food do not, in most European Member States, live a natural life. Their quarters are cramped and the farmers who rear them are short of money. The faster they put on weight, the better their health, the more quickly they can be sold. Feeding livestock is a technologically sophisticated activity. For years farmers in Europe (and elsewhere) have given their animals feed containing tiny quantities of antibiotic growth promoters[3] to ensure they digest their food efficiently, avoid intestinal diseases and put on

---

[1] From Thomas Middleton's additions to Shakespeare's *Macbeth*.
[2] A devil is the trainee of a 'junior' advocate at the Scots Bar.
[3] One kilo of antibiotic is enough for 50,000 kilos of animal feed.

weight quickly. In 1968 a new antibiotic was identified in Belgium and named virginiamycin, after the American state where it was wrongly believed to have been previously identified. The substance turned out to be disappointing for treating human disease, since it was not soluble in water and could not be 'delivered' to sites of infection in the body. However, it was discovered to be a valuable contributor to the rearing of animals. Pigs which ate waste from the laboratory thrived (so I was told), as the antibiotic improved their digestion and reduced minor ailments which commonly affected livestock.

In 1970, nineteen antibiotic growth promoters, including virginiamycin and bacitracin zinc, were authorised for use as a feedstuff additive in farms in the European Community. The registrations of the two products were regularly updated and remained in force, with various adaptations, until they were banned by a Council Regulation[4] whose legality was challenged before the Court of First Instance.[5] The Court received lengthy and detailed written submissions on the law, and the facts, and the science. The oral argument lasted two days (ending after 10.00pm on the evening of the first day.) The Court's judgment, issued on 11 September 2002, offered some language which offered general comfort for the industry, but also raised a number of troubling questions. I was one of the counsel involved in those cases. There was no appeal, and the litigation concerning the ban is now over. All antibiotic feed additives are now being phased out in Europe. The Belgian factory which makes virginiamycin has been sold by Pfizer Animal Health, and now supplies feed manufacturers outside the European Union. This article will reflect on some of the broader legal and regulatory questions presented.[6]

1. THE VOCABULARY: RISKS, PREVENTION AND PRECAUTION

'Words are the daughters of earth and . . . things are the sons of heaven'[7]

Regulations govern many aspects of our lives: directly or indirectly, there are controls over the brakes on our cars, the wrapping of frozen food, the feed given to cattle, the polyurethane foam in household chairs. Some of these regulations stipulate standards to be adhered to by all products, other regulations permit the

---

[4] Council Regulation No 2821/98 amending, as regards withdrawal of the authorisation of certain antibiotics, Directive 70/524/EC concerning additives in feeding stuffs, OJ 1998 L 351/4.

[5] Case T-13/99 *Pfizer Animal Health* v. *Commission* [2002] ECR II-3305, with respect to virginiamycin; Case T-70/99 *Alpharma Inc.* v. *Council* [2002] ECR II-3495, with respect to bacitracin zinc. The manufacturers of two other banned products did not appeal. Interim measures to suspend the effectiveness of the Regulation were refused by Order of the President on 8 June 1999 in Case T-13/99 R [1999] ECR II-1961 (upheld on appeal by the President of the Court of Justice on 18 November 1999 in Case C-329/99 P (R) [1999] ECR I-8843).

[6] I express thanks to Professors Casewell, Majone, Joerges, Philips, Pugh and others who have attempted to instruct me in the relevant science and in risk management, and to Messrs. Gale-Batten, Killick and McCarthy with much appreciation for their contribution during the litigation.

[7] Dr. Samuel Johnson, *Dictionary*.

sale of products only once they have been specifically tested and approved. Some chemicals and all pharmaceuticals are subject to especially stringent checks. Many standards are set at European level. The common market functions more easily if discrepancies in national standards for the same products are eliminated. It is politically and materially impossible for European Commission officials to decide these matters, so there are scores of Council working groups and committees which meet regularly, usually in Brussels, to consider the merits of new products, discuss controversial products, issue recommendations, or take decisions. Although they pursue consensus, these committees sometimes encounter disagreement along national lines (Belgium considers the product desirable, Finland considers it undesirable), or along technical lines (evidence convincing to Portuguese representatives, evidence unconvincing to Irish representatives). The manufacturer of a product or the national government to which it is most sympathetic may argue that the product is excellent and should be authorised for sale (or that its authorisation should remain valid). Critics may say the product should be banned or should not be authorised. A number of scientific committees exist to offer advice and technical guidance to the decision-makers. That advice is usually, but not always, accepted.

Committees, working groups and administrative hierarchies depend on words recorded in writing. Overly colourful use of words can significantly distort sober analysis. It is easy to say 'safety first', 'take no risks', 'do not play roulette with human health', and difficult to disagree with such sentiments. In ordinary speech, words like chance, odds, likelihood are often used casually, imprecisely. In the world of risk analysis, there is a special lexicon: risk, hazard, danger, threat, adverse outcome, uncertainty, proof, confidence, doubt, and even precaution, can each be used casually or precisely. A controversy arises. Is there a danger, a risk, a threat? How to analyse and how to decide? When looking at a supposed danger, gravity and probability should be separately considered. Risk is a combination of hazard and likelihood. If the hazard is not severe and the likelihood of occurrence is remote, the risk factor is low and acceptable; no action is needed. If the likelihood of occurrence is high, then action is appropriate, the more so if the event would be serious. If the event may be dire but the likelihood of occurrence is remote, action is unnecessary (an asteroid of one kilometre in diameter striking the Earth). These are easy challenges for the regulator. Unfortunately, debates about the precautionary principle usually involve a dire hazard and a hotly-debated likelihood. The proponent of 'safety first' calls for a prohibition on the ground that the worst might happen, the manufacturer says the fears are exaggerated, lobbyists of various hues opine vigorously, the public reads the newspapers and the authorities have to take a position.

'Prévention routière' is a common term for road safety policies in French-speaking countries. Prevention in this sense means the taking of measures to avoid already established dangers or lessen their frequency: speed limits, prohibitions on driving while intoxicated, hygiene requirements in restaurants and food factories.

Precaution means something different: the taking of action, always negative action, to prevent the possibility that harm may occur due to a threat whose nature and severity are not known. Precautionary policies bite before it is sure that action is necessary and, by definition, bite in the absence of proof. Thus precaution implies in this context the taking of legal or regulatory or policy steps to prevent the occurrence of a danger, even when it is not known that the danger will or can materialise.[8]

2. THE RISKS WE RUN

King Richard: '*I have set my life upon a cast,
And I will stand the hazard of the die.*'[9]

As ordinary citizens, we are irrational in our decision-making about the risks we are willing to run and those we consider it essential to avoid. The likelihood that a pedestrian who crosses the road when the traffic lights are against him will suffer harm thereby is considerably higher than the risk of contracting Creuzfeld-Jakobs Disease (*CJD*) through eating contaminated meat: but we all do the former, and few of us would object to a ban on all meat as a way of reducing the risk of the latter. On 1 May 2003 the inhabitants of Beijing did not congregate to celebrate Labour Day; they stayed at home lest they catch SARS. Probably Beijing's smokers smoked as many cigarettes as usual on that day, and few Beijing inhabitants modified their behaviour to reduce the risk of contracting HIV/AIDS. Yet fewer than two thousand Chinese have died of SARS, while the country is the victim of an AIDS epidemic which has already killed thousands; and the incidence of smoking-induced diseases is rising rapidly throughout Asia. But a new disease with, as yet, no known remedy, is perceived as much more threatening than (or at least changes citizens' behaviour more than) a by now familiar disease with no known remedy, or an attractive habit whose danger has been known for some years. Thus the universe of citizens is not well-equipped to make these delicate choices and it makes them in a manner which is not logical.

An admirable book entitled 'Living with Risk'[10] explains the statistical likelihood of death while engaged in certain common activities such as playing

---

[8] There is a considerable literature on this topic. One of the most accessible surveys is C Joerges 'Integrating Scientific Expertise into Regulatory Decision-Making. Scientific Expertise in Social Regulation and the European Court of Justice: Legal Frameworks for Denationalized Governance Structures' (1996) *European University Institute Working Paper RCS No. 96/10*; likewise G Majone 'The Precautionary Principle and its Policy Implications' (2002) 40 *Journal of Common Market Studies* 89. For the views of a scientist who is also a European civil servant and quotes Shakespeare, read MD Rogers 'Risk analysis under uncertainty, the Precautionary Principle, and the new EU chemicals strategy' *Regulatory Toxicology and Pharmacology* 37, 370-381, 2003 Elsevier Science (USA). For a one-page thoughtful survey by a US official, see IM Goklany 'From precautionary principle to risk-risk analysis' (2002) *Nature Publishing Group* 1075, http//:www.nature.com/nature-biotechnology.

[9] Shakespeare: *Richard III*, Act V.

[10] Michael Henderson (ed.) *The BMA Guide to Living with Risk* (Penguin Books, 1990).

football, being a professional fisherman and being a miner. There is a 6,000 to one chance of dying in a car crash each year for a UK driver who covers an average mileage. This means 17 deaths per year among 100,000 people (or 170 deaths per year per million of the population). Playing football is less dangerous: 25,000 to 1 or 4 deaths per 100,000 each year. Non-smoking women under 35 who take the contraceptive pill face even better odds: 77,000 to 1, or 1.3 deaths per 100,000. Some will abstain even though they have 69,999 chances out of 70,000 of surviving. As we will see, it is difficult to decide wisely controversies where the statistical threat to the population is 1 per million or less. The threat is not non-existent, and the hazard may be horrid, yet the chances of harm materialising are far more remote than other harms to which society probably does not devote enough preventive effort.[11]

3. THE PRECAUTIONARY PRINCIPLE

'Our watchword is security'[12]

This brings us to the precautionary principle, which is an attempt to offer an intellectually and politically defensible framework for deciding controversies when the science is disputed. There seems to be no single authoritative version of the words which encapsulate it. Professor Per Sandin claims to be able to identify 19 versions.[13] One of its precursors was the German notion of *Vorsorgung* or *Vorsorgeprinzip* (taking care in advance). It was referred to in international agreements on the environment such as the Rio Declaration[14] (which is in turn evoked in Article 1 of the Cartagena Protocol on Biosafety[15]):

> *'In order to protect the environment, the precautionary approach shall be widely applied by States according to their capabilities. Where there are threats of serious or irreversible damage, lack of full scientific certainty shall not be used as a reason for postponing cost-effective measures to prevent environmental degradation.'*

---

[11] There is a debate in the UK about whether it is preferable to spend millions of pounds on railway safety in order to reduce the odds of a small number of railway fatalities, whereas the same sum spent on road safety would save more lives.
[12] Prime Minister William Pitt, the Elder.
[13] P Sandin 'Dimensions of the Precautionary Principle' (1999) 5 *Hum. & Ecological Risk Assessment* 889. See the many other sources (criminal, sociological, political) set forth in J Wiener 'Whose Precaution After All: A comment on the comparison and evolution of risk regulatory systems' (Special Issue 2003) 13 *Duke Journal of Comparative and International Law* 202.
[14] Declaration of 12 August 1992 on Environment and Development, following the United Nations Conference on Environment and Development held at Rio de Janeiro from 3 to 14 June 1992.
[15] *'In accordance with the precautionary approach contained in Principle 15 of the Rio Declaration on Environment and Development, the objective of this Protocol is to contribute to ensuring an adequate level of protection in the field of the safe transfer, handling and use of living modified organisms resulting from modern biotechnology that may have adverse effects on the conservation and sustainable use of biological diversity, taking also into account risks to human health, and specifically focusing on transboundary movements.'*

The Commission issued a Communication on the Use of the Precautionary Principle[16] and justifies recourse to the precautionary principle where,

'... *scientific evidence is insufficient, inconclusive or uncertain and there are indications through preliminary objective scientific evaluation that there are reasonable grounds for concern that the potentially dangerous effects on the environment, human, animal or plant health may be inconsistent with the chosen level of protection.*'

Article 174(2) of the EC Treaty as amended mentions the precautionary principle as a doctrine relevant in the environmental field.[17] The Commission has stated that the precautionary principle *'has been progressively consolidated in international law and so it has since become a full-fledged and general principle of international law.'* Thus it seems clear enough that Community law and policy recognise and respect, even honour, the precautionary principle. Aware of the doubts relating to the principle's possible abuse, when announcing the adoption of its Communication on 2 February 2000, the Commission said:

'... *the precautionary principle is neither a politicisation of science or the acceptance of zero-risk but [that] it provides a basis for action when science is unable to give an answer. The Communication also makes it clear that determining what is an acceptable level of risk for the EU is a political responsibility. It provides a reasoned and structured framework for action in the face of scientific uncertainty and shows that the precautionary principle is not a justification for ignoring scientific evidence and taking protectionist decisions.*'[18]

I will be submitting that these commendable sentiments have not been observed consistently in actual practice. The first thing to say is that the meaning of the principle is not precise.

'*Few legal concepts have achieved the notoriety of the precautionary principle. Praised by some, disparaged by others, the principle is deeply ambivalent and apparently infinitely malleable ... an instrument of reconciliation between popular and expert government it becomes apparent that the principle may operate to conceal rather than resolve such tensions.*'[19]

---

[16] COM(2000) 1 Communication on the Use of the Precautionary Principle, 10.

[17] '*Community policy on the environment shall aim at a high level of protection taking into account the diversity of situations in the various regions of the Community. It shall be based on the precautionary principle and on the principles that preventive action should be taken, that environmental damage should as a priority be rectified at source and that the polluter should pay.*'

[18] Press release IP/00/96.

[19] J Scott and E Vos (authors) 'The Juridification of Uncertainty: Observations on the Ambivalence of the Precautionary Principle within the EU and the WTO' in C Joerges and R Dehousse (eds) *Good Governance in Europe's Integrated Market* (Oxford University Press, 2002). See also such polemical pieces as GH Smith 'Beware The 'Precautionary Principle'' (December 2000) *McClane Publications*, http://www.mclane.com/publications/environmental/030.htm; and HI Miller 'Precautionary Principle Raises Blood Pressure' (25 June 2002) *Health Facts and Fears.com*, http://www.healthfactsandfears.com/high_priorities/ipriorities/2002/precautionary062, attacking a proposed ban on a diagnostic device because it used mercury.

Certain formulations favoured by those who are sceptical about the use of technology would shift the burden of proof:

> '... the applicant or proponent of an activity needs to demonstrate to the satisfaction of the public and the regulatory community that ... public health will be safe. The proof must shift to the party or entity that will benefit from the activity and is most likely to have the information.'[20]

If 'safe' means 'guaranteed not to be in any circumstances unsafe', then this prescription is unrealistically severe, as cars, pharmaceuticals, vaccines and many other products bring dangers to health and safety as well as advantages. (Cheeses and alcohols bring pleasures as well as dangers.) If 'safe' means 'appropriately safe', then the principle is incapable of being disagreed with, but not very helpful for the resolution of specific controversies. Likewise, we are told that lack of full scientific certainty shall not be used as *'a reason for postponing measures to prevent environmental degradation'*. Since scientific certainty is almost never present in any controversy, this formulation would justify measures everywhere or nowhere to prevent environmental degradation. The principle then is like a slogan, not an intelligible prescription for action.

European Institutions are not immune from extravagant formulations which cannot mean exactly what they say. In its Defence in the *virginiamycin* case noted above, the Council stated: *'the Community decided to withdraw the products until it can be demonstrated conclusively that they pose no present or future risks to human health.'* The Council made a similar statement in its Observations in the Interim Measures proceedings. The Commission does not routinely advance such arguments: in the case of *Nancy Olivieri* v. *Commission*,[21] an expert argued that the Commission had wrongly handled the process for authorising a medicine which she regarded as unsafe, and the Commission successfully defended itself at the interim measures stage. The President of the Court of First Instance stated in his Order:

> *'The Commission further points out that, in so far as no medicinal product is entirely without risk, the degree of acceptable risk will depend on the therapeutic value and uniqueness of the medicinal product in question.'*[22]

4. LOOKING AT THE BEST AND THE WORST

> 'Science is nothing but trained and organised common sense, differing from the latter only as a veteran may differ from a raw recruit.'[23]

---

[20] Wingspread Statement on the Precautionary Principle, Racine, Wisconsin, 25 January 1998. This is one of many 'green' versions of the principle.
[21] Case T-326/99R *Nancy Olivieri* v. *Commission* [2000] ECR II-1985.
[22] Ibid., *Nancy Olivieri*, para. 90.
[23] TH Huxley.

A person without knowledge is likely to be ready to believe that each of two possible outcomes is equally probable. The more arcane the field of knowledge, the more difficult it is for the layman to make an intelligent or prudent decision as to an outcome's likelihood. We are almost always uncertain about whether a supposed risk is real and how serious it is. Uncertainty may relate to cause, or to effect, or to both. Pitching a tent in Central Africa close to standing or slow-moving water is likely to lead to mosquito bites and, unless the camper has been taking a prophylactic anti-malaria medicine, there is a measurable risk of being infected by a serious blood-borne malady. There may be uncertainty as to effect: does extensive use of a mobile telephone increase the incidence of brain tumours? There may be uncertainty as to both, as in the case of a medicine which is said to be statistically associated with certain health problems.

The best approach for rational decision-making is to look at all possible outcomes, not only the worst outcome, and to consider the likely consequence of action, including the risks associated with a prohibition. The entire problem should be examined taking into account every available piece of information. This should involve considering all probable events, all available regulatory decisions, and all the combinations of decisions and events which might occur. Moreover, the decisions should be capable of being rationally up-dated from time to time.

Read calmly, the foregoing ideas are likely not to be very controversial. How we apply the doctrine in disputes is controversial: however, encouraging prohibition in the presence of doubt implies either that huge numbers of products which are not acceptably unsafe would be banned; or that the selected few unlucky products would be chosen for prohibition in an arbitrary and unpredictable manner.

The precautionary principle preaches that where scientific knowledge is 'insufficient, inconclusive or uncertain', society may properly act conservatively to eliminate the 'danger' provisionally; whereas if scientific knowledge were complete, a formal risk assessment could be completed and an informed decision taken definitively. But real life does not correspond to these chosen alternatives: the normal condition of the well-informed expert is to be neither perfectly knowledgeable nor perfectly ignorant. The normal condition is to have some data about which not all experts will agree.[24] If the level of knowledge is characterised as imperfect, the precautionary principle may be applied and it will be legitimate to be 'tough', cautious, conservative, risk-averse, protective of public health, and so on. In this climate, it will seem reasonable to ban the product until matters become clearer. A ban in such circumstances will be based on the assertion that knowledge is 'inadequate', when that inadequacy may reflect an ideological debate rather than an incomplete picture. Worse, perfect know-

---

[24] The molecules fenfluramine and dexfenfluramine, anti-obesity medicines developed by Les Laboratoires Servier, have been the subject of over 6,000 articles in medical literature, and are probably the most copiously examined and commented pharmaceuticals in history, yet there is still controversy about their risk/benefit ratio.

ledge is virtually unattainable (and only a fool would believe he had attained it). This means that for many, many products it will be impossible to show that there are no risks; *ergo*, knowledge is not adequate; *ergo*, a ban might be reasonable. The ban may be described as provisional, but in many cases its application will be permanent. A product once prohibited can hardly ever be rehabilitated.

5. TWO EXAMPLES OF POSSIBLY EXCESSIVE CAUTION

The precautionary principle has the potential to open the field to decisions driven by discretionary caprice. I offer two amateur doubts about the dangers of well-intentioned regulation.

Justified by reducing the danger of liver cancer, from which 35,000 Europeans die each year, a ban was proposed on nuts and grains from a number of African countries, for fear that they might contain aflotoxins which could involve a risk of 1.4 deaths per billion, or one life every two years in the European continent (a billion is one second in 37 years). The likely cost was estimated at 670,000,000 dollars, and endangered the livelihood of hundreds of thousands of African farmers.[25]

A second example is the pesticide DDT which has been largely eliminated as a chemical in most countries because of its effect on the reproductive process of birds of prey. DDT was extremely successful in controlling the mosquitoes which carry the malaria parasite. In countries where malaria was endemic, spraying was a cheap and effective means of suppressing the danger. Donor countries frown on the use of DDT, and poor countries have tried to suppress its use. Cases of malaria are rising: there were over 300 million last year, and a million deaths. As DDT has been phased out, the great strides in controlling malaria in the 1940s, 1950s and 1960s have been reversed. There is a fiercely debated literature,[26] and I have no conclusion to offer, but I submit that the matter deserves to be considered calmly.

6. THE RESOLUTION OF DISPUTES

'... *where ignorant armies clash by night*'[27]

Scientific method typically involves the advancing of several different theories, followed by a cautious adaptation of those theories in light of greater knowledge.

---

[25] T Otsuki, JS Wilson and M Sewadeh (2000) 'Saving Two in a Billion: A Case Study to Quantify the Trade Effect of European Food Safety Standards on African Exports', Mimeo (Washington DC: World Bank).
[26] For example, R Tren and R Bate 'When Politics Kills: Malaria and the DDT Story' (2001) *Competitive Enterprise Institute*, http://www.fightingmalaria.org).
[27] Matthew Arnold: *Dover Beach*.

The incorporation of new evidence and new data which is processed intelligently should normally lead to convergence of opinions. Science is a discipline which pursues unanimity in the form of concepts, laws, and principles which are agreed and accepted as axioms upon which subsequent scientific research is built. The notion of public knowledge connotes the emergence of doctrines and theories which are the best reconciliation of diverging opinions which scientific method can deliver on the basis of available data. But some of these axioms are not yet capable of being demonstrated as universally valid under laboratory conditions. If uncertainty's presence justifies a departure from normal scientific method, we will rarely follow scientific method. It is regrettable that when confronting diversity of opinion, the process of decision-making, both at institutional level and before the European Courts, changes (even degenerates?) from the characteristic of academic scientific debate which involves the pursuit of convergence between different observers of known phenomena. It becomes a process of advocacy, in which the scientist is deployed as an advocate propounding the rightness of one approach or the other approach.

During the debate about the use of antibiotic growth promoters in European farming, Scandinavian government officials took the position that as a matter of high policy, such products are undesirable, potentially harmful and deserving of prohibition. On the other side were scientists asserting that the risks were hypothetical, that a full risk analysis should be made, that ongoing enquiries would reveal useful information, that there was not no risk, but that such risk was rather trivial and that the evidence advanced (by Denmark, whose national ban triggered the subsequent Council ban) did not reveal any emergency justifying the prohibition of a product. Each side was in good faith. Each side had defensible scientific arguments to deploy. The European Court of First Instance in Cases T-13/99 (*Pfizer Animal Health: virginiamycin*) and T-70/99 (*Alpharma: bacitracin zinc*) was confronted with two groups of learned professors of medicine. Each sounded convincing, and each endorsed one side of the debate. They spoke partly as expert witnesses and partly, in a sense, as advocates for one view or the other.

Unfortunately, the Court did not take the preliminary step of inviting the experts of each side to sit together and produce a common document recording the points as to which they agreed and the points as to which they disagreed. Nor was the Court able to benefit from the proper testing of one expert's theories by questioning from counsel educated by another expert.[28] The legal submissions therefore tended, on the one side, to emphasise grave danger ('*bodies in the streets*', '*nightmare reality*', '*ultimate spectre*', and the need to '*run no risk with public safety*'), whereas on the other side the manufacturers emphasised the need for further enquiry, due process, the exhaustive enquiries and checks already carried out, 30 years of trouble-free use, and similar notions.

---

[28] The Court's tradition does not lend itself to, but I would submit the Court's rules do not preclude, such a mode of enquiry.

The process of litigation does not enhance the likelihood of scientific consensus: to the contrary, it can make scientists into advocates arguing that their side is right and the other side is wrong, whereas if the scientists had been invited to do so they could have produced a helpful explanation of where they disagreed, how significant was that disagreement, and might also have been able to reach consensus on statistical probabilities.

7. THE US JUDICIAL EXPERIENCE OF SCIENTIFIC CONTROVERSIES

'Perfect safety is a chimera; regulation must not strangle human activity in the search for the impossible'[29]

In the United States there have been a number of judgments of superior courts concerning scientific controversies. Two strands seem noteworthy, both pertaining to scientific rigour, one as to minority scientific theories, and the other as to standard-setting. The US litigation system creates huge economic incentives for lawyers and their clients to win cases where damage awards are pronounced by juries of laymen. The role of the expert scientist as a paralegal litigation asset has given rise to an extensive literature and numerous attempts, sometimes successful, to invoke before American courts the so-called *Daubert* Principle to prevent juries being confused by scientific opinion which lies very much in the minority.

In *Daubert* v. *Merrell Dow Pharmaceuticals*,[30] the Supreme Court confirmed that a trial judge was under a duty to ensure that scientific testimony was not just relevant to the controversy, but also reliable enough to be advanced to the jury. Among the factors to be considered in examining whether proffered testimony is 'junk science'[31] are whether the theory can be tested or demonstrated, whether it has been subject to peer review and publication, whether it seems to be prone to errors and exceptions, and its general acceptance by the scientific community. In *Kumho Tire Co* v. *Carmichael*,[32] the court extended the *Daubert* 'gatekeeping' constraint to include a prior check upon all expert testimony, whether from scientists or those who claim technical or practical experience (in that case, the excluded testimony came from a man who could identify why tyres had failed by looking at their physical characteristics). Thus, the Supreme Court stated that it was legitimate for a trial judge to decline to allow the advancing of 'scientific evidence' which did not correspond to recognised scientific doctrines.

---

[29] Chief Justice Burger, concurring in *Industrial Union Department, AFL-CIO* v. *American Petroleum Institute et al*. 448 US 607 (1980) at 664 (the *Benzene* case).
[30] 509 US 579 (1993).
[31] A contemptuous term commonly used by those who defend companies against claims based on novel technical theories.
[32] 526 US 137 (1999).

Thus the US courts have endorsed the principle that scientific input should be in the mainstream of opinion in order to be cognisable during the course of a trial. By contrast, the European Court of First Instance has stated that the Institutions were entitled to rely on a minority opinion, although that opinion should not be fanciful or hypothetical. We will also note below various WTO controversies in which world trade bodies have favoured a more robust standard of confidence based upon mainstream scientific opinion.

It is equally interesting to note how the US courts have dealt with the setting of standards of exposure. In such early cases as *Tennessee Valley Authority* v. *Hill*,[33] the Supreme Court reluctantly endorsed the taking of action in precautionary circumstances at a time when there was acute anxiety in the US about degradation of the environment. It sharply reversed direction in the *Benzene* case noted above, where it chastised the agency[34] for setting the standard for the presence of a dangerous contaminant by reference to mere conjecture about possible risks. The Occupational Health and Safety Administration had set 1 part per million (1ppm) as the acceptable maximum exposure of workers to benzene.[35] There was of course no certainty as to what would be a safe standard, but on the other hand there had been no quantification of the number of illnesses which would have been prevented by the new standard. The agency felt that the appropriate threshold for carcinogens ought to be the lowest feasible level of exposure. The agency should have shown there was 'significant risk',[36] and the Court noted that 'safe' is not the same as 'risk-free'.[37]

On the basis of conversations with various specialists and experts,[38] I have the impression that US regulation today corresponds more closely to mainstream scientific opinion, whereas European regulation is more unpredictable once

---

[33] 437 US 153 (1978): This was the celebrated *Snail Darter* case, where the construction of a dam on the Little Tennessee River was halted for fear of damaging the habitat of a population of snail darter fish (which subsequently have been found to thrive elsewhere), there being 90 other species of darter fish in the State of Tennessee. '*It may seem curious to some that the survival of a relatively small number of three-inch fish among all the countless millions of species extant would require the permanent halting of a virtually completed dam for which Congress has expended more than $100 million. The paradox is not minimized by the fact that Congress continued to appropriate large sums of public money for the project, even after congressional Appropriations Committees were apprised of its apparent impact upon the survival of the snail darter. We conclude, however, that the explicit provisions of the Endangered Species Act require precisely that result.*' (p. 172) See also Justice Powell's dissent: '*Here the District Court recognized that Congress, when it enacted the Endangered Species Act, made the preservation of the habitat of the snail darter an important public concern. But it concluded that this interest on one side of the balance was more than outweighed by other equally significant factors.*' (p. 213).

[34] '*These assumptions are not a proper substitute for the findings of a significant risk of harm required by the Act.*' (Benzene, above n 29, at p. 662). Likewise, '*When the administrative record reveals only scant or minimal risk of material health impairment, responsible administration calls for avoidance of extravagant, comprehensive regulation.*' (Benzene, p. 664).

[35] One part per million is 1 inch in 16 miles, 1 centimetre in 10 kilometres.

[36] Above n 29, *Benzene*, p. 655.

[37] Above n 29, *Benzene*, p. 642.

[38] There was an interesting discussion of these questions at the European Policy Centre's conference on 'The US, Europe, Precaution And Risk Management,' 19–21 June 2003, Berlin, when

controversies arise. This seems particularly true with respect to procedure, methodology and judicial review. However, as to the substance of what is being guarded against, the picture is not consistent.

The admirable article by Jonathan Wiener[39] mentioned earlier shows that the United States is sometimes very cautious, even precautionary, sometimes not; and that Europe and North America do not always agree as to what they should be worrying about. Wiener notes that the United States severely limits the use of diesel engines in passenger cars in order to reduce suspended particulate matter from exhaust emissions, whereas Europe promotes diesel engines to reduce CO_2 emissions. Both sides of the Atlantic are acting to protect the environment, but they are doing so in a very different manner. Likewise, various public authorities in the United States have imposed severe restrictions on the donation of blood there by those who have been living in Europe, for fear that European residents who offer blood may have contracted variant CJD due to eating beef products contaminated by Bovine Spongiform Encephalopathy (BSE). New York bans European blood donors even though no one has yet been shown to have contracted CJD via a blood transfusion. In Europe, the consequences of refusing blood donations from all European residents for fear of CJD infection would, naturally, be regarded as excessively severe by comparison to the modest public health advantage. However, some 200 articles confirm that the hazard is not hypothetical.[40]

8. CONSTITUTIONAL PROBLEMS

A further reason for an EC lawyer to be uneasy about the precautionary principle is constitutional, both internal and external.

The internal dimension

There is often a spectrum of opinion, extending from passionate zealotry at one extremity to true scientific confidence (as taught in high school chemistry lessons) at the other. Official policy is made by individuals whose collective sentiment is likely to lie between these poles. There is rarely no evidence which the zealot can deploy, and very few scientists can be totally confident about safety

---

specialists in various disciplines compared and contrasted approaches in very diverse areas (environment, penology, food standards, and even foreign policy).

[39] J Wiener, above n 13.
[40] See for example, PG Smith 'The Epidemics of Bovine Spongiform Encephalopathy and Variant Creutzfeldt-Jakob Disease: Current Status and Future Prospects' (2003) *Bulletin of the World Health Organization* 81(2). WK Hoots, C Abrams, D Tankersleydagger 'The Impact of Creutzfeldt-Jakob Disease and Variant Creutzfeldt-Jakob Disease on Plasma Safety' (2001) *Transfusion Medical Review* 15 (2 Supplement 1). There are many others.

in every circumstance. We will now note how the European Court has dealt with such controversies, where one Member State sees danger and another Member State (or the Commission, or a citizen) sees a hindrance to free movement.

The European Court of Justice and the Commission used to be confronted repeatedly with justifications offered by Member States for maintaining national standards on flimsy grounds of public health. Blackcurrant liqueur, blood sausages and beer were only some of the many cases.[41] In some, the European Court looked at the specific facts and circumstances and was able to reject the national arguments as unfounded. Indeed, it is not difficult to mock the suggestion that German beer as liquid bread[42] is important to the health of the labour force. However, not every case was easy. In the *Nisin* case,[43] the European Court was confronted with a cheese additive: some countries banned it, some did not. Opinions varied. The Court declined to interfere with the application of a national prohibition on the use of the product. In other cases where the concern about public health appeared genuine, even if Member States' opinions varied, the Court was willing to uphold the prohibition. See, for example, *Mirepoix*[44] and *Melkunie*,[45] both concerning safety levels of extraneous matter in food.

On the other hand, in *Commission v France*,[46] the Court rejected French essentially precautionary arguments against allowing the sale in France of British beef after the winding down of the BSE crisis. This is to be contrasted with the Court's rejection of appeals by the UK meat industry against a ban which addressed anxiety about BSE.[47] Nevertheless, in *Denmark v. Commission*,[48] the Court held that a Member State is entitled to decline to follow Community harmonisation legislation on the grounds that the risk to public health appears to be more severe than contemplated when the harmonisation measure was adopted. Denmark lost a Council vote in 1995 on certain food additives, and in 1999 informed the Commission that it proposed not to respect the standards adopted, and requested the Commission's approval. The Commission refused the request on the grounds that Denmark's measures were disproportionately burdensome, having regard to the needs of public health. Denmark challenged that decision, successfully, before the European Court of Justice. The Court found that:

'... the applicant Member State may, in order to justify maintaining such derogating national provisions, put forward the fact that its assessment of the risk to public health

---

[41] 170 pages of Peter Oliver's *Free Movement of Goods in the European Community* (Sweet & Maxwell, 4th ed, 2003) are devoted to cases involving justifications based on Article 30 of the EC Treaty.
[42] Case 17/84 *Commission v Germany (beer)* [1987] ECR 1227.
[43] Case 53/80 *Officier van Justitie v. Koninklijke Kaasfabriek Eyssen* [1981] ECR 409.
[44] Case 54/85 *Ministère public v. Xavier Mirepoix* [1986] ECR 1067.
[45] Case 97/83 *Criminal proceedings against CMC Melkunie BV* [1984] ECR 2367.
[46] Case C-1/00 *Commission v. France* [2001] ECR I-9989.
[47] Case C-157/96 *National Farmers' Union and Others* [1998] ECR I-2211, para. 64.
[48] Case 3/00 *Denmark v. Commission* (judgment of 20 March 2003, not yet reported)

is different from that made by the Community legislature in the harmonisation measure. In the light of the uncertainty inherent in assessing the public health risks posed by, inter alia, the use of food additives, divergent assessments of those risks can legitimately be made, without necessarily being based on new or different scientific evidence.

A Member State may base an application to maintain its already existing national provisions on an assessment of the risk to public health different from that accepted by the Community legislature when it adopted the harmonisation measure from which the national provisions derogate....'[49]

As to sulphites, the Commission's decision survived scrutiny, but as to nitrites and nitrates, the decision was annulled. There are genuine differences of policy and opinion between experts and between governments: the *Danish Nitrite* judgment suggests that Member States on the losing side in Council votes where public health questions are genuinely debated may disregard the Community norm and retain a national standard, even if this standard is based on opinions outwith the scientific mainstream.

It is very difficult to reconcile the mass of European Court judgments which confront the challenge to a common market of sincerely held opposing national opinions. There are many cases, and with ingenuity they can be fitted into a coherent mass,[50] any imperfections in which are made more palatable by the popularly recognised importance of the Court's role as a reconciler of contradictory European and national values. Scientific rigour was given less importance than the constitutional goal of building a rationale which favoured free movement while not dishonouring local preoccupations.

Many of the difficult cases did not involve great sums of money or big constitutional principles. The Court gave an answer (sometimes it changed course) and life moved on. But the external environment seems less forgiving. More harsh in analysing science, less courteous in respecting national anxieties.

9. THE EXTERNAL DIMENSION

Hamlet: '*We defy augury*'[51]

There are many situations where countries in the world trading system have elected to exclude or limit other countries' goods on the grounds of public health. WTO members are not compelled to align their domestic policies, but they are compelled to act in a transparent and non-discriminatory manner in

---

[49] Ibid., paras 63 and 64.
[50] Roman lawyers are familiar with the efforts of mediaeval glossators who devoted huge creativity and diligence to reconciling inconsistencies in Justinian's *Digest*, a work even longer than the Bible: perhaps future generations will look similarly at the first forty years of the European Court's jurisprudence on free movement of goods.
[51] Shakespeare, *Hamlet*, Act V.

their treatment of foreign goods as compared to domestic goods. What level of scientific confidence is necessary in order to exclude, on grounds of public health or the environment, products which are unwelcome as a matter of domestic policy?

Hormones have been controversial both internally and externally. A 1985 Directive prohibiting the use of hormones in the rearing of food animals was challenged by the UK as having been brought under the wrong legal basis, and as being based on flawed science. The UK noted that the official scientific experts of the Institutions had not endorsed a ban. Further consultations of these experts were discontinued and the rationale moved—genuinely—from the confident ground of public health to the slippery one of consumer interest. A measure which was originally criticised by mainstream scientific opinion survived challenge in Luxembourg when re-branded as a measure which corresponded to the widespread will of the population.[52]

However, the measure did not survive challenge under the WTO rules. In *Hormones*,[53] the Appellate Body stated that it was not enough to rely on an *'identifiable risk'* since *'science can never provide absolute certainty that a given substance will not ever have adverse health effects'*. The *Hormones* Panel Report was polite but sceptical about whether a 'risk assessment' occurred: *'an assessment of risk is, at least for risks to human life or health, a scientific examination of data and factual studies; it is not a policy exercise involving social value judgments made by political bodies.'*[54] The evidence was too general and non-specific to justify a ban. After a risk assessment has been carried through, WTO members can choose their appropriate level of sanitary or phytosanitary protection.[55] There are several Panel Reports along similar lines. The *Salmon*[56] Appellate Body report confirmed that it is *'not sufficient that a risk assessment conclude that there is a possibility of entry, establishment or spread of diseases and associated biological and economic consequences.'*

In a very recent case about apples from the United States the Panel found that Japan had gone too far in limiting apple imports to avoid the danger of fire blight.[57] In violation of the WTO Agreement on the Application of Sanitary and Phytosanitary Measures, the Japanese measure was *'maintained without sufficient scientific evidence'* and was not *'based on'* a risk assessment. The Agreement says that where *'relevant scientific evidence is insufficient'*, a

---

[52] Case 68/86 *United Kingdom* v. *Council* [1988] ECR 855.

[53] *European Communities-Measures Concerning Meat and Meat Products (Hormones)*, Report of the Appellate Body, WT/DS26/AB/R (16 January 1998).

[54] *European Communities-Measures Concerning Meat and Meat Products (Hormones)*, Complaint by the United States, Report of the Panel, WT/DS26/R/USA (18 August 1997), §8.94.

[55] The Panel Report does not acknowledge the fact that *'appropriate level of sanitary or phytosanitary protection'* had already been interpreted in Annex A in a way that essentially condones regulatory diversity.

[56] *Australia-Measures Affecting Importation of Salmon*, Report of the Appellate Body, WT/DS18/AB/R (20 October 1998), 123.

[57] *Japan-Measures Affecting the Importation of Apples*, Report of the Panel, WT/DS245/R (15 July 2003).

Member may '*provisionally adopt*' measures on the basis of '*available pertinent information*', provided that it seeks to obtain '*the additional information necessary for a more objective assessment of risk*' and reviews the measure within a reasonable period of time. The '*additional information*' which Japan had gathered demonstrated why the measure was not necessary in the first place: there was already in existence a large amount of scientific evidence demonstrating that the risk of transmission of fire blight through apples was negligible.

The Japanese risk assessment was conducted on the basis of a '*general assessment*' of possibilities of introduction of fire blight into Japan through a variety of routes, including—but not limited exclusively to—apples. It was '*not sufficiently specific to the matter at issue to constitute a proper risk assessment*'.[58]

In each of these cases, we can see strongly-held sentiments coming to grief in the absence of rigorous scientific support.[59] An even bigger controversy looms. On 13 May 2003 the United States formally initiated its complaint against the EU moratorium on granting approvals for new agricultural products created via biotechnology. Several Member States have imposed bans on the planting or sale of GMO (genetically modified organisms) crops, and these bans have not been challenged by the European Commission. A significant percentage of consumers in Europe believe GM foods are unsafe, or less safe than conventional foods (how different GM foods are from others, and indeed what is and is not a GM food, are each indeed a topic of debate). Once again, we see passion and some science on one side of the debate, reassurances on the other side, and a doubtful public.

Bio-tech producing countries argue that the moratorium violates WTO disciplines prohibiting imposition of sanitary and phytosanitary measures without demonstrating clear scientific evidence of risk. Developing countries also resist cultivation of biotech products, for fear that their exports to the EU (a large market for poor countries' exports) will be resisted if 'tainted' by bio-engineering techniques. More specifically, it is said that the EU's moratorium is inconsistent with WTO rules, including the Agreement on Sanitary and Phytosanitary Standards (the SPS Agreement), the Agreement on Technical Barriers to Trade (the TBT Agreement), the Agriculture Agreement and GATT 1994, in that Europe's own scientific studies have not produced adequate risk assessments that biotech products are harmful to human health or the environment. The SPS Agreement, for example, recognises that countries are entitled to regulate food products to protect human health and the environment, but requires measures imposed to carry out these non-trade objectives to be based on 'sufficient scientific evidence', and approval procedures to be carried out without 'undue delay'. The allegation is that SPS measures, if not based on a proper assessment of risk and function, are disguised barriers to trade.

---

[58] Ibid.
[59] For an American view, see White Paper *Looking Behind The Curtain, The Growth of Trade Barriers That Ignore Sound Science* (2003) National Foreign Trade Council, Inc., Washington DC.

Howse & Mavroidis in an interesting article[60] consider how restrictions on genetically modified organisms would be judged by a WTO panel. It remains to be seen whether their analysis will be prescient. What is sure is that the European Union has not been convincingly successful in arguing before international fora that prohibitory measures were legitimately based on science, but that its efforts in Luxembourg have been more successful.

10. THE ANTIBIOTICS LITIGATION IN LUXEMBOURG

This brings us to the recent controversy about the banning of four antibiotic feed additives. I repeat that as an advocate involved in those cases, my views are unreliable; I am perfectly content to cook meat from chicken which has been reared without the use of virginiamycin (although other antibiotics may have been used, either because the bird was reared in the United States or because authorised antibiotics had been used in its production); and no citizen can object to society's reaching a policy decision after mature and frank debate. It is also quite possible that the controversy has been salutary, and that the Institutions have learned from it: on 22 July 2003 (long after this book should have gone to press), the Commission announced that the four remaining antibiotic growth promoters (monensin sodium, salinomycin sodium, avilamycin, flavophospholipol) would be phased out, not as an emergency measure but as part of a general food strategy.

11. CAMPAIGN TO REDUCE THE USE OF ANTIBIOTICS, NOTABLY IN SCANDINAVIA

The Nordic countries have a commendable commitment to high environmental standards. For some years they have pursued a policy of encouraging the phasing out of antibiotic growth promoters, as part of a general scheme to make animal husbandry more wholesome. The results of this policy were not consistently positive: the therapeutic use of antibiotics on herds and flocks rose (prophylactic use in tiny doses helped avoid common diseases, as well as making the animals thrive), and there was an increase in the use of alternative treatments, which have their own adverse environmental consequences. However, the policy enjoyed broad popular support. During their accession negotiations, the governments of Sweden and Finland obtained a prolongation, until January 1999, of the deadline by which they would have to accept the use of antibiotic growth promoters, or the Community regime would be adapted, or an extension of the temporary ban would be made. It was expected that by January 1999 the Community would have reached a definitive view on the products.

---

[60] R Howse & PC Mavroidis 'Europe's evolving regulatory strategy for GMOs – the issue of consistency with WTO law: of kine and brine' (2000) 24 *Fordham International Law Journal* 317.

Critics asserted that the use of antibiotic growth promoters in animal husbandry might have the effect of hindering the delivery of effective medical care to patients infected by an organism resistant to the antibiotics fed to animals, as that organism would also be resistant to other powerful antibiotics in the same chemical family. (Antibiotics exist in families, and public health policy has been to discourage the use of antibiotics in the same family both for human use and for animal non-therapeutic use. Virginiamycin is in the streptogramin family). There was a robust debate in which one side said there was a danger and the other said there was no need to change as the risks had been taken into account when the products were authorised, and were in any event remote, whereas the benefits to farmers were certain.

Each of us has inside our body millions of *Enterococci faecium*—not resistant to antibiotics—which help to digest our food. It is possible that in the gut of some human beings today dwell colonies of *E. faecium* which acquired resistance to the antibiotic virginiamycin. Such resistant *E. faecium* might have entered those intestinal tracts through the presence, on undercooked chicken meat, of living enterococci from chicken faeces dropped on the surface of that meat after slaughter. This eventuality cannot be disproved. Someone could in 1998 have bought frozen chicken which had been reared on a farm in Spain that used virginiamycin as a feedstuff additive, and the meat could have contained some *E. faecium* resistant to antibiotics of the streptogramins family, so that the consumer, when having a liver transplant operation, then fell victim to an infection which could not be cured other than by the use of another streptogramin such as the human medicine synercid. If the patient had acquired resistance to all streptogramin antibiotics, they would be ineffective to cure the infection. Nevertheless, in recorded human medical science, no patient's treatment has ever been compromised due to resistance attributable to virginiamycin. The products have been used in Europe for approximately thirty years.[61] No one fell ill, so far as is known. In France, the streptogramin antibiotic pristinamycin was used for decades in human medicine, and virginiamycin was used in animal feed, with no significant change in either the incidence of the effectiveness of the human medicine, or the incidence of resistance in humans to streptogramins.[62] Researchers have sought such proof of harm, but they have not found it.

It is not disputed that the principal cause of the grave medical problem of human antibiotic resistance is the excessive use of antibiotics in human medicine.[63] There is a whole branch of medical science devoted to preventing and

---

[61] The danger of acquiring a resistance to antibiotics, called 'a hazard of enormous severity . . . a nightmare . . .' was eliminated as to purchases of European chicken meat by the Regulation. However, this danger continues to haunt chicken meat imported from Hong Kong or the United States, perhaps because of the very fact that WTO standards as to scientific proof are stricter than EU standards.

[62] A major study was under way in 1999 in several Member States to ascertain the level of resistance in food animals to particular antibiotics due to the use of antibiotic feed additives, but the study was not completed due to the ban.

[63] US consumption of one antibiotic was 1000% higher than that of the Netherlands per head of the population.

controlling hospital-borne infections. Professor Casewell, one of the scientists who gave evidence for the producers, was a founder and Chairman of the Hospital Infection Society, and could describe from personal knowledge and experience how hospitals (where patients are most at risk from opportunistic infections by bacteria which have grown stronger and stronger through unsuccessful efforts to kill them) have analysed and responded to multiple-resistant organisms. For example, washing the walls of operating theatres with antibiotic liquid and using antibiotic soap each turned out to make hospital infections more difficult to manage. No friend of laxity in the use of antibiotics, he criticised the scientific rigour of the challenges to antibiotic feed additives in 1998 and earlier years.

The prohibition of the four products covered by the contested Regulation started with a Danish prohibition in January 1998 of virginiamycin feedstuffs, taken on the basis of the emergency procedure under Article 11 of Directive 70/524/EEC. The Danish ban lacked technical evidence, and the Commission requested data. In February 1998 the Kingdom of Sweden requested to be allowed to maintain its ban after December 1999. The Danish authorities produced further evidence in March and April 1998 which was again challenged by the industry. There was no consensus among the Member State delegates on the working group responsible for deciding animal feed controversies.

The matter was submitted to the Scientific Committee on Animal Nutrition (*SCAN*), which gave its opinion that, as to virginiamycin, the evidence advanced for its consideration did not justify a prohibition of the products. An additional piece of evidence offered in the course of 1998, an experiment on germ-free rats, demonstrated that resistant *E. faecium* would conjugate in the intestinal tract of a germ-free rat, and could transfer resistant characteristics to other enterococci. The European Commission relied upon this rat experiment as 'major fresh evidence' as to virginiamycin which obliged it to act quickly for the protection of public health. The SCAN was not asked to opine upon this new evidence. The SCAN was not consulted on whether the use of bacitracin zinc as a feed additive presented a threat to public health. The Commission recommended a ban to the Council, which adopted that recommendation after a vote.

The Court of First Instance considered the matter in detail from January 1999 to September 2002. The manufacturers argued that the Regulation had several vices. Firstly, the authorities chose to ignore official scientific advice whose contents were unwelcome (virginiamycin), or they did not seek advice (bacitracin zinc); secondly, the Regulation justifying action and imposing a ban failed to present the scientific evidence fairly; thirdly, the debate and the decision improperly mingled the policy discussion as to the desirability of the products with whether an emergency existed, and failed to follow proper procedures. (If the Regulation had recorded all the material evidence on both sides and then announced that a ban would be phased in over a period of time, the decision would have been almost immune from judicial review.) Those arguments were rejected in a very lengthy judgment of 519 paragraphs which offered some admirable statements of principle that will doubtless be invoked in future cases:

> '172. . . . a scientific risk assessment carried out as thoroughly as possible on the basis of scientific advice founded on the principles of excellence, transparency and independence is an important procedural guarantee whose purpose is to ensure the scientific objectivity of the measures adopted and preclude any arbitrary measures.'

12. HOW TO HANDLE OFFICIAL SCIENTIFIC ADVICE

'It is the customary fate of new truths to begin as heresies and to end as superstitions.'[64]

When considering how the precautionary principle should be applied, there are no 'proof on the balance of probabilities' or 'proof beyond a reasonable doubt' evidentiary standards on which civil and criminal courts might rely. That is understandable. The Court found that the Community Institutions were entitled not to follow the advice of their own scientists in the virginiamycin case (they were not even consulted as to bacitracin zinc). It was only advice, and of course was not binding. The Institutions are entitled to prefer a minority view to a majority view, provided the minority view has at least some evidentiary basis and is not pure hypothesis. There is no filtration mechanism or standard of respectability which must be satisfied before evidence against a product can lawfully be relied upon. The constraint that a ban cannot be founded on 'mere hypotheses that have not been scientifically confirmed' is helpful, but may not represent much of a restriction since many hypotheses have some confirming evidence. Officials may decide whether they will pick mainstream or sidestream sentiment as the scientific basis of an administrative decision or recommendation.

Tens of thousands of the Internet's websites deal with medical matters. Having studied the information provided by some of these medical websites the President of South Africa, Mr. Mbeki, believes that there is no proven link between HIV and AIDs. This may be a minority view, but it cannot be definitively proved wrong. The public health policy of his country appears to have been damaged or at least adversely affected by his espousal of this opinion. Administrative decisions affecting public health have been taken as a result of this eminent politician's minority view of medico-scientific issues.

13. THE SELECTION OF THE LEVEL OF RISK AS A POLICY, NOT A SCIENTIFIC, CHOICE

The decisive factor for determining whether the threat is serious enough is not a scientist's choice, but the Institutions' political judgment of what risks society

[64] TH Huxley.

should accept. Although the Institutions must not base their decision on zero risk, they must take account of their obligation to ensure a level of human health protection which *'does not necessarily have to be the highest that is technically possible'*. While setting zero risk as a target would be unacceptable, even the lowest imaginable level of risk from a product – or the technical inadequacies of the Member States in handling its problems—would justify banning it. The ban might be necessary to pursue the highest technically feasible levels of safety.

Thus considerations labelled 'scientific' (not religious, not humanitarian, not trade-related) and based on some assertions in the scientific literature can justify a prohibition on precautionary grounds. No distinction need be made between such a prohibition as an emergency step or as a long-term legislative choice. Whether it is temporary or permanent elimination of a product that is contemplated, the same levels of hypothesis or anxiety based on scientific opinions may suffice. The scientific risk assessment must merely allow the politicians to conclude that there is a risk to human health, even if it is small. The politicians can then determine that as a matter of public policy this level of risk is too high to be acceptable, and ban the product.

Much depends on how the public authority assesses the acceptable level of risk in a complex scientific matter where it clearly lacks scientific expertise. The Institutions have created new scientific committees to assist the Commission in assessing the quality, safety and efficacy of pharmaceutical and veterinary products; yet they themselves do not treat those committees' opinions and findings as *a priori* reliable, and do not always even take advantage of their expertise. Instead, the scientifically demonstrated[65] existence of not fanciful risks is enough. Then it is a policy, and a political, decision whether this level of risk is acceptable or not.

14. FREEDOM TO SELECT FROM A RANGE OF OPINIONS

'Lest men suspect your tale untrue, keep probability in view'[66]

The Institutions are free to disregard a scientific opinion, in whole or in part, if they can find *'other evidence, whose probative value is at least commensurate with that of the opinion concerned'*.[67] They can do the same to other opinions also. There was debate during the case as to whether government scientists could themselves constitute the scientific input which the Court says is necessary.[68] In *Alpharma*, where there was no SCAN opinion, the Court goes fur-

---

[65] Or alleged, or suggested.
[66] John Gay, *The Painter who pleased everybody or nobody*.
[67] Above n 5, *Pfizer*, para 199.
[68] Reference was made to Case C-212/91 *Angelopharm GmbH* v. *Freie und Hansestadt Hamburg* [1994] ECR I-171, in which the Court of Justice held that, pursuant to the Cosmetics Directive, the Commission was obliged to consult the Scientific Committee on Cosmetology before taking a decision as it lacked the necessary scientific resources itself.

The Dangers of too Much Precaution 225

ther⁶⁹ to allow reliance on the report of the scientists from the country which wished to impose the ban. This seems difficult to reconcile with what the Court said to the effect that a scientific risk assessment should be founded on scientific advice which is in turn founded on '... *independence* ... *to ensure the scientific objectivity of the measures adopted and preclude any arbitrary measures*'.⁷⁰

It would be a pity if scientific considerations, and scientific anxieties as felt by amateur or non-mainstream scientists, became subservient to policy considerations. There can be no constitutional objection to the proposition that scientists analyse, consult, report and advise on what the risks are, while political decision-makers decide. But by what standard should they decide? The less a decision to ban is informed by science according to well-defined parameters, the more likely it is to be bad. For regulated industry products (and for those who depend on those products), the risk that a decision to ban if a controversy arises will be bad is particularly high. Once there is some evidence (albeit challenged by other scientists) of a degree of risk, the political class may act on that evidence if the unacceptable level of risk is set at a sufficiently low level.

15. THE ROLE OF THE EUROPEAN COURTS

Judges are not equipped to make social or policy choices, and understandably refrain from doing so. It was no surprise that the Court stated that judicial review must be limited given the highly complex scientific controversies. 'Light judicial review' is a familiar feature of the case-law of the European Courts: judges examine *légalité* not *opportunité*. The Court also found that the Commission needed the assistance of the relevant scientific committee (save in exceptional circumstances) because of the complexity of the facts.⁷¹ Thus the Institutions cannot be expected to work out the science themselves and need scientists to guide them. But they nevertheless have a very wide discretion to decide how they will interpret that science (and which science to select) to reach decisions. The discretion which the authorities enjoy is particularly wide when read in the light of the limited amount of scientific literature needed before a ban can be considered. Those decisions should be subject to only limited judicial review because judges, even if they can understand such controversies, are not equipped to settle them. If two professors of medicine disagree on a scientific point, either European Court will be reluctant to decide that point if public health is said to be at stake. I observe that national courts decide cases on medical negligence and that both European Courts are ready to challenge expert economists in competition cases, so more judicial boldness might emerge!

While the comitology regime compels close consultation between governments and their regular cooperation with the EU, it reserves them the right to

---

⁶⁹ Ibid., *Alpharma*, paras 299-302.
⁷⁰ This had been clarified in *Angelopharm*, but bears repetition.
⁷¹ Above n 5, *Pfizer*, para 270.

act independently in emergencies. Let us imagine that some (national) scientific experts identified a (non-hypothetical) risk—for example, that cheese made from the milk of cows which had consumed genetically modified grasses poses a threat to biodiversity. If one government scientist considers that such a product presents risks for the public, and his view becomes government policy, it will offer a basis for a policy/political decision to impose a ban at least nationally, even if a large majority of other government scientists are of a different view. This is not to argue that a lone voice should be disregarded; but the scientific world's practices of peer review and replication of experimental findings ensure that in the field of scientific discovery a lone voice whose results are sound will soon cease to be a lone voice. The Court considered such a Member State authority sufficiently knowledgeable to be able to pick which parts of which scientific advice it wishes to follow. On this basis, the Commission did not disregard the experts' opinion, but rather adopted a different opinion on the science. The Commission need not offer reasons of commensurate scientific weight with the advice of its own scientists when deciding to disregard their advice, or to follow alternative scientific views.

16. THE DISTORTION OF SCIENTIFIC EVIDENCE

The terms in which the Regulation was drafted were offensive to a number of members of the SCAN. They communicated their displeasure to the Secretariat of the Committee, suggesting that the Regulation misrepresented their scientific advice. The Vice-Chairman of the SCAN was so stirred that he offered to give testimony on behalf of the manufacturer of virginiamycin, Pfizer Animal Health, to the European Court in support of the challenge to the legality of the ban on virginiamycin. He wrote a fourteen-page critique of the Regulation, asserting that it distorted and misrepresented what the SCAN scientists had said in their report to the Commission, and that the ban was precipitate and disproportionate, based on speculation and weak evidence. His subsequent comments to the Court were also extensive. The Vice-Chairman was then summoned to Brussels and dismissed from his position for having publicly criticised the Council's decision. One of the linguistic distortions complained of was recital 9: the Regulation stated the SCAN said '*[the risk] could be expected to be demonstrated*' when the sense of the SCAN's words was in fact the opposite: if there really was a risk '*it could be expected to be demonstrated*', yet no demonstration had been forthcoming. The Court did not need to address this question in its judgment, as the alleged distortion concerned another product whose producer did not appeal.

17. RISKS FROM BANNING RISKS

In the event that a product is eliminated, there are consequences for society. Jobs are lost. Costs go up or go down. Alternatives are used. New products emerge. Former modes of operating change or disappear. Foretelling these consequences is almost impossible. Proponents and opponents will each envisage dire things if their view is rejected. It is wrong to assume society will be better off for the banning of a controversial product. It may be, but this is not sure. Justifying a ban by looking at the elimination of one hypothetical danger is incomplete, even if it is understandable. There are a number of sources which indicate animals are in worse health following the ban.[72]

The precautionary principle is a reaction to the necessity for officials or political leaders to make decisions in controversial disputes in which public safety is said to be involved and almost always is involved. The most prudent (speaking sociologically and politically) reaction of the regulator is to ban the product. That will lead to fewer criticisms, most of those emanating from discontented manufacturers who can be criticised as profiteers uninterested in public health. Lost opportunity costs are not easily demonstrated.

One problem of the precautionary principle relates to the setting of standards. A standard may mean selecting a maximum level of a dangerous substance in a product used frequently in daily life; it may mean choosing whether to accept any presence of that substance; or it may mean deciding to ban a product in light of dangers possibly associated with it. The decision-maker has to choose whether to allow products which contain some level of a substance deemed harmful. What level to allow? Should cadmium or dioxin or aflatoxin be wholly absent, or should a certain presence be tolerated? Ill-applied, the precautionary principle could deny society access to valuable products which might prolong active life, make work easier, improve food production or enhance enjoyment.

Sometimes European Community policy in an area serves a hidden agenda. Competition law has served, or been said to serve, industrial policy. Fisheries policy has not done very much to help fisheries conservation, but it has probably helped regional integration by offering Southern European fishermen the chance to catch fish in northern waters where conservation policies have been stricter. I speculate whether the precautionary principle too may serve a hidden agenda, perhaps by responding to the techno-sceptic 'green' wing of society which doubts what we are told by industry and government about the impact of man upon our environment. Appearing to take action which appears to protect the

---

[72] To quote Professors Casewell, Friis, Marco, McMullin and Phillips in 'Consequences of ban of growth promoters' (2003) *Journal of Antimicrobial Chemotherapy* 'The theoretical and political benefit of the widespread ban of growth promoters needs to be more carefully weighed against the increasingly apparent adverse consequences'. For an alternative view, see the brochure entitled 'Antibiotic Resistance: A Growing Health Threat to You and Your Family', *Keep Antibiotics Working: The Campaign to End Antibiotic Overuse*, Washington D.C., KeepAntibioticsWorking.com.

public is not an illegitimate government activity. The higher levels of environmental, health and other protection applied in Sweden and Finland were the subject of special attention during the negotiations leading to those countries' accession. They are free to pursue especially high standards in those areas, and very properly commend them in policy-making debates. Can such standards be 'exported' to the rest of Europe? The difficult question is to decide when a controversy relates to conflicting policies where reasonable men may reasonably differ, or to a concrete threat where decisive action is indeed necessary.

18. TO BAN OR NOT TO BAN? THE DIFFICULTY OF QUANTIFYING HOW BAD THE RISKS ARE, AND SIMPLICITY OF DECIDING TO BAN LEST WORSE HAPPEN

'If we wait for threats to fully materialize, we will have waited too long'[73]

'Are there new and definite findings and facts? Does the threat assessment justify taking a very high risk?'[74]

It seems inevitable that the final decisions will be taken by non-scientists. The universe of preoccupations which non-scientists bear in mind when making a decision is different from the universe of those who look at matters from a purely scientific point of view. Unfortunately, a non-scientist will have difficulty in quantifying or digesting evidence or reports or press articles when scientific issues are involved, the more so as the debate is likely to be coloured, or at least nurtured, by factions, such as those which make or sell the product, and environmental, consumer, press and other groups.[75] The risk of media pressure on the political decision-makers is high; at best, it will make it harder for them to examine the matter soberly and assess the risk objectively. Pressure of this kind is especially relevant to procedural scrupulousness. Hence the requirement for transparency. Scientific input is essential, but it will be wasted if the decision-maker is then allowed to manipulate the scientific contribution. The only acceptable standard of decision-making is one which neutrally seeks input, assesses it, and then describes fairly what it has been told.

It seems that constitutionally, Europe would not be willing to allow European scientists to make decisions without political supervision, and it is not yet ready to ascribe to them as much weight as they are accorded in rule-making in the United States. The precautionary principle is here to stay. This should not, however, deter lawyers and those engaged in other disciplines from drawing attention to its implications and possible weaknesses.

---

[73] President George W. Bush, speech to the graduating class at West Point, 1 June 2002.
[74] German Foreign Minister Joschka Fischer to the UN General Assembly, 14 September 2002.
[75] The Royal Society, the national academy of sciences in the UK, has launched an enquiry chaired by Professor Sir Patrick Bateson about how and when scientists communicate their research results to the public, and whether scientists should check each other's work before it is published.

The precautionary principle has a built-in tendency to favour the banning of a product which is controversial. The evidence may not be fairly presented, it may have been poorly compiled, or the statistical conclusions drawn from it may be exaggerated, but there will not usually be no evidence at all. The decision-maker will be encouraged to ban the product and thereby protect human health and safety. Because of public attitudes, politicians risk less if they prohibit and more if they refuse to do so. The administrator who has to make the final decision will feel safer and more prudent if he elects to ban than if he elects not to ban.[76] Assuaging public concern is one of the functions of a political leader. Unfortunately, being told that experts are confident in a product does not assuage public concern.

Civil servants and lawyers may have a role to play in assisting the decision-maker to reach a decision. The civil servant's role should be to endeavour to enhance the quality of the political decision which he is helping to prepare. Civil servants sometimes receive a political mandate from the decision-maker with the instruction to produce grounds to support that conclusion.

The European Courts control the legality of the administrative process, and have a tradition of not substituting their own sentiment for the lawfully-exercised discretion of politicians and civil servants. This would not, though preventing the European Courts from demanding the same level of scrupulousness and rigour in fact-gathering and fact-describing from the European Institutions as would be required in competition cases, and from being equally ready to disagree with the Institutions in competition cases.

19. HIGHLY REGULATED PRODUCTS

What about products which were subject to heavy regulatory control before they reached the market? Should they be deemed liable to be banned on precautionary principle grounds? Should they be immune from the precautionary principle altogether? Would the problem of the precautionary principle be solved if it was not applied to products whose putting on the market involved exhaustive regulation? To what extent does exhaustive pre-marketing regulation *ipso facto* involve the application of the precautionary principle? May one argue that regulated products represent a special case, the very expression, as it were, of the observance of the precautionary principle? Such products reach the marketplace only after passing through an elaborate and exhaustive series of tests to demonstrate their safety and efficacy: years of testing in the laboratory, on animals, on healthy human volunteers, on selected volunteer patients, and on hundreds or thousands of patients in clinical trials. It will have side effects in some cases and

---

[76] Moreover, banning involves exercising his authority, which accepting the *status quo* does not; and the exercise of authority is often not disagreeable, since taking action is commonly preferable to not taking action.

the potential for causing harm. It will never offer society unalloyed and unequivocally benign consequences—indeed, in many cases its deleterious effects are a necessary counterpart of its therapeutic benefits. The merits and demerits of the product will have been appraised and balanced by those who have the scientific, technical, social or other knowledge for this essential task, and authorisation granted only after they have carried it out.

Prohibiting such a product, after it has passed through this elaborate process, may reflect either society's conclusion that the original balance of risk and benefit needs to be recalibrated, or society's concern that the product, contrary to its original appraisal, presents an urgent danger. Prohibition on the first ground may indeed be justified—everyone makes mistakes, and science can offer clarity—but its passage should not be smoothed by claiming that it was required by the second ground.

This critic of the Commission's approach to the precautionary principle would regret that it is not the scientific substance of the fears that triggers the ban, but the political decision that what is feared offers a serious threat to society. Scientific input is therefore presented as one of several equally valid 'readings' of the world. The precautionary principle should return to its roots: the idea that action should not wait until concrete proof of causality is present, rather than allowing minimal evidence of a risk to justify action. Whereas critics are not under any serious obligation to substantiate their allegations, the innovators are often faced with enormous costs.

20. CONCLUDING REMARKS

The subject of this article has been extremely difficult for this author to grasp. The disciplines of the scientist, the epidemiologist, the civil servant, the judge and the lawyer are each relevant. I offer no magic formula for the future for the taking of decisions in precautionary principle controversies, but I do modestly submit that how decisions have been taken in the past is imperfect. The European Institutions appear particularly vulnerable, because of a variety of factors, to media pressure and imperfectly robust analysis of genuinely painful choices. I do not expect that in the foreseeable future we will have a world where scientists alone are given the right to decide on whether a product should be banned or not banned; anyway, scientists are not immune to error, policy preoccupations, obstinacy or naivety. It would appear that decisions are going to continue to be made on the basis of recommendations from civil servants to political leaders. I offer some suggestions.

There should be greater clarity as to what is the role of the civil servant with a scientific training: is he an advocate or an advisor or a decision maker to be guided by other experts?

There should be continued judicial rigour in demanding scrupulous respect for applicable procedures.

The European Courts may reconsider whether it is desirable that the political class set the standard of risk which they deem society should be willing to accept, without ensuring that such level corresponds to an opinion shared by mainstream scientific opinion.

The precautionary principle should not become an excuse for failing to address controversy fairly; nor should it be invoked where no other doctrine fits.

There is a vast body of literature on this subject, which is of interest and importance, and I regret that very few lawyers in their regular practice have the privilege of becoming involved in such controversies. I also regret never having had the chance to argue one of these cases before Judge Edward, the person in whose honour this book has been compiled.

17

Different but (Almost) Equal—The Development of Free Movement Rights under EU Association, Co-Operation and Accession Agreements

ELEANOR SHARPSTON QC

For centuries, there have been population movements over the continent of Europe, often although not invariably from East to West. The 'barbarian hordes' of Vandals, Franks and Visigoths battered at the crumbling frontiers of the Roman Empire for about 150 years before Alaric and his Visigoths finally sacked Rome itself in 410 AD. The Vikings (before their descendants acceded to the EU) were noted and feared for their annual migratory habit of sailing their longships out of their home fjords and archipelagos in Scandinavia and running them up onto any coastline (in France . . . in England . . . in Ireland . . .) in search of summer work of the pillage and plunder variety. Turkish expansion into the West spread down into the Balkans and was halted twice at Vienna, in 1529 and again in 1683. There have also, of course, been the reactive population movements of the unarmed and non-violent: the Huguenots fleeing France after the revocation of the Edict of Nantes in 1685; the Irish moving out[1] in desperation at the successive potato famines of the 1840s; economic migrants of every kind and quality looking for better prospects, career advancement and a better lifestyle;[2] the Jews moving everywhere and anywhere in response to who was trying to exterminate them and who would leave them in peace at any particular point.[3]

---

[1] Not all to the USA.
[2] At every level, from prominent migrant artists (such as Michaelangelo and Leonardo da Vinci) and composers (Bach, Haydn, Mozart, Beethoven . . .) to the nameless and forgotten itinerant craftsmen and labourers.
[3] For example: into Spain under the relatively benevolent rule of the Caliphs; out of Spain in 1492 when 'los Reyes Catolicos' (Ferdinand and Isabella) decided (to mix centuries and languages) to make Spain 'Judenrein'; into England, then expelled, then back in again under Cromwell in 1656; into the Germany of the Enlightenment and the Lithuania, Poland and Russia of the Tsars, out in response to the 19th century pogroms; stuffed by loving parents into Kindertransporte; or destroyed in the Shoah.

Small wonder, then, that free movement of persons has formed an integral part, both of the EC Treaty itself and of the various association agreements, pre-accession agreements and accession agreements signed between the European Economic Community (and later the EC, and later the EU) and various third countries bordering (or embedded in) the continental European landmass.

In developing its jurisprudence on the interpretation of these agreements, the Court of Justice has had to grapple with a series of dilemmas. First, did it in fact have jurisdiction to interpret them at all? Secondly (assuming that it did), what were the principles of interpretation that it should apply? Thirdly, was it conceivable that the doctrine of direct effect—that essential vehicle for conferring individual enforceable rights—could be extended to certain terms in such agreements? Fourthly (assuming that it could be), were such directly effective rights co-extensive with their 'parent' Treaty rights?

One can readily guess at the different forces at play within the court itself. Obviously one must attribute some meaning to such agreements—but how much meaning, and how much legal force of the kind that grants rights to individual third country nationals? It was already settled law (for example) that the provisions of GATT, although binding on the Community itself, were not directly effective within the Community system.[4] Was there anything different (and if so, exactly what?) about these detailed bilateral accords between the Community and specific third countries? How far is it wise, politically, to go in interpreting an agreement (EEC-Turkey) and its associated protocols and decisions[5] that envisaged a three-stage route to Turkish accession that has now been stalled for decades; or the rather muddled texts of the 'Europe Agreements' that emerged out of smoky corridors in the wee small hours, as the most tangible expression of post-Berlin Wall euphoria?

As advocate and later as judge, David Edward has been closely involved in the evolution of the court's case law in this area. Perhaps there will be a soft Scots chuckle at some of the strands here identified (or misidentified!).[6]

---

[4] Joined Cases 21 to 24–72 *International Fruit Company NV et al* v. *Produktschap voor Groenten en Fruit* [1972] ECR 1219 at paras 19–28, confirmed in Case 266/81 *Società Italiana per l'Oleodotto Transalpino (SIOT)* v. *Ministero delle Finanze, Ministero della Marina mercantile, Circoscrizione doganale di Trieste and Ente Autonomo del Porto di Trieste* [1983] ECR 731 at para 28.

[5] Agreement establishing an Association between the European Economic Community and Turkey signed at Ankara on 12 September 1963 (revised text published in OJ 1977 L361/29); Additional Protocol and Financial Protocol signed at Brussels on 23 November 1970 (revised text published in OJ 1977 L 361/59); see also in particular the following Decisions of the EEC-Turkey Association Council (not published in the OJ, and correspondingly difficult to track down and access): Decision 1/80, Decision 2/76 and Decision 3/80.

[6] This contribution does not pretend to be an exhaustive survey of either case law or literature. It seeks merely to highlight certain ideas and ask a few questions.

1. JURISDICTION

Perhaps it is not surprising that this issue was raised at an early stage by the Member States—specifically, in the EEC-Turkey context, by Germany and by the United Kingdom[7]—in Case 12/86 *Meryem Demirel* v. *Stadt Swäbisch Gmünd* [1987] ECR 3719. After all, in Case 26/62 *Van Gend en Loos* v. *Nederlandse Administratie der Belastingen* [1963] ECR 1, the first part of the judgment is taken up with the discussion of whether the Court had jurisdiction to answer the Article 177 reference at all.[8] In Case C–170/96 *Commission* v. *Council* [1998] ECR I–2763 (airport transit visas), the United Kingdom tried (unsuccessfully) to argue that because the contested act was adopted on the basis of Article K.3(2) of the TEU, the court's jurisdiction to hear the application was ousted by Article L of the TEU.[9] Jurisdictional challenges are an excellent way of trying to get a problem to disappear altogether, thus avoiding the potential awkwardness of an unexpected substantive ruling.

In Case 181/73 *Haegeman* v. *Belgium* [1974] ECR 449, the court had already ruled that an agreement concluded by the Council under Articles 228 and 238 of the Treaty is, as far as the Community is concerned, an act of one of the institutions within the meaning of Article 177(1)(b) and, as from its entry into force, the provisions of such an agreement form an integral part of the Community legal system. Within the framework of that system the court has, of course, jurisdiction to give rulings under Article 177 concerning the interpretation of such an agreement.

Nothing daunted, in *Demirel* the United Kingdom and Germany contended that, in the case of a mixed agreement (such as the EEC-Turkey Agreement and its Additional Protocol) the court's interpretative jurisdiction did not extend to 'provisions whereby Member States have entered into commitments with regard to Turkey in the exercise of their own powers', which is the case of the provisions on freedom of movement for workers'.[10]

The court gave that nuanced version of the jurisdiction argument short shrift. Since the agreement in question was an association agreement 'creating special, privileged links with a non-Member country which must, at least to a certain extent, take part in the Community system,'[11] Article 238 'must necessarily empower the Community to guarantee commitments towards non-member

---

[7] Represented at the hearing by Professor David Edward. The court identifies the jurisdiction point as having been raised in the written observations. One would love to know how much emphasis counsel placed on it in his speech.
[8] See pp10–11 of the judgment.
[9] Paras 12–18. Since the substantive issue was whether the contested measure fell within, and thus should have been based upon, Article 100c EC rather than Article K.3(2) in the first place, it is hardly surprising that the court was unimpressed by this argument.
[10] Para 8.
[11] Para 9.

countries in all the fields covered by the Treaty.'[12] In that context, it made no difference that the task of laying down the necessary rules to give effect to the Agreement's free movement provisions, or to decisions to be adopted by the Association Council, fell to the Member States. The Court had already held in Case 104/81 *Hauptzollamt Mainz* v. *Kupferberg & Cie KGa.A.* [1982] ECR 3641 that:

> [i]n ensuring respect for commitments arising from an agreement concluded by the Community institutions the Member States fulfil an obligation . . . in relation to the Community which has assumed responsibility for the due performance of the agreement.[13]

It followed that (of course) the court had jurisdiction to interpret the provisions of the Agreement and the Additional Protocol.

With more persistence than realism, the German Government tried to run a jurisdictional argument again in Case C–192/89 *SZ Sevince* v. *Staatssecretaris van Justitie* [1990] ECR I–3461.[14] Unsurprisingly, the court held that, since it had jurisdiction to rule on the interpretation of the Agreement and the Additional Protocol, it also had jurisdiction to rule on the interpretation of decisions of the Association Council.

2. PRINCIPLES OF INTERPRETATION

The court had explained as long ago as Case 270/80 *Polydor Limited and RSO Records Inc.* v. *Harlequin Records Shops Limited and Simons Records Limited* [1982] ECR 329 that the mere fact that an association agreement shares a form of wording with the Treaty is insufficient to warrant interpreting it in the same way. Emphasising that 'it is necessary to analyse the provisions [of the association agreement] in the light of both the object and purpose of the agreement and of its wording,'[15] the court there proceeded to stress the differences between an Association Agreement and the Community established by the EEC Treaty (rather than their similarities). Trade liberalisation within a free trade area was the aim of the EEC-Portugal Agreement at issue in that case[16]—a much more limited aim than the EEC arrangements under which 'the Treaty, by establishing a common market and progressively approximating the economic policies of the Member States, seeks to unite domestic markets into a single market having the characteristics of a domestic market.'[17] In consequence, the court could

---

[12] Para 9.
[13] Para 13 of *Kupferberg*, cited at para 11 of *Demirel*. The detailed analysis at paras 9–27 of *Kupferberg* is a classic examination of the interaction of international law and Community law.
[14] See paras 7–12.
[15] Para 8.
[16] The case was decided prior to the negotiations leading to Portugal's entry into the Community. At para 18 the Court stated that 'although it [the Agreement] makes provision for the unconditional abolition of certain restrictions on trade . . . , it does not have the same purpose as the EEC Treaty.'
[17] *Polydor* at para 16.

(and did) conclude in *Polydor* that identical wording in the Agreement to the EEC provisions on free movement of goods led to the opposite result:

> in the context of the Agreement restrictions on trade in goods may be considered to be justified on the ground of the protection of industrial and commercial property in a situation in which their justification would not be possible within the Community.[18]

Similarly, when the court came to consider the first 'Europe Agreement' cases (*Gloszczuk*,[19] *Kondova*[20] and *Barkoci & Malik*[21]), it was careful to reject the applicants' arguments that, because one finds the principle of freedom of establishment in both the EC Treaty and the Europe Agreements, the court's EC case law on establishment should be transposed lock, stock and barrel into the world of the Europe Agreements. Thus, in *Kondova*, the court stated:

> The Association Agreement is designed simply to create an appropriate framework for the Republic of Bulgaria's gradual integration into the Community, with a view to its possible accession, whereas the purpose of the Treaty is to create an internal market.[22]

In consequence:

> [T]he rights of entry and residence conferred on Bulgarian nationals as corollaries of the right of establishment are not absolute privileges, inasmuch as their exercise may, where appropriate, be limited by the rules of the host Member State concerning entry, stay and establishment of Bulgarian nationals.[23]

It followed that 'the interpretation of Article 52 of the Treaty, as reflected in the Court's case law, cannot be extended to . . . the Association Agreement.'[24]

To stop there defines by reference to a negative. We know what rights of free movement under association agreements are not. So, what are they as rights?

---

[18] *Ibid* at para 19.
[19] Case C–63/99 *R v. Secretary of State for the Home Department, ex parte Wieslaw Gloszczuk and Elzbieta Gloszczuk* [2001] ECR I–6369.
[20] Case C–235/99 *R v. Secretary of State for the Home Department, ex parte Eleanora Ivanova Kondova* [2001] ECR 6427.
[21] Case C–257/99 *R v. Secretary of State for the Home Department, ex parte Julius Barkoci and Marcel Malik* [2001] ECR I–6557.
[22] Above n20 at para 53; equivalent passages are to be found in *Gloszcuk* (above n 19 at para 50) and in *Barkoci & Malik* (above n21 at para 53).
[23] *Ibid* at para 54.
[24] *Ibid* at Para 55. Note the application of the same reasoning with the opposite result in the judgment of the CFI in Case T–115/94 *Opel Austria GmbH v. Council* [1997] ECR II–39. There, at paras 100–110, the CFI held that Article 10 of the EEA Agreement was identical in substance to Articles 12, 16 and 17 of the EC Treaty and should therefore (in accordance with Article 6 of the EEA Agreement), 'be interpreted in conformity with the relevant rulings of the Court of Justice and the Court of First Instance prior to the date of signature of the agreement' (para 111). Cf also the references in Case C–434/93 *Ahmed Bozkurt v. Staatssecretaris van Justitie* [1995] ECR I–1475 to going 'one stage further' (para 19) towards securing freedom of movement for workers: 'In order to ensure compliance with that objective, it would seem to be essential to transpose, so far as possible, the principles enshrined in [Article 48, 49 and 50 of the Treaty] to Turkish workers who enjoy the rights conferred by Decision No. 1/80' (para 20).

3. DIRECT EFFECT

In its ruling in *Demirel*, which was concerned with family reunification, the court concluded that Article 12 of the Agreement and Article 36 of the Protocol 'essentially serve to set out a programme and are not sufficiently precise and unconditional to be capable of governing directly the movement of workers.'[25] There was no separate decision of the Association Council that addressed the issues of family reunification, so Mrs Demirel was unsuccessful. In arriving at that conclusion, however, the Court highlighted the existence of Decision 1/80 which:

> [w]ith regard to Turkish workers who are already duly integrated in the labour force of a Member State, prohibits any further restrictions on the conditions governing access to employment.[26]

Consciously or unconsciously, the court displayed remarkable prescience; for the series of EEC-Turkey references with which it would be concerned over the succeeding years were indeed to be concerned with 'workers who are duly integrated into the labour force' and the proper interpretation of Decision 1/80.

In its next two judgments—in *Sevince* and Case C-237/91 *Kazim Kus v. Landeshauptstadt Wiesbaden* [1992] ECR I-6781 – the court gave effective teeth to the provisions of the Association Council's decisions. In *Sevince*, the court applied exactly the same test for direct effect to the articles of Decisions of the Association Council as is applied to provisions of the Agreement itself and to 'ordinary' provisions of Community law, namely whether:

> [H]aving regard to its wording and the purpose and nature of the agreement itself, the provision contains a clear and precise obligation which is not subject, in its implementation or effects, to the adoption of any subsequent measure.[27]

The court concluded that the key provisions—Article 2(1)(b) of Decision 2/76 and Article 6(1) of Decision 1/80:

> [u]phold in clear, precise and unconditional terms the right of a Turkish worker, after a number of years' legal employment in a Member State, to enjoy free access to any paid employment of his choice.[28]

By the same token, Article 7 of Decision 2/76 and Article 14 of Decision 1/80 contained unequivocal 'standstill' clauses regarding the introduction of new restrictions on access to employment of workers legally resident and employed in the territory of the contracting States. 'Gastarbeiter', provided they watched their step, were here to stay at their choice rather than that of the host Member State, or (ultimately) their original employer.

[25] Para 23.
[26] *Ibid* at para 22.
[27] Para 15.
[28] *Ibid* at para 17.

In *Kus* the court reaffirmed Sevince, holding that a Turkish worker must be authorised to reside in the territory of the host Member State[29] and must have [legal] employment', which 'presupposes a stable and secure position as a member of the labour force'[30] during the periods of time that are to be accounted for under Article 6(1) of Decision 1/80. Acquisition of rights means that the worker must keep on the right side of pertinent legislation; and appeal time cannot be counted in his favour.[31] Provided the worker is legally resident—for whatever reason[32]—the time spent in employment in that Member State will count. And—crucially—the right to employment also connotes a right to residence:

> [E]ven though [Article 6(1) of Decision 1/80] governs the situation of the Turkish worker only with respect to employment and not to the right of residence, those two aspects of the personal situation of a Turkish worker are closely linked . . . by granting to such a worker, after a specified period of legal employment in the Member State, access to any paid employment of his choice, the provision in question necessarily implies—since otherwise the right granted by it to the Turkish worker would be deprived of any effect—the existence, at least at that time, of a right of residence for the person concerned.[33]

Kus also adds an interesting gloss as to the role of national legislation vis-à-vis the rights conferred by Article 6 of Decision 1/80:

> Article 6(3) of Decision No. 1/80 merely clarifies the obligation incumbent upon the Member States to take such administrative measures as may be necessary for the implementation of that provision, without empowering them to make conditional or restrict the application of the unconditional right which the provision grants to Turkish workers.[34]

In consequence, a Turkish worker who is able to rely upon the provisions of Article 6(1), first or third indent, of Decision 1/80 may rely directly on those provisions in order to obtain the renewal not only of his work permit but also of his residence permit.[35]

It is difficult to overstate the importance of this ruling. Traditionally, Member States retain the right to determine, not only access to their territory, but also the right to stay and reside there. That right had already disappeared in relation to EC nationals exercising rights of free movement.[36] Now, the court was saying that third country nationals claiming rights under an association agreement may also acquire entrenched rights, which defeat the ordinary immigration policy of the Member State concerned.

---

[29] Para 10.
[30] Para 12, citing *Sevince* para 30.
[31] Paras 12–18.
[32] Paras 22–23.
[33] Para 29, building on para 29 of *Sevince*.
[34] Para 31.
[35] Para 36.
[36] See Case 157/79 R v. *Stanislaus Pieck* [1980] ECR 2171 at paras 4–10. The Pontypridd Magistrates Court thereby made a significant contribution to Community law.

It was against that background that the court came to construe the freedom of establishment provisions of the 'Europe Agreements'. In a trilogy of cases (*Gloszczuk, Kondova, Barkoci & Malik*)[37] it brushed aside the argument that, because Member States had expressly retained the right to apply their immigration rules, the core provisions of these Agreements granting freedom of establishment could not be directly effective and generate a derived right of residence.[38]

4. THE EXTENT OF THE RIGHTS CONFERRED

Once the court had made it clear that certain provisions of both association agreements themselves and of 'decisions' made under such agreements by legislative Association Councils are capable of having direct effect, the obvious question then became: is there or is there not a material difference between rights under an association agreement and rights under the EC Treaty itself?

The cases dealing with Article 6(1) of Decision 1/80 show that those rights are more extensive than, perhaps, Member States had thought. Once a Turkish worker successfully enters the country and completes his first year of employment, he will in due course obtain access to the entire labour market provided that he follows carefully the programmatic structure of Article 6(1).[39]

'Clocking up the necessary time' is taken seriously. The Turkish worker must have had a contractual relationship lasting for a year in order for this to be considered to be 'expressive of employment relations stable enough to guarantee the Turkish worker continuity of employment with his employer'.[40] Those who have accumulated the necessary service, however, are free to seek work in other sectors. Thus in Case C-171/95 *Recip Tetik* v. *Land Berlin* [1997] ECR I-329, the court held that a Turkish worker who had four years' qualifying employment had the right, under the third indent of Article 6(1) of Decision 1/80, to leave his employment on personal grounds and for a reasonable period seek new employment in the same Member State.[41] Member States cannot adopt legislation that,

---

[37] Above nn 19–21 respectively.

[38] See eg *Gloszczuk* (above n 19) at paras 29–38, para 47 and paras 54–55. The drafting of the Agreements is of the kind that calls for a cold towel around the temples. Establishment rights are expressly conferred; then Member States expressly retain the right to apply all their usual immigration rules; but that retained right is then itself subject to a proviso: 'provided that in so doing they do not nullify or impair the benefits accruing to any Party under the terms of a specific provision of this Agreement' (Article 58(1) Poland Agreement: a similar provision appears in the other agreements).

[39] Precise respect for the structure is essential: see eg the answer to the first question referred in Case C–355/93 *Hayriye Eroglu* v. *Land Baden-Württemberg* [1994] ECR I–5131 (paras. 9–15 of the judgment). See also, e.g., the fact that time spent whilst an appeal is being processed does not 'count' towards time under Article 6(1) of Decision 1/80: *Sevince* at paras 27–33 (third question referred).

[40] Case C–386/95 *Süleyman Eker* v. *Land Baden-Württemberg* [1997] ECR I–2697 at para 22; at para 31, the court concluded that the extension of a residence permit was contingent upon the Turkish worker having been legally employed continuously for one year with the same employer.

[41] Para 31.

at the outset, excludes whole categories of Turkish migrant workers from the benefit of the three indents of Article 6(1) of Decision 1/80.[42] Similarly, advance limitation of the maximum period of residence by the Member State is ineffective.[43] Nor can a Member State expel a Turkish national who is duly registered as part of the labour force on general preventive grounds.[44]

In the context of the Europe Agreements, the court has adopted a mixed proportionality/remedies-style test:

> [w]hether the immigration rules applied by the competent national authorities are appropriate for achieving the objective in view or whether they constitute, in regard to that objective, measures which would strike at the very substance of the rights which Article 44(3) of the Association Agreement grants to Polish nationals by making exercise of those rights impossible or excessively difficult.[45]

5. RIGHTS ONLY WHEN ACTIVE IN THE LABOUR FORCE

The rights conferred are for active 'gastarbeiter' within the labour force, not for former workers, however meritorious. Thus in *Bozkurt*,[46] the court declined to say that a lorry driver permanently incapacitated from further work by an accident (sustained during his work) had a right to continue to reside in the host Member State.[47] It held that:

> [I]n the absence of any specific provision conferring on Turkish workers a right to remain in the territory of a Member State after working there, a Turkish national's right of residence, as implicitly but necessarily guaranteed by Article 6 of Decision No 1/80 as a corollary of legal employment, ceases to exist if the person concerned becomes totally and permanently incapacitated for work.[48]

---

[42] Case C–98/96 *Kasim Ertanir* v. *Land Hessen* [1997] ECR I–5179.

[43] *Ibid*, at paras 45–47. See also Case C–36/96 *Faik Günaydin, Hatice Günaydin, Grünes Günaydin and Seda Günaydin* [1997] ECR I–5143 at paras 52–55 and Case C–1/97 *Mehmet Birden* v. *Stadtgemeinde Bremen* [1998] ECR I–7747.

[44] Case C–340/97 *Omer Nazli, Caglar Nazli and Melike Nazli* v. *Stadt Nürnberg* [2000] ECR I–957 (cf Article 3 of Council Directive 64/221/EEC and Case 30/77 R v. *Pierre Bouchereau* [1977] ECR 1999 at paras 25–30). See further Case C–188/00 *Bülent Kurz, né Yüce* v. *Land Baden-Württemberg* [2002] ECR I–10691.

[45] *Gloszczuk* (above n19) at para 56. Interestingly, this test would appear to be more favourable towards Member States than the actual wording of the proviso (which required Member States not to 'nullify or impair' benefits). The detailed application of such immigration rules to the world's oldest profession was deliciously examined in Case C–268/99 *Aldona Malgorzata Jany et al* v. *Staatssecretaris van Justitie* [2001] ECR I–8615.

[46] Above n25.

[47] An EU national would have a right of residence in equivalent circumstances by virtue of Article 39(3)(d) of the Treaty, and Regulation (EEC) No 1251/70 of the Commission of 29 June 1970 on the right of workers to remain in the territory of Member State after having been employed in that State (OS 1970 L142/24).

[48] *Bozkurt* (above n24) at para 40.

6. UNLAWFUL CONDUCT

The court is unimpressed by applicants who fraudulently seek to evade the application of national immigration rules. In Case C–285/95 *Suat Kol* v. *Land Berlin* [1997] ECR I–3069, the court had little difficulty in deciding that a Turkish worker could not count periods of employment after a residence permit had been obtained by fraudulent conduct leading to a conviction as 'legal' employment for the purposes of Article 6(1) of Decision 1/80.[49] A more nuanced approach is evident in Case C–37/98 *R* v. *Secretary of State for the Home Department, ex parte Abdulnasir Savas* [2000] ECR I-2927. There the court (having held that Article 41(1) of the Additional Protocol was an unequivocal standstill clause having direct effect[50]) went on to rule that Mr Savas, being unlawfully present in the Member State concerned, could not claim a right of establishment or a right of residence derived directly from Community provisions.[51] However, the national court was still required to assess whether the new version of the national immigration rules (which breached Article 41(1)) had the effect of worsening his position compared to the previous version of those rules.[52]

This case law clearly affected the Court's approach to the first batch of Europe Agreement cases. In both *Gloszczuk* (an overstayer) and *Kondova* (an illegal entrant), the court specifically held that a person who 'gets round' the relevant national controls by making false declarations 'places himself outside the sphere of protection afforded to him under the Association Agreement.'[53]

7. RIGHTS OF FAMILY MEMBERS

Article 7 of Decision 1/80 is (like Article 6(1) of that Decision) a clear, precise and unconditional provision. It therefore permits:

> [C]hildren of Turkish workers who have completed a course of vocational training in the host country to respond to any offer of employment there, irrespective of the length of time they have been resident in that Member State, provided one of their parents has been legally employed in the Member State concerned for at least three years.[54]

---

[49] Paras 25–29. Compare and contrast the answer to the second question referred in *Günaydin* (above n 44), where the court seems to accept the likelihood that there was an honest change of intention (see paras 56–61).
[50] Paras 46–54.
[51] *Ibid*, paras 61–67, especially para 67.
[52] *Ibid*, paras 68–70: a real twist in the tail of the judgment.
[53] *Gloszczuk* (above n 19) at para 75; *Kondova* (above n 20) at para 80.
[54] *Eroglu* (above n 39) at para 17.

Because 'the right of residence is essential to access to and the pursuit of any paid employment, . . . the right [under Article 7] . . . necessarily implies the recognition of a right of residence for that [child].'[55]

If the family member behaves reasonably (eg, if he is absent from the family residence for reasonable periods for legitimate reasons, or for reasons beyond his control), such interruptions will not count against him in the reckoning up of residence for the purposes of Article 7 of Decision 1/80: see Case C–351/95 *Selma Kadiman* v. *Freistaat Bayern* [1997] ECR I–2133. A similarly friendly approach was adopted in Case C–65/98 *Safet Eyüp* v. *Landesgeschäftsstelle des Arbeitmarktservice Vorarlberg* [2000] ECR 4747. There, the Court proved as indulgent towards separating, divorcing, co-habiting and then remarrying Turkish workers as the press traditionally is towards Hollywood couples whose marriages follow a similar pattern. Mrs Eyüp was held to have acquired the necessary rights under Article 7 of Decision 1/80. Further examples of a liberal approach are to be found in Case C–210/97 *Haydar Akman* v *Oberkreisdirektor des Rheinisch—Bergischen-Kreises* [1998] ECR I-7519 and Case C–329/97 *Sezgin Ergat* v. *Stadt Ulm* [2000] ECR I–1487.

In the absence, under the Europe Agreements, of 'secondary legislation' equivalent to the decisions of the EEC-Turkey Association Council, applications seeking secondary rights for family members have so far foundered at national court level without generating a reference under Article 234.

8. NON-DISCRIMINATION

In the light of this discussion, it seems important to draw a distinction between the principle of non-discrimination, on the one hand (a classic self-executing directly effective provision which is already a key component of EC law), and other principles whose scope might require some form of extension, extrapolation or implementation in order to give the necessary protection in a particular case, on the other hand. This is, one feels, the way of reconciling the decisions of the court in Case C–277/94 *Z Taflan Met, S Altun-Basar and E Andal-Bugdayci* v. *Bestuur van de Sociale Verzekeringsbank and O Akol* v. *Bestuur van de Nieuwe Algemene Bedrijfsvereniging* [1996] ECR I–4085 and Case C–262/96 *Sema Sürül* v. *Bundesanstalt für Arbeit* [1999] ECR I–2685.[56]

In *Taflan Met*, the court was confronted with interpreting a decision (Decision 3/80) which sets out to coordinate Member States' social security schemes with a view to enabling Turkish workers employed in the Community, members of their families and their survivors to qualify for benefits in the traditional branches of social security. The court was prepared to imply a date of entry into force even though the Decision had failed to specify one.[57] However,

---

[55] *Ibid*, para 20.
[56] There are two Opinions of Advocate General La Pergola in this case.
[57] *Taflan Met*, paras 8 and 12–22.

unfortunately for those applicants, Decision 3/80 was, by its nature 'intended to be supplemented and implemented in the Community by a subsequent act of the Council'[58] and it proved impossible to construe Articles 12 and 13 of Decision 3/80 as having direct effect.[59]

In *Sürül*, the court distinguished *Taflan Met*.[60] It held that Article 3(1) of Decision 3/80 embodied the principle of equal treatment[61] and satisfied the established classic conditions for direct effect.[62] The court drew on its decisions under other Association Agreements, such as the EEC-Morocco and EEC-Algeria agreements where non-discrimination/equal treatment provisions had similarly been held to be directly effective.[63] Linking across to its decision in Case C-85/96 *Maria Martínez Sala v. Freistaat Bayern* [1998] ECR I-2691, the court held that Mrs Sürül would have the status of a worker even if she were only covered in respect of a single risk, on a compulsory or optional basis, by a general or special social security scheme, irrespective of the existence of an employment relationship;[64] and that the national requirements constituted unequal treatment on grounds of nationality.[65]

Pursuing that thought, it may well be that there is a degree of intellectual parallelism between the court's treatment of non-discrimination in the area of rights for third country nationals—an area where (if anything) one would expect rights to be lesser rather than greater—and the fast-developing (and politically sensitive) area of the rights of 'citizens of the Union'. Certainly, the cases that have advanced citizens' rights thus far are ones in which the applicants have relied upon citizenship rights (Article 17 EC and Article 18 EC) read in conjunction with the general prohibition on discrimination contained in Article 12.[66] It is relatively straightforward, when the only obstacle to someone getting what they need is the discriminatory application to them of a rule that does not apply to

---

[58] *Ibid*, para 33. There had been a proposal for such a regulation since 1983. The Court coyly notes (para 36) that the proposal 'has not yet been adopted'. A brief recollection of accessions to the Community since then may help to explain why.

[59] See *Ibid*, paras 23–38.

[60] After reopening the oral procedure, obtaining two opinions from Advocate General La Pergola, and giving Member States the benfit of a temporal limitation as to the effects of the Judgment.

[61] *Sürül*, paras 55–59.

[62] *Ibid*, paras 60–62.

[63] *Ibid*, para 65. The line of authority was already quite long.

[64] *Ibid*, para 86, citing *Martínez Sala* at para 21. It was for the national court to decide whether Mrs Sürül was covered, either in her own right or through her husband (para 95).

[65] *Ibid*, paras 101–103, again implicity echoing *Martínez Sala*. For a subsequent application of Article 3(1) of Decision 3/80 that resulted in a finding of non-discrimination, see Joined Cases C–102/98 and C–211/98 *Ibrahim Kocak v. Landesversicherungsanstalt Oberfranken und Mittelfranken* (C–102/98) and *Ramazan Örs v. Bundesknappschaft* (C–211/98) [2000] ECR I–1297.

[66] See Case C–274/96 *Criminal proceedings against Horst Otto Bickel and Ulrich Franz* [1998] ECR I–7637, *Martinez Sala*, Case C–184/99 *Rudy Grzelczyk v. Centre public d'aide social d'Ottignies-Louvaine-la-Neuve* [2002] ECR I–6193 and Case C–224/98 *Marie-Nathalie D'Hoop v. Office national de l'emploi* [2002] ECR I–6191. It remains to be seen how the Court will approach Case C–138/02 *Brian Francis Collins v. Minister of State for Works and Pensions* (pending), where the issues are less straightforward. Will it follow Advocate General Ruiz-Jarabo Colomer (opinion delivered 10 July 2003) and conclude that no community law rights are engaged?

nationals of the host Member State (or which such nationals can more readily fulfil), to strike that rule down. The consequence of that approach—even in the absence of further detailed measures whose adoption may run into political difficulties—is often to grant a useful degree of protection to individuals.[67]

9. CONCLUSION

In its treatment of cases involving rights for third country nationals, the court has on the whole proved careful but generous. Judge Edward has been an important part of that difficult balancing act. As he leaves the court, one hopes that the tradition will continue.

---

[67] In the Europe Agreement context, see further Case C–162/00 *Land Nordrhein-Westfalen* v. *Beata Pokrzeptowicz-Meyer* [2002] ECR I–1049 for the successful application of the equal treatment principle.

18

Diplomas and the recognition of professional qualifications in the case law of the European Court of Justice

DIETER KRAUS

1. ELEMENTA BRITANNICAE

IN A CONTRIBUTION to the *Festschrift* dedicated to David Edward it may be permitted to mention that the British members of the European Court of Justice have always played a particularly significant role in the development of the Court's case law on the recognition of diplomas and professional qualifications. The secrecy of the Court's deliberations and the rule under which judgments are never given by one judge alone certainly make it difficult to draw any particular conclusion from the fact that in many of the cases concerning students and their diplomas or, more generally, the recognition of professional qualifications, British members, both past and present, acted as *Judge Rapporteur*. Also, many of the influential Opinions delivered in those cases have been prepared by British Advocates General. One might even be tempted to think that this practice amounts to an unwritten jurisprudential principle that has emerged, in a very 'British' way indeed, over the last ten or fifteen years. David Edward has played a very prominent part in this tradition and the modest purpose of this article is to make some few comments on the state of Community law and, more particularly, on the Court's case law in that area.

2. THE INTERNAL MARKET, FREE MOVEMENT OF PERSONS AND COMMUNITY LEGISLATION FACILITATING THE MUTUAL RECOGNITION OF DIPLOMAS AND PROFESSIONAL QUALIFICATIONS

The fundamental objective, as stated in the preamble to the EC Treaty, of bringing about an ever closer union among the peoples of Europe could not be attained if the Community failed to realise that the success of its internal market required the concept of free movement of persons to go beyond the mere physical move of persons and to extend to their diplomas and professional qualifications as well. Indeed, the right to take up employment or to establish oneself in another Member State or to provide cross-border services would be quite meaningless if those who wish to exercise these fundamental freedoms could not make use of their diplomas and professional qualifications abroad. On the other hand, the protection of the consumer or, more generally, the public interest calls for mechanisms to ensure that certain professions or activities cannot be exercised unless the person concerned posseses the appropriate specialised qualifications. But to require anyone wishing to exercise such a profession or activity in another Member State to hold all the professional qualifications prescribed by the law of that State, without taking into account the professional qualifications that person has acquired elsewhere, would seriously impede the achievement of one of the Treaty's most prominent objectives.

On the Treaty level, Community law provides for the Community legislator to adopt measures intended to facilitate the taking-up and pursuit of activities covered by the fundamental freedoms (see, in relation to workers, self-employed persons and services, Articles 40, 47, 55 EC, respectively). Exercising the competence thus conferred on it, the Community legislator adopted, mainly over a ten year period beginning in the late 1970s, a number of directives covering various professions, including those of doctor, general care nurse, dental practitioner, veterinary surgeon, midwife, pharmacist and architect (so-called sectoral directives).[1] Hence, with respect to the medical profession, Directive 93/16 provides that each Member State is to recognise the diplomas, certificates and other evidence of formal qualifications awarded to Community nationals by the other Member States in accordance with the conditions laid down in that directive, by giving such qualifications, so far as the right to take up and pursue the activities of doctor is concerned, the same effect in its territory as those which it itself awards. Thereby, Community law makes the award of a doctor's diploma subject to certain specific requirements, in order that the diploma is capable of being recognised automatically and unconditionally throughout the Community. Those requirements entail a degree of harmonisation and coordination at Community level of both basic and specialist medical training (the harmonisation aspect) and of the rules for taking up and pursuing the activities of a doctor in the Member States (the coordination aspect).[2]

However, since it had shown to be a rather difficult and lengthy process to provide for a Community regime on a profession by profession basis, the leg-

[1] The most important of those directives is the one on doctors: Council Directive 93/16/EEC of 5 April 1993 to facilitate the free movement of doctors and the mutual recognition of their diplomas, certificates and other evidence of formal qualifications (OJ 1993 L 165, 1), replacing Directives 75/362/EEC and 75/363/EEC. The other directives are Directives 77/452/EEC and 77/453/EEC (nurses responsible for general care), Directives 78/686/EEC and 78/687/EEC (dentists), Directives 78/1026/EEC and 78/1027/EEC (veterinary surgeons), Directives 80/154/EEC and 80/155/EEC (midwives), Directives 85/432/EEC and 85/433/EEC (pharmacists), Directives 85/384/EEC (architects), all as amended.

[2] See Case C–110/01 *Malika Tennah-Durez* v. *Conseil national de l'ordre des médecins*, judgment of 19 June 2003, not yet reported, para 31.

islative technique pursued in the following years favoured a more general approach, leading to (by now) three so-called 'general system' directives (Directives 89/48/EEC, 92/51/EEC and 1999/42/EC).³ Those directives put in place another method of mutual recognition of diplomas and professional qualifications, a method that is based on the idea that the conditions upon which the practice of the professions concerned is dependent are to be broadly equivalent. Accordingly, persons holding a diploma authorising them to exercise a regulated activity in the Member State of origin should in principle be able to pursue the same activity in other Member States where that activity is regulated by the legislation of that State. If the activity is not regulated in the Member State of origin, the fact that it has been pursued there for a reasonable and sufficiently recent period of time should be regarded as a suitable qualification for taking up equivalent activities in Member States which regulate such activities. Nevertheless, the general system directives permit the host Member State to require the applicant, subject to certain conditions, to take compensation steps (adaptation period or aptitude test), notably where substantial differences exist between the theoretical and/or practical education and training undergone and that covered by the qualification required in the host Member State.

The 'SLIM' Directive 2001/19/EC amending and simplifying all these directives has achieved a remarkable consolidation of the legal and procedural regime for professional recognition.⁴ With a view to further facilitating the rules on the recognition of professional qualifications, the Commission recently suggested replacing both the sectoral and the general system directives by a single text, in order to have a clearer and simpler set of rules applicable in that area.⁵

3. THE JUDGMENTS IN VLASSOPOULOU, HAIM AND HOCSMAN

As regards the case law, the judgment in *Vlassopoulou*⁶ is certainly the leading case and this landmark decision pronounced in 1991 has soon become and still

---

³ Council Directive 89/48/EEC of 21 December 1988 on a general system for the recognition of higher education diplomas awarded on completion of professional education and training of at least three years' duration (OJ 1989 L 19, 16), as amended; Council Directive 92/51/EEC of 18 June 1992 on a second general system for the recognition of professional education and training to supplement Directive 89/48/EEC (OJ 1992 L 209, 25), as amended; Directive 1999/42/EC of the European Parliament and of the Council of 7 June 1999 establishing a mechanism for the recognition of qualifications in respect of the professional activities covered by the Directives on liberalisation and transitional measures and supplementing the general systems for the recognition of qualifications (OJ 1999 L 201, 77).
⁴ Directive 2001/19/EC of the European Parliament and of the Council of 14 May 2001 amending Council Directives 89/48/EEC and 92/51/EEC on the general system for the recognition of professional qualifications and Council Directives 77/452/EEC, 77/453/EEC, 78/686/EEC, 78/687/EEC, 78/1026/EEC, 78/1027/EEC, 80/154/EEC, 80/155/EEC, 85/384/EEC, 85/432/EEC, 85/433/EEC and 93/16/EEC concerning the professions of nurse responsible for general care, dental practitioner, veterinary surgeon, midwife, architect, pharmacist and doctor (OJ 2001 L 206, 1).
⁵ Com(2002)119 final. Proposal for a Directive of the European Parliament and of the Council on the recognition of professional qualifications (document dated 7 March 2002).
⁶ Case C–340/89 *Irene Vlassopoulou* v. *Ministerium für Justiz, Bundes- und Europaangelegenheiten Baden-Württemberg* [1991] ECR I–2357.

is the foundation of the Court's case law in the area of recognition of diplomas and professional qualifications. In *Vlassopoulou* the Court was faced with the problem of how to deal with the refusal of the German authorities to admit a Greek lawyer, of the Athens Bar and with a German doctorate in law, to the legal profession in Germany. When the case started (in 1989), no measure had yet been adopted under Article 47(2) EC concerning the harmonisation of the conditions of access to the legal profession; Directive 89/48 did not apply to the facts of the case.[7] The Court stated that, even if applied without any discrimination on the basis of nationality, national requirements concerning qualifications may have the effect of hindering nationals of the other Member States in the exercise of their right of establishment guaranteed to them by Article 43 EC. That could be the case if the national rules in question took no account of the knowledge and qualifications already acquired by the person concerned in another Member State.[8] The Court's conclusion was that:

a Member State which receives a request to admit a person to a profession to which access, under national law, depends upon the possession of a diploma or a professional qualification must take into consideration the diplomas, certificates and other evidence of qualifications which the person concerned has acquired in order to exercise the same profession in another Member State by making a comparison between the specialised knowledge and abilities certified by those diplomas and the knowledge and qualifications required by the national rules.[9]

Thus, it was in this judgment that the Court established the principle that in situations where no Directive on recognition of professional qualifications applies the Treaty obliges the national authorities to compare, on the one hand, the professional qualifications the host Member State requires for the exercise of the regulated profession concerned with, on the other hand, the professional qualifications the migrant Community national has. In so far as the applicant's qualifications correspond to those required, the host Member State must recognise the diploma of the person concerned.

Since then, the *Vlassopoulou* principle has proved to be very useful and beneficent. It has been applied to various other professions, such as those of doctor, dentist and architect, thereby being restated and refined. Today it can be said to be of general application.[10] The rulings in *Haim*[11] and *Hocsman*[12] provide good examples for it.

[7] *Vlassopoulou*, paras 11, 12. Now see Directive 98/5/EC of the European Parliament and of the Council of 16 February 1998 to facilitate practice of the profession of lawyer on a permanent basis in a Member State other than that in which the qualification was obtained (OJ 1998 L 77, 36).

[8] *Vlassopoulou*, para 15.

[9] *Vlassopoulou*, para 16.

[10] Apart from the judgments referred to in the text, see eg Case C–234/97 *Teresa Fernández de Bobadilla v. Museo Nacional del Prado* [1999] ECR I–4773, para 29 to 31; Case C–232/99 *Commission v. Spain* [2002] ECR I–4235, para 21.

[11] Case C–319/92 *Salomone Haim v. Kassenzahnärztliche Vereinigung Nordrhein* [1994] ECR I–425.

[12] Case C–238/98 *Hugo Fernando Hocsman v. Ministre de l'Emploi et de la Solidarité* [2000] ECR I–6623.

In its judgment in *Haim*, the Court transposed the *Vlassopoulou* principle to the situation of an Italian national holding a diploma in dentistry awarded in 1946 by the University of Istanbul. Mr Haim had subsequently worked as a dental practitioner in Belgium where his Turkish diploma had been recognized as equivalent to a Belgian dentist's diploma. Having moved to Germany, he applied without success to the German authorities to be considered eligible for appointment as a dental practitioner of a social security scheme. The Court confirmed that recognition by a Member State of qualifications awarded by a third country, even if they have been recognised as equivalent in one or more Member States, does not bind the other Member States.[13] However, the Court went on to say that Article 43 EC prohibits Member States from refusing access to a regulated profession of a Community national whose diploma is not eligible for automatic recognition but who has been authorised to practise, and has been practising, his profession in the Community, without examining whether and, if so, to what extent, that person's professional experience corresponds to that required by the national legislation of the host Member State.[14]

The judgment in *Hocsman* clarified two points. First, doubts had been raised as to whether the *Vlassopoulou* principle is or should be limited to professions for which there is no sectoral directive. The argument put forward was that the Court's case law in this area concerned professions such as the profession of lawyer (at issue in *Vlassopoulou*) or estate agent (see *Aguirre Borrell*[15]) which at the time when those judgments were delivered had not (yet) been covered by Community legislation on the mutual recognition of diplomas. Some governments concluded that those judgments are therefore of no relevance to the freedom of movement of doctors, which is regulated (exhaustively) by Directive 93/16. The Court, however, followed the Commission's reasoning according to which it would be paradoxical if the existence of a directive aimed at mutual recognition of diplomas had the effect of depriving Community nationals whose diplomas did not meet the requirements set out in that directive of the possibility of relying on the *Vlassopoulou* principle, when they would certainly have been able to do so in the absence of such a directive. Moreover, the Court firmly asserted that the *Vlassopoulou* line of judgments is merely the jurisprudential expression of a principle which is inherent in the fundamental freedoms of the Treaty.[16] The second point relates to the extent as to which professional qualifications have to be taken into account when the *Vlassopoulou* principle is being applied. In that respect, the Court held that not only diplomas and related work experience obtained in a Member State but also every such qualification

---

[13] *Haim*, para 21, referring to Case C–154/93 *Abdullah Tawil-Albertini* v. *Ministre des Affaires Sociales* [1994] ECR I–451, para 13.

[14] *Haim*, para 29.

[15] Case C–104/91 *Colegio Nacional de Agentes de la Propiedad Inmobiliaria* v. *Aguirre Borrell and Others* [1992] ECR I–3003.

[16] *Hocsman*, para 24. See also Case C–31/00 *Conseil national de l'ordre des architectes* v. *Nicolas Dreessen* [2002] ECR I–663, para 25.

acquired in a third country have to be considered.[17] This appears to be a logical consequence of the fact that the *Vlassopoulou* principle stems from freedom of establishment, on which, as a fundamental freedom, all Community citizens can rely and which does not discriminate between professional qualifications originating within or outside the European Union. It is noteworthy that this formula seems to go beyond what Directive 2001/19 inserted into the sectoral directive on doctors. In effect, the new Article 42c of Directive 93/16 stipulates that Member States shall examine diplomas, certificates and other evidence of formal qualifications in the field covered by this Directive obtained by the holder outside the European Union in cases where those diplomas, certificates and other evidence of formal qualifications have been recognised in a Member State, as well as evidence of training undergone and/or professional experience gained in a Member State.[18]

In 2002, the Court effectively summarised this case law as follows:

> [T]he authorities of a Member State to which an application has been made by a Community national for authorisation to practise a profession, access to which depends, under national legislation, on the possession of a diploma or professional qualification or on periods of practical experience, are required to take into consideration all of the diplomas, certificates and other evidence of formal qualifications of the person concerned and his relevant experience, by comparing the specialised knowledge and abilities so certified and that experience with the knowledge and qualifications required by the national legislation.[19]
>
> That obligation extends to all diplomas, certificates and other evidence of formal qualifications as well as to the relevant experience of the person concerned, irrespective of whether they were acquired in a Member State or in a third country, and it does not cease to exist as a result of the adoption of directives on the mutual recognition of diplomas.[20]

4. TWO MAIN METHODS OF MUTUAL RECOGNITION OF PROFESSIONAL QUALIFICATIONS

Generally speaking, two main methods of recognition of diplomas and professional qualifications can be distinguished: automatic and unconditional recognition on the sole basis of Community law and case-by-case recognition on the basis of a comparison of the actual qualifications with the qualifications required. Those methods are significantly different.

Automatic and unconditional recognition means that Member States must accept the equivalence of certain diplomas and cannot require the persons concerned to comply with obligations other than those laid down by the relevant directives. That type of recognition is governed by Community law alone.

---

[17] *Hocsman*, para 40.
[18] Article 14 No 17 of Directive 2001/19.
[19] *Dreessen*, para 24.
[20] *Commission* v. *Spain*, para 22.

Community law determines which are the minimum or other training requirements that need to be satisfied in order that the diploma qualifies for Community-wide recognition. Community law determines that every Member State has to treat such diplomas as if they were delivered by its own authorities. Community law determines in what way the professional title can be used. The effects of automatic and unconditional recognition are identical in all Member States. Automatic and unconditional recognition therefore presupposes some (minimal) harmonisation of the training leading to the grant of such a diploma. Otherwise the Member States' mutual trust in the adequacy of the diplomas awarded by other Member States might be at risk, such trust to be based on a training system the standards of which are determined by mutual agreement.

In contrast, recognition on a case-by-case basis compares professional qualifications: on the one hand those the migrant possesses with those the host Member State requires for the taking up and pursuit of the regulated activity. It is in principle the host Member State that determines according to its own legislation which professional qualifications are required to exercise the profession concerned. However, Community law provides a number of rules for the above-mentioned comparison: for instance that the exercise of a regulated activity in the home Member State for a certain period should generally suffice and provide sufficient guarantees for the host Member State to authorise the exercise of that activity on its own territory; or the obligation to take into account the migrant's diplomas as well as his experience in the area concerned and his relevant professional qualifications. The result of that comparison may, however, vary according to the Member State that carries out the comparison. Furthermore, it is possible that the host Member State may require the migrant person to complete a period of adaptation or to pass an aptitude test.

It is important to realise that no legal obligation for automatic and unconditional recognition can be found in the Treaty itself. Whereas the rules applicable to the case-by-case recognition can be derived from the Treaty, most notably the fundamental freedoms, and, therefore, apply whether there is a directive (further) facilitating recognition of professional qualifications or not, automatic and unconditional recognition necessarily presupposes the existence and applicability of Community legislation putting in place that method of recognition.

In most cases, automatic recognition is more advantageous for the person concerned since this method leaves no discretion to the host Member States' authorities.[21] It makes it possible to know precisely and in advance if a particular diploma gives the right to take up and pursue the corresponding profession in other Member States whereas the migrant has much less certainty as to what will be result of any case-by-case comparison.[22] A diploma that qualifies for

---

[21] This does not exclude the possibility that the host Member State requires the migrant person to have the language skills needed to practise the profession. In that regard and as to the limits the principle of proportionality imposes on the Member States, see Case C–424/97 *Salomone Haim* v. *Kassenzahnärztliche Vereinigung Nordrhein* [2000] ECR I–5123, paras 59, 60.

[22] See *Commission* v. *Spain*, para 25.

automatic and unconditional recognition amounts to a 'passport' enabling its holder to exercise the professional qualifications attested to by the diploma throughout the European Union, without their being open to challenge in the host Member State except in specific circumstances laid down by Community law.[23]

Since the mechanism of automatic and unconditional recognition has such far-reaching effects, it can only apply where its conditions are clearly and fully met. The judgment in *Erpelding*[24] provides an useful example.

Dr Erpelding, a Luxembourg national, had obtained a diploma of doctor and a diploma of specialist in internal (general) medicine in Austria. Both diplomas had been recognised by the competent Luxembourg authorities so that he could practise internal (general) medicine there. After having further qualified, again in Austria, as a specialist in 'internal medicine, cardiology practice', he wished, some years later and back in Luxembourg, to devote himself exclusively to the practice of cardiology. However, the Luxembourg authorities refused him the right to use the professional title of cardiologist. Indeed, under Directive 93/16, automatic recognition of a medical specialty requires that the specialty exists— as a specialty—in both Member States concerned. Since cardiology is regarded in Austria as a branch of internal medicine, cardiology did not appear, for Austria, on the list of medical specialties in Directive 93/16. For that reason, Dr Erpeldings's diploma in cardiology was not eligible for automatic recognition in Luxembourg where cardiology is a medical specialty. Accordingly, and although his Austrian diploma of cardiology might have been the standard Austrian qualification in cardiology, he had no automatic right, on the basis of that diploma, to use the professional title of cardiologist in Luxembourg.[25] This was a fairly obvious and inevitable result on the basis of Directive 93/16.[26]

If the judgment in *Erpelding* serves to illustrate the limitations of the system of automatic and unconditional recognition under Directive 93/16, the recent judgment in *Tennah-Durez* demonstrates the strength of that mechanism.

Mrs Tennah-Durez, of Algerian and then Belgian nationality, obtained a diploma of doctor in medicine from the Algiers faculty of medicine in 1989. The University of Ghent in Belgium recognised her six years of training and consequently authorised her to enrol for the seventh and final year of medicine, on

---

[23] See *Tennah-Durez*, para 57.
[24] Case C–16/99 *Ministre de la Santé v. Jeff Erpelding* [2000] ECR I–6821.
[25] *Erpelding*, paras 26, 27. The Luxembourg Minister of Health had (only) authorised Dr Erpelding to use the academic title of the Austrian diploma in the language of the State where that diploma had been obtained, namely 'Facharzt für Innere Medizin, Teilgebiet Kardiologie'.
[26] The application of the *Vlassopoulou* principle might well have led to a different solution. In order to avoid the (erroneous) impression that that principle could not apply in the present case, the Court pointed out that it had neither been mentioned in the order for reference nor discussed in the hearing (*Erpelding*, paras 20, 21). After the first *Dreessen* case (C–447/93), where no such statement had been included in the judgment that simply held that Mr Dreessen's diploma in architecture did not qualify for automatic recognition under Directive 85/384, it took many years until the issue was referred again, this time to ascertain whether the *Vlassopoulou* principle applies to Mr Dreessen's situation (see the second judgment in *Dreessen*, [C–31/00] paras 21, 22).

completion of which she was awarded the Belgian diploma of doctor in 1995. In addition, she qualified and was authorised to practise in Belgium as a general medical practitioner in 1998. Having moved to France, the question arose whether her Belgian diploma of doctor qualified for automatic and unconditional recognition in the other Member States, notwithstanding the fact that six out of seven years of the training had been received outside the European Union. The argument which was put forward against automatic recognition was that automatic recognition requires the medical training to be received predominantly in a university in a Member State or under the supervision of such a university. The Court, however, did not accept that argument. It stressed that Directive 93/16 does not specify either expressly or by implication the extent to which the medical training required by Directive 93/16 may comprise training received in a third country. The reason for this, as explained by the Court, was that for the purposes of recognition under Directive 93/16 the relevant aspect is not where the training leading to the diploma has been provided but whether the training complies with the qualitative and quantitative requirements laid down by Directive 93/16.[27] Consequently, provided that the competent authority in the Member State awarding the diploma is in a position to validate medical training received in a third country and to conclude on that basis that the training duly complies with the training requirements laid down by Directive 93/16, that training may be taken into account in deciding whether to award a doctor's diploma.[28] The Court stressed that the responsibility for ensuring that the training requirements, both qualitative and quantitative, are fully complied with falls wholly on the competent authority of the Member State awarding the diploma. In exercising its powers that authority must bear in mind that a doctor's diploma will enable its holder to move around and practise throughout the European Union as a result of its being recognised automatically and unconditionally.[29] The Court also pointed out that such a diploma is in fact not a diploma awarded in a third country but a diploma awarded by a university in a Member State.[30]

That last point is the key difference between *Tennah-Durez* and *Hocsman*. In *Hocsman*, the migrant doctor also held a third country diploma in medicine, went to Spain, had his Argentinean diploma recognized as equivalent to the Spanish degree in medicine and surgery so allowing him to practice medicine in Spain and to train there as a specialist in urology. He then moved to France where his various applications to register with the *Ordre National des Médecins* with a view to practising in France were rejected on the ground that the Argentinean diploma did not satisfy the conditions required in that respect. In effect, unlike Dr Tennah-Durez, he had not obtained a—new—doctor's diploma under Directive 93/16, but—only—a certificate of equivalence. His

[27] *Tennah-Durez*, para 53.
[28] *Tennah-Durez*, para 60.
[29] *Tennah-Durez*, para 56.
[30] *Tennah-Durez*, para 69.

situation therefore was not covered by the automatic and unconditional recognition available for a diploma awarded under Directive 93/16. All that the Court could do was to invite the national authorities to consider, when applying the *Vlassopoulou* principle, whether the equivalence accorded in Spain was based on criteria comparable to those whose purpose, in the context of Directive 93/16, is to ensure that Member States may rely on the quality of the diplomas in medicine awarded by the other Member States.[31] That might facilitate the recognition of his Argentinean diploma.[32]

5. CONCLUSION

Automatic recognition of diplomas and professional qualifications has proved to be a very powerful tool that appreciably facilitates the free movement of those professionals entitled to benefit from it. As the case law shows, the applicability of that mechanism and, more particularly, its unconditional effect is linked to and coupled with a rather strict handling of the requirements the various sectoral directives set out. However, once a diploma eligible for automatic recognition has been delivered in accordance with the relevant directive, the effects of its recognition by virtue of Community law cannot easily be put into question. The general system directives are of a greater scope than the sectoral directives but their effects are more limited since the recognition mechanism they create is partly national in nature such that outcomes are liable to vary from Member State to Member State. The principle established in *Vlassopoulou* and further developed since then underpins and strengthens both mechanisms, in that this principle constantly acts as a reminder of the Treaty dimension of mutual recognition of diplomas and professional qualifications.

---

[31] *Hocsman*, para 39.
[32] It seems that Dr Hocsman eventually was granted recognition of his Argentinean diploma.

19
The Transformation of the Rome Convention

RICHARD PLENDER QC

1. INTRODUCTION

THE ROME CONVENTION on the Law Applicable to Contractual Obligations[1] is one of the few texts related to Community law on which David Edward was not called upon to rule in the period, approaching twelve years, that he spent as judge of the Court of Justice of the European Communities. Admittedly he had cause to refer to it in conjunction with the Brussels Convention.[2] In *Groupe Concorde*[3] he sat as a member of the full court which found support in the Rome Convention for the conclusion that it is for the applicable law to determine the place of performance of the obligation for the purposes of Article 5(1) of the Brussels Convention. In *Coreck Maritime GmbH* v. *Handelsveem BV*[4] he presided over the Fifth Chamber when it reasoned that a court situated in a contracting state must assess the validity of a jurisdiction clause according to the applicable law, including conflict of laws rules, when applying Article 17 of the Brussels Convention. He was however denied the opportunity to rule on the meaning of the Rome Convention directly since the protocols on its interpretation remain to be ratified by one of the contracting states, almost a quarter of a century after the Convention's conclusion.[5]

As a former holder of the Salvesen Chair at Edinburgh, he would know better than most that the shipping company of that name contributed to the development of Scottish private international law as litigant in a seminal judgment of

---

[1] Convention on the Law Applicable to Contractual Obligations, Rome, 19 June 1980, OJ 1980 L266.
[2] Convention on Jurisdiction and the Enforcement of Judgments in Civil and Commercial Matters, 27 September 1968, OJ 1972 of L299/32 as amended by the Convention of Accession of 9 October 1978 of the Kingdom of Denmark, of Ireland and of the United Kingdom, OJ 1978 L304, the Convention of 25 October 1982 on the Accession of the Hellenic Republic, OJ 1982 L388 and the Convention of 26 May 1989 on the Accession of the Kingdom of Spain and the Portuguese Republic, OJ 1989 L285.
[3] Case C–440/97 *GIE Groupe Concorde and Others* v. *Master of the vessel 'Suhadiwarno Panjan'* [1999] ECR I–6307, paras 26 and 32.
[4] Case C–387/98 *Coreck Maritime GmbH* v. *Handelsveem BV and others* [2000] ECR I–9337.
[5] Belgium has yet to ratify the two Protocols on Interpretation, 19 June 1980, OJ 1980 L266/1.

1927.[6] He might have welcomed the opportunity to make a personal contribution to the private international law of contracts at a time when the European rules on the subject are in some disorder. In the absence of guidance from Luxembourg, courts in the contracting states have occasionally given divergent interpretations to the Rome Convention;[7] and as the Conventions of Funchal[8] and Rome[9] concerning the accession of Spain and Portugal and Austria, Finland and Sweden, have modified the Rome Convention in certain respects but have not yet been ratified by all the contracting states,[10] two different versions coexist.

The Commission now proposes to address this situation. In January 2003 it published its Green Paper proposing to transform the Rome Convention into a Community instrument and to modernise it.[11] The Commission's initiative is welcome; but conversion of the Rome Convention to a Community instrument will present some difficulties of its own. A few of these are identified in this essay.

2. THE TREATY OF AMSTERDAM

The legal basis for a an instrument transforming the Rome Convention into Community legislation is to be found in Article 61(c) of the EC Treaty, inserted by the Treaty of Amsterdam.[12] This provides that in order to secure progressively an area of freedom, security and justice, the Council shall adopt measures in the field of judicial cooperation in civil matters as provided for in Article 65. The latter provides that:

> Measures in the field of judicial cooperation in civil matters having cross-border implications, to be taken in accordance with Article 67 and in so far as necessary for the proper functioning of the internal market shall include . . .
> (b) promoting the compatibility of the rules applicable in the Member States concerning the conflict of laws and of jurisdiction.

---

[6] *Salvesen (or Van Lorang)* v. *Austrian Property Administrator* [1927] AC 641.

[7] Compare the view of Hobhouse LJ that the presumption created by Article 4(2) was 'very weak': *Crédit Lyonnais* v. *New Hampshire Insurance Company* [1997] 2 Lloyd's Rep 1 with the view of the Hoge Raad, observing that such presumptions should be discarded only in exceptional circumstances: *Société Nouvelle des Papéteries de l'Aa v BV Maschinenfabriek BOA* Hoge Raad, NJ1992/750. See further O Lando, 'The Eternal Crisis' in *Festschrift für Ulrich Drobnig zum 70 Geburtstag* (Tubingen, Mohr Siebeck, 1998).

[8] OJ 1992 L333/1.

[9] OJ 1997 C15/10.

[10] The amendment made by the Funchal Convention mainly concerned the deletion of Article 27 on the geographical scope of the Convention.

[11] COM (2002) 654, 14 January 2003. See also the Commission's Action Plan *A More Coherent Contract Law* which aims to remove obstacles to intra-Community trade arising from differences in national and regional rules governing contracts (COM (2003) 68, 12 February 2003). On the latter subject see u Drobnig, 'The UNIDROIT Principles in the Conflict of Laws' [1998] *Uniform LR* 3(2/3) 385.

[12] OJ 1997 C340/1.

Article 67 provides for a special legislative procedure to be applied in adopting relevant Community legislation:

> During a transitional period of five years following the entry into force of the Treaty of Amsterdam, the Council shall act unanimously on a proposal from the Commission or on the initiative of a Member State and after consulting the European Parliament.

After the expiry of those five years:

> [T]he Council, acting unanimously after consulting the European Parliament, shall take a decision with a view to providing for all or parts of the areas covered by this title to be governed by the procedure referred to in Article 251 and adapting the provisions relating to the powers of the Court of Justice.

Thus, on the expiry of the transitional period Member States are to lose their power of initiative and the Council is to take a decision with a view to the application of the co-decision procedure and adaptation of the jurisdiction of the Court of Justice.[13]

On the basis of Article 61(c), the Community has adopted several new Regulations for judicial cooperation in civil matters, including the 'Brussels II' regulation on matrimonial matters,[14] and regulations on bankruptcy,[15] service of documents[16] and evidence.[17] On the same basis it has converted the Brussels Convention of 1968 into a Regulation[18] and it is preparing a Community instrument on the law applicable to non-contractual obligations.[19] For the European Parliament, at least, the new treaty basis for Community legislation presents attractions, since the co-decision procedure provides for a greater participation of the Parliament in the legislative process in civil matters, except for family law.

Nevertheless some problems arising from the application of Article 61(c) have yet to be resolved. What is to happen if, by the end of the transitional period, the

---

[13] The Vienna Action Plan of the Council and the Commission, adopted by the Council in 1998, refers specifically to the compatibility of the conflict rules: OJ 1999 C19/1, point 51(c). Point 40(c) calls for 'revision, where necessary, of certain provisions of the Convention on the Law applicable to contractual obligations, taking into account special provisions on conflict of law rules in other Community instruments.' The Mutual Recognition Programme specifies that measures to harmonise conflict of laws rules constitute supporting measures, facilitating implementation of the principle of mutual recognition of judgments in civil and commercial matters: OJ 2001 C12/1.

[14] Council Regulation (EC) 1347/2000 of 29 May 2000 on jurisdiction and the recognition and enforcement of judgments in matrimonial matters and matters of parental responsibility for children of both spouses, OJ 2000 L160/19.

[15] Council Regulation (EC) 1346/2000 of 29 May 2000 on insolvency proceedings, OJ 2000 L160/1.

[16] Council Regulation (EC) 1348/2000 of on 29 May 2000 on the service in the Member States of judicial and extrajudicial documents in civil or commercial matters, OJ 2000 L160/37.

[17] Council Regulation (EC) No 1206/2001 of the Council of 28 May 2001 on cooperation between the courts of the Member States in the taking of evidence in civil or commercial matters, OJ 2001 L 174/1.

[18] Council Regulation (EC) No 44/2001 of 22 December 2000 on jurisdiction and the recognition and enforcement of judgments in civil and commercial matters, OJ 2001 L12/1.

[19] On 3 May 2002 the Commission launched a consultation on a preliminary draft proposal for a Council Regulation on the law applicable to non-contractual obligations. The text is available at: http://europa.eu.int/comm/dgs/justice_home/unit/civil/consultation/index_en.htm.

Council fails to achieve unanimity on the application of the co-decision procedure and the adaptation of the powers of the European Court? The prospect is not fanciful: the co-decision procedure prescribed by Article 251 entails qualified majority voting, and Member States are at present far from agreement on the identification of the courts and tribunals from which the Court of Justice should be competent to receive references for preliminary ruling.

In the event of the Council's failure to adopt a decision on the co-decision procedure, it is probable that Article 67(2) applies independently so as to authorise use of the co-decision procedure. That is the view of Basedow[20] and of Besse[21] and it appears justified by the precision with which the obligation is expressed in Article 67(2).

If that is right, the same cannot be said in the event of a failure by the Council to make a decision on the adaptation of the jurisdiction of the Court of Justice. Too many options present themselves. Article 68(1) envisages that a reference for preliminary ruling may be entertained where a question on the interpretation of Title IV, or of the validity or interpretation of Community acts adopted thereunder, is raised in a court or tribunal of a Member State against whose decisions there is no remedy under national law. In derogation from the rule prescribed by Article 234 of the EC Treaty, references for preliminary ruling will not be admissible from lower courts. By Article 68(3):

> The Council, the Commission or a Member State may request the Court of Justice to give a ruling on a question of interpretation of this title or of acts of the institutions of the Community based on this title. The ruling given by the Court of Justice in response to such a request shall not apply to judgments of courts or tribunals of the Member States which have become *res judicata*.

A decision of the Council under Article 67(2) is necessary to determine whether references are to be admissible from lower courts and to decide whether references may be made, somewhat anomalously, by the Council, the Commission or a Member State.[22]

A difficulty of a different kind is presented by the words which qualify the application of Article 65. Measures to be adopted thereunder must relate to matters having 'cross-border implications' and they are to apply 'in so far as necessary for the proper functioning of the internal market.' One of the enduring disputes under the Brussels Convention is whether the jurisdictional rules prescribed thereby, particularly in Article 2, apply in the absence of a factor

---

[20] J Basedow, 'The Communitarisation of the Conflict of Laws under the Treaty of Amsterdam' (2000) 37(3) *CMLRev* 687 at 693–4.

[21] D Besse, 'Die Justitielle Zusammenarbeit in Zivilsachen nach dem Vertrag von Amsterdam und das EuGVÜ' (1999) 7 *ZEuP* 107 at 114.

[22] It is not difficult to perceive the Member States' interest in limiting references to courts of final appeal in cases governed by Articles 62 and 63 of the EC Treaty, which deal with rules on visas and measures on asylum. It is no doubt for such cases that provision is made for requests for preliminary ruling to be made by the Council, the Commission and Member States; but in the case of measures in the field of judicial cooperation in civil matters those considerations do not apply.

connecting the case to any of the situations envisaged by Community law. The judgment of the Court of Appeal in *Re Harrods (Buenos Aires)*[23] suggests that those rules do not apply in such a case; but academic commentary is divided[24] and the Court of Justice is currently seised of the question.[25]

Despite some initial doubts,[26] courts in the United Kingdom have consistently applied the Rome Convention even in the absence of an effect on trade between Member States. In the words of Article 1, the Convention applies 'in any situation involving a choice between the laws of different countries.'[27] In his opinion in *Caledonia Subsea Ltd v Micoperi Srl*,[28] Lord Hamilton quoted those words from Article 1 and continued:

> It is thus immaterial, albeit the Rome Convention is an instrument of what is now the European Union, that one of the laws in question is the law of a country outside the Union.

In that case the choice was between Scottish and Egyptian law. In *Marodi Service di D Mialich & Co sas v Mikkal Myklesbuthaug Rederi A/S*[29] a temporary judge in the Court of Session considered the Rome Convention to resolve a jurisdictional question arising in a suit initiated by an Italian company against a Norwegian company, owners of a vessel flying the Panamanian flag, in respect of bunker fuel obtained by Cypriot charterers in Turkey and Sicily. Where the choice is between English and Scottish law (and has no implications for trade between one Member State and another) the Scottish courts apply the rules in

---

[23] *Re Harrods (Buenos Aires) Ltd* [1992] Ch 72 at 97C.
[24] Sir Lawrence Collins argued that '[t]he Contracting States were setting up an intra-Convention mandatory system of jurisdiction. They were not regulating relations with non-Contracting States' (L Collins, 'Forum non conveniens and the Brussels Convention Again' (1991) 107 *LQR* 180. Cf P Kaye, 'The EEC Judgments Convention and the Outer World: Goodbye to Forum Non Conveniens?' [1992] *Journal of Business Law* 47 at 75; A Briggs and P Rees (eds), *Civil Jurisdiction and Judgments* (Lloyd's of London, 3rd edn 2002) at paragraph 2.216; P North and J Fawcett, *Cheshire and North's Private International Law* (Butterworths, 13th edn 1999) at pages 264–66; G Droz, 'Compétence Judiciaire et Effets des Jugements dans le Marché Commun' (1972) 13 *Bibliothèque de droit international privé* 429.
[25] Case C–281/02 *Jackson and Others v. Owusu*.
[26] In the course of the Parliamentary debate on the Bill that matured into the Contracts (Applicable Law) Act 1990, Lord Wilberforce contended that the Convention applies only to a choice of law affecting intra-Community trade; and proposed that the Bill should be confined accordingly. His proposal was not accepted: 513 HL Deb, cols 1472–80.
[27] According to the *Giuliano-Lagarde Report*, OJ 1980 C282/1, '[t]he uniform rules are to be applied in all cases where the dispute would give rise to a conflict between two or more legal systems'. That view is shared by the editors of *Dicey and Morris on the Conflict of Laws* (Sweet & Maxwell, 12th edn 1993, Vol II) at 1193. It is also endorsed by C Wadlow, 'Intellectual Property and the Rome Contracts Convention' (1997) 19(1) *European Intellectual Property Review* 11: '[T]he Rome Convention applies in full whether or not there is any connection at all with a Member State of the European Communities'. See further A Diamond, 'Harmonisation of private international law relating to contractual obligations' (1986) 199(4) *Recueil des Cours de l'Académie de droit international de la Haye* 241 at 246.
[28] [2001] SC 716.
[29] [2002] GWD 13–398.

the Rome Convention.[30] Similar but more numerous examples may be found in case-law of the larger jurisdiction south of the river Tweed.[31]

Those who seek to confine the Brussels Regulation to cases involving a 'connection with one of the situations envisaged by Community law'[32] commonly rely on the wording of Article 65 of the EC Treaty, with its references to 'cross-border implications . . . in so far as necessary for the proper functioning of the internal market.' But what is good for the goose must be good for the gander. If the Brussels Regulation were so confined, the Rome Convention would be subject to a similar constraint. That is not the Commission's aim. In its words:

> The Convention has a very wide scope of application in view of the fact that the Courts of the Contracting States will always have to apply it whenever they have to decide which substantive law is applicable in an individual case, whether the choice is between the laws of several Contracting States or of several non-Contracting States or of both Contracting States and non-Contracting States.[33]

3. OPTIONAL PROVISIONS IN THE ROME CONVENTION

While transformation of the Rome Convention into a Community instrument will present the advantage of uniformity it will also present a corresponding difficulty. As matters stand, contracting parties are entitled under Article 22 of the Convention to enter reservations relating to Articles 7(1) and 10(1)(e). The former permits the courts of contracting states, when applying the law of a country, to give effect to the mandatory rules of the law of another country with

---

[30] See for example the opinion of Lord MacFadyan in *Tullis Russell & Co Ltd v Eadie Industries Ltd* [2001] GWD 28–1122.

[31] In the last twelve months English courts have applied the rules prescribed by the Rome Convention to choices between the laws of Illinois and Texas, *American Motor Insurance Co v. Cellstar Corporation and another* [2003] EWCA Civ 206; English and Chilean law, *Import Export Metro Ltd and another v Compañia Sud Americana de Vapores SA* [2003] EWHC 11 (Comm); the laws of England, the Ukraine and Switzerland, *Welex AG v. Rosa Maritime Ltd* [2002] EWHC 2033 (Comm); English law and the law of Lesotho, *Lesotho Highlands Development Authority v. Impreglio SpA and others* [2002] EWHC 2435 (Comm); and between the laws of England and those of Mongolia, *Marubeni Hong Kong and South China Ltd v. Mongolian Government* [2002] 2 All ER (D) 09 (Aug).

[32] The expression is frequently used by the Court of Justice in the context of free movement of persons and services. See among other examples Case 27–6/69 *Caisse de maladie des CFL 'Enrt'aide medicale' and Société nationale des chemins de fer luxembourgeois v. Compagnie belge d'assurances générales sur la vie et contre les accidents* [1969] ECR 405 at para 4; Case C–108/98 *RI.SAN. Srl v. Comune di Ischia, Italia Lavro SpA and Ischia Ambiente SpA* [1999] ECR I–5219 at para 22; Case C–206/91 *Ettien Koua Poirrez v. Caisse d'allocations familiales de la region parisienne* [1992] ECR I–6685 at paras 10, 11 and 12; Case C–60/00 *Mary Carpenter v Secretary of State for the Home Department* [2002] ECR 1–6279 at para 28; Case 61–65 *Vaassen-Göbbels v. Management of the Beambtenfonds voor hat Mijnbedrif* [1966] ECR 261, 277; Joined cases C–95/99 to C–98/99 and C–180/99 *Mervett Khali and others v. Bundesanstalt für Arbeit, Mohammad Nasser v. Landeshauptstadt* and *Meriem Addou v. Land Nordrhein Westfalen* [2001] ECR 7413 at para 51; and Case 459/99 *MRAX v Belgian State* [2002] ECR I–6591 at para 39.

[33] Opinion of 17 March 1980, OJ 1980 L 94/39.

which the situation has a close connection. The latter states that the applicable law shall determine 'the consequences of nullity of the contract'.[34]

The rule now contained in Article 7(1) has its origin in the *Sonderstatut* theory, developed in Germany during the Second World War as a defence to proceedings brought in the United States against German borrowers of United States bonds which ceased to be serviced after the introduction of exchange controls.[35] Although the theory has come to be recognized in some continental States[36] it is not easily reconciled with the purpose of the Rome Convention, as explained by the writers of the Jenard Report.[37] In their words:

> the purpose of the Convention is . . . , by establishing common rules of jurisdiction, to achieve . . . in the field which it was required to cover, a genuine legal systematization which will ensure the greatest possible degree of legal certainty.

Article 7(1), on the other hand, produces unpredictability, not only by making provision for the application of rules derived neither from the applicable law nor from the law of the forum but also by leaving it to the appreciation of the judge to determine whether the rules of that extraneous jurisdiction are mandatory and if so, whether they shall be applied in the instant case. The draftsmen of a new Community instrument must give careful consideration to the question whether a rule such as Article 7(1) is to be retained.

A different difficulty is presented by Article 10(1)(e). It has long been established that the remedies for which English and Scottish law provide in the event of unjust enrichment or unjust benefit, in the form of restitution or recompense, are separate from the law of contract.[38] In *Baring Brothers & Co. Ltd* v. *Cunninghame District Council*[39] the Outer House of the Court of Session was required to identify the law governing recompense in the event of the illegality of one of the 'swaps' arrangements into which local authorities entered with banks. Lord Penrose, giving judgment, identified four possibilities. The first was the proper law of the putative contract as determined by the rules laid down in the Rome Convention. On that view, the parties' choice of law, express or implied, would govern the claim for recompense, although the contract itself was void. The second was the law governing the putative contract, as determined by the law with which the obligation has the closest connection, ignoring

---

[34] See T Hartley, 'Mandatory rules in international contracts: the common law approach' *Recueil des Cours de l'Académie de la Haye* (1997) 206 at 337–426.

[35] Mann, 'The Effect of Mandatory Rules' in Lipstein (ed) *Harmonisation of Private International Law by the EEC* (Institute of Advanced Legal Studies, London 1978) at 32.

[36] See the judgment of the Hoge Raad in *Van Nievelt, Goudrian and Co's Stromvaartmij v NV Hollandische Assurantie Societeit and Others* (1967) 56 *Rev. crit. Dr.int.priv.* 522; Article 13 of the Benelux Treaty concerning a Uniform Law on Private International Law, (1970) 18 *Am Jo Comp L* 420; and Article 16 of the Hague Convention of 14 March 1978 on the Law Applicable to Agency, Cmnd 7020.

[37] OJ 1979 C 59/1.

[38] Lord Wright in *Branwhite* v. *Worcester Works Finance Ltd* [1968] 3 All ER 104.

[39] *The Times*, 30 September 1996. The case was a sequel to *Hazell* v. *Hammersmith and Fulham LBC* [1992] 2 AC 1.

any choice by the parties. The third was the law which determines the nullity of the contract. That would not necessarily be the same as the law which would govern contractual issues generally had the contract been valid, since a contract may be rendered void by incapacity (governed by the *lex personae*) or by the public policy of the forum. The fourth was the proper law of the obligation: that is, the law with which the critical events have their most real and substantial connection. He held that the fourth of these governed recompense.

That judgment been subjected to some criticism on the ground that 'the system of law which declares the contract to be a nullity should determine the consequences of nullity.'[40] That this criticism appears misplaced. The law that declares the contract a nullity is by no means necessarily the same as the applicable law: it may well be the *lex fori* or the *lex personae*. The interest that a legal system has in rendering a contract null by reason of public policy or personal capacity may well be insufficient to warrant submitting to that law the consequences of the invalidity on a transaction which is most intimately connected with another jurisdiction. The suggestion that the proper law of the putative contract should govern recompense has little to commend itself where, as in Scotland, recompense is not a branch of the law of contract at all.

It is of course appreciated that for the majority of the contracting parties, the consequences of the nullity of contract are governed by the law of contract; but the application of such a rule in England and Scotland would produce profound consequences exceeding the subject-matter of the Rome Convention. In the conversion of that Convention into a Community instrument, the safest course would be to delete the present Article 10(1)(e).

4. PROLIFERATION OF SECTORAL INSTRUMENTS

The rules of private international law affecting contracts within the Community are now complicated by the proliferation of rules in sectoral instruments that have an impact on the applicable law. There are Community instruments containing isolated conflict rules in Directives dealing with such matters as the return of cultural property,[41] posted workers[42] and consumer contracts;[43] and various other Directives instruments have an impact on the applicable law by determining the territorial application of Community rules.[44] Harmonisation of

---

[40] R Stevens, *Restitution and the Rome Convention* (1997) 113 *LQR* 249 at 252.

[41] Eg Council Directive 93/7/EEC of 15 March 1993 on the return of cultural objects unlawfully removed from the territory of a Member State, OJ 1993 L74/74.

[42] Directive 96/71/EC of the European Parliament and of the Council of 16 December 1996 concerning the posting of workers in the framework of the provision of services, OJ 1997 L18/1.

[43] Directive 99/44/EC of the European Parliament and of the Council of 25 May 1999 on certain aspects of the sale of consumer goods and associated guarantees, OJ 1999 L171/12.

[44] Directive 93/13/EEC of 5 April 1993 on unfair terms in consumer contracts, OJ 1993 L95/29; Directive 94/47/EC of the European Parliament and of the Council of 26 October 1994 on the protection of consumers in respect of timeshare contracts, OJ 1994 L280/83; Directive 97/7/EC of the European Parliament and of the Council of 20 May 1997 on the protection of consumers in respect

the provisions affecting private international law in these instruments would promote clarity and predictability.

Many of the conflicts rules prescribed by the Community's existing legislation serve the purpose of protecting the weaker party. The same purpose is served by the provisions in the Rome Convention governing mandatory rules. As experience shows, difficulty may arise not only in determining whether a particular rule of national law is to be characterised as mandatory but also in deciding whether rules of Community law may possess that quality. It appears from *Ingmar GB Ltd v Eaton Leonard Technologies Inc*[45] that rules of Community law may indeed be mandatory. In that case the Court of Justice ruled that:

> Articles 17 and 18 of [Council] Directive [86/653/EEC][46] which guarantee certain rights to commercial agents after termination of agency contracts, must be applied where the commercial agent carried on his activity in a Member State although the principal is established in a non-member country and a clause of the contract stipulates that the contract is to be governed by the law of that country.

The Court of Justice adopted similar reasoning, but *sub silentio*, in *Davidoff v Levi Strauss, Tesco Stores and Others*.[47] It may be inferred from that judgment that Directive 89/104/EEC[48] which harmonised trade mark protection at Community level, is to be applied regardless of the national law governing the contract. Thus the freedom to choose an applicable law, in accordance with the Rome Convention, is subjected to the principle of Community exhaustion. In view of these judgments, it may be prudent to include in the instrument transforming the Rome Convention more detailed provisions to define both the source of mandatory rules and the core elements giving them their essential character.

What the Commission will propose to replace the Rome Convention and what the Council and Parliament will make of it remain to be seen. One point is clear. When the Court of Justice is required to interpret the emerging instrument, it will require judges with the intellectual energy and clarity that David Edward brought to that institution in his years as judge.

---

of distance contracts, OJ 1997 L144/19; Directive 99/44/EC of the European Parliament and of the Council of 25 May 1999 on certain aspects of the sale of consumer goods and associated guarantees, OJ 1999 L171/12; Directive 2002/65/EC of the European Parliament and of the Council of 23 September 2002 on distance sales of financial services, OJ 2002 L271/16.

[45] Case C–381/98 *Ingmar GB Ltd* v. *Eaton Leonard Technologies Inc* [2000] ECR I–9305.
[46] Council Directive 86/653/EEC of 18 December 1986 on the coordination of the laws of the Member States relating to self-employed commercial agents, OJ 1986 L382/17.
[47] Joined Cases C–414/99 to C–416/99 *Zino Davidoff SA* v *A&G Imports Ltd* and *Levi Strauss & Co et al* v. *Tesco Stores Ltd et al* [2001] ECR I–8691.
[48] First Council Directive 89/104/EEC of 21 December 1988 to approximate the laws of the Member States relating to trade marks, OJ 1989 L40/1.

20
Standard of Review in WTO Law

CLAUS-DIETER EHLERMANN AND NICOLAS LOCKHART*

1 A PERSONAL TRIBUTE

DAVID PERSONIFIES, for me, one of the most admirable and successful aspects of the judicial system in the United Kingdom, namely the selection and appointment of judges. The European Union has greatly benefited from this practice as the UK government has always applied it in nominating judges to the Court of Justice in Luxembourg.

Unlike Nicolas, who was of invaluable help while I was in Geneva, I have never had the chance to work with David. We first met in the late seventies. David was then a brilliant young Scottish advocate who had been co-opted as a member of the 'dream-team' that assisted IBM in its difficult dealings with DG IV and before the Court of Justice. After taking up the chair previously held by the late John Mitchell, David brought me to his University in Edinburgh where he enthusiastically taught European Community law. Finally, our professional paths crossed again when David joined the Court of First Instance and—later—the Court of Justice in Luxembourg.

The following thoughts on standard of review are devoted to a subject of common interest. This subject intrigued me profoundly during my relatively short experience as a member of the Appellate Body of the WTO. I am sure that it has also preoccupied David during his many years as a judge in Luxembourg.

Claus-Dieter Ehlermann

I had the very great privilege to work with David during nearly four years of his time at the Court. David is that rare person who has an extraordinary professional ability that is matched by his integrity and human qualities. As every good judge does, David knows his own mind and is ready to make tough decisions. However, he is also a man who seeks out the views of others. He is

---

* Claus-Dieter Ehlermann is Senior Counsel, Wilmer, Cutler & Pickering, Brussels. He was a Member and, during his last year of office, Chairman of the Appellate Body of the WTO. Before that, he was Director-General of Competition and of the Legal Service at the European Commission.

Nicolas Lockhart is on leave of absence from the WTO Secretariat. He was a counsellor with the Appellate Body Secretariat of the WTO and a *référendaire* to David Edward at the European Court of Justice.

willing to challenge—and relishes being challenged on—his own ideas. He also cares a lot about people and he always took a great deal of interest in fostering my development. That made it a pleasure to be part of David's team.

Before heading off for my Master's, David told me that what counts in a legal education is not just what you learn, but from whom you learn it. 'Go and learn', he said, 'at the feet of great men and women.' In my case, I will always be grateful to David for giving me the chance to learn at his feet. And, of course, for the chance to be part of the extended Edward 'family', with the rest of the cabinet, under Elizabeth's thoughtful guidance. I have also been lucky enough to learn at the feet of another great man, my co-author, Claus.

Nicolas Lockhart

1. INTRODUCTION

Standard of review is a key issue for any court or tribunal that devotes time to the business of reviewing legislation or administrative decisions. Routinely, a court will have to address questions like: to what extent should it second-guess the work of a first decision-maker; does a court have the tools and experience to carry out a full-scale re-examination of legal and factual issues already examined by a first decision-maker; is it ever appropriate for a court to 'roll-over-and-play-dead' in the face of choices made by a first decision-maker?

The answers to these questions are intimately linked with the separation and balance of powers among the legislative, executive and judicial branches of government. In an international setting, the answers also affect the division of powers between a State and a multilateral entity, such as the World Trade Organization ('WTO') or the European Union ('EU'). Perhaps because of this, the answers to these questions can be controversial when a judicial institution is said to have interfered in the political arena.

David is, of course, no stranger to these questions. Far less is he a stranger to the criticism that is, from time-to-time, heaped upon courts by politicians and the media. Indeed, David's time at the European Court of Justice ('ECJ' or 'Court') saw a considerable upsurge in criticism of the institution and its role in the development of the EU. In a speech to the European-Atlantic Group in July 1996, David remarked, with characteristic modesty, that when he embarked on his Luxembourg adventure in 1989, 'few people had the least idea of what I was going to do'.[1] Yet, as he observed in the same address, the Court has since become a 'hot topic', accused of judicial activism and of eroding the national sovereignty of the EU Member States.

---

[1] 'The European Court of Justice—Friend or Foe?', address by Judge David Edward, 18 July 1996 (transcript available at http://www.eag.org.uk/speech%20edward.htm).

David is no shrinking violet and it has been a feature of his time at the Court that such criticism has not gone unanswered.[2] Confronting head-on charges of political interference, David has explained that the role of the Court is limited to the sphere of law, even if the Court works in a necessarily political environment. Many of the decisions that the Court is asked to review are, in a sense, 'political' and involve questions of policy. Yet, that does not mean that the judges are politicians, reaching 'political' compromises for 'political' reasons. To the contrary, the proper role of a judge is to eschew political considerations and reach a decision on purely legal standards.

In many cases, inevitably, the judicial decision must land on one side or the other of a political divide; inevitably, also, judicial decisions have political consequences and they will be criticised by some who would have preferred an alternative outcome. But the decision will nevertheless be based on legal considerations.

In legal theory, there is a bright line that separates the judicial from the political. That bright line marks the separation of powers in government: on the one side, there is the judicial branch; and on the other, the legislative and executive branches, themselves separated by another bright line. In practice, however, the path traced by these lines is not always easy to see, and their position may move over time. Indeed, in different legal systems the location of the lines can also be quite different.

In any legal system, including both EU and WTO law, standard of review is one of the mechanisms used to guarantee the separation of powers. Standard of review refers to the nature and intensity of a court's scrutiny of the legal validity of a legislative or administrative decision. It provides the answers to the questions we posed at the outset about the degree of deference judges should accord legislators and regulators. Essentially, standard of review defines the parameters within which judges work and, correspondingly, within which legislators and regulators work. It establishes 'no go' areas for judges, requiring them to respect the choices made by legislators or regulators. Within these 'no go' areas, the first decision-maker has discretion to make choices that the judge cannot reconsider. Beyond the 'no go' areas, the judge has the authority to verify the legal—but not political—validity of the decision. Standard of review is, therefore, an important part of the system of checks and balances in government, helping to ensure the accountability of decision-makers. It should also function to allocate decision-making authority and resources in an efficient fashion among the different branches of government.

There is, though, no single or 'right' standard of review. Each legal system must develop a standard that suits its own needs. Further, within a single system, the standard may well differ depending upon the decision under review, and it is likely to evolve over time. Perhaps the most important objective of

---

[2] See also D Edward 'Judicial Activism—Myth or Reality?' in Campbell and Voyatzi (eds) *Legal Reasoning and Judicial Interpretation of European Law: Essays in honour of Lord Mackenzie-Stuart* (Trenton, 1996).

standard of review is that it should enhance the quality and legitimacy of the governmental decision-making process as a whole.

The tensions that exist in government among the judiciary, legislature and executive play out, therefore, in standard of review. These tensions take on an additional dimension where international tribunals review the acts of sovereign States. International scrutiny of this type can be problematic at the national level because it may be perceived as unwarranted interference with State sovereignty. A national authority is no longer responsible just to a local court but rather to an 'alien', 'foreign', court that is said to know nothing of domestic needs. Yet, the effectiveness, and even viability, of an international regime depends on a degree of international scrutiny to maintain the cohesiveness of the regime across its membership.

In the WTO system, standard of review has become a 'hot topic', with panels and the Appellate Body being criticised for the level of their scrutiny of national measures, particularly trade remedy measures.[3] Critics have suggested that panels and the Appellate Body have not respected the proper discretion of national authorities and, in so doing, they are said to have usurped the powers of the WTO Members.

2. STANDARD OF REVIEW IN WTO LAW—IN GENERAL

Article 3.2 of the *Understanding on Rules and Procedures Governing the Settlement of Disputes* (*DSU*) sets forth objectives for the WTO dispute settlement system. It states that this system 'is a central element in providing security and predictability to the multilateral trading system'. The same provision also stipulates that the dispute settlement system serves to 'preserve' the balance of WTO Members rights and obligations. The pursuit of these goals indicates that the WTO Membership attaches a great deal of importance to a cohesive and stable trading regime where WTO rules are applied in the same way from Member to Member. In turn, these core goals influence the standard of review applied by panels, and as appropriate the Appellate Body, in providing international scrutiny of contested national measures. That scrutiny must, however, respect the prerogatives which the WTO agreements leave to the individual Members.

When the Appellate Body addressed standard of review for the first time, in *EC—Hormones*, it explicitly referred to this link between standard of review and the balance of powers between WTO Members and the WTO.[4] The Appellate Body acknowledged that:

[3] For instance, in July 2003, the United States General Accounting Office ('GAO') produced a report for the United States' Senate Finance Committee, entitled 'World Trade Organization—Standard of Review and Impact of Trade Remedy Rulings' (USGAO Report). In the introductory page, explaining why the study was conducted, GAO notes that '[t]here is congressional concern that the WTO . . . is interfering with [the] ability' of WTO Members to rely on trade remedies and 'there is also congressional concern that the WTO is not treating the United States fairly in resolving trade remedy disputes.' For some of the conclusions reached in the *USGAO Report*, see footnotes 20 and 29 below.

[4] Appellate Body Report, *European Measures Concerning Meat and Meat Products (Hormones)* (*EC—Hormones*), WT/DS26/AB/R, WT/DS448/AB/R, adopted 13 February 1998, Dispute Settlement Reports ('DSR') 1998:I, 135.

The standard of review ... must reflect the balance established in [the particular WTO agreement] between the jurisdictional competences conceded by the Members to the WTO and the jurisdictional competences retained by the Members for themselves....[5]

In striking this 'finely drawn balance', the Appellate Body turned to Article 11 of the DSU.[6] This provision states that 'a panel should make an *objective assessment* of the matter before it, including an objective assessment of the facts...' (emphasis added). In *EC—Hormones*, the Appellate Body said that Article 11 articulates a standard of review that is generally applicable to all WTO disputes.[7] It added that, under Article 11, 'the applicable standard is neither *de novo* review as such, nor "total deference"'.[8]

However, even if generally applicable, the standard of 'objective assessment' is couched in rather broad terms that do little to provide substantive guidance on the nature and intensity of the review which panels should apply to national measures. To illustrate, take two different possible standards of review. One requires a panel to review a national measure to determine whether a national authority's decision is *reasonable*; the second requires the panel to review whether the authority's decision conforms to the panel's view of what is *correct*. In both cases, the panel could perform an 'objective assessment of the matter', whilst respecting the different standards of review. However, as the degree of deference in the two examples is different, it is perfectly possible that the outcome of the 'objective assessment' could be different. Thus, requiring panels to make an 'objective assessment' does not indicate specifically what panels are expected to do by way of review. In other words, the requirement for an 'objec-

---

[5] Appellate Body Report, *EC—Hormones*, para 115. The Appellate Body has also said that standard of review 'goes to the very core of the integrity of the WTO dispute settlement process itself'. (Appellate Body Report, *European Communities—Measures Affecting the Importation of Certain Poultry Products* (*EC—Poultry*), WT/DS69/AB/R, adopted 23 July 1998, DSR 1998:V, 2031, para. 133)

[6] Appellate Body Report, *EC—Hormones*, para 115.

[7] Art 17.6 of the *Anti-Dumping Agreement* provides special standards of review for disputes concerning anti-dumping measures that apply in conjunction with Art 11 of the DSU. These special standards were introduced into the *Anti-Dumping Agreement* after prolonged negotiations that proved to be among the most contentious issues in the Uruguay Round. Some negotiators sought to have the standards of review in Art 17.6 applied to all WTO agreements. In the end, a Ministerial Decision was adopted that requires WTO Members to review the standards of review in Art 17.6, after three years, 'with a view to considering the question of whether it is capable of general application.' (*Decision on the Review of Article 17.6 of the Agreement on Implementation of Article VI of the General Agreement on Tariffs and Trade 1994*) To date, the WTO Members have not conducted the review envisaged in the Decision. Thus, the standards of review in Art 17.6 of the *Anti-Dumping Agreement* continue to apply only to disputes concerning anti-dumping measures. (See Appellate Body Report, *United States—Imposition of Countervailing Duties on Certain Hot-Rolled Lead and Bismuth Carbon Steel Products Originating in the United Kingdom* (*US—Lead and Bismuth II*), WT/DS138/AB/R, adopted 7 June 2000, DSR 2000:V, 2601, para 50) For a detailed history of the negotiations on Art 17.6 of the *Anti-Dumping Agreement*, see Steven P Croley and John J Jackson, 'WTO Dispute Procedures, Standard of Review, and Deference to National Governments', *American Journal of International Law*, Vol 90 (April, 1996), 193, at 199.

[8] Appellate Body Report, *EC—Hormones*, para 117.

tive assessment' must function with another, more detailed, underlying standard of review.[9]

Moreover, Article 11 seems to adopt a 'one-size-fits-all' approach to standard of review: every question relating to standard of review is to be answered by resort to the notion of 'objective assessment'. Yet, in practice, standard of review has raised a series of questions that have not received a uniform response. Certainly, panels perform an 'objective assessment'; but the scope and intensity of the panel's assessment is not the same for every issue, in every dispute.

In exploring standard of review, a number of considerations should be borne in mind. First, the work of a panel, like other tribunals, comprises three different, basic activities. Panels make findings that: (a) are purely legal in nature; (b) are purely factual; and (c) involve the application of the facts to the law. This last activity is the most difficult to pin down. It involves the weighing and appreciation of the facts and their characterisation in terms of the legal rules. In WTO law, notwithstanding the generality of Article 11 of the DSU, the nature and intensity of review differs depending on which of these three activities a panel is engaged in.

Second, the nature of review also appears to change with the subject-matter of the dispute. For instance, a public health measure examined under the *Agreement on the Application of Sanitary and Phytosanitary Measures* (*SPS Agreement*) appears to be subject to a different kind of review from that applied to a measure taken under the *Agreement on Safeguards*.

Third, the process by which the contested national measure was adopted at national level can also influence the nature of review. Thus, if the measure resulted from a treaty-mandated investigative procedure, conducted at national level, that may dictate a different review from that applied to a measure where no similar national procedure is required.

3. STANDARD OF REVIEW IN WTO LAW—SPECIFIC ISSUES

Legal Determinations

According to Article 11 of the DSU, the requirement for panels to conduct an 'objective assessment' relates to a panel's overall consideration of the 'matter'. The word 'matter' includes both factual and legal issues that arise in examining a contested national measure.[10] Thus, irrespective of whether panels are mak-

---

[9] The Appellate Body has indicated that the requirement for panels to conduct an 'objective assessment' can apply in conjunction with different underlying standards of review. In examining the special standards of review in Art 17.6(i) of the *Anti-Dumping Agreement*, the Appellate Body has said that 'it is inconceivable that Art 17.6(i) should require anything other than that panels make an *objective* 'assessment of the facts of the matter'. (Appellate Body Report, *United States—Anti-Dumping Measures on Certain Hot-Rolled Steel Products from Japan* (*US—Hot-Rolled Steel*), WT/DS184/AB/R, adopted 23 August 2001, para 55)

[10] The term 'matter' has been defined as a reference to the contested national measure and the legal basis of a complaining party's complaint regarding that measure. (Appellate Body Report,

ing legal findings, factual findings, or mixed findings on the application of the facts to the law, they must make an 'objective assessment'.

Although Article 11 applies to all these different determinations, the character of the review is not the same in each case. In *EC—Hormones*, the Appellate Body was careful to distinguish its consideration of the review applicable to 'the determination and assessment of the facts' from the review applicable to legal determinations.[11] In particular, the Appellate Body prefaced its oft-quoted statement—that 'the applicable standard is neither *de novo* review as such, nor "total deference"'—with the words '[s]o far as fact-finding is concerned'.[12]

In the next paragraph, the Appellate Body addresses 'legal questions' separately, stating that panels have a 'duty to apply the customary rules of interpretation of public international law', as required by Article 3.2 of the DSU.[13] Thus, although a panel must 'objectively assess' interpretive questions, its review of a national authority's legal determinations is different from its review of factual determinations.

Legal questions arise in every dispute and, each time, panels and the Appellate Body approach the questions from first principles, as if they were the first to address the legal issue. In many cases, panels and the Appellate Body will, indeed, be the first to interpret the WTO rules because national authorities generally apply *national* rules, albeit often implementing WTO rules. However, even in cases where national authorities have applied rules that are the same as, or similar to, WTO rules, panels and the Appellate Body reach their own independant conclusions as regards interpretive questions.[14]

As the Appellate Body said in *EC—Hormones*, this approach is dictated by the text of the DSU, which requires panels and the Appellate Body to follow the customary rules of interpretation of public international law. The Appellate Body has stated that the relevant customary rules are codified in the *Vienna Convention on the Law of Treaties* (**Vienna Convention**).[15] In terms of Articles 31 and 32 of this Convention, the treaty interpreter must seek out the ordinary

---

Guatemala—Anti-Dumping Investigation Regarding Portland Cement from Mexico (***Guatemala— Cement I***), WT/DS60/AB/R, adopted 25 November 1998, DSR 1998:IX, 3767, para 72) Art 11 of the DSU states explicitly that the objective assessment includes 'the applicability of and conformity with the relevant covered agreements'.

[11] Appellate Body Report, *EC—Hormones*, para 116. See also paras 112, 114, and 117. The European Communities appeal on standard of review related solely to the panel's treatment of the facts.

[12] Appellate Body Report, *EC—Hormones*, para 117.

[13] As already mentioned, Art 17.6(ii) of the *Anti-Dumping Agreement* provides special standards of review for anti-dumping disputes. See below.

[14] We are, of course, referring to the interpretation of WTO law by panels and the Appellate Body in disputes concerning the WTO consistency of national measures. The treatment of national law by panels and the Appellate Body raises issues beyond the scope of this article.

[15] Done at Vienna, 23 May 1969, 1155 UNTS 331; 8 International Legal Materials 679; Appellate Body Report, *United States—Standards for Reformulated and Conventional Gasoline* (*US— Gasoline*), WT/DS2/AB/R, adopted 20 May 1996, DSR 1996:I, 3, at 17; Appellate Body Report, *Japan—Taxes on Alcoholic Beverages* ('*Japan—Alcoholic Beverages II*'), WT/DS8/AB/R, WT/DS10/AB/R, WT/DS11/AB/R, adopted 1 November 1996, DSR 1996:I, 97, at 104.

meaning of the text. The treaty interpreter cannot set aside what it considers is the ordinary meaning of the text even in the event that, for example, the national authority's decision is based on an alternative reasonable reading of the text.[16]

For purely legal questions there is, therefore, *de novo* review of a national authority's legal determination, whereas for factual determinations there is not. Yet, in both cases, panels must conduct an 'objective assessment'. This stark difference in approach to legal and factual questions is explained by the distinct roles of the national authorities and the panel.

The WTO dispute settlement system has exclusive jurisdiction to hear disputes between WTO Members relating to the WTO agreements. In that system, panels and the Appellate Body have a unique responsibility for interpreting, or as the DSU says 'clarifying', the WTO agreements.[17] Moreover, as we said, under Article 3.2 of the DSU, the dispute settlement system seeks to guarantee 'security and predictability' to the trading system, and to 'preserve' the WTO Members' balance of rights and obligations. Panels and the Appellate Body play an important part in achieving these goals by providing for a uniform interpretation of WTO law. If individual WTO Members were afforded discretion to interpret WTO law, the uniform interpretation would be lost. It would lead to what Palmeter and Spak have described as a 'Tower of Legal Babel.'[18] The obligations assumed by WTO Members, and the rights acquired, would differ from Member to Member, undermining the core objectives of the rule-based system. There is, therefore, considerable justification for requiring panels and the Appellate Body to conduct an original, *de novo* review of a national authority's legal determinations, using the rules of the *Vienna Convention*.

'Permissible' Legal Interpretations—Special Rules for Anti-Dumping

The only context in which panels are called upon to apply different rules to the interpretation of WTO law is under Article 17.6(ii) of the *Agreement on Implementation of Article VI of the General Agreement on Tariffs and Trade 1994* (the '*Anti-Dumping Agreement*'). It is worth quoting this provision in full:

> [T]he panel shall interpret the relevant provisions of the Agreement in accordance with customary rules of interpretation of public international law. Where the panel

---

[16] This may be contrasted with the special standard of review in Article 17.6(ii) of the *Anti-Dumping Agreement*. Under this provision, panels and the Appellate Body will accept a national authority's decision if it rests upon a 'permissible' interpretation of the *Anti-Dumping Agreement*. See below.

[17] Under Article IX:2 of the *WTO Agreement*, the Ministerial Conference and the General Council have 'the exclusive authority to adopt interpretations' of the WTO agreements. These interpretations must be adopted by three-fourths majority of the WTO membership. The interpretations are thereafter binding upon all WTO Members in a uniform manner.

[18] David Palmeter and Gregory J Spak 'Resolving Anti-Dumping and Countervailing Duty Disputes: Defining GATT's Role in an Era of Increasing Conflict' *Law and Policy in International Business*, Vol. 24 (1993), 1145, at 1158.

finds that a relevant provision of the Agreement admits of more than one permissible interpretation, the panel shall find the authorities' measure to be in conformity with the Agreement if it rests upon one of those permissible interpretations.[19]

Under this provision, a panel's primary interpretive responsibility is the same as it is under the other WTO agreements. The first sentence of Article 17.6(ii) reiterates the requirement in Article 3.2 of the DSU for panels to rely upon the customary rules of interpretation. As we have said, this means that, under both Article 3.2 of the DSU and Article 17.6(ii) of the *Anti-Dumping Agreement*, panels must interpret treaty text according to Articles 31 and 32 of the *Vienna Convention*.[20] In so doing, panels must make an 'objective assessment' of the relevant legal provisions, consistent with Article 11 of the DSU.[21]

The added twist in Article 17.6(ii) comes in the second sentence of the provision. It states that where a national authority's anti-dumping measure rests upon a *'permissible'* interpretation of a WTO norm, panels and the Appellate Body must accept the measure as WTO-consistent. This standard of review 'presupposes' that provisions of the *Anti-Dumping Agreement* 'admit of more than one permissible interpretation'.[22] In light of the requirement to interpret WTO law according to the *Vienna Convention*, the Appellate Body has emphasised that the multiple permissible interpretations of a provision must each result from the application of the rules embedded in that *Convention*.[23]

Some suggest that reading the two sentences of Article 17.6(ii) together creates certain difficulties for the treaty interpreter. Article 31 of the *Vienna Convention* is intended to elicit what the convention describes as '*the* ordinary meaning' of the treaty (emphasis added). Article 32 of the *Convention* also refers, three times, to 'the meaning' of the treaty (emphasis added). Article 32,

---

[19] At the time of the conclusion of the Uruguay Round this provision continued to provoke disagreement. Some negotiating parties sought to have the phrase 'reasonable interpretation' included instead of the word 'permissible interpretation'. This standard of 'reasonableness' would appear to be drawn from the *Chevron* doctrine in United States administrative law (see *Chevron USA., Inc* v. *Natural Resources Defense Council, Inc*, 467 U.S. 837 (1984)). The word 'reasonable' was opposed by others, with agreement finally being reached on the word 'permissible' in the closing days of the Round. For a detailed history of the negotiations on this point see Steven P Croley and John J Jackson 'WTO Dispute Procedures, Standard of Review, and Deference to National Governments' *American Journal of International Law*, Vol 90 (April, 1996), 193, at 199.
In the *USGAO Report* to the Senate Finance Committee, GAO notes that '[a] majority of the experts [GAO consulted] maintained that the United States was not successful in getting the standard of review it wanted in the Anti-Dumping Agreement . . .' (p 30).

[20] Appellate Body Report, *US—Hot-Rolled Steel*, para 57.
[21] Appellate Body Report, *US—Hot-Rolled Steel*, para 62. The Appellate Body stated that the special standard of review in Article 17.6(ii) does not replace the requirement to make an 'objective assessment' but supplements it. There is, therefore, no conflict between Art 11 of the DSU and Art 17.6(ii) of the *Anti-Dumping Agreement*.
[22] Appellate Body Report, *US—Hot-Rolled Steel*, para 59.
[23] Appellate Body Report, *US—Hot-Rolled Steel*, para 60. See also Panel Report, *United States—Anti-Dumping Duty on Dynamic Random Access Memory Semiconductors (DRAMS) of One Megabit or Above from Korea* (***US—DRAMS***), WT/DS99/R, adopted 19 March 1999, DSR 1999:II, 521, para 6.53, fn 499.

in fact, provides rules to enable the interpreter to arrive at 'the meaning' of a treaty even where the text is 'ambiguous or obscure'.

In other words the rules of the *Vienna Convention* are designed, it is argued, to produce a single meaning for a text, and not the multiple 'permissible' meanings envisaged in the second sentence of Article 17.6(ii). This has led commentators to question when there might be multiple permissible interpretations of a provision of the *Anti-Dumping Agreement*. In particular, Professors Croley and Jackson have said that 'it is not clear in light of [the *Vienna Convention*] whether or how a WTO panel could ever reach the conclusion that provisions of an agreement admit of more than one interpretation'.[24]

Although the Appellate Body has accepted that there are provisions of the *Anti-Dumping Agreement* which admit of multiple permissible interpretations, some still argue that there is a tension between the first and second sentences of Article 17.6(ii)[25]. Under the first sentence, panels must follow Articles 31 and 32 of the *Vienna Convention* which instruct the treaty interpreter to find a single meaning of the treaty. Yet, Article 17.6(ii) 'presupposes' that there are provisions of the *Anti-Dumping Agreement* that admit of more than one permissible interpretation under the rules of the *Vienna Convention*.[26]

The text of the *Anti-Dumping Agreement* does little to assist the treaty interpreter in resolving this perceived tension. There is no guidance as to which provisions admit of multiple permissible interpretations nor is there any guidance on how to read the first and second sentences of Article 17.6(ii) so as to give proper meaning to both. In particular, there is nothing in the *Anti-Dumping Agreement* to suggest that parts of the *Vienna Convention* do not apply to interpretation under Article 17.6(ii).[27] It may be that the perceived tensions between the first and second sentences of Article 17.6(ii) of the *Anti-Dumping Agreement* are clarified in subsequent negotiations.[28]

---

[24] Steven P Croley and John J Jackson 'WTO Dispute Procedures, Standard of Review, and Deference to National Governments' *American Journal of International Law*, Vol. 90 (April, 1996), 193 at 200. Bill Davey has also said 'The provisions [of Art 17.6] are worded in such general terms, however, that it remains to be seen whether they will have much impact on the results of panel decisions.' (William J Davey 'The WTO/GATT World Trading System: An Overview' in Pierre Pescatorre, William J Davey and Andreas F Lowenfeld (eds), *Handbook of WTO/GATT Dispute Settlement* (Transnational Publications, 1995) 7).

[25] Appellate Body Report, *US—Hot-Rolled Steel*, paras 60 and 61.

[26] Appellate Body Report, *US—Hot-Rolled Steel*, para 60.

[27] Croley and Jackson consider whether the existence of ambiguities in the text of the *Anti-Dumping Agreement* could lead to multiple permissible interpretations (p. 201). The different possible ambiguous readings of the text might each be 'permissible' interpretations. However, they point out that '[o]nce a panel has invoked Articles 31 and 32 of the Vienna Convention, it presumably will have already settled on a nonambiguous, nonabsurd interpretation.' (p 201) Yet, they also note that 'Article 17.6(ii) does, at least on the surface, suppose that a panel could somehow reach the conclusion that a provision admits of more than one permissible interpretation . . .'(p 201).

[28] In the latest negotiations, the United States has called upon Members to consider whether Art 17.6 of the *Anti-Dumping Agreement* should be addressed 'to ensure that panels and the Appellate Body properly apply it.' The United States considers that panels and the Appellate Body 'have not accepted reasonable, permissible interpretations' of the *Anti-Dumping Agreement*, and they 'have reached the unwarranted conclusion that applying the customary rules of interpretation of inter

Factual Determinations

For the assessment of facts, the Appellate Body has held that the standard of review is one of 'objective assessment'.[29] As we noted, this broad formulation does not go far towards defining a operable standard of review. Any assessment of the facts, whether it is highly deferential, marginally deferential, or not deferential at all, can be 'objective'. Article 11 of the DSU is, therefore, not the end of the road in the search for a standard of review for the facts.

In defining the appropriate standard, the Appellate Body has generally expressed what is *not* the WTO standard of review. Indeed, there are few statements setting out positively the nature of the standard of review that is applied to facts—beyond the generic reference to 'objective assessment'.

In *EC—Hormones*, the Appellate Body rejected two possible standards: there is no *de novo* review of the facts nor is there total deference. In this vein, panels and the Appellate Body have fleshed out what is not permitted under the WTO standard of review, in particular by adding meaning to the exclusion of '*de novo*' review.

In *US—Lamb*, the Appellate Body opined that 'the phrase '*de novo* review' should not be used loosely.'[30] For the Appellate Body, *de novo* review envisages the situation where the panel redoes an investigation into the facts that has already been done by a national authority, with the panel also assuming for itself the 'complete freedom' to substitute its own analysis and judgment for that of the national authority.[31] In other words, the panel would do a new investigation without affording any measure of deference to the first, national investigation.

The Appellate Body has said that, instead of performing a *de novo* review, a panel must 'put itself in the place of [the national authority] at the time it made its determination'.[32] It is implicit in this description of the panel's function that the panel should accord a considerable degree of discretion to national authorities in the determination and assessment of facts. The panel should not seek to

---

national law results in a single permissible interpretation of most provisions' of the *Anti-Dumping Agreement*. (Document TN/RL/W/130, 20 June 2003).

In the *USGAO Report* to the Senate Finance Committee, GAO states that 'no expert [GAO consulted] pointed to a clear instance in which a panel first applied the Vienna Convention, found several permissible interpretations, and then upheld the agency determination because it was consistent with-one of them' (28). The United States agencies 'most involved in trade remedy activities' told GAO that 'article 17.6(ii) has been improperly applied in some trade remedy cases, mainly because the WTO has not applied article 17.6(ii) in a way that allows for upholding permissible interpretations of WTO members' domestic agencies' (27). A 'majority' of the experts consulted by GAO 'believed that the WTO had not exceeded its authority in applying the standard of review in the trade remedy cases'. (27) GAO also recorded that 'almost all of the experts believed that the United States and other WTO Members have received the same treatment in trade remedy cases' (27).

[29] Appellate Body Report, *EC—Hormones*, para. 117.
[30] Appellate Body Report, *United States—Safeguard Measure on Imports of Fresh, Chilled or Frozen Lamb Meat from New Zealand and Australia* (*US—Lamb*), WT/DS177/AB/R, WT/DS178/AB/R, adopted 16 May 2001, para 107.
[31] Appellate Body Report, *EC—Hormones*, para 111.
[32] Appellate Body Report, *United States—Transitional Safeguard Measure on Combed Cotton Yarn from Pakistan* (*US—Cotton Yarn*), WT/DS192/AB/R, adopted 5 November 2001, para 78.

displace the national authority by doing its own factual investigation; nor should it reject factual findings by the national authority because it prefers other findings. It is also implicit in this description that the panel's work must respect the parameters of the national authority's own investigation. This constraint influences the temporal scope of the panel's factual review. To remain in the 'place' of the national authority, the panel is not entitled to examine new facts that were not, or could not, have been included in the national authority's investigation. We will return to these issues below.

The exclusion of such *de novo* review makes sense, at least under some of the WTO agreements. In practical terms, it would be almost impossible for the panel to conduct a wholly new inquiry as it does not have the resources or technical expertise to do so. In the WTO context, the panel is also likely to be operating in a different country, or even continent, and to be working in a different language from that of the national authority.[33] More importantly, in terms of the separation and balance of powers, it would usurp the treaty-mandated role of the national authority for panels to conduct a fresh inquiry, imposing their own assessment of the facts.

There is, of course, an assumption built into the exclusion of *de novo* review. That assumption is that the contested national measure results from a national investigation. If there is no national investigation, the panel cannot put itself into the 'place' of a national authority nor can it grant deference to an authority for its factual findings. In that event, the exclusion of *de novo* review has no meaning. The panel is confronted by a situation where the only possibility is for it to conduct an original or *de novo* review. This may equally be true, under some WTO agreements, where a rather limited national investigation has taken place. In that event, issues might arise before the panel that call for an original factual inquiry by the panel.

In WTO law, there are some agreements that mandate that a measure must result from a national investigation. However, there are other agreements that do not require, or otherwise envisage, that a national measure should result from an investigation. Although panels always conduct an 'objective assessment', the underlying nature and indentity of a panel's review cannot be the same in these quite different situations. The review for factual issues must, therefore, be analysed from the perspective of each WTO agreement, taking into account the structure and specific obligations of the agreement. We do not propose to examine the standard of review under each WTO agreement. Instead, we have selected three different situations that present different characteristics, and we offer thoughts on the standard of review in each situation. The three situations we will explore are: (a) the trade remedy agreements;[34]

---

[33] The WTO has, at 1 September 2003, 146 Member States and three official and working languages: English, French and Spanish.

[34] The trade remedy agreements are: the *Anti-Dumping Agreement*; the *Agreement on Safeguards*; and the *Agreement on Subsidies and Countervailing Measures* (**SCM Agreement**). Safeguard measures may also be taken under the *Agreement on Agriculture* and the *Agreement on Textiles and Clothing* (**ATC**).

(b) the *Agreement on Technical Barriers to Trade* ('*TBT Agreement*') and the *SPS Agreement*; and (c) Articles III and XX of the *General Agreement on Tariffs and Trade 1994* (the GATT 1994).

4. STANDARD OF REVIEW UNDER SPECIFIC WTO AGREEMENTS

Trade Remedy Agreements

Anti-Dumping Agreement

Under the *Anti-Dumping Agreement*, an anti-dumping measure may only be adopted by a Member following an investigation that is to be conducted at national level by a specially-designated investigating authority.[35] For anti-dumping measures, which are adopted pursuant to this national investigation, Article 17.6(i) of the *Anti-Dumping Agreement* provides a special standard of review for factual matters. Like the special standard of review in Article 17.6(ii) for interpretive matters, the standard in Article 17.6(i) does not appear in other WTO agreements.[36]

Article 17.6(i) explicitly confers broad discretion upon the national authority for its 'assessment' of the facts. The provision provides two separate standards, the first applying to the national authority's 'establishment' of the facts and the second to its 'evaluation' of the facts.

As regards the former, Article 17.6(i) states that a panel must respect the authority's 'establishment' of the facts if it is 'proper'. This standard seeks to prevent the panel rejecting factual findings made at national level just because the panel prefers an alternative finding. Indeed, under this provision, the focus of the panel's review should not be on the facts themselves, but rather on whether the process of establishing those facts was 'proper'. If that process was 'proper', the facts found as a result of the process should be accepted, 'even though the panel might have reached a different conclusion'. There is, therefore, no *de novo* review and panels cannot substitute their own analysis for that of the national authority. Only in cases where there is, perhaps, a manifest or egregious impropriety is a panel likely to interfere with a national authority's establishment of the facts under Article 17.6(i). In short, the word 'proper' carries with it a considerable margin of discretion.

Article 17.6(i) also requires that the evaluation of the facts be 'unbiased and objective'. Again, this provision is designed to prevent panels from making their own independent assessment of the facts. Instead, panels should consider whether the national authority conducted the factual evaluation in an appropriate way—

---

[35] On the extensive role of the national authorities in an anti-dumping determination, see, for instance, Art 3, 5, 6, and 9–12 of the *Anti-Dumping Agreement*. Under Art 17.4 of the *Anti-Dumping Agreement*, anti-dumping measures are anti-dumping duties or price undertakings.

[36] However, see above n 9 concerning the Ministerial Decision on Art 17.6 of the *Anti-Dumping Agreement*.

are the authority's factual conclusions based on an 'unbiased and objective' evaluation of the record? This equates to something akin to whether the authority was balanced, impartial and open-minded in its evaluation of the facts.

Article 17.6 of the *Anti-Dumping Agreement* seeks to draw a bright line between a panel's review of the national authority's assessment of the facts and its review of the authority's legal determination. In Articles 17.6(i) and 17.6(ii), the Agreement has two separate 'boxes', one with a standard of review for factual questions and the other with a standard for legal questions.

In practice, this division between legal and factual issues is not so clear cut. Many of the most difficult questions that confront a panel are mixed questions of fact and law. In particular, where a panel is characterising the facts in terms of the legal rules, the panel is engaged simultaneously in an assessment of the facts and also in an interpretation of the rules.

Take, for example, a panel's review of an injury determination under Article 3 of the *Anti-Dumping Agreement*. First, the panel must determine the factual basis for its review, namely the relevant economic data. Second, it must interpret the treaty provisions relating to injury. These two tasks are clearly factual review, in the first case, and legal interpretation, in the second. However, finally, the panel must review the national authority's determination that the particular set of facts constitutes a situation of injury. That is not just a question of evaluating all the economic data. Simply reviewing the data, in isolation, does not indicate whether the data amounts to injury. Nor is it simply a question of interpretation of the injury provisions in the abstract. Rather, the panel must make a judgment that combines, inseparably, an appreciation of the facts with an interpretation of legal norms. It is, perhaps, the interpretation of legal rules *in concreto* rather than *in abstracto*. As this characterisation process is very much a mixed question of fact and law, it is difficult to decide which of the two 'boxes' in Article 17.6 applies because, in a sense, both do.[37]

We mentioned earlier that, under Article 3.2 of the DSU, the core objectives of the dispute settlement system include providing security and predictability to the trading system, and also ensuring that the balance of Members' rights and obligations is preserved. If WTO Members had a broad discretion as regards the legal characterisation of a given set of facts, there would be a considerable risk that these goals would not be achieved because the uniform application of WTO law might well fragment. In very similar fact situations, one Member may determine that it has the right to apply an anti-dumping measure, while another may determine that it does not. For this to be avoided, panels would have to apply a more intensive review of these mixed characterisation questions that would ensure the predictability and balance that stems from uniformity.[38]

---

[37] The situation is all the more complex because the process of making a final determination does not just involve an injury determination. National authorities will typically make a large number of sub-determinations on the way to making a final determination.

[38] We will examine further below panel's review of 'substantive' obligations in the trade remedy agreements.

The two paragraphs of Article 17.6 define the degree of deference which panels should accord to national authorities. Another feature of the review process relates to the scope of the panel's factual inquiry. Article 17.5(ii) states that the panel's examination is to be 'based upon . . . the facts made available' to the national authority during its investigation. The panel in *Guatemala—Cement II* deduced from this that 'we are not to examine *any new evidence* that was not part of the record of the investigation' (emphasis added).[39]

Article 17.5(ii) imposes a temporal constraint on the scope of the panel's factual review that stems from the exclusion of *de novo* review. If the panel is to put itself in the 'place' of the national authority, it must respect the timeframe of that investigation. The reason is that, if the panel's review extends beyond that timeframe, it is the panel that becomes the investigator for the extended period—and this would amount to a form of *de novo* review.

The reading that the panel in *Guatemala—Cement II* gave to Article 17.5(ii) would prevent a panel reviewing 'any new evidence', even new evidence of, or relating to, data that the national authority could, and maybe should, have examined as part of its investigation.[40] The Appellate Body has not yet examined the meaning of Article 17.5(ii), but it has addressed a similar question in reviewing trade remedy measures under other WTO agreements. The Appellate Body drew a distinction between new evidence that is based on 'old' data and new evidence that is based on 'new' data. Thus, in *US—Cotton Yarn*, a safeguard case brought under the *ATC*, the Appellate Body held that the panel erred by considering United States' census data that was not yet published when the national authority reached its decision.[41] In other words, the panel could not review the decision of the national authority in light of 'new' data that did not exist at the time of the national authority's decision. For the *ATC*, that leaves open whether a panel may be entitled to review a measure in light of 'old'

---

[39] Panel Report, *Guatemala—Definitive Anti-Dumping Measures on Grey Portland Cement from Mexico* (*Guatemala—Cement II*), WT/DS156/R, adopted 17 November 2000, DSR 2000:XI, 5295, para 8.19.

[40] Art 17.5(ii) could be read to mean that panels should examine only facts that were 'made available' to the national authority by a third party. This reading would mean that national authorities have no independent investigative responsibilities. However, the panel in *European Communities—Anti-Dumping Duties on Malleable Cast Iron Tube or Pipe Fittings from Brazil* (*EC—Tube and Pipe Fittings*) held that, 'while the investigating authority must consider all information submitted to it by interested parties in an investigation, it may also supplement such information, where necessary, in order to ensure that its investigation is comprehensive.' (Panel report, WT/DS219/R, adopted as modified by the Appellate Body Report (WT/DS219/AB/R) on 18 August 2003, para 7.328) This suggests that, in some circumstances, national authorities do have an independent investigative responsibility and should include, in the investigation, information not 'made available' by the interested parties. This is consistent with the position under the *Agreement on Safeguards*. (See Appellate Body Report, *United States—Definitive Safeguard Measures on Imports of Wheat Gluten from the European Communities* (*US—Wheat Gluten*), WT/DS166/AB/R, adopted 19 January 2001, para 55; see also fn 56 below.)

[41] Appellate Body Report, *US—Cotton Yarn*, para 78. The holding in *US—Cotton Yarn* was made under the *ATC* which does not include a provision similar to Art 17.5(ii) of the *Anti-Dumping Agreement*. The holding was based on the principles underlying the exclusion of *de novo* review. We will consider this further below.

data that did exist when the investigation was conducted. We return to this question in examining review under the *Agreement on Safeguards* and the *SCM Agreement*.

If the wording of Article 17.5(ii) were to prevent a panel from examining certain new evidence relating to 'old' data, panels might nonetheless be entitled to examine whether the national authority failed in its investigative duties by not properly examining existing data.

The rationale for the discretion granted to national authorities through Articles 17.6(i) and 17.5(ii) lies in the structure of the *Anti-Dumping Agreement* itself. As we mentioned at the beginning of this section, an anti-dumping measure may only be adopted by a Member following an investigation conducted at national level by a specially designated investigating authority. The Agreement sets out, in great detail: when the national authority may open an investigation; when it must terminate an investigation; how the investigation is to be conducted by the authority, including publication and notification requirements, specific issues to be examined and opportunities for interested parties to be heard. The agreement also provides a series of procedural guarantees to protect the interests of parties likely to be affected by an anti-dumping measure. Further, although an anti-dumping measure can be maintained only if it is still necessary, the Agreement stipulates that the determination of on-going necessity is to be made by the national authority in a second investigation.[42]

The *Anti-Dumping Agreement* has, therefore, established very clearly that, in the first instance, the determination of the need and justification for anti-dumping measures is to be carried out at national level. It is for the national authority to gather and analyse the evidence, to make factual findings, and to determine whether the conditions permitting the application of an anti-dumping measure are, and continue to be, present. The Agreement, therefore, gives a pre-eminent position to the national investigation.

The nature of a panel's review, as directed by the provisions of Articles 17.5 and 17.6, take into account that the *Anti-Dumping Agreement* gives national authorities the responsibility for investigating the facts and making an initial determination. The role of the panel is, therefore, confined to reviewing the investigation and determination that has been carried out at national level. To respect the structure that the Agreement creates, the Agreement requires panels to show deference to the national investigative process.

Yet, even without Articles 17.5(ii) and 17.6(i), the structure of the Agreement would seem, to us, to dictate that national authorities should be accorded a considerable degree of deference in fact-finding. Any other standard of review would disregard the division of responsibility between national authorities and panels, and would undermine the treaty-mandated role of the national authority.[43]

---

[42] See Articles 11.1 and 11.2 of the *Anti-Dumping Agreement*.

[43] We note with interest that several commentators have suggested that Art 17.6(i) of the *Anti-Dumping Agreement* was not novel but simply codified the existing practice of GATT panels. In other words, according to these commentators, even in the absence of Art 17.6(i), panels accorded

Agreement on Safeguards and the SCM Agreement

The *Anti-Dumping Agreement* is not the only WTO agreement that envisages that national measures be based on a treaty-mandated investigation conducted at national level. The *Agreement on Safeguards* and the *SCM Agreement* also require a national authority to conduct a comprehensive investigation, with WTO-mandated procedural guarantees, before a WTO Member can adopt either a safeguard or countervailing measure.[44] Similarly, under these agreements, national authorities also have responsibility for determining, in a new investigation, whether there is on-going need for such measures.[45] The structure of these two agreements, therefore, replicates the structure of the *Anti-Dumping Agreement*. In all three agreements, a national investigating authority is given a pre-eminent position in the decision-making process.[46]

As with the *Anti-Dumping Agreement*, this structure influences the respective roles of the panel and national authorities. In disputes under these agreements, the panel must recognise that responsibility for the investigation and determination lies, in the first place, with the national authority. The role of the panel is to review, not redo, what has been done at national level.

Formally, the standard of review for all the WTO agreements, other than the *Anti-Dumping Agreement*, is the general 'objective assessment' standard under Article 11 of the DSU. The well-established rule excluding *de novo* review has been held to apply, under Article 11, to trade remedy disputes, other than anti-dumping disputes.[47]

---

a very similar level of deference to national authorities for fact-finding, in anti-dumping disputes, under the earlier Tokyo Round Anti-Dumping Code. See GN Horlick and PA Clarke 'Standards for Panels Reviewing Anti-dumping Determinations under the GATT and WTO' in *International Trade Law and the GATT/WTO Dispute Settlement System*, E-U Petersmann (ed) (Kluwer, 1997), 6, 11, and 13; and HJ Bourgeois 'GATT/WTO Dispute Settlement Practice in the Field of Anti-Dumping Law' in Petersmann *International Trade Law and the GATT/WTO Dispute Settlement System*, 52–53. See also n 58.

[44] See Art 2–4 of the *Agreement on Safeguards* and Articles 11–20 of the *SCM Agreement*.

[45] See Art 7 of the *Agreement on Safeguards* and Article 21 of the *SCM Agreement*.

[46] Art 6 of the *ATC* provides rules on safeguard measures concerning these products. The Agreement does not, however, specify either the organ or the procedure through which a Member makes a safeguard determination. The Appellate Body has ruled that the principles of standard of review under Art 11 of the DSU that are applicable to the *Agreement on Safeguards* apply equally to a review of a safeguard determination under the *ATC*. (Appellate Body Report, *US—Cotton Yarn*, para 76.)

[47] For the *Agreement on Safeguards* see Appellate Body Report, *US—Lamb*, paras 106–107. For the *ATC*, see Appellate Body Report, *US—Cotton Yarn*, para 74. For countervailing measures under Part V of the *SCM Agreement*, see Appellate Body Report, *US –Lead and Bismuth II*, para 51. Although the Appellate Body held that the standard of review in Article 11 of the DSU applies to disputes concerning countervailing measures, it did not refer explicitly to the exclusion of *de novo* review. Nonetheless, it cited approvingly *EC—Hormones*, where the exclusion of *de novo* was mentioned by the Appellate Body (para 46).

By definition, the exclusion of *de novo* review means that panels afford a considerable measure of discretion to Members for fact-finding. Thus, as in anti-dumping disputes, panels do not have the freedom to conduct a fresh inquiry nor to substitute their own judgment for that of a national authority. It is not open to panels to reach their preferred factual conclusion. This also reflects that, as with anti-dumping disputes, panels are not the appropriate bodies to conduct factual investigations as they do not have the necessary resources or expertise. As a result, panels are very likely to be disposed to accept the national authority's establishment of the facts, unless there is some clear flaw in those findings. Indeed, in all of the disputes to date, panels have accepted the national authority's establishment of the facts, without ever imposing alternative factual conclusions.

As with anti-dumping disputes, the most difficult issues for a panel relate to the characterisation of the facts in terms of legal rules—for instance, does a particular set of facts constitute 'serious injury' under the *Agreement on Safeguards*? As we said in looking at the *Anti-Dumping Agreement*, this characterisation process involves mixed questions of fact and law. We will explore in the next section how these questions have been approached. In general, though, panels have sought to leave national authorities a margin of discretion, whilst at the same time attempting to preserve the uniform application of WTO law. This balance is, however, delicate and not easy for panels and the Appellate Body to strike.

Another feature of panel's deferential approach to national investigations relates to the scope of the factual inquiry. We noted that Article 17.5(ii) of the *Anti-Dumping Agreement* requires panels to 'base' their examination on facts made available to the national authority. This has been read by one panel to exclude any new evidence from the panel process.[48] For the other trade remedy agreements, the position appears to be more nuanced. In *US—Cotton Yarn*, the Appellate Body held that panels could not examine data which did not exist at the time of the national investigation. This ruling constrains the factual scope of a panel's review and guarantees that panels respect the temporal limits of a national investigation.

However, although *de novo* review excludes consideration of new *data*, it has not been held to preclude a panel from hearing new *arguments* that were not put to the national authority.[49] Further, panels may well also be able to examine new *evidence* that was not before the national authority, provided the new evidence does not involve new data that the national authority could not have examined. For instance, a panel might be able to consider new expert testimony, not

---

[48] Panel Report, *Guatemala—Cement II*, para 8.19.
[49] See Appellate Body Report, *US–Lamb*, paras 113 and 114. See also Appellate Body Report, in *Thailand—Anti-Dumping Duties on Angles, Shapes and Sections of Iron or Non-Alloy Steel H-Beams from Poland* ('*Thailand—H-Beams*'), WT/DS122/AB/R, adopted 5 April 2001, para 94.

presented to the national authority, on the significance of 'old' data.[50] New testimony of this kind could and, perhaps, should have formed part of the national authority's investigation.[51] Without recourse to new arguments, and certain new evidence, the panel would be restricted largely to determining whether the national authority's decision is internally coherent—which could allow deficiencies in the original decision to escape review.

There are also important institutional reasons for allowing the panel to look beyond the arguments and, possibly also, the evidence submitted to the national authority. Most importantly, in domestic proceedings, the national authority applies the domestic rules implementing WTO rules, and not the WTO rules themselves. Moreover, the WTO Members participating in a WTO dispute as complainant or third parties may not have participated in the national investigation. Accordingly, WTO Members are 'not confined merely to rehearsing arguments that were made' to the national authorities.[52]

In sum, therefore, panels' approach to review of factual matters for safeguard and countervailing measures appears to be rather close to the deferential approach under Articles 17.5(ii) and 17.6(i) of the *Anti-Dumping Agreement*.[53] There is, however, still insufficient dispute settlement case-law to draw hard-and-fast conclusions.

Procedural v Substantive Review of Trade Remedy Measures

The fact that panels defer to national authorities in factual matters does not mean that panels do not provide meaningful scrutiny of national trade remedy

[50] In *US—Lamb*, New Zealand submitted new expert econometric analysis, to the panel, of market data that was before the United States national authority. The panel did not expressly address this analysis. In light of the factual record, the Appellate Body did not find 'it necessary to examine the significance of this [analysis]'. (para. 116) In *US—Cotton Yarn*, the Appellate Body expressly distinguished between new data (excluded, it said, from judicial review) and other forms of new evidence, such as 'new' econometric analysis, 'that is based on data which existed' when the decision was made. The Appellate Body did not rule upon whether such new analysis is admissible. (Appellate Body Report, *US—Cotton Yarn*, para. 78, fn 51). The Appellate Body has, therefore, left open the possibility that new evidence relating to 'old' data is admissible before panels.

[51] The Appellate Body has held that, under Art 3.1 of the *Agreement on Safeguards*, the national authority has, in some circumstances, an independent investigative duty that requires it to look beyond the facts made available by interested parties. (See Appellate Body Report, *US—Wheat Gluten*, para 55.)

[52] Appellate Body Report, *US—Lamb*, para 113.

[53] This conclusion, perhaps, bears out the suggestion of some commentators that the standard of review applied in anti-dumping disputes, prior to the adoption of Art 17.6(i) of the *Anti-Dumping Agreement*, was rather similar to the standard that now applies under that provision. It seems that panels apply a similarly deferential standard of review to factual matters in all trade remedy disputes and this standard has been codified in Art 17.6(i) for anti-dumping disputes. See n 48. Our conclusion that, in practice, there appears to be a similar standard of review for factual matters in all trade remedy disputes is also consonant with the Uruguay Round *Ministerial Declaration on Dispute Settlement Pursuant to the Agreement on Implementation of Article VI of the General Agreement on Tariffs and Trade 1994 or Part V of the Agreement on Subsidies and Countervailing Measures* that recognises 'the need for consistent resolution of disputes arising from anti-dumping and countervailing duty measures.'

measures—be it anti-dumping, safeguard or countervailing measures. In particular disputes, the precise character of a panel's review depends on the specific obligations that are at issue.[54] Under the trade remedy agreements, national authorities are generally subject to obligations of two different types. The first are procedural obligations regarding the conduct of national investigations, while the second are substantive obligations relating to the content of their determinations. In reviewing trade remedy measures, the Appellate Body has drawn a distinction between these procedural and substantive aspects of the decision-making process at national level.[55]

The review of whether procedural obligations have been respected implies no judgment on the substance of the decision. It is a 'check-list' approach to review that avoids consideration of the often more controversial substantive aspects of a decision. Nevertheless, a rigorous procedural review is important as there is potentially a significant link between the formal process and the final determination because a procedural failure can have repercussions for that determination.

There have, though, been relatively few cases where national authorities have failed to follow the required procedures. One example is *Argentina—Footwear (EC)*, where it was held that Argentina had not examined one of the economic factors listed in the *Agreement on Safeguards*.[56] This did not imply that there was, or could be, no substantive justification to impose a safeguard measure. Rather, the ruling meant that the WTO Member in question had not satisfied the procedural requirements that entitled it to impose such a measure.

The review of the legality of trade remedy measures is not, however, confined to such formal analysis. The trade remedy agreements impose a number of substantive conditions that determine whether, and when, a measure can be imposed. Even if the national authority has fully respected the procedural obligations in an agreement, it might (wrongly) determine that a measure can be applied even though the required legal conditions have not been fulfilled.

A 'check-list' approach to review, which looked only at the procedural issues, would not test compliance with the substantive conditions required by the WTO agreements. Such an approach would obviously not be satisfactory in a rule-based system that seeks to provide 'security and predictability'. Thus, in *EC—Tube and Pipe Fittings*, the panel rejected a 'check-list' approach to review, holding that the provision of the *Anti-Dumping Agreement* at issue 'require[d] substantive, rather than purely formal, compliance.'[57] A good statement of the nature of the substantive review was given in *US—Lamb*:

---

[54] Appellate Body Report, *US—Lamb*, para. 105.
[55] Appellate Body Report, *US—Lamb*, para. 103.
[56] Appellate Body Report, *Argentina—Footwear (EC)*, para 137. Argentina failed to examine capacity utilisation and productivity (see para 134). In *EC—Tube and Pipe Fittings*, the Appellate Body held that, in some circumstances, it is permissible to discern from the record of an anti-dumping investigation that a particular factor has been evaluated, even if there is no separate record of that evaluation (para 161).
[57] Panel Report, *EC—Tube and Pipe Fittings*, para. 7.310.

The substantive aspect [of the review] is whether the competent authorities have given a *reasoned* and *adequate explanation* for their determination. . . . [A] panel can assess whether the competent authorities' explanation for its determination is reasoned and adequate only if the panel critically examines that explanation. . . . Panels must, therefore, review whether the competent authorities' explanation fully addresses the nature, and, especially, the complexities of the data, and responds to other plausible interpretations of that data (emphasis added).[58]

This aspect of review is rooted in the trade remedy agreements themselves. Under each of the agreements, national authorities are required to publish a detailed explanation for their findings and conclusion on all legal and factual matters.[59] These reports must, therefore, address the substantive conditions for imposition of a trade remedy measure, with the precise explanation required depending upon the specific substantive obligations at issue. As the Appellate Body said in US—Lamb, the character of panel's review 'is mandated by the specific obligations' imposed.[60]

By scrutinising the explanation given by the national authority for its findings, the panel can review whether the national authority's determination complies with the substantive obligations of the agreement. In practice, this aspect of review has usually been applied to mixed questions of fact and law, in particular the national authority's characterisation of the facts in legal terms.

A good example is US—Lamb, where the Appellate Body held that the national authority's explanation of the facts was insufficient to support a finding of threat of injury.[61] The Appellate Body accepted the factual record of the investigation, but ruled that the national authority had not properly explained how these facts could fall within the meaning of the term 'threat of serious injury'. Although the Appellate Body ruled that the explanation did not support the determination, it did not rule that the facts did not, or could not, amount to a threat of injury. Its conclusion was 'simply that the [national authority] has *not* adequately explained how the facts relating to prices support its determination'.[62]

The standard of an 'adequate and reasoned' explanation for the substantive findings falls far short of requiring panels to decide whether the national authority's determination is 'right' or 'wrong'. Instead, the notion of an adequate explanation carries with it a margin of discretion for the national authority. Thus, even if a panel would have preferred a different determination, it should treat the substantive explanation as adequate if the authority provides a coherent and logical set of reasons that address the key features in the data. In US—Lamb, the explanation was not adequate because it did not deal, among other

---

[58] Appellate Body Report, US—Lamb, paras 100 and 106.
[59] Art 12.2 of the *Anti-Dumping Agreement*; Art 22.3 of the *SCM Agreement*; and Art 3.1 of the *Agreement on Safeguards*.
[60] Appellate Body Report, US—Lamb, para 104.
[61] Appellate Body Report, US—Lamb, paras 140, 141, and 153–161.
[62] Appellate Body Report, US—Lamb, para 160.

things, with an apparent contradiction in the data on prices that suggested that the domestic industry could have been in the process of recovery, rather than on the verge of serious injury.

There are not yet enough cases to know exactly what degree of discretion will be afforded to national authorities in their characterisation of the facts in terms of the legal norms. However, where such mixed findings of fact and law are reviewed, as opposed to purely factual findings, the degree of discretion afforded to national authorities should be influenced by the need to preserve the 'security and predictability' of the system through the uniform application of WTO law.

TBT and SPS Agreements

TBT Agreement

The cornerstone of the standard of review for fact-finding that has been developed under the trade remedy agreements is the exclusion of *de novo* review. We have argued that this exclusion, and the deference it confers upon national authorities, stems from the treaty-mandated national investigation. The very idea of excluding *de novo* review is that there has already been a first investigation to which panels should defer, rather than repeat or redo. Although trade remedy measures are following a national investigation, the same is not true for national measures covered by all other WTO agreements. In other words, under many WTO agreements, Members adopt measures that do not result from a formal national investigation. In these cases, the notion of *de novo* review does not arise in the same way as there is no treaty-mandated, first investigation that panels can reprise.

The *TBT Agreement* contains largely substantive obligations regulating technical regulations and standards that constitute barriers to trade. The Agreement creates few procedural rules on the process a Member should follow in developing such regulations.[63] The *TBT Agreement* certainly does not require a national authority to carry out a formal investigation, with fact-finding. Nor does the justification for a TBT measure need to be explained in a detailed report.[64] In addition, although TBT measures can only be applied so long as justified, the *TBT Agreement* does not require that the determination of this on-going justification be made, in the first place, by a national authority in a

---

[63] See Art 2.1–2.8 of the *TBT Agreement*. Under Art 2.9–2.12, Members are, *inter alia*, obliged to notify proposed technical regulations to other Members and take account of comments they may have. Members must also publish proposed technical regulations to enable interested parties to become acquainted with them.

[64] Under Art 2.9.2 of the *TBT Agreement*, a Member must provide a 'brief indication of the objective and rationale' for a proposed technical regulation. This falls far short of the 'detailed', 'adequate', 'reasoned' explanation that is expected of national authorities in trade remedy investigations.

national investigation. The structure of the *TBT Agreement* is, therefore, very different from the trade remedy agreements.

In our view, this difference influences the nature of the review that a panel should conduct under Article 11 of the DSU. The *TBT Agreement* does not establish a marked division of responsibility between a national authority and the panel. A panel can review the consistency of a TBT measure without having to defer to, or wait for, any formal national investigation—because none is foreseen in the Agreement. In such a situation, the exclusion of *de novo* review has no meaning because the panel is, under the WTO agreements, the first body formally to engage in fact-finding.

Although the *TBT Agreement* does not prescribe a formal process for the adoption of TBT measures, a Member may elect to adopt TBT measures on the basis of a formal process. It is not clear what degree of deference panels and the Appellate Body would accord to formal fact-finding in such an elective process. If the national process incorporated the range of procedural guarantees provided in trade remedy investigations, national authorities might be accorded deference as they are in the trade remedy context. This would be consistent with a strict application of the rule against *de novo* review. However, the rationale for the deference accorded in the trade remedy setting lies in the balance the WTO Members have struck, in the agreements, between the respective 'jurisidictional competences' of the Members and of the WTO.[65] The trade remedy agreements prescribe that national authorities are to make the initial determination, and subsequent re-determinations, and the agreements prescribe, in detail, how that is to be done. Panels are constrained to respect that process by according deference both as regards the scope of the factual inquiry and the nature and intensity of review. Under the *TBT Agreement*, no formal national process is prescribed and panels are not, therefore, subjected to the same constraints by the structure of the agreements. Moreover, as the WTO agreements do not prescribe a formal process for national authorities to apply, it may be doubted whether panels should apply a lower level of scrutiny to a Member because it chooses to apply a formal process.

As regards the scope of a panel's review of a TBT measure, we see no reason in the *TBT Agreement* to exclude any data or other evidence from the enquiry. The justification for the exclusion of new data in trade remedy cases seems to be that panels are obliged to respect the temporal limitations of the national investigation and cannot examine, for the first time, new data that the national authority has not yet examined. Under the *TBT Agreement*, there is no formal investigation which must precede the panel's examination of the WTO-consistency of a TBT measure. Article 2.3 of the *TBT Agreement* precludes Members from 'maintain[ing]' TBT measures if 'changed circumstances' mean the measure is no longer justified in its present form. Unlike the trade remedy agreements, the *TBT Agreement* imposes this on-going obligation

---

[65] See Appellate Body Report, *EC–Hormones*, para. 115.

without prescribing that a national authority should assess the 'changed circumstances' before the panel does.⁶⁶ Instead, there do not appear to be any qualifications, in the Agreement, on the factual scope of a panel's assessment of the WTO-consistency of TBT measures. Accordingly, we believe that a panel's examination may include any evidence of 'changed circumstances'.

SPS Agreement

The *SPS Agreement* allows WTO Members to adopt measures to protect human, animal or plant life or health. In many respects, the *SPS* and *TBT Agreements* have a similar structure, although the *SPS Agreement* has an additional wrinkle that the *TBT Agreement* does not have. Article 5.1 of the *SPS Agreement* requires that an SPS measure must be 'based on an assessment . . . of the risks to human, animal or plant life or health'.

The significance of this requirement was examined in *EC—Hormones*, where the panel found that:

> . . . there is a *minimum procedural requirement* contained in Article 5.1. In our view, the Member imposing a sanitary measure needs to submit evidence that at least it actually *took into account* a risk assessment when it enacted or maintained its sanitary measure in order for that measure to be considered as *based on* a risk assessment (emphasis added).⁶⁷

The existence of minimum procedural requirements might be taken to suggest that a Member has to conduct a formal national process before adopting an SPS measure. However, the Appellate Body reversed the panel's finding and rejected the existence of 'minimum procedural requirements' for a risk assessment.⁶⁸ In reaching this finding, the Appellate Body emphasised the 'substantive requirements' that regulate the adoption of SPS measures, essentially that an SPS measure must be justified by science.⁶⁹ The Appellate Body also drew on Article 2.2 of the *SPS Agreement*, which requires that there be 'sufficient' scientific evidence to justify an SPS measure. The Appellate Body also held that, absent national procedural requirements, a Member may rely on a risk assessment conducted by another Member or by an international organisation.⁷⁰

---

⁶⁶ In examining whether Article 2.4 of the *TBT Agreement* applies to measures that existed before the *TBT Agreement* was adopted, the Appellate Body observed that 'the use of the present tense [in Article 2.4] suggests a continuing obligation for existing measures . . .'. (*European Communities—Trade Description of Sardines* ('*EC–Sardines*') WT/DS231/AB/R, adopted 23 October 2002, para. 205) In our view, the grammatical structure of Article 2.3 ('Technical regulations shall not be maintained . . .') is equally indicative of an on-going or continuing obligation.
⁶⁷ Panel Report, *EC–Hormones (US)*, WT/DS26/R/USA, adopted 13 February 1998, as modified by the Appellate Body Report, WT/DS26/AB/R, WT/DS48/AB/R, DSR 1998:III, 699, para 8.113.
⁶⁸ Appellate Body Report, *EC–Hormones*, para 189.
⁶⁹ Appellate Body Report, *EC–Hormones*, para 193.
⁷⁰ Appellate Body Report, *EC–Hormones*, para 190. In *Australia–Measures Affecting Importation of Salmon* ('*Australia–Salmon*'), WT/DS18/AB/R, adopted 6 November 1998, DSR 1998:VIII, 3327, para. 121, the Appellate Body set out the substantive requirements for a risk assessment.

Thus, although the Agreement identifies the substantive issues to be addressed in the assessment, it does not lay down any procedures for how the risk assessment is to be conducted. There is no requirement to conduct an investigation, to engage in formal fact-finding, or to publish a report explaining how the SPS measure is justified. The structure of the *SPS Agreement*, therefore, differs markedly from the trade remedy agreements and is much closer to the *TBT Agreement*.

The standard of review that applies under the *SPS Agreement* reflects this. The standard is an 'objective assessment' under Article 11 of the DSU; in practice, though, the 'objective assessment' applied under the *SPS Agreement* does not appear to be the same as the assessment applied under the trade remedy agreements.

Like the *TBT Agreement*, the panel will often be the first body to engage in formal fact-finding, for instance concerning scientific justification. The panel will not be able to defer to a national authority's fact-finding because, absent 'procedural requirements', there may be none. Again similar to the *TBT Agreement*, this might be different only where a Member elected to conduct a formal process, with adequate procedural guarantees, for determining the need for an SPS measure. However, as we said earlier, it is open to question whether the scope, nature and intensity of a panel's review should change simply because a Member opts to apply a formal process that is not required by the WTO agreements.

Also consistently with the *TBT Agreement*, we believe that the *SPS Agreement* does not prevent a panel from examining any data or other new evidence in reviewing SPS measures. Under Article 2.2, Members must have sufficient scientific evidence to 'maintain' an SPS measure. Similarly, under Article 5.6, in 'maintaining' an SPS measure, a Member must ensure that the measure is no more trade-restrictive than necessary. Both these obligations are on-going and require Members with SPS measures to keep abreast of the latest scientific developments. Consistent with the absence of 'minimum procedural requirements', the *SPS Agreement* does not qualify the obligations in Article 2.2 and 5.6 by indicating that the determination of on-going justification must first be made at national level in a new risk assessment.[71] It seems, therefore, that panels can review, at any time, whether an SPS measure is justified by the latest scientific information. Thus, in the recent panel report in *Japan—Apples*, the panel examined a claim under Article 2.2 of the *SPS Agreement* in light of very recent scientific evidence that had not yet been taken into account in a national risk assessment.[72]

---

[71] This may be contrasted with Art 5.7 of the *SPS Agreement* which indicates that, for provisional SPS measures, adopted without sufficient scientific evidence, a Member should 'review the [SPS] measure . . . within a reasonable period of time', in light of the latest information. In the case of provisional measures, the Agreement apparently envisages a periodic national review and allows a reasonable period for that review.

[72] Panel Report, *Japan–Measures Affecting the Importation of Apples* (*Japan–Apples*), WT/DS245/R, 15 July 2003, para 8.124. The contested SPS measure dates from 1994 and Japan carried out risk assessments in 1996 and 1999. The panel considered evidence from a 2003 scientific study.

Although the panel may not be able to defer to national *fact-finding*, panels do accord deference in reviewing *policy choices* made by Members in the adoption of SPS measures. First, Members have absolute freedom to determine their own individual 'level of protection' (ie, the level of health risk they are willing to take).[73] Second, although Article 2.2 requires that an SPS measure be justified by 'sufficient scientific evidence', Members are entitled to rely on a divergent or minority scientific opinion.[74] Sufficiency, therefore, need not refer to the quantity of the evidence but may refer equally to its quality. Third, in *EC—Hormones*, the Appellate Body appears to endorse an approach of examining whether the scientific evidence is '*reasonably* sufficient' to justify the SPS measure (emphasis added).[75] There is, therefore, considerable scope for Members to adopt SPS measures tailored to their own needs, provided that they can point to some sound scientific evidence to support the measures.[76, 77]

In sum, therefore, the obligations and structure of the *TBT Agreement* and the *SPS Agreement* indicate that panels are less constrained in their fact-finding than they are under the trade remedy agreements.[78] Neither of these agreements provides for a formal national procedure prior to the adoption of a measure. The exclusion of *de novo* review is unlikely, therefore, to arise because there has been no formal fact finding at national level. Moreover, in light of the specific obligations in these agreements, the review of a TBT or SPS measure appears to be open-ended and contemporaneous, with panels entitled to examine whatever scientific and technological evidence is relevant. This may be contrasted with the trade remedy agreements, where the review is limited and historical, as it respects the parameters of the national investigative process. The nature and intensity of review under the *TBT* and *SPS Agreements* seems, therefore, to be different from review under the trade remedy agreements.

The GATT 1994

Articles III and XX of the GATT 1994 provide yet another perspective on the standard of review. Broadly, Article III of the GATT 1994 imposes a non-

---

[73] Appellate Body Report, *Australia—Measures Affecting Importation of Salmon* (*Australia–Salmon*), WT/DS18/AB/R, adopted 6 November 1998, DSR 1998:VIII, 3327, para. 199. The sole constraint on this freedom is found in Art 5.5 of the *SPS Agreement*, which provides that a Member 'shall avoid arbitrary or unjustifiable distinctions in the levels [of protection] it considers to be appropriate in different situations, if such distinctions result in discrimination or a disguised restriction on international trade.'

[74] Appellate Body Report, *EC–Hormones*, para 194.

[75] Appellate Body Report, *EC–Hormones*, para 198.

[76] Article 5.7 of the *SPS Agreement* provides a temporary exception to the need for SPS measures to be justified by scientific evidence. See footnote 71 above.

[77] Although these issues have not been addressed in dispute settlement cases under the *TBT Agreement*, it would seem likely that the *TBT Agreement* will be found to give similar discretion to Members in pursuing 'legitimate objectives' under that agreement.

[78] For legal determinations, we have already noted that panels engage in an interpretation of the relevant WTO rules, using the *Vienna Convention*, on a *de novo* basis.

discrimination rule that requires imported goods to be treated no less favourably than domestic goods. Article XX creates a series of 'general exceptions' from general WTO rules, such as Article III, for interests such as public policy and health.

Members have complete freedom in the way in which they adopt rules covered by these provisions of the GATT 1994, as no national procedures whatsoever are prescribed. In other words, Articles III and XX govern solely the substantive aspects of relevant national rules. This feature of the WTO obligations influences, again, the nature of a panel's review.

Certainly, the general requirement for an 'objective assessment' applies; but, in a context where there is unlikely to have been much, if any, national fact-finding, the standard of review cannot be the same as in the trade remedy context.[79] By definition, absent a national fact-finding process, the panel is engaged in an original or *de novo* review of the facts. As such, the usual rule that panel's cannot conduct a *de novo* review does not apply. Moreover, there is no basis to exclude any evidence from the panel's review.

A good example is *Chile—Alcoholic Beverages*, where the panel had to determine whether a Chilean beverage, pisco, was 'like' certain other beverages, such as whisky, gin and tequila.[80] In addressing this issue, the panel made a series of factual findings on the competitive relationship between the different beverages. The panel's inquiry was entirely *de novo* as there was no prior national investigation of this question. Furthermore, there were no limitations on the data, or other evidence, which the panel could examine. The panel's inquiry was, therefore, *de novo*, open-ended and contemporaneous. In essence, the panel examined, in absolute terms, whether Chile's tax afforded protection to pisco, under Article III:2 of the GATT 1994.

The position is similar under Article XX of the GATT 1994. As mentioned, this provision allows Members to adopt measures that derogate from WTO rules, provided certain conditions are respected. In reviewing whether a measure complies with these conditions, a panel must inquire into facts that are unlikely to have been formally examined before. Again, in this situation, the panel conducts a *de novo* review of those facts because no one else has examined them before. Moreover, there is no reason for the panel to exclude any evidence from its review that it considers relevant.

In *EC—Asbestos*, the panel reviewed whether a ban on the use of chrysotile asbestos was justified by the need to protect health, under Article XX(b).[81] The

---

[79] As with TBT and SPS measures, it is possible that a Member elects to adopt a measure after engaging in a formal process that includes fact-finding. In this situation, it may also be questioned whether panels and the Appellate Body should accord considerable deference to a national process that is neither required nor regulated by the WTO agreements.

[80] Panel Report, *Chile–Taxes on Alcoholic Beverages* (***Chile–Alcoholic Beverages***), WT/DS87/R, WT/DS110/R, adopted 12 January 2000, as modified by the Appellate Body Report, WT/DS87/AB/R, WT/DS110/AB/R, DSR 2000:I, 303.

[81] Panel Report, *European Communities–Measures Affecting Asbestos and Asbestos-Containing Products* (***EC–Asbestos***), WT/DS135/R and Add 1, adopted 5 April 2001, as modified by the Appellate Body Report, WT/DS135/AB/R.

panel examined the evidence submitted on this point in order to determine whether the ban was justified under Article XX. The panel did not need to defer to any national authority's factual findings because it was the panel that conducted the first and, therefore, *de novo* review of the issues.

Similar to the *SPS Agreement*, although there is very limited scope for deference to national *fact-finding*, panels do show deference in assessing *policy choices* made by Members under Article XX. Each Member decides for itself whether, and to what extent, it will protect the interests identified in Article XX. For instance, in examining Article XX(b), the Appellate Body has stated that 'WTO Members have the right to determine the level of protection of health that they consider appropriate in a given situation.'[82] Further, in making policy choices under Article XX, a Member need not rely on the 'majority scientific opinion' but may rely on a divergent opinion.[83] Accordingly, the panels leave Members considerable margin for making policy choices in pursuing the interests covered by Article XX.

5. CONCLUSION

Although panels are always obliged to conduct an 'objective assessment of the matter' under Article 11 of the DSU, there is no generally applicable approach to review for all WTO disputes. The phrase 'objective assessment' does not indicate precisely the nature and intensity of review that a panel should apply. It does not indicate the degree of deference, if any, to be accorded to any formal fact-finding at national level nor does it shed light on the scope of a panel's factual inquiry. Instead, it dictates that, whatever the specific nature and intensity of review, the panel should approach its task in an 'objective' fashion.

To identify precisely the nature and intensity of review to be applied in a particular WTO dispute, it is, therefore, necessary to look beyond the phrase 'objective assessment'. If the panel is reviewing a purely legal issue, the panel conducts an original or *de novo* interpretation of the WTO agreement, using the rules of interpretation of the *Vienna Convention*. This task must, of course, be conducted 'objectively'. If Article 17.6(ii) of the *Anti-Dumping Agreement* applies, the panel must also determine whether an anti-dumping measure is based on a 'permissible' interpretation of the *Anti-Dumping Agreement*.

Where the panel is addressing the establishment or evaluation of facts, the decisive factor in identifying the nature of the review is the particular WTO agreement, and specific provisions of that agreement, that are at issue. We have seen that, under the trade remedy agreements, panels review measures which result from a national investigation that is prescribed by the WTO agreements. The panel's 'second tier' review of the national measure is constrained by the earlier 'first tier' national investigation, which has a privileged place in the process. The limitations on the panel relate both to the degree of deference

---

[82] Appellate Body Report, *EC–Asbestos*, para 168.
[83] Appellate Body Report, *EC–Asbestos*, para 178.

accorded to the national authority's establishment and evaluation of the facts, and also to the scope of the panel's factual inquiry. As we have said, the panel's review of trade remedy measures is historical and constrained.

At the other end of the spectrum are disputes where a panel is reviewing measures that did not result from any formal investigative process at national level. The panel is the 'first-tier' of review and it is not, therefore, constrained in the same way. The panel's examination is original, open-ended and contemporaneous. There is no formal fact-finding at national level to which the panel can defer. We have suggested that disputes under Articles III and XX of the GATT 1994 fall into this category.

There are also WTO agreements that do not fit neatly into one or other of these two 'boxes'. We view the *TBT Agreement* and *SPS Agreement* in this light. Under these agreements, there is no treaty-mandated investigation of the type required by the trade remedy agreements. Nonetheless, these two agreements both call for some scientific or technological evaluation at national level prior to the adoption of a measure. As the prescribed national process is extremely limited, with very few formal procedural requirements, the agreements place fewer constraints on a panel's review. The panel is not, in short, required to defer to any formal national investigation. Unlike in trade remedy cases, panels can assess the on-going justification for TBT and SPS measures on the basis of the latest information, without any need to await a new national process. The review is, therefore, more akin to review under the GATT 1994 in that it is both open-ended and contemporaneous, and often original.

It is also significant that where the WTO agreements allow Members to pursue other policy goals, such as health and the environment, that result in trade restrictions, the agreements give Members a margin of discretion in making policy choices that panels and the Appellate Body respect. The role of panels and the Appellate Body is to ensure that, in exercising this discretion, Members respect the legal conditions in the WTO agreements that govern when and how trade restrictions may be adopted. The WTO standard of review, therefore, seeks to strike a balance between the 'political' choices left to Members and the legal requirements that set the parameters for Members' action.

Perhaps the most striking feature of the WTO rules on standard of review is that, beneath the overarching requirement for an 'objective assessment', there are several underlying approaches to review that apply in different contexts. This suggests that panels and the Appellate Body have attempted to give practical effect to the divergent approaches in the various WTO agreements to the role and prerogatives of Members *vis-à-vis* the WTO.[84]

It is clear, though, that there is a tension between granting discretion to Members and ensuring the 'security and predictability' of the trading system

---

[84] It is worth recalling a statement from the Appellate Body that we mentioned earlier (Appellate Body Report, *EC–Hormones*, para. 115): 'The standard of review ... must reflect the balance established in [the *SPS Agreement*] between the jurisdictional compctences conceded by the Members to the WTO and the jurisdictional competences retained by the Members for themselves.'

through the uniform application of WTO law. It is a tension between the interests of one Member in pursuing its own sovereignty and the collective interests of all WTO Members—including the one—in preserving the multilateral rule-based system. For the long-term success of the system, both these interests are important. As the WTO dispute settlement system is still relatively new, and as the WTO agreements are being re-negotiated, it is likely that the rules on standard of review will evolve over time. It is also to be hoped that, over time, panels and the Appellate Body will continue to find the 'right' balance between affording discretion to WTO Members and preserving the uniformity of WTO law.

In so doing, panels and the Appellate Body—like the ECJ—are unlikely to escape criticism. But, as David has said on many occasions, that does not mean that the decisions are not based on sound legal principles.

VI. EU Remedies Issues

21

Approaches to Interpretation in a Plurilingual Legal System

FRANCIS G JACOBS*

IN AN ESSAY celebrating David Edward's service as a judge of the Court of Justice,[1] it may be appropriate to recall at the outset the contribution of Scottish judges to international courts, to European courts and to supreme courts. For specific examples, reference need only be made to McNair at the International Court of Justice, to Jack Mackenzie Stuart at the European Court of Justice and to Lord Reid in the House of Lords. More generally, the law reports abound with eloquent and distinguished judgments by Scottish judges.

The contribution of David Edward to the case-law of the ECJ, however weighty, cannot be quantified. In contrast to English (and Scottish) courts, and even to international courts such as the International Court of Justice and the European Court of Human Rights, the European Court of Justice delivers a single collective judgment in every case. No minority opinions, separate opinions or dissenting opinions are allowed. Indeed every judge, before taking up his duties, takes an oath to preserve the secrecy of the deliberations of the Court. It may be mentioned in passing that the same oath is taken by Advocates General, although they are spared from taking part, except in rare instances, in the deliberations of the Court.

The institution of the single collective judgment, although unusual from a common law perspective, is in my view appropriate to the character and functions of the Court of Justice. If individual opinions were permitted, then judges when deliberating would no longer be compelled to fuse the national perspectives from which they come, and the process of jurisprudential integration would be likely to suffer. Although it cannot be demonstrated, the probability must be that the success with which the ECJ has performed its role is to a large extent due to the institution of the single judgment.

This does not entail that judges on the ECJ are anonymous ciphers—which would be a particularly inappropriate description of David Edward. His interrogations from the Bench may have sometimes seemed no less fearsome than the

---

* My thanks to Alan Baillie for his help with the preparation of this essay.
[1] And, from 1989–1992, of the Court of First Instance.

legendary interventions of Lord Reid in the House of Lords. At the other extreme, his hospitality, and that of Elizabeth, in the rural retreat of Flaxweiler has charmed a huge circle of visiting judges, lawyers and many others. One may conjecture that his contributions to the deliberations of the ECJ have been occasionally fiery, but generally persuasive.

While carrying the Scottish flag in the Court, David has always been the United Kingdom judge, and has not sought to maintain the romantic notion of a special relationship between Scots law and the 'civil law' systems. Generalisations of that kind are quickly refuted at the Court, and perhaps one of the best examples of that is the topic of this essay, the approach to interpretation.

Moreover, the approach of the Court of Justice also illustrates exceptionally well, in my view, the advantages of the single judgment. This Court's approach has been, over the years, remarkably consistent, as well as being particularly appropriate, as I shall suggest, to the Community legal system.

Since space precludes a discussion of all aspects of that approach, I will focus on one aspect only: the plurilingual aspect. Other aspects are perhaps less distinctive. It is well known that the Court often relies on the 'teleological' approach, seeking to give effect to the object and purpose of the measure. It relies often also on the context of the provision, seeking to ensure that the interpretation makes sense in the scheme of the piece of legislation as a whole, and where necessary in the scheme of European law more generally. Occasionally it relies on preparatory materials.

In all these respects the Court's approach does not seem greatly out of line with the general rule laid down in the Vienna Convention on the Law of Treaties. Article 31(1) of the Convention states:

> A treaty shall be interpreted in good faith in accordance with the ordinary meaning to be given to the terms of the treaty in their context and in the light of its object and purpose.

And *travaux préparatoires*, under Article 32, may be used in order to confirm the meaning resulting from the application of Article 31 or to remove ambiguity or absurdity.

There are, it is true, differences of degree which may prove important. The Court is more willing to depart from the text of a provision, in order to give effect to its aim and purpose, or to reconcile it with the scheme and context of the provision, than an English court would be.[2] But such differences of degree might be partly explained by differences in the ways in which legislation is drafted: Community legislation, it might be conjectured, may more often contain conscious inconsistencies, which are, consciously or not, left to the Court to resolve.

---

[2] For a striking recent example, see Case C–292/00 *Davidoff* v. *Gofkid*, judgment of 9 January 2003, not yet reported.

The plurilingual aspect of the Community legal system, by contrast, raises some novel issues. How are legal texts authentic in many languages to be applied by unilingual national courts, or even by the plurilingual Court of Justice? The questions become even more acute with the number of languages set to rise from the current eleven to no fewer than twenty with effect from 1 May 2004.

Before turning to Community Treaties and Community legislation, we should look at other treaties which provide examples of plurilingual texts. The rules laid down by Article 33 of the Vienna Convention on the Law of Treaties for the interpretation of treaties authenticated in two or more languages include a general rule in Article 33(4) that, when a comparison of the authentic texts discloses a difference of meaning:

> [T]he meaning which best reconciles the texts, having regard to the object and purpose of the treaty, shall be adopted.

That rule has been invoked by the European Court of Human Rights in interpreting the European Convention on Human Rights, of which the English and French texts are equally authentic. Thus the Court referred to the rule in the *James* case,[3] where the applicants challenged provisions of the United Kingdom leasehold enfranchisement legislation as contrary to their property rights under Article 1 of the First Protocol. The Court had to consider whether the deprivation of property suffered by the freeholders who were compelled under the legislation to sell their freehold at artificially low prices to often wealthy tenants could be said to be 'in the public interest'/*'pour cause d'utilité publique'*. The French text, in particular, might seem not to cover such a compulsory sale to a private beneficiary. Seeking to reconcile the two concepts, the Court adopted a broad view of the public interest and of the State's margin of appreciation in assessing what is justified in the public interest. It has indeed been suggested that, in the Court's case-law on property rights, there is almost a presumption that a national measure is in the public interest.

A different approach has been followed in the GATT and in the WTO Agreement, whose provisions bear some comparison with the central provisions of the Community Treaties. Under the WTO dispute settlement procedures, in particular, which now provide for compulsory semi-judicial settlement of trade disputes by the panels and the Appellate Body, there seems in practice a tendency to apply the English-language texts although the English, French and Spanish versions of the WTO Agreement are each authentic. In some cases however the three versions have been compared and the above rule in Article 33(4) of the Vienna Convention applied.[4]

Two competing approaches to legislative drafting and interpretation—for the approach to drafting and the approach to interpretation must always go hand

---

[3] *James and others* v. *UK*, judgment of 21 February 1986, Series A No 98 (1986) 8 EHRR 123.
[4] See for example Report of panel on Argentina—safeguard measures on imports of footwear, WT/DS121/R, 1999, para 8.166.

in hand—have been identified as 'fuzzy' and 'fussy', the former being thought of as rooted in the civilian tradition, the latter in the common law, although that distinction must be regarded as a very approximate generalisation.

In the 'fuzzy' approach, legislation tends to be drafted in simpler, broader and more general language, which the courts then have appreciable freedom to interpret and apply in each case, often relying in that task on the overall purpose of the legislation as it may be inferred from various statements of intent and from its place in the overall scheme of the law.

The 'fussy' approach, by contrast, involves an attempt by the legislature to 'attain if possible a degree of precision which a person reading in bad faith cannot misunderstand. It is all the better if he cannot pretend to misunderstand it.'[5] This is accompanied by a reluctance on the part of the courts to look beyond the words used when interpreting the legislation, an attitude encapsulated by Lord Mildew in *Scott v The Thames Conservancy*: 'If Parliament does not mean what it says it must say so'.[6]

(Precision here is not to be equated with clarity, or 'fuzziness' with a lack of it. On the contrary, a greater degree of precision may well be accompanied by a greater degree of incomprehensibility, as the language used increases in quantity and complexity in the quest to nail down every conceivable situation to which the law may apply. A simpler, more general provision, on the other hand, whilst perhaps a model of clarity to the 'man in the street', may prove unhelpfully vague when it has to be applied to specific facts.)

Even in common-law jurisdictions, a 'fuzzy' approach may be taken to ascertaining legislative intent, particularly where it is necessary to interpret an international agreement or treaty but also, increasingly, in general.

Courts in the United Kingdom, which traditionally would depart from a literal interpretation only when that led to a result that was wholly unreasonable or absurd, have moved far in recent years. Indeed the increasing readiness of the United Kingdom courts to depart from the literal approach to statutory interpretation and to adopt a more purposive approach may be partly explained by the influence of European law itself.

First, Community law requires national courts to take all possible steps, where a Community directive has not been fully implemented in national law, to construe all national legislation to give effect to the directive. Thus the ECJ has held, notably in *Marleasing*, in 1990,[7] that, in applying national legislation, a national court is required to interpret it 'as far as possible' in the light of the

---

[5] Stephen J in *Re Castioni* [1891] 1 QB 149.
[6] Although the fictional utterance of an entirely fictional judge, this dictum so accurately reflects the approach taken that it appears to have been relied on in all seriousness by some courts in Texas: see *Brazos River Authority v. City of Graham* 354 SW 2d 99 (Tex 1961), *Railroad Commission of Texas v. Miller* 434 SW 2d 670 (Tex 1968) and *State ex rel Vance v. Hatten* 600 SW 2d 828 (Tex Cr App 1980). In *Flores v. Workmen's Compensation Appeals Board* (1974) 11 Cal 3d 171, however, the Supreme Court of California recognised it as an 'unforgettable quip' by AP Herbert.
[7] Case C–106/89 *Marleasing v. La Comercial* [1990] ECR I–4135.

wording and purpose of the directive in issue, and to do so even where the legislation was not enacted in order to implement the directive.

Secondly, a similar obligation has been imposed on United Kingdom courts in relation to the European Convention on Human Rights which has an unquestionably broader impact on their day-to-day practice. Reflecting the language of the above case-law of the European Court of Justice, the Human Rights Act 1998 provides that:

> So far as it is possible to do so, primary legislation and subordinate legislation must be read and given effect in a way which is compatible with the Convention rights.

That interpretative obligation has notoriously led United Kingdom courts to adopt constructions impossible to reconcile with the literal meaning of the legislation.

Yet as long ago as 1981 Lord Hailsham had said in a House of Lords debate:

> I always look at Hansard, I always look at the Blue Books, I always look at everything I can in order to see what is meant . . . If you were to go upstairs and you were a fly on the wall in one of those judicial committees that we have up there, where distinguished members of the Bar . . . come to address us, you would be quite surprised how much we read . . . The idea that we do not read these is quite rubbish . . . if you think that they did not discuss what was really meant, you are living in a fool's paradise.[8]

Such practices (which Lord Mildew considered to be 'looking under the bed') have since been judicially acknowledged and endorsed, to a certain extent, in *Pepper* v. *Hart*.[9]

There is a common perception in the common-law world that European Union legislation is drafted and interpreted in a 'fuzzy' manner and it is sometimes thought in that regard that the Court of Justice has accorded itself exceptional freedom from the constraints of textual analysis, giving rise to some interpretations that seem to go beyond the intention of the legislators.

Yet those constraints can be gruelling, even in a single language. Following a particularly difficult analysis, Lord Justice Scrutton once said: 'I regret that I cannot order the costs to be paid by the draftsman of the Rent Restriction Acts, and the members of the Legislature who passed them, and are responsible for the obscurity of the Acts.'[10] When legislation is drafted in 11 or more languages, the difficulties are multiplied.

The characteristic features of European legislation were famously pointed out by the Court of Justice in *CILFIT*.[11] First, it is drafted in several languages and the different language versions are all equally authentic; interpretation thus involves a comparison of those different versions. Second, even where the different language versions entirely agree, Community law uses its own terminology and legal

---

[8] 26 March 1981; 1981 HL Rep (5th series) co 1346.
[9] [1993] AC 593.
[10] In *Roe* v. *Russell* [1928] 2 KB 117.
[11] Case 283/81 *CILFIT* v. *Ministry of Health* [1982] ECR 3415, at paras 17 ff.

concepts, which do not necessarily have the same meaning as in the laws of the Member States. Finally, every provision of Community law must be placed in its context and interpreted in the light of that law as a whole, having regard to its objectives and to its state of evolution at the date on which the provision in question is to be applied.

Perhaps the second of those points is the most fundamental. Whatever the philosophical approach to interpretation and even if there were only one language among 15 or 25 Member States, European Union law would still be in danger of disintegration if it were applied in individual cases only after examination through the very different lenses of 15 or 25 or more different systems of judicial interpretation.[12]

Even a single-language version of a single legislative text within a single State may give rise to differing interpretations by different jurisdictions using (more or less) the same language: see, for example, with regard to the objective or subjective nature of 'recklessness' for the purposes of Section 2 of the Road Traffic Act 1972, *Allan v. Patterson*[13] in Scotland and *R v. Murphy*[14] in England (the Scottish, objective, approach was subsequently endorsed—by substituting the concept of dangerousness for that of recklessness—by Parliament in the Road Traffic Act 1991).

Yet the existence of numerous different authentic versions of the same legislative text clearly introduces a further dimension, or series of dimensions, to the problem, akin to standing in a hall of distorting mirrors. What is a court to do when those mirrors reflect two or three or many conflicting images?

The type of solution adopted in Ireland—'In case of conflict between the texts of a law enrolled ... in both the official languages, the text in the national language shall prevail'[15]—is not available in a Community or Union of sovereign States, each with its own national or official language or languages.

Where a measure is enacted in 11 or more different language versions, it is however not realistic to assume that the legislature itself—the Council, with or without the European Parliament, or the Commission—has in fact devoted its collective attention to the wording of each of those versions.[16] The reality is that a text is drafted originally in one of the (major) official languages, then translated into the others. Whilst those translations are diligently coordinated by a team of extremely competent legal and linguistic experts and whilst different

---

[12] An interesting apparent exception to this principle may be found in the realm of butchery. In Case 327/82 *EKRO v. Produktschap voor Vee en Vlees* [1984] ECR 107, at para 7 ff, the Court considered that a single term ('thin flank' in Commission Regulation No 2787/81) could be assumed to refer to different cuts of meat in different Member States. It had no uniform precise anatomical definition but depended on various cutting and boning methods, themselves varying according to consumer habits and trade practices. In those circumstances, it was not for the Court to give a uniform Community definition.

[13] 1980 JC 57.

[14] [1980] QB 434.

[15] Constitution of Ireland—*Bunreacht na hÉireann*, Art 25(4)(6).

[16] And if it is deemed to have done so, one might be tempted to feel—again with Lord Mildew—that there may be 'too much of this damned deeming'.

individual legislators will be considering the text in different language versions, it is decidedly a fiction to say that the legislature as a whole has approved all the language versions together.

Such fiction becomes even stranger if one considers a text adopted before 1 January 1973 in the then four official languages, and which remains in force unamended—now in 11 languages, soon in 20.[17] By stages, it has come about that an increasing majority of the language versions are translations which the legislature as such has never considered. To what extent should a translation, drawn up 30 or more years after the enactment of the original, be relevant to the interpretation of such a text?

And if that fiction of equal plurilingual authority is accepted, courts are faced with the task of examining all the language versions before being able to reach a conclusion as to meaning. Such a task may not be insuperable for the Court of Justice in Luxembourg, with members from all Member States and with its numerous multilingual and multinational staff, learned in both national and Community law—though it is undoubtedly arduous even in those circumstances. But Community legislation is not interpreted by the Court of Justice alone—far more cases are resolved directly in the national courts of the Member States.

In *CILFIT*, the Court made it clear that a national court—at least one against whose decisions there is no appeal—may not resolve an issue of Community law itself, but must refer a question to the Court of Justice, unless the correct answer is so obvious as to leave no scope for any reasonable doubt. Before it comes to that conclusion, however, that court must be convinced that the matter is equally obvious to the courts of the other Member States and to the Court of Justice.[18]

Even in 1982, when the Community had seven official languages, that was a rather exacting requirement. To what extent will it be possible, in 2004, to expect a Portuguese court to be satisfied that a matter is obvious to an Estonian court, or a Hungarian court to verify that the same interpretation flows from the Dutch or Greek version of a regulation? Should such a court obtain, as one English court has done, certified translations into its own language of all the other—soon perhaps 19—versions?

But even if the relevant court is in a position to perform such a task, how is it then to proceed when the language versions conflict?

Some guidance might be derived from Article 33 of the Vienna Convention on the Law of Treaties, cited above: terms are presumed to have the same meaning in each authentic text, but when a comparison of those texts discloses a difference of meaning, the meaning which best reconciles the texts, having regard to

---

[17] For example, Art 2 of the First Council Directive of 11 April 1967 on the harmonisation of legislation of Member States concerning turnover taxes, OJ 1967 L71/1301, which still sets out the most fundamental principles of the system of VAT in the Community—and which is a good example of 'fuzziness'.

[18] At para 16 of the judgment.

the object and purpose of the treaty, is to be adopted. In the field of plurilingual—or bilingual—legislation in a national context, Section 8 of Canada's Official Languages Act 1969 introduced a rather 'fussier' set of rules under which, essentially, it was first necessary to exhaust all possibilities of linguistic reconciliation before giving preference to the version which:

> [A]ccording to the true spirit, intent and meaning of the enactment, best ensures the attainment of its objects.[19]

That latter criterion has been adopted in other plurilingual or bilingual States; it is, for example, the only criterion in Vanuatu.[20]

A conflict between language versions can only rarely be resolved by purely linguistic means, and the greater the number of languages involved the rarer the opportunities will be. Unless there really is some clear common meaning which has simply been expressed differently as a result of differing semantic and syntactical constraints—so that there is in fact no conflict at all—some other approach must be found. One based on pure arithmetic might be dangerous, possibly even leading to the absurdity that some legislation would have to be interpreted differently before and after an enlargement of the Union, simply by reason of the increase in number of official languages and change in spread of language versions. As Advocate General Lagrange pointed out in *De Gens* v. *Bosch*,[21] the fact that all language versions are authentic means that no single one of them is authentic. Nor thus can a simple (or even qualified[22]) majority claim authenticity.

That is not to say that the Court will never take numerical considerations into account—where they support what appears on other grounds to be the best interpretation. In particular, it has often relied on the consistency of a majority of the language versions to justify the conclusion that the version or versions in the minority contained drafting errors,[23] or that the ambiguity inherent in those versions must be resolved in a particular way.

In general, however, whether the legislation itself be 'fussy' or 'fuzzy', regard will be had to the purpose it seeks to achieve.

The features summarised above perhaps provide the key to what otherwise would be an intractable problem.

The approach of the Court seems to reflect the character of the provisions to be interpreted.

---

[19] Now formally repealed, though apparently still used by the courts. S 10 of the present Official Languages Act 2002—a much 'fuzzier' enactment—simply states: 'The English and French versions of legislation are equally authoritative'.

[20] Interpretation Act 1981, s 17(2).

[21] Case 13/61 [1962] ECR 45 at 710.

[22] In Case C–296/95 *The Queen* v. *Commissioners of Customs and Excise*, ex parte *EMU Tabac and Others* [1998] ECR I–1605, at para 36, the Court noted that, 'all the language versions must, in principle, be recognised as having the same weight and this cannot vary according to the size of the population of the Member States using the language in question.'

[23] Case 19/67 *Sociale Verzekeringsbank* v. *Van der Vecht* [1967] ECR 345, one of the earliest cases in which the Court considered conflicting language versions, is a case in point.

Approaches to Interpretation in a Plurilingual Legal System 305

In the case of Treaty provisions of a general character—some even of a quasi-constitutional character—a broad and purposive approach to interpretation will be recognised as appropriate in many legal systems. National constitutions, the constituent instruments of international organisations, charters and conventions on human rights will be given an evolutionary interpretation, even where reference is occasionally made to the supposed 'original intent'.

In the case of Community legislation of a more technical character, which now forms the main diet of the Court, the approach may turn on the subject-matter and on the nature of the legislation, as is the case in national law. But even where the legislation is detailed and the text apparently clear, the Court may feel less constrained by a textual approach. Here too, a purposive approach may be justified, and the Court shows itself concerned to reach a solution which will be effective and appropriate.

The result of such an approach is to make less significant textual discrepancies between different language versions of Community provisions, and to make it unnecessary in the normal case for national courts to feel constrained to examine umpteen different language versions. It will be more useful to focus on the way in which the Court generally approaches provisions of the type in issue, as national courts have often shown themselves well able to do.

To put the matter in a metaphorical nutshell, it will not generally be fruitful to focus on differences between different language versions, since generally the Court's approach will be as expressed in *Bouchereau*:

> The different language versions of a Community text must be given a uniform interpretation and hence in the case of divergence between the versions the provision in question must be interpreted by reference to the purpose and general scheme of the rules of which it forms a part.[24]

---

[24] Case 30/77 *Régina* v. *Bouchereau* [1977] ECR 1999, para 14 of the judgment.

22

Private Enforcement—A Complete System of Remedies?

ANNELI HOWARD AND DEOK JOO RHEE

1 INTRODUCTION

FIFTY YEARS ago, when the Community was first established, it was widely assumed that the Treaty of Rome was like any other international treaty with its scope limited to determining the relationships between the contracting Member States and the institutions to which they had transferred their sovereign powers. It did not take the Court of Justice long to disabuse the Member State governments of this impression, with its seminal 1964 judgment in *Van Gend en Loos*:[1]

> the EEC Treaty has created its own legal system, which is integrated into the legal systems of the Member States and which their courts are bound to apply. The subjects of that legal system are not only the Member States but also their nationals. Just as it imposes burdens on individuals, Community law is also intended to give rise to rights which become part of their legal patrimony. Those rights arise not only where they are expressly granted by the Treaty but also by virtue of obligations which the Treaty imposes in a clearly defined manner both on individuals and on the Member States and the Community institutions.

With the benefit of hindsight, private enforcement seems a natural progression. However, the Court could easily have decided the other way. It could simply have followed Advocate General Roemer, dismissing the notion of individual rights by affirming that the Treaty was addressed to Member State governments only and set out adequate enforcement mechanisms through the infringement and annulment procedures (now set out in Articles 226 and 230 EC).

If it had done so, Community law would be a very different animal today. The enfranchisement of private parties and national courts has pivoted the Community into a rights-driven society as opposed to a purely obligations-based one. It has inspired the doctrinal development of direct effect, Member State liability and the protection of fundamental rights. Perhaps more importantly, it has focused the development of the internal market on the interests of

---

[1] Case 26/62 *Van Gend en Loos* [1963] ECR 1.

those most affected on an everyday basis by employment policies, restrictions to free movement and anti-competitive practices—the Community's citizens.

Fifty years later, private enforcement is on the verge of moving into pole position within the Community's system of remedies. In its recent case law, the Court appears keen to promote the merits of private enforcement and has recognised its significant contribution to the practical effectiveness of Community law throughout the Union.[2] Given the vagaries of the Article 226 infringement procedure, with its political compromises and lack of immediate sanctions, it has become all the more imperative for individuals to be able to invoke Community law before their national courts. This is not just to reproach the failures of their Member State governments but also to assert their positive Community law rights against other private parties. Further, the Court has recently emphasised the key role of national court proceedings within the 'complete system of legal remedies and procedures' designed by the Treaty to ensure judicial review of the legality of Community legislation.[3]

The decentralisation of Community law enforcement powers to the national courts is not new.[4] Promoting private enforcement should increase the awareness and effectiveness of Community rights and disseminate a litigation culture within the Community. However, in practice, it remains questionable whether the Community judicial network has indeed reached the requisite stage of maturity to guarantee a complete system of legal remedies and procedures, let alone one which meets the requirements of effective judicial protection as enshrined in Articles 6 and 13 of the ECHR and Article 47 of the Charter. The authors submit that the Court of Justice has embarked upon a long journey, which will lead to a new judicial system of checks and balances and a volume of judge-made procedural harmonisation.

It is not possible within the constraints of this article to provide an encyclopaedic review of the Community's system of remedies. Part A of this Article will highlight some shortcomings within the system at Community level whereas Part B will analyse the impact of Community law on the principle of domestic procedural autonomy. Drawing on practical examples at both Community and domestic level, the authors would like to finish with some possible pointers for future reform.

---

[2] Case C-453/99 *Courage* [2001] ECR I-6297, paras 26 and 27, and Case C-253/00 *Muñoz* [2002] ECR I-7289, para 31.

[3] Case 50/00 P *Unión de Pequeños Agricultores* ('UPA') v. *Council* [2002] ECR I-6677, para 41.

[4] A similar exercise is being conducted by the Commission in the realm of competition law under Regulation 1/2003, which acknowledges the essential part that national courts have to play in applying the Community competition rules and in protecting subjective rights under Community law.

PART A: GAPS IN THE COMMUNITY'S SYSTEM OF REMEDIES

2. OUTLINE OF THE TREATY ENFORCEMENT MECHANISMS

The Treaty provides for three levels at which a private individual may invoke Community law—the choice of level will often determine the forum and remedy available:

(i) at Community level, before the Court of First Instance, by:
   a. challenging the validity of Community legislation or administrative acts or omissions under Articles 230 and 232 EC; or
   b. pleading the invalidity of regulations under Article 241 EC; or
   c. seeking damages from a Community institution under Article 288 EC for a sufficiently serious infringement of a rule of law intended to confer rights on individuals.
(ii) at 'vertical' Member State level, before the national administrative courts—if necessary with an Article 234 EC reference to the Court of Justice—by:
   a. challenging measures adopted by a Member State government or public authority[5] which contravene Community law;[6] or
   b. seeking damages against a Member State for its failure to implement or consistently apply Community law.[7]
(iii) at 'horizontal' grassroot level, before the ordinary domestic courts—if necessary with an Article 234 EC preliminary reference to the Court of Justice—by:
   a. asserting positive Community rights as a 'sword' against another private individual to force them to comply with their Community obligations; or
   b. invoking Community law as a 'shield' to defend a claim lodged by another private individual which is unfounded from a Community law perspective.[8]

i) Source of rights and their horizontal enforceability at 'grassroot level'

Due to the inter-governmental focus in the drafting of the original Treaty, there are limits to the 'user-friendliness' of its procedural mechanisms for private parties. In several respects, the Treaty's enforcement procedures are based on conciliatory dispute resolution between Member States and/or the institutions.

---

[5] Within the meaning of the test laid down by Case C-188/89 *Foster* v. *British Gas* [1990] ECR I-3313.

[6] Including the exercise of the Member State's discretion in implementing Community law: see Case 51/76 *Verbond van Nederlandse Ondernemingen* v. *Inspecteur der Invoerrechten en Accijnzen* [1977] ECR 113, paras 22, 23 and 24, Case C-72/95 *Kraaijeveld and Others* v. *Gedeputeerde Staten van Zuid-Holland* [1996] ECR I-5403, para 56, and Case C-287/98 *Grand Duchy of Luxemburg* v. *Berthe Linster and others* [2000] ECR I-6917, para 32.

[7] Cases C-6/90 and C-9/90, *Francovich* [1991] I-5357 and Joined Cases C-46/93 and C-48/93 *Brasserie du Pêcheur/Factortame* [1996] ECR I-1029.

[8] See Cases C-194/94 *CIA Security* [1996] ECR I-2201 and C-443/98 *Central Foods* v. *Unilever* [2000] ECR I-7535.

That explains the lack of direct sanctions for a Member State's failure to implement legislation and the limited action for declaratory relief where an institution oversteps the limits of its powers.

The original *Van Colson* conundrum has evolved—the Treaty is not a mere international treaty but neither is it a citizen's charter. There are some provisions which are intended to concern only the contracting Member States and the institutions. The Court has to tread a tightrope between recognising individual rights and promoting the effectiveness of Community law on the one hand, and, on the other, keeping within its jurisdictional confines of interpreting and applying the Treaty under Article 220 EC.

The horizontal direct effect debate is a keen example of the conflict of interests between effective judicial protection and the institutional balance in the legislative process. The layers of legislation in Article 249 EC are carefully designed to preserve Member State autonomy and the principle of subsidiarity. The choice of measure and Treaty base reflects the relative competences between the Community institutions. The measure is often couched in wording that has more to do with political compromise than private enforcement. The impact of the measure, as a source of individual rights, often seems an after-thought which is left to the Court of Justice to elucidate.

It is now settled that directives cannot be directly invoked by private individuals in horizontal disputes before their national courts.[9] Instead, private litigants have to rely on their domestic implementing legislation or, if none is forthcoming, wait until the implementation deadline has expired before asserting action against the Member State itself, or where appropriate, relying on the latter's default by way of defence to private proceedings.[10]

Given the prevalence of Directives as a legislative tool and the high infringement rate by Member States, the lack of a positive cause of action against other individuals is a major flaw in the Community system of procedures. However, in its recent case law, the Court of Justice has been at pains to promote the horizontal direct effect of other measures whose terms are clear and unconditional, such as regulations[11] and the Treaty articles themselves.[12]

---

[9] See Cases 152/84 *Marshall* v. *Southampton and South-West Hampshire Health Authority* [1986] ECR 723, para 48 and C-91/92 *Faccini Dori* [1994] ECR I-3325. The Court held that as a directive is binding only in relation to 'each Member State to which it is addressed', it cannot of itself impose obligations on an individual and cannot therefore be relied upon as such against an individual. Any other construction would equate to the Community having the power to enact obligations for individuals with immediate effect, contrary to limited competence conferred by the Treaty, confined to situations where the legislator is empowered to adopt regulations.

[10] See *CIA Security* and *Central Foods* v. *Unilever* at n 8 above.

[11] Case C-253/00 *Muñoz* [2002] ECR I-7289 at n 2 above.

[12] Article 28 EC (free movement of goods) in Case C-108/01 *Consorzio del Prosciutto di Parma v Asda Stores Ltd and Hygrade Foods Ltd* [2003] ECR (unpublished); Article 29 EC (freedom of exports) in Case C-469/00 *Ravil* [2003] ECR (unpublished); Article 39 EC (free movement of workers) in Case C-415/93 *Bosman* [1995] ECR I-4921, paras 82-84; Article 81 EC (competition law) in

The horizontal assertion of these rights, reinforced by flexible remedies such as mandatory injunctions[13] and the prospect of group action[14] will be a major impetus for the achievement of the internal market. The Community cannot be expected to legislate for every eventuality—it is only by individual challenge that restrictive commercial practices will be detected and eradicated.

There are two paradoxes to this development. First, the Community legislator is unlikely to increase the use of regulations as a legislative tool, given the degree of resistance to the rigid and anti-subsidiarity nature of this type of harmonisation. Secondly, it is ironic that the horizontal direct effect filter only recognises 'directly applicable' legislation which has no implementing measures to bring the content of such rights and obligations to the attention of those individuals likely to be affected. In such circumstances, as highlighted by the recent *Parma Ham* case,[15] individual rights are nothing but a hollow shell.

If Community legislation is going to take individual rights seriously rather than merely paying them lip service, it will have to be drafted with right-holders in mind. That means, as the Court signalled so long ago in *Van Gend en Loos*, indicating the creation of individual rights in a 'clearly defined manner' so that private individuals can adjust their conduct in line with the expectations demanded of them.[16] Secondly, in the same way as it has done with competition and employment law, the Commission should disseminate legal information to the public at large, if necessary with the co-operation of national authorities. Lastly, regulations should set out detailed publication and enforcement mechanisms to ensure that the rights receive effective protection before the national courts of each Member State.[17] Failing that, Member States should be required, as part of their duty of loyal co-operation under Article 10 EC, to ensure the promulgation of information regarding the rights and obligations

---

Case C-453/99 *Courage* [2001] ECR I-6279 paras 26 and 27 and Article 141 EC (equal pay and discrimination) in Case 43/75 *Defrenne v SABENA* [1976] ECR 455, para 24.

[13] The availability of injunctive relief to support private enforcement has recently been accepted by AG Jacobs in his Opinion in Joined Cases C-264/01, C-306/01, C-354/01 and C-355/01 *AOK Bundesverband* [2003] ECR (unpublished).

[14] The possibility of collective action for enforcing Community law was accepted by AG Jacobs in his Opinion in Case C-195/98 *Österreichischer Gewerkschaftsbund, Gewerkschaft öffentlicher Dienst v. Austria* [2000] ECR I-1497, paras 47-48. He noted that rights of collective group were a common feature of most modern legal systems and further private enforcement of rules adopted in the public interest and support individual complainants who are often badly equipped to face well organised and financially stronger opponents.

[15] Case C-108/01 *Consorzio del Prosciutto di Parma v. Asda Stores Ltd and Hygrade Foods Ltd* [2003] ECR (unpublished), para 89 and Case C-469/00 *Ravil* [2003] ECR (unpublished) at n 12 above.

[16] See the requirements of legal certainty and transparency set down by the ECHR in *Rekvényi v. Hungary* [1999] EHRLR 114, para 34.

[17] The authors submit that this could be achieved by the inclusion of a provision in the legislation requiring Member States to adopt measures as part of their national legal systems which enable all persons who consider themselves to be victims of a breach of Community law to pursue their claims by judicial process. See, by analogy, the discussion of Article 6 of the Equal Treatment Directive 76/207/EEC in Case C-185/97 *Belinda Jane Coote* [1998] ECR I-5199.

flowing from directly applicable Community provisions as well as their effective judicial protection.[18]

ii) Gaps at the Community level—challenging Community legislation

Article 230 EC shows a clear bias in favour of challenges brought by Member States and the Community institutions over those brought by individuals who must satisfy the requirements of direct and individual concern if they want to challenge a regulation. The Court has interpreted this criterion strictly, requiring applicants to demonstrate that the measure,

> affects their legal position by reason of certain attributes peculiar to them, or by reason of a factual situation which differentiates them from all other persons and distinguishes them individually in the same way as the addressee.[19]

Despite the criticisms in Advocate General Jacobs' *UPA* opinion and the Court of First Instance in *Jégo-Quéré*[20] that the wording of Article 230 does not strictly require such a restrictive standing test, the Court of Justice refused to adopt an 'evolutionary' interpretation of the Treaty to take account of the increasing competences transferred to the Community over the years and their increasing impact on individuals' interests. One can only surmise the policy reasons behind its confirmation of the *Plaumann* test—perhaps the desire to shelter the developing Community legal order from anxious scrutiny and/or to dam the floodgates. In any event, the Court considered that it did not have authority to change the system of remedies and procedures established by the Treaty by judicial interpretation.[21]

In the Court's view, the principle of effective judicial protection did not require it to change its stance, given that the individual has a remedy before his national courts. The Treaty envisages that where individuals do not meet the standing requirements in Article 230 EC, they can plead the invalidity of the measure before the national courts and ask them to make a reference to the Court of Justice for a preliminary ruling on validity.[22]

---

[18] See, by analogy, Case C-326/88 *Hansen* [1990] ECR I-2911, where the Court held that where Community legislation, in that case Regulation No 543/69 on the harmonisation of certain social legislation relating to road transport, does not specifically provide any penalty for an infringement or refers for that purpose to national laws, regulations and administrative provisions, Article 10 EC requires the Member States to take all measures necessary to guarantee the *application* and effectiveness of Community law (emphasis added).

[19] See Case 25/62 *Plaumann* v. *Commission* [1963] ECR 95.

[20] Case T-177/01 *Jégo-Quéré* v. *Commission* [2002] ECR II-02365.

[21] *UPA*, para 45 at n 3 above. See also Case C-87/95 P *CNPAAP* v. *Council* [1996] ECR I-2003, para 38 and Case C-300/00 P-R *Federación de Cofradías de Pescadores de Guipúzcoa and others* [2000] ECR I-8797, para 37.

[22] National courts have no competence to declare Community acts invalid—see Case 314/85 *Foto-Frost* [1987] ECR 4199, para 20.

In practice, now that the private party's ability to challenge EC measures of general application is effectively blocked at Community level, it has to divert its claim through the domestic courts instead. Rather than the Court of First Instance assessing the claim under Article 230 EC, the Court of Justice will assume control of the challenge following an Article 234 EC reference from the national court. However, it is not clear that this funnelling of primary responsibility to the national courts will necessarily ensure access to a court let alone effective protection of the applicant's substantive rights.

In terms of access, the *UPA* diversion assumes that: (i) a dispute will arise at national level on this point in the near future; (ii) the party has a cause of action; and (iii) the national court will be able and willing to comply with the Article 234 reference procedure. In reality, the chances of a dispute arising may be remote. As regulations are directly applicable, there will be no domestic implementing legislation that the individual can challenge at Member State level. As AG Jacobs points out, only a very altruistic private party would consider violating the rule in question just to obtain an opportunity to assert the invalidity of those rules by way of defence. At grassroots level, it would be an uphill struggle to launch a horizontal claim, whose foundation is flatly contradicted by directly applicable and apparently valid Community legislation.[23] Although another individual may seek to enforce the terms of the Regulation against him,[24] the would-be proactive challenger will then be relegated into the position of a reactive defendant, with the mainstay of his defence being to assert the invalidity of supreme Community rules—not the most attractive submission to make to a national judge.

In terms of remedies, as AG Jacobs observes,

> proceedings before national courts do not, however always provide effective judicial protection of individual applicants and may, in some cases, provide no legal protection whatsoever.

Compared to the 'one-stop' Art 230 EC procedure before the Court of First Instance, the challenger will now have to endure the delay and expense of a triple loop of procedures before the national court and the Court of Justice before he succeeds on his point of principle. Even then, there is no guarantee that the national court will agree to make a reference in the first place[25] or comply with the ruling when it returns from Luxembourg,[26] which will spark off a

---

[23] In the English courts, such a tactic would be likely to encounter an application for strike out or summary judgment as the apparent validity of the Community measure would be a powerful indicator that the claimant had no real prospect of success in the main action.

[24] The direct effect of regulations has been confirmed by the Court in Case C-253/00 *Muñoz* [2002] ECR I-7289, at n 2 above.

[25] See the recent reference in Case C-491/01 *Imperial Tobacco Ltd and British American Tobacco Ltd.* [2002] ECR (unpublished) which was appealed all the way to the House of Lords before the reference was made.

[26] See the December 2002 judgment by Mr. Justice Laddie in *Arsenal v. Football Club v. Matthew Reed* (2003) 1 All ER 137 which disregarded the ECJ's judgment on the ground that the ECJ had exceeded its jurisdiction. The Court of Appeal reversed the judgment in May 2003.

further string of appeals through the domestic courts. Given the difficulties in obtaining interim relief, it would be a tough cost-benefit decision for even a seasoned commercial litigator.

The Court of Justice was not blind to these problems. Its response was to impose, as part of the Article 10 EC duty of loyal co-operation, a requirement on Member States to establish a system of legal remedies and procedures that ensures respect for effective judicial protection. National courts are obliged to interpret and apply their national procedural rules so as to ensure that individuals can plead the invalidity of a Community act which underpins the legality of a national measure applicable to them.

What happens if the Member State, as a result of the refusal of its national courts to entertain such a claim, disregards its duty and in so doing violates a Community law right? At the moment, the sanction is purely declaratory: a more incisive answer may be provided by the pending *Köbler* reference.[27] AG Léger has relied specifically upon the *Van Gend en Loos* dicta to justify an extension of the *Francovich* doctrine[28] to breaches by national supreme courts. In his view,

> the principle of State liability constitutes the necessary extension of the general principle of effective judicial protection or of the right to challenge a measure before the courts [and] helps to ensure the full effectiveness of Community law through effective judicial protection of the rights which individuals derive from the Community legal order.[29]

Member States could therefore be liable in damages if their supreme courts fail to afford adequate protection to individuals' Community rights.

By analogy with the Court's case-law on Article 10 EC, national courts are obliged to interpret their national law, as far as possible, in the light of the wording and purpose of Community law in order to achieve its intended result.[30] As they are under a duty to give full effect to the provisions of Community law, they must, if necessary, refuse of their own motion to apply any conflicting provision of national legislation, even if adopted subsequently. It is not necessary for the court to request or await the prior setting aside of such provision by legislative or other constitutional means.[31] The court will be expected to substitute the incompatible domestic norms for Community law, unless that would aggravate the legal liability of one of the parties.[32]

---

[27] See the Opinion of Advocate General Léger of 8 April 2003 in Case C-224/01 *Gerhard Köbler v. Austria* [2003] ECR (unpublished).

[28] Joined Cases C-6/90 and C-9/90 *Francovich* [1991] ECR I-5357 and Joined Cases C-46/93 and C-48/93 *Brasserie du Pêcheur Factortame* [1996] ECR I-1029.

[29] *Ibid*, para 35.

[30] Case C-106/89 *Marleasing* [1990] ECR I-4135, para 8; Case C-91/92 *Faccini Dori* [1994] ECR I-3325, para 26 and Case C-62/00 *Marks & Spencer* [2002] ECR I-6325, para 24.

[31] Case C-168/95 *Arcaro* [1996] ECR I-4705, paras 16 and 24.

[32] Case 80/86 *Kolpinghuis Nijmegen* [1987] ECR 3969, paras 13 and 14.

Since *Factortame*[33] and *Verholen*,[34] it is clear that Article 10 EC does not just require national courts to review all national substantive legislative measures but also their own procedural rules. They will be obliged to grant interim relief and to grant individuals standing to bring proceedings, even where they would be unable to do so under national law. AG Léger envisages three situations in which a supreme court could be liable for a sufficiently serious breach of Community law: (i) if it gives a decision contrary to provisions of Community law despite their clear and unambiguous meaning; (ii) if it inexcusably disregards the Court of Justice's case law; or (iii) refuses to make a reference to the Court of Justice in spite of its obligation as a court of last resort. There is not much of a quantum leap to the case where a supreme court interprets its national procedural rules in such a way so as to block an applicant from access to justice in breach of the fundamental principle of effective protection.

How would this work in practice? As in *Köbler*, the private litigant would have to exhaust his domestic remedies on his main substantive action challenging the validity of the Community measure ('the validity issue'). Unless he was astute enough to raise the incompatibility of the domestic procedural law ('the procedural issue') as part of his substantive appeal before the supreme court, he would have to start a separate claim in damages against the Member State for the loss suffered as a result of the impasse resulting from the supreme court's interpretation of its national procedural requirements.

If the national court does not feel able to rectify the breach itself, it will have to make an Article 234 reference to the Court of Justice. Although, turning the reference procedure into a 'tell-tale licence' would have worrying implications for the Court's case load, it would enable the Court to oversee the standards of protection afforded by domestic legal regimes and to lay down minimum requirements. Gradually, a body of case law would evolve, amounting to de facto binding judicial harmonisation as result of the Article 10 EC duty of loyal co-operation. This would deepen the understanding between the Community and national courts, in spite of the 'judicial veil' envisaged by the separation of powers in Article 234 EC, and, as Part B of this article shows, would make further inroads into national procedural autonomy.

Moreover, as a judicial innovation, the *Köbler* concept is likely to suffer from important limitations regarding the quality of the eventual remedy. There is no guarantee that the question(s) referred will extend beyond the compatibility of the interpretation of the domestic procedural law and enable the litigant to continue his quest on the underlying validity issue.[35] Even if it is raised, the validity of the Community legislation will only be addressed in the context of characterising the

---

[33] Case C-213/89 *Factortame* [1990] ECR I-2433, paras 19 to 22.
[34] Joined Cases C-87/90, C-88/90 and C-89/90 *Verholen* [1991] ECR I-3757, paras 23 to 24.
[35] This is particularly the case where the *Köbler* reference is made in a separate set of proceedings after the supreme court rejected the challenge of the Community legislation purely on the basis of domestic procedure e.g. standing requirements/time limits without assessing its obligations of loyal co-operation under Article 10 EC.

national court's dismissal of the claim as sufficiently serious. The litigant will not necessarily obtain his copper-bottomed declaration of invalidity. There will be no 'closure' for his legal position in pending and future disputes.

Further, any damages awarded against the Member State are unlikely, as a matter of causation, to extend to the total loss flowing from the continued application of the invalid Community measure. As AG Léger notes in *Köbler*, the direct causal link from the supreme court's breach may be limited to the notional loss of opportunity. Even if it extends to material loss, it will be difficult for the claimant to prove that the supreme court would have upheld his claims if it had referred a question for preliminary ruling. The *Köbler* concept (assuming it is accepted by the Court of Justice) is unlikely to confer adequate redress for the damages and costs that the claimant should have been awarded in the unsuccessful domestic proceedings.

Therein lies the rub. After two rounds of domestic proceedings, a third round before the Court of Justice, the litigant will have to start a further set of proceedings before a third court, the Court of First Instance, to obtain full redress for his loss from the responsible Community institution under Article 288 EC. He may obtain redress in the end but only after a circuitous and time-consuming route.

Although the Treaty provides a complete system of procedures, the Court's application of the principle of effective protection to date has largely focused on the availability of causes of action and access to a court. To be fair, this is due to the declaratory nature of the Treaty, which focuses on prescribing rights and obligations. In line with the principles of subsidiarity and procedural autonomy, the Court has left the procedural and remedial mechanisms to the various domestic legal orders. However, this means that the Community courts have paid limited regard to the actual quality of the eventual remedy and the efficiency of the enforcement procedure as a whole. The next section will demonstrate the extent to which the requirements of effective judicial protection are making inroads on the application of domestic procedural law by the national courts.

PART B: IMPACT OF COMMUNITY LAW ON DOMESTIC PROCEDURAL RULES

i) **An overview**

It is the national courts that have provided the main arena for the growth in the enforcement of Community law rights by private litigants. Yet, the absence of procedural and remedial harmonisation at Community level has meant that a Community right, once validly invoked, runs the risk of running aground on the vagaries of national procedural rules. Indeed, the principle of national procedural autonomy as initially declared by the Court appeared to leave all matters of procedure to national courts, subject to the seemingly minimal provisos that the national rules of procedure should be applied no less favourably than to comparable domestic law actions, and further that the Community law right should not be rendered impossible in practice to exercise.[36]

However, in line with the development of direct effect of Community law provisions, and the enfranchisement of private individuals and national courts in the integration and application of Community law, considerable inroads have been made to this principle of national procedural autonomy, as initially declared.[37] That is, the increasing power afforded to individuals to assert their Community law rights before their national courts has entailed, as a corollary, an increased focus on the adequacy of national procedural rules governing the exercise of those rights. From this perspective, a simple demarcation between 'substance' and 'procedure' could not bear up to scrutiny, when procedural rules could have the effect of rendering illusory the effective exercise of Community law rights.

Whilst an inescapable factor on which the principle of national procedural autonomy is founded has been the absence of Community harmonising legislation in the field of remedies,[38] the requirement that the exercise of a Community law right should not be rendered impossible in practice, or excessively difficult, has seen itself transformed from being a somewhat negatively expressed proviso (indicating the presumptive legitimacy of the national procedural rule), to being a positive requirement that national procedural rules should allow for the *effective protection* of rights conferred by Community law and should provide where necessary for an effective remedy.

In this way, the mantra of effectiveness of protection of rights derived from Community law has proved a powerful tool in filling the legislative vacuum on remedial harmonisation. It has (i) in the first instance, required national courts to give 'full effect' to community legislation intended to confer rights on individuals—through the provision of adequate redress in case of breaches of those rights,[39] (ii) required the setting aside of national legislation restricting the right to an effective remedy,[40] (iii) ensured the protection of rights intended to be conferred (or in fact conferred) by Community directives by requiring Member

---

[36] Case 33/76 *Rewe-Zentralfinanz* [1976] ECR 1989; Case 45/76 *Comet* [1976] ECR 2043.

[37] The enfranchisement of national courts has taken place not only through the development of the Article 234 EC reference procedure, where the Court has been keen to foster a spirit of horizontal cooperation, but also through the emphasis by the Court on the Article 10 EC duty of cooperation in the application by national courts of Community law.

[38] There have of course been discrete instances of harmonisation. See for example, Directive 89/665/EEC (OJ 1989 L 395/33)—the remedies directive in the field of public procurement.

[39] See Case 14/83 *Von Colson and Kamann v. Land Nordrhein-Westfalen* [1984] ECR 1891, where the Court, relying in particular on the 'specific enforcement' provisions contained in Article 6 of the Equal Treatment Directive, held that in the absence of adequate remedies for discrimination, the rights conferred by the Directive would not be 'fully effective, in accordance with the objective that it pursues.'

[40] Case C-213/89 *R v. Secretary of State, ex parte Factortame Ltd.* [1990] ECR I-2433, where the national rule prohibiting the award of interim relief against the Crown was required to be set aside.

States to provide damages in case of non-implementation[41] and (iv) has thereby established the general principle of state liability for breach of Community law,[42] which, should the Court in *Köbler* follow the opinion of Advocate General Leger,[43] would also encompass breaches of Community law by national courts of last resort. It should also be mentioned that the Court has recently held that the principle of liability for damage for breach of Community law is available against a private party for breach of Article 81 EC,[44] although to what extent this principle will be extended to other directly effective provisions of the Treaty remains to be seen.

As a consequence, the dynamic between the two provisos to the principle of national procedural autonomy—equivalence and effectiveness—has been a continuously evolving one, serving to shape and reshape the reach of Community law as applied in the domestic courts. The authors submit that it is through this interplay that the Court has been able to achieve a greater degree of harmonisation in the field of remedies and national procedural rules.

In the initial absence of remedies on a Community level, the principle of equivalence acted more as an impediment to a unitary system of remedies, as the reality of the Community derived right was simply shaped by the applicable national procedural rules.[45] However, through the Court's development of a Community system of remedies through the landmark cases of *Von Colson*,[46] *Factortame I*,[47] *Francovich*,[48] *Brasserie du Pecheur/Factortame*[49] it has often been the new Community law remedies that have required a more innovative comparative approach to the question of equivalence. The authors submit that this emerging, newer aspect or role to the principle of equivalence has provided a further tool for integrating the Community and national legal orders. However, commensurate with its enhanced role, the application of this principle has been the source of some uncertainty, as demonstrated by the *Preston* litigation,[50] and further remains the potential source of considerable disparities between the level of protection afforded to Community rights across the Member States.

By contrast, the principle of effectiveness, having played a large part in the creation of a Community system of remedies, has adopted a meeker role when

---

[41] See Joined Cases C-6/90 and C-9/90 *Francovich* [1991] ECR I-5357 where the Member State was held liable in damages for the failure to implement a directive.
[42] See further Joined Cases C6/93 and C48/93 *Brasserie du Pêcheur/Factortame* [1996] ECR I-1029 in which the Court outlined the conditions giving rise to state liability.
[43] Case C-224/01, at n 27 above.
[44] Case C-453/99 *Courage* v. *Crehan*, at n2, where the action for compensation was extended to breach by a private individual of article 81 EC.
[45] See for example, Case 158/80 *Rewe-Handelsgesellschaft* [1981] ECR 1805.
[46] Above, n 39.
[47] Above, n 40.
[48] Above, n 41.
[49] Above, n 42.
[50] *Preston* v. *Wolverhampton NHS Trust* [1998] 1 WLR. 280 (HL); Case C-78/98 [2000] ECR I-3201; [2001] 2 WLR 408 (HL), discussed below.

assessing the impediments caused to the exercise of Community rights by the national procedural rules—such as time limits and limits on compensation—which circumscribe, but do not preclude, the right to relief.[51]

ii) Remedies—damages and interim relief

Before turning to the principle of equivalence, however, some brief comments follow on the Court's development of Community law remedies for breach of Community law. First, not only has the Court developed its remedies jurisprudence, encompassing the award of both interim relief as well as damages for breach of Community law, it has also outlined for both cases the conditions giving rise to liability, thereby ensuring a greater degree of uniformity than had the conditions of liability been left to be determined by a particular national law vehicle.

Secondly, from the perspective of a unitary system of remedies, whilst an individual may have difficulties directly challenging the validity of Community legislation,[52] it may be of some (albeit rather conceptual) consolation that the conditions of Member State liability are drawn from those for the Community's own liability under Article 288 EC (ex Article 215).[53] Perhaps of more comfort to the individual litigant is the fact that, whilst of course national courts cannot determine the validity of a Community law measure, they may, however, suspend its operation, pending final determination in Luxembourg, a year (or so) later.[54]

Analogous to the position in respect of damages liability, the Court has drawn from the conditions for the grant of interim relief under direct actions at Community level (under Articles 242 and 243 EC—ex Articles 185 and 186),[55] and further held that the conditions for the grant of interim relief (in the national arena) should be the same irrespective of whether, on the basis of a Community law right, it is a Community norm or a national measure which is sought to be set aside.[56] The caveat however is that the Court, perhaps wary of

---

[51] As to this distinction, see Case C-246/96 *Magorrian v. Eastern Health and Social Services Board* [1997] ECR I-7153.

[52] See discussion of *UPA*, above.

[53] See Joined Cases C-46/93 and C-48/93, *Brasserie du Pecheur/Factortame*, above n 42.

[54] Case 314/85 *Foto-Frost* [1987] ECR 4199.

[55] The conditions of relief in the case of direct actions are that there must be a prima facie case, and urgency resulting from the likelihood of irreparable damage to the applicant, which is then balanced against the possibility of irreparable damage to the Community should the act be suspended but the applicant's case fail (see Joined Cases C-143/88 and C-92/89 *Zuckerfabrik Süderdithmarschen and Zuckerfabrik Soest* [1991] ECR I-415).

[56] Cases C-143/88 and C-92/89 *Zuckerfabrik*, above n54. See also the observation by Lord Slynn in R v. *Secretary of State, ex parte Imperial Tobacco & ors* [2001] 1 WLR 127, that the fact that the Court did not, in the pre-*Zuckerfabrik* case of *Factortame I* (above n 38), stipulate the criteria to be applied for the grant of interim relief was simply because the question as posed to the Court did not make it necessary to do so. (On the return of the reference in *Factortame I*, the House of Lords, having set aside the national rule prohibiting the grant of interim relief, applied the *American Cyanamid*

the power of national courts to set aside (even temporarily) Community legislation was, whilst drawing from the conditions for relief in the case of direct actions, keen to vary the test for the grant of interim relief at national level. Hence, in *Zuckerfabrik* the Court substituted for the 'prima face case' requirement applicable under direct actions, the tougher condition that the national court must be satisfied that 'serious doubts' exist as to the validity of the Community act in question—this test therefore also applying to the suspension of a national measure. The Court's protective attitude to Community legislation has therefore by parity of treatment been extended to national measures, the suspension of which is sought on grounds of Community law.[57]

iii) The principle of equivalence

The harmonisation in the field of remedies carried out by the Court is dependent, to a certain extent, on the proper integration of Community law by the national courts into their own legal systems. For example, in *Palmisani*, the Court was called upon to consider the question of equivalence in relation to a rule of national law which fixed a one year limitation period in respect of actions for reparation of loss or damage sustained as a result of the belated implementation of a Community directive relating to the protection of employees in the event of insolvency of their employer.[58] The Court rejected as comparable to a claim for damages for belated implementation, a claim for compensation as introduced under the Directive in question, instead preferring to look to the ordinary system of non-contractual liability, under which claims are 'directed against public authorities which have failed to act or have committed an unlawful act for which they can be held responsible in the exercise of their powers.'

In relation to such 'vertical' actions for damages, the concept of state liability is one that sits uneasily within the English legal system, under which there is in principle no equation of public law illegality with damages liability.[59] Whilst the Court has been at pains to stress that the vagaries of national legal systems should not determine the effectiveness of protection to be afforded to

---

v. *Ethicon Ltd* [1975] AC396 test for the relief: *R* v. *Secretary of State for Transport, ex p. Factortame (No.2)*, (1991) 1 AC 603. However, notwithstanding the subsequent clear ruling of the Court in *Zuckerfabrik*, a mistaken distinction appears to have emerged at domestic level according to which applications, based on a Community right, for the interim suspension of *national* measures have nonetheless been determined according to the domestic/*American Cyanamid* test: see for example, *R* v. *Secretary of State, ex parte Trade Union Congress* (2000) IRLR 565 (CA)).

[57] In any event, the actual difference between the *Zuckerfabrik* and *American Cyanamid* tests for the grant of interim relief may not be that evident. See in this respect the observations of Lord Slynn in *Imperial Tobacco* (above n 55), and further D Wyatt, "Injunctions and Damages against the State for Breach of Community Law—a Legitimate Judicial Development" in *European Community Law in the English Courts* (Clarendon, London, 1998) M Andenas and FG Jacobs (eds).

[58] Case C-261/95 *Palmisani* v. *INPS* [1997] ECR I-4025.

[59] French law, by contrast, does in fact recognise the principle of administrative liability in damages for loss caused by unlawful action.

Community rights,[60] nonetheless the approach to be adopted has not always been evident to the national courts. Hence, whilst the conditions giving rise to state liability have been laid down by the Court in *Brasserie du Pêcheur/Factortame*, the procedural rules circumscribing the liability remain dependent on the identification of an appropriate national law cause of action.[61] A similar exercise is also being undertaken in relation to the action for damages against private individuals.[62]

In a similar vein, the question of identifying the comparable domestic law action has been playing out in the field of sex discrimination, a field in which the requirement of an adequate remedy has long been established. On the return of *Preston* from the Court of Justice, the House of Lords was required, inter alia, to identify the domestic law action comparable to a claim of sex discrimination under Article 141 EC for the purpose of assessing the equivalence of the six month limitation rule under Section 2(4) of the Equal Pay Act 1970, which governed the claimants' claims.[63] The Court had in this respect, in line with its decision in *Levez*,[64] rejected as a comparable domestic law action, a claim under the 1970 Act itself.[65] In *Levez*, it had observed that the Equal Pay Act 1970 was the domestic legislation which gave effect to the Community principle of non-discrimination on grounds of sex in relation to pay, as enshrined in Article 141 EC and the Equal Pay Directive. As such the fact that identical time limits applied to both claims, one relying on a right conferred by Community law and the other a right acquired under domestic law, was not enough to ensure compliance with the principle of equivalence, since one and the same action was involved.[66]

The key, according to the Court, was to identify an action that is similar as to its 'purpose, cause of action and essential characteristics'. The potential breadth of this inquiry was indicated by AG Leger, who reiterated his view given in *Levez* that neither the Sex Discrimination Act 1975 nor the Race Relations Act 1976 could usefully be compared to Article 141. Over and above the identity of the Community and domestic law actions in the case of sex discrimination, he further stated, '[s]uch an approach would savour of an approach in which the problem of discrimination—whether based on sex or race—remains the central issue.'

---

[60] The Court stated in *Brasserie du Pêcheur/Factortame*, that national law may not make liability in damages dependent on proof of fault (whether intentional or negligent) to the extent that such a requirement is more restrictive than the concept of sufficiently serious breach, above n 7 at paras 75–80. See further the approach of the Court in Case C-410/98 *Metallgesellschaft & Hoechst v. Inland Revenue* [2001] ECR I-1727.

[61] English law has now settled on the tort of breach of statutory duty as the appropriate domestic law vehicle: *R v. Secretary of State for Transport, ex parte Factortame (No 5)* [1999] 3 WLR 1062.

[62] See judgment of Park J. of 26 June 2003, in *Courage v Crehan* [2003] EWHC 1510 (Ch), also *Garden Cottage Foods v. Milk Marketing Board* [1984] AC 130.

[63] *Preston*, n 50 above. The claimants who were part-time workers alleged that their exclusion from membership of an occupational pension scheme was contrary to Article 141 EC.

[64] Case C-326/96, *Levez v. TH Jennings (Harlow Pools) Ltd.* [1998] ECR I-7835.

[65] Above, n 50.

[66] The Court treated as irrelevant the fact that the Equal Pay Act 1970 was enacted prior to the UK's accession to the Community.

Applying the criteria set out by the Court in *Levez*, the House of Lords held that a claim for breach of contract may be the appropriate domestic law comparison to the claim in question. In this respect, Lord Slynn reasoned:

> The essential matter here is that moneys have not been paid to the trustees of a pension fund to purchase pension rights on eventual retirement or on reaching the prescribed age. A successful claim under article 119 obtains retroactively full access to the scheme so that the necessary contributions to obtain the appropriate pension rights for that individual have to be paid. A claim in contract would be for damages for the failure to pay those sums to the trustees leading to a total or in some cases a partial loss of the pension rights. In form they are plainly different but in substance the eventual benefit to the employee is sufficiently similar for present purposes. To adopt the words of the Court of Justice . . . the 'right of action available under domestic law is a domestic action similar to proceedings to give effect to the rights conferred by article 119 of the Treaty . . .' This is so whether the contractual term is express, implied or imposed by statute.[67]

However, and again drawing from the judgment of the Court in *Levez*, the House of Lords ruled that in any event the differences between an action under the Equal Pay Act and one for breach of contract, the six month time limit did not offend the principle of equivalence.[68] The approach adopted by Lord Slynn in the identification of a comparable action in particular illustrates the somewhat transcendental nature of the analysis to be adopted by the national court, which is required to sit somewhere above the Community and national legal orders in order to fix on, where possible, the appropriate comparison. The potential for difficulty and uncertainty in the application of the equivalence principle is evident. However the development marked by this case is to be welcome as it provides a further means of entrenching the protection of Community law rights within the mainstream of national legal systems. Surely a valiant development in the absence of legislative procedural harmonisation?

---

[67] Above, n 50, at para 22.

[68] There are . . . factors to be set against the difference in the limitation periods. As has already been seen the claim under a contract can only go back six years from the date of the claim whereas a claim brought within six months of the termination of employment can go back to the beginning of employment . . . Moreover the claimant can wait until the employment is over, thus avoiding the possibility of friction with the employer if proceedings to protect her position are brought within the period of employment, as will be necessary since the six-year limitation runs from the accrual of a completed cause of action. It is in my view also relevant to have regard to the lower costs involved in the claim before an Employment Tribunal and if proceedings finish there the shorter time-scale involved. The period of six-months itself is not an unreasonable short period for a claim to be referred to an Employment Tribunal. The informality of the proceedings is also a relevant factor. I am not satisfied that in these cases it can be said that the rules of procedure for a claim under section 2(4) does not breach the principle of equivalence.' (*per* Lord Slynn, at paras 30-31, above n).

iv) Some remaining 'gaps'

A *uniform* system of remedies and procedures applicable across all Member States is clearly not yet a reality. Indeed where the principle of equivalence has a role to play, the issue will be one of non-discrimination by reference to the comparable national law action.[69] Nonetheless, seen from the perspective of an individual litigant, with a foot in both his own national and Community legal orders, the principle of equivalence may help bring about a more *complete* or coherent system of remedies and procedures.[70]

Within this framework there remains scope for the further deployment of the effectiveness requirement. Indeed, as independent requirements, the principle of effectiveness may, in a given case, take a litigant further than the equivalence principle, and vice versa. The relationship between equivalence and effectiveness can perhaps be (loosely) compared to the twin considerations of discrimination and market access which characterise the debate in the free movement of goods arena. How far considerations of effectiveness (or market access) are applied, in the absence of discrimination, to further the development of Community law will depend on a number of policy factors.

At present, difficulties of course remain for the individual litigant: time limits per se, being a facet of legal certainty, are not precluded by the principle of effectiveness of protection,[71] and further may begin to run, when perhaps through the failure of Member State to implement in time, an individual litigant may remain ignorant of his cause of action.[72] Questions of degree also enter into the equation: time limits on the retroactivity of a claim which limit but not preclude altogether a remedy may also slip under the net,[73] as may limits on the amount of compensation payable.[74] The scope for a nuanced application of the effectiveness principle, depending on the nature of the right at issue, may be one direction that the Court may pursue further.[75]

---

[69] Where 'similar' domestic law actions are identified within the mainstream of national legal systems, there is perhaps more possibility of a certain rapprochement between the procedural rules in place across the Member States.

[70] The absence of legislative harmonisation in this field may be explained in part by the desire to avoid the inevitable instances of reverse discrimination that would arise in the case of harmonised rules of procedure applying to actions based on Community law rights.

[71] See, for example, Case C-126/97 *Eco Swiss China Time Ltd.* v. *Benetton International NV* [1999] ECR I-3055.

[72] The decision in Case C-208/90 *Emmott* v. *Minister for Social Welfare* [1991] ECR I-4269, where the Court held that the an action based on an unimplemented Directive would not begin to run until the date of implementation by the Member State is now seen as confined to the particular facts of that case. See, for instance, Case C-410/92 *Johnson* v. *Chief Adjudication Officer* [1994] ECR I-5483, para 26.

[73] See for example, Case C-338/91 *Steenhorst-Neerings* [1993] ECR I-5475, Case 246/96, above at n 51, and *Preston*, above at n 50 (in relation to the s 2(5) of the Equal Pay Act 1970).

[74] Case C-66/95 *R* v. *Secretary of State for Social Security, ex parte Sutton* [1997] ECR I-2163.

[75] See for example, Case C-240-244/98 *Océano Grupo Editorial* [2000] ECR I-4491 and Case C-126/97, above at n 71.

Seen from this perspective, there is a certain logic to this complex and seemingly contradictory area of law. Whilst falling short of a uniform system of remedies (an objective which may be hard to realise in the absence of legislative harmonisation not only of national procedural rules but of private law itself), the developments have by and large represented positive steps towards the creation of a complete system of remedies. The requirement of effectiveness has focused not solely on a given national procedural rule, but has also brought under its gaze the role of national courts in the enforcement of Community law. Combined then with the principle of equivalence and its newer more extended role, the Court has managed to afford a more structured arena for the private enforcement of Community law rights.

3. CONCLUSION

This article has attempted to show the way in which the enforcement of individual rights fits into the overall inter-governmental structure of the Treaty. Often, the issue of private enforcement is overlooked during the legislative process where attention is diverted by squabbles over institutional competences, Member State autonomy and political compromise. Instead, the Community and national courts play a vital role in ensuring the protection of individual rights. It is often left to the Court of Justice to flesh out the content of Community rights and the mechanics for their enforcement through judge-made principles. In turn, the Court of Justice, having laid down general principles governing the right to an effective remedy is devolving responsibility for effective protection to the national courts, pursuant to their domestic system of remedies.

The doctrines of direct effect, Member State liability and the remedial principles of equivalence and effectiveness have contributed to the effectiveness of the Community system of legal remedies and procedures. However, the system is by no means complete. The Treaty constraints and the limits of the Court's powers of judicial interpretation have left gaping holes, particularly regarding standing and horizontal direct effect. Notwithstanding the Court's development of fundamental procedural principles, the absence of legislative harmonisation inevitably bears its marks. Although the system dictates procedures, there is a huge difference between mere access to a court and the guarantee of adequate and effective redress for a breach of Community rights. It is time to concentrate on completing the system of *effective* remedies.

The achievement in practice of a complete system of legal remedies and procedures will depend on several shifts in attitude by both the Community institutions and domestic courts:

First, provisions that are intended to have horizontal effect will have to be drafted with individual rights in mind. The existence, scope and content of the right/obligation will have to be set out in clear unqualified language.⁷⁶ Secondly, detailed notification and enforcement mechanisms will have to be provided, if necessary through harmonisation.⁷⁷ Another option would be for the increased use of Regulations, rather than Directives, in complex areas—however this would represent a step back from mutual co-ordination to more detailed harmonisation and may upset Member State autonomy.

Failing that, there should be effective sanctions under the Article 226 infringement procedure to penalise and deter Member States' failure to implement Directives or to set up enforcement mechanisms for Regulations;

Thirdly, as the enforcement of private rights rests largely with national courts, their judicial procedures and remedies will have to evolve to keep pace with the demands of commercial litigation. The litigation landscape may have to expand to include arbitration, ADR and class actions.

If national court procedures are defective and cannot be rectified at domestic level, there must be an effective means of recourse to correct any denial of justice. The *Köbler* concept may provide a means for judge-made procedural harmonisation at the risk of the Article 234 EC reference procedure becoming clogged with tattletale. Even then, it does not guarantee an effective means for challenging Community legislation.

In relation to national procedural rules, national courts should not be deterred from undertaking the somewhat novel comparative exercise involved in identifying a comparable domestic law action as illustrated by the case of *Preston*. Such exercises will strengthen the interpenetration of the national and Community legal orders, which, in the absence of procedural harmonisation, can only be seen as a laudable development towards the creation of a complete system of remedies.

Against the developments outlined in this paper, the principle of effectiveness should be viewed as a useful valve in controlling and carefully extending the reach of Community law, taking into account the nature of the Community law right at stake.

Most importantly, there has to be an effective working relationship between national courts and the Court of Justice, with increased co-operation and dialogue to make the 'judicial veil' under Art 234 EC more transparent.⁷⁸ If citizens

---

⁷⁶ This is particularly the case for some of the rights set out in the Charter of Fundamental Rights—see the difficulties experienced by the Court in interpreting Article 18 EC (citizenship) due to the legislative caveats imposed by the Treaty wording.

⁷⁷ The language used by the Court in its remedies jurisprudence has borne fruit in certain fields. For instance, article 9 of the 2001 TUPE directive obliges Member States to introduce 'such measures as are necessary to enable all employees and representatives of employees who consider themselves wronged by failure to comply with the obligations arising from this Directive to pursue their claims by judicial process'. In the same way, the Framework Employment Equality Directive requires Member States to 'ensure that judicial and/or administrative procedures, including where they deem it appropriate conciliation procedures, for the enforcement of obligations under this Directive are available to all persons who consider themselves wronged by failure to apply the principle of equal treatment to them, even after the relationship in which the discrimination is alleged to have occurred has ended.'

⁷⁸ This will be especially important with the 2004 accession, where Community judges will be unfamiliar with 10 new legal systems and the new plenary formation will not guarantee the presence of a 'home State' judge to clarify national procedure.

are to have faith in their legal system, it is crucial that **all** Community courts (whether in Luxembourg or Member States) work together to ensure that the principle of effective judicial protection does not just mean access to a court but also a guarantee of adequate redress within a cost-effective timeframe.

23
Article 234: A Few Rough Edges Still

ROBERT LANE

1. INTRODUCTION

READERS OF a collection of essays dedicated to David Edward will require no persuasion of the importance, and achievement, of the preliminary ruling procedure of Article 234. It is through Article 234 that the great 'constitutional' cases came before the Court—first and foremost the triumvirate of cases which established the direct effect of Community law,[1] the primacy of Community law[2] and a remedy in reparation when deprived of a Community law right.[3] It is Article 234, in tandem with the direct effect created through the medium of Article 234, which makes the national judge a Community judge and all national courts Community courts of first instance: by 'injecting' the Court of Justice into national proceedings it makes the meanest, as well as the highest, court in the land, in effect, a constitutional court. And it is through Article 234 that the Court has required, and enabled, the national judge to cast off burdens of national design, to ignore his or her own judicial code,[4] and even constitutional bars to the court's jurisdiction,[5] if necessary to give effect to a Community law right. This 'constitutionalisation' of a Community judiciary, and the place of the Court of Justice within it, was always going to be a gamble, but it is one which has met with astonishing success. Maybe it is precisely because it allows the *Pretore di Nessun Posto* to become a constitutional judge for a day that so many have embraced it. But except for an extended spat with the French *Conseil d'Etat*,[6] now resolved, it has also won the consistent acquiescence and support of the high courts. Article 234 is, in short, a success story.

---

[1] Case 26/62 *NV Algemene Transport- en Expeditie Onderneming van Gend en Loos* v. *Nederlandse Administratie der Belastingen* [1963] ECR 1.
[2] Case 6/64 *Costa* v. *ENEL* [1964] ECR 585.
[3] Joined Cases C–6 & 9/90 *Francovich & Bonifaci* v. *Italy* [1991] ECR I–5357; Joined Cases C–46 & 48/93 *Brasserie du Pêcheur SA* v. *Germany* and *R* v. *Secretary of State for Transport, ex parte Factortame and ors* [1996] ECR I–1029.
[4] Case 106/77 *Amministrazione delle Finanze dello Stato* v. *Simmenthal SpA* [1978] ECR 629.
[5] Case C–213/89 *R.* v. *Secretary of State for Transport, ex parte Factortame Ltd and ors* [1990] ECR I–2433; Case C–462/99 *Connect Austria Gesellschaft für Telekommunikation GmbH* v. *Telekom-Control-Kommission*, judgment of 22 May 2003, not yet reported.
[6] On the matter of the *Conseil d'Etat* refusing to recognise the direct effect of directives (CE, 22 décembre 1978 (*Ministre de l'Intérieur c./ Cohn-Bendit*) Rec p. 524) and so to refer questions on

But it is now a victim of that very success. The Court of Justice is reeling under the weight of its workload, the major part of which is now Article 234 references. In the early years it positively encouraged and welcomed references: a great many national judges will recall enjoying the ample hospitality of the Court, an exercise in proselytisation a purpose of which was to attune them to its existence and purpose, and to drum up business. The exercise is no longer necessary: the work has multiplied severalfold and continues to multiply, with new Treaties (appearing now with alarming frequency), new legislation, and, within a year, references from the courts of ten more member states.

It is appropriate to visit Article 234 once again in this volume, for a number of reasons. There is a vast literature on the procedure,[7] to which David himself has recently added.[8] He also hails from that jurisdiction which, by any measure, has made least use of it, Scottish courts having lodged a very niggardly ten references in over 30 years;[9] compare the 223 (and counting) references from Austrian courts since accession in 1995. This may of course simply serve as testament to the excellence of the Scottish judiciary, requiring the assistance of Luxembourg only very sparingly; but it does now hint at questions of effective judicial protection in Scotland. Third, a number of outstanding issues have come to light in recent cases, in which the Court is giving off mixed signals. It is proposed to look at two of them, the admissibility of Article 234 references and the blurring of the jurisdiction of the Court of Justice; it would be well if they could be clarified, or at least understood, before the Union absorbs (the courts

the matter to the Court of Justice. There was a similar rebellion from the German *Bundesfinanzhof* (BFH, 16. Juli 1981 (6. *Mehrwertsteuer Richtlinie*), BFHE 133, 470), but it was even more short-lived.

[7] See most recently, in English, the encyclopaedic and authoritative D Anderson and M Demetriou, *References to the European Court* 2nd edn. (London, Sweet & Maxwell, 2002). For issues discussed in this essay see C Barnard and E Sharpston, 'The Changing Face of Article 177 References' (1997) 34 *Common Market Law Review* 1113.

[8] DAO Edward, 'Reform of the Article 234 Procedure: The Limits of the Possible', in D O'Keeffe (ed.), *Judicial Review in European Union Law: Liber Amicorum in Honour of Lord Slynn of Hadley* (The Hague, Kluwer, 2000).

[9] Of the ten, one (from the Court of Session on the Brussels Convention) was promptly recalled: Case C–126/96 *Marie Brizard & Roger International SA v. Wm Grant and Sons (International) and anor*; removed from the Register by Order of 25 February 1997. Of the remaining nine:

—One was from the House of Lords: Case C–394/96 *Brown v. Rentokil Ltd* [1998] ECR I–4185. Another House of Lords case (*Litster v. Forth Dry Dock Ltd* 1989 SC 96) ought probably to have been referred by virtue of a duty to do so under Art. 234(3), but was not; doubtless their Lordships found David's submissions (acting for the winning side) to have rendered the matter *acte clair*.

—Three were from the High Court of Justiciary: Case 24/83 *Gewiese & Mehlich v. MacKenzie (PF Stornoway)* [1984] ECR 817; Case 79/86 *Hamilton (PF Dunfermline) v. Whitelock* [1987] ECR 2363; Case 370/88 *Walkingshaw (PF Stranraer) v. Marshall* [1990] I–4071;

—Three were from the Court of Session: Case 197/86 *Brown v. Secretary of State for Scotland* [1988] ECR 3205; Joined Cases C–20 & 64/00 *Booker Aquaculture Ltd and Hydro Seafoods GSP Ltd v. The Scottish Ministers*, judgment of 10 July 2003, not yet reported; and

—Two were from the sheriff court: Joined Cases C–251 & 252/90 *Wither (PF Elgin) v. Cowie & Wood* [1992] ECR I–2873.

Closer examination will reveal that, of the nine cases which proceeded to judgment, six were about fish.

of) ten new member states and we enter a new phase of judicial geometry created by the Treaty of Nice. It should become apparent that the thrust of reform, or development, is directed less at discouraging the use of Article 234 than at making that use more efficient.

2. ADMISSIBILITY OF REFERENCES

The success of the Article 234 procedure has led to some efforts to stem the tide. National courts of last instance were absolved of the (apparently absolute) duty of Article 234(3) to refer questions in *CILFIT*,[10] but arguably only in circumstances so burdensome that it has produced the opposite effect. Swings and roundabouts, the Court at the same time claims sole jurisdiction to invalidate (or annul) an act of a Community institution;[11] this is perfectly sound, and would result in significant chaos had the Court said otherwise, but it means that all actions in which the validity of a Community act is raised before any national court must, if the national court is minded to agree, be referred, unless invalidated (or annulled) by the Court in other proceedings.[12] The Rules of Procedure allow for a reference on a question which is identical to one upon which the Court has already ruled or which admits of no reasonable doubt to be disposed of by reasoned order[13] (which can be rendered much more speedily than a formal judgment), and this is happening with increasing frequency. The accelerated procedure was introduced in 2000, to be used where circumstances require a judgment as 'a matter of exceptional urgency';[14] but this serves only to allow a case to jump the queue. The Court now habitually draws the attention of a referring national court to existing or intervening case law and invites it to consider whether it wishes to maintain the reference in light of it; although compliance with the invitation may prove costly.[15]

More substantial reform has been urged by the Court *extra cathedra*: the 'Reflection Group' of past and present judges has argued that the number of references could and should be reduced by the adoption of a number of reforms, primarily a formal removal of the obligation of courts of last instance to refer under Article 234(3) and some additional means of discouraging references

---

[10] Case 283/81 *Srl CILFIT and anor* v. *Ministero della Sanità* [1982] ECR 3415.
[11] Case 314/85 *Foto-Frost* v. *Hauptzollamt Lübeck-Ost* [1987] ECR 4199.
[12] Case 66/80 *SpA International Chemical Corporation* v. *Amministrazione delle Finanze dello Stato* [1981] ECR 1191.
[13] Rules of Procedure of the Court of Justice, Art. 104(3).
[14] *Ibid.*, Art. 104a. See e.g. Case C–189/01 *Jippes* v. *Minister van Landbouw, Natuurbeheer en Visserij* [2001] ECR I–5689, the exceptional urgency being a function of measures to combat the spread of foot and mouth disease; the case took a remarkable 77 days from arrival at the Registry to judgment.
[15] See Case C–224/01 *Köbler* v. *Republik Österreich*, pending; Opinion of A-G Léger delivered 8 April 2003, in which the Austrian *Verwaltungsgerichtshof* withdrew a reference at the invitation of the Court of Justice, disposed of the case as it saw fit, and, it is now argued (and A-G Léger agrees), left Austria liable in damages for getting it badly wrong.

which are 'unimportant' in Community law terms or to which the answer is relatively clear.[16] Both Advocates-General[17] and academic writers[18] have argued for the adoption of some form of 'docket control' by which the number of references could be limited. But that way of course lies some peril: who can say that a case before a *giudice conciliatore* involving a failure to pay a 1,925 *lire* electricity bill[19] would have made it to a Court which discourages questions on 'unimportant' matters? In any event, the only action which has been taken is one to be approached with great circumspection: jurisdiction in Article 234 references—prior to the Treaty of Nice the only head of the Court's jurisdiction reserved by the Treaty to the Court of Justice[20]—may now be conferred upon the Court of First Instance (or the 'High Court', if M. Giscard gets his way)[21] in specific areas (yet) to be laid down by the Statute of the Court.[22]

One other way in which the Court may dissuade references, or, alternatively, seek to make them better, is by refusing to hear them. And this has given rise to some debate. The premiss of Article 234 is straightforward: there must be a dispute in an action raised before a national court or tribunal in which a decision upon the issue(s) of Community law raised is 'necessary' to enable the national court to determine the dispute. That question may be referred to the Court of Justice, or must be referred if (a) the proceedings take place before a court of final instance,[23] or (b) the question is one requiring invalidation of an act of a Community institution, so falling within the exclusive jurisdiction of the Court.[24] Since the very early years[25] the Court has emphasised that it has no jurisdiction with respect to facts, and that the decision to refer (so implicitly the determination of whether there is a 'necessary' question of Community law to answer), the timing of the reference, the formulation of the question(s), and of course the ultimate application of the ruling to the resolution of the dispute in the 'main proceedings', are matters exclusively for the national court. Hence, in *Costa* v. *ENEL*:

---

[16] *The Future of the Judicial System of the European Union (Proposals and Reflections)*, submitted to the Council on 10 May 1999.

[17] See the opinion of A-G Jacobs in Case C–338/95 *Wiener SI GmbH* v. *Hauptzollamt Emmerich* [1997] ECR I–6495.

[18] See e.g. H Rasmussen, "Issues of Admissibility and Justiciability in EC Judicial Adjudication of Federalism Disputes under Article 177 EEC", in HG Schermers *et al.* (eds.), *Article 177 EEC: Experiences and Problems* (Amsterdam, North-Holland, 1987).

[19] Being the subject matter in Case 6/64 *Costa* v. *ENEL* [1964] ECR 585.

[20] EC Treaty, Art. 225(1) (pre-Nice).

[21] Draft Treaty establishing a Constitution for Europe, Art. I–28.

[22] EC Treaty, Art. 225(3).

[23] EC Treaty, Art. 234(3); subject to the dispensation considered by the Court in Case 283/81 *Srl CILFIT and anor* v. *Ministero della Sanità* [1982] ECR 3415. As to what constitutes a court of final instance, see Case 6/64 *Costa* v. *ENEL* [1964] ECR 585; Case C–99/00 *Criminal proceedings against Kenny Roland Lyckeskog* [2002] ECR I–4839.

[24] Case 314/85 *Foto-Frost* v. *Hauptzollamt Lübeck-Ost* [1987] ECR 4199.

[25] See e.g. Case 26/62 *NV Algemene Transport- en Expeditie Onderneming van Gend en Loos* v. *Nederlandse Administratie der Belastingen* [1963] ECR 1; Joined Cases 28–30/62 *da Costa en Schaake NV and ors* v. *Nederlandse Belastingsadministratie* [1963] ECR 31.

Since Article 177 . . . is based upon a clear separation of functions between national courts and the Court of Justice, it cannot empower the latter either to investigate the facts of the case or to criticize the grounds and purpose of the request for interpretation.[26]

Subsequently,

Its [the national court's] assessment must be respected even if, as in this case, it is difficult to see how the answers which the Court is asked to give can influence the decision in the main proceedings.[27]

Dicta to this effect have hardened into a standard formulation—for example, most recently:

[I]t should be remembered that, in proceedings under Article 234 EC, which is based on a clear separation of functions between the national courts and the Court of Justice, any assessment of the facts in the case is a matter for the national court. Similarly, it is solely for the national court before which the dispute has been brought, and which must assume responsibility for the subsequent judicial decision, to determine in the light of the particular circumstances of the case both the need for the preliminary ruling in order to enable it to deliver judgment and the relevance of the questions which it submits to the Court. Consequently, where the questions submitted by the national court concern the interpretation of Community law, the Court of Justice is, in principle, bound to give a ruling[28]

and have been employed repeatedly and consistently.

But no longer universally. Fissures have begun to appear, the veil of the reference put forward by the national court pierced. In a number of cases—not many, but on a slow increase—the Court now refuses jurisdiction to answer a question. The result, on one view, is that the 'spirit' of Article 234 is 'under attack'.[29] If so, it is appropriate to ask if the Court is attacking Article 234 capriciously; and therefore to attempt to classify the grounds upon which it may (or must) refuse jurisdiction, or otherwise refuse, to respond to a reference.

The referring court is not a 'court or tribunal of a member state'

There is an increasingly complex body of case law on what constitutes a 'court or tribunal' for purposes of Article 234.[30] It may be desirable to apply the relevant

---

[26] Case 6/64 [1964] ECR 585, at 593.
[27] Joined Cases 98, 162 & 258/85 *Bertini and ors v. Regione Lazio and anor* [1986] ECR 1885, at para. 8.
[28] Case C–326/00 *Idryma Koinonikon Asfaliseon v. Ioannidis*, judgment of 25 February 2003, not yet reported, at para. 27.
[29] D O'Keeffe, 'Is the Spirit of Article 177 under Attack? Preliminary References and Admissibility' (1998) 23 *European Law Review* 509.
[30] See the extensive discussion of A-G Ruiz-Jarabo Colomer in Case C–17/00 *de Coster v. Collège des Bourgmestres et Echevins de Watermael-Boitsfort* [2001] ECR I–9445, in which he urged a significant shift in the Court's approach, which plea fell upon deaf ears.

tests, as regards the accession member states, with a degree of suppleness lest the 'courts' there which betray hybrid judicial/administrative characteristics (as was the case in Finland) be frightened off using the procedure. It is established that the Court of Justice cannot question the competency of the action in the main proceedings or whether the national court is improperly constituted or otherwise acting outwith its jurisdiction as a matter of national law.[31] The general question will acquire a new complexity with the 'variable judicial geometry' introduced by the Treaty of Amsterdam whereby the 'normal rules' of Article 234 have been set aside for references relating to matters falling within (the new) Title IV of the EC Treaty and those made under Article 35 of the Treaty on European Union: there are likely to be instances of references from what is clearly a court or tribunal of a member state, but not one competent to invoke Article 234 in the particular context.[32]

The question of whether the referring court or tribunal is one 'of a member state' has, hitherto, not troubled the Court. Whilst it must find a reference from a court outwith the Community to be inadmissible, even if that court is applying Community law and may reasonably require advice upon its interpretation or validity,[33] it has extended Article 234 to be available to courts or tribunals in other countries or territories in which the Treaty applies, so has admitting references from French Polynesia,[34] the Isle of Man[35] and Jersey.[36] Although not strictly a court of 'a member state', a reference from the Benelux Court of Justice is admissible.[37]

The matter falls outwith the jurisdiction of the Court of Justice

This question may arise in a number of ways.

—By virtue of its phrasing of the question may invite the Court to interpret, or rule upon the validity of, a provision of national law, which it has no jurisdiction to do in Article 234 proceedings. But it has long been the art of the Court to re-cast maladroit questions so as to bring them within its juris-

---

[31] Case 65/81 *Reina & Reina* v. *Landeskreditbank Baden-Württemberg* [1982] ECR 33; Case C–116/00 *Criminal proceedings against Claude Laguillaumie* [2000] ECR I–4979.

[32] Case C–24/02 *Marseille Fret SA* v. *Seatrano Shipping Co Ltd* [2002] ECR I–3383 (request for a ruling on the interpretation of the Brussels Convention from a court incompetent to seek it).

[33] See discussion in Joined Cases T–377, 379 & 380/00 & 260 & 272/01 *Philip Morris International Inc and ors* v. *Commission*, judgment of 15 January 2003, not yet reported.

[34] Cases C–100 & 101/89 *Kaefer & Procacci* v. *French State* [1990] ECR I–4647; Case C–260/90 *Leplat* v. *Territory of French Polynesia* [1992] ECR I–643.

[35] Case C–355/89 *Department of Health and Social Security* v. *Barr & Montrose Holdings Ltd* [1991] ECR I–3479.

[36] Case C–171/96 *Pereira Roque* v. *HE The Lieutenant Governor of Jersey* [1998] ECR I–4607; Case C–293/02 *Jersey Produce Marketing Organisation* v. *The States of Jersey*, pending.

[37] Case C–337/95 *Parfums Christian Dior SA and anor* v. *Evora BV* [1997] ECR I–6013.

diction.³⁸ This is seen to be unobjectionable, provided the question is not re-cast into one which is not there.³⁹

—The question referred is not one of Community law: absent a Community element requiring to be resolved, the Court has nothing to say. If the question is genuinely one of interpretation or validity of national law with no Community law element, the Court will, and must, refuse jurisdiction to answer it.⁴⁰ An exception is a dispute in the main proceedings involving solely national law, but national law which expressly incorporates, or refers to, Community provisions, in which case the Court may furnish a ruling, if requested, not on the national law but on the Community provisions relevant to its interpretation.⁴¹ The general issue of 'Community element' will be considered in greater detail below.

—The dispute does not fall within the scope *ratione materiae*⁴² or *ratione temporis*⁴³ of Community law.

—the Court is invited to interpret a provision of an instrument which is not justiciable⁴⁴ or which, whilst normally justiciable, is to be applied in a context over which the Court is afforded no jurisdiction.⁴⁵

—the question referred is palpably off the wall, without the remotest discernable tangency to Community law, or to logic.⁴⁶

The question is premature

It is a function of the national court's exclusive jurisdiction to determine the necessity and timing of a reference. So, a reference as to the validity of a

---

³⁸ Eg Case 6/64 *Costa* v. *ENEL* [1964] ECR 585; Case 14/86 *Pretore di Salò* v. *Persons Unknown* [1987] ECR 2545.
³⁹ See discussion *infra*.
⁴⁰ Case C–346/94 *City of Glasgow District Council* v. *Kleinwort Benson* [1995] ECR I–615; Case C–30/95 *Max Mara Fashion Group Srl* v. *Ufficio del Registro di Reggio Emilia* [1995] ECR I–5083.
⁴¹ Case 297/88 & 197/89 *Dzodzi* v. *Belgium* [1990] ECR I–3763; Case C–28/95 *Leur-Bloem* v *Inspecteur der Belastingdienst/Ondernemingen Amsterdam 2* [1997] ECR I–4161; Case C–130/95 *Giloy* v. *Hauptzollamt Frankfurt am Main-Ost* [1997] ECR I–4291; Case C–306/99 *Banque Internationale pour l'Afrique Occidentale SA* v. *Finanzamt für Großunternehmen in Hamburg*, judgment of 7 January 2003, not yet reported.
⁴² Case C–299/95 *Kremzow* v. *Austria* [1997] ECR I–2629; Case C–355/97 *Landesgrundverkehrsreferent der Tiroler Landesregierung* v. *Beck Liegenschaftsverwaltungsgesellschaft mbH and anor* [1999] ECR I–4977, *per* A-G La Pergola at paras. 7–11 of his opinion.
⁴³ Case C–355/97 *Beck, ibid., per* A-G La Pergola at para. 7 of his opinion.
⁴⁴ Case 93/78 *Mattheus* v. *Doego Fruchtimport und Tiefkülkost eG* [1978] ECR 2203; Case C–253/94P *Roujansky* v. *Council* [1995] ECR I–7; Case C–167/94 *Criminal proceedings against Juan Carlos Grau Gomis and ors* [1995] ECR I–1023. The Court may have declined jurisdiction in *Mattheus* v. *Doego* at least in some measure because of the political sensitivity adhering to it; see Rasmussen, cited at n. 18 *supra*.
⁴⁵ Case C–321/97 *Andersson & Wåkerås-Andersson* v. *Svenska Staten* [1999] ECR I–3551.
⁴⁶ See eg Case 105/79 *Preliminary Ruling by the Acting Judge at the Tribunal d'Instance, Hayange (No. 1)* [1979] ECR 2257; Case 68/80 *Preliminary Ruling by the Acting Judge at the Tribunal d'Instance, Hayange (No. 2)* [1980] ECR 771; Joined Cases C–95 & 96/96 *URSSAF des Bouches-du-Rhône* v. *Clinique Florens SA*, Order of 12 June 1996, unreported.

Community act may be made even if it has yet to produce legal effects (a regulation which is not yet in force,[47] or a directive the time limit for implementation having not yet passed and no national legislation, even in draft, having been adopted[48]) so long as there is a genuine dispute in which the question of validity is competently raised. But a request for an interpretative ruling upon a directive in the absence of implementing measures and prior to the final date for implementation is premature and so inadmissible.[49]

The question referred is too vague

This is related to other grounds of inadmissibility considered below but can be seen as logically distinct: the question may well betray a Community law context and point to be determined, but it is for the national court to make it reasonably clear what it is and why it is so; with the Court of Justice no longer scrabbling for work, it has no duty to divine a question which may be, but is not clearly, there.[50]

The reference amounts to an abuse of process

A reference amounts to an abuse of process if the questions are hypothetical or disclose no real legal dispute. This, determined in 1980 in *Foglia* v. *Novello*,[51] was the first instance in which the Court directly and incontrovertibly declined jurisdiction. So stunned was the referring national court that it re-referred a question, asking whether the Court had not misapprehended its jurisdiction, and duty, under Article 234. The Court replied that it had not:[52] its duty was to assist in the administration of justice, not to resolve (non-)disputes orchestrated by the parties in order to procure from the Court its view on a matter upon which they were agreed—in other words, to deliver 'advisory opinions'. This, said the Court, was not trespassing upon the jurisdiction of the national court, rather it was preventing the application of Article 234 to purposes other than that for which it was intended.

---

[47] Case C–306/93 *SMW Winzersekt GmbH* v. *Land Rheinland-Pfalz* [1994] ECR I–5555; Joined Cases C–27 & 122/00 *R* v. *Secretary of State for the Environment, Transport and the Regions*, ex parte *Omega Air Ltd and ors* [2002] ECR I–2569.
[48] Case C–74/99 *R* v. *Secretary of State for Health and ors*, ex parte *Imperial Tobacco and ors* [2000] ECR I–8599, per A-G Fennelly at 8436–8439; Case C–491/01 *R.* v. *Secretary of State for Health*, ex parte *British American Tobacco (Investments) Ltd and anor* [2002] ECR I–11453.
[49] Case C–165/98 *Criminal proceedings against André Mazzoleni & Inter Surveillance Assistance* [2001] ECR I–7823.
[50] See e.g. Case C–157/92 *Pretore di Genova* v. *Banchero* ('*Banchero I*') [1993] ECR I–1085; Case C–387/93 *Criminal proceedings against Giorgio Domingo Banchero* ('*Banchero II*') [1995] ECR I–4663; Case C–116/00 *Criminal proceedings against Claude Laguillaumie* [2000] ECR I–4979.
[51] Case 104/79 *Foglia* v. *Novello* (No 1) [1980] ECR 745.
[52] Case 244/80 *Foglia* v. *Novello* (No 2) [1981] ECR 3045.

Foglia met with significant criticism.⁵³ It is widely thought that the view of the Court was coloured by questions referred from a court of one member state (Italy) on the validity of the law of another member state (France), although that surely goes too to the jurisdiction of the national court. It wasn't deployed again for some ten years, until the redoubtable Mr Meilicke bought his one share in a German company in order to contrive a reference (the text of the questions alone spanning eight pages in the ECR) to test his hobby horse (one upon which he had written a book) on capitalisation in German company law. The Court declined to play the game: it was 'not appropriate' to answer the questions submitted by the national court.⁵⁴ Since *Meilicke* the Court has rebuffed references in a number of similar circumstances.⁵⁵

An Article 234 reference is also an abuse of process if a party which had *clear* title and interest to raise annulment proceedings against a Community act under Article 230, but failed to do so, subsequently challenges its validity in national proceedings, and a reference made to assist in this purpose will be inadmissible.⁵⁶ This will of course require the Court to delve into the main proceedings in order to identify the party putting forward the plea.

The questions asked bear no relation to the subject matter of the dispute

Whilst it is for the national court to identify the issues and frame the questions, the Court of Justice has assumed jurisdiction to test the relevance of those questions to the dispute at issue in the main proceedings, and to interfere with the assessment of the national court there is insufficient tangency between the two.⁵⁷ The reference will be rejected 'only if it is quite obvious' that the link is not there.⁵⁸ The Court of Justice may now call upon he referring court to explain why it requires an answer to the questions referred in order to resolve the dispute before it,⁵⁹ but apprehends no duty to do so.

---

⁵³ E.g., G Bebr, 'The Existence of a Genuine Dispute: An Indispensable Precondition for the Jurisdiction of the Court of Justice under Article 177 EEC Treaty' (1980) 17 *Common Market Law Review* 525.
⁵⁴ Case C–83/91 *Meilicke v. ADV/ORGA AG* [1992] ECR I–4871.
⁵⁵ Case C–111/94 *Job Centre Coop. arl* [1995] ECR I–3361; Case C–86/00 *HSB-Wohnbau GmbH* [2001] ECR I–5353; Case C–153/00 *Criminal proceedings against Paul der Weduwe* [2002] ECR I–11319; Case C–318/00 *Bacardi-Martini SAS and anor v. Newcastle United Football Company Ltd*, judgment of 21 January 2003, not yet reported.
⁵⁶ Case C–188/92 *TWD Textilwerke Deggendorf GmbH v. Germany* [1994] ECR I–833; Case C–178/95 *Wiljo NV v. Belgium* [1997] ECR I–585; Case C–241/01 *National Farmers' Union v. Secrétariat Général du Gouvernement* [2002] ECR I–9079.
⁵⁷ Case 286/88 *Falciola Angelo SpA v. Comune di Pavia* [1990] ECR I–191; Case C–343/90 *Lourenço Dias v Director da Alfândega do Porto* [1992] ECR I–4673; Case C–83/91*Meilicke v. ADVORGA AG* [1992] ECR I–4871; Case C–297/93 *Grau-Hupka v Stadtgemeinde Bremen* [1994] ECR I–5535; Case C–415/93 *Union Royale Belge des Sociétés de Football Association ASBL v. Bosman* [1995] ECR I–4921; Cases C–430 & 431/99 *Inspecteur van de Belastingdienst Douane, Rotterdam v Sea-Land Service Inc & Nedlloyd Lijnen BV* [2002] ECR I–5235; Case C–318/00 *Bacardi-Martini*, above, n 55.
⁵⁸ Case 126/80 *Salonia v. Poidomani and anor* [1981] ECR 1563, at para. 6.
⁵⁹ Rules of Procedure of the Court of Justice, Art. 104(5).

Insufficient context

The Court will reject a reference where the referring national court has failed to provide sufficient information as to the factual and legal background to the case to enable the Court adequately to identify the issues.[60] This has become the most commonplace of grounds for finding a reference inadmissible.

If these are the grounds by which the Court declines to provide a preliminary ruling, they may depart from the spirit of Article 234; but so long as they are widely understood, and applied consistently, a national judge will know where he or she stands. But a major problem is one of inconsistency. For example, *Vaneetveld*[61] was a reference begging to be knocked back for insufficiency of background information. But the Court said, tersely,

> that requirement is less pressing where the questions relate to specific technical points and enable the Court to give a useful reply even where the national court has not given an exhaustive description of the legal and factual situation[62]

and contented itself with the case file forwarded from the national court and the submissions of the parties which

> have given the Court enough information to enable it to interpret the rules of Community law in respect of the situation which is the subject of the main proceedings.[63]

But it provided no guidance, certainly no guidance which would inform another national judge, as to why this was so. Inconsistency is also discernable in a more gentle disposition (or deference?) shown to higher courts: a 1997 reference from the Austrian *Oberster Gerichtshof* offended just about every count of admissibility, Advocate-General La Pergola recommended it be shown the door, yet the Court bent over backwards to answer it.[64] This may be explained in part by a 'honeymoon period' afforded the courts of new(ish) member states; otherwise the irony is that a supreme court such as the *Oberster Gerichtshof* might reasonably be expected to get it better than a lower or provincial judge.

A general pattern can be seen to develop, then out of the blue it seems to get knocked on its head. For example, there has appeared in a number of recent cases, each involving a matter wholly internal to a member state, what might be called, in the context, the '*Angonese* clause'. The judgment in *Angonese*[65] is of

---

[60] Case C–320/90 *Telemarsicabruzzo SpA and ors* v. *Circostel and ors* [1993] ECR I–393; Case C–157/92 *Pretore di Genova* v. *Banchero* ('*Banchero I*') [1993] ECR I–1085; Case C–386/92 *Monin Automobiles—Maison du Deux-Roues* (No 1) [1993] ECR I–2049; Case C–378/93 *La Pyramide SARL* [1994] ECR I–3999; Case C–176/96 *Lehtonen & Castors Canada Dry Namur-Braine ASBL* v. *Fédération Royale Belge des Sociétés de Basket-ball ASBL* [2000] ECR I–2681; Case C–190/02 *Viacom Outdoor Srl* v. *Giotto Immobilier SARL* [2002] ECR I–8289.
[61] Case C–316/93 *Vaneetveld* v. *Le Foyer SA* [1994] ECR I–763.
[62] *Ibid*, at para. 13.
[63] *Ibid*, at para. 14.
[64] Case C–355/97 *Landesgrundverkehrsreferent der Tiroler Landesregierung* v. *Beck Liegenschaftsverwaltungsgesellschaft mbH and anor* [1999] ECR I–4977.
[65] Case C–281/98 *Angonese* v. *Cassa di Risparmio di Bolzano SpA* [2000] ECR I–4139.

course best known for its recognition of the horizontal direct effect of Article 39. But Mr Angonese was in fact an Italian national seeking to invoke a Treaty right in Italy, his adventures in another member state (Austria) having occurred largely prior to Austrian accession and having failed to produce a qualification. His was therefore a situation which was 'wholly internal' to a member state, and so one which, upon the basis of well established (if increasingly contentious) case law, falls outwith the application of Community law. And if it falls outwith the application of Community law, the Court of Justice has no jurisdiction in the matter. Advocate-General Fennelly discussed this point at some length. But the Court did not; it said simply:

> Whether or not the reasoning of the order for a reference ... is well founded, it is far from clear that the interpretation of Community law it seeks has no relation to the actual facts of the case or to the subject-matter of the main action.
> In those circumstances, the question submitted must be answered.[66]

This formula has been reapplied since. In *Guimont*,[67] involving the application of Article 28 to French labelling requirements in the context of the sale of French cheese in a French shop, the Court recognised that

> it is clear from the Court's case-law that such a rule falls under Article 30 of the Treaty only in so far as it applies to situations that are linked to the importation of goods in intra-Community trade[68]

but cited *Angonese* with approval and managed to embellish it, saying

> [a] reference for the preliminary ruling from a national court may be rejected *only if it quite obvious* that the interpretation of Community law sought by the court bears no relation to the actual nature of the case or the subject-matter of the main action.[69]

In *Reisch*[70] it cited both *Angonese* and *Guimont* in their turn, with approval, and answered a question on whether Community rules on the free movement of capital applied to formalities attached to the acquisition by Austrians of heritable property in Austria. And all three were cited in *Salzmann*,[71] in which the Court found it was not 'quite obvious' and 'not evident' that the rules on capital could not apply to the registration of heritable property bought by an Austrian, from an Austrian, in Austria.

This is well and good. It cleaves to the original 'spirit' of Article 234, recognising the authority of the national court to identify the issue of Community law and questioning it only in the most exceptional circumstances. If it is applied

---

[66] *Ibid.*, at paras. 19–20.
[67] Case C–448/98 *Criminal proceedings against Jean-Pierre Guimont* [2000] ECR I–10663.
[68] *Ibid*, at para. 21.
[69] *Ibid*, at para. 22; emphasis added.
[70] Joined Cases C–515 etc/99 *Reisch and ors v. Bürgermeister der Landeshauptstadt Salzburg and ors* [2002] ECR I–2157.
[71] Case C–300/01 *Doris Salzmann*, judgment of 15 May 2003, not yet reported.

consistently, the national judge knows his or her ground. But it is not. *Bacardi-Martini*[72] was a dispute involving a contract with Newcastle United FC for the advertising of alcoholic beverages on the 'display panels' around the touchline at St James' Park. They were all above board in terms of English law, but because a Newcastle-Metz UEFA Cup tie was to be broadcast live by Canal+ in France, Newcastle instructed the relevant display panels to be removed or, in the alternative, that they not appear in the live broadcast (contrary to the terms of the contract, which provided for lingering views of the relevant panels). This was in order to comply with the *Loi Évin* on the prohibition of advertising of alcoholic products in France.[73] Disgruntled, Bacardi-Martini raised proceedings in High Court seeking damages and an injunction. The High Court took the view that it was necessary to consider the compatibility of the *Loi Évin* with the Treaty rules on provision of services (and even the French courts had produced conflicting views on its application to cross-frontier broadcasting of sporting events), and referred two questions to the Court of Justice to that effect.

This was not an *Angonese* case involving the wholly internal rule, rather it was a part *Foglia* point, involving the testing for compatibility with Community law of the law of one member state in a court of another. The Court responded:

> In order that the Court may perform its task in accordance with the Treaty, it is essential for national courts to explain, when the reasons do not emerge beyond any doubt from the file, why they consider that a reply to their questions is necessary to enable them to give judgment.[74]

And it must exercise 'special vigilance'[75] when a national court in one member state considers the law of another. In the result, the High Court having failed to clarify the issues (in response to a request to do so) to the satisfaction of the Court, the reference was declared inadmissible.

Where does this high hurdle ('beyond any doubt') come from, and how does it square with the generosity shown in the *Angonese* cases? Granted the *Foglia* element of the case in part, it was at the same time very un*Foglia*-ish in that there was no question of the existence of a genuine dispute; and the question of Community law was in all likelihood pivotal to its resolution. Is it therefore desirable that the High Court resolve the issue, of which it was competently seised and so bound to resolve, without the assistance, and wisdom, of the Court of Justice? *Bacardi-Martini* was decided by the full Court (11 judges) and so cannot be considered a rogue judgment. Unless it displays a requirement of especial sensitivity in the narrow *Foglia* context, it does seem to betray the spirit of Article 234. If the High Court goes against Newcastle, the sole consolation may subsist in having won the match 2-0.

---

[72] Case C–318/00 *Bacardi-Martini SAS and anor v. Newcastle United Football Company Ltd*, judgment of 21 January 2003, not yet reported.
[73] Loi n° 91/32 du 10 janvier 1991, JORF du 12 janvier 1991, p. 615.
[74] Above n72, at para. 44.
[75] *Ibid*, at para. 45.

Article 234: A Few Rough Edges Still   339

The problem arises if admissibility is, or seen to be, a lottery. It may be (but oughtn't to be) so if it varies depending upon the composition of the Court of Justice. But there is probably a discernable differentiation depending upon the member state(s) the courts of which submit the questions. It is to be hoped that there be a reasonable honeymoon period as, say, Hungarian and Latvian judges are coaxed into the game.

It has particular resonance for references not on interpretation but on invalidity of a Community act. The Court of Justice recently (and unexpectedly?) declined the opportunity to expand the title and interest available to natural and juristic persons seeking the annulment of a Community act under Article 230.[76] The present rules are adequate to afford the individual sufficient judicial protection, although they necessarily impose upon the member states a burden to establish a system of legal remedies and procedures which ensure respect for the right to effective judicial protection[77]—which will (and must, if the system is to work) lead to invalidity references under Article 234. However, we know from *Foglia* case law that the Court does not like contrived or orchestrated actions. And this was one of the (many) criticisms Advocate-General Jacobs levelled at present rules, that the individual barred from proceeding under Article 230 would require to act in a manner contrary to the Community measure and await national enforcement proceedings, possibly criminal, to be directed against him. This

> does not offer the individual an adequate means of judicial protection. Individuals clearly cannot be required to breach the law in order to gain access to justice.[78]

Well, yes they can. And now must. And since their purpose is to orchestrate a reference, does it not fall foul of *Foglia* principles? It is to be hoped, and is anticipated, that the Court would dig very deeply into even the most unfortunate invalidity reference before knocking it back; and even then, it might be barred by *Union de Pequeños Agricultores* from doing so. But the Court cannot rule upon the validity of a Community act it does not encounter, and the lottery element is alive here as well: is it really conceivable that a serious question as to the validity of a Community act has arisen only twice in Scotland since 1973,[79] but many dozens of times in Austria since 1995?

---

[76] Case C–50/00P *Union de Pequeños Agricultores v. Council* [2002] ECR I–6677; Case C–263/02P *Commission v. Jégo-Quéré et Cie SA*, pending; Opinion of A-G Jacobs delivered 10 July 2003.
[77] Case C–50/00P *Union de Pequeños Agricultores, ibid.*, at para. 41.
[78] *Ibid*, per A-G Jacobs at para. 43 of his Opinion.
[79] Of the ten references from Scottish courts to date (see above n 9), only two (Case 370/88 *Walkingshaw (PF Stranraer) v. Marshall* [1990] I–4071; Case C–64/00 *Hydro Seafoods GSP Ltd v. The Scottish Ministers*, judgment of 10 July 2003, not yet reported) raised questions of the validity of a Community act.

3. EXCEEDING JURISDICTION

The Court has stressed from the beginning that questions of fact are exclusively for the national court; the Court of Justice may only interpret the appropriate rule(s) of Community law to those facts. But in a number of cases the court has blurred the distinction. And it has done so without apology. For example, in the first *B & Q* case on the compatibility with Article 28 of the (then) rules in England and Wales on Sunday trading,[80] the Court furnished what was, it must be said, a fairly cryptic ruling on the tests to be applied. National courts promptly made a hash of applying that ruling. In response to a second *B & Q* reference from the House of Lords, the Court therefore

> considered that it had all the information necessary for it to rule on the question of the proportionality of such rules and that it had to do so in order to enable national courts to assess their compatibility with Community law in a uniform manner since such an assessment cannot be allowed to vary according to the findings of fact made by individual courts in particular cases.[81]

In other words, leaving questions of fact to the national courts may imperil the uniform application of Community law, that is undesirable, and we shall therefore remedy the problem by determining questions of fact ourselves. This may indeed remedy the problem (although the Court did not justify why it was a problem: why, for example, it is offensive for Sunday trading legislation to apply differently in deepest, sabbatarian Pembrokeshire than in sinful London), but the Court ought not to exceed its jurisdiction in order to do so. Even more striking, in *Semararo Casa Uno*,[82] an Article 28 case on shop hours, the referring national court had established that the relevant Italian legislation produced effects different as between domestic and imported goods, so failing the *Keck & Mithouard* test of affecting them 'in the same manner, in law and in fact'.[83] The Court of Justice invited the referring court to withdraw the reference, which it declined to do, and the Court went on to rule that Article 28

> does not apply to national rules on the closing times of shops applicable to all traders exercising an activity on national territory and affecting in the same way in law and in fact the marketing of national products and products from other Member States[84]

—not only determining questions of fact, which it has no jurisdiction to do, but, in effect, overruling the national court in its (exclusive) determination of fact.

---

[80] Case 145/88 *Torfaen Borough Council* v. *B & Q plc* [1989] ECR 3851.

[81] Case C–169/91 *Council of the City of Stoke-on-Trent and anor* v. *B & Q plc* [1992] ECR I–6635, at para. 14.

[82] Joined Cases C–418 etc/93 *Semeraro Casa Uno Srl and ors* v. *Comune di Erbusco and ors* [1996] ECR I–2975.

[83] Joined Cases C–267 & 268/91 *Criminal proceedings against Bernard Keck & Daniel Mithouard* [1993] ECR I–6097, at para. 16.

[84] Joined Cases C–418 etc/93 *Semeraro Casa Uno*, above n82, at para. 28.

The risk here of course is that it may diminish the authority of the Court; and this is best illustrated by a recent judgment of the English High Court. The ruling delivered in Article 234 proceedings is binding for the referring national court, which must apply it in disposing of the case in the main proceedings.[85] It may re-refer the same question if it encounters difficulties in understanding or applying the ruling or where other circumstances have come to light which might lead the Court of Justice to decide the reference differently,[86] but is otherwise bound by it. But bearing in mind there is a division of jurisdiction between the referring national court and the Court of Justice, it is possible that the Court of Justice may misapply or exceed its jurisdiction, so absolving the national court of the obligation to apply the ruling rendered. Thus it was that the High Court refused to apply a preliminary ruling[87] on the interpretation of a directive on the ground that the Court of Justice had strayed into findings of fact (and findings inconsistent with those of the national court), the Court had therefore exceeded its jurisdiction under article 234, and the referring court was, as a consequence, relieved of the obligation to apply the ruling:

> The ECJ [sic] has disagreed with the conclusions of fact reached at the trial. . . . If this is so, the ECJ has exceeded its jurisdiction and I am not bound by its final conclusion. I must apply its guidance on the law to the facts as found at the trial.
>
> This is a most unattractive outcome. . . . [N]ational courts do not make references to the ECJ with the intention of ignoring the result. On the other hand, no matter how tempting it may be to find an easy way out, the High Court has no power to cede to the ECJ a jurisdiction it does not have.[88]

This does not happen often; and, in the event, the High Court has now been overruled by the Court of Appeal.[89] But the response of the High Court—one, it is submitted, which was open equally to the *Pretura Circondariale* in *Semararo Casa Uno*—may be taken as a shot across the Court's bow, an occasional warning of the limits of its jurisdiction and a (re-)assertion of that of the national court.

A related circumstance is if and when the Court responds to questions not asked; it is best illustrated by a (now dated) series of cases in the French administrative courts. In 1979 the Court responded to a reference from a French administrative court on the validity of a Commission regulation by declaring the regulation invalid *and*, exercising a jurisdiction it had assumed in the interests of legal certainty, limiting the temporal effect of that declaration.[90] The French

---

[85] Case 52/76 *Benedetti* v. *Munari* [1977] ECR 163; Case 69/85 *Wünsche Handelsgesellschaft GmbH & Co* v. *Germany* [1986] ECR 947.
[86] Case 69/85 *Wünsche*, ibid; Case C–466/00 *Kaba* v. *Secretary of State for the Home Department*, judgment of 6 March 2003, not yet reported.
[87] Case C–206/01 *Arsenal Football Club plc* v. *Reed* [2002] ECR I–10273.
[88] *Arsenal Football Club plc* v. *Reed* [2002] EWHC 2695 (Ch), [2003] 1 All ER 137 at 146.
[89] *Arsenal Football Club plc* v. *Reed* [2003] EWCA Civ 96 (CA), [2003] All ER (D) 289.
[90] Case 109/79 *Sàrl Maïseries de Beauce* v. *Office National Interprofessionnel des Céréals* [1980] ECR 2883.

court refused to apply the second part of the ruling because it had not asked the question, and the Court of Justice therefore, in its view, had no jurisdiction to give it;[91] it was upheld by the *Conseil d'Etat*.[92] Now this is certainly not the first time the Court has answered a question not asked.[93] To the Court, the need to provide a 'satisfactory', 'helpful' or 'useful' answer to the referring court may justify consideration of provisions of Community law not addressed in the question;[94] but then it must be for the referring court to decide whether or not the provisions thus interpreted are applicable to the main proceedings.[95] And measured against occasions in which the Court responds to questions not asked is when reformulation of a question neuters it, resulting, by design or otherwise, in a question which was perfectly clear, and possibly important, not being answered. Most students of Community law will have their favourite, maddening, example; I shall put forward only one, *Courage* v. *Crehan*[96]—an important question on civil liability in reparation and/or restitution for breach of Article 81(1), put in a manner clear as a bell, but a bullet dodged rather than bitten.

4. CONCLUDING REMARKS

As David himself noted,[97] much of the literature addresses the flaws of Article 234, not its achievements. And this is perhaps not fair, for its achievements have been wholly remarkable. But it is important to seek to ensure its continued success, which requires its peripheries to be understood. The near future is likely to see the conferral of *some* jurisdiction in preliminary rulings upon the Court of First Instance. If done deftly, it will bring advantages: the Community constitutional order is unlikely to be imperilled by determination by the Court of First Instance of whether a nightdress ceases to be a nightdress, for customs classification purposes, if it might be worn to take a cup of tea in the evening.[98] Even deftly, there are serious issues to be addressed: the appropriate subject-areas; the role of (new) Advocates-General; when a case is to be referred up to the Court of Justice because it 'requires' (*appelle*) a decision of principle likely

---

[91] Tribunal Administratif, Orléans, 23 février 1982, Rec p. 471. Other lower administrative courts did likewise.

[92] CE 26 juillet 1985, Rec p. 233.

[93] For example, the entire basis of the dichotomy of the existence/exercise of intellectual property rights and the protection of their specific subject matter under Arts. 28 and 30 arose in a reference from a German court (Case 78/70 *Deutsche Grammophon Gesellschaft mbH* v. *Metro-SB-Großmärkte GmbH & Co KG* [1971] ECR 487) which had restricted its questions to the requirements of Arts. 10, 81 and 82.

[94] Case 35/85 *Procureur de la République* v *Tissier* [1986] ECR 1207; Case C–265/01 *Criminal proceedings against Annie Pansard and ors*, judgment of 16 January 2003, not yet reported.

[95] Case 35/85 *Tissier*, ibid.

[96] Case C–453/99 *Courage Ltd* v. *Crehan* [2001] I–6297.

[97] DAO Edward, 'Reform of the Article 234 Procedure: The Limits of the Possible', in D O'Keeffe (ed.), *Judicial Review in European Union Law: Liber Amicorum in Honour of Lord Slynn of Hadley* (The Hague, Kluwer, 2000).

[98] Case C–338/95 *Wiener SI GmbH* v. *Hauptzollamt Emmerich* [1997] ECR I–6495.

to affect the unity or consistency of Community law;[99] or when, if not referred, they are under 'serious risk' so justifying 'exceptional' review by the Court of Justice.[100] If not deftly, the procedure may fall, if not into disrepute, into disfavour. And that will bring no benefit to the present Union, never mind its new eastern half. What the near future will also, incontrovertibly, bring is ten new judges. In the last ten to fifteen years the Court has begun to go through judges with increasing rapidity: David arrived in 1989, moved upstairs in 1992, but by September 2003 ranks fourth in the Court's seniority. There is therefore some risk to the continuity of the institution, all the more so for its growth and restructuring. For that too, a degree of consolidation, rather than adventurism, may be wise.

---

[99] EC Treaty, Art. 225(3).
[100] *Ibid.*

24

Discretionary References: To Refer or not to Refer?

MARK HOSKINS

1. INTRODUCTION

I FIRST MET David Edward in 1991 when I competed as a student in the European Law Moot Court competition. Our team did very well and my prize was a week's visit to Luxembourg. After the competition, David came to seek me out and invited me to spend a week in his Chambers. I like to think that he spotted my raw potential, but the truth is that he was probably attracted to a fellow Scottish accent. I obviously did not do too badly during my week's stay, because some time later, David invited me to become a *référendaire*. When my time came to leave Luxembourg, I said at my leaving party that I had learned more from David about law, and particularly the practice of law, than from any other person. Eight years on, that statement holds good. I will always bear a huge personal debt to David for setting me on my way as a practising lawyer.

Given that background, it seemed appropriate that my contribution to his book should focus on an issue of practical significance. It is for that reason that I chose to write about the English courts' approach to the exercise of discretion by a national court in deciding whether to seek a preliminary ruling under Article 234 EC. This issue will be of great significance to the national courts of the new Member States following enlargement. It will also be of significance for David's successor, because if national courts make too many references, the ability of the EC Courts to deal with them efficiently will be seriously impaired.

2. THE EXISTENCE OF A DISCRETION TO REFER

Not all courts[1] have discretion whether to make a reference. That depends upon whether the court is a court of last resort or not and whether the issue before it is a matter of interpretation or validity.

---

[1] References to 'courts' in this essay should be understood as covering 'any court or tribunal' within the meaning of Article 234 EC.

Under Article 234 EC, second paragraph, a court other than a court of last resort has discretion whether to seek a preliminary ruling. However, as a result of the judgment in Case 314/85 *Foto-Frost*,[2] even a court which is not a court of last resort must make an order for a reference where a substantial doubt has been raised concerning the validity of a Community measure. A national court may find that a Community act is valid, however only the Court of Justice has power to declare that such acts are invalid.

Under Article 234 EC, third paragraph, a court of last resort must seek a preliminary ruling on questions of both interpretation and validity (subject to the limited exceptions recognised in Case 283/81 *CILFIT*[3]).

It follows that the discretion to make a reference applies to questions of interpretation that arise before courts which are not courts of last resort.

3. NECESSITY

Article 234 EC, second paragraph, establishes that a court may seek a preliminary ruling 'if it considers that a decision on the question is necessary to enable it to give judgment'. In *Bulmer Ltd* v. *Bollinger SA (No 2)*,[4] Lord Denning MR held that this meant that the issue of Community law must be 'conclusive' so that, whichever way the point is decided, nothing more will remain for the national court but to give judgment. However, such an approach is unduly restrictive and has not been followed in subsequent cases. In contrast, it is clear that the word 'necessary' is stronger than 'desirable' or 'convenient'.[5] The proper approach lies somewhere in between. At the very least, an issue of Community law will be 'necessary' when it is relevant to the issues before the national court, even where it may not in itself be determinative of the case.

4. WIDE DISCRETION

Even where a Community law issue of interpretation is 'necessary' for the determination of a case, the national court retains the 'widest discretion' in deciding whether or not to refer questions to the Court of Justice.[6] This discretion cannot be fettered by any national rules or judicial authority.[7] For example, the fact that, under domestic law, a court is bound on points of law by a ruling of a

---

[2] [1987] ECR 4199 paras 11–20.
[3] [1982] ECR 3415.
[4] [1974] Ch 401 at 422D–E.
[5] *An Bord Bainne* v. *Milk Marketing Board* [1985] 1 CMLR 6 at 10, per Neill J.
[6] Case 166/73 *Rheinmülen* [1974] ECR 33 paras 2–4.
[7] Case C–312/93 *Peterbroeck v Belgium* [1995] ECR I–4599 para 13; Joined Cases C–430/93 and C–431/93 *van Schijndel v SPF* [1995] ECR I–4705 para 18.

superior court cannot prevent the inferior court from seeking a preliminary ruling from the Court of Justice.[8]

It follows that a national court, when deciding whether to make a reference or not, is entitled to have regard to any factors that it considers relevant. These might include the following (which are by no means intended to be exhaustive):

Delay

In 2002, the average time (from lodging to judgment) taken by the Court of Justice to deal with a reference was just over two years. If a case is time-sensitive, this may be a reason for a national court to decide the issue itself. Whilst Article 104a of the Rules of Procedure of the Court of Justice now provides for the possibility of an accelerated procedure for dealing with preliminary rulings, it is clear from its express terms that this power will only be used in exceptional cases.

Cost

In order to minimise costs, it may be best for a national judge to decide a case without seeking a preliminary ruling. However, where a reference appears inevitable at some stage, it may be beneficial (in terms of both time and expense) to seek a reference at an early stage of proceedings, rather than permitting the case to proceed through one or more domestic appeal stages.

Importance of the issue

Where the issue raised is of general importance for the Community as a whole, this will militate in favour of making a reference.

Difficulty

The more difficult the issue of Community law, the more likely that a reference will be made.

Language/purposive approach to interpretation

Where consideration of different language versions and/or the need for a purposive approach to interpretation are likely to be significant, the Court of

---

[8] Case 166/73 *Rheinmülen*, above.

Justice will generally be better placed than a national court to carry out that exercise.

Wishes of the parties

The parties have no right to demand a reference to the Court of Justice; the right to make a reference belongs to the national courts.[9] However, if both parties want a point to be referred, the national court should certainly have regard to their wishes, without treating them as being decisive of the issue.

5. A DISCRETIONARY STRAITJACKET?

In *R v. Stock Exchange, ex parte Else Ltd*, Sir Thomas Bingham M.R. held:

> I understand the correct approach in principle of a national court (other than a final court of appeal) to be quite clear: if the facts have been found and the Community law issue is critical to the court's final decision, the appropriate course is ordinarily to refer the issue to the Court of Justice unless the national court can with complete confidence resolve the issue itself. In considering whether it can with complete confidence resolve the issue itself the national court must be fully mindful of the differences between national and Community legislation, of the pitfalls which face a national court venturing into what may be an unfamiliar field, of the need for uniform interpretation throughout the Community and of the great advantages enjoyed by the Court of Justice in construing Community instruments. *If the national court has any real doubt, it should ordinarily refer.* I am not here attempting to summarise comprehensively the effect of such leading cases as *H.P. Bulmer Ltd. v. J. Bollinger S.A.* [1974] Ch. 401, *C.I.L.F.I.T. (S.r.l.)* v. *Ministry of Health* (Case 283/81) [1982] E.C.R. 3415 and *Reg.* v. *Pharmaceutical Society of Great Britain, Ex parte Association of Pharmaceutical Importers* [1987] 3 C.M.L.R. 951, but I hope I am fairly expressing their essential point.[10]

The approach suggested in *ex parte Else* is too restrictive for two reasons. First, it elevates one factor in the exercise of discretion, the difficulty of the question, above all other potentially relevant factors. Second, its approach to that factor, particularly the suggestion that 'If the national has court has any real doubt, it should ordinarily refer', is unduly restrictive. Indeed, this approach is very close to the obligation to make references imposed on courts of last resort. Pursuant to Article 234, third paragraph, as interpreted in Case 283/81 *CILFIT*, a court of last resort is obliged to make a reference to the Court of Justice save where the Community law issue raised is irrelevant or has been dealt with by a previous judgment of the Court of Justice, or where the answer is so obvious as to leave

---

[9] Case 5/72 *Fratelli Grassi* [1972] ECR 443 para 4.
[10] [1993] QB 534 at 545C–G (emphasis added).

no scope for any reasonable doubt (*acte clair*). It is telling that Sir Thomas Bingham expressly relied on *CILFIT* as part of the basis for his analysis.

The approach adopted in *ex parte Else* can be contrasted (unfavourably) with the approach adopted by Lord Denning M.R. in the earlier case of *Bulmer Ltd v. Bollinger SA*.[11] Lord Denning identified the difficulty and importance of a point as being merely two factors amongst many others which are relevant to the exercise of discretion to make a reference and stated that, 'Unless the point is really difficult and important, it would seem better for the English judge to decide it himself.' This approach encourages national courts to grapple with and to decide Community law issues on their own. It encourages them to see Community law as part of their own legal order, rather than something distinct that is best decided by the Court in Luxembourg.

Not surprisingly, given the eminence of the judge concerned, *ex parte Else* became the leading authority on the exercise of discretion when deciding whether to make a reference. However, in practice, the approach to that authority has varied. Some judges, perhaps those with more experience of dealing with Community law issues, whilst paying lip service to *ex parte Else*, have adopted an approach closer to that suggested in *Bulmer Ltd v. Bollinger SA*. In terms of legal certainty, it is clearly undesirable to have a dichotomy between legal precedent and practical reality, and also between the approaches adopted by different judges.

6. A NEW APPROACH?

In his Opinion in Case C-338/95 *Wiener v. Hauptzollamt Emmerich*,[12] Advocate-General Jacobs suggested that, given the increasing number of references, and given the more developed state of Community law, both the national courts and the Court of Justice should show 'a greater measure of self-restraint' in relation to preliminary references. In the absence of such restraint, he suggested that:

> the Court could be called upon to intervene in all cases turning on a point of Community law in any court or tribunal in any of the Member States. It is plain that if the Court were to be so called upon it would collapse under its case-load.

In relation to courts which are not courts of last resort, Advocate-General Jacobs therefore expressed the following view.

> A reference will be most appropriate where the question is one of general importance and where the ruling is likely to promote the uniform application of the law throughout the European Union. A reference will be least appropriate where there is an established body of case-law which could readily be transposed to the facts of the instant

---

[11] Above, at 424F.
[12] [1997] ECR I–6495.

case; or where the question turns on a narrow point considered in the light of a very specific set of facts and the ruling is unlikely to have any application beyond the instant case. Between these two extremes there is of course a wide spectrum of possibilities; nevertheless national courts themselves could properly assess whether it is appropriate to make a reference, and the Court of Justice, even if it continued to maintain that the decision to refer was exclusively within the discretion of the national courts, could perhaps give some informal guidance and so encourage self-restraint by the national courts in appropriate cases.

The Court of Justice did not deal in its judgment with the general issues raised by Advocate-General Jacobs. However, the call for self-restraint was heard by the English courts, in particular, the Court of Appeal.

In *Trinity Mirror plc* v. *Commissioners of Customs and Excise*,[13] Chadwick LJ, delivering the judgment of the Court of Appeal, held that the approach to be adopted in deciding whether to seek a preliminary ruling was that set down in *ex parte Else*. However, he indicated that it was also important 'to have in mind' the observations of Advocate-General Jacobs in *Wiener*. In the event, the Court of Appeal declined to make a reference because there was not 'any real doubt' how the question should be answered. The words 'any real doubt' are of course taken from the judgment in *ex parte Else*.

In *Customs and Excise Commissioners* v. *Littlewoods Organisation plc*,[14] Chadwick LJ, delivering the judgment of the Court of Appeal, again indicated that the approach to be adopted was that explained in *ex parte Else*, but that it was also important to have in mind the observations of Advocate-General Jacobs in *Wiener*. In the particular case, the Court of Appeal declined to make a reference stating:

> we are satisfied that there is ample guidance on the question of principle in the existing decisions of the Court of Justice. We feel confident that we can apply the principle to the particular facts of the appeals which we have to decide.

It is interesting to note that the language used here was not as restrictive as that in *ex parte Else*. *Ex parte Else* uses the expression 'complete confidence'. In contrast, the Court of Appeal in *Littlewoods* was content not to seek a reference because it was 'confident' as to the proper outcome.

In *Professional Contractors' Group* v. *Commissioners of Inland Revenue*,[15] Robert Walker LJ, delivering the judgment of the Court of Appeal, declined to order a reference on the following basis:

> The principles stated by Sir Thomas Bingham MR in *Queen* v. *International Stock Exchange ex parte Else* [1993] QB 534 still hold good. But in applying them the court must also take account of the guidance given by the court (following European authority) in *Trinity Mirror plc* v. *Commissions of Customs & Excise* [2000] 2 CMLR 759, 783-5. The latter case has drawn attention both to the very heavy case-load of the

---

[13] [2001] 2 CMLR 33 paras 48–55.
[14] [2001] EWCA Civ 1542, [2001] STC 1568, paras 116–18.
[15] [2001] EWCA Civ 1945 paras 90–91.

Court of Justice and also to the greater familiarity with Community law which domestic courts now have. In this case as in many others, the real difficulty is not in ascertaining the relevant principles of Community law but in applying them to the facts; and that is a task for the national court.

In *Customs and Excise Commissioners* v. *BAA plc*,[16] Sir Andrew Morrit V-C, delivering the judgment of the Court of Appeal, made reference to the need for judicial self-restraint urged by Advocate-General Jacobs in *Wiener*, and held that there was no need to order a reference as the existing case-law of the Court of Justice provide a sufficient basis for the resolution of the case. No express reference was made to *ex parte Else*.

The current state of the case-law before the Court of Appeal is therefore that the correct approach to the exercise of discretion is still that laid down in *ex parte Else*, but that it is necessary to bear in mind the comments of Advocate-General Jacobs in *Wiener*. The attempt to 'water down' the approach in *ex parte Else* is welcome. However, the unduly restrictive approach to the exercise of discretion that *ex parte Else* imposes will clearly remain so long as the Court of Appeal continues to invoke it. This is not simply a theoretical issue. There is a gap between the proper approach required by Community law, ie unfettered discretion, and the unduly restrictive approach established by *ex parte Else*. Whilst, as I have already indicated, the detrimental effects of *ex parte Else* may be ameliorated in practice by judges who are experienced in dealing with Community law matters, it is confusing to have one approach suggested by the leading authority, whilst some judges in fact follow a different approach in practice.

The confusion engendered by continuing to cite *ex parte Else* is demonstrated by a comparison of two Chancery Division judgments: *Centralan Property Ltd v. Customs and Excise Commissioners*,[17] decided on 23 January 2003, and *Vtech Electronics (UK) plc v. Commissioners of Customs & Excise*,[18] decided on 29 January 2003. In *Centralan Property*, the Court made an order for a preliminary reference. Sir Andrew Morrit V-C followed the approach adopted in the Court of Appeal judgments referred to above by stating that the correct approach is established by *ex parte Else*, but that it is also necessary to bear in mind the Opinion of Advocate-General Jacobs in *Wiener*. In contrast, in *Vtech Electronics*, Lawrence Collins J, when refusing to order a preliminary ruling, did not make any reference to *ex parte Else*, but rather adopted the following approach:

> The discretion to refer is broad and unfettered: Case 166/73 *Rheinmuhlen* [1974] ECR 33. Recent guidance from the Court of Appeal (referring to the Opinion of Advocate General Jacobs in Case C-338/95 *Wiener SI GmbH v Hauptzollamt Emmerich* [1997] ECR I-6495, who suggested 'a greater measure of self-restraint' on the part of national courts: paras 18-21) warns against too great a readiness to refer, particularly in cases

---

[16] [2002] EWCA Civ 1814, [2003] STC 35, paras 47–48.
[17] [2003] EWHC 44 (Ch), [2003] All ER (D) 186, paras 20–25.
[18] [2003] EWHC 59 (Ch) paras 117–19.

in which 'the real difficulty is not in ascertaining the relevant principles of Community law but in applying them to the facts; and that is a task for the national court' *R (on the application of the Professional Contractors' Group)* v. *Commissioners of Inland Revenue* [2002] EWCA Civ. 1945, [2002] STC 165 at para 91; cf. *Trinity Mirror* v. *Commissioners of Customs and Excise* [2001] EWCA 65; [2001] 2 CMLR 759, paras 48–55.

The approach adopted in *Vtech Electronics* properly reflects the position in Community law and avoids the unduly restrictive fetter on the general discretion to refer that is to be found in *ex parte Else*. It would be highly desirable if that position were recognised in the case-law and for the courts to depart expressly from *ex parte Else*. *Ex parte Else*, decided in 1993, should be seen as a product of its times. However, the situation has changed since then. If one looks at the nature of the cases that now come before the Court of Justice, it is clear that many are of a detailed, technical nature. Community law has matured and fundamental issues of general importance are now much rarer than before. In addition, the English courts have become well versed in the particular approach required to Community law issues. The greater maturity of the Community legal system, and the greater experience of the national courts in Community law matters, should encourage the English courts expressly to abandon the strictures of *ex parte Else* and exercise their general discretion with confidence.[19]

---

[19] Under the English doctrine of precedent, both the High Court and the Court of Appeal are bound by previous decisions of the Court of Appeal on questions of law (see *Halsbury's Laws*, Vol 16, *Practice and Procedure*, para 1242). However, even if the guidance set down in *ex parte Else* is properly to be classified as a question of law, as indicated earlier in this essay, Community case-law establishes that a court's discretion to refer cannot be fettered by any national rules or judicial authority. Both the High Court and the Court of Appeal would therefore be entitled expressly to depart from *ex parte Else*.

25

Direct Applicability or Effect

JOXERRAMON BENGOETXEA*

DIRECT EFFECT AND direct applicability are two of the main foundations of European Community law. It may seem highly unimaginative to write about these subjects in a collection of essays in honour of one of the persons and jurists I admire and respect the most. Direct effect is a subject of Community law on which many articles and theses are written. Sacha Prechal, one of the authors who has most extensively written about the subject was recently suggesting that there was nothing new to be said about it.[1] Yet, in a way, when the idea of dedicating to David Edward a collection of essays from his closest assistants and colleagues was put to me by the editors, I knew that I had to write about direct effect. David Edward and direct effect were a natural couple! Our views about the subject have been intertwining since 1993, when we gave a seminar for local judges at the Oñati International Institute for the Sociology of Law, in the Basque Country. *Faccini Dori*[2] was being discussed at the time at the court, and already then, many of us were struggling to move away from a simplistic language of rights when considering the horizontal direct effect of directives, trying to escape from a blunt analysis which was being urged upon the court by some of its Advocates General (Lenz, Jacobs and van Gerven). What about judicial obligations: were judges, as organs or emanations of the state, not bound by full, clear norms contained in a directive?

When, a year later, the solution to *Faccini Dori* was rounded up with consistent interpretation and Member State liability, many commentators sighed in relief. For some, perhaps the minority, it was clear that directives could not possibly have horizontal direct effect, and orthodoxy had to prevail. For others, the case illustrated the unfairness of not recognising such effect since individuals were deprived of rights and footdragging legislators were getting away with it; Member State liability was, at least, an antidote. The solution seemed to settle the matter for some time, it was a well reasoned judgment with a solomonic solution, a good example of fairness in judicial adjudication and coherent

---

* Many thanks to Jose Palacio for comments.
[1] S Prechal, 'Direct Effect Reconsidered, Redefined and Rejected' in JM Prinssen and A Schrauwen (eds), *Direct Effect, Rethinking a Classic of EC Legal Doctrine* (University of Amsterdam, 2002).
[2] Case C–91/92 *Faccini Dori v. Recreb Srl* [1994] ECR I–3325.

development of the legal system. If I may disclose one of the secrets, not of *délibéré*, but of the corridors of the third floor of the old *Palais*, I shall always remember hearing from my office the soft voice of Judge Mancini congratulating the rapporteur, Judge Joliet, for a fantastic draft. I am quite certain that, had they had the opportunity to read David Edward's contribution to the *Mancini Festschrift*,[3] they would have both agreed with the views. Now that I see the old *Palais* building de-asbestised and reduced to its bare metallic structure I cannot but help thinking that one always has to re-examine and reconstruct from the foundations of Community law. There is some indescribable beauty, solidity and dynamism in the delphic nudity of the building's rusty system.

The next serious opportunity to turn our minds to direct effect was with the occasion of the deliberation of *GrossKrotzenburg*,[4] *Kraaijeveld*[5] and *CIA Security International*.[6] The discussions at the time led to the abovementioned article in the *Mancini Festschrift*. We had very interesting discussions on the subject and carried out some research. I remember rediscovering the pellucidly clear views of Professor Winter[7] and struggling not to be contaminated by infant diseases[8] of confusing applicability and effect, a risk to which even the court was not, should I say is still not, entirely immune.[9]

The next time our minds met on this topic was at a joint seminar at the University of Oxford in October 2001, under the initiative of John Gardner, Otto Pfersmann and Steve Weatherill who had organised a series of seminars on the legal theoretical issues of EC law. I tested out these ideas again in the LLM course at the University of Stockholm in 2001 and 2002 with the encouragement of Ola Wiklund, and they seemed to go down quite well. It became clear to me that my analysis required going back to the foundations of Community law in order to present the system in a new perspective. The analysis of direct effect had to include direct applicability if it were to move away from the lofty discourse of norms from which individual rights are derived and into the heftier domains of the legal order and its instruments.

In a nutshell, my theory is that the jurisprudential distinction between provisions or instruments and norms is the key to understanding the distinction between direct applicability and direct effect. In other words, direct applicability is a character of the instruments that make up the legal order, direct effect is a character of the norms contained in those instruments and which make up the

---

[3] DAO Edward, 'Direct Effect, the Separation of Powers and the Judicial Enforcement of Obligations' in *Scritti in onore di Giuseppe Federico Mancini* (Milan, Giuffrè, 1998).

[4] Case C–431/92 *Commission v. Germany* [1995] ECR I–2189.

[5] Case C–72/95 *Aannemersbedrijf pk Kraaijeveld BV v. Gedeputeerde Staten van Zuid-Holland* [1996] ECR I–5403.

[6] Case C–194/94 *CIA Security International SA v. Signalson SA & Securitel SPRL* [1996] ECR I–2201.

[7] JA Winter, 'Direct Applicability and Direct Effect. Two Distinct and Different Concepts in Community Law' (1972) 9 *CLM Rev* 425.

[8] P Pescatore, 'The Doctrine of Direct Effect: an infant disease of Community Law' (1983) 8 *EL Rev* 155.

[9] See Case C–253/00 *Antonio Muñoz y Cia SA and Superior Fruiticola SA v. Trumor Ltd and Redbridge Produce Marketing Ltd* [2002] ECR I–7289.

legal system. The distinction between provisions (instruments) and norms and that between the legal order—the body or corpus of valid provisions, the set of signs, *les paroles*—and legal system—the structured network of norms, *la langue*—help us grasp the semiotics of law. I shall try to explain this, and do so refraining from indulgence in a discussion of the extensive literature and the many cases on direct effect, save where strictly necessary.

1. THE DISTINCTION BETWEEN PROVISIONS AND NORMS IN LEGAL THEORY

The distinction between provisions and norms is a classic in many theories of law.[10] It is not a universally accepted distinction, especially when one adopts the perspective of norm-making and legislation,[11] but it is a widespread distinction in theories of judicial adjudication and interpretation. Let us postulate as a provisional hypothesis that a provision is a piece or an item of written law as it is found in constitutions, treaties, statutes, acts of parliament, regulations and the like, whereas the norm is the meaning assigned to those items following their interpretation or construction. Legal provisions, in Roman languages 'dispositions', are found in those instruments which are considered to be official sources of law.[12]

Legal provisions are sometimes called 'articles', sometimes 'paragraphs' or 'sections' of articles, and they are normally identifiable as complete and self-standing sentences. Reference to such texts are normally performed using the quotation marks and separate, hyphenated text to indicate their literal existence. They need not have a particular structure or verbal mode, indeed they can be imperative, subjunctive or indicative, active or passive; instead, their normativy is derived from the fact that they belong to a legal instrument that is institutionally recognised as valid law according to some *rule of recognition* of the legal system.

Norms, on the other hand, are the meaning or meanings of provisions. In the normal, easiest and clearest cases a provision will contain one, and only one, norm which will quite naturally follow from a literal interpretation; there will be a *univocal* relationship between 'provision' and 'norm'. But in other cases, a provision may allow more than one interpretation, its terms and grammar may

---

[10] The clearest work elaborating on this distinction is, in my opinion, R. Guastini, *Dalle Fonti Alle Norme* (Torino, 1st edn, 1990). 'Provision' is any statement which is part of a normative document, any statement of the discourse of the sources whereas 'norm' is any statement which contains the meaning or the sense ascribed to a provision or to a fragment of a provision, or to a combination of provisions or to a combination of fragments of provisions. The provision is part of text to be interpreted, the norm is part of an interpreted text (at p 17).

[11] Universal norms adopted by the legislator become provisions before the eyes of the judge who will extract new indivudal norms for the purpose of applying the law to specific situations. Ideally the norm adopted by the legislator and that distilled by the judge coincide: the latter being the individual formulation of the former. When they do not, there is a development of the law.

[12] See J Bengoetxea, 'Introduction. Sources and Resources of Law' in E. Attwooll and P. Comanducci (eds), *Sources of law and Legislation* (ARSP Beiheft 69, Stuttgart 1998), at pp 19–29.

potentially convey more than one meaning and may thus contain more than one norm; or it may actually contain none at all if it means nothing; or contain only part of a norm if the provision is combined with other provisions in order to construct the norm they jointly contain. The relationship between 'provision' and 'norm' will then be multivocal or even *equivocal*. Of the different possible meanings that may be attached to one (ambiguous or multisemic) provision, one may become authoritative, it will then become the norm contained in the provision.

Thus take the following provisions, paragraphs 1 and 2 of Article 234 on the preliminary ruling procedure:

The Court of Justice shall have jurisdiction to give preliminary rulings concerning:

(a) the interpretation of this Treaty;
(b) the validity and interpretation of acts of the institutions of the Community and of the ECB;
(c) the interpretation of the statutes of bodies established by an act of the Council, where those statutes so provide.

Where such a question is raised before any court or tribunal of a Member State, that court or tribunal may, if it considers that a decision on the question is necessary to enable it to give judgment, request the Court of Justice to give a ruling thereon.

Interestingly, since the *Foto-Frost*[13] judgment, a norm was derived from this provision paragraph 2, which could hardly be considered as a meaning of the provision. It turned a permission into an obligation, a 'may' into a 'must', whenever a question of validity is raised. Thus something like the following became a norm, one of the several norms contained in Article 234: 'whenever a question of validity of secondary Community law is raised before the court of a Member State, this court will request the Court of Justice to give a preliminary ruling on the question of validity'. Of course, arguments of interpretation other than the textual or linguistic were resorted to in order to justify that interpretation of the provision, in order to justify the creation of that particular norm.

Let us mention **a few examples of provisions** in order to illustrate the point. Take Article 18 EC (ex article 8a importantly modified in paragraph 2, and with a new paragraph 3). It provides:

1. Every citizen of the Union shall have the right to move and reside freely within the territory of the Member States, subject to the limitations and conditions laid down in this Treaty and by the measures adopted to give it effect.
2. If action by the Community should prove necessary to attain this objective and this Treaty has not provided the necessary powers, the Council may adopt provisions with a view to facilitating the exercise of the rights referred to in paragraph 1. The Council shall act in accordance with the procedure referred to in Article 251.
3. Paragraph 2 shall not apply to provisions on passports, identity cards, residence permits or any other such document or to provisions on social security or social protection.

[13] Case 314/85 *Foto-Frost* v. *Hauptzollamt Lübeck-Ost* [1987] ECR 4199.

Direct Applicability or Effect 357

This article has three different provisions. They are contained in a particular instrument of EC law, in the Treaty establishing the European Community. Their validity is dogma because the validity of the Treaties goes unquestioned, provided they are in force and have not been repealed, denounced or replaced. The provisions above have been in force since the Treaty of Nice entered into force on 1 February 2003. These provisions contain different norms. Here is a list of possible norms contained in that provision:

Norm 1: 'Every citizen of the Union has the right to move freely within the territory of the Member States, subject to limitations.'
Norm 2: 'Every citizen of the Union has the right to reside freely within the territory of the Member States, subject to limitations.'
Norm 3: 'Limitations and conditions on citizen's right of residence in the territory of the Member States are laid down in the Treaty establishing the EC and in the measures adopted to give effect to this Treaty.'
Norm 4: 'Limitations and conditions on citizen's right to move freely within the territory of the Member States are laid down in the Treaty establishing the EC and in the measures adopted to give effect to this Treaty.'
Norm 5: 'If necessary, and if no specific power has been foreseen by the Treaty establishing the EC, the Council, following the procedure referred to in Article 251 of the Treaty, may adopt provisions other than on passports, identity cards, residence permits, or any such document or on social security or social protection, with a view to facilitating citizens' rights of residence and movement.'
But Norm 5 could be split into more specific norms e.g.
Norm 5.1: 'the Council may not adopt provisions on social security with a view to facilitating Union citizens' rights of residence and movement' or
Norm 5.2: 'the Council may not adopt provisions on residence permits with a view to facilitating Union citizens' right of residence in the territory of the Member States,' etc.

Consider next a well-known provision like the following:

> Article 12
> Member States shall refrain from introducing between themselves any new customs duties on imports or exports or any charges having equivalent effect, and from increasing those which they already apply in their trade with each other.

This is no longer a valid provision forming part of the legal system of EC law because it belongs to an instrument which ceased being in force when the Treaty of Amsterdam entered into force in May 1999. The norm or norms—Norm 1: 'Member States may not introduce between themselves any new customs duties on imports'; Norm 2: 'Member States may not introduce between themselves any charges having an effect equivalent to customs duties on imports'; Norm 3: 'Member States may not increase any custom duty they already apply in their trade with each other'; Norm 4 up to Norm N—which this provision may contain are no longer valid norms of the legal system. They have been replaced by other, rather similar, norms contained in new provisions (Article 25 EC).

> In Article 12 of Regulation 1612/68 reads as follows:
> The children of a national of a Member State who is or has been employed in the territory of another Member State shall be admitted to that State's general educational, apprenticeship and vocational training courses under the same conditions as the nationals of that State, if such children are residing in its territory.
> Member States shall encourage all efforts to enable such children to attend these courses under the best possible conditions.

Two provisions are contained in Article 12 which potentially contain several norms. The extent and scope of those norms depend on the interpretation of several concepts like that of residence in the territory, the question whether the worker or former worker still has to reside in the Member State, the very notion of child of a worker, the length of time required for a worker to have worked in another Member State, and the question whether the right can only be enjoyed in order to carry out studies in the Member State where the child resides or a scholarship to study in a different Member State, thus implying a change of residence, etc. The case law of the Court of Justice has clarified many of these questions and as a result the number and extent of the norms contained in this provision has expanded and has gained in determinacy.

The normative character of the second paragraph of Article 12 is particularly interesting: it is normatively weak but is contained in an instrument, the Regulation, which is normatively strong, since it is directly applicable. It is difficult to see exactly what norm is contained in this provision or how it may produce any legal effect: a wish or the formulation of a desire addressed to Member States so that they encourage (to what degree, with what consequences?) efforts (by whom?) to enable such children to attend courses (which courses?) under the best possible conditions (which are those? Are they better than the conditions offered to the children of nationals?) The indeterminacy of the provision leads to an absence of norm, not in the sense that there is a gap, but in the sense that it is almost impossible to know or detect the norm contained therein. The discourse of this provision is typical of instruments of a non-binding nature.

Finally, take the following provisions found in Directive 64/221:

> Article 3
> 1. Measures taken on grounds of public policy or of public security shall be based exclusively on the personal conduct of the individual concern.
> Article 10
> 1. Member States shall within six months of notification of this Directive put into force the measures necessary to comply with its provisions and shall forthwith inform the Commission thereof.
> Article 11
> This Directive is addressed to the Member States.

These provisions are worded in normatively strict or strong terms, as compared to the text of the Regulation above, but they are contained in an instrument, the directive, which is normatively weak, in that it is not directly applicable. The scope of interpretation is undeniable especially as regards the meaning of 'personal conduct', but also as regards 'public policy' and 'public security' and the effect of the disjunctive 'or' in the syntagma 'public policy or of public security'. As regards the meaning of measures and the type of measures which may be involved, an interpretation based on the context and system of the provision, ie the rest of the Directive, may provide further clues. Thus, Article 2 clarifies that these are measures to restrict entry into the territory of a Member State.

The meaning of that provision, and the strict text it contained were taken seriously in the *Van Duyn*[14] case, where the fact of belonging to a given religious confession was considered not to be the personal conduct of the individual concerned. If the similar, I believe correct and reasonable, interpretation was followed today, belonging to a banned political party would equally not count as personal conduct of the individual. Yet, in spite of the possibility of discerning the norms contained in the provision, the fact that this provision belongs to a particular instrument, ie the directive, implies that the norms it contains are to be developed in new provisions adopted by Member States. Similarly a recommendation may contain language that resembles closely that used by provisions contained in regulations or in the Treaties, although they will tend to look more like the second provision of Article 12 of Regulation 1612/68 mentioned above. Yet, the fact that they belong to an instrument which is not part of binding sources of law is crucial when it comes to determining its normativity.

According to this view, legal norms are no more and no less than constructs, interpretations or meanings of legal provisions. Their construction will be more or less complex and difficult, and there is no a priori certainty that the construct, the norm-contention is correct, they are no more than interpretations and can be confirmed or rejected by an official interpretation by the courts of highest resort. On the other hand, the provisions are fixed text, they are items to be found in instruments and can be altered or removed from the law-book.

We have just mentioned some instruments that are found among the outputs of EC institutions. Some of these provisions are recognised as legal provisions which are considered as containing valid and binding norms of Community law. Others are not. Yet they may all look the same and have similar language structure. Indeed some of those that lack legal bindingness—recommendations, communications, resolutions, opinions, reports, white papers, even statistics!—may look more binding than proper legal provisions contained in formally binding instruments like Treaties, international agreements, regulations, directives or decisions. Thus the definition of an SME (small and medium enterprise) or the de minimis rule in the field of state aid are 'norms' that are found (or were initially contained) in so-called soft law instruments. They regulate the behaviour

---

[14] Case 41/74 *Van Duyn* v. *Home Office* [1974] ECR 1337.

of actors and bind their authors but they are not strictly integrated in the legal system. They are borderline cases. But in order to recognise them as instruments likely to contain legal norms valid in a given legal system we make use of some implicitly accepted rule of recognition of such legal system which tells us which instruments constitute official sources of law and which do not. In Community law, this rule of recognition is Article 249 EC.

2. THE CO-EXISTENCE OF SYSTEMS OF LAW

One of the interesting features of Community law is that it constitutes a system of law that is superimposed on previously existing systems of law, as though it was grafted onto them. Community law does not replace existing legal systems of the Member States; rather, it consists in a set of provisions found in instruments which contain norms that are uniform and common to all those systems. The question is then by what mechanisms does Community law enter or penetrate the law of the Member States so as to become, officially, part of that internal law and be treated exactly like internal law. There are two principal mechanisms: *direct penetration* or automatic integration and *indirect incorporation* through ratification.

The regulation is a perfect example of automatic integration into internal law directly creating norms of universal application. The decision is also an example of automatic integration producing individual norms. These instruments need no process of recognition or ratification. They apply directly and automatically from the moment of their publication in the official journal or their notification to the addressees. In international legal jargon these instruments are said to be self-executing. In Community law, they are said to be directly applicable. On the other hand, the directive follows the classic example of international law: the instrument has to be ratified in domestic law in order to integrate the law and be applicable in the same way internal law is applicable to all persons under its jurisdiction. In international law, the directive would be a non-self-executing instrument and in Community law, we say that the directive is not directly applicable. Also in international law categories it could be said that the regulation is a classical monist instrument (the valid adoption and publication of the instrument produces its immediate validity in all the domestic laws) and the directive is a classical dualist instrument since its adoption and formal incorporation into the legal system of the EC does not imply its existence in the domestic laws, but it requires an act of incorporation.

The particularities of regulations and directives cannot be understood unless the co-existence and simultaneous validity of different systems is assumed. The question is how to ensure that instruments produced according to one particular body of law, Community law, which is common and uniform across Member States, get to be integrated in or become part of internal, domestic law so that they apply directly: sometimes this is done automatically (regulations are directly applicable), sometimes through an act of incorporation (the transposition of directives, which are not directly applicable). The distinction between provisions and norms acquires tremendous impact, from a pragmatic point of view, in the operation of directives. Directives contain norms dressed in provisions. The transposition of a directive into domestic law does not consist or does not require the verbatim reformulation of the provisions of the directive. When they are transposed into domestic law, the norms of the directive can be cloaked in different provisions, indeed they may already be part of domestic law with the consequence that no formal transposition is necessary. The control of the correctness of the transposition consists in an examination of legal norms: the norms of the directive and the norms of domestic law. The provisions in question may look different but the norms they contain should be the same.

3. DIRECT APPLICABILITY AND THE OFFICIAL JOURNALS

One of the most important but difficult ideological dogmas or principles in our legal culture is the presumption (and obligation) that citizens know the law. This postulate is of a normative nature and has important variations: citizens are obliged to know the law, citizens are expected to behave according to the law, ignorance of the law is no excuse for non-compliance. Whether from a descriptive or sociological perspective this is untrue is of no importance to the normative claim. Another interesting variation is that the law must be accessible for citizens to know it, and secret law cannot possibly bind the citizens and impose obligations on them. All the variations of this principle are related to the rule of law or Rechtstaat.

The condition for citizens to know the law is that the law is public or made public. The means of making law available to citizen knowledge is through publication in the official journal. Each legal system or sub-legal system has its own official journal, even if it is only a virtual one available not in paper but electronically. An obligation can only be imposed on a citizen when such obligation has been made accessible to that citizen in an instrument which is meant to regulate the conduct or behaviour or the legal relations of that citizen. Any instrument published in the official journal of the Member State (or the region) where that citizen operates will fulfil such function. Any regulation published in the Official Journal of the EU will also fulfil such function.

As we have just explained, Community law is unique in that it operates by penetrating the legal and judicial systems of the Member States. Some instruments of Community law need a code or a password in order to enter the legal territory of the internal legal systems: directives are such special instruments. They are just like classical international treaties: they need to be ratified in order to make it into the internal legal system. If they are not incorporated into the official journals of the Member States (and/or its regions), they will only exist in the Official Journal of the EU and they will bind according to EC law. DAOE refers to this issue as the problem of the firewall, the issue as to how Community law can penetrate internal law. A citizen cannot be expected to know of any obligations which may be contained in a directive if that directive has not been translated into the law of the State. It is a question of citizens knowing the law or the law being accessible to the citizens: since directives are addressed to Member States and require them to incorporate into their legal systems the norms contained in those directives, then it would be a gross violation to extend that obligation to ordinary citizens. The directive may indeed be addressed to any manifestation of the Member State or any public administration and public undertaking, or any venture in which a public administration is a part or in which they hold control.

Whereas a regulation which is published in the Official Journal of the EU makes it directly into the law of the Member States because it is an instrument that applies directly or automatically in internal law as if it were internal law itself, a directive which is published in the Official Journal of the EU does not make it automatically into the law of the Member States. It requires a process of incorporation in order to become part of internal law. Of course, from the moment the directive is published in the Official Journal of the EU, it becomes part of Community law and produces effects in that law, even if it is never transposed. The directive forms part of EC law in any case, and even after its correct, full implementation in internal law, the norms contained in the directive will still be norms of Community law as long as they are not revoked or their validity has not expired. This point is very important; the fact that a directive has not been transposed into the internal law of a Member State only means that whatever norms it may contain cannot be applied to a private individual in that jurisdiction. This does not mean that the norms of the directive cannot operate; they do operate in EC law and they bind their addressees, the Member States, and they do so even before the expiry of the deadline for implementation.[15]

The principle that only the law which is made accessible to the citizens can be opposed against them has been pushed to its logical consequences in the recent judgments of 20 May 2003.[16] The condition that *Grana Padano* cheese must be grated and packaged in the region of production or that Parma ham must be sliced and packaged in the region of production cannot be relied on against economic operators, as those conditions were not brought to their attention or their knowledge by adequate publicity in Community legislation, which could have been done by mentioning those conditions in Regulation No 1107/96. However, the importers of the goods did not know about those requirements and limitations. It may be that in order to get to this interesting issue, the judgments had to go through rather unconvincing and excessively protectionist arguments

---

[15] Case C–129/96 *Inter-Environnement Wallonie ASBL v. Région Wallone* [1997] ECR I–7411.

[16] Case C–469/00 *Ravil SARL v. Bellon import SARL and Biraghi SpA,* judgment of 20 May 2003, not yet reported and Case C–108/01. *Consorzio del Prosciutto di Parma and Salumificio S Rota SpA v. Asda Stores Ltd and Hygrade Foods Ltd* judgment of 20 May 2003, not yet reported at paras 87 to 99.

based on the poor logic of the *Rioja II* judgment which is unfaithful to the principle that exceptions are to be construed narrowly.[17]

This is exactly the same rationale that has led to the conclusion that a directive cannot be opposed to an individual who is not expected to know the obligations contained in the norms of that directive. Miss Faccini Dori could not invoke the directive against Recreb Srl since the latter could not possibly know of the requirements or limitations imposed by that directive which had not been incorporated into Italian law. If I may put this in a provocative way, from the point of view of legal obligations, a citizen can ignore a directive and EC law expects the citizens to ignore directives! The question was and is normally analysed as horizontal direct effect of directives but this is somehow incorrect, it is in the very nature of the instrument that it cannot break through the firewall built into Community law: the norms of the directive operate through provisions of internal law and the citizen cannot be expected to know the obligations contained in a directive.[18] The rule of law would suffer a serious blow if citizens were made responsible for not knowing the law contained in instruments which are only addressed to public authorities.

4. DIRECT EFFECT

If the features of direct applicability are generally predicated about the sources or instruments of Community law—a regulation is directly applicable because it is a specific type of source and the directive is not because it is a source that requires domestic incorporation—the features of direct effect are predicated about the norms contained in the provisions of those instruments. Some norms are capable of governing legal relationships fully, others are incomplete and can only guide certain aspects of legal relations. It is not because a norm is contained in a directive, that it will be imperfect nor will it be perfect and capable of governing legal relations just because it is contained in a regulation. Paragraph 2 of Article 12 of Regulation 1612/68, discussed above, is a very good example. For a norm to operate fully or have full effects, it will have to fulfil certain conditions: clarity, completeness, unconditionality, no scope for discretion, possibility of defining the main features of the normative relationship: holder of an obligation, holder of a right, time and place, content and extent of the obligation, etc.[19] And the extent of the effectiveness of norms is always a pragmatic

---

[17] Case C–388/95 *Belgium* v. *Spain* [2000] ECR I–3123.

[18] 'Comme la Cour l'a relevé dans une jurisprudence constante depuis l' arrêt du 26 février 1986, Marshall (152/84, Rec. p. 723, point 48), une directive ne peut pas par elle-même créer d'obligations dans le chef d' un particulier et ne peut donc pas être invoquée en tant que telle à son encontre' (paragraph 20 of *Faccini Dori*), above n 2.

[19] The standard formulation runs along these lines: 'Disposition inconditionnelle et suffisamment précise pour pouvoir être invoquée à l'encontre de l' État par les particuliers. Ceux-ci sont dès lors fondés à sen prévaloir devant les juridictions nationales et . . . tous les organes de l'administration, y compris les autorités décentralisées, telles les communes, sont tenus d'en faire application.' See Case 103/88 *Fratelli Costanzo SpA* v. *Comune di Milano* [1989] ECR 1839.

question. Normally one expects norms contained in regulations to satisfy those conditions and norms contained in directives will normally be incomplete because they will recognise a scope for discretion of Member States to define more precisely some of the features of the legal relationship.

The question of direct effect in Community law arises because some norms are capable of governing legal relationships. If they are contained in instruments that are directly applicable—regulations or the Treaties—then there is no problem, but if they are contained in instruments that require incorporation—directives—then the particular legal features of the instrument apply: the directive being addressed to the Member States, the complete norm contained in the directive can be invoked directly against any organ of the state or the public administration from the moment the deadline for implementation has expired. But even if the norm is complete and capable of defining all imaginable aspects of a legal relationship, it will not be possible to invoke it against an individual unless it has trespassed the firewall of domestic law. This does not mean that the norm will have no effect at all. It will still be a norm of EC law and domestic law will still have to be interpreted in conformity with the untransposed directive. Legislators at the domestic level will not have the authority to adopt new norms that contradict those of EC law, including the untransposed directive, and even if the deadline for implementation has not expired.[20]

5. TYPES OF NORMS. ISSUES OF INTERPRETATION

Perhaps one should talk about about the different intensity of effects produced by norms in any legal order and also in EC law: from full intensity of effect to a lesser intensity of the EC law norm as an aid to interpretation of Community law, or even of domestic law (the duty to interpret internal law in conformity with Community law).[21] Full or complete norms will contain no conditional terms they will not be be time-bound, they will not allow for further discretion from the legislator.[22] The effectiveness of norms is a matter of degree; as we said above it is a pragmatic question.

Since the norm is always the result of an interpretation of one or more provisions contained in instruments recognised as sources of law, the characteristics or features of a norm, the degree or effect of this norm will also be a consequence of the interpretation performed. There is a principle of interpretation (a second order or metalinguistic principle) in Community law according to which provisions are to be interpreted usefully with a view to obtaining the maximum

---

[20] *Inter-Environnement Wallonie* (above n 15).

[21] C–106/89 *Marleasing SA v. La Comercial Internacionale de Alimentacion SA* [1990] ECR I–4135.

[22] This is probably what Justice Marshall had in mind when speaking about norms that had not left the realm of the legislator to enter the realm of the judge, an idea David Edward has elaborated upon when relating the doctrine of direct effect to the separation of powers.

effect of which they are capable (*effet utile*) so that the obligations and rights following from such norms are effective in regulating the behaviour of actors, and citizens can guide and justify their actions according to those norms. In order to define the different aspects of the legal or juridical relation governed by the norm, other elements may come in handy: the context or *sedes* of the provision, the logical relationships between norms of the system, the dynamic aspects of the law: the purpose, aims or the consequences they seek, etc. This does not mean distilling effective norms from provisions which yield very little because of their indeterminacy, their conditionality, their incompleteness, their obscurity or their ambiguity. There are limits to interpretation and the need to justify chosen interpretations according to more or less accepted standards is one of those important limits. Just as in the case of consistent interpretation, a provision of domestic law cannot be made to say something it clearly does not say. Although the syntagma *interpretatio contra legem* is circular, it does convey an interesting idea from a metalevel of interpretation.

To finish this contribution, I would like to recall one of the ideas dearest to David Edward in relation to direct effect of Community law, that is its close connection with the theory of obligations and *pacta sunt servanda*: third parties can derive rights from clear and unconditional obligations undertaken by primary players, in this case the Member States. Since the Member States undertook a standstill obligation in the old Article 12 of the EC Treaty mentioned above, then individuals could invoke those obligations before national courts and prevent Member States from increasing customs duties. The germ of this revolutionary and liberating idea is to be found in the very balanced use of discretion by the ECJ as far back as *van Gend en Loos*.[23] The Treaties had created rights which became part of the legal heritage or patrimony of the citizens. The Member States could no longer invoke their classical view of international law and their ascendancy over their subjects in order to hinder the operation and invokeability of EC law; the citizens (technically, the individuals) could directly rely on EC law in order to derive rights and defend those rights in the courts.

The court seems to be gestating new ways of understanding judicial protection and access to justice. There have been new developments of the theory of direct effect in cases like *Linster*,[24] or *Unilever*,[25] and previously in *CIA Security, Kraaijeveld* or *Inter-Environnement Wallonie*.[26] An individual can invoke a norm contained in a directive (a norm of Community law) even if untransposed into domestic law, in order to leave aside an incompatible norm of domestic law or in order to control its validity. Arguably these are not cases on direct effect in the classical sense, but they do have important elements in common: the possibility to rely on EC law before national courts even where direct individual

---

[23] Case 26/62 *Van Gend en Loos v. Nederlandse Administratie der Belastingen* [1963] ECR 1.
[24] C–287/98 *Luxembourg v. Berthe Linster, Aloyde Linster and Yvonne Linster* [2000] ECR I–6917.
[25] C–443/98 *Unilever Italia Spa v. Central Food SpA* [2000] ECR I–7535.
[26] Above n 15.

interest is weak and even if the norms relied upon are contained in instruments that are not directly applicable, in order to control the validity of domestic law. They are interesting examples of the effects that norms of Community law produce in the different legal systems where they apply. A new right of the citizen seems to be in the making, a right to rely on the rule of law in order to make sure the Community legal order is respected by all the Member States (even if no subjective right is directly derived from it). The citizen, and the associations and organisations of civil society thus become new custodians of the rule of EC law, new curators of the *ius civile europaeum*, a new, fascinating dimension of European citizenship. It is only to be hoped that there will be recognised an equally wide access to the court in order to control the validity of instruments of EC law,[27] opening up the heretofore restrictive jurisprudence on locus standi (Article 230, paragraph 4), which requires direct and individual concern interpreted in a way which strides against the criteria based on active citizenship. However, this development, which has heretofore been rejected by the Court, may first require a re-examination of the instruments of Community law, and especially of the regulation.

---

[27] Instruments which suffer from a greater democratic deficit than the instruments of internal law, the validity of which it encourages the citizens to control.

26

Du concept de l'effet direct à celui de l'invocabilité au regard de la jurisprudence récente de la Cour de justice

JUDGE MELCHIOR WATHELET

CE N'EST PAS un hasard qu'en hommage à David Edward, je consacre cet article à l'effet direct. L'article qu'il avait lui-même consacré à cette problématique suite à l'arrêt *Kraaijeveld*[1] et nos nombreuses discussions à ce sujet, jusque dans les couloirs ou par notes interposées auxquelles s'associait mon premier référendaire, Sean Van Raepenbusch, m'ont incité à tenter cette synthèse. Au-delà des raisons scientifiques, c'est aussi l'amitié et le plaisir d'avoir travaillé ensemble qui ont inspiré ces lignes, auxquelles Sean Van Raepenbusch a largement contribué, ce dont je le remercie.

Je ne doute pas du plaisir que nous aurons David Edward et moi-même de reparler de l'effet direct et de bien d'autres choses encore après notre départ de la Cour.

1. L'INTRODUCTION

L'applicabilité directe n'est pas une notion propre au droit communautaire.[2] Toutefois, les conditions dans lesquelles une disposition est susceptible de produire un effet direct (expression plus fréquemment utilisée que celle d'application directe) dans l'ordre juridique communautaire interne sont fondamentalement plus libérales qu'en droit international.[3]

---

[1] Affaire C–72/95 *Aannemersbedrijf P K Kraaijeveld BV v. Oedeputeerde Staten vai zuid Holland* [1996] ECR I–5403

[2] L'expression a été utilisée par la Cour permanente de Justice internationale dans l'affaire Ville libre de Danzig (avis consultatif n° 15 du 3 mars 1928, *Publication de la Cour permanente de Justice internationale*, Série AB, n° 28, p 17).

[3] Voy L-J Constantinesco, *L'application directe dans le droit de la CEE* (Paris, LGDJ, 1970); Kovar, *L'applicabilité directe du droit communautaire* (Clunet, 1973), p 219.

L'on se souviendra, de façon générale, que l'applicabilité directe d'un traité s'entend de son aptitude à produire directement, c'est-à-dire sans mesures d'exécution internes, des droits et des obligations dont les particuliers peuvent se prévaloir devant les tribunaux ou toute autre autorité nationale.[4] Certes, nul ne conteste aujourd'hui que les traités internationaux peuvent directement conférer aux particuliers des droits et des obligations invocables devant les juges internes et ne se cantonnent pas à produire des effets de droit à l'égard des États cocontractants, sujets classiques du droit international.

La grande majorité des traités ne revêtent cependant pas ce caractère. L'on ajoutera que, si un traité est dépourvu de caractère directement applicable, il n'en perd pas pour autant son caractère juridiquement obligatoire dans l'ordre interne, puisqu'il fait partie des règles de droit présentant un caractère obligatoire à l'égard de l'administration.[5]

Toute la difficulté réside alors dans l'analyse à laquelle il convient de se livrer pour établir si telle ou telle règle de droit international conventionnel possède ce caractère. Il semble bien que la *volonté des Parties contractantes* soit toujours une condition nécessaire et même suffisante pour la reconnaissance de l'effet direct.[6] Cela n'empêche cependant pas que les caractéristiques objectives du

---

[4] Le professeur J Velu a défini comme suit une norme ayant des effets directs dans l'ordre juridique national: 'La norme claire d'un traité, juridiquement complète, qui impose aux États contractants soit de s'abstenir, soit d'agir de manière déterminée, et qui est susceptible d'être invoquée comme source d'un droit propre par les personnes relevant de la juridiction de ces États ou de soumettre ces personnes à des obligations' ('Les effets directs des instruments internationaux en matière de droits de l'homme', in *L'effet direct en droit belge des traités internationaux en général et des instruments internationaux relatifs aux droits de l'homme en particulier* (Bruylant, Éditions de l'ULB, 1981), p 56).

[5] Ainsi, le Conseil d'État belge pourrait valablement être saisi d'un reCours en annulation concernant la légalité d'un acte administratif au regard d'un tel traité, sans devoir vérifier si celui-ci a pour objet de faire naître des droits ou des obligations pour le requérant, dès lors que le contrôle de la juridiction administrative est objectif (voir, en ce sens M Waelbroeck, «*Traités internationaux et juridictions internes dans les pays du marché commun*» CIDC 1969, n° 161 M Verhoeven, JT, 1969, p 697). Le Conseil d'État a ainsi jugé, à propos de l'article 13, paragraphe 2, du pacte international relatif aux droits économiques, sociaux et culturels, en matière d'accès à l'enseignement, 'que la question ainsi posée n'est pas de savoir si le pacte . . . a conféré aux particuliers des droits subjectifs dont ils pourraient se prévaloir devant les tribunaux, mais de vérifier si la législation belge est compatible avec l'objectif inscrit dans la règle claire et précise de l'article 13,2, a), du pacte' (arrêts du 6 septembre 1989, n° 32 989 et 32 990, RACE, 1989 pp 66 et 71).

La Cour d'arbitrage belge s'est prononcée dans le même sens en censurant des normes législatives violant l'obligation, fondée sur l'article 13 du pacte, d'assurer progressivement la gratuité dans divers secteurs de l'enseignement, alors même que cette disposition n'est pas revêtue d'effet direct (arrêt n° 40/94, du 19 mai 1994, APM, juin 1994, p 109; M Melchior et P Vandernoot, rapport de la Cour d'arbitrage de Belgique au colloque des Cours constitutionnelles des États de la Communauté européenne (Paris, septembre 1997), ayant pour thème: 'Contrôle de constitutionnalité et droit communautaire dérivé', p 3).

[6] Voir l'avis Compétences des tribunaux de Dantzig, précité, de la CPJI; J Verhoeven, 'Applicabilité directe des traités et 'intentions des parties contractantes', in *Liber Amicorum E. Krings*, (Brussel 1991), p 895.

traité (caractère précis et juridiquement achevé) puissent être prises en compte pour dégager l'intention des Parties.[7]

A la différence de ce qui prévaut encore à l'égard des traités internationaux, il existe une présomption en faveur de l'effet direct dans l'ordre juridique communautaire. La question n'est pas purement d'ordre quantitatif: elle est d'ordre qualitatif dès lors que le droit communautaire, dans son ensemble, en ce compris les traités fondateurs, nonobstant leur qualité de traités internationaux, est comme tel apte à produire des effets qui affectent immédiatement la situation personnelle et matérielle des particuliers, dans la mesure où le droit communautaire est au service d'un projet d'intégration.[8] La Cour de justice, après avoir constaté que la norme se suffit à elle-même (est complète et précise), est donc 'justiciable', vérifie simplement si elle 'concerne' les particuliers, si, 'par sa nature, elle est prête à produire des effets directs dans les relations juridiques entre les États membres et leurs justiciables'[9] (effet direct vertical) et, le cas échéant, entre les particuliers eux-mêmes (effet direct horizontal).

En somme, le fondement de l'effet direct, en droit communautaire, est la spécificité même de l'ordre juridique communautaire: 'c'est la finalité d'intégration qui postule l'applicabilité de principe'.[10] Ce qui est visé, c'est, selon R LeCourt, 'le droit pour toute personne de demander à son juge de lui appliquer traités, règlements, directives ou décisions communautaires. C'est aussi l'obligation pour le juge de faire usage de ces textes, quelle que soit la législation du pays dont il relève'.[11]

Compte tenu précisément de l'étendue des obligations qui pèsent, à divers égards, sur le juge national en vue d'assurer l'efficacité des normes communautaires et, en particulier, de protéger les droits que ces normes confèrent aux particuliers, la question se pose de savoir s'il est encore approprié de reCourir au seul concept de l'effet direct pour désigner l'aptitude d'une disposition de droit communautaire à être invoquée par un particulier devant le juge national.

A vrai dire, la règle communautaire peut être invoquée devant le juge national avec différentes finalités: pour déterminer ou orienter l'interprétation d'une norme nationale, écarter une norme nationale contraire, obtenir réparation

---

[7] Ainsi, dans un arrêt du 4 novembre 1999, la Cour de cassation belge a jugé que les dispositions de l'article 3 de la Convention de New-York du 20 novembre 1989 relative aux droits de l'enfant, qui prévoit notamment que l'intérêt de ce dernier doit être une considération primordiale dans toute décision le concernant, ne sont pas 'suffisamment précises et complètes pour avoir un effet direct, dès lors qu'elles laissent à l'État plusieurs possibilités de satisfaire aux exigences de l'intérêt de l'enfant'. La Cour d'appel de Gand, dont l'arrêt a été cassé, avait estimé que, lorsqu'une demande concernant la filiation d'un enfant est introduite, quelle que soit la personne qui l'introduit, le droit international oblige le juge à tenir compte de l'intérêt des enfants (*Pasicrisie belge*, 1999, 588).

[8] Voir D Simon, 'Le fondement de l'autonomie du droit communautaire', colloque de Bordeaux, Droit international et communautaire, perspectives actuelles, texte polycopié, 44.

[9] Voy. à ce propos, les commentaires de P. Pescatore, 'International Law and Community Law. A comparative Analysis', 6 *CML Rev* (1970) 167, p 174–5.

[10] G Isaac, *Droit communautaire général* (Masson, 1989), p 157.

[11] R LeCourt, *L'Europe des juges* (Bruylant, Bruxelles, 1976), p 248.

d'un dommage subi du fait de la violation du droit communautaire par un État membre, ou encore pour être appliquée en lieu et place d'une règle nationale contraire, voire en l'absence de toute règle nationale. La doctrine française a fort judicieusement qualifié ces différentes hypothèses d'invocabilité d'interprétation conforme, d'exclusion, de réparation et de substitution.[12] La question se pose de savoir dans lesquelles de ces hypothèses la norme communautaire, pour pouvoir être invoquée devant un juge national, doit satisfaire aux conditions minimales de précision et de caractère inconditionnel requises pour se voir reconnaître un effet direct. Je suis d'avis que seule l'invocabilité de substitution requiert cette exigence dès lors que, dans cette hypothèse, c'est la règle communautaire et uniquement elle que le juge national est invité à appliquer pour garantir le droit conféré par l'ordre juridique communautaire au justiciable. Mais, la jurisprudence de la Cour, en son état actuel, semble l'imposer également pour l'invocabilité d'exclusion.

Il n'est pas inutile de faire le point de la jurisprudence à cet égard.

Nous terminerons par quelques considérations relatives à l'effet direct des accords internationaux conclus par la Communauté, à propos desquels la grille d'analyse qui précède n'est pas pleinement transposable.

2. L'INTERPRÉTATION CONFORME

C'est à propos des directives, en particulier lorsqu'elles n'ont pas été transposées ou correctement transposées, que la Cour a dégagé le principe dit de 'l'interprétation conforme'.

L'effectivité du droit communautaire requiert évidemment que les mesures nationales prises pour la mise en œuvre d'une directive soient interprétées et appliquées conformément aux exigences du droit communautaire.[13] Dans l'arrêt *Von Colson et Kamann*,[14] à propos de la nature des sanctions d'une discrimination fondée sur le sexe, la Cour, après avoir considéré qu'aucune obligation inconditionnelle et suffisamment précise n'était prévue par la directive 76/207/CEE[15]—celle-ci laissant aux États membres "la liberté de choisir parmi les différentes solutions propres à réaliser son objet", a cependant ajouté qu'il appartenait :

---

[12] Voir D Simon, *Le système juridique communautaire* (2ème édition, PUF, 1998), p. 308 et suiv; Y Galmot et J-C Bonichot, 'La Cour de justice des Communautés européennes et la transposition des Directives en droit national' (1998) *RFDA* 16, spéc 10, arrêt Affaire 14/83 *von Colson et Elisabeth Kamman* v. *Land Nordstein-Westfalen* [1984] ECR 1891. Voy également T Tridimas, 'Black, White, and Shades of Grey: Horizontality of Directives Revisited' (2002) *YEL*.

[13] Voir arrêts du 12 novembre 1974 Affaire 32–74 *Friedrich Haagen GmbH* [1974] ECR 1201; du 20 mai 1976, Affaire 11–75 *Impresa Costruzioni comm Quirino Mazzalai* v. *Ferroria del Penon* [1976] ECR 657, point 10.

[14] Voy. Supra n 11.

[15] Directive du Conseil, du 9 février 1976, relative à la mise en œuvre du principe de l'égalité de traitement entre hommes et femmes en ce qui concerne l'accès à l'emploi, à la formation et à la promotion professionnelles, et les conditions de travail (JO 1976 L39 40).

à la juridiction nationale de donner à la loi prise pour l'application de la directive, dans toute la mesure où une marge d'appréciation lui est accordée par son droit national, une interprétation et une application conformes aux exigences du droit communautaire (point 28).

A cet égard, la Cour a estimé que, si un État a choisi le versement d'une indemnité par l'employeur fautif, son montant devait être adéquat par rapport au préjudice subi et devait donc aller au-delà d'une indemnisation purement symbolique.

L'exigence d'une interprétation conforme joue également lorsque la transposition d'une directive fait tout simplement défaut: les juridictions nationales, lorsqu'elles interprètent toute disposition de droit national, antérieure et postérieure, sont tenues :

> de le faire dans toute la mesure du possible à la lumière du texte et de la finalité de la directive pour atteindre le résultat visé par celle-ci et se conformer ainsi à l'article 189 du traité [devenu article 249 CE].[16]

Il est clair que cette obligation s'impose au juge national, même et surtout si la norme communautaire en cause n'est pas suffisamment précise et inconditionnelle pour être directement appliquée.[17] Évidemment, l'interprétation conforme a ses limites; elle ne permet pas d'écarter une règle nationale littéralement contraire au droit communautaire.

Ce qui vaut pour les directives vaut d'ailleurs pour tout acte communautaire producteur d'effet juridique et même non contraignant. Ainsi, la Cour a jugé, dans son arrêt du 13 décembre 1989, *Grimaldi*[18] que :

> les juges nationaux sont tenus de prendre les recommandations en considération en vue de la solution des litiges qui leur sont soumis, notamment lorsque celles-ci éclairent l'interprétation de dispositions nationales prises dans le but d'assurer leur mise en oeuvre, ou encore lorsqu'elles ont pour objet de compléter des dispositions communautaires ayant un caractère contraignant.

Ce n'est, certes, pas 'l'interprétation conforme' à proprement parler, mais il s'agit incontestablement d'une obligation découlant, de façon générale, du devoir de coopération loyale, inscrit à l'article 10 CE.

---

[16] Arrêt du 13 novembre 1990, Affaire C06/89 *Marleasing SA v. La Comercial Internacional de Alimentacion SA* [1990] ECR I–4135 point 26. Voir également arrêts du 16 décembre 1993, Affaire C–334/92 *Teodoro Wagner diret v. Fondo de garantia Salarial* [1993] ECR I–6911, point 20; du 30 avril 1998, Affaire C–215/97 *Barbara Bellene v. Yokohama SpA* [1998] ECR I–2191; du 22 septembre 1998, Affaire C–185/97 *Belinea Jane Cooke v. Granada Hospitality Ltd* [1998] ECR I–5199, point 18; du 27 juin 2000, Affaires jointes C–240/98 à C–244/98 *Océano Grupo Editorial SA v. Roció Murciano Quintero et Editores Sa v. José m Sánchez Alcón Prades et al* [2000] ECR I–4941, point 30.
[17] Voir arrêts du 14 juillet 1994, Affaire C–91/92 *Paola Faccinin Dori v. Recreb Srl* [1994] ECR I–3325, point 26, et du 15 juin 2000, Affaire C–365/98 *Brinhmann Tabafabriken GmbH v. Hauptzollamt Bielefeld* [2000] ECR I–4619, point 40.
[18] Affaire C–322/98 *Salvatore Grimaldi v. Fonds des maladies professionnelles* [1989] ECR 4407, point 19.

3. L'EXCLUSION DES REGLES NATIONALES CONTRAIRES

L'on se souviendra, à cet égard, du célèbre arrêt *Simmenthal*.[19]

Interrogée sur la compatibilité avec le droit communautaire, et spécialement, avec la notion d'effet direct, du monopole que s'était réservé la Cour constitutionnelle italienne pour vérifier la compatibilité des actes législatifs internes avec le droit communautaire et, donc, avec l'article 11 de la constitution italienne, la Cour, dans son arrêt *Simmenthal*, répond on ne peut plus clairement:

> Le juge national chargé d'appliquer, dans le cadre de sa compétence, les dispositions du droit communautaire, a l'obligation d'assurer le plein effet de ces normes, en laissant au besoin inappliquée, de sa propre autorité, toute disposition contraire de la législation nationale, même postérieure, sans qu'il ait à demander ou à attendre l'élimination préalable de celle-ci par voie législative ou par tout autre procédé constitutionnel.

Cette obligation, qui pèse sur le juge national, doit le conduire à écarter tout obstacle, même de nature constitutionnelle, que le droit national pourrait opposer à l'accomplissement du plein effet de la règle communautaire.

La jurisprudence *Simmenthal* s'inscrit parfaitement dans le cadre de la mission générale dévolue aux juridictions internes, lesquelles sont appelées à se prononcer 'en première ligne' sur les questions d'interprétation et d'application du droit communautaire eu égard au système de l'administration indirecte qui caractérise l'ordre juridique communautaire.[20]

Ceci ne transforme nullement le juge national en juge exerçant une compétence communautaire, ainsi que le souligne Louis Dubouis,[21] mais lui impose, 'comme à tout organe de l'État', d'assurer la satisfaction du droit communautaire. Sa mission, à cet égard, est d'autant plus cruciale que, 'face au stade ultime de l'exécution de la règle', il est le garant du respect de celle-ci.

Or, pour écarter une norme nationale contraire, point n'est besoin, pour le juge national, de lui reconnaître un effet direct.

A cet égard, la jurisprudence de la Cour a connu une évolution remarquable ces dernières années à la faveur d'un renforcement de la protection juridictionnelle des particuliers et de l'efficacité des normes communautaires, spécialement celles contenues dans des directives. Voyons plutôt.

---

[19] Arrêt du 9 mars 1978, Affaire 106/77 *Administration des finances de Etat* v. *Société anongre Simmenthal* [1978] ECR 629, point 21. Voy déjà les arrêts du 4 avril 1968, Affaire 34/67 *Firma Gebrüden Lück* v. *Hauptzollamt Köln-Rheinau* [1968] ECR 359, spéc 370; du 7 mars 1972, Affaire 84/71 *Spot Marmet* v. *Ministero delle Finaze* [1972] ECR 89; du 17 mars 1972, Affaire 93/71 *Orsohl Lenesio* v. *Ministero dell'agricoltura e foreste* [1972] ECR 287; du 4 avril 1974, Affaire 167/73 *Commission* v. *France* [1974] ECR 359.

[20] Voy A Barav, 'La plénitude de compétence du juge national en sa qualité de juge communautaire', in *l'Europe et le droit, Mélanges en hommage à Jean Boulouis* (Dalloz, 1991), p 1.

[21] L Dubois, 'La responsabilité de l'État pour les dommages causés aux particuliers par la violation du droit communautaire' (1992) *RFDA*, spéc 9.

L'arrêt du 30 avril 1996, *CIA Security International SA*,[22] qui porte sur les conséquences d'un défaut de notification d'une règle technique au sens de la directive 83/189,[23] constitue un bon point de départ pour notre analyse.

On rappellera que, afin de favoriser la libre circulation des marchandises, cette directive prévoit une procédure de contrôle préventive en obligeant les États membres à communiquer tout projet de règle technique à la Commission, qui porte aussitôt le projet à la connaissance des autres États membres. La Commission ou un autre État membre peut ensuite émettre un avis circonstancié selon lequel la mesure envisagée devrait être modifiée afin d'éliminer ou de limiter les entraves à la libre circulation des biens qui pourraient éventuellement en découler. L'adoption du projet est automatiquement reportée de trois mois pour permettre son examen et le report est de six à douze mois dans l'hypothèse où des objections ont été émises sur sa compatibilité avec le traité ou lorsque la Commission indique son intention d'adopter une directive sur le sujet (voir articles 8 et 9 de la directive).

Dans une communication de 1986,[24] la Commission en avait déduit que, si un État membre adoptait une règle technique au sens de cette directive sans la notifier, ladite règle ne pouvait être rendue exécutoire à l'égard des tiers.

Cette position, contestée par certains États membres, déjà débattue devant la Cour sans que celle-ci ne se soit prononcée,[25] a été entérinée par la Cour dans son arrêt *CIA Security International SA*.

En l'occurrence, CIA Security, ayant pour activité la fabrication et la vente de systèmes et de centraux d'alarme, reprochait à deux sociétés concurrentes (Signalson SA et Securitel SPRL) de l'avoir diffamée en prétendant notamment qu'un système anti-effraction qu'elle commercialisait ne remplissait pas les conditions de la législation belge en matière de systèmes de sécurité. A titre reconventionnel, ces deux dernières sociétés faisaient valoir que CIA Security n'était pas agréée en tant qu'entreprise de sécurité et qu'elle commercialisait un système d'alarme non approuvé, de telle sorte qu'elle devait se voir interdire la poursuite de ses activités. Se posait, à cet égard, la question de savoir si la législation belge en cause, prétendument méconnue par CIA Security, constituait des règles techniques qui auraient dû, préalablement à leur adoption, être notifiées à la Commission conformément à l'article 8 de la directive 83/189.

Avant de se prononcer sur les conséquences du défaut de notification, à l'égard d'un particulier, la Cour a pris soin de constater que les dispositions en

---

[22] Affaire C-194/94 *CIA Security International* v. *Signelson St Et Securities SPRL* [1996] ECR I-2209.

[23] Directive 83/189/CEE du Conseil, du 28 mars 1983, prévoyant une procédure d'information dans le domaine des normes et réglementations techniques (JO 1989 L109 8), telle que modifiée par la Directive 94/10/CE du Parlement européen et du Conseil, du 23 mars 1994, portant deuxième modification substantielle de la Directive 83/189 (JO 1994 L100 30).

[24] JO 1986 C 245/4 (1er Octobre 1986).

[25] Arrêts du 27 octobre 1993 Affaire C-69/91 *Procédure penade contre Franicine Decoster* [1993] ECR I-5335 et du 14 juillet 1994, Affaire C-52/93 *Commission* v. *Pays-Bas* [1994] ECR I-3591.

cause de la directive étaient inconditionnelles et suffisamment précises de sorte que les particuliers pouvaient s'en prévaloir devant un juge national.

La Cour a estimé, en effet, que :

> les articles 8 et 9 de la directive 83/189 prescrivent une obligation précise pour les États membres de notifier à la Commission les projets de règles techniques avant leur adoption. Étant, par conséquent, du point de vue de leur contenu, inconditionnels et suffisamment précis, ces articles peuvent être invoqués par les particuliers devant leurs juridictions nationales (point 44).

Ce n'est qu'ensuite que la Cour a jugé qu'il incombe au juge national 'de refuser d'appliquer la règle technique nationale qui n'a pas été notifiée conformément à la directive' (point 55).

Au soutien de cette dernière conclusion, elle relève que :

> l'objectif de la directive est la protection de la libre circulation des marchandises par un contrôle préventif et que l'obligation de notification constitue un moyen essentiel pour la réalisation de ce contrôle communautaire. L'efficacité de ce contrôle sera d'autant renforcée que la directive est interprétée en ce sens que la méconnaissance de l'obligation de notification constitue un vice de procédure substantiel de nature à entraîner l'inapplicabilité des règles en cause aux particuliers (point 48).[26]

Il apparaît ainsi, à la lecture de cet arrêt, que même l'invocabilité d'exclusion (dès lors qu'il s'agit non pas d'appliquer directement une règle communautaire, mais uniquement d'écarter une règle technique nationale qui n'a pas été préalablement notifiée à la Commission conformément à la directive 83/189) serait subordonnée à l'examen préalable des caractéristiques de la règle communautaire appliquée (caractère précis et inconditionnel), ce qui, à notre avis, ne se justifie pas dès lors qu'il ne s'agit pas pour le particulier de se prévaloir d'un droit subjectif directement conféré par la norme communautaire et qui n'existe pas dans l'ordre juridique national. Et ce d'autant plus que l'effet direct même dérivé de la disposition en cause serait inopérant, puisque l'effet direct horizontal n'est pas reconnu aux directives.

---

[26] Dans son arrêt du 16 juin 1998 (Affaire C–226/97 *Procédure penale contre Johannes Martinus Lemmens* [1998] ECR I–3711), la Cour a précisé la portée de sa jurisprudence CIA dans le cadre d'une procédure pénale engagée à l'encontre de M. Lemmens pour excès de vitesse en état d'ivresse. L'examen d'alcoométrie avait été effectué sur le prévenu au moyen d'un éthylomètre répondant aux normes d'un arrêté imposant à la police judiciaire l'utilisation d'appareils aux caractéristiques techniques précises, normes qui n'avaient pas été notifiées à la Commission conformément à la Directive 83/189. La juridiction de renvoi demandait donc si le prévenu pouvait invoquer l'inapplicabilité dudit arrêté pour ce motif. La Cour répond par la négative: 'Si l'absence de notification des règles techniques, constituant un vice de procédure dans leur adoption, rend ces dernières inapplicables en tant qu'elles entravent l'utilisation et la commercialisation d'un produit non conforme à ces règles, elle n'a par contre pas l'effet de rendre illégale toute utilisation d'un produit qui est conforme aux règles non notifiées' (point 35): 'Or, l'utilisation du produit par les pouvoirs publics, dans un cas comme celui de l'espèce, n'est pas susceptible de créer une entrave aux échanges qui aurait pu être évitée si la procédure de notification avait été suivie' (point 36).

La Cour limite ainsi, par cet arrêt, l'inopposabilité de règles techniques non notifiées aux situations d'entraves aux échanges, contraires aux objectifs de la Directive violée.

A noter que la Cour s'est référée à l'arrêt *Enichem Base* du 13 juillet 1989[27] qui concernait l'obligation pour les États membres, prévue par la directive 75/442,[28] de communiquer à la Commission tout projet de réglementation nationale en matière de déchets et où la Cour n'avait reconnu aucun droit, dans le chef des particuliers, d'obtenir, devant les juridictions nationales, l'annulation ou l'inapplication d'une réglementation nationale qui aurait été adoptée sans avoir été communiquée au préalable à la Commission. La Cour a constaté, à cet égard, que la directive ne fixait pas de procédure de contrôle communautaire des projets de réglementation et ne subordonnait pas leur mise en vigueur à l'accord ou à la non-opposition de la Commission, l'obligation de communication visant uniquement à permettre à la Commission d'être informée sur les mesures nationales envisagées dans le domaine de l'élimination des déchets afin de pouvoir évaluer les nécessités d'une harmonisation communautaire ainsi que d'examiner si les projets étaient ou non compatibles avec le droit communautaire. En conséquence, selon la Cour, l'obligation de communication préalable concernait les relations entre les États membres et la Commission, mais n'engendrait aucun droit dans le chef des particuliers qui soit susceptible d'être lésé (points 21 à 23 de l'arrêt *Enichem Base*).

S'agissant, en revanche, de la directive 83/189, le but de celui-ci n'est pas, selon la Cour, simplement d'informer la Commission, mais d'éliminer ou de restreindre les entraves aux échanges dans le cadre de dispositions claires, subordonnant la date de mise en œuvre des réglementations nationales à l'accord ou à la non-opposition de la Commission (points 49 et 50 de l'arrêt *CIA Security*).

A vrai dire, la différence de solution entre l'arrêt *CIA Security* et l'arrêt *Enichem Base* ne nous paraît pas découler de l'existence ou non d'un droit subjectif dans le chef des particuliers susceptible d'être lésé, ni du caractère précis et inconditionnel des dispositions communautaires en cause, mais du mécanisme même mis en place par les directives: dans un cas, la directive avait pour seul objectif de garantir que la Commission fût tenue informée des mesures nationales adoptées (en l'occurrence, dans le domaine de l'élimination des déchets), sans que leur prise d'effet eût pu dépendre du respect de cette obligation d'informer; dans l'autre cas, c'est la mise en œuvre des réglementations nationales envisagées qui était subordonnée à la notification préalable.

Si l'arrêt *CIA Security* a été considéré comme constituant une contribution importante de la Cour pour garantir l'effet utile de la directive, il a aussi suscité de profondes inquiétudes dans tous les États membres ayant omis de notifier des règles techniques, au point qu'avait été fortement envisagée l'introduction d'un protocole dans le traité d'Amsterdam dans le but d'éviter ou de réduire les effets rétroactifs de cette jurisprudence sur l'ensemble des règles non notifiées. Tel ne

---

[27] Affaire 380/87 *Enichen Base ea* v. *Comme di Cinisello Balsamo* [1989] ECR 2491.
[28] Directive 75/442 du Conseil, du 15 juillet 1975, relative aux déchets (JO L 194, p 47).

fut finalement pas le cas. Les États membres ont notifié les règles techniques qui auraient dû l'être, sous forme de nouveaux projets et une 'opération de rattrapage' a été lancée.

C'est à nouveau la directive 83/189 qui était en cause dans l'affaire *Unilever*[29] arrêt du 26 septembre 2000, mais cette fois dans le cadre d'un litige entre parties contractantes, l'un fournisseur, l'autre acheteur, et non plus entre particuliers dans le cadre d'un procès en concurrence déloyale, comme dans l'affaire *CIA Security*.

On rappellera, en exergue, que les directives ne peuvent jamais produire un effet direct horizontal, c'est-à-dire qu'elles ne sont jamais opposables, en tant que telles, aux justiciables, qui ne peuvent donc jamais, par leur effet, être obligés à l'égard de l'État ou à l'égard d'autres particuliers: leur caractère contraignant n'existe qu'à l'égard de 'tout État membre destinataire'.[30] Selon la Cour, étendre l'invocabilité des directives non transposées entre particuliers 'reviendrait à reconnaître à la Communauté le pouvoir d'édicter avec effet immédiat des obligations à la charge des particuliers, alors qu'elle ne détient cette compétence que là où lui est attribué le pouvoir d'adopter des règlements' (arrêt *Faccini Dori*, précité supra n 17, point 23).[31]

En l'occurrence, la société Unilever Italia SpA avait fourni à Central Food SpA, en exécution d'une commande, 648 litres d'huile d'olive extra-vierge. Central Food a cependant refusé de régler le prix au motif que l'huile n'était pas étiquetée conformément à la loi italienne, laquelle, cependant, avait été pro-

---

[29] Affaire C–443/98 *Unilever Italia Spf* v. *Central Food SpA* [2001] ECR I–7535.

[30] Voir arrêts du 26 février 1986, Affaire 152/84 *Marshall* v. *Southampton and South-West Hampshire Area Health Authority (Teaching)* [1986] ECR 723; du 12 mai 1987, Affaires jointes 372 à 374/85 *Ministére public* v. *Oscar Traen et autres* [1987] ECR 2141; du 22 février 1990, Affaire C–221/88 *CECA* v. *Fillite Acciaierie e Ferriere Busseni SpA* [1990] ECR I–495, et surtout *Faccini Dori*, précité supra n 17. et, plus récemment, arrêt du 16 juillet 1998, Affaire C–355/96 *Silhouette International Selmied GmbH & Co KG* v. *Hartlauer Handelsgesellschaft GmbH* [1998] ECR I–4799. Cette jurisprudence est constante malgré les conclusions des avocats généraux Van Gerven, Jacobs et Lenz, favorables à la reconnaissance d'un effet horizontal respectivement dans les affaires Affaire C–262/88 *Douglas Harvey Barber* v. *Guardian Royal Exchange Assurance Group* [1990] ECR I–1889; Affaire C–316/93 *Nicole Vaneetveld* v. *SA Le Foyer* et *SA le Foyer* v. *Fédération des mutualités socialistes et syndicates de la province de Lis socialistes et syndicates de la province de Lièse* [1994] ECR I–763, et *Faccini Dori*, précitée. Pour une analyse critique de cette jurisprudence, voy F Emmert et M Fereira de Azevedo, 'Les jeux sont faits: rien ne va plus ou une nouvelle occasion perdue par la CJCE' (1995) *RTDE*, 11; T Tridimas, 'Horizontal Effect of Directives: A Missed Opportunity', 19 *EL Rev* (1994) 621.

[31] De même, une autorité nationale ne peut se prévaloir, à charge d'un particulier, d'une disposition d'une Directive dont la transposition nécessaire en droit national n'a pas encore eu lieu (arrêts du 8 octobre 1987, Affaire 80/86 *Procédure finale contre Kolpinghuis Nijmeja BV* [1987] ECR 3969, point 9; du 26 septembre 1996, Affaire C–168/95 *Procédure finale contre Luciano Arcaco* [1996] ECR I–4705, point 36). Toutefois, une Directive est opposable à l'encontre de toute autorité publique, quelle qu'elle soit (même l'État), lorsqu'elle agit en tant qu'employeur (arrêt *Marshall*, précité supra n 29), y compris les organes décentralisés, telles les communes (arrêt du 22 juin 1984, Affaire 103/88 *Fratelli Costazzo SpA* v. *Commune di drilano* [1989] ECR 1839).

mulguée en violation de la directive 83/189. En effet, la Commission avait demandé à la République italienne de reporter l'adoption de la loi de douze mois, compte tenu de son intention de légiférer en la matière, ce qui n'a pas empêché le législateur italien de voter la loi litigieuse et de la publier.

Le juge national, saisi du litige entre Unilever et Central Food, a donc posé à la Cour la question de savoir s'il était en droit d'écarter l'application d'une règle technique nationale qui a été adoptée pendant une période de report d'adoption prévue par la directive 83/189.

La Cour a rappelé son arrêt, *CIA Security*, précité supra n 28, dans lequel, ainsi qu'on l'a vu, elle a déjà jugé que la méconnaissance de l'obligation de notification des règles techniques entraîne leur inapplicabilité, de sorte qu'elles ne peuvent pas être opposées aux particuliers. Ces derniers peuvent donc se prévaloir des articles 8 et 9 de la directive 83/189 devant le juge national, auquel il incombe de refuser d'appliquer une règle technique nationale qui n'a pas été notifiée conformément à ladite directive.

Dans son arrêt *Unilever*, la Cour a traité de la même façon les cas de méconnaissance des obligations de report d'adoption, prévues à l'article 9 de la directive, conformément à l'objectif de celle-ci, y compris en ce qui concerne la possibilité pour les particuliers d'invoquer l'inapplicabilité des règles techniques adoptées en méconnaissance de ces obligations dans une procédure civile les opposant au sujet de droits et d'obligations d'ordre contractuel.

Cet arrêt franchit ainsi une étape supplémentaire par rapport à l'arrêt *CIA Security*, où la Cour, avant d'inviter le juge national à écarter la règle technique adoptée en méconnaissance de la directive, avait vérifié si les dispositions pertinentes de celles-ci satisfaisaient aux conditions minimales de l'effet direct, c'est-à-dire de précision et de caractère inconditionnel, ce qu'elle ne fait pas dans la présente affaire. Or, ici, plus clairement encore que dans l'affaire *CIA Security*, nous sommes en présence d'un litige entre deux opérateurs économiques à l'encontre desquels une directive ne saurait, en tout état de cause, être invoquée. La Cour précise, à cet égard:

> S'il est vrai . . ., qu'une directive ne peut pas par elle-même créer d'obligations dans le chef d'un particulier et ne peut donc pas être invoquée en tant que telle à son encontre (voir arrêt du 14 juillet 1994, Faccini Dori, C–91/92, Rec. p. I–3325, point 20), cette jurisprudence ne s'applique pas dans une situation, où le non-respect de l'article 8 ou de l'article 9 de la directive 83/189, qui constitue un vice de procédure substantiel, entraîne l'inapplicabilité de la règle technique adoptée en méconnaissance de l'un de ces articles (point 50).
>
> Dans une telle situation, et contrairement à l'hypothèse de la non-transposition des directives couverte par la jurisprudence [Faccini Dori], la directive 83/189 ne définit nullement le contenu matériel de la règle de droit sur le fondement de laquelle le juge national doit trancher le litige pendant devant lui. Elle ne crée ni des droits ni des obligations pour les particuliers (point 31).

Bel exemple d'invocabilité d'exclusion d'une directive: qu'elle ait ou non un effet direct ne changerait rien à cette invocabilité.

Une autre illustration nous est donnée par l'arrêt du 18 septembre 2000, *Linster*,[32] cette fois à propos de la directive 85/337.[33]

En vue de la réalisation de la liaison autoroutière avec la Sarre, l'État luxembourgeois avait introduit devant le juge national une demande d'expropriation de terrains à l'encontre des consorts Linster, propriétaires de ces terrains. Pour leur défense, ces derniers avaient notamment fait valoir que le projet en cause n'avait pas été précédé d'une étude des incidences sur l'environnement ni d'une enquête publique conformément à la directive 85/337. Or, cette directive n'avait pas été intégralement transposée en droit luxembourgeois.

La question posée alors à la Cour de justice, dans cette affaire, était de savoir si le juge national pouvait néanmoins prendre en considération la directive afin de contrôler si certaines formalités prescrites par cet acte avaient été respectées.

La réponse de la Cour a été positive. Rappelant ce qu'elle avait déjà jugé dans ses arrêts du 1er février 1977, *Verbond van Nederlandse Ondernemingen*,[34] points 22 à 24, du 24 octobre 1996, *Kraaijeveld e.a.*, precite, supra n 1, point 56 et du 16 septembre 1999, *WWF ea*,[35] , point 69, la Cour a jugé qu'il serait incompatible avec l'effet contraignant de la directive (voir art. 249, al. 3, CE)

> d'exclure en principe que **l'obligation qu'elle impose** puisse être invoquée par des personnes concernées. Particulièrement dans les cas dans lesquels les autorités communautaires auraient, par voie de directive, obligé les États membres à adopter un comportement déterminé, l'effet utile d'un tel acte se trouverait affaibli si les justiciables étaient empêchés de s'en prévaloir en justice et les juridictions nationales empêchées de le prendre en considération en tant qu'élément du droit communautaire pour vérifier si, dans l'exercice de la faculté qui lui est réservée quant à la forme et aux moyens pour la mise en œuvre de la directive, le législateur national est resté dans les limites de la marge d'appréciation tracée par la directive (point 32; c'est nous qui soulignons).

La directive est ainsi invoquée pour **écarter la norme nationale contraire**, en l'occurrence une procédure d'expropriation pour cause d'utilité publique, dans le cadre de la réalisation d'une autoroute, lorsque l'évaluation préalable des incidences du projet sur l'environnement n'a pas été effectuée, que les informations recueillies aux termes de l'article 5 de la directive 85/337 n'ont pas été mises à la disposition du public et que le public concerné n'a pas eu la possibilité d'exprimer son avis avant que le projet ne soit entamé, contrairement aux prescriptions de l'article 6, paragraphe 2, de la directive.

Force est de constater que la Cour n'a pas préalablement vérifié, comme elle l'avait fait dans son arrêt *CIA Security*, si les dispositions en cause de la

---

[32] Affaire C–287/98 *Luxembourg v. Berthe Linster, Algose Linster et Yvonne Linster* [2000] ECR I–6917.

[33] Directive 85/337/CEE du Conseil, du 27 juin 1985, concernant l'évaluation des incidences de certains projets publics et privés sur l'environnement (JO 1985 L175, 40).

[34] Affaire 51/76 *Verbone van Nederlandse Onderneminge v. Inspecteur der Invoerrechten en Accijnzen* [1977] ECR 113

[35] Affaire C–435/97 *World Wildlife Fund ea v. Auton one Provinz Bozen ea* [1999] ECR I–5613.

directive étaient inconditionnelles et suffisamment précises pour être invoquées par les particuliers devant le juge national. Alors même qu'elles laissent une marge d'appréciation aux États membres, la Cour a jugé que celle-ci n'exclut pas 'qu'un contrôle juridictionnel puisse être effectué afin de vérifier si les autorités nationales ne l'ont pas outrepassée' (point 37).

Dans son arrêt *Brinkmann*, précité supra n 17, la Cour reprend fidèlement la grille d'analyse qu'elle avait suivie dans l'affaire *CIA Security*. La question était de savoir si un particulier pouvait se prévaloir de l'article 3, paragraphe 1, de la directive 92/80 sur les accises minimales générales pour les tabacs manufacturés autres que les cigarettes.[36] Cette disposition laisse aux États membres le choix entre trois formules de taxation (soit ad valorem, soit spécifique, par quantité, soit mixte, comprenant un élément ad valorem et un élément spécifique).

En l'occurrence, le législateur allemand ayant opté pour une formule de taxation non prévue par l'article 3, paragraphe 1, de la directive, la question se posait de savoir si un assujetti pouvait invoquer cette disposition en vue d'écarter l'application à son égard de cette formule de taxation et d'être frappé uniquement d'une taxe ad valorem. La Cour a jugé que l'article 3, paragraphe 1, de la directive, en raison même de la marge d'appréciation qu'il laisse aux États membres, ne peut être invoqué par les assujettis devant une juridiction nationale, la formule ad valorem ne correspondant qu'à l'une des options prévues et le juge national ne pouvant se substituer au législateur national auquel il appartient seul de faire un choix (points 36 à 39).

A vrai dire, l'arrêt *Brinkmann* ne concernait pas uniquement un cas d'invocabilité d'exclusion, car, non seulement il était demandé au juge national d'écarter la règle fiscale nationale contraire à la directive (invocabilité d'exclusion), mais également d'y substituer un autre formule de taxation, directement sur la base de la directive (invocabilité de substitution), ce qui était impossible en raison de la marge d'appréciation laissée par celle-ci aux États membres.[37]

Enfin, l'arrêt *Océano Grupo*, précité supra n 16, ne manque pas non plus d'intérêt, puisqu'il y est question de la possibilité pour le juge national, saisi d'un litige entre particuliers, de faire d'office application d'une directive en vue d'écarter une stipulation contractuelle contraire, nonobstant, une fois encore, l'absence d'effet direct horizontal.

En l'occurrence, la clause litigieuse, qui figurait dans un contrat d'achat à tempérament d'une encyclopédie, attribuait compétence aux juridictions de la ville du siège du vendeur, dans laquelle aucun des consommateurs en litige ne résidait. La Cour a jugé que la juridiction nationale pouvait d'office apprécier le caractère abusif de cette clause au regard de la directive 93/13:[38]

---

[36] Directive 92/80/CEE du Conseil, du 19 octobre 1992, concernant le rapprochement des taxes frappant les tabacs manufacturés autres que les cigarettes (JO 1992 L316/10).

[37] Une solution plus radicale pour la Cour aurait été d'inviter la juridiction nationale à se limiter à écarter la règle fiscale nationale contraire, ce qui aurait impliqué l'absence de tout impôt, mais ce n'est pas ce que l'assujetti concerné avait, en l'occurrence, demandé au juge national.

[38] Directive 93/13/CEE du Conseil, du 5 avril 1993, concernant les clauses abusives dans les contrats conclus avec les consommateurs (JO1993 L95, 29).

la faculté pour le juge d'examiner d'office le caractère abusif d'une clause constitue un moyen propre à la fois à atteindre le résultat fixé à l'article 6 de la directive, à savoir empêcher qu'un consommateur individuel ne soit lié par une clause abusive, et à contribuer à la réalisation de l'objectif visé à son article 7 [obligation pour les États membres de mettre en œuvre des moyens adéquats et efficaces afin de faire cesser l'utilisation des clauses abusives], dès lors qu'un tel examen peut avoir un effet dissuasif conCourant à faire cesser l'utilisation de clauses abusives dans les contrats conclus avec les consommateurs par un professionnel (point 28).

En conclusion, même si, dans l'affaire *CIA Security*, la Cour a pris soin de vérifier si les dispositions invoquées de la directive 83/189 étaient directement applicables, alors même qu'il s'agissait uniquement pour le particulier de les invoquer afin d'écarter une réglementation nationale contraire, il semble bien que la jurisprudence récente de la Cour ne fasse plus dépendre l'invocabilité d'exclusion du caractère d'effet direct des dispositions communautaires en cause (cas *Linster, Océano Grupo, Unilever*). Bien sûr, l'exclusion de la règle nationale contraire ne suffit pas toujours pour assurer la protection juridictionnelle des justiciables, en particulier lorsque la mise à l'écart de la règle nationale contraire entraîne un vide juridique sur le plan national.[39]

L'invocabilité de substitution peut alors s'avérer nécessaire. Or, celle-ci requiert l'effet direct de la règle communautaire, laquelle doit répondre aux conditions minimales de précision et de complétude pour être appliquée par un juge national.

4. LA RESPONSABILITÉ EXTRACONTRACTUELLE DES ÉTATS MEMBRES

Autre volet important de la mission dévolue au juge national: la mise en œuvre de la responsabilité des États membres pour violation du droit communautaire.[40] De fait, la pleine efficacité des normes communautaires serait mise en cause et la protection des droits qu'elles reconnaissent serait affaiblie si les particuliers n'avaient pas la possibilité d'obtenir réparation lorsque leurs droits sont lésés par une violation du droit communautaire imputable à un État membre. C'est dans son arrêt du 19 novembre 1991, *Francovich et Bonifaci ea*,[41]

---

[39] Tel n'est pas toujours le cas. Ainsi, dans l'affaire *Bernáldez* (arrêt du 28 mars 1996, Affaire C–129/94 *Procédure penale contre Rafael Ruiz Bernàldez* [1996] ECR I–8129), la mise à l'écart d'une exception contenue dans la législation espagnole, jugée incompatible avec le droit communautaire (en l'occurrence, notamment la Directive 72/166/CEE du Conseil, du 24 avril 1972, concernant le rapprochement des législations des États membres relatives à l'assurance de la responsabilité civile résultant de la circulation de véhicules automoteurs et au contrôle de l'obligation d'assurer cette responsabilité, JO 1972 L103/1), permettait de faire application de la règle générale espagnole, laquelle était conforme à la Directive.

[40] Sur cette question, voy M Wathelet et S Van Raepenbusch, 'La responsabilité des États membres en cas de violation du droit communautaire. Vers un alignement de la responsabilité de l'État sur celle de la Communauté ou l'inverse?' (1997) *CDE* 13.

[41] Affaires jointes C–6/90 et C–9/90 *Andrea Francovich et Danila Bonifac ea* v. *Republique italienne* [1991] ECR I–5357.

que la Cour a consacré pour la première fois avec netteté le principe de la responsabilité de l'État membre pour les dommages causés aux particuliers par un manquement au droit communautaire. Ainsi, 'le principe de la responsabilité de l'État pour les dommages causés aux particuliers par des violations du droit communautaire qui lui sont imputables est inhérent au système du Traité' (point 35). A défaut, 'la pleine efficacité des normes communautaires serait mise en cause et la protection des droits qu'elles reconnaissaient serait affaiblie' (point 33). 'La possibilité de réparation à charge de l'État membre est particulièrement indispensable lorsque, comme en l'espèce, le plein effet des normes communautaires est subordonné à la condition d'une action de la part de l'État' (point 34).[42]

On sait que l'arrêt *Francovich* concernait précisément un cas de non transposition d'une directive dont les dispositions pertinentes n'avaient pas d'effet direct.[43] Mais, la Cour a, par la suite, estimé que la responsabilité de l'État pouvait également être engagée en cas de violation d'une norme directement applicable (que les particuliers étaient précisément en droit d'invoquer devant les juridictions nationales).[44]

Même si l'arrêt *Francovich et Bonifaci* énonce déjà des conditions de mise en oeuvre de la responsabilité de l'État,[45] il convient de se référer surtout à l'arrêt

---

[42] Voy notamment F Schockweiler, 'La responsabilité de l'autorité nationale en cas de violation du droit communautaire' (1992) *RTDE* 27.

[43] L'Italie s'était abstenue de transposer la Directive 80/987/CEE du 20 octobre 1980 sur la protection des travailleurs salariés en cas d'insolvabilité de leur employeur (JO 1980 L283/23). Cette Directive impose aux États membres l'obligation de 'prendre les mesures nécessaires afin que des institutions de garantie (à créer ou à désigner par eux) assurent le paiement des créances impayées des travailleurs salariés résultant de contrats de travail ou de relations de travail'.
En l'absence de mesures de transposition nécessaires, des salariés d'entreprises en faillite ne pouvaient pas pour autant se prévaloir directement de la Directive devant les juridictions nationales afin de récupérer leurs créances. En effet, les dispositions en cause de la Directive n'étaient pas inconditionnelles ni suffisamment précises, l'État disposant d'une grande marge d'appréciation quant à la façon d'organiser les institutions de garantie qu'il devait mettre en place et à la façon d'assurer leur financement. En revanche, la Cour a jugé que les salariés étaient en droit d'obtenir de l'État réparation du préjudice qu'il leur avait causé en ne mettant pas en place les institutions qui devaient garantir le paiement de leurs salaires. Dans ces conditions, l'action en réparation permettait de pallier les conséquences dommageables, pour les destinataires d'une Directive, du défaut de transposition de celle-ci par un État membre.

[44] Voy l'important arrêt du 5 mars 1996, Affaires jontes C–46/93 et C–48/93 *Brasserie du Pêcheur SA* v. *Bundesrepublik Deutschland* et *The Queen* v. *Secretary of State for Transport, ex parte Factortame Ltd ea* [1996] ECR I–1029, qui concernait la violation d'une norme communautaire d'effet direct (en l'occurrence, les articles 30 et 52 du traité CE) dans un contexte général où les États membres jouissaient d'un large pouvoir d'appréciation pour opérer des choix normatifs (en l'occurrence, le domaine des denrées alimentaires et celui des activités de pêche).

[45] S'en tenant à la situation de l'espèce (non transposition d'une Directive dans le délai imparti), la Cour de justice a estimé que les conditions suivantes suffisaient pour ouvrir un droit à réparation. Outre bien entendu la violation de l'obligation qui incombe à l'État, il y a lieu d'établir: (a) l'existence d'un dommage consistant en l'atteinte portée à un droit du particulier, ce qui suppose, en l'occurrence, que 'le résultat prescrit par la Directive comporte l'attribution de droits au profit de particuliers' et 'que le contenu de ces droits puisse Ltre identifié sur la base des dispositions de la Directive'; *et (b)* un lien de causalité entre la violation de l'obligation qui incombe à l'État et le dommage (point 40). Sans doute le principe de l'autonomie procédurale est-il également réaffirmé dans l'arrêt: 'c'est dans le cadre du droit national de la responsabilité qu'il incombe à l'État de réparer les

Brasserie du Pêcheur et Factortame où la Cour a cherché à élaborer un régime général, valant pour tous les cas de manquements étatiques.

La Cour a considéré qu'un droit à réparation était reconnu par le droit communautaire dès lors que trois conditions étaient réunies, à savoir:

- que la règle de droit violée ait pour objet de conférer des droits aux particuliers,
- que la violation soit suffisamment caractérisée,
- enfin, qu'il existe un lien de causalité direct entre la violation de l'obligation qui incombe à l'État et le dommage subi par les personnes lésées (point 51).

La deuxième condition, à savoir l'existence d'une violation du droit communautaire suffisamment caractérisée, constitue le point névralgique de l'appréciation du comportement qui est reproché à l'État. Il doit s'agir d'une méconnaissance manifeste et grave des limites qui s'imposent à son action (point 55). En cela, la Cour transpose dans le contexte de la responsabilité des États membres un critère d'appréciation utilisé dans la jurisprudence relative à la responsabilité extra-contractuelle de la Communauté.

S'il appartient au premier chef au juge national de vérifier cette condition, la Cour a cependant dégagé plusieurs éléments qu'il peut prendre en considération à cet effet, à savoir le degré de clarté et de précision de la règle violée, l'étendue de la marge d'appréciation que cette règle laisse aux autorités nationales ou communautaires, le caractère intentionnel ou involontaire du manquement commis ou du préjudice causé, le caractère excusable d'une éventuelle erreur de droit, la circonstance que les attitudes prises par une institution communautaire ont pu contribuer à l'infraction (voir point 56).

Par ailleurs, en ce qui concerne l'étendue matérielle de la réparation, la Cour estime qu'elle doit être adéquate, c'est-à-dire de nature à assurer une protection effective des droits des particuliers lésés. Cette question est importante car, ainsi que le relève L Dubois,[46] elle domine 'la mesure de l'effectivité de la protection des droits à laquelle les victimes peuvent s'attendre'. Il apparaît ainsi que la Cour ne formule aucune exigence en ce qui concerne la 'gravité' ou la 'spécialité' du dommage, ainsi qu'il était requis sur le terrain de la responsabilité extra-contractuelle de la Communauté. S'il est encore trop tôt pour tirer des conséquences à cet égard, force est de reconnaître que cette 'omission' laisse

conséquences du préjudice causé. En effet, en l'absence d'une réglementation communautaire, c'est à l'ordre juridique interne de chaque État membre qu'il appartient de désigner les juridictions compétentes et de régler les modalités procédurales des reCours en justice destinés à assurer la pleine sauvegarde des droits que les justiciables tirent du droit communautaire' (point 42). Mais, en réalité, l'autonomie ainsi reconnue est fort réduite, car elle est assujettie à une obligation de résultat: celle de garantir pleinement le droit à réparation lorsque le droit communautaire en reconnaît le bénéfice aux particuliers.

[46] L Dubois, 'La responsabilité de l'État législateur pour des dommages causés aux particuliers par la violation du droit communautaire et son incidence sur la responsabilité de la Communauté' (1996) *RFDA* 583, spéc 598.

augurer une évolution de la jurisprudence en la matière,[47] puisque l'arrêt Brasserie du Pêcheur avait clairement indiqué (point 42) que:

> [L]es conditions de mise en œuvre de la responsabilité de l'État pour des dommages causés aux particuliers en raison de la violation du droit communautaire ne doivent pas, en l'absence de justification particulière, différer de celles régissant la responsabilité de la Communauté dans des circonstances comparables.

Du reste, cette exigence n'apparaît dans aucun arrêt postérieur, que ce soit à propos de la responsabilité de la Communauté ou des États membres.[48]

En l'absence de dispositions communautaires en ce domaine, le juge national fera application des critères retenus par son droit interne, à la condition qu'ils ne soient pas moins favorables que ceux concernant des réclamations semblables fondées sur le droit interne et qu'ils ne rendent pas en pratique impossible ou excessivement difficile la réparation (principe de l'autonomie procédurale).

Le juge national pourra vérifier, à cet égard, si la victime a fait preuve d'une diligence raisonnable pour éviter le préjudice ou en limiter la portée et si, notamment, elle a utilisé en temps utile toutes les voies de droit qui étaient à sa disposition.

Les principes dégagés dans l'arrêt Brasserie du Pêcheur ont été confirmés:

- à propos d'une transposition erronée d'une directive (voir arrêts du 26 mars 1996, *British Telecommunications*,[49] du 17 octobre 1996, *Denkavit*[50] et du 15 juin 1999, *Rechberger*:[51] il ressort de ces arrêts qu'une transposition incorrecte d'une directive ne saurait être considérée comme une violation suffisamment caractérisée du droit communautaire s'il y avait place pour des fautes excusables [découlant, par exemple, de l'imprécision de la disposition en cause, qui supportait raisonnablement, outre l'interprétation donnée par la Cour dans son arrêt, celle qu'avait donnée, de bonne foi, l'État mis en cause et qui n'était manifestement pas contraire au texte de la directive ni à l'objectif qu'elle poursuit (arrêt

---

[47] Autre signe d'un rapprochement entre le régime de la responsabilité de l'État membre et de celui de la responsabilité de la Communauté, la Cour, dans son arrêt du 4 juillet 2000, Affaire C–352/98 *Laboratoires pharmaceutiques Bergaderm SA et Jean-Jacques Goupil* v. *Commission* [2000] ECR I–5291, relatif à la responsabilité de la Communauté, a souligné que, lorsque l'État membre ou l'institution en cause ne disposent que d'une marge d'appréciation considérablement réduite, voire inexistante, la simple infraction au droit communautaire peut suffire à établir l'existence d'une violation suffisamment caractérisée (point 44), confirmant ainsi la position dégagée dans l'arrêt *Brasserie du Pêcheur et Factortame*.

[48] Dans ses conclusions dans les affaires *Brasserie du Pêcheur et Factortame*, point 92, M Tesauro a d'ailleurs fait valoir la thèse selon laquelle la condition du dommage spécial doit être réservée à des cas de responsabilité objective (voir également en ce sens, les conclusions de M. Mischo dans l'affaire C–104/97 P *Atlanta* v. *Commission* [1999] ECR I–6983.

[49] Affaire C–392/93 *The Queen* v. *HM Treasury, ex parte British Telecommunications plc* [1996] ECR I–1631.

[50] Affaires jointes C–283/94, C–291/94 et C–292/94 *Denkavit* ea v. *Bundesamt für Finazen* [1996] ECR I–5063.

[51] Affaire C–140/97 *Walter Rechberger ea* v. *Republik Österreich* [1999] ECR I–3499.

British Telecommunications, point 43) de l'absence d'indications dans la jurisprudence de la Cour sur l'interprétation à donner à la disposition en cause, de ce que l'interprétation condamnée par la Cour était adoptée par la quasi-totalité des États membres intéressés (arrêt *Denkavit*, points 51 et 52)[52]];
- à propos d'une interdiction claire prescrite par le traité laissant place à une marge d'appréciation très réduite (voir arrêt du 23 mai 1996, *Hedley Lomas*[53]), concernant le refus non justifié de délivrance d'une licence d'exportation en violation de l'ex-article 34 du traité (devenu article 29 CE);
- à propos du défaut de transposition d'une directive (voir arrêt du 8 octobre 1996, *Dillenkoffer ea*);[54]
- sur l'étendue de la réparation en cas de transposition tardive: voir arrêts du 10 juillet 1997, *Bonifaci ea et Berto ea*,[55] *Palmisani*,[56] et *Maso ea*.[57]

Il ressort de ce qui précède que l'invocabilité de réparation est totalement déconnectée de toute exigence d'effet direct des dispositions communautaires en cause. Il n'est donc pas nécessaire qu'elles soient précises et inconditionnelles. En revanche, elles doivent avoir pour objet de conférer des droits aux particuliers.

5. LES ACCORDS EXTERNES

Force est de constater que les considérations exposées ci-dessus à propos du droit communautaire 'interne' et qui font apparaître la spécificité de l'ordre juridique communautaire, en raison de ses caractéristiques intrinsèques, ne sont pas transposables automatiquement aux accords externes dont les caractéristiques (l'objet et le but, notamment la nécessité de maintenir une réciprocité des avantages et inconvénients, particulièrement dans les accords de libre échange) ne sont pas forcément les mêmes que celles du traité de Rome.

---

[52] En revanche, l'arrêt *Rechberger* offre l'exemple d'une violation suffisamment caractérisée d'une disposition d'une Directive par l'Autriche.

[53] Affaire C–5/94 *The Queen* v. *Ministry of Agriculture, Fisheries and Food, ex parte Hedley Lomas (Ireland) Ltd* [1996] ECR I–2553

[54] Affaires jointes C–178/94, C–179/94, C–188/94, C–189/94 et C–190/94 *Erich Dillenkofer ea* v. *Bundesrepublik Deutschland* [1996] ECR I–4845. Ce dernier arrêt est intéressant dans la mesure où la problématique est proche de celle sur laquelle a porté l'arrêt *Francovich*. Or, au lieu de reprendre purement et simplement la motivation de l'arrêt du 19 novembre 1991, la Cour, après avoir reconnu l'existence de la responsabilité de l'État en cause, a transposé le régime dégagé dans l'arrêt *Brasserie du Pêcheur et Factortame*.

[55] Affaires jointes C–94/95 et C–95/95 *Danila Bonifaci ea* [1997] ECR I–4006.

[56] Affaire C–261/95 *Rosalba Palmisani* v. *Istituto nazionale della previdenza sociale (INPS)* [1997] ECR I–4025.

[57] Affaire C–373/95 *Federica Maso ea* [1997] ECR I–4051.

De façon générale, deux observations s'imposent à titre liminaire:[58]

- d'une part, les normes issues des engagements externes des Communautés ne bénéficient pas de la présomption d'applicabilité directe posée par l'arrêt *Van Gend & Loos*;[59]
- d'autre part, 'conformément aux principes du droit international, les institutions communautaires, qui sont compétentes pour négocier et conclure un accord avec des pays tiers, sont libres de convenir avec ceux-ci des effets que les dispositions de l'accord doivent produire dans l'ordre interne des parties contractantes'. L'intention des parties est donc un élément d'appréciation important conformément à la pratique internationale. 'Ce n'est que si cette question n'a pas été réglée par l'accord qu'il incombe aux juridictions compétentes et en particulier à la Cour, dans le cadre de sa compétence en vertu du traité CE, de la trancher au même titre que toute autre question d'interprétation relative à l'application de l'accord dans la Communauté.'[60]

Dans cette dernière hypothèse, la Cour, de façon générale, examine d'abord l'accord dans sa globalité, sa nature ou son économie ('*à la lumière tant de l'objet et du but de l'accord de son contexte*'), pour déterminer, ensuite, si la disposition spécifique peut se voir reconnaître un effet direct (arrêts *Kupferberg* et *Portugal/Conseil*, précités).

On peut donc constater que la Cour suit les méthodes générales d'interprétation des traités en recherchant, au premier chef, la volonté des Parties.[61]

L'avocat général Darmon a bien synthétisé dans ses conclusions sous l'affaire *Demirel*[62] la méthode suivie par la Cour dans ce domaine:

[D]e façon plus générale, il résulte de votre jurisprudence que, pour reconnaître à un accord externe un effet direct, vous recherchez, comme pour l'application des normes communautaires stricto sensu, les caractéristiques de la disposition à appliquer. Mais, alors qu'en droit communautaire, la volonté des parties contractantes d'attribuer par les traités des droits subjectifs est maintenant considérée comme toujours acquise, l'applicabilité directe dépendant seulement du caractère précis et complet de la norme à appliquer, pareille intention ne peut être présumée pour l'appréciation d'un accord international. Ainsi, en pareille matière, vous commencez par vérifier si la nature et l'économie de l'accord font obstacle à l'invocabilité directe d'un de ses stipulations.

---

[58] Voir S Van Raepenbusch, *Droit institutionnel de l'Union et des Communautés européennes* (De Boeck Université, 2001, 3ème éd), p 378.

[59] Affaire 26/62 *Van Gend & Loos* [1963] ECR 1. Voir, par exemple, arrêt du 9 février 1982, Affaire 270/80 *Polydor Limited et RSO Records Inc* v. *Harlequin Records Shops Limited et Simons Records Limited* [1982] ECR 329), points 14 et s, à propos de l'accord de libre échange avec la Grèce.

[60] Arrêt du 23 novembre 1999, Affaire C–149/96 *Portugal* v. *Conseil* [1999] ECR I–8395, point 34; voir également arrêt du 26 octobre 1982, Affaire 104/81 *Hauptzollant Mainz* v. *CA Kupferberg & Cie KG aA* [1982] ECR 3641, point 17.

[61] Voir Ph Manin, 'L'influence du droit international sur la jurisprudence communautaire', colloque de Bordeaux, précité supra n 8, texte polycopié, 13.

[62] Arrêt du 30 Septembre 1987, Affaire 12/86 *Meryem Demirel* v. *Ville de Schwäbisch Gmünd* [1987] ECR 3719

Pour répondre ensuite à la question de savoir si une telle stipulation est inconditionnelle et suffisamment précise pour produire un effet direct, vous considérez qu'il faut d'abord l'analyser à la lumière tant de l'objet et du but de cet accord que de son contexte (point 8).[63]

S'il apparaît ainsi que les conditions de reconnaissance de l'effet direct des accords externes conclus par la Communauté sont plus strictes que celle concernant les actes internes, il reste encore la question de savoir si l'invocabilité d'une disposition contenue dans un accord externe devant le juge national postule toujours qu'elle doive avoir un effet direct.

Il doit assurément en être ainsi, à l'instar de ce qui prévaut pour les actes internes, en cas d'invocabilité de substitution, c'est-à-dire, lorsqu'il s'agit, pour un particulier, d'invoquer le bénéfice d'un droit conféré par une norme conventionnelle.[64]

Bien que, à notre connaissance, cette question n'ait pas encore été tranchée par la Cour, il semble que la condition relative à l'effet direct doive également être remplie dans l'hypothèse où la règle conventionnelle est invoquée uniquement pour écarter une règle nationale ou communautaire interne contraire. En effet, compte tenu des missions qui lui sont dévolues et des réalités économiques internationales, la Cour s'est plus attachée à garantir la pleine efficacité du droit communautaire dans les ordres juridiques des États membres que des traités internationaux, dans leur ensemble, dans l'ordre juridique communautaire et dans les ordres juridiques nationaux.

S'agissant, enfin, de l'invocabilité de réparation, les arrêts du 30 septembre 2003, *Biret International*[65] et *Établissements Biret*[66] (non encore publiés au Recueil) méritent réflexion. Ces arrêts sont d'autant plus intéressants qu'ils concernent l'accord OMC et ses annexes à propos desquels la Cour a jugé que, pas plus que les règles de l'accord général sur les tarifs douaniers et le commerce (GATT) de 1947, ils ne figurent pas en principe, compte tenu de leur nature et de leur économie, parmi les normes au regard desquelles la Cour et le Tribunal contrôlent les actes des institutions communautaires en vertu de l'article 230,

---

[63] Pour plus de développements, voy. M Wathelet et S Van Raepenbusch, 'Quelques considérations sur l'interprétation par la Cour de justice des accords externes conclus par la Communauté européenne' in *Mélanges en hommage à C.N. Kakouris*, à paraître.

[64] Par exemple, la règle de l'égalité de traitement dans le domaine de la sécurité sociale (voir arrêts du 31 janvier 1991, Affaire C–18/90 *Office national de l'enploi* v. *Bhaia Kziber* [1991] ECR I–199 à propos de l'article 41, paragraphe 1 de l'accord de coopération entre la CEE et le Maroc, ou du 4 mai 1999, Affaire C–262/92 *Sema Sürül* v. *Bunlevanstalt für Arbeit* [1999] ECR I–2685, à propos de l'article 3, de la décision 3/80 du Conseil d'association CEE/Turquie, ou encore du 27 septembre 2001, Affaire C–63/99 *The Queen* v. *Secretary of State for the Home Department, ex parte Wieslaw Gloszczuk et Elzbieta Gloszczuk* [2001] ECR I–6369, à propos de l'article 44, paragraphe 3, de l'accord européen CE/Pologne; voir également les arrêts de même date, Affaire C–235/99 *The Queen* v. *Secretary of State for the Home Department, ex parte Eleanora Ivanova Kondova* [2001] ECR I–6427), et Affaire C–257/99 *The Queen* v. *Secretary of State for the Home Department, ex parte Julius Barkoci et Marcal Malik* [2001] ECR I–6557.

[65] Affaire C–93/02P *Biret International*.

[66] Affaire C–94/02P *Etablissements Biret et Cie*.

premier alinéa, CE et qu'ils ne sont pas de nature à créer pour les particuliers des droits dont ceux-ci pourraient se prévaloir en justice.[67]

On rappellera que, selon la Cour, les accords OMC ont pour objet le règlement et la gestion des relations entre États ou organisations régionales d'intégration économique, et non pas la protection des particuliers. Ils restent fondés sur le principe de négociations entreprises sur une base de réciprocité et d'avantages mutuels, et se distinguent ainsi des accords conclus par la Communauté avec des pays tiers qui instaurent une certaine asymétrie des obligations (arrêt *Portugal/Conseil*, précité supra n 61, point 42). En outre, la question de l'effet direct des accords OMC ne peut être dissociée de celle de la reconnaissance d'un tel effet par les parties contractantes qui sont, du point de vue commercial, les partenaires les plus importants de la Communauté. En effet, l'absence de réciprocité à cet égard, 'risque d'aboutir à un déséquilibre dans l'application des règles de l'OMC' (point 45).

Ce n'est que dans l'hypothèse où la Communauté a entendu donner exécution à une obligation particulière assumée dans le cadre de l'OMC, ou lorsque l'acte communautaire renvoie expressément à des dispositions précises des accords OMC, qu'il appartient au juge communautaire de contrôler la légalité de l'acte communautaire en cause au regard des règles de l'OMC (voir, pour ce qui concerne le GATT de 1947, arrêts de la Cour du 22 juin 1989, *Fediol*,[68] points 19 à 22, et du 7 mai 1991, *Nakajima*[69] point 31).

Dans les affaires *Biret International* et *Établissements Biret*, les requérantes avaient introduit devant le Tribunal de première instance, à l'encontre du Conseil un reCours en réparation du préjudice qu'elles prétendaient avoir subi du fait de l'adoption et du maintien de plusieurs directives[70] par lesquelles avait été interdite l'importation dans la Communauté, en l'occurrence en provenance des États-Unis, de viande et de produits carnés provenant d'animaux traités avec certaines hormones.

L'organe de règlement des différends de l'OMC (l'ORD) avait précisément, par décision du 13 février 1998, à l'issue d'une procédure initiée par les États-Unis et le Canada, considéré que la Communauté avait, du fait de cette

---

[67] Voir arrêts de la Cour du 23 novembre 1999, *Portugal v. Conseil* (precité, supra n 61); du 14 décembre 2000, Affaires jointes C–300/98 et C–392/98 *Parfums Christian Dior SA v. TUK Consultancy BV et Assco Gerüste GmbH et Ros Van Dijk v. Wilhelm Layher GmbH & Co KG et Layter BV* [2000] ECR I–11307; et du 9 octobre 2001, Affaire C–377/98 *Pays Bas v. Parlement et Conseil* [2001] ECR I–7079 ; et ordonnance de la Cour du 2 mai 2001, Affaire C–307/99 *OGT Fruchthandelsgeselhschanft mbH v. Hauptzollamt Hamburg- St Annen* [2001] ECR I–3159.
[68] Affaire 70/87 *Fediol v. Commission* [1989] ECR 1781
[69] Affaire C–69/89 *Nakajima All precision Co Ltd v. Conseil* [1991] ECR I–2069.
[70] Directive 81/602/CEE du Conseil, du 31 juillet 1981, concernant l'interdiction de certaines substances à effet hormonal et des substances à effet thyréostatiques (JO 1981 L222/32), la Directive 88/146/CEE du Conseil, du 7 mars 1988, interdisant l'utilisation de certaines substances à effet hormonal dans les spéculations animales (JO 1988 L70 16), et la Directive 96/22/CE, concernant l'interdiction d'utilisation de certaines substances à effet hormonal ou thyréostatique et des substances ß-agonistes dans les spéculations animales et abrogeant les Directives 81/602, 88/146 et 88/299/CEE (JO 1996 L125/3).

interdiction, violé plusieurs dispositions de l'accord sur l'application des mesures sanitaires et phytosanitaires (SPS), annexé à l'accord OMC, essentiellement au motif de l'absence d'une analyse scientifique suffisamment spécifique des risques de cancer associés à l'utilisation de certaines hormones en tant que promoteurs de croissance.

La Communauté ayant finalement indiqué qu'elle entendait respecter ses obligations au titre de l'OMC mais que, pour ce faire, elle devait disposer d'un délai raisonnable, conformément à l'article 21, paragraphe 3, du mémorandum d'accord sur les règles et procédures régissant la réglementation des différends,[71] elle s'était vu accorder à cette fin un délai de quinze mois, expirant le 13 mai 1999.

Le Tribunal, après avoir rappelé la jurisprudence de la Cour sur l'absence d'effet direct des règles de l'OMC, a constaté que les circonstances de l'espèce ne correspondaient manifestement à aucune des deux hypothèses dans lesquelles il serait possible pour le juge communautaire de contrôler la légalité d'un acte communautaire au regard des règles de l'OMC (c'est-à-dire lorsque la Communauté a entendu donner exécution à une obligation particulière assumée dans le cadre de l'OMC, ou dans l'occurrence où l'acte communautaire renvoie expressément à des dispositions précises des accords OMC) (voir arrêts du 11 janvier 2002, *Biret International*[72] et *Établissement Biret*[73]).

En effet, selon le Tribunal, les directives en cause ayant été adoptées plusieurs années avant l'entrée en vigueur de l'accord SPS, le 1er janvier 1995, elles ne pouvaient logiquement ni donner exécution à une obligation particulière assumée dans le cadre de cet accord ni renvoyer expressément à certaines de ses dispositions (point 64). De plus, la décision de l'ORD du 13 février 1998 étant nécessairement et directement liée au moyen tiré de la violation de l'accord SPS, elle ne pouvait être prise en considération 'que dans l'hypothèse où l'effet direct de cet accord aurait été consacré par le juge communautaire dans le cadre d'un moyen tiré de l'invalidité des directives en cause' (point 67).

Dans ses arrêts du 30 septembre 2003, la Cour a estimé, pour l'essentiel, que le Tribunal avait insuffisamment motivé ses arrêts. En effet, il lui incombait encore de répondre à l'argument selon lequel les effets juridiques à l'égard de la Communauté européenne de la décision de l'ORD du 13 février 1998 étaient de nature à remettre en cause son appréciation quant à l'absence d'effet direct des règles de l'OMC et à justifier l'exercice par le juge communautaire du contrôle de la légalité des directives 81/602, 88/146 et 96/22 au regard de ces règles, dans le cadre de l'action en indemnité introduite par les requérantes. En somme, c'est la question de l'invocabilité de réparation des règles de l'OMC qui était au centre de l'argumentation développée par les requérantes devant le Tribunal, comme elle l'a été devant la Cour au stade du pourvoi.

---

[71] OJ 1994 L336/234.
[72] Affaire T–174/00 *Biret International SA* v. *Conseil* [2002] ECR II–17.
[73] Affaire T–210/00 *Etablissements Biret et Cie SA* v. *Conseil* [2002] ECR II–47.

C'est donc une question qui était restée ouverte après, notamment, le prononcé de l'arrêt *Portugal/Conseil* et qui nécessitait une réponse spécifique.

Toutefois, l'erreur de droit commise par le Tribunal au regard de l'obligation de motivation n'a pas été de nature à invalider l'arrêt attaqué dès lors que le dispositif de celui-ci, et en particulier le rejet du moyen de première instance trié de l'accord SPS, pouvait valablement être fondé pour d'autres motifs de droit (voir, en ce sens, arrêt du 2 avril 1998, *Sytraval*,[74] point 47).

A cet égard, la Cour n'a pas abordé le fond de la question, en particulier les éventuelles conséquences indemnitaires que pourrait avoir pour des particuliers l'inexécution par la Communauté d'une décision de l'ORD constatant l'incompatibilité d'un acte communautaire avec les règles de l'OMC. Elle s'est limitée à constater que, compte tenu du délai que la Communauté s'était vu accorder, afin de mettre en œuvre la décision de l'ORD du 13 février 1998 et qui a expiré le 13 mai 1999, le juge communautaire ne pouvait, sous peine de priver d'effet l'octroi d'un tel délai, exercer un contrôle de la légalité des actes communautaires en cause pour la période antérieure au 13 mai 1999, en particulier dans le cadre d'un reCours en indemnité introduit au titre de l'article 235 CE (point 62). En outre, s'agissant de la période postérieure à cette date, la Cour a constaté que Biret International avait fait l'objet d'une procédure de liquidation judiciaire par jugement du 7 décembre 1995 du Tribunal de Commerce de Paris, lequel avait fixé provisoirement la date de cessation de paiement au 28 février 1995. Cela signifiait qu'il était exclu que des effets dommageables prétendument causés à la requérante par le maintien en vigueur, après le 1er janvier 1995, des directives 81/602 et 88/146 ainsi que par l'adoption, le 29 avril 1996, de la directive 96/22 aient pu se produire au Cours de la période postérieure au 13 mai 1999 (point 63 de l'arrêt *Biret International*).

Il n'empêche que la Cour n'a pas exclu, par principe, toute indemnisation d'un dommage causé à un particulier du fait d'une violation d'une règle de l'OMC, constatée par décision de l'ORD, nonobstant l'absence d'effet direct des règles de l'OMC. Il est vrai qu'elle ne l'a pas admise non plus. La question reste ouverte.

Cela étant, il est probable qu'à terme, les mêmes possibilités pour les particuliers d'invoquer devant le juge national ou communautaire les accords externes conclus par la Communauté, que celles admises en droit communautaire interne, soient consacrées par la Cour justice, indépendamment de la question de savoir si les dispositions conventionnelles en cause sont revêtues ou non de l'effet direct, même si cette dernière condition sera toujours requise lorsqu'il s'agira de faire directement application de l'accord externe en lieu et place d'une règle—nationale ou communautaire interne—contraire, voire en l'absence de toute règle nationale ou communautaire interne.

---

[74] Affaire C–367/958 *Commission v. Sytraval et Brink's France SARL* [1998] ECR I–1719.

Index

Any references to footnotes are indicated by page number followed by 'n' and note number

abuse by undertakings,
   collective dominance, 164
Accession Negotiations,
   conclusion, 108–9
   draft Common Position (DCP), 103–4
   first ten, 103–9
   opening of, 102–3
   principles governing, 105–7
   provisional closure concept, 106
   re-opening a chapter, 106
   screening, 103
   working methods/language, 105
Accession Treaty (Union enlargement), 107, 109–11
   ratification, 111–12
acquis communautaire, 100
acquis jurisprudentiel, 79
administrative law,
   development, 32
admissibility, preliminary rulings *see* preliminary ruling procedure (Article 234): admissibility of references
Advocate General Opinion, Community law, 92–8
   Article 6 letter, 95
   Article 230, annulment action, 96–7
   Article 232 action,
      admissibility issues (*Asia Motor France*), 97, 98
      conversion to annulment (Article 230 of Article 6 letter), 96–7
      use to compel Commission to act, 95
   Commission,
      compulsion to act (Art 232), 95
      duty to investigate complaint, 93–6
      justification of inaction, 95–6
   facts, 92–3
   issue of principle, 93–6
      Art 232, use of to compel Commission to act, 95
      Commission's duty to investigate complaint, 94
      inaction, justification of, 95–6
   procedural issues, 96–7
   structure and style, 97–8
AIDs, 206, 223
amicus curiae, 148, 149
Amsterdam Treaty (1997),
   norms, 357
   and Rome Convention, 258–62

subsidiarity, 59
Amtsgericht (Prussia), 14
antibiotics,
   bacitracin zinc, 204, 222
   campaign to reduce use (Scandinavia), 212, 220–3
   growth promoters/feed additives, 204, 212
   Luxembourg litigation, 220
   virginiamycin, 204, 220, 221, 222, 223
Association Agreements (free movement rights), 236, 237
   EEC-Algeria, 244
   EEC-Morocco, 244
   see also Europe Agreements; free movement rights
Association Councils,
   free movement rights, 236, 238, 240
      EEC-Turkey, 243

Balak massacre (1876), 82
beef, dangers of eating, 215
Berlin European Council,
   Union enlargement, 101
bias, danger of,
   judicial process, 22, 23
Brussels European Council,
   Union enlargement, 109
Bundeskartellamt, West Berlin, 99
burden of proof,
   merger control decisions, 122

CAP (common agricultural policy), 57
CAT (Competition Appeal Tribunal), 187–91
   Guide to Appeals under Competition Act (1998), 189
CCBE (Council of the Bars and Law Societies of the European Union), 11, 154–5, 157, 158
CFI (Court of First Instance) *see* Court of First Instance (CFI)
Charter of Fundamental Rights, 74, 75
   and European Human Rights Convention, 77
CILFIT case,
   admissibility of references, 329
   discretionary references, 348, 349
   limited exemptions recognised in, 346
   linguistic issues, 301–2, 303
co-decision procedure, 259, 260

392 *Index*

collective dominance, 119, 120
  abuse by undertakings, 164
  Article 82 EC, 162–75
    abuse by one or more undertakings, 164
    economic links, 167, 172–5
    non-collusive parallel behaviour, 163
    relationship with Article 81 EC, 164–6
    see also merger control decisions: case law development, and non-collusive parallel behaviour, 163
  ECMR, under, 162, 175–86
    Commission guidelines on horizontal mergers, 185–6
  economic links, 167, 172–5
  European courts, 161–86
    Article 82 EC, 162–75
    case law, 167–72
    ECMR, 175–86
  merger control decisions, 119–23
    CDP (collective dominant position), 119, 120
    MCR (Regulation), 119, 120, 122
    see also merger control decisions
  non-collusive parallel behaviour and development of, 163
comitology regime, 225–6
Commission, European *see* European Commission
Committee of the Regions (COR), consultation, 60
common agricultural policy (CAP), 57
Common Market, 193
Common Position (Union enlargement), candidate commitments, 107
  draft (DCP), 103–4
  opening of negotiations, 102
Community law,
  in devolution settlements, 48–53
    restraint on devolved powers, 48–50
  domestic procedural rules, impact on, 316–24
    equivalence principle, 319, 320–2
    remedies, 319–20
  as driving force, 50–1
  EC policy, legislation imposed on new institutions, 51–3
    debates and inquiries, 53
    guarantees for involvement with EU affairs, 52–3
  judges' role, 83
  CFI member, Opinion *see* Advocate General Opinion (Community law)
  Memorandum of Understanding (UK Government/Scottish Ministers), 52
  national courts, generally applied by, 75
  place of devolved institutions, 53–66
    challenge of Community legislation, 61–6

impact of integration on internal structure of Member States, 55–8
Member States as main protagonists, 54–5
strategy to gain power, 58–61
professional qualifications/diplomas, mutual recognition, 248, 252–3, 254, 256
ratification, 360
systems of, direct penetration or automatic integration, 360–1
Competition Appeal Tribunal (CAT), 187–91
  collective dominance *see* collective dominance
  judicial panel candidate, 89
  merger control decisions *see* merger control decisions
  procedure, 187–91
  Regulation 1/2003,
    preliminary observations, 145–51
    and Regulation 17, 145, 146
  Rules, 190
  uniform application of EC Rules, national courts, 145–51
concordats, 52
  modification, 64
conglomerate/portfolio effects,
  merger control decisions, 125–31
Constitution for Europe,
  Convention,
    Court of Justice (ECJ), role, 70, 76, 78
    proposals of, 69
  draft Treaty (2003), 69n2
    Court of Justice (ECJ), future, 78, 79
    fundamental rights, 75, 77
    subsidiarity principle, 72, 73
consultation,
  and devolved institutions, 60–1
Copenhagen criteria,
  enlargement of Union, 101
COR (Committee of the Regions), consultation, 60
Council of Ministers, devolved institutions' access to, 60
Court of First Instance (CFI),
  Advocate General, appointment of, 91
  antibiotic use, 204, 222
  competition law,
    and CAT (Competition Appeal Tribunal), 189
  confidentiality issues, 159
  judicial panels, 89
Court of Justice (ECJ), division of jurisdiction, 70
direct action jurisdiction, 83, 85
exceptional review of rulings, 85
fast-track procedure, 117–18

role, 70
  major redefinition of, 84–7
  scientific controversy/dispute resolution, 212, 214, 225–6
Court of Human Rights,
  and Court of Justice (ECJ), 77
  impartiality, 23
  plurilingual texts, 299
Court of Justice (ECJ),
  access to, truncated test, 76
  admissibility issues, 332–3, 339
  appeal to, 83
  character, 70
  Community objectives, conflicts between, 193
  competition law,
    confidentiality issues, 153, 154
    uniform application, EC Rules, 145, 147, 150, 151
  constitutional reform proposals, 69–70
  Court of First Instance, division of jurisdiction, 70
  direct action jurisdiction, 89
  discrimination, mandatory requirements case law, 198, 199
  discussion circle on, 70, 76
  environmental protection, 197
  and European Court of Human Rights, 77
  free movement rights, 194, 234
  fundamental rights, 74, 75–6
  future, 78–79
  linguistic issues, 301, 303
  preliminary rulings,
    admissibility of references, 332–3, 339
    exclusive jurisdiction, 83–4
    provisions/norms distinguished, 356
  professional qualifications/diplomas, mutual recognition, 247–56
    case law, 249–52
    directives, 248, 249
    free movement of persons, 247–8
    internal market, 247–8
    methods, 252–6
  role, 69, 73, 84–7
  scientific controversy, 225–6
  single collective judgments, 297
  subsidiarity principle, 72, 73
  workload, 84, 328
Court of Session (Scotland),
  judges,
    chosen from Faculty of Advocates, 16
    salary, 16
    working time, 17
  judicial review, 40
  jurisdiction monopoly, 14, 17, 33
  law making, 19
Cyprus problem,
  Union enlargement, 112

damages,
  community law, impact on domestic rules, 319–20
DDT pesticide, 211
Declaration 23 (future of Europe),
  and Court of Justice (ECJ), 70
  fundamental rights, 74
  subsidiarity principle, 71
devolution (and Community law),
  challenging of legislation, 61–6
    case law, 63–4
    co-operation with other devolved institutions, 65–6
    individual decisions, 62
    measures of general application, 63
    Member States only as privileged applicants, 61–2
    modification of concordats, 64
    'rights' dimension, 65–6
  consultation, 60–1
  Council of Ministers, access to, 60
  Member States,
    integration, impact on internal structure of, 55–8
    as main protagonists, 54–5
    as privileged applicants, 61–2
  place of devolved institutions, 53–66
    challenging of Community legislation, 61–6
    impact of integration on internal structure of Member States, 55–8
    Member States as main protagonists, 54–5
    strategy to gain power, 58–61
  restraint on devolved powers, 48–50
    limitations on legislative competence, 48–49
    limitations on Scottish Ministers, 49–50
  settlements, law in, 48–53
    restraint on devolved powers, 48–50
    strategy to gain power, 58–61
  subsidiarity, 58–9
diplomas, mutual recognition see professional qualifications/diplomas, mutual recognition
direct action jurisdiction,
  CFI, 83, 85
  Commission, 89
  ECJ, 89
direct applicability, 353, 354
  official journals, 361–3
direct effect, 353, 354–5, 363–4
  enforcement mechanisms, 317, 324
  Faccini Dori, 353
  free movement rights, 238–40
  horizontal, 309–12, 353

directives,
    professional qualifications/diplomas, mutual recognition, 248, 249
    systems of law, 360–1
discrimination,
    non-discrimination principle, 243–5
dispute resolution,
    precautionary principle, 211–13

Edward, David (Judge),
    as Advocate General, 92–8
    case law, contribution to, 297–8
    and direct effect, 353
    on draft Treaty (future of Europe), economic provisions, 79
    European-Atlantic Group, speech to (1996), 268
    and free movement rights, case law, 234
    on judgments, 29
    and judicial review, 31, 34, 35
    and preliminary ruling procedure, 328
    professional qualifications/diplomas, mutual recognition, 247
    publications by, 153
    qualifications, 24
    retirement from office, 11, 45, 144
    and Rome Convention (1980), 257
    on Scottish legal system, 20
    tale telling, 1–7
    tributes, 267–8
effectiveness principle,
    enforcement, 318–19
employment,
    free movement rights, 239–42
        and qualifications, mutual recognition, 248
enforcement, private, 307–26
    Community law, impact on domestic procedural rules, 316–24
    damages, 319–20
    effectiveness principle, 318–19
    equivalence principle, 318, 319, 320–2
    Francovich doctrine, 314, 318
    horizontal direct effect, 309–12, 353
    Köbler concept, 314, 315, 316, 325
    remedies, 319–20
    Rome Treaty, 307, 309–16
        gaps at Community level, 312–16
        horizontal direct effect, 309–12
        Plaumann test, 312
        source of rights, and horizontal direct effect, 309–12
enlargement of EU, 99–115
    Accession Conferences, 102, 104–5
    Accession Treaty, 107, 109–11
        ratification, 111–12
    acquis chapters, discussions, 102
        re-opening, 106

'boiler room perspective', 115
Common Position,
    candidate commitments, 107
    draft (DCP), 103–4
    opening of negotiations, 102
continuing process, 114
Cyprus problem, 112
enlargement process, 100
interim period, 112–14
negotiations,
    conclusion, 108–9
    draft Common Position (DCP), 103–4
    for first ten, 103–9
    opening of, 102–3
    principles governing, 105–7
    provisional closure concept, 106
    re-opening a chapter, 106
    screening, 103
    working methods/language, 105
new neighbourhood initiative (Commission), 115
political process, 101
pre-accession strategy, 101
Working Group, 102, 103, 110
environmental protection, 195–7
    and free movement of goods, 197–200
    mandatory requirements case law, 198, 199
equal treatment principle, 244
equivalence principle, 318, 319, 320–2
equivalent effect concept,
    free movement of goods, 194
'Eurodevils', 20
Europe Agreements,
    free movement rights, 234, 237, 240, 241, 242
European Commission,
    competition cases,
        EC Rules, uniform application, 147–51
        judicial panels, 89
    direct action jurisdiction, 89
    duty to investigate complaint, 93–6
        compulsion to act (Art 232), 95
        inaction, justification of, 95–6
        methodology, 94
    enlargement process,
        new neighbourhood initiative (2003), 115
        roadmap for conclusion of negotiations, 108
    merger control decisions *see* merger control decisions
    precautionary principle,
        Communication on Use, 208
        products, risk assessment, 205
European Convention on Human Rights,
    and Charter of Fundamental Rights, 77
    enforcement, decentralisation, 308
    European Union acceding to, 74, 76, 77
    High Contracting Parties, 77

Index   395

and limitations on Scottish Ministers, 49–50
linguistic issues, 301
public hearing, right to, 27
European Council,
  Observations in the Interim Measures proceedings, 209, 212
European Union (EU),
  constitutional reform proposals, 69–79
    acquis jurisprudentiel, 79
    Court of Justice (ECJ), future, 78–9
    fundamental rights, 74–7
    subsidiarity principle, 71–4
  enlargement *see* enlargement of EU
  European Human Rights Convention, accession to, 74, 76, 77
  Foreign and Security Policy, competences, 82
  judicial architecture, 83, 84, 85–6, 89
  Official Journal, 361, 362

Faculty of Advocates (Scotland), 15, 16
fair trial rights, 27–8
fire blight danger,
  Japan, 218–19
France,
  antibiotic use, 221
  Second Republic, 82
free movement of goods, 194–5, 201, 237
  and environmental protection, 197–200
free movement of persons,
  professional qualifications/diplomas, mutual recognition, 247–8
free movement rights, 233–45
  Agreements, 234, 235, 236, 237, 238, 240, 242
    absence of 'secondary legislation', 243
    proportionality/remedies test, 241
  case law, 235–42, 244
  direct effect, 238–40
  employment, 239–42
  extent conferred, 240–1
  family members, 242–3
  history, 233
  interpretation principles, 236–7
  jurisdiction, 235–6
  non-discrimination, 243–5
  only when active in labour force, 241
  population movements, 233
  'standstill clauses', 238, 242
  unlawful conduct, 242
  see also free movement of goods
freedom of establishment, 237, 240
fundamental rights, 74–7
  Working Group, 75, 76, 77

GMO (genetically modified organisms) crops, 219

Gothenburg European Council,
  Union enlargement, 108

Helsinki six,
  Union enlargement, 102
High Court of Justiciary (Scotland), 15, 18, 19
hormones,
  scientific controversies, 218

IGC (Inter-Governmental Conference),
  Community law, and devolved institutions, 61, 66
  competition law, 89
  Court of Justice (ECJ), future, 78
  at Nice, 84
  impartiality requirement,
    judicial process, 22, 23, 24
Interim Committee,
  Union enlargement, 113
interpretatio contra legem, 365
ius civile europaeum, 366

judges,
  appointment system, 25–6
  Community, 83
    CFI member, Opinion of, 92–8
  impartiality requirement, 22–4
  Scottish,
    chosen from Faculty of Advocates, 16
    contribution to international courts, 297
    salary (Court of Session), 16
    working time, 17
  see also Edward, David (Judge) ; judicial panels; judicial process; lawyers
Judicial Appointments Commission,
  Scotland, 25
judicial architecture,
  European Union, 83, 84, 85–6, 89
judicial geometry,
  preliminary ruling procedure (Article 234), 329, 332
judicial panels,
  candidates, 87–9
  proposals for creation, 70, 84
judicial process, 21–30
  bias, danger of, 22, 23
  blindfolding, 21
  composition of bench, 26–7
  fair trial rights, 27–8
  impartiality/partiality, 22–4
  judgments, pronouncements of, 28–9
  'justice seen to be done', 21–2
  transparency, need for, 22, 26, 27, 29, 30
  see also Judges
judicial review,
  development in United Kingdom, 32
  ex post, subsidiarity principle, 72, 73
  merger control decisions, 117–18

judicial review (cont.):
  scientific controversy, 225
  Scotland, 31–45
    homelessness, 33
    local government bodies, competence, 33
    Rules of Court, 37, 39, 41
    substantive law, 37–8
    ultra vires decisions, 32, 41, 43, 45
    'unfinished business', 37, 40

Laeken Declaration (2001),
  future of Europe, 70, 78
    fundamental rights, 74, 77
    subsidiarity principle, 71
Laeken European Council,
  Union enlargement, 108, 109
Lamassoure report,
  Court of Justice (ECJ), 73
lawyers,
  employed, 154, 155–7, 158
  non-European Union, 154, 157–8, 159
  see also judges
legal theory,
  provisions, norms distinguished, 354, 355–60
leveraging, merger control decisions, 125, 126
lex personae, 264
Lord Advocate, 15, 16
Luxembourg,
  antibiotics litigation, 220
Luxembourg six,
  Union enlargement, 102, 108

malaria, 211
MCR (Merger Control Regulation), 118, 144
  ancillary restraints, 133, 134
  case law, 137, 138, 139
  collective dominance, 119, 120, 122
  conglomerate/portfolio effects, 129
  one-stop regulatory procedure, 131, 132
medical profession,
  mutual recognition of qualifications, 248
merger control decisions, 117–44
  ancillary restraints, 133–4
  burden of proof, 122, 136–44
  collective dominance, 119–23
  see also collective dominance
  conditional positive decisions, implementation of commitments, 134–6
  conglomerate/portfolio effects, 125–31
  horizontal mergers, 123–5, 185–6
  judicial review, 117–18
  leveraging, 125, 126
  'one-stop shop' regulatory procedure, 131–3
  review (Phases), 133, 137–8
  trans-national factors, 124

New Zealand,
  impartiality of judges, 22–3

Nice Treaty,
  CFI competence, direct actions, 85
  constitutional reform proposals, 69–70
    fundamental rights, 74
    subsidiarity principle, 71
  IGC,
    ECJ backlog, 84
    Final Act, 87
  judicial geometry created by, 329
  judicial panels *see* judicial panels
norms,
  examples, 357
  interpretation issues, 364–6
  provisions distinguished, legal theory, 354, 355–60

OHIM (Office for Harmonisation in Internal Market), 87, 88
ope exceptionis,
  judicial review, 35, 36, 39, 41

pacta sunt servanda, 365
Paris Treaty,
  role of Community judges, 83
patent cases,
  judicial panel candidate, 88
plurilingual legal system, interpretation approaches, 297–305
  'fuzzy'/'fussy', 300, 301, 304
  public interest, 299
  Scottish judges, 297
precaution, 203–31
  antibiotics *see* antibiotics
  constitutional problems,
    external dimension, 217–20
    internal dimension, 215–17
  meaning, 206
  possibly excessive, examples, 211
  precautionary principle *see* precautionary principle
  'prévention routière', 205
  products, highly regulated, 229–30
  regulations, 204–5
  risk, 206–7
    banning of, 227–9
    selection of level as policy choice, 223–4
  vocabulary, 204–6
  see also precautionary principle; scientific controversies
precautionary principle,
  assessment, 209–11
  banning of products, 227, 228
  Communication on Use of (Commission), 208
  constitutional problems, 215–17
    external dimension, 217–20
    internal dimension, 215–17
  EC Treaty, 208

excessive caution, examples, 211
hidden agenda, 227
products,
  banning, 227, 228
  highly regulated, 229–30
proof, 223
standard setting, 227
Vorsorgung/Vorsorgeprinzip, 207
see also precaution; scientific controversies
preliminary ruling procedure (Article 234), 327–43
  admissibility of references, 329–39
    abuse of process, reference as, 334–5
    insufficient context, 336-9
    matter falls outside ECJ jurisdiction, 332–3
    premature question, 333–4
    referring court not 'court or tribunal of member state', 331–2
    Rules of Procedure, 329
    subject matter of dispute, question bearing no relation to, 335
    vague question, 334
  judicial geometry, 329, 332
  jurisdiction, exceeding, 340–2
  Rome Convention, transforming, 260
  success, 327–8
preliminary rulings,
  admissibility, 260
professional qualifications/diplomas, mutual recognition, 247–56
  automatic/unconditional recognition, 252–3, 254, 256
  case-by-case recognition, 252, 253
  free movement of persons, 247–8
  'general system' directives, 249
  internal market, 247–8
  sectoral directives, 248
  'SLIM' Directive, 249
proportionality principle,
  Constitution for Europe draft Treaty, 72, 73
provisional closure concept,
  Union enlargement, 106
provisions, legal,
  examples, 356–7
  norms distinguished, 354, 355–60

reasonable man test,
  impartiality, 22, 23
references,
  admissibility, 329–39
    abuse of process, reference as, 334–5
    insufficient context, 336–9
    matter falls outside ECJ jurisdiction, 332–3
    premature question, 333–4
    referring court not 'court or tribunal of member state', 331–2

Rules of Procedure, 329
subject matter of dispute, question bearing no relation to, 335
vague question, 334
discretionary, 345–52
  cost, 347
  delay, 347
  difficulty, 347
  existence of discretion to refer, 345–6
  importance of issue, 347
  language, 347–8
  necessity, 346
  new approach, 349–52
  purposive approach to interpretation, 347–8
  wide discretion, 346–8
  wishes of parties, 348
Restrictive Practices Court,
  and Competition Appeal Tribunal, 191
review, standard of, 268–96
  appropriate questions, 268
  de novo, 273, 274, 277, 278, 294
    TBT Agreement 288, 289
    trade remedy agreements, 283, 284
  objective of, 269–70
  particular needs, 269
  separation of powers, 269
  WTO law, 270–96
    anti-dumping rules, 274–6, 279–82
    de novo review see Review, standard of:
      de novo review
    dispute settlement system, 270, 274, 283, 289, 291, 294
    factual determinations, 277–9
    generally, 270–2
    legal determinations, 272–4
    'objective assessment', 271, 272, 274, 278, 294
    'one-size-fits-all' approach, 272
    'permissible' legal interpretations, 274–6
    specific agreements, 279–92
Rio Declaration (1992), 207
risk, 206–7
  banning of,
    assessment of decision, 228–9
    dangers, 227–8
  selection of level as policy choice, 223–4
Roman Empire,
  free movement rights, 233
Rome Convention on Law Applicable to Contractual Obligations (1980), 257–65
  and Amsterdam Treaty, 258–62
  civil matters, judicial co-operation, 259
  co-decision procedure, 259, 260
  'cross-border implications', 260, 262
  optional provisions, 262–4

Rome Convention on Law Applicable to
    Contractual Obligations (cont.):
  sectoral instruments, 264–5
  UK application, 261
Rome, Treaties of (1957),
  changing structure, 194–7
    environmental protection, 195–7
    free movement of goods, 194–5
    and Convention on future of Union, 69
  EC competition law,
    collective dominance (Art 82), 162–75
    merger control restraints (Article 81), 133
    uniform application (Articles 81 and 82),
      145, 147, 148, 149, 150
  enforcement mechanisms, 307, 309–16
    gaps at Community level, 312–16
    horizontal direct effect, 309–12
    Plaumann test, 312
  freedom of establishment, 237
  independence of judges, 24
  non-EU lawyers, legal services by (Art 230),
    159
  precautionary principle, 208
  preliminary rulings *see* preliminary ruling
    procedure (Article 234)
  role of Community judges, 83
  and Rome Convention, 258
rule of law, 70–1

Schuman Declaration (1950), 78–9
Schuman, Robert, 81, 83, 89
scientific controversies, 213–15
  advice, handling, 223
  case law, 213, 214
  Daubert principle, 213
  dispute resolution, 211–13
  European courts, role, 225–6
  evidence, distortion, 226
  hormones, 218
  knowledge, insufficient, inconclusive or
    uncertain, 210
  method, 211–12
  opinions, selecting from, 224–5
  USA on, 213–15
Scotland,
  Judicial Appointments Commission, 25
  judicial review, 31–45
  judiciary process, danger of bias, 22
  legal system, 11–20
    case law nature, 19–20
    lower and higher courts, 15
    overlapping jurisdiction, 17–18
    Sheriffs, chosen from Faculty of
      Advocates, 16
    Supreme Court jurisdiction, 31–2
  unjust enrichment, 263–4
  see also Court of Session (Scotland); judges:
    Scottish

Scottish Ministers,
  limitations on actions, 49–50
  Memorandum of Understanding (UK
    Government), 52
Scottish Parliament (SP),
  restraint on powers, 48
separation of powers,
  standard of review, 269
Sonderstatut theory, 263
staff cases,
  judicial panel candidates, 87
'standstill clauses', free movement rights, 238,
    242
Structural Funds Programme, 62
subsidiarity principle,
  devolution, and Community law, 58–9
  and future of Europe, 70, 71–4
  Working Group, 72, 73
Supreme Court jurisdiction,
  Scotland, 31–2
systems of law,
  co-existence, 360–1

TEU (Treaty of European Union),
  and co-operation with devolved institutions,
    65
  Community policies, precedence issues, 193
  environmental protection, 196–7
  free movement of goods, 195
  free movement rights, 235
  subsidiarity, 58
  see also Rome, Treaties of (1957)
Thessaloniki, European Council meeting
    (2003),
  Constitution for Europe, 69n, 72, 78
  European enlargement, 114
trade mark cases,
  judicial panel candidate, 87–8
trade remedy agreements (WTO), 279–88
  Anti-Dumping, 274–6, 279–82
    case law, 281
  procedural v substantive review of measures,
    285–8
    case law, 286–8
TRADOS translation system,
  Accession Treaty (Union enlargement), 111
transparency, need for,
  judicial process, 22, 26, 27, 29, 30
travaux préparatoires, 298

United Kingdom,
  judicial appointments, 25
  judicial review, growth, 32
  Rome Convention, application of, 261
United States,
  judiciary process,
    judgment pronouncements, 30
    judicial appointments, 25

Index   399

United States (cont.):
  scientific controversies, judicial experience, 213–15
unjust enrichment, 263–4
unlawful conduct,
  free movement rights, 242

Vienna Action Plan (1998), 259n13
Vlassopoulou principle,
  mutual recognition of qualifications, 249–50, 251, 252, 256

WTO (World Trade Organisation),
  Agreements,
    Agriculture, 219
    Anti-Dumping, 274–6, 279–82
    Application of Sanitary and Phytosanitary Measures (SPS), 218–19, 272, 279, 290–2
    General Agreement on Tariffs and Trade (GATT), 234, 292–4
    Safeguards/SCM Agreement, 272, 282, 283, 284, 286
    Technical Barriers to Trade (TBT), 219, 279, 288–90, 292
    trade remedy, 279–88
  Appellate Body,
    Anti-Dumping Agreement, 276
    factual determinations, 277
    general review, 270–1
    legal determinations, 273, 274
  dispute settlement system, 270, 274, 283, 289, 291, 294
  linguistic issues, 299
  non-EU lawyers, legal services by, 158–9
  public health, action against other countries' goods, 217–20
  review, standard of, 268–96
    anti-dumping rules, 274–6
    dispute settlement system, 270, 274, 283, 289, 291, 294
    EC-Hormones case, 270–1, 273, 277, 290
    factual determinations, 277–9
    generally, 270–2
    legal determinations, 272–4
    'objective assessment', 271, 272, 274, 278, 294
    'one-size-fits-all' approach, 272
    'permissible' legal interpretations, 274–6
    separation of powers, 269
    specific agreements, 279–92
    specific issues, 272–9
  trade remedy measures, procedural and substantive review, 285–8